ONE PARTY
AFTER ANOTHER

ONE PARTY
AFTER ANOTHER

The Disruptive Life of Nigel Farage

MICHAEL CRICK

**SIMON &
SCHUSTER**

London · New York · Sydney · Toronto · New Delhi

First published in Great Britain by Simon & Schuster UK Ltd, 2022

Copyright © Michael Crick, 2022

The right of Michael Crick to be identified as the author
of this work has been asserted in accordance with
the Copyright, Designs and Patents Act, 1988.

1 3 5 7 9 10 8 6 4 2

Simon & Schuster UK Ltd
1st Floor
222 Gray's Inn Road
London WC1X 8HB

www.simonandschuster.co.uk
www.simonandschuster.com.au
www.simonandschuster.co.in

Simon & Schuster Australia, Sydney
Simon & Schuster India, New Delhi

The author and publishers have made all reasonable efforts
to contact copyright-holders for permission, and apologise
for any omissions or errors in the form of credits given.
Corrections may be made to future printings.

A CIP catalogue record for this book
is available from the British Library

Hardback ISBN: 978-1-4711-9229-6
eBook ISBN: 978-1-4711-9231-9

Typeset in Perpetua by M Rules
Printed and bound by CPI Group (UK) Ltd, Croydon, CR0 4YY

MIX
Paper from
responsible sources
FSC
www.fsc.org   FSC® C171272

Also by Michael Crick:

Militant
Scargill and the Miners
Manchester United: The Betrayal of a Legend (with D. Smith)
Jeffrey Archer: Stranger than Fiction
The Complete Manchester United Trivia Factbook
Michael Heseltine: A Biography
The Boss: The Many Sides of Alex Ferguson
In Search of Michael Howard
Sultan of Swing: The Life of David Butler

CONTENTS

INTRODUCTION

Sweating heavily, the pilot put out a Mayday call. His passenger awaited his fate, having decided there was nothing he could do, or say, to help. He considered calling or texting his 'nearest and dearest', but didn't see how that would assist much either. He thought about lighting a cigarette, but then remembered how a lot of fuel might be spilt if the aircraft had to crash-land.

Which it soon did.

It was early morning on the day of the British general election of 2010. In its final moments, the two-man plane had plummeted to earth at 80 miles an hour. 'The impact separated the engine from its mounts and collapsed the landing gear,' an official report found later. 'As the fuselage hit the ground, the front section dug in and the aircraft pivoted forwards, coming to rest inverted.'[1]

'It's strange,' Nigel Farage reflected years later. 'Initially, you're filled with fear, and as the ground rushes up, a sort of sense of resignation, kind of feeling, "Well, if this is it, let's hope it's all over quickly."'[2]

Farage opened his eyes. 'There is light. Good God. I am still here,' he thought to himself.

Still strapped into his seat, he could see the grass right in front of his nose. His face was almost touching it. His blood was dripping onto the turf.

Another few inches and the former, and future, leader of the UK Independence Party would surely have been dead. And the momentous decade which enveloped British politics after 2010 might have been very different. It's not just a matter of whether or not the United Kingdom would still be a member of the European Union: the Brexit battle has also transformed our politics in ways which may be permanent. We may soon see the end of the United Kingdom itself, even if such repercussions were never intended by those like Farage who had long fought to leave the European Union.

This is the extraordinary story of one of the most important politicians of modern British history; he's been a more significant player than most leaders of the traditional political parties, more influential than quite a few prime ministers. Nigel Farage is the only man ever to have won a nationwide election as leader of an insurgent party. And he managed that astonishing feat twice, five years apart, leading two different parties. Yet Farage has never been elected to the House of Commons, never served as a government minister and will almost certainly never achieve either role. He will go down as one of the great political communicators of our age, a man with a rare instinctive feel for public opinion, yet someone who managed to fall out with many of those, in his parties and beyond, who were committed to the very same cause.

Nigel Farage has written two what one might loosely call auto-biographies – *Fighting Bull* (2010) and *The Purple Revolution* (2015).[3] He features heavily in a couple of early histories of UKIP, and Owen Bennett has written two highly readable chronicles of Farage during the referendum period.[4] But surprisingly, until now nobody has published a biography in traditional book form (though in 2015 a Kindle and audio biography was published by Matthew Lynn).[5] In 2019, when a sympathetic former UKIP candidate Nigel Jones took Farage to lunch and announced he'd like to write a book, Farage made it clear that he wasn't keen, and so Jones dropped the idea.

I have written six previous biographies, mostly on political sub-jects, and in a strange way this one has been harder to research and write than any before. In part, this has been due to the 2020-21 Covid restrictions which hindered face-to-face interviews and visits to archives, but largely because, like one of my early subjects, Jeffrey Archer, no aspect of Nigel Farage's life is ever dull – not even his years trading metal futures in the City of London. His 2010 polling day air crash was one of three occasions on which Farage has come close to death; his political career is regularly punctuated with spectacular bust-ups; every move in his two main parties – UKIP and the Brexit Party – seems to involve intrigue. And he's made an impact beyond the UK, admired by Donald Trump and publicly vilified by Hillary Clinton. In Europe, adversaries who initially derided this English upstart came to fear and have a sneaking regard, almost an affection, for him. Top that with a highly colourful personal life and the biographer is deluged with a wealth of material. And with Farage's new career as a presenter with GB News, the stream of Farage opinions and interventions is unlikely to subside.

I have frequently interviewed Farage over the years, yet oddly I can't recall when I first met him. During the Labour government of Gordon Brown, continuing into the Coalition of David Cameron and Nick Clegg, I like to think I was one of the first broadcasters to spot that UKIP represented a significant, and expanding, body of opinion in British politics which deserved proper coverage. This was not a view shared by all my colleagues at the BBC, ITN or Channel 4, many of whom thought it was wrong to boost UKIP by giving them publicity.

To interview Nigel Farage in front of a camera was always a challenge, always fun, never dull. On one occasion we enjoyed what's fondly called a PFL – a Proper Farage Lunch (or Proper Fucking Lunch) at his favourite lunchtime haunt, Boisdale in Victoria, with beer, the seasonal grouse and plenty of red wine, though my guest did insist on regular fag breaks in the restaurant's upstairs open-air smoking area. Farage seemed rather disappointed and unimpressed when I announced around 4 p.m. that I had to get back to work. But we had the odd row over the years, too, including one occasion when he publicly called me 'despicable'.

This is an independent biography. He has not helped beyond answering the odd question on one or two occasions when we've met for other reasons. It is certainly not 'authorised' – that horrible term – or likely to be endorsed by the subject. In a free democratic society, journalists have not just a right but a duty to explore and understand the lives of politicians, and those who aspire to lead us. I told Nigel Farage about this book at the very start, and he was wary about it, understandably perhaps. Many of his friends sensibly took the view that they had a duty to speak up for him, though a few were so cautious as to be a waste of time. Quite a few people wanted nothing to do with this project, in some cases because Farage was an experience they wanted to forget.

The book could not be written without first-class research by Henry Dyer – a young journalist with a great future. My former wife Margaret Crick also made a substantial contribution with her skills at tracking people down and getting them to talk. Lucia Henwood did a great job wading through many of the numerous UKIP blogs, and also in fact-checking. My former TV colleague Philip Braund was extremely generous in supplying the fruits of his UKIP and Farage research over many years. I am grateful also to Seth Thevoz and Sophie Brokenshire for their research contributions.

I was also the beneficiary of a big suitcase and two large crates of documents from the early years of UKIP, supplied by the Conservative MP Craig Mackinlay, which was an astonishingly generous act given relations between us in the not-too-distant past. The former UKIP MEP Jim Carver also supplied scores of editions of the party magazine *Independence*. Stuart Dunbar was assiduous in helping with Dulwich College lists.

Another huge contributor wishes to remain anonymous, but I couldn't have done without their meticulous UKIP archive. They were incredibly patient with my regular queries, and helped add a huge amount of extra UKIP colour and detail. Thank you also to Lewis Baston, David Cowling, Christopher Wilson, Gary Gibbon, Phil Hornby, Anamaria Townley and Caroline Morgan for their help in various ways. Jackie Mayes did a splendid job exploring the genealogy, based on previous work by John Hitchcock. Beverly Hetherington and Moira Hall transcribed several interviews.

My partner Lucy Hetherington put huge care into reading my manuscript and suggested substantial improvements. My daughter Catherine picked up numerous flaws and inconsistencies in the text. Every biography needs a family tree, and Catherine drew the Farage pedigree on pages 544–5.

I am especially grateful to Ian Chapman and Ian Marshall at Simon & Schuster, and to Kat Ailes, Polly Curtis and the rest of the team for their diligence and extreme patience, and to Martin Soames for his wise legal advice.

The book involved around 300 interviews, just a fraction of which are cited in the footnotes. A big thank you to all those who gave of their time and memories, and in many cases fished out valuable material. My big disappointment is that the pandemic greatly restricted my ability to visit places which are key to the story, and I wasn't able to meet more of my sources in person. You can only go so far with Zoom.

There will inevitably be one or two errors. These are entirely my fault. If you let me know about them, I will try to correct them in future editions.

MICHAEL CRICK
London, November 2021

DOWNE HIS WAY

If you walk the London Loop, the 140-mile long-distance footpath round the edge of Greater London, it's striking how swathes of outer London are very rural. You might be strolling through one of the remote English shires.

Downe, about a mile or so south of the Loop, in the Borough of Bromley, is a good example. To the visitor, Downe has all the characteristics and institutions of a classic English country village – a thirteenth-century church, a village hall, a primary school, a cricket club, two patriotically named pubs – the George and Dragon, and the Queen's Head – and a grand residence, Down House, with its ample grounds and splendid gardens.

Through woodland and across local farmland, you're within walking distance of the North Kent Downs – hence the name Downe (the 'e' was added in 1940 to avoid confusion with Co. Down in Northern Ireland). Winston Churchill's country home, Chartwell, is six miles south of here; and above Downe, barely half a mile away, is the historic runway at Biggin Hill. From here, RAF Hurricanes and Spitfires helped Churchill achieve Britain's 'finest hour' in the skies above southern England in the hot summer of 1940: the Battle of Britain.

Few places feel more traditional, or more English. Downe still seems like an idyllic 1950s picture of rural Kent, the county of cricket and orchards and hops grown to brew English ale. The only giveaway feature is the occasional distinctively red London bus trundling through. Downe has officially been part of Greater London since 1965, though thanks to the green belt policy it's protected from the capital's suburban sprawl.

This is Nigel Farage country. He grew up here. He walked the
local fields and fished the local streams. He still drinks here, and to
this day lives a mile down the road. Through all the turmoil of his
life, personal and political, this part of England – which he still calls
Kent – has always been home.

Downe is natural Conservative territory, of course. But it wasn't
always. In March 1962, this constituency, Orpington, saw one of
the greatest by-election upsets of all time, when a Tory majority of
almost 15,000 was turned into a Liberal majority of almost 8,000.
The new Liberal MP, Eric Lubbock, had been a last-minute choice
as candidate after their previous nominee was found technically to
have committed bigamy. Lubbock, who immediately became known
as 'Orpington Man', was a local councillor whose aristocratic
ancestors had long lived at another local grand house, High Elms.
Lubbock's shock victory prompted a late twentieth-century revival
of the Liberals – as a third party in British politics, a party not of
government but of protest.

Two years later, on 3 April 1964, Nigel Paul Farage, a master of
political upsets in the twenty-first century, was born at Farnborough
Hospital, a couple of miles from Downe.

As a boy, Farage lived in a semi-detached Victorian cottage which
used to belong to the Down House estate, the grounds of which it
backed onto. The gardens were his playground. Now run by English
Heritage and open to the public, Down House was for forty years
home to a great Victorian who challenged the conventional wisdom
of his day and outraged his contemporaries. It was here that Charles
Darwin developed his revolutionary ideas, wrote his historic work
On the Origin of Species By Means of Natural Selection, and conducted
biological experiments in the gardens. The locals took pride in their
illustrious forebear, who had employed some of the villagers' grandparents. 'We were aware of him and loyal to his memory, much as
many Christians grew up with unthinking loyalty to creationism,'
Farage recalls. 'In Downe he was ours.'[1]

The young Farage would wander through the grounds of Down
House and nearby parkland, chatting away to both the people
and the animals he met, and foraging with a fork and trowel for

'treasure' – collecting, as Darwin did. He still keeps some of his booty, including clay pipes, coloured glass bottles, fragments of pottery and coins. Farage acquired a detailed knowledge of local flora and fauna, following almost literally in Darwin's footsteps. He was also inspired by his father, Guy, who loved collecting butterflies and moths.

The flamboyantly named Guy Justus Oscar Farage was twenty-nine years old when Nigel was born in 1964. He had married Barbara Stevens, five years his junior, the previous year. They were a lively and good-looking couple, both local to the area. She was a shorthand typist, whose father and grandfather had both served as CID officers with the Metropolitan Police – her father Robert was a detective superintendent by the time he retired, having specialised in murder and fraud cases. Guy was the son of a stockbroker's clerk and worked as a stockbroker himself. Though smaller in stature, Guy bore a striking similarity to the future Nigel and was always dapper in appearance – with expensive pin-stripe suits from Savile Row, handmade, highly polished shoes, silk ties, a bowler hat and umbrella. He was, says Nigel, remembered 'as the best-dressed man on the Stock Exchange at that time'.[2] Guy was also known as a great talker, a storyteller, and full of charm.

Both sides of the family were traditional Conservatives, patriotic people who were hugely influenced by Britain's role in two world wars. 'When I was small, you could never spend time with my grandparents without them talking about the past,' Farage has said.[3] His grandfather, Harry Farage, signed up within weeks of the outbreak of war in 1914, but was injured in both thighs at Vimy Ridge near Arras in 1915, in a dangerous engagement for which his corporal was awarded the Victoria Cross. Harry later returned to action and became a lance corporal.

Nigel's father Guy was a young schoolboy during the Second World War, and in later life would no doubt have loved to have been in action. Guy's early adult life was blighted by the drinking culture which pervaded the financial institutions of the City of London. The young Nigel adored his father, but saw little of him when he was small. Whether working or drinking, Guy would spend nearly all his time and much of his money in the Square Mile, causing strains in the marriage as Barbara was left to bring up Nigel and his younger brother Andrew, pretty much on her own.

Barbara was as big a character as her husband, vivacious, outgoing and fun. 'Both of my parents are very dynamic people,' Farage once said. 'They get involved; they get stuck in.'[4] And his mother was 'exceptionally glamorous' in the eyes of the young Nigel.[5] Years later, in her late sixties and early seventies, Barbara would slightly embarrass Nigel by stripping off and posing several times for fund-raising calendars. Flowers or other items were placed in key positions, of course, to save Nigel even more blushes, and once she even had pink roses painted over much of her body. The calendars raised more than £42,000 for charity. She also gave lectures on local and natural history topics, including the survival of the fittest.

Barbara has said that as a boy Nigel was never one for toys. He was too busy foraging the area on his own for fossils, bottle tops and the like. It's interesting that in his fond reminiscences in two sets of memoirs, Farage makes little mention of childhood friends. 'Weird child', he says of his young self.[6]

In 1968, as Europe was suddenly opening up as a holiday destination for English families, the Farage family flew to Portugal for a fortnight on the Algarve, which at that time was only just starting to be a popular tourist destination. He was only four at the time, but Nigel was enchanted by the foreign food – exotic items included tuna steaks, sardines and spicy sausages. It was his first trip to a continent that would come to dominate his life, though it would be another two decades before Portugal joined the European Community. The holiday was meant to put things right between his parents, but it didn't work. The following year Guy Farage left his family, and the two young boys were told their parents were getting a divorce.

Even though Guy Farage is still alive, and now in his late eighties, Nigel has always been remarkably frank and open about his father's alcoholism. For a while, things got so bad that the boys were prohibited from seeing their father; he lost his job on the Stock Exchange and tried to fend for his family by trading antiques.

'In fact,' Nigel has written, 'Guy Farage did at last prove a hero worthy of my mum and even of my illusions. In 1971, at the age of just thirty-six, he knocked the booze and started afresh.'[7] He kept his pledge not to drink, and the following year was readmitted to the Stock Exchange.

Barbara quickly married again, to a local shop owner, Richard Tubb, who became Nigel's stepfather and also his golf instructor, introducing him to the game and patiently coaching him. Nigel soon acquired a half-sister – Melanie, born in 1971 (another future calendar girl) – and a half-brother, Julian, born four years later. In 1980 Guy also married again – to Carol Hyatt. He didn't retire until 2010, when he was seventy-five.

The evolution of the Farage family can be traced back through British soil to roots sixty miles due west of Downe, just south of Reading in Berkshire. Swallowfield is a village of about 2,000 people, whose most notable historic resident was Henry Hyde, the second Earl of Clarendon, who briefly – from 1685 to 1687 – was Lord Privy Seal and a close adviser to the Catholic king, James II.

It was in Swallowfield twenty years later, in 1706, that Mary Cowdery, a girl from a long-established Berkshire family (which was more often spelt Cowdrey), married a newcomer called George Farridge in the local Anglican church. George and Mary Farridge were Nigel Farage's great-great-great-great-great-grandparents. But the question of where George Farridge came from is something of a mystery. There is no sign of him being born in Swallowfield, or of any previous relatives in the village.

In the summer of 2013 Nigel Farage was asked at a meeting organised by the *Jewish Chronicle* whether he was opposed to refugees. 'Not at all,' he replied. 'I myself am a descendant of refugees, French Huguenots who came here to avoid being burned at the stake!'[8] Farage is remembered to have made a similar claim when he was a schoolboy. It sounds slightly exotic to be descended from French Protestants, but it may not be true.

Earlier in 2013, the *Mail on Sunday* had said that George Farridge was born in 1681 as Georgius Ferauge in France – in Fumay in the Ardennes, in a finger of France that sticks into Belgium. The newspaper claimed that Ferauge was a Huguenot who had fled to Britain to escape the persecution of Louis XIV, though the article included no evidence for this.

The story seems unproven and improbable. Georgius Ferauge was actually baptised in a Catholic church in France, so it is unlikely that he would have been a Huguenot. And why would a Huguenot refugee, who probably didn't speak much English, choose to flee to rural Berkshire when there seems to be no record of other Huguenots living in the vicinity? Indeed, the Clarendon connection with Swallowfield makes this account even more improbable, since the local estate was owned by one of them, a former adviser to a Catholic king, and Clarendon remained a life-long Jacobite who supported the Stuart pretenders to the throne.

At other times in the past, Nigel Farage has dismissed the idea that his name was originally French. 'Don't think so, no,' he said when asked about it in 2009. 'Thought it might have been Huguenot. No problem with that – great people, the Huguenots.'[9] And in 2020, in conversation with this author, he also expressed scepticism about the idea. His theory was that the earlier spelling of the name was English, a combination of the words 'far' and 'ridge', perhaps denoting someone who came from or lived on a distant ridge.[10]

Over subsequent generations the surname went through several variations – Feridg, Ferridge and eventually Farage. The family moved from Berkshire to Mitcham in Surrey, where his great-great-grandfather Edward Farage was a police constable for 20 years in the mid-nineteenth century – so Nigel Farage has police ancestors on both sides. Over the generations, the family moved to Croydon, then Sutton, and onto Penge. Nigel's great-grandfather, Daniel Farage, worked successively as a labourer, shopman, clothier's outfitter, collector for the Singer Sewing Machine Company and then as a boot-maker. By the 1911 census, Nigel Farage's grandfather, Harry Farage, was employed as a stockbroker's clerk. Harry's son, Guy Justus Oscar Farage – Nigel's father – was born in Bromley in south-east London, in 1935.

As the rather exotic middle names suggest, there are other, much firmer, continental roots on the paternal side of Nigel Farage's family tree. Around 1861, a young couple, Nicholas and Bena Schrod, both aged about twenty-three, arrived in this country from the German city of Frankfurt. Nigel Farage has said he suspects the name 'Schrod' had been shortened from 'Schroder', to make it sound more Germanic and less Jewish.[11]

The Schrods found rented accommodation in Frances Street, which ran between Tottenham Court Road and Gower Street in central London, and is now Torrington Place. Today the area is dominated by University College and other parts of the University of London, but in the nineteenth century it was run-down and impoverished, and a popular quarter for working-class immigrants from Germany. Many had arrived from the economic and political turmoil of the loose federation of German states, which would not become the unified modern Germany until 1871. At that time, Britain imposed no restrictions on immigration; many Europeans were welcomed here, especially if they had skills. In the mid-nineteenth century there was religious and political persecution in Germany, but the Schrods almost certainly came to London for a better life – as economic migrants.

Nicholas had learned his trade as a cabinetmaker in Frankfurt, and set up in business in London making wooden cases for pianos, both upright and grand models. He'd latched onto a trend. During the nineteenth century, pianos became more popular as middle-class families grew in number and became more prosperous, and people enjoyed the pastime of singing together round the piano. Meanwhile, Bena Schrod worked as a dressmaker and doing needlework.

In 1870, Nicholas Schrod appeared at Bow Street police court in London charged with assaulting two young men. It was the time of the Franco-Prussian War, and according to the *Globe* newspaper, Schrod had been leaning out of an upstairs window when he overheard the two men discussing the conflict in the street below. When one of the men boasted that '40 Englishmen could beat 80 Germans', Schrod reportedly 'came downstairs, charged the complainants with improper conduct, and assaulted them'. Farage's German great-great grandfather was fined twenty shillings, and paid it at once.[12]

Nicholas Schrod was only forty-four when he died, and the

couple's only child, Carl Justus, who later adopted the more Anglicised first name of Charles, was Nigel's great-grandfather. He was born in 1863, shortly after his parents arrived in London, and grew up to become a messenger with the General Post Office's new telegraph network. The family later moved out to Brixton and Herne Hill, then to a three-bedroom semi-detached house in the growing suburb of Beckenham in north-west Kent, where he worked as a post office letter sorter. Nigel's grandmother Gladys Schrod was born in Beckenham in 1900.

As well as these German forebears, and the possible French Huguenot connection, Nigel Farage has a strain of Irish ancestry. His great-grandfather Daniel Farage married Lucy Susannah Moynihan, whose grandfather was an immigrant from Ireland, and Farage is distantly related to the abstract painter Rodrigo Moynihan.

Three generations of the Farage family had lived in the suburbs and outer parts of south-east London since the start of the twentieth century. Nigel's father, grandfather and maternal great-grandfather would travel by train each day from the Bromley area into the City of London. His grandfather Harry Farage, born in 1890, began life as a stockbrokers' clerk and remained in the business for forty years – almost as long as his son Guy. His grandsons, Nigel and his brother Andrew, were also destined for City jobs, but first they needed an education.

Despite their separation and financial problems, Guy and Barbara Farage were keen to send their sons to independent, fee-paying schools. Nigel's first was Greenhayes School for Boys, a day school opposite large playing fields on Corkscrew Hill in West Wickham, about five miles from the family home in Downe. Farage was just four and a half when he started, and would have had to turn up in school uniform – green, of course – with a green, red and blue school cap. 'Very like *Just William*,' says Martin Young, a Greenhayes pupil some years earlier.[13]

It was unfortunate that, shortly after Farage arrived there, his parents divorced. It may have been the Swinging Sixties, but in respectable middle-class suburbs like Bromley and Beckenham in south-east London, divorce was still unusual. It was frowned upon, even seen as a matter of shame, and schoolchildren suffered disapproval from fellow pupils. 'It was as if the taint might rub off on them,' Farage later wrote. So he fought back, telling schoolmates that divorce was quite normal, if not compulsory, among 'clever' and 'top people'.[14] The experience probably nurtured a tough resilience.

Greenhayes was very traditional, with lots of learning 'by heart' – important dates in history, the kings and queens of England, the times tables – and pupils had to live with the violent perils of flying board-rubbers or punishment by slipper. After just two years, when he was only six, Farage was moved from Greenhayes because his parents had heard an unfortunate rumour that the headmaster was up to 'the usual thing'.[15]

They sent their son instead to Eden Park, a small preparatory school – mixed this time – a couple of miles away in Upper Elmers End Road, Beckenham. It was based on an old farm with a large main house with plenty of rooms, a loft converted into classrooms, and which still had the old servants' bells. Three outbuildings had been turned into a nursery, a hall and a classroom; the lavatories had been converted from pigsties, and next to the playground ran the Beck, a small stream where the boys and girls sometimes played. Lunch was often eaten in a hut with long tables and benches. The school was run by the legendary and formidable Alice Mallick, who had lost her husband during the war and set up the school for local children who hadn't been evacuated. 'She made it very cheap for people who wanted to pay for education, but didn't have a lot of money,' one former teacher explains. She was 'a real fireball and war horse,' says the former sports master Roy Thompson: 'Very strict indeed, but a great teacher. The kids used to love her and she loved the kids. She brought the school up from nothing. When I first went there I was in complete awe of her. She frightened the life out of me!'[16] Thompson was actually a postman who finished his shift at noon, then took games lessons in the afternoon and often evening practice sessions, too.

Nigel Farage has described Alice Mallick as a 'fearsome' woman who 'killed wasps with her bare hands'.[17] Another old teacher,

Pam Taylor, has similar memories: 'I was terrified of her.' The curriculum was 'quite narrow', she says. 'It was a reading, writing, arithmetic sort of school, very formal.' Very few of the teachers were properly trained or qualified, and 'teachers' pay was disgusting', says one former member of staff – 'the cleaner got paid more'.[18] Alice Mallick would cook the school lunches herself.

The classes, one for each year, were small – between a dozen and twenty, and a lot of the pupils went on to good private secondary schools in the area such as Whitgift, St Dunstan's and Dulwich College. 'They always had elocution lessons, certain amounts of physical activity at a local sports ground,' says Pam Taylor. 'There was French on the agenda and music. Mrs Mallick played the piano, and at a very fast speed. She was a real character.'[19]

Academically, Farage did reasonably well, though he struggled with maths. A year early, at the age of nine, he took the entrance exam for Dulwich College, with which his family had connections on both sides. Nigel's maths may have been ropey, but he apparently impressed the examiners with his essay entitled 'What I Did Last Weekend', in which he described feasting on fine and fancy food – 'sweetmeats from furthest Araby' – as well as losing his wellies in mud.[20]

He was accepted.

2

REBEL WITHOUT A CAUSE

Dulwich College was founded as the 'College of God's Gift' in 1619 by Edward Alleyn, the celebrated Jacobean actor and contemporary of William Shakespeare. Hence, former pupils are Old Alleynians (though confusingly the college was divided in the late nineteenth century with the formation of two other local schools – Alleyn's and the girls' school James Allen's). The son of an innkeeper, Edward Alleyn established his reputation as the great celebrity performer of late Elizabethan theatre, but made much of his fortune from property and business – including theatres such as the Rose on the South Bank – and, some think, a group of brothels along the Thames. Edward Alleyn also owned the Bear Garden, a bear-baiting site in Southwark, and even personally baited lions in a show performed for James I. Alleyn craved a long-term legacy – hence Dulwich College – but he never received the knighthood he always sought.

A flamboyant, powerful performer; a man of great energy; raffish yet spectacularly successful; provocative yet keen to keep in with the establishment. In all, an appropriate founder for a school which would one day be attended by Nigel Farage.

In most political biographies, the years at secondary school are worth only a page or two, yet Nigel Farage's time at Dulwich College was not only colourful, but illuminates his subsequent life and career. Dulwich shows many of the contradictions in Farage's character – the ultra-rebel who tries to provoke, stand out and show off, yet is also keen for recognition by those in authority – the man who wants both to join the established order, and yet also bring much of it down.

In Britain, taking an interest in your schooldays and joining

Old Boys' events is regarded by many as a bit naff, yet Farage loves Dulwich College. He sent one of his sons there, and regularly went to watch him play rugby on Saturday mornings. He recently served as President of the Old Alleynian golf club, and is an assiduous attender of alumni events where he sometimes turns up in an OA blazer with its garish stripes and brass buttons. The school, though, has a delicate love-hate relationship with Nigel Farage. On the one hand, he's their most famous Old Boy these days, fiercely proud of his Dulwich past and admired for the way he turns up when he must be so busy, mingles with everyone and doesn't try to press his politics upon them, or embarrass the school. On the other hand, the school can't hide some discomfort with Farage's public reputation and record, and how he represents an outlook and politics which many Dulwich staff and Old Boys abhor.

In September 1974, at the age of ten, Nigel arrived outside the imposing Gothic edifice. Designed by the same family of architects as the Palace of Westminster, Dulwich College is situated in extensive grounds in an affluent and leafy area of south-east London.

> As you ascend into the Great Hall, portraits of great former pupils hang on the walls, including Sir Ernest Shackleton. On entering the school for the first time, Dulwich was a frightening and intimidating place . . . it looked and felt like one of the great classical public-school institutions such as Westminster School or Eton College. But Dulwich was different.[1]

Nigel arrived at Dulwich and caught the tail end of what was called the 'Dulwich Experiment', a scheme which from the 1940s to 1975 meant local councils paid the fees of boys who passed both the 11-plus and the school's own tough entrance exam – so more than half the school's intake of 1,400 boys didn't have to pay. The result was a much more diverse population than at most other public schools, in terms of both class and ethnicity. The school had a couple of hundred boarders, but Farage was a day boy, and from Downe caught a bus to Bromley South station, then the train to West Dulwich, which took about an hour door-to-door.

Farage – or 'Farridge' as he pronounced it then – made an immediate impact. One contemporary remembers him giving a talk on
collecting old bottles. 'I thought at the time what an odd thing for
somebody of nine to be doing, but also quite interesting, and that
stood out. They were bottles like old-fashioned Pepsi bottles with
an extra glass ball in the top to keep it fizzy. From the '20s and '30s.
I don't know where he found them. Maybe digging in rubbish tips.'
The same boy remembers Farage telling how his mother made him
brush his teeth until the gums bled, 'and I thought "That's not right."'

'He was very confident, articulate, forthright, a real character, not particularly academic,' says Peter Petyt, a classmate from
Farage's first two years in the main school. 'You could tell he would
be someone in life.' Farage was already used to political discussions
over Sunday lunch at home, so together he and Petyt formed a
debating team. 'We won virtually everything,' says Petyt. 'He was
quite a good foil. Both of us were reasonably confident and outgoing
people, so we were able to get our points across. I remember him
as quite an entertaining, witty chap. I really enjoyed being on the
stand with him. There was one motion about trying to prove or
disprove the existence of the Bermuda Triangle. I think quite a lot
of the time he spoke without notes. He'd speak and be questioned
by the audience.'[2]

And Farage was willing to argue any case. Their English master,
Laurie Jagger, had to suppress Farage from speaking all the time
in class debates, another contemporary recalls. When the English
master called a volunteer to propose a motion Farage would invari-
ably raise his hand. 'No, not you, Nigel,' Jagger insisted, hoping to
find someone new to do the job. And when Jagger then sought an
opposition speaker, Farage, undeterred, would volunteer again. 'To
my mind, if you wanted to support something you couldn't oppose
it, too,' says this classmate. 'I realised how mature and self-assured
he was.'

Farage wasn't much good at running or athletics but was a
keen cricketer, and during Test matches he'd walk round school
with a transistor radio pressed to his ear for the live commentary.
The teacher who picked him for the Under-11 squad, Gardner

Thompson, recollects how Farage 'never stopped talking' on the cricket field, 'to the extent that on one occasion I was moved to banish him from the vicinity of where I stood as umpire to the deepest of deep-fielding positions, so that I no longer had to listen'.[3]

Farage's extra-curricular activities extended beyond the school gates, as the listener to his bottle-top lecture recalls:

> We got into all sorts of trouble, and he also smoked very heavily, from a very early age. I think we were about eleven. I was quite in awe of him, because at West Dulwich station we would all crowd onto the platform, and he could spit across the double rails and get people on the opposite platform who were going north to Victoria. As a nine-, ten-, eleven-year-old boy I was quite impressed with that. I thought it was quite an achievement. I think possibly we all tried it.

Stuart Dunbar, another classmate in Farage's first year, also travelled into Dulwich every day by train: 'He was the sort who kept getting into trouble and that always involved me.'

Dunbar came from a station further down the line, and Farage encouraged him to catch a later train so they could travel with all their Dulwich mates. At that time the electric trains through Dulwich were often divided into separate compartments which the boys called 'dog-boxes'. 'You could take the light bulbs out,' another of the regular Dulwich train party recalls, 'and then during the Sydenham Hill tunnel, you could have a massive punch-up in the dark, obviously hilariously funny.'

Stuart Dunbar remembers:

> They used to find an empty, single compartment and wait until they got into a tunnel and just throw the light bulbs out of the window, throw the cushions out – that sort of thing! I promise you it happened, on a regular basis. And then there was a big thing at school assembly. British Rail had contacted the school saying there was vandalism, and they believed it was Dulwich boys who were doing it. I think it probably stopped then.

These rail journeys were almost as formative as school life, says Tim France. 'The train was where we did our own (and each other's!) homework. It was where we experimented with smoking and swearing and chatting up girls.'[4]

One of Stuart Dunbar's other memories from this early period is how Farage would join his mates in the groundsman's hut at lunchtime and sit smoking or drinking beer, which one of the boys would steal from his father. But the threat of expulsion came after one of the teachers failed to turn up for a lesson and four of them, including Farage and a friend of theirs called Paul Cousins, ended up in a water fight in the lavatories, 'just absolutely soaking each other'. 'And the head of the lower school came in and just went absolutely mad and said to me, and I think to Paul, but not Nigel: "I'm surprised at you two: your future at the school is on my desk at the moment, and I can tell you now you won't be coming back next year." So that really scared me. So the next year I thought I don't want to be friends with him, I just end up in trouble.'

Dunbar remembers Farage as being highly political, even at the age of eleven or twelve. 'He knew so much about politics and was very Conservative.' And Dunbar will never forget the day Harold Wilson resigned as prime minister in 1976, when Farage was just eleven. He 'came into class singing "The Sun Has Got His Hat On" at the top of his voice. He was just so happy and he came and sat down and said: "Wilson's just resigned." And I thought, *Why would you even bother about that?* It didn't even occur to me.'

The mid-1970s were a period when the neo-fascist and racist National Front became prominent, especially after clashes with antifascist protestors in central London in 1974 when a student, Kevin Gately, was killed in Red Lion Square. As the decade wore on, the tensions were probably greatest on the streets of south-east London. In 1977, there were violent scenes just down the road from Dulwich in 'The Battle of Lewisham' in which fifty-six police officers were injured, weighing in between National Front marchers and antifascist counter-demonstrators.

In 1981 the death of thirteen young Black people in a fire at a house at New Cross exacerbated the tension. Many in the Black community suspected the fire wasn't an accident but a racist attack. Protests were held under the slogan 'Thirteen Dead, Nothing Said'. Local police were accused of not investigating the incident properly, and of being racist for not bringing anyone to justice over the fire.

The late '70s and early '80s were a turbulent time in British politics, with the advent of Thatcherism, huge industrial struggles, mass unemployment and social unrest. In the spring of 1981, some of that unrest occurred only a couple of miles from Dulwich College on the streets of Brixton, where mostly Black youths rioted against aggressive policing, racism, the lack of jobs, and poverty. For several nights running, they burned cars, looted shops and attacked the police. And during these troubles Dulwich College allowed the Metropolitan Police to use the school grounds as a base to park their armoured vans and for officers in riot gear to recuperate and regroup.

Dunbar says that even though their mutual friend Paul Cousins was Black, Nigel Farage could sometimes be 'racist'.

> Whether that was attention-seeking, just to wind people up, I don't know. He had this thing about the National Front, and would run into classrooms and chalk NF on the board, but obviously that was his initials as well. But also, he got on really well with Paul Cousins, the Black kid, so he didn't have a problem with that at all . . . I'd come from a much more multi-cultural school in south London where there were instances of people being called names, but I'd never seen that level of someone being so fixated on it. It really was a major thing for him. I do remember asking him once why he said those things, why he didn't like Black people? 'And what about Paul?'[5]

Sadly, Stuart Dunbar can't remember Farage's response.

Farage's main activities outside class were cricket and golf, and the army section of the college's Combined Cadet Force (CCF), in which Farage always tried to be the smartest cadet. 'I remember you spending hours with spit and polish producing what were unquestionably the brightest pair of CCF army boots in school,' one contemporary told Farage years later.[6]

While the CCF showed the conformist side of his character, Farage's rebellious streak was often to the fore. In his fourth year, he and other members of his form clubbed together to buy a bottle of whisky which they brought into school and drank behind the cricket pavilion before morning assembly. 'We bellowed "Jerusalem" with unwonted fervour,' Farage recounted. 'All save Winterbourne [whose] internal organs were evidently more fragile and startled than ours . . . To our horror, the boy turned white, clutched at his stomach, winced, lurched and collapsed like a stringless puppet.'

In the subsequent enquiry, the boys had to see the head of middle school, D. V. Knight, one by one. Farage explained how cold it had been that morning. There had been some whisky around, so he thought it a good idea to have a 'couple of nips' before 'plunging into the fray'. As for who had supplied the whisky, Farage refused to say.

His classmates were horrified when they heard what he'd said. They'd denied it all. That evening, after the rest were caned one by one, Farage was last to visit Knight for punishment. Because he'd owned up, he was spared the thrashing and told to go out and 'develop some sort of brain'.[7]

Similar honesty came to Farage's rescue on a CCF field trip when, on a very hot day, he and a colleague were assigned as emergency back-up at a location right next to a welcoming pub. The result was inevitable, and on the return journey Farage and his fellow beer-drinker vomited over the seats of the coach and colleagues' smart CCF kit. Farage claims he explained to the master in charge how they'd been unable to resist the temptation placed in their way. The master accepted their excuse and let them off. 'Drink providently, boys,' he advised them. 'And do not run before you can walk, or, in your case, stagger before you can march.'[8] Dangerous territory, though, for the son of an alcoholic. For a while in his mid-teens, Farage seriously considered joining the army, and even had an interview for a three-year short-service commission. He knew, however, that he'd be hopeless at obeying orders.

Although the college was only five miles from central London, it enjoyed an outer London atmosphere. 'Dulwich had the air of a great public school,' says one pupil who was in Farage's year. 'The grounds had been painted by [Camille] Pissarro [in 1871]. But it was small-minded suburban. There were more kids from small towns and villages around Kent than from central London. It was a very different population from that at Westminster or St Paul's. It's not the same now.'

Located so near to Westminster, it was not difficult for the college to attract top-rank politicians to speak. In 1978, the school was addressed by one of Margaret Thatcher's closest advisers, the cerebral Sir Keith Joseph. He attacked the Callaghan Labour government, and argued that people and the market could look after themselves. 'I had never joined anything in my life,' Farage claims, 'but the following day I joined my local Conservative party.'[9] He was never a very active member, but celebrated the following year when Thatcher became prime minister.

The former Conservative prime minister Edward Heath visited Dulwich; and Farage also recalls assailing the new left-wing leader of the Greater London Council, Ken Livingstone. But most significant was a visit by Enoch Powell, only a few weeks before Farage left the school in 1982. Powell had been a long-standing opponent of Britain joining the European Community in 1973, but was probably even better known for public opposition to non-white immigration, as exemplified by his notorious Rivers of Blood speech in 1968. Powell 'dazzled me for once into awestruck silence', Farage later said. He instantly became one of Farage's great political heroes.[10]

In his memoirs, Farage has described how he, too, loved championing unfashionable causes, and challenging conventional wisdom:

> Whenever I encountered interventionist authority, I was at the forefront of the dissidents. Whenever I encountered unthinking acceptance of doctrine, whether about the news or history, I challenged it fiercely. Whatever my own views, I would champion any neglected damsel in distress amongst ideas against the dragons of prejudice. I fought fiercely for anarchy, CND doves and warmongering hawks, Christianity, atheists, the pro- and anti-abortion (NOT pro-choice and pro-life) factions, feminism, chauvinism . . .

This was not mere puppy play-fighting. I had discovered in myself a passionate loathing for received opinion.[11]

Farage was confirmed in the Church of England when he was thirteen – 'a voluntary thing' – but slowly lost his faith: 'I think by the time I was eighteen I was pretty much a non-believer.'[12]

Then he claims that one lunchtime, aged fourteen, he discovered in the college library John Stuart Mill's great work *On Liberty*, and this passage in particular:

The only purpose for which power can be rightfully exercised over any member of a civilised community, against his will, is to prevent harm to others. His own good, either physical or moral, is not a sufficient warrant . . . Over himself, over his own body and mind, the individual is sovereign.[13]

'These instantly became sacred words,' Farage has said (in a very rare reference to reading any book). 'Self-determination,' he says, 'remains at the heart of my moral beliefs and was to become the core principle of my politics.'[14]

In his later years, around the age of sixteen, the spitting, yobbish Farage of the Bromley train developed into a smart, well-dressed figure – a 'dandy' almost, in the style of his father Guy, at a time when the ITV series *Brideshead Revisited* and the film *Chariots of Fire* had come to influence public school culture. One account has Farage hiding his box of snuff from teachers, and walking round with an old-fashioned cane. Another recollects him carrying round a rolled-up umbrella 'like he'd just stepped out of the stockbrokers'.[15]

'He suddenly started wearing a striped blazer and wearing a boater,' says a third classmate. 'I just thought it was very strange. Why would he become this very public schoolboy – round about our O-level time? I didn't get it, didn't understand what made him change. He went from being messy, tie down and scuffed shoes to suddenly the model of looking like he went to Eton. He put "blakeys" [steel heel protectors] on his shoes – they made you click as you walked. It seemed to be an overnight transformation from being one of the naughty boys.' Indeed, Farage seemed almost to go in the reverse direction to his contemporaries. 'The rest of us, becoming teenagers, would slightly adapt our uniform. We'd turn our ties round to make them really thin, carrying army bags rather than briefcases, and he went totally the opposite way, and we all just thought "What's he doing?"'

Another Old Alleynian says:

> People generally wore black jackets and occasionally blue blazers, particularly in summer, and didn't take trouble with their appearance, but Nigel Farage was rather distinctive. He wore a dark blue double-breasted blazer that was extremely smart and very well fitting and obviously expensive, and immaculately pressed trousers, and his black shoes were always very highly polished. He most reminded me of the Secretary of an upmarket golf club – that kind of official air. But the most distinctive thing, to top it all off, he had a rose in his buttonhole. Even then he gave off the air of someone of 17 or 18 going on 40 or 50. He was very mature.

The same Old Boy recalls playing rugby with Farage on a 'wet and muddy winter's day' in a house match, 'and we were all dishevelled at the end of the game but Farage, his kit was as clean at the end as it was at the beginning. You wouldn't have guessed he'd been playing in a match – he must have been standing by the edge most of the time. There were 29 very dirty boys, and Nigel Farage.'

A senior boy who helped out in the school library also remembers a boorish arrogance about him:

> I was on the front desk stamping people's books in and out and telling people to be quiet, and Farage came in and started just being a bit loud and noisy, and refused to be quiet, with a kind of, 'What are you going to do about it, then?' attitude. I seem to remember he was wearing a Union Jack handkerchief as well, and at the time I thought 'What an idiot!' I got the impression he was trying to draw a bit of attention to himself, just enjoying

sticking two fingers up at the rules, and of course 40 years on I see the same behaviour. Sometimes I wonder if it's provocation for provocation's sake.

As Farage got older so his rebellious streak grew. 'I always questioned authority,' he says. 'I suppose I was a bit of a wind-up merchant, really.'[16]

Despite all this, in the spring of 1981, not long after Farage's seventeenth birthday, David Emms, the Master of Dulwich College – the school's traditional name for the head teacher – appointed him a prefect for his final year.

The decision caused uproar among the teachers. In the teaching body – known as the Common Room – Farage's appointment was debated at length in the annual gathering to discuss the proposed new prefects. 'The meeting became enormously heated,' former English master Bob Jope has recalled. 'A significant number of staff, young and old, from various departments, expressed concern at Nigel Farage being made a prefect . . . The accusation from some staff was that Nigel had voiced views that were not simply right-wing, but views that were racist . . . not the views that a school should tolerate.'[17]

Allies of Farage say that Jope's criticism stemmed from his personal left-leaning outlook. He was a 'lovable hippy type, a crusty of his time', one old boy recalls, and Jope sang in a teachers' rock band called Breaking Class, which performed occasionally at school. 'He was a cool teacher, and we all liked him,' remembers another old boy. 'He sounded like Elvis, but sang Bob Dylan.'[18] Indeed, Jope was undoubtedly one of those whom Farage meant by the 'Bob Dylan set' among the Dulwich staff.[19]

Yet it wasn't Bob Jope who led the protests about Farage's promotion, but Chloe Deakin, an even younger, female colleague in the English department. She was so shocked by what she'd heard that when it was clear that the Master was pressing ahead with Farage's appointment regardless, she wrote the following letter to David Emms:

Dear Master

I am happy to say that I am not acquainted with NP Farage . . . — happy, because judging from the reports I have received he is not someone with whom I would wish to be acquainted . . .

You will recall that at the recent, and lengthy, meeting about the selection of prefects, the remark by a colleague that Farage was a ' fascist, but that was no reason why he would not make a good prefect' invoked considerable reaction from members of the Common Room. Another colleague, who teaches the boy, described his publicly professed racist and neo-fascist views; and he cited a particular incident in which Farage was so offensive to a boy in his set, that he had to be removed from the lesson. This master stated his view that that behaviour was precisely why the boy should not be made a prefect. Yet another colleague described how, at a CCF camp organised by the College, Farage and others had marched through a quiet Sussex village very late at night shouting Hitler youth songs; and when it was suggested by a master that boys who expressed such views 'don't really mean them', the College chaplain himself commented that, on the contrary, in his experience views of that kind expressed by boys of that age are deep-seated, and are meant.

At the end of that meeting I had not a scintilla of doubt that after the facts disclosed to you, Farage's nomination would no longer be considered. Nor, I imagine, had my colleagues: otherwise, we would have expressed ourselves even more strongly.

But yesterday I was told by a senior boy, in terms of disgust, that Farage was indeed to be selected; and today, of course, his appointment was announced in Assembly — an announcement, I gather, which was met with disbelief and derision. To say that it is too late to reverse this decision, or that Farage's activities will be restricted to particular areas of College life, or that he will be supervised within them, is futile . . .

You will appreciate that I regard this as a very serious matter. I have often heard you tell our senior boys that they are the nation's future leaders. It is our collective responsibility to ensure that these leaders are enlightened and compassionate. As you know, the national and educational press has recently given much prominence to

the growing concern at the exploitation of school pupils by extremists
of all kinds. A school of the stature and high reputation of Dulwich
College which openly condemned the recent troubles in Brixton, and
offered its facilities freely to the forces of law and order, ought not
to be seen inside or outside its confines to be giving its endorsement,
expressly or by implication, to budding extremists of the opposite
kind.

I am by disposition, tolerant; and in politics, moderate. But as a
member of the Common Room, I find it distasteful that a boy such
as Farage should have bestowed upon him the prestige of office and
authority: were I a parent or a pupil, I would find it profoundly so.

In view, as I am aware, of the wide concern within the College
about this matter, I am sending a copy of this letter to the chairman
of the Common Room.

Yours very sincerely,
Chloe Deakin[20]

It was a very strong letter, and brave of Chloe Deakin to challenge
the Master's decision, especially when she was only twenty-four
and had only been teaching for a couple of years. And Deakin was
rather different from some English teachers at the school, not easy
to dismiss as trendy or left-leaning. Neat and elegantly dressed,
Deakin lived with her fiancé in Albany, the exclusive mansion block
off London's Piccadilly. She later left teaching to become a senior
civil servant in the Education Department.

Her letter made no difference. David Emms stuck to his decision.
'I was responsible for his salvation,' Emms told me in 2013, when
extracts from Deakin's letter were first revealed on Channel 4.

I saw potential in him. I thought of him as a naughty boy who
had got up the noses of the teaching staff for reasons that are his
chirpiness and cheekiness. They wanted to expel him. I think
it was naughtiness rather than racism. I saw good in him and he
responded to being made a prefect. I saw considerable potential
in this chap and I was proved right.[21]

Emms died in 2015. His deputy Terry Walsh, who has also since died, told me that Farage liked to provoke left-wing teachers. Walsh agreed that Farage might sometimes express support for the National Front, or the even more extreme neo-Nazi British Movement, 'among his contemporaries, and probably to some members of staff, because he knew it would rile them'.

> Like most schools there was quite a strong left-wing element among the staff . . . I think at times he adopted a sort of façade . . . You know: 'If you think I'm that sort of chap, then I am that sort of chap,' and so on. But I don't think he ever, ever believed that. You know, he was too caring and considerate of other people.

It was merely 'a joke', Walsh recalled, and claimed to have said so back in 1981. 'Like a lot of those people, they didn't have a sense of humour. You can't deal with the Farages of this world if you haven't got a sense of humour, or a sense of the ridiculous.'[22]

In *Fighting Bull*, published before the Deakin letter became public, Farage said the 'outrage' among some staff was because they 'particularly deplored my spirited defence of Enoch Powell'.[23] When the Channel 4 film was broadcast, Farage dismissed the accusation about Hitler youth songs as 'completely silly'. He didn't know 'the words' of such songs, he said. As for racist remarks: 'Yes, of course, I said some ridiculous things . . . not necessarily racist things . . . it depends how you define it.' Yes, he had been excluded from class 'dozens of times' and, he said, he might simply have been winding up his critics. 'Was I a difficult, bolshie teenager who pushed the boundaries of debate further than perhaps I ought to have done? Yes . . . Have I ever been a member of any extremist organisation, left or right? No.'[24]

Many of Nigel Farage's contemporaries concur that he was simply a Conservative right-winger, an admirer of Margaret Thatcher, Enoch Powell and Keith Joseph. But there are several people whose memories go well beyond that. They accuse Farage of being significantly racist or anti-Semitic, particularly in his early years at Dulwich.

One Jewish pupil recalls a climate in which it wasn't unusual to hear anti-Semitic or racist comments in school. 'I got it,' he says. 'Kids from India or Pakistan got it.' He specifically remembers how Farage would sidle up to him and say, 'Hitler was right', or 'Gas 'em' – in obvious reference to the Nazi concentration camps. 'I think I felt my tactic was to affect not to care, and to keep my head down, and show that it hadn't got to me.'

This Jewish contemporary remembers Farage explaining how his name was originally Huguenot:

> And I remember saying to him afterwards: 'So you are also from a family who came to this country under threat of genocide? That's interesting.' And he said: 'Yes.' And I said: 'Isn't your attitude to Jews and Blacks out of kilter?' And he said: 'I suppose so.' He was quite capable of being reflective, and intelligent and quite charming. And you see that now, absolutely.

The boy had relatives who were murdered in the Holocaust. He 'despised' Farage, he says, but he 'never entirely hated him' as a person. 'I was thirteen at the time, and we went our separate ways, and I just avoided him thereafter.' And Farage didn't seem that threatening because he carried out the abuse on his own.

> I didn't feel bullied, and I might have done if he had acolytes bearing down on me as a group. Of course, he was provocative. He was provocative to everyone – he was eccentric. But he had no clique; he wasn't a classic bully with his gang. He was very much a loner. I kind of thought he was slightly mad, a nutter, as David Cameron later said, or a 'fruit-cake'.

Strangely, more than forty years on, he now feels more strongly about what happened than he did at the time. Revisiting the experience recently 'made me realise quite how much I'd bottled up'. His memories of Dulwich College are quite 'foggy', but not what Farage said to him. 'Those words, that voice, retain an icy clarity to this day – in part I guess due to his ubiquity in the UK media.'

In 2019, the website of the former *Independent* newspaper published an anonymous article from a Dulwich Old Boy who spoke in similar vein. It was in the form of a letter addressed to Nigel Farage. The former Dulwich pupil claimed that he and Farage had been 'close friends', and that he'd once stayed at Farage's home, where 'your mother did do a fantastic great British breakfast for us'. And he added: 'I remember the way you enchanted people at school, senior teachers and fellow pupils alike. Your English project on fishing enthralled everyone.'

Yet the anonymous correspondent also recalled the 'keen interest' Farage had in the fact that the initials of his name – NF – were the same as the National Front, and how he doodled on his school books with the NF's symbol (which involved the 'N' and 'F' merged together). 'Nigel Farage, NF, National Front. I remember watching you draw it,' he told Farage. 'Just a laugh, eh, Nigel?' The letter writer remembers Farage frequently crying 'Send 'em home', his citing the name of the former British fascist leader Oswald Mosley, and singing a song which went 'gas them all, gas 'em all, gas them all', to the chorus of the wartime song 'Bless 'em all' made famous by George Formby.

'I can't forget the words,' the anonymous letter writer told Farage, but they were so 'vile' that 'I can't bring myself to write the rest of it'. It would be easy to dismiss this 'letter' as a political opponent attacking Farage under cover of anonymity. Yet the writer said he was a '51 per cent reluctant Remainer' who had thought Farage had been 'absolutely right to challenge the EU' robustly, and he had thought 'Good on Nigel' in the past for the amusement provided by Farage's speeches in the European Parliament.[25]

Bob Jope thinks he was probably the master referred to in the second pararaph of Chloe Deakin's letter, who threw Farage out of class for yelling 'anti-Semitic abuse'. 'I can see the room in my mind's eye,' says Jope. 'English area, downstairs, year 11 (as we'd now say): "Shut up, you Jew!" I forget what prompted him: I guess he *wanted* to be thrown out – the only occasion in my teaching career that I did that, I think.'[26] The Jewish victim of the abuse is thought to have been Peter Ettedgui, who says that around the age of thirteen and fourteen he did suffer 'frequent anti-Semitic verbal abuse by Farage'.[27]

'He was seventeen, going on sixty,' another contemporary, Nick Gordon Brown, has said. 'He looked like a middle-aged man when he was a sixth-former. He was a very vocal National Front supporter. There was no hiding it at all. He always referred to "our black and brown friends". He used to talk about voluntary repatriation. He saw me as someone he wanted to provoke ... There was a Jewish lad at school whom he was horrible to. With Jewish schoolmates, he made no secret of his distaste for them. What you see now, is what he was like then.'[28]

'He was a deeply unembarrassed racist,' says David Edmonds, who was in the same class as Farage when they were about fifteen. 'He used words like "wogs" and "Pakis". He didn't like Jews very much and came out with the usual anti-Semitic tropes. We could never be friends, but although I am Jewish – and this may seem odd, and I would feel very differently today – I didn't dislike him. He relished rubbing people up the wrong way. But I think that his far-right politics, his racism and English nationalism were also quite firmly ingrained. He had the sense that England was being destroyed by waves of immigrants. I think his main racist feelings were against what he called "wogs" – Blacks. The idea that he wasn't a racist is 100 per cent incorrect. He was a racist. Wherever you draw the line, by whatever definition, he was a racist.'[29]

Tim France says Farage openly 'supported the British Movement [BM]', the extremist group which later called itself the British National Socialist Movement. He recalls Farage as 'very vocal', how he chanted 'BM, BM. We are British Nazi men', and how he even did Nazi salutes. France also remembers a repetitive chant similar to the song mentioned by the anonymous letter writer: 'gas them all, gas 'em all, gas them all.' 'He just used to go round chanting that. He consciously and vocally positioned himself as a very extreme right-winger. This was when he was eighteen.'[30]

But the picture is confused. Old Boys from his time probably divide fairly equally. For everyone who recalls Farage voicing extreme views, another will say they heard nothing untoward. 'I would never have said he said anything racist or insulting to people,' says Jonathan Mayne. 'He was larger than life and also quite self-deprecating in his humour. I don't think he was seen to be malicious. He was unconventional. He said things that were not everyone's cup of tea.'[31]

Nor does Jon Benjamin think Farage was anti-Semitic. 'Being Jewish, I think I'd remember that.'[32] Ian Oakley Smith says, 'Nigel's views at the time wouldn't be exceptional, so they probably didn't stand out as much as they would today.'[33]

Nigel Farage responded to these allegations of racism and anti-Semitism:

> Let's get one thing straight. I joined the Conservative party in 1978, and thought all of the far right parties/movements to be ludicrous/barmy/dangerous. There were some hard left class-of-1968 masters [who] joined the College and several of us thoroughly enjoyed winding them up. Terms of abuse thrown around between fifteen-year-olds were limitless; there were no boundaries. I think red-haired boys fared especially badly.[34]

Despite his own record as a miscreant, Farage actually thought Dulwich should be tougher on boys who misbehaved. This was an era when corporal punishment was still legal, though the cane was rarely applied at Dulwich. Fellow prefect Roger Gough, who is now Conservative leader of Kent County Council, recalls one of the get-togethers which the Master held with the prefects every year. Once David Emms had delivered his address, he called for questions. 'Nigel sort of sprang to attention,' Gough says, 'heels clicked, back straight, and said: "Sir, there is a growing problem with indiscipline within the school. We should use the cane more." And David Emms said: "I'm not sure where it is, actually." And Terry Walsh, the chain-smoking deputy Master and head of the cadet force said: "I've got about six of them in my study!" The rising tide of anarchy wasn't evident to the rest of us. It's almost a measure – like all things with Nigel – of how much of it was an act.'[35]

Farage's promotion to be a prefect partly stemmed from his success at golf. Back in Downe, he and his brother Andrew often worked in the shop at the golf course on Saturday mornings, then played in the afternoon. Meanwhile, Nigel was picked for the three-man Dulwich team who in 1981 reached the finals of the national Schools Golf Championship in Surrey. They finished equal ninth overall in a contest held in terrible conditions which had to be reduced to nine holes. 'We owe our fairly high position,' the college magazine reported, 'to the excellent performance of Nigel Farage who, had he not faltered at the last, could so easily have won the individual prize.'[36] Farage needed a par four on the last hole, only for the wind to carry his ball up away into the scrub, and he needed six strokes to complete the hole. The individual prize would have been worth winning, for traditionally it entailed a golf scholarship to Arizona College in America.

Farage also took part in an initiative to encourage boys to take more interest in financial matters. The Investment Society required boys to decide which public companies were worth backing, and then small blocks of shares were bought and sold on the stock market. The trading was carried out by Farage's father Guy, through his City firm.

As Farage neared the end of his time at Dulwich, most of his contemporaries were planning to go to university, and many were about to take Oxbridge entrance exams, at a time when around a third of the Dulwich sixth form ended up at Oxford or Cambridge. Nigel's mother Barbara feared the thought of him following his father into the City, and urged him to consider university too. He would make an excellent barrister; the bar could be well paid, she suggested, and left open the possibility of other careers, such as politics.

Farage was certainly clever enough to go to university. 'He didn't work very hard, frankly – like a lot of boys of seventeen,' says one former master who taught him in the sixth form. He estimates Farage was in the third quartile at the school academically, but then Dulwich was extremely selective in its intake. Farage was adamant, however, that higher education wasn't for him. He'd decided that after A levels at eighteen he wanted to follow his father into the City of London, and make lots of money. Even at school he'd shown business acumen – by running a shoe-shining business. 'He paid the juniors to clean shoes,' says classmate Nick Owen, 'and then skimmed a commission off the top.'[37] 'There were ... one or two rackets going on,' Farage once said.[38] Another business involved buying and selling physical silver, at a time when the price was soaring.

In those days, quite a few Dulwich boys skipped university and headed straight for the Square Mile. 'I couldn't wait to get cracking,' Farage once said. 'I don't want to be a scruffy student', he thought. 'I want to be out there.'[39]

The former Labour transport secretary Lord (Andrew) Adonis recalls being guest of honour at a Dulwich speech day when he was schools minister in the Blair/Brown government. As Adonis spoke, he spotted Farage in the front row, and later learned he was there to watch his son Sam receive a rugby prize. Afterwards the two politicians spent a long time chatting, even though their politics could hardly be more different. Adonis was struck by how Dulwich College took 'an odd pride' in the fact that Farage took them so seriously. 'It shows a very upper middle-class and middle-class Englishness,' Adonis says, 'and tells you how good he is at getting on with these people when he's plotting their downfall.'[40]

At one Dulwich event, around 2009, the former Master David Emms would delight Farage by quietly confessing that he'd voted for him in the recent European elections.

'Life at the school will not be the same without him,' Emms had apparently written in Farage's report the summer he left.[41]

Nigel Farage got A levels in economics, geography and history, but his fairly mediocre grades didn't matter much since he wasn't applying to university. A contemporary recalls how at that year's leavers' event, held on 12 July 1982 – the Twelfth in Northern Ireland, or Orangemen's Day – Farage was as flamboyant and provocative as ever. He turned up with an orange rose in his buttonhole.

Teacher Neil Fairlamb says he told his pupil on the day of his departure in 1982: 'Nigel, I have a feeling you will go far in life, but whether in fame or infamy, I don't really know.' Fairlamb adds that Farage looked back at him and replied: 'Sir, as long as it's far, I don't care which.'[42]

3

CITY TRADER

A 'yuppie' – that's what Nigel Farage said he wanted to be – the 1980s term for young, upwardly mobile professionals who came to symbolise the Thatcher era. 'I was fiercely ambitious when I was 18,' Farage later said. 'Fiercely ambitious. And that ambition was to succeed in business and make a lot of money.'[1] And for him the City was the obvious route.

He didn't fancy the Stock Exchange, however. His father was too well known there, and he didn't like the idea of people thinking he'd exploited the family connection. A solution arose one weekend just before Christmas 1980 while playing at West Kent Golf Club. Between holes, Farage explained his City ambitions to Bob McPhie, one of the older members with whom he was playing – a Scot who was then in his late fifties. They continued the conversation over a few beers back at the clubhouse.

Farage hardly knew McPhie, though he'd frequently seen him around the club. The older man explained how he was managing director of Maclaine Watson & Co., a firm on the London Metal Exchange (LME). It might be the sort of thing Nigel was looking for. Perhaps he would like to come and visit the business in a week or two.

Farage researched the background. Maclaine Watson & Co., he would have discovered, was among the last remnants of a trading firm which had been founded by two Britons in 1827 on the island of Java, then one of the Dutch colonies in the Far East. From cotton, coffee and opium, the firm had expanded into other commodities across the Far East and had become one of Asia's biggest trading companies.

One morning around the start of 1981, Farage got up early, put on his suit and polished brogues and took the train to London Bridge. His day with Maclaine Watson was a great success, and Bob McPhie suggested that a job would be available once Farage had completed his A levels. Naturally, he accepted the offer.

The London Metal Exchange was – and still is – a global institution. It was founded in 1877, but the market dates back 300 years before that when trading was conducted in London coffee houses. The LME's job is to oversee and regulate the fluctuating and risky worldwide industrial markets in several non-ferrous metals – copper, lead, zinc, aluminium and nickel, at the time Farage joined Maclaine Watson in 1982. Subsequently tin, aluminium alloys, steel and cobalt were added to the list.

The most visible part of the Exchange is The Ring, with its 'open-outcry' trading. With phones pressed to their ears – often both ears – traders sit or stand round a circle of padded benches shouting out prices and details of what they want to buy and sell, or making tic-tac signals with their fingers. The Ring – said to be the last exchange in Europe where 'open-outcry' trading still occurs – is surrounded by traders' booths, with large electronic boards above them showing the latest prices. It operates from 11.40 a.m. to 5 p.m. each day, in five-minute trading spells. But business in The Ring is now a relatively small part of the twenty-four-hour electronic trading which LME members carry on away from the floor.

Some LME business is for immediate delivery, but much of it is in futures – officially for delivery in three months' time, a period chosen back in 1877, when it took that long for ships to transport copper from ports in Chile to London. It's now about securing the price in advance of physical need for the client so they can plan ahead. And the LME owns a network of approved warehouses around the world where the metals can be delivered or collected.

Having passed his A levels, Farage took the summer off to play golf and go fishing – a lifelong passion. He joined Maclaine Watson on 1 September 1982 at their offices in Old Broad Street, where the firm had its own trading room. The City of London, like several other great British institutions – such as horse racing, the army and boxing – was a successful mixture of upper-class public schoolboys and working-class barrow boys.

Farage found it to be:

> a mixture of an old gentlemen's club and very aggressive young men; the Green Suit Brigade with white socks who lived in places such as Basildon and Southend – 'Sarf End', as they would say. It was a cross-section of different parts of society . . . But the vast majority of the men on the trading floor (they were exclusively men in 1982) were from the Essex Marshes. I liked the mix in the City – nobody cared how posh or how rough you were; you were rated on how much money you could make.[2]

Farage, unlike many middle-class people, has always felt very comfortable with people from other classes. And his time in the City helped develop his skills in communicating with people of all backgrounds and nationalities. He started work in the Square Mile at a historic time. It was the end of an era – many City institutions and practices hadn't changed since the nineteenth century. 'It was the dying days of a gentlemen's club,' he recalled in 2011, 'magnificent, socially wonderful but going nowhere – there was still a whiff of P. G. Wodehouse about people who toddled off to the City all day and did things that nobody understood at all.'[3]

A huge change had been heralded in October 1979 with Margaret Thatcher's decision to abolish exchange controls on foreign currency transactions. This not only greatly reduced the government's ability to run the economy but also paved the way for a global economy. Hundreds of staff at the Bank of England lost their jobs but the rest of the City prospered greatly from the decision.

Maclaine Watson had enjoyed membership of the LME for decades, though by 1982 it was no longer independent, having just been taken over by the highly aggressive American investment bank Drexel Burnham Lambert. Later that decade, Drexel would achieve notoriety and bankruptcy through scandals involving the junk bond trader Michael Milken, the model for Gordon Gekko in Oliver Stone's 1987 film *Wall Street*.

At first, Farage was allowed none of the excitement of high-adrenaline commodities trading. He was confined to a backroom office with the tedious task of processing paperwork for transactions agreed by colleagues. He was paid £4,000 a year, with a bonus at the end of his first twelve months of £300. 'I was very chuffed,' he says.[4] And he got his bonus, despite one day losing a silver warrant worth £90,000, 'which was never found despite a thorough ransacking of the building'.[5]

It wasn't long, however, before Farage became a trader. 'The pressure of being a market-maker in a busy market,' he once said, 'when you've got people all around you screaming and shouting at you, and you're dealing in numbers, and it's like that, that, that, that – that's pretty pressurised. That's why it's a young man's job. You don't get many fifty-year-old money-brokers: they can't do it anymore.'[6] 'When it was busy, my goodness me, it was busy. You can't imagine the pressure,' he has also said.[7]

'At the age of eighteen,' he later wrote, 'I was handling millions, and drinking more or less continuously . . . throughout the day and night, but youth and adrenaline sustained me.'[8]

Judge the market right and the profits could be huge; read it incorrectly and his firm would have suffered big losses. 'It taught you how to really hold your nerve, as well as admit when you had messed up. They were lessons that I would need for a career in politics.'[9] The City in the 1980s may have been 'enormous fun', but sometimes if you lost money 'you were out of the door', Farage once explained. 'I've seen people asked to leave the office immediately. And don't tell me that we were earning a lot of money for doing nothing!'[10]

'The good old days,' says trader Steven Spencer, who dealt with Farage at that time and got to know him well.

It was great fun. The brokers made money. The world was happy. Regulation hadn't started yet. It was free. It was the Wild West. We had the best time of our careers from the late '70s to the early '90s. There was a lot of money to be made, with deals to be done everywhere and it was highly competitive. Some of the best brains in the City were working at the Metal Exchange.[11]

The prospect of becoming rich was one reason Farage found the City attractive; the other was the lifestyle – one which had almost destroyed his father. And Nigel Farage's first five years in the City seem to have been one long party. After an early start, the commodities traders would work hard all morning, then often enjoy a long, alcohol-fuelled lunch.

The favourite venue was the eighteenth-century Simpson's Tavern, in Ball Court, a narrow alleyway off Cornhill, which served traditional steaks and chops, and spotted dick for pudding, and which boasts of being 'the oldest chophouse in London'. When he takes journalists back to his old City haunts, Farage loves showing them an even older watering hole only a few yards away in St Michael's Alley. The front steps of the Jamaica Wine House have been worn by the centuries: the very first coffee house in London, dating from 1652, it was mentioned by Pepys.

Other favourites were another ancient institution, Sweetings, a fish restaurant on Queen Victoria Street. If trading was busy and he was pressed for time, he'd enjoy a couple of pints of Young's and a beef roll in the fourteenth-century Lamb Tavern by the cobblestones of the indoor Leadenhall Market. Both also served up very traditional British food, and plenty of it.

In the 1980s the City of London, like Fleet Street and broadcasting, was awash with alcohol. As a result, Farage has often said, huge, costly mistakes were often made in trades struck after lunch, when a zero might be left off or added, a purchase mixed up with a sale, or someone might buy the wrong metal. Yet the errors weren't always punished. It could be 'chaos' in the afternoons. 'I remember once there was a really big cock-up,' Farage has recalled. 'I remember the boss saying, "So when did this happen?" "Half-past four yesterday afternoon." "Oh well, there we are then." The boss accepted this!'[12]

'It was unbelievable,' Farage said in 2012. 'The booze culture was mega. The drugs culture was huge. I left the drugs culture alone completely, thank goodness . . . If I had smoked cannabis I probably would have done it to excess. There was enough trouble with the booze culture, and I am one of the lucky ones. Because I really enjoy going for a drink, but I don't need it.'[13]

He'd seen with his father, drink can be very dangerous, as he acknowledged some years ago: 'Some people who go through that lifestyle are lucky and some are desperately unlucky, and you never know which you're going to be. Lots of people who were my drinking mates in the City have been through the most disastrous downward spirals, and a lot of them are dead . . . I lived through all of that and I'm very candid: I say I am lucky. I am lucky.'[14] Surprisingly, what he consumed most was port, a drink associated with eighteenth-century London, gout and after-dinner cigars. 'We'd all go back to work, all crimson,' he told the *FT* in 2016. 'That's just what we did! No one cared. I don't drink port at all now, ever.'[15]

The culture was very male and testosterone-driven – 'laddish' would be the word now – and would today be considered very politically incorrect, as he would later admit:

> I liked girls – the wicked and the tiny variety – but as extra-cur-ricular diversions . . . Somewhere at the back of my mind was the awareness that one day I would want children and a country house, and that a woman would presumably be necessary for both, but my idea of fun was trading, drinking and trading some more. I wanted life to be one long boys' club jamboree with occasional bouts of conkers on the Exchange.
>
> I was, in short, a puerile sexist in a puerile sexist world.[16]

Racism and bullying were also rife. 'There were elements of crude-ness in the City,' Farage has admitted, in 'language and behaviour' and 'things we said and did then . . . values change'. People were 'routinely abused', he says, in every way, including racially. 'That was the culture,' he admits, without condoning what happened.[17]

These were heady days. Electronic trading was transforming and globalising world markets, and the Thatcher government would famously deregulate the City with the so-called Big Bang in 1986. Long-standing rules were overturned; restrictions lifted on who was allowed to buy and sell what. Sleepy, old-fashioned, gentlemanly British firms were suddenly taken over by brash American institutions, or by European banks. 'You've ruined the best gentlemen's club in the world,' Guy Farage reportedly told Sir Nicholas Goodison, the then-chairman of the Stock Exchange, when he bumped into him one day in a lift.[18]

Yet young men in their twenties were suddenly making huge sums, as parodied by Harry Enfield's 1980s character Loadsamoney. Farage wanted his share of this revolution. 'It was just the most incredibly exciting period of time,' he says. 'And the pop stars even dressed like City brokers. I absolutely loved it.'[19]

The Big Bang saw the City cement its place as the world's foremost financial capital, ideally placed in terms of time zones between the markets of the Far East and the East Coast of America. Yet surprisingly perhaps, for someone committed to free-market capitalism, Farage is ambivalent about the 1980s financial revolution. On the one hand he said in 2011 that 'what I saw in the Eighties and Nineties was London becoming in many ways a genuine global centre for entrepreneurial flair, for innovation, for very hard work – and for creating profits'.[20] Yet he's also admitted that the Big Bang did not change the City for the better. It gave huge power to big overseas banks, most of them American. And ultimately the City would be increasingly subject to regulation by the European Community (or the European Union as it became in 1993).

In addition, the 1986 Financial Services Act which accompanied the Big Bang brought new regulators in the form of the Securities and Investments Board (later the Financial Services Authority). 'But the vast majority of those regulators (God, I hate those people) had failed in the City – they frankly did not understand what bankers and brokers were up to,' Farage says. 'The new culture beckoned in massive banks that dominated the market place, and hapless regulators simply couldn't see the wood for the trees.'[21]

Farage claims that by 1985 – when he was twenty-one – he was earning £20,000 a year, about £55,000 today. But his blossoming career was suddenly interrupted one night in November when he arrived back at Orpington station. It was late, as usual. He'd enjoyed a long lunch at an Indian restaurant that day, and then spent the evening arguing in the pub about the new Anglo-Irish Agreement which Margaret Thatcher had just signed. Farage felt it was a betrayal of the Unionists in the North.

It was a wet autumn evening. Farage lit a cigarette and walked along to the pelican crossing. 'I grasped the lamp's stalk and swung myself into the street,' he wrote in his memoirs. 'I remember nothing more.'[22] A Volkswagen Beetle braked, but it was too late. The car hit Farage and he was thrown into the air, over the vehicle and onto the kerb. He landed on his head and woke up in Bromley General Hospital with head injuries and his left leg suspended in traction. He might lose the lower leg, Farage was warned, and he would spend two months in hospital. His left leg recovered, though with a large lump of bone always sticking out, and thereafter Farage also suffered tinnitus, the condition whereby one hears ringing or noises in the ears.

It was during those two months that Farage met Clare Hayes, one of the nurses looking after him. A few months older than him, Clare had been born in Chatham in Kent, where her father worked as a charge nurse, and was actually christened Gráinne, indicative of her family's Irish roots. It undoubtedly helped their relationship that when Farage returned to work his leg remained in plaster for almost a year, so he couldn't resume his former lifestyle. There was no late-night drinking, and no commuting by train. His brother Andrew (now also working in town) drove Nigel to and from London each day in his Citroën 2CV, which gave Nigel more time with his new girlfriend. 'She was a great girl who was to make me happy for several years,' Farage has written. But he admits he was still 'immature', and 'unfit for marriage and would surely never have considered it had it not been for my brush with death'.[23]

Then, remarkably, came his second brush within a year. In the Queen's Head in Downe the following Boxing Day, Farage had ordered his customary pint only to be struck suddenly by an excruciating pain on his left side; it shot from near his kidney, through his stomach and into his groin.

Farage endured two days of pain before realising something was seriously wrong. Back at Bromley Hospital, doctors concluded that he had testicular torsion, whereby the spermatic cord twists and cuts off the blood supply to the testicle. It's treated by untwisting the testicle, followed by surgery. But just as Farage was about to be taken into the operating theatre at nearby Farnborough Hospital, a doctor challenged the diagnosis. It was merely an infection, he said. There was no need for an operation; it could be treated with antibiotics.

Yet the pain persisted. Farage's testicle swelled bigger than a lemon and grew harder, and Farage found it hard to walk or go into work. His GP referred him to a consultant who merely prescribed more antibiotics. Farage was very distressed, but his boss at Maclaine Watson advised he could get a second opinion via the firm's health insurance scheme. A private GP immediately recommended he see the Harley Street groin specialist Jerry Gilmore, who arranged an ultrasound scan. 'Oh, Mr Farage,' Gilmore announced afterwards, 'I do hope you're not planning to go anywhere too quickly . . .'[24]

Testicular cancer sounds grim, but nineteen out of twenty men survive it. However, Farage's left testicle would have to be removed, in an operation at Princess Grace Hospital in Marylebone. 'I didn't need two,' he wrote later in *Fighting Bull*, 'but I had quite liked the sense of security which the extra one had provided . . . Nonetheless, when they offered me an artificial one to supply me with greater social confidence, I refused.'[25] But removing the testicle wasn't the end of his troubles.

Jerry Gilmore told Farage that, as a result of the blood tests, 'it was almost inconceivable that I would not have secondary tumours in my stomach and lungs. I was terrified.' He thought he was being told he was 'almost certainly riddled with cancerous tumours'. He would need a full CAT scan.

For forty-eight hours, Farage feared the worst – that at twenty-two his life would end before it had barely started. 'It was a horrendous experience,' Farage once said. 'There was an overwhelming feeling of it being so unfair. I hadn't done any of the things I had wanted to do. Those two days were like torture.'

Eventually, his oncologist turned up in Farage's room to find him smoking, drinking 'a glass of something' and on the phone placing bets as he watched the racing on TV. He brought good news. The cancer hadn't spread:

And he came in and sort of stared at me, and he said, 'Well, Mr Farage, after an experience like this, many of my patients spend the rest of their life drinking carrot juice, and some go the other way. And I suspect you're a member of the latter category.' He grins at me and lets out his surprisingly endearing laugh, a sort of spluttering hiss that sounds like a steam train leaving the station.[26]

Instead of a course of highly unpleasant chemotherapy, Farage would have to attend London Bridge Hospital twice a week for blood tests, which was 'psychologically worse'.[27] If his protein count rose, he would have to have chemotherapy after all. All went well. The tests became less frequent, and the cancer didn't return, and having only one testicle made no difference. 'He just couldn't get over the fact that he *was* able to have children,' his mother Barbara told a TV audience thirty years later.[28]

For the biographer searching for what fired Nigel Farage's rockets and propelled him into politics, it was probably these two occasions, a few months apart, when he stared death in the face. 'No one who's been through what I went through could ever say that it is out of their mind totally. I'm very much a fatalist. Life's for the living. You've got to follow your heart and I won't pretend that didn't shape my decision to leave business and enter politics.'[29]

Nigel and Clare bought a small, modern, two-bedroom terraced house in Farnborough, three miles from Downe, and married in July 1988. Their first son, Sam, was born the following January, and a second, Tom, at the end of 1991.

Farage had left Maclaine Watson after four years, around 1986, to join a small trading firm called R. J. Rouse & Co., part of Mercantile House Holdings, in what was another golf course appointment. He was tempted by the offer of a much broader portfolio. The firm was run by a very traditional character, John Barkshire, a colonel in the Territorial Army, but very soon Rouse was also subject to the Big Bang revolution, and was bought up by the French bank Crédit Lyonnais, to become Crédit Lyonnais Rouse.

It was while still working in the City in his early twenties that

Farage founded a group called Farage's Foragers. The 'foraging' was a sort of extension of his childhood habit of combing the country-side around Downe for artefacts of any kind – old bottles, the lids of pots or ancient clay pipes – much of it discarded from the grand old houses round the area (and some of which he still has). Only now Farage's foraging involved trips to First World War battlefields in France and Flanders – it made him a bit of a 'geek', Farage once admitted, on the 'outskirts' of what was considered a suitable hobby. It was a hobby inherited from his father – 'a combination of my passion for First World War history and the knowledge gleaned from years of study, together with my other passions for a good, well-cooked meal, a pint of ale (or three) and the company of friends, old and new'.[30] They became known as 'bottlefield tours' says fellow forager, and future political colleague, Godfrey Bloom. 'I remember we were in Ypres. It was about three in the morning. We must have drunk the restaurant completely dry. It was one hell of a session, and I called time. I staggered up into bed, and Farage shouted at me: "Lightweight!" And that really sums him up.'[31]

It was a period when there were still quite a few surviving veterans from the Great War, and Farage would occasionally invite one of them to enliven the trip with first-hand testimony. City colleague Steven Spencer remembers Farage displayed an early sign of his politics when they took with them a British army veteran who was Canadian (or possibly Australian) – and the group had to pass through passport control on the return trip. Immigration officials wanted the Commonwealth veteran to go through a different gate. 'He confronted the border guards,' says Spencer. 'German, French and Belgians were going through the EU citizens' gate and this Canadian had to go somewhere else. He was passionately pro-ally, pro-Commonwealth, anti-Europe. Nigel was really sensitive about it and said: "This man won a medal in the war for us, you know." Nigel was pretty annoyed.'[32]

Though his interest in military history was largely confined to the 1914–18 war, he was also fascinated by one aspect of the Second World War. His childhood home, at 4 West Hill Cottages in Downe, was just over half a mile, across the West Kent golf course, from the main runway at Biggin Hill. And every May or June in his late teens and early twenties, Farage would attend the Biggin Hill Air Fair. It was an era when many Battle of Britain pilots were still alive, so Farage says he 'always headed for the veterans' tent where men of "The Few" were selling and signing their autobiographies. So I was lucky to meet many of the famous names that helped save our country.' The Air Fair gave Farage the 'added spice' of meeting German veterans, among them Adolf Galland, who was credited with victories against more than a hundred Allied aircraft.[33]

In the City, in 1989, Farage also founded a lunching group for people who shared his increasingly Eurosceptic politics. The Column Club met on the first Monday of every month at Simpson's Tavern off Cornhill. 'The criteria for membership,' he's said, 'were an appreciation of things British (with particular reference to cricket), a resilient liver, and a hearty appetite, and a deep mistrust of the European Union.'[34] Others, however, recall that the politics of some members of Farage's Column Club were on the extreme right of politics, sympathisers with or members of the British National Party.

Farage had been increasingly unhappy at Rouse, whose foreign owners interfered a lot more than he'd been used to during his early days. The French might also enjoy long wine-filled lunches, but Farage's new bosses weren't so tolerant of the City's old drunken ways. One day he took out to lunch at Sweetings an old friend and client called Joe Corazza. It turned into a long meal, and a very expensive one – several pints of beer, various fish courses, Chablis and a couple of decanters of port. 'It may just be,' Farage later wrote, 'that our intake that afternoon was a trifle excessive by the standards of the modern City.'[35]

Corazza came up with the suggestion that Farage might like to take him as a guest onto the trading floor of the London Metal Exchange. But when they got there, Corazza proceeded to insult brokers and had to be escorted out by staff. Farage was in big trouble, not least because Rouse was at that point involved in a serious dispute with the LME. He was sacked on the spot.

'I knew that I was unemployable,' Farage has said. So, at the start of 1994, he set up on his own. 'I was henceforth to be my own boss.'[36] Farage Futures rented space from Refco, an American commodities company, who also let Farage use various facilities at their City offices. But now he had the independence which provided a platform for subsequent events. 'So the EU Commission can add Joe Corazza to its blacklist of "Those Who made Farage Possible",' he joked in his memoirs.[37] And those who made Brexit possible, too.

Farage Futures issued one share to his mother Barbara and Farage held the rest. The firm was officially registered in Chatham, at the offices of a young accountant called Craig Mackinlay (of whom more later). Farage was earning a lot more than he was at the LME, but he had to work much harder, too. His new business involved plenty of foreign travel, notably to the United States, and to Italy. And Farage Futures, which also involved his younger brother Andrew and employed five staff, seems to have been a contented crew. The office had a drinks cabinet, and there were none of the modern City rules of behaviour. His long-standing trading customer Steven Spencer recalls: 'I would wander into a smoke-filled room, with tobacco smoke about four feet from the floor, with a bunch of very happy traders [and] good chemistry around Nigel.'[38] Farage himself smoked a pipe. 'One of my largest expenses was suit dry-cleaning,' says Malcolm Freeman, one of his traders.[39]

'He had a good team of very good brokers who knew the market backwards,' Spencer adds. 'He was very professional; he was very outspoken, and very straight. If he didn't like what was going on in the market, he would say. Nigel has many faults but lack of integrity is not one of them.'[40]

'Everything they were doing – there was no front running or insider trading – Nigel played with a very straight bat,' says Malcolm Freeman:

Occasionally he could get a little bit invisible when it was his round, but whatever your pay or agreement was with him, I would say and the other guys would too, he met it absolutely to the penny. If he said 'Your percentage was X' – because we worked on commission – you got exactly what you thought it was. He was very, very straight on that one. Was he the best dealer in the world? No. You wouldn't put him down as a naturally talented trader, I don't think. But he was a superb clients' man. The company in many ways punched above its weight because he just had a way with people. I know he's chalk and cheese, but he has a superb way with clients. He does have a cranky but infectious sense of humour.[41]

Freeman recalls how, under the rules, Farage Futures had to be in a separate office from the main Refco dealing room, cut off by an opaque glass window. And people would hear 'shrieking laughter' from inside and go in to find what lay behind it.

'He was a natural-born salesman,' says Alex Heath, another commodities broker. 'Setting up on your own requires backing and it requires people who believe in you, and Nigel is very good at getting people to believe in him.'[42]

One colleague remembers:

Although we had hysterical fun, we did it always 100 per cent on the right side of what you should be doing. It was his company, and that's the way he chose to run it. Accounts were correct, taxes were paid; it was all done properly and above board. Looking back on it you think, 'It was because you wanted to go into politics, you don't want to be found out for paying everyone in cash or numbered bank accounts in Switzerland.' Certainly none of that happened. Everyone had a UK account and paid all their own taxes.

The business lasted eight years and some have questioned just how successful Farage Futures was financially. 'The suggestion that he was a very wealthy man in the City is probably a bit of a misnomer,' one metals broker told the *Financial Times*. 'I don't think he was anywhere near as successful as some people are portraying.'[43]

In the early noughties, Farage Futures would run into trouble. So Nigel and Andrew Farage moved under the umbrella of Natixis Metals, a subsidiary of the French bank, Natexis Banque Populaire. One of the bank's employees wasn't impressed with Farage's demands and apparent ingratitude. 'There was a sense of entitlement about him,' says Stephen Ayme:

> Independence from the bank, doing it his way, rather than the bank's way, on the basis of his own rules, not the group's principles. I remember thinking 'What a prat!' He had his demands. It had to be like this, and like that. My opinion was that it was a firm led by a guy who turned up at ten, made a few calls and had a few meetings and then would go out to lunch. It struck me that the arrangement would only be temporary, not a long-term relationship.

But Ayme quietly noted, and with some dismay, how much the political views that Farage expressed increasingly openly seemed to strike a chord with his colleagues in the metal-trading world. 'He was remarkably popular with the metal people. A lot of them lapped up his political leanings and apparent hatred of the European Union. Many thought he was right.'[44]

And his views were about to get a boost which would propel Nigel Farage into the public limelight.

4

HOOKED BY POLITICS

It was 5 October 1990. Nigel Farage was enjoying Friday evening drinks with his chums at Corney & Barrow, a wine bar on Old Broad Street, when the news came through. Margaret Thatcher and her chancellor, John Major, had decided to take the pound sterling into the Exchange Rate Mechanism (ERM), the system which tied many currencies in the European Economic Community (EEC) to each other and so limited fluctuations in exchange rates.

The decision received almost universal approval in political and economic circles, and was backed by Labour, the Liberal Democrats, the trades unions and most business organisations. Many saw Britain joining the ERM as a step towards joining the single currency that was planned by most leaders of the European Community. Thatcher had only agreed to the ERM under considerable pressure from senior colleagues – her foreign secretary Douglas Hurd and, most notably, the new and relatively unknown chancellor, John Major.

'I was incandescent,' Nigel Farage remembers. 'I am told that I spent the rest of the evening fuming and spitting like a very hot fire of green timber. "What sort of stupid, asinine moron *is* this Major . . . ?" This *cannot* work . . .! This *will* not work . . .! This will be a *disaster* . . .! Yes. Another pint please . . . This Major man is *certifiable* . . .! What does he think he is *doing* . . . ?'[1]

The question of Britain's relationship with Europe still dogged British politics seventeen years after the country joined the Community in 1973. Labour had opposed Ted Heath's decision, and insisted on revisiting the issue when the party returned to power in 1974. After a superficial renegotiation of the terms of

British membership, the government held a referendum in 1975 in which people decided by a margin of more than two to one for the UK to remain members. That didn't satisfy many Labour activists, however, among them the left-wing leader Tony Benn for whom it was a matter of British 'sovereignty'. Only eight years after the referendum, Labour fought and lost the 1983 general election on a policy of outright withdrawal, without even suggesting there should be a second plebiscite.

But the Conservatives, too, always had a small band of MPs who remained opposed to Britain's membership, among them Teddy Taylor and Peter Tapsell. Margaret Thatcher, who had famously campaigned for a Yes vote in 1975 wearing a jumper adorned with flags from all the member states, fought tenaciously as prime minister for Britain's interests, but never suggested it was time to leave. In the mid-1980s, Thatcher and her ministers played a key part in creating the single market within the Community, to encourage free trade, break down protectionist barriers and harmonise rules and regulations. When finally introduced at the start of 1993, it entailed the famous four freedoms – free movement of people, of capital, of services and of goods.

Meanwhile, the president of the European Commission from 1985 onwards, the French socialist Jacques Delors, led the charge for a single European currency – the euro – to replace individual currencies across the Community. Margaret Thatcher began to become publicly more sceptical about the speed and extent of future integration and urged radical reform of the EEC in its current form. She was an early 'Eurosceptic', as the term soon became known.

Thatcher increasingly feared that Germany and France, guided by Helmut Kohl, François Mitterrand and Jacques Delors, along with other European leaders, wanted to turn the European Community into a political project, which would see power sucked away from the individual states to the formation of a federal Europe. In 1988, Margaret Thatcher famously took aim at them in a speech in Bruges (delivered at the city's medieval watchtower): 'Let me say bluntly on behalf of Britain: we have not embarked on the business of throwing back the frontiers of the state at home, only to see a

European super-state getting ready to exercise a new dominance from Brussels.'[2]

But leading Conservatives such as Michael Heseltine, Ken Clarke and Douglas Hurd broadly supported many of the moves towards greater European integration, and the Conservatives grew increasingly divided. Labour, meanwhile, had radically changed course under Neil Kinnock, after Jacques Delors persuaded the British trades unions, in a rousing speech to their annual Congress, that the Community could help protect workers' rights against the excesses of free-market capitalism.

Until this point Nigel Farage had barely dipped a toe into political waters. Officially he was still a member of the Conservative Party, and had worked for them once or twice in local campaigns. But remarkably, in the 1989 elections to the European Parliament, Farage voted for the Green Party. One might think that the Greens stood for everything that Farage didn't, but he has always been a keen conservationist (inspired no doubt by foraging in Darwin's garden). More important, the Greens were not the fervent pro-EU group they are today; like most British left-leaning parties at that time, they were hostile to the EEC and saw it as too centralised and dominated by big business, though the Greens didn't go as far as wanting to withdraw. When he told Bob Brett, his local Tory agent, that he'd voted Green, Farage jokes that 'he very nearly collapsed and had to be revived with ardent spirits'. Farage felt that 'My vote was, personally, a hugely significant break with the past. I was striking out on my own, no longer finding refuge in the compromises offered by conventional parties.' He saw this as a direct result of his accident and illness a few years before.[3]

The Greens didn't win any seats in 1989, because Britain still used the first-past-the-post voting system for European elections. But their astonishing 14.5 per cent of the vote was almost three times that of the Liberal Democrats, in a period when green issues were becoming more prominent (following the 1986 Chernobyl disaster and early concerns about climate change). Had Britain used a proportional voting system in 1989, the Greens would have gained about a dozen seats in Brussels, and probably many more since voters would have realised that their votes could translate more directly into seats. The 1989 election showed for the first time how British voters might treat European elections as a chance to protest on a nationwide scale, and give the established parties an occasional kick.

Margaret Thatcher was ousted by Conservative MPs in 1990, only a few weeks after Britain joined the ERM, but her successor, John Major, continued to resist much of the so-called Delors plan for Europe. At their summit in Maastricht in December 1991, European leaders agreed a whole series of measures to codify employment and social regulations, and to start progress towards creating the single currency, the euro, though John Major secured important British opt-outs from these measures.

Two main groups had already taken up the Eurosceptic cause – the Bruges Group, named after Thatcher's 1988 speech, which largely comprised Conservatives; and the Campaign for an Independent Britain, which was more cross-party. Ahead of the Maastricht summit, the Campaign for an Independent Britain advertised in the London *Evening Standard* a forthcoming meeting at Methodist Central Hall in Westminster. Top billing was given to two long-standing former Cabinet ministers, the Conservative John Biffen and Labour's Peter Shore.

In questions after their speeches, there was debate about whether things could really be reformed from inside the Community, and some began asking why Britain couldn't simply withdraw from the EEC. John Harvey, a maths teacher from Sussex, got a small cheer when he stood up and volunteered to stand as an independent on a policy of withdrawal. Then Dr Alan Sked, a historian from the London School of Economics, rose to his feet and went further. 'And I intend to start a party which will lead Britain out of the EU,' John Harvey recalls him saying to the senior figures on the platform. 'If you will not take that responsibility, we will.' That was met with even louder cheers.[4]

Nigel Farage claims to have been in the audience at Westminster Central Hall, attracted there by the ad in the *Evening Standard*. He says he was also among those who crowded round Sked afterwards to learn more about his plans. Sked can't remember meeting Farage.

Although he was a university lecturer, Alan Sked was as well dressed as Farage, almost dapper, and stood out for his shock of wavy jet-black hair and his refined Scottish accent. He was a former Liberal, who'd even stood for the party, aged just twenty-two, in Paisley in the 1970 general election. And he saw his new venture not as a right-wing party, but as a 'centre mainstream liberal democratic party'.[5] A student of A. J. P. Taylor, Sked had made his name working on European history, especially the Habsburg dynasty, though many knew him for his classic Penguin book, *Post-War Britain: A Political History* (written with Chris Cook).

Following the Central Hall meeting, Sked sent out a letter to members of the Bruges Group, and recruited the first 150 members of what he called the Anti-Federalist League (AFL). He then announced that the AFL would stand several candidates at the next general election, which was legally due by the summer of 1992.

The historian in Sked had named his Anti-Federalist League after Richard Cobden and John Bright's successful mid-nineteenth-century campaign against the corn laws. 'Just as the Anti-Corn Law League converted [Robert] Peel to free trade,' Sked later claimed, 'the Anti-Federalist League would convert the Tory Party to Euroscepticism and to British Independence.'[6] It was a ludicrous, cumbersome title which failed to sum up the party's aspirations, and few voters would have known what 'federalist' meant. Some people, Sked now says, assumed the party's name meant 'it was akin to right-wing fascist organisations'.[7]

In the April 1992 general election the AFL fielded just seventeen candidates, and Sked himself stood in Bath against the Conservative chairman Chris Patten, a close ally of John Major. Despite getting just 117 votes (0.2 per cent) in Bath, Sked claims credit for Patten's dramatic defeat in the city (though nationally, and against expectations, Patten had helped Major achieve a small Commons majority, and more than 14 million votes, the highest total ever secured in Britain). Farage appears to have limited his support for the AFL in the 1992 election to a cheque for £50. Despite Maastricht, and despite problems with the ERM, the AFL did woefully – a total of just 4,383 votes in the seventeen seats it fought. Per candidate, that was worse than the Monster Raving Loony Party, or the two extreme right-wing parties, the National Front and the British National Party. Farage wasn't one of those candidates and doesn't appear to have campaigned for Sked or any other AFL contender. He thought the party's name silly and wasn't impressed either by the AFL founder. 'Sked seemed bright, sincere and affable, but soft, unworldly and strangely spoiled,' he wrote. 'He was autocratic in style and a seriously bad organiser.'[8]

Despite the election setback, Sked pressed on. He claims he first met Nigel Farage after a Bruges Group meeting at the Reform Club, a few weeks after the election. 'He was respectfully dressed, and said could he join the AFL, and I said "Yes, of course."'[9] Sked then convened an AFL meeting at his workplace, the LSE, the institution founded by some of the giants of Fabian socialism – Sidney and Beatrice Webb and George Bernard Shaw. Until then, the Anti-Federalist League had been pretty much a one-man show, but now Sked wanted to create some of the structure of a proper party. This post-election meeting was the first AFL gathering which Farage attended, but he didn't join the new National Executive Committee. He didn't do much, in fact, until a year later when Sked stood in the May 1993 Newbury by-election. Sked had persuaded Farage's schoolboy hero Enoch Powell to come and address a public meeting. He had no trouble enlisting Farage to drive Powell down to Berkshire, for what was one of Powell's last public appearances.

Sked's memory is that Powell said nothing on the journey in Farage's Mercedes, a company car belonging to his employers, Crédit Lyonnais Rouse. 'There was complete silence all the way, and we never exchanged a word. He had nothing in common with Farage, and never spoke to Farage. We drove back to Eaton Square and he simply thanked Farage.'[10] Farage claims that Powell not only gave him detailed instructions on how to reach the M4, but then, after dinner in a local pub, told him not to worry about not being on time for the meeting. 'Better to be a little late. It is all part of the act,' he reportedly said.[11]

As they arrived outside Newbury racecourse, the venue for the meeting, they encountered a small demonstration. Farage says one protestor hit the back of his car with a wooden stake, but Powell was used to such violence. He advised Farage to drive as close to the door as possible, and they got in without further mishap. Powell's speech – given to several hundred people 'was fiery and colourful, logical and persuasive', Farage would recall. It 'awoke all sorts of aspirations in me which I had not even acknowledged before. It inspired me. Public service was not just about kowtowing to a party line.'[12]

Farage spent more than a week in Newbury campaigning for Sked, canvassing homes, chatting to voters in pubs, helping arrange meetings in village halls and driving the candidate round Newbury in a turquoise pickup truck adorned with yellow Sked posters. Farage found he loved talking to ordinary people and seemed good at it. And Newbury was an exciting campaign in good weather, in the era when by-elections were still covered extensively by the media (with this reporter there almost full-time for BBC *Newsnight*). The Conservatives were on the defensive after sterling had crashed out of the ERM the previous September, and huge tax rises were announced in Norman Lamont's 1993 Budget. Nonetheless, the result was a shock. The Tories' 12,357 majority was turned into one of 22,055 for the Liberal Democrats. Farage hadn't made much of an impact, though. Sked got just 601 votes.

Nonetheless, the whole election experience – especially the Enoch Powell event – had thrilled and energised Farage. He wanted more. He loved the selling and persuasion of the campaign, trying to charm and convince total strangers on the street. Politics would now be his life. 'I was hooked,' he says.[13]

In Christchurch, Dorset, twelve weeks later, in July 1993, Sked stood at a second by-election. The final days of the contest were conducted against the dramatic background at Westminster of John Major trying to get his Maastricht legislation through the Commons as sixty-one days of debate drew to a climax. A group of Eurosceptic Tory rebels joined with Labour to defeat the government over the Social Chapter, and Major then called a Vote of Confidence, which he duly won. But this high drama in London seemed to have little impact in Dorset, and again the Anti-Federalist League didn't click with voters. Alan Sked's leaflets included a picture of Enoch Powell, which illustrated one of the AFL's problems during that era. Sked liked the intellectual Powell as an opponent of the European project, but the populist Powell must also have attracted voters who admired him for his opposition to non-white immigration, an issue which Sked would adamantly not touch. Sked got just 878 votes in Christchurch, an improvement on Newbury, but negligible nonetheless.

The Liberal Democrats still remained the obvious choice for people who wanted to cast a protest vote, and they pulled off an even bigger shock than Newbury, with an astonishing swing of 35 per cent. This reduced Major's majority to just seventeen, which gave Tory Eurosceptics even more clout. The rebels caused trouble for Major on European issues for the rest of the Parliament, and at one point nine Conservative MPs – the so-called Maastricht rebels – were suspended from the parliamentary party, which theoretically wiped out Major's majority altogether.

Euroscepticism was slowly gaining strength, but, eight days after Christchurch, senior figures in the Anti-Federalist League gathered at the LSE and decided they wouldn't get far in advancing the anti-EU cause with an incomprehensible name. So in September 1993, again at the LSE, the UK Independence Party was born. But that was quite a mouthful, too. People soon called it 'the UKIP', and later simply 'UKIP'. Farage was on one of his battlefield tours, so didn't attend this historic first meeting, but now he did join the National Executive.

His colleagues included the teacher John Harvey; Hugh Moelwyn-Hughes, a Welsh solicitor; Anthony Scholefield, who owned tourist shops in central London; and Gerard Batten, a sales executive with British Telecom. The only woman was Helen Szamuely, a fellow historian whom Sked had met and recruited after they'd both been invited to tea with A. J. P. Taylor's widow in Oxford.

Farage, at twenty-nine, was one of two youngsters. The other was Craig Mackinlay, a 27-year-old accountant from Kent, who had contacted Sked after hearing him on a BBC politics programme. Indeed, Mackinlay had also stood for election in 1992, but not under the AFL banner. 'I wasn't keen on this posh, nineteenth-century-style name,' he says, and he stood instead as an Independent opposed to EEC membership and to Maastricht. Farage and Mackinlay were obvious rivals as the bright, young, rising stars in a party which was predominantly elderly, but they became friends too. They often went out drinking together, Mackinlay says, and Farage recruited Mackinlay as the accountant for Farage Futures.

The new UKIP decided that their first big goal would be the next elections to the European Parliament, due in June 1994, though their prospects weren't very promising since European elections in Britain – as in 1989 – were still contested on the traditional first-past-the-post system, with eighty-four large single-member constituencies of just over half a million voters, on average. Sked was adamant, however, that in the highly unlikely event that any UKIP candidate were to be elected an MEP, they should adopt an 'absten-tionist' position similar to Sinn Féin's long-standing policy that its MPs should boycott the Westminster Parliament. But senior UKIP figures were far from agreed on this. The question of how much they should participate in an institution they despised would cause wran-gles for the next quarter of a century. Those who feared UKIP MEPs would be corrupted by living in Brussels and Strasbourg, and unable to resist the European gravy train, would feel vindicated by events.

John Harvey suggested their MEPs should turn up in Brussels or Strasbourg just once, and make a speech declaring they would only return once UK independence had been secured. Sked incorrectly said that joining the Parliament would require UKIP MEPs to swear an oath of allegiance to the EU. Moreover, Sked argued, it would be seen as legitimising the Parliament and the European Union itself. Farage believed in participation, though for several years the issue was merely hypothetical.

Farage was adopted as candidate for the European seat of Itchen, Test and Avon – what he called 'the angler's celestial constituency', though he had little time to pursue his passion for fishing.[14] It com-prised the city of Southampton and five surrounding Westminster seats in Hampshire, Dorset and Wiltshire. On the same day there was also scheduled a by-election in one of those constituencies – the railway town of Eastleigh in Hampshire. It made obvious sense for

Farage to be UKIP's nominee for the Westminster seat, too, and he
subsequently boasted of being 'the first candidate ever to stand for
UKIP'.[15] That's not really true. Unusually, there were five parliamentary by-elections on 9 June 1994, and UKIP also stood in three
other Westminster seats in east London – Newham North East,
Dagenham and Barking.

Farage put all his effort into Eastleigh. No doubt hoping to rekin-
dle memories of nearby Newbury the year before, he wrote to Enoch
Powell asking for further help:

> I have everything in place to fight a good, aggressive campaign but
> a voice from you could transform things and put the issue to the
> forefront. Please give us the help you can. As your performance
> at Newbury showed the electorate are beginning to wake from
> that long sleep. Come and give them another jog . . .
>
> I will hold several public meetings during the campaign and I
> would like you to come and speak at the Town Hall in Eastleigh at
> some point during the week preceding Polling Day. If you agree
> to this I will, of course, organise transport, dinner and whatever
> you need. I might take a break from the driving this time!
>
> . . . the manifesto for the European elections states clearly that
> if elected, UKIP candidates will not take their seats. I know that
> you approve of this policy.

Farage, of course, didn't tell Powell that he himself opposed this
abstentionist stance. But Powell's response was rather disappointing:
'I have given very serious consideration to the request,' he wrote,
'but have concluded that I do not feel I can contribute further to
the campaign by speaking on your behalf at the by-election. Recent
developments seem to show that opinion in the United Kingdom
is consolidating against membership of the European Union.'[16] In
subsequent years, before Powell's death in 1998, several other UKIP
members wrote to Powell, begging him to stand as a UKIP candidate. He always declined.

A film clip from the Eastleigh campaign on YouTube shows the
30-year-old Farage in a cream linen summer jacket, pinning a red,

white and blue UKIP rosette to his lapel.[17] His voice is more nasal, more hesitant and less fluent than the Farage of later years. And he calls his party 'the U-K-I-P', spelled out in letters rather than as an acronym. He did slightly better in Eastleigh, though, than Alan Sked had in the Newbury and Christchurch by-elections – with 952 votes, or 1.7 per cent. But the three UKIP candidates who stood in the East End of London that day all performed a bit better – a sign of the party's potential in working-class areas with high levels of immigration.

The result for the European seat, Itchen, Test and Avon, was declared three days later, and here Farage could claim some success, with 12,423 votes – 5.4 per cent. This was UKIP's best result in the UK, and Farage was one of only two UKIP candidates to retain his deposit. 'There's a new party in British politics,' Farage declared in his speech at the count. 'I came to this constituency without a single member of my party here when we began, with no money at all, and still we get 5 per cent.'[18]

Following the success of the Greens in 1989, it was clear that increasing numbers of voters saw the European elections as a chance to experiment with other parties. Before long, that would become ever more prevalent.

UKIP had opened a ramshackle campaign office in Eastleigh, and Farage told a TV interviewer they would keep it open for an extra month to handle all the enquiries from the public they'd had as a result of the TV election broadcast which UKIP had been allowed for the European election. Farage himself soon ventured to another of the Westminster seats within his 1994 Euro constituency, the cathedral city of Salisbury, where a local farmer, Tony Gatling, had approached him about standing at the next election (due by the spring of 1997). A notice in the *Salisbury Journal* declared that Farage had been announced as their candidate by the Wiltshire branch of UKIP, during a 'wine and cheese party' in the village of Compton Chamberlayne.[19]

Salisbury's sitting MP, Robert Key, was a left-leaning Conservative who had once been an adviser to Edward Heath, the prime minister who'd taken Britain into Europe, and had later helped Heath find a home in the city. Farage and Tony Gatling put huge effort into campaigning, even though the election was probably two years away. Farage increasingly devoted his weekends to UKIP activity and saw little of his family at a time when his marriage was falling apart.

In Wiltshire, he and Gatling and a growing band of helpers would hand out leaflets on the streets, knock on doors and hold public meetings. It was all based on very old-fashioned techniques at a time when the mainstream parties were increasingly canvassing by telephone, or reaching voters by direct mail. Farage would usually stay at the Gatlings' farmhouse, but it was gruelling and sometimes demoralising work. On one occasion they advertised a meeting and nobody turned up, though that was perhaps rather less embarrassing than having to address an audience of just one or two. Gatling observed how with each meeting Farage improved as a speaker and grew in confidence.

By October 1996, *UK Independence News* was reporting that in Salisbury 'their local newsletter has a circulation of 2,300 sympathisers and the PPC [Prospective Parliamentary Candidate] Nigel Farage has spoken at twenty-four meetings throughout the constituency'. More important, Alan Sked came down to open a branch office in the city, and the event got several minutes on the local ITV news, including shots of the UKIP battle bus outside Edward Heath's grand Georgian house in the Cathedral Close. Symbolically, UKIP's new Salisbury office also took over some of the administrative burden handled by national headquarters.[20]

Gradually, Farage expanded his UKIP activity beyond Salisbury. While he was content to let Alan Sked handle national media opportunities – pretty limited at that time – he began building UKIP at the grassroots – in village halls, in upstairs rooms in pubs, in people's sitting rooms. Locals would organise and advertise a meeting. Farage would be billed as star speaker, and his increasingly fluent oratory would inspire the formation of another local branch. Every speech ended with the same peroration, which regular listeners soon learned to mouth in sync: 'We seek an amicable divorce from the political European Union and its replacement with a genuine free trade agreement, which is what we thought we signed up to in the first place!'[21]

The journalist and environmentalist Richard North, who became involved in the early UKIP, says that even at this stage, in the mid-'90s, Nigel Farage was effectively running the party. 'Sked was an academic, very gentle, an intellectual. He didn't have the "street cred", the nous; he wasn't a thug in a way Farage was. You needed somebody out there to bruise people, beat people up, get them motivated and moving.'[22] Farage was the best speaker the party had, and happy to campaign night after night after night, with long car journeys to each location, which meant he saw even less of Clare and his two young sons.

But Farage wasn't just building up the local party member by member, branch by branch, he was also making his name and becoming popular. For many local activists, he was the only senior UKIP figure they had ever met. Tony Scholefield, one of the founding NEC members and a long-standing critic of Farage, nonetheless acknowledges this early contribution. 'Nigel was good. Going round setting up branches was a job which most people didn't want to do. Who would want to do that? In those five years he would establish a few dozen branches.'

In tactics, though not politics, Richard North compares Farage with the historic insurgents of 1920s Germany. 'It was as if intuitively he had adopted the same strategy as the Nazis did in the early days, by-passing the media. It went under the radar and he did hundreds of meetings in church halls and pubs. He was there, building a support base of public recognition that was invisible to the media. He worked for it, and he worked his socks off.'[23]

When Farage stood for re-election to the UKIP NEC in June 1996 against ten other contenders, he topped the poll by a comfortable margin – 634 (82 per cent) of the 773 voters supported him, compared with 550 (71 per cent) for his closest rival.

But Tony Scholefield says it soon seeped back to other people in the leadership that Farage was also using these semi-public UKIP meetings to make no secret of his contempt for Alan Sked and other senior figures. He wouldn't refer to them by name but talk, for instance, of 'when we get the right people in charge'. Scholefield says this meant that when, around 1996, the party started to hold larger conferences, with several hundred members, 'there were a lot of people primed that Sked, Scholefield, Mackinlay etc were all no good.'[24]

Relations between Alan Sked and Nigel Farage grew ever more strained, and the UKIP leader says he got written complaints from Salisbury voters about Farage's leaflets, saying things such as: 'I'm very happy that your candidate in Salisbury believes in education, but I will not vote for him until he learns to spell.' Sked adds: 'One day, I said: "Nigel, I'm going to have to teach you the rudiments of English spelling and grammar." After an hour, he flounced out and said: "I don't understand words."'[25] It may seem an odd remark for a former Dulwich College schoolboy, yet while Farage has always been brilliant with the spoken word, he's never shown much skill as a writer.

Alan Sked also alleges that he admonished Farage for turning up drunk to National Executive meetings. Given Sked's subsequent bitterness towards Farage and UKIP, one should take his claims with caution. On the drunkenness allegation, however, there is corroboration. The NEC minutes for February 1997 report that during one discussion 'Dr Sked rebuked Nigel Farage for constantly repeating himself, and for coming to the meeting under the influence of alcohol.'[26]

The former UKIP leader also says that after a meeting of the NEC, Farage took some of his colleagues to a Mayfair strip club. 'The place was decorated like a Victorian brothel. It was incredibly sleazy,' Sked says. 'It was full of these hatchet-faced women wearing nothing but G-strings, selling drinks. Nigel was buying the drinks. I think we had champagne. The rest of us had one drink and in that time Nigel had half a dozen. He was completely blotto. As I left, I saw Nigel's head was wedged between one woman's breasts. He confessed later he had no idea how he got home.'[27]

Far more serious is a claim which Sked has repeated in print on many occasions, but which Nigel Farage has always vehemently denied. Sked says that just before the 1997 election, Farage suggested it was time to drop the policy on banning former National Front members from being UKIP candidates. 'Don't be so daft!'

Sked recalls him saying. 'We're a liberal party, committed against racism. The National Front is fascist. And he then said: "You needn't worry about the nigger vote. Nig-nogs will never vote for us." There was nobody else there, so there is no witness.'[28]

Sked's numerous accounts of this conversation vary in small details, but not in the overall thrust of what Farage reportedly said, nor in his alleged use of the highly offensive words 'nigger' and 'nig-nogs'.[29] Hundreds of people were interviewed during the research for this book – including dozens who dealt with him during the 1990s – yet nobody else recalls Nigel Farage using such racist language at any time since he left Dulwich College in 1982. Nor do any of the interviewees recollect Farage saying anything even close to such words – yet many of them dislike him and are highly critical in numerous other ways. It seems probable that either Sked's memory is at fault, or that if Farage did say what Sked alleges, it was a one-off instance – though once would be bad enough.

The Eurosceptic journalist Richard North, who subsequently fell out with Farage, denies that he's an 'out-and-out' racist. But Farage was 'locked in aspic' from the time of the Great War, he says:

> He was racist in a Churchillian sense. He believed in the superiority of the white Englishman – King and Empire. He was really interested in the First World War. He'd done his battlefield tours. His knowledge was incredibly limited to the British front. He knew nothing about the French. He wasn't interested in the Second World War. Just the First World War. In a sense he's a white supremacist on a King and Country basis, rather than overt hatred of coloured people. He would have made a wonderful subaltern in the Indian Army, that was his demeanour. As an Englishman he'd won first place in the lottery of life.[30]

Throughout the 1990s the political tide was slowly moving in UKIP's direction. Margaret Thatcher had made Euroscepticism more acceptable within the Conservative Party and the former PM gave her tacit approval when some Tory MPs opposed the Maastricht Treaty and other moves towards further EU integration.

Within government, hardline Eurosceptic Cabinet ministers John Redwood, Michael Portillo and Peter Lilley became known as 'the bastards' after John Major was caught on camera calling them that.

A sign of how things were moving so rapidly was seen with the former chancellor Norman Lamont, who had run John Major's leadership campaign, and suffered the humiliation of Black Wednesday in 1992 when Britain was forced out of the ERM. Privately, Lamont told the Conservative Philosophy Group in 1994 that withdrawal from the EU should be restored to the range of 'serious possibilities'.[31] A few months later, Lamont told a Conservative conference fringe meeting, 'When we come to examine the advantages of our membership today of the European Union they are remarkably elusive . . . I cannot pinpoint a single concrete advantage that unambiguously comes to this country because of our membership . . . I do not suggest that Britain should today unilaterally withdraw from Europe. But the issue may well return to the political agenda.'[32]

UKIP had competition on the right of British politics, however. Serious competition. In the 1994 European elections, the controversial billionaire businessman Sir James Goldsmith had secured election to the Brussels parliament from a seat in France as a candidate for French Eurosceptic party L'Autre Europe.

Sir James, a member of the German-Jewish Goldsmith banking family, was a flamboyant and buccaneering financier who made his considerable fortune through high-stakes takeovers and asset-stripping. He had a colourful love life, three wives and several homes. Goldsmith's hostility towards the EU stemmed from his belief that it was a back-door way for Germany to take control of Europe. Although his father had been a Conservative MP, Goldsmith was knighted in 1976 in the notorious resignation honours list of the Labour prime minister Harold Wilson. Goldsmith had won favour with Wilson, and achieved considerable public attention, with his long-running feud against *Private Eye* which almost bankrupted the satirical magazine. The *Eye* had accused Goldsmith of trying to help his friend Lord Lucan escape justice after the murder of Lucan's family nanny and the peer's mysterious (and still unresolved) disappearance.

In 1993, Goldsmith delivered a television lecture explaining his hostility to the European Union – on Channel 4 of all places. So later that year the first national secretary of the brand-new UK Independence Party wrote to Goldsmith seeking his financial support. 'Dear Gerard Batten,' Goldsmith replied. 'Thank you for your letter which has just reached me in Europe . . . I am grateful for your suggestions. However, I will continue to fight for the cause, but on a non-party-political basis.'[33]

And yet within five months of the European elections in 1994, Sir James reversed that stance. He was a friend of the TV presenter Sir David Frost, and the two men agreed the format of an interview on Frost's Sunday morning BBC programme, to allow Goldsmith suddenly to announce, with maximum impact, that he would now form a new party in Britain. The Referendum Party, as the name suggests, had the single policy of campaigning for a public vote on Britain's continued membership of the European Union, a softer goal than UKIP's aim of outright withdrawal. And unlike UKIP, the new Referendum Party had the benefit of Goldsmith's huge wealth, which he promised to spend liberally. The new party looked bound not just to grab far more media attention than UKIP, but to crush its poorer rival in the process.

James Goldsmith recruited some high-profile candidates. These included Margaret Thatcher's former economic adviser Sir Alan Walters; the entrepreneur Peter de Savary; the TV botanist David Bellamy; and the zoo-owner and gambling impresario John Aspinall. Goldsmith himself decided to stand in Putney against the former Cabinet minister David Mellor. The party fielded 547 candidates in the 1997 election, and avoided seats where the sitting MP – of whatever party – was known to be Eurosceptic.

The story of the Referendum Party in the mid-1990s is worth a book in itself. Sir James Goldsmith was said at the time to have spent £20 million on the campaign, but according to Goldsmith's then political chief-of-staff Patrick Robertson, the real tally was around £28 million. It was easily the largest sum any individual has ever spent on a British election, and one of the largest that any political party has ever expended in the UK. It enabled the Referendum

Party to be highly professional in comparison with the ramshackle amateurs of UKIP.

Goldsmith recruited a hundred local election agents and set up ten regional offices. Candidates were vetted by a security firm and checked with the World Jewish Congress in case they had shown anti-Semitic or fascist views in their past, and candidates received professional training. The Referendum Party had no actual members – just registered supporters – since Goldsmith said that because he was wealthy he didn't think it right to ask people to pay subscriptions. Nor was there any internal democracy: it was entirely Jimmy Goldsmith's show. But the party attracted some interesting names of the future. These included a University of Essex politics graduate, then in her early twenties, who'd left a job at Conservative HQ to run the Referendum Party press office. She was the future home secretary Priti Patel.

Goldsmith's millions were largely spent communicating with voters on a grand scale in the run-up to the general election. The party placed numerous advertisements in national and local newspapers, and Goldsmith arranged for a professionally made film, on 5 million VHS cassette tapes, to be posted out to voters. The tapes were produced in America and had to be flown in on two jumbo jets, but because of election spending rules the VHS mailing couldn't be confined to the most promising constituencies: they had to be spread evenly around the UK, to roughly 8,000 households per seat, chosen randomly from the electoral register. John Major and his party did their best to spike Goldsmith's guns. Sir James was offered a peerage to withdraw, but refused the bribe. And in 1996 the Major government blunted Goldsmith's message – and sole policy – by conceding at last that they would hold a referendum if the Conservatives decided to take Britain into the proposed European single currency. Labour felt obliged to match Major's pledge, and the Liberal Democrats advocated a referendum, too.

UKIP's campaign, in contrast, was weak and chaotic. The only 'name' they could claim was the actor Leo McKern, famous for playing the title role in the TV series *Rumpole of the Bailey*. He was employed to introduce UKIP's sole party election broadcast sitting alongside Alan Sked in a formal room with a photo of Winston Churchill on the wall. It was almost comic. 'We are not a one-issue party,' Sked insisted, 'but a potential party of government.' 'Thank you, Dr Sked,' McKern replied, 'I, for one, was most impressed.' McKern then turned to viewers and added, 'No doubt, you were as well.'[34]

UKIP fielded just 193 candidates in 1997 – in less than a third of the seats, mostly in Conservative parts of southern England. In all but twenty-five seats they were competing directly with a Goldsmith candidate. UKIP didn't bother standing in most of the Midlands and the North: they had no candidates, for example, in Hartlepool, Boston & Skegness, or Grimsby, or Harwich in East Anglia, all of which would be prime UKIP targets twenty years later.

In part, of course, this reflected the UKIP membership, which was heavily concentrated across the South. In the 1990s, UKIP was regarded – internally and externally – very much as a middle-class and lower middle-class alternative to the Conservatives – a party of golf clubs in the home counties, and crusty retired colonels. Nigel Farage used to say that in the early days you could always tell you were at a UKIP meeting by the number of Bomber Command ties in the audience. Farage, the public school-educated City trader from the borders of London and Kent – a man who loved golf, cricket and fishing, and pottering about First World War battlefields – fitted that southern middle-class profile perfectly.

The Referendum Party got 811,849 votes in 1997, well short of their 1 million target, and all but forty-two of Goldsmith's candidates lost their deposits. It worked out at about £35 per vote, though Goldsmith could at least claim he had forced the major parties to pledge a referendum on the single currency. But their presence may have caused quite a few Conservative MPs to lose their seats – nineteen Tories lost by a smaller margin than the vote for the Referendum Party contender. Among those probably defeated by the presence of a Goldsmith candidate were Cabinet ministers Roger Freeman and Tony Newton, and the former Olympic gold medallist Sebastian Coe.

Goldsmith's tally – though disappointing – dwarfed UKIP's meagre 105,722 votes and there were severe recriminations within Sked's party. Why hadn't UKIP tried to strike a pact with Goldsmith? Farage later claimed that Sked had told him the two leaders did meet. He has also said he was 'reliably' told that Goldsmith offered Sked a deal – that the Referendum Party would stand down in seventy-five seats in favour of a joint 'UKIP/Referendum' candidate, and meet the campaign costs in those seats.

Yet Sked, according to Farage, rejected this offer. 'This,' Farage says, 'would, alas, have been entirely characteristic. Aside from his insistence on being top dog, Sked displayed a quite unreasonable dislike for Goldsmith and the Referendum Party, who were, after all, natural allies.'[35] Yet Sir James Goldsmith had publicly said he wanted Britain to stay in the EU, while UKIP wanted to withdraw.

Sked denies Farage's claims completely. 'I never met Jimmy Goldsmith,' he says. 'Farage went round saying that I met Goldsmith personally and that I turned down a deal to his face.' Sked does admit, however, that he wrote to Sir James on two occasions seeking some form of co-operation. The first letter was in 1994, when Goldsmith said he'd give financial backing to parties who supported a referendum. Sked immediately faxed him, but merely received a standard reply, he says, and only a year later. When he wrote a subsequent letter to Goldsmith, 'I never got a response,' he says. And at the UKIP conference in 1996, Sked appealed publicly for Goldsmith to give financial backing to the party. Again there was no reply. Sked believes Goldsmith never saw his letters and claims that they were intercepted by the businessman's chief adviser, Patrick Robertson. 'Patrick was getting the letters and destroying them.'[36]

Robertson firmly denies this. If Sked had made a formal approach, he argues, Goldsmith would naturally have considered it, but he explains that it didn't help relations that Sked had often attacked Goldsmith publicly in the most personal way, decrying him as a 'billionaire'.[37]

The rivalry between the two leaders and the two parties, and their unequal strengths, was shown when the Referendum Party met in the Brighton conference centre in 1996, and UKIP mounted a fringe event in a nearby hotel. 'I'm told they are going to be parading some so-called defectors from our lot,' one Goldsmith ally remarked. 'But why would anybody want to leave to eat sausage rolls and drink poor white wine with the likes of Dr Alan Sked when we can drink as much champagne as we like, and look at Jemima' – a reference to Goldsmith's daughter, who had just married the former Pakistan cricket captain Imran Khan.[38] But UKIP boasted that the Brighton event prompted three dozen defectors from Goldsmith's party.

Nigel Farage enjoyed a rather more successful campaign in 1997 than most of his Eurosceptic colleagues. At his pre-election rally at Salisbury City Hall, he was backed by a brass band and endorsed by the journalists Christopher Booker and Simon Heffer, and by Norris McWhirter, the TV commentator and co-founder of the *Guinness Book of Records*. Farage also got support from the leader of the seven-strong independent group on Salisbury Council. But during the campaign an extraordinary anonymous letter was received by the editor of the *Salisbury Journal*, with a copy also sent to the incumbent MP Robert Key. It was on UKIP head office notepaper, and the author claimed to be 'writing from within the UK Independence Party about our candidate Nigel Farage. I don't want to see him elected MP for Salisbury. He would be a disaster. He is a drunk . . .'

The writer then made several serious allegations against Farage and members of his family which are almost certainly untrue. These included a claim that his father, Guy, was a member of the extreme right-wing National Front in the 1960s and '70s. This claim has often surfaced over the years, but despite extensive research this author has found no evidence for it, and Guy Farage firmly denies it. The anonymous letter continued:

> Nigel himself had to start his own business after he was sacked from his previous job for collapsing drunk with a friend on the floor of the commodities exchange. He is totally disloyal to Dr Sked, our party leader, whose education he bitterly resents – Nigel being an O-level man – and because Dr Sked apparently rebuked him for turning up blotto to the UKIP National Executive meetings – something which, I'm told, is recorded in that body's

minutes. (I'll try to get you a copy.) Having developed a half-hour nationalist rant, Nigel now thinks he is a new Churchill.[39]

The letter then suggested a series of questions to ask Farage, based on the various allegations. It was signed by 'An ex-Tory' who gave no name. Much of its contents were similar to allegations which Alan Sked would make about Farage to journalists in the years ahead, and its mention of 'educational qualifications', and of Farage 'being an O-level man', suggest it may have been written by Sked himself (though he is not an 'ex-Tory'), and he adamantly denies doing so. Or perhaps it came from somebody very close to Sked. An article in *Spearhead*, the magazine of the British National Party in 1999, would accuse Sked of sending such a letter. The editor of the *Salisbury Journal* did nothing with it; it never cropped up during the 1997 campaign; and until now it has never been published.

Salisbury, with its famous medieval cathedral, market square and fine buildings, has the air of an Anthony Trollope novel, and people were rather old-fashioned in their ways. 'He didn't fit into Barchester,' says Robert Key:

> He was from the start, brash and abrasive. He was rude to people all the time. His literature was really rubbish. There was not a word in it about the constituency, or jobs for local people, and it suggested he had no interest in being a constituency MP. They were fly-posting – telegraph poles, and council offices, and bridges and so on – road signs. That went down very badly with people. He broke the rules. He was a dirty campaigner. He didn't play cricket.[40]

Key is correct. Farage's main election address didn't mention a single local issue and yet he got 5.7 per cent in Salisbury – 3,332 votes – while UKIP candidates elsewhere averaged around one per cent. Indeed, he was the sole UKIP candidate in 1997 to retain his deposit. 'I was the only one who tried,' Farage said afterwards. 'The rest were all intellectuals. They thought it all happens in coffee houses.'[41]

But Farage had the huge benefit that Salisbury was one of the few southern English seats which James Goldsmith chose not to fight, and so the Eurosceptic vote wasn't divided. But why did Goldsmith stand aside? The reason was simple. Robert Key, despite being pro-EU, was in favour of a referendum on British membership, and had actually voted for a Referendum Bill proposed in the Commons by the arch-Eurosceptic Tory backbencher Bill Cash. In 1996, Goldsmith wrote to all sitting Conservative MPs to announce that his party was thinking of standing against them, unless they could supply evidence of support for an EU referendum. So Robert Key was able to oblige, though Nigel Farage was probably the bigger beneficiary.

Alan Sked, in contrast, did face Referendum Party opposition in the neighbouring constituency of Romsey. Sked managed only 3.5 per cent, but, of all the 176 constituencies where UKIP and Goldsmith's party faced each other, Romsey was one of just two where UKIP beat their Referendum rival.

Nevertheless, so long as Sir James Goldsmith's party remained on the stage, UKIP looked doomed. Sked and Farage's party seemed set to suffer the fate of so many other anti-EU parties over recent decades.

But, as so often in politics, there came an unexpected turn.

5

TREACHERY

For about five years UKIP's first headquarters was at 80 Regent Street, just north of Piccadilly Circus in central London. It sounds like a grand address, but in reality the offices were above one of those many tourist shops which are sprinkled round the West End. The shop, simply called 'Scotland', was a rival to the Edinburgh Woollen Mill chain, and sold Scottish clothes and knitwear – Harris tweed, cashmere scarves, patterned jumpers, kilts, socks, hats and teddy bears. The office accommodation above was spartan, scruffy and cramped – about 700 square feet, with a main room and two side rooms, but UKIP was also allowed to store leaflets in the basement, alongside the shop's supplies of clothing.

The offices had been let to UKIP for free by Anthony Scholefield, the businessman who owned the shop. Scholefield sat on the UKIP NEC and had stood as candidate in Harrow East, where the Referendum Party – in line with the wider trend – beat UKIP by more than three to one. As Scholefield and UKIP volunteers toiled in Regent Street in those early days following Tony Blair's New Labour landslide victory, the prospects must have looked bleak.

But rescue would come from the most improbable source – just a few doors away, at 68 Regent Street, amid the luxury and spacious splendour of the five-star Hotel Café Royal, one of London's top locations for champagne-fuelled dinners and events. Here, a fortnight after the election, Sir James Goldsmith had invited to lunch his main lieutenants from the Referendum Party campaign, and many of his leading candidates.

It was time for another party.

Following his vast spending on the contest, Goldsmith had finished election night in a famous televised spat with David Mellor at
the count in Putney. As Mellor, who'd been defeated by Labour,
used his results speech to dismiss the 'derisory' 1,500 votes which
Goldsmith had achieved and declared his party was 'dead in the
water', the billionaire fought back, jeering 'out, out, out!', while he
delivered a slow handclap to the defeated MP.[1] Goldsmith and his
team consoled themselves that they had prompted a major change in
policy by all three leading parties, and that the Blair government was
pledged not to join the proposed single currency without consulting
the electorate. And they felt the campaign had helped educate the
British public about the nature of the European Union.

Yet when Goldsmith rose at the Café Royal two weeks later,
he seemed to reflect Mellor's jibe by delivering a shock. The
Referendum Party would no longer fight elections. It would become
the Referendum Movement, he explained, run by his wife, Lady
Annabel Goldsmith. Sir James announced that he himself would
now withdraw from the battlefield of politics. He left a similar message on the party's phone answering service. It was all so sudden.

'It is very sad,' said a young member of the party staff. 'We are
dismantling everything. Sir James has left a message and gone away.
There is no longer a Referendum Party as such.' And what would
the staff member now do herself, an *Evening Standard* reporter asked.
'Join the ranks of the unemployed,' replied Priti Patel.[2]

Only those close to Goldsmith knew why. For several years, he
had been suffering from pancreatic and liver cancer. Indeed, his
illnesses had restricted his movements during the campaign. He
took a doctor everywhere he went, together with medicines, and
had to limit himself to one major appearance per day.

After the Café Royal lunch, Goldsmith flew off on holiday. On 18
July 1997, eleven weeks after the election, the news came through
from Spain. Sir James Goldsmith was dead.

Both his wife and his mistress were at his bedside.

Yet before the election result, and before the Café Royal lunch,
Goldsmith still had big plans for the Referendum Party. In particular, he had his eye on the European elections in 1999, for which

Labour's manifesto had committed the government to a new proportional voting system, as demanded by most EU leaders. If that happened, minor parties might start winning seats. Goldsmith was still only sixty-four, and, had he lived, he might have remained active in British and European politics for another ten or twenty years. Given the 7:1 ratio in votes between the two Eurosceptic parties, and the vast gulf in resources, the logical move for a famous corporate raider like Goldsmith would have been to swallow up the smaller entity.

In which case the world might have long forgotten UKIP and never heard of Nigel Farage.

The UK Independence Party would have found it difficult to resist such a takeover. The party was in post-election turmoil. Alan Sked saw no reason to stand down from the leadership, but his internal critics had had enough. Sked was too dictatorial, they said, and too intellectual – he didn't have enough of the common touch. He was too egotistical; too prone to outbursts of anger. Sked was a good lecturer, and often witty, but lacked passion and the ability to inspire ordinary people. 'He was slick and quick,' said Nigel Farage, 'but he left audiences impressed rather than moved. He saw the theoretical dangers, but could not make them real to his listeners.'[3]

Some years later, one of UKIP's founders, Hugh Moelwyn-Hughes, would describe Sked as a 'child':

> A charming, bright child, but petulant and sometimes surprisingly silly. He had done all that he could. He was the world's worst organiser. He could so early have recognised this, and could still be the honoured leader emeritus to this day. His tragedy was not that he could not organise a piss-up in a brewery but that he did not know or acknowledge the fact. Such a shame.[4]

Sked could be 'totally aloof', recollects Tony Stone, who often worked as a volunteer in the Regent Street office, doing menial tasks. 'He would come in and never once did he even acknowledge me. I was just a worker and beneath his attention. This was no way to run a democratic party.'[5]

'Sked saw the party as his own personal fiefdom,' said David Rowlands, a Welsh farmer and activist. Helen Szamuely, whom Sked expelled for opposing the 'abstentionist' policy for putative UKIP MEPs, warned her old colleagues: 'Alan will make sure that you all toady to him.'[6] Sked was also criticised for wanting to hog the media limelight, and not letting others do TV and radio appearances. Nigel Farage has said Sked made it clear to a colleague, 'that he resented my small successes as a speaker around the country. "L'Etat, c'est moi," was Sked's attitude. He wanted no rising stars.'[7]

Yet such criticisms of the then UKIP leader and founder would find echoes in those levelled at Nigel Farage in the years ahead.

Farage decided to act, and began working in league with two colleagues, Michael Holmes and David Lott. Holmes, a business-man, who coincidentally had been born in the same hospital in Farnborough as Farage, had become a multi-millionaire by publish-ing free newspapers. Lott was a former RAF jet-fighter pilot and squadron leader who later flew commercially for Britannia Airways. A few weeks after retiring at the age of fifty-three, Lott had read an article about UKIP by a columnist in the *Daily Mail*, which, remarkably, had Sked's phone number printed underneath. Lott had rung and was astonished when Sked immediately recruited him as a candidate for the 1997 election – in Hexham, in Northumberland, where he lived.

Lott devoted his new retirement to UKIP and became famous within the party for his 7-ton Luton horsebox, which he converted into a UKIP mini-office and drove around the country to fight elections, recruit new members and establish new branches. Having arranged a visit with local activists, Lott would typically set up in the local market square, put out a few fold-up chairs, plonk some leaflets on a table and chat to passers-by. Together Lott and Farage had taken on the brunt of the work establishing UKIP as a grassroots organisation.

Farage, Holmes and Lott convened a meeting, to be held in Basingstoke in Hampshire in early June 1997. The invitation list included candidates who had performed well at the election, and, crucially, the trio also approached the most successful candidates from the Referendum Party. Top of the agenda was the formation of a 'New Alliance', with the long-term aim of a merger. The date of the meeting appears to have been chosen to clash with a long-planned meeting in London which would tie up Sked and most of the NEC.

To Alan Sked, this Basingstoke gathering was a plot, an act of treachery. He took the implied criticism of his regime very personally. He retaliated immediately by urging all UKIP members to join the official party event in London that day, forcing activists to declare where their loyalties lay. Sked quickly expelled Farage, Holmes and Lott from the party. Farage and his allies took this as a declaration of 'open war'.[8]

Michael Holmes who, according to Farage, was 'by nature vengeful and had money to burn', instituted legal action against Sked over the expulsion, and for libel over a letter to David Lott in which Sked had called Holmes a 'poisonous liar' and a 'reptile'.[9] Sked then upset UKIP colleagues by spending £15,000 of party funds on fighting the legal actions without consulting them.

Sked was soon thwarted. He conceded the legal cases, and Farage, Holmes and Lott were readmitted to membership and the NEC. Battered, bewildered and feeling betrayed, Sked resigned as leader. He appointed the thirty-year-old Craig Mackinlay in his place, pending a contest for a new leader. 'I have no wish to lead a lunatic fringe in which temporary divisions are fought to the bitter end,' Sked wrote in a valedictory article for *UK Independence News*. 'Reluctantly, therefore, I have decided to return to my ivory tower.' Thanking colleagues, Sked named Mackinlay and Tony Scholefield among possible successors, and credited fourteen others by name for helping build UKIP in its first four years. Pointedly, Nigel Farage wasn't mentioned.[10] More than twenty years later, Farage would come to describe Alan Sked as the 'biggest enemy' he ever faced.[11]

By July 1997 UKIP was in a dire state, highlighted by the Uxbridge by-election in north-west London, where the party came tenth out of eleven candidates and got just thirty-nine votes, less than a tenth of the support garnered by Screaming Lord Sutch and his Monster Raving Loony Party. Some parties might have called it a day – as David Owen did when his Social Democrats were similarly humiliated by Sutch in the Bootle by-election seven years earlier. But UKIP's barely flickering flame would soon be rekindled.

Although James Goldsmith's Referendum Movement survived as a pressure group (and still exists as the Democracy Movement), his decision to withdraw from elections gave UKIP a golden opportunity. Without Goldsmith's presence and the force of his personality, much of what had been the Referendum Party was swallowed up by its much smaller rival – the kind of reverse takeover for which Goldsmith was once famous in his business days. Having come close to destroying UKIP in the May general election, Goldsmith's party suddenly gave UKIP an extraordinary lifeline.

Surprisingly perhaps, given his grassroots popularity and growing influence within UKIP, Nigel Farage chose not to contest the leadership election caused by Alan Sked's departure. He would subsequently say that at thirty-three he was too young for the job (the Tories' newly elected leader William Hague was only thirty-six, though perhaps that would prove Farage's point). But 1997 also saw Nigel and Clare Farage divorce.

The year before, Nigel had met Kirsten Mehr, a German bond broker whom he would marry in 1999. In an ITV programme twenty years later, Farage explained to Piers Morgan how he had travelled to Germany. 'I was always out on the road; always punting; always looking for new clients; always looking for new business.' But it was also a time, Farage admitted, when he was looking for a new wife. He spotted Kirsten, a curvaceous blonde, when he and a colleague walked into a trading room in Frankfurt around eight or nine in the morning, not feeling too good after flying in and some heavy drinking the night before. 'She was a bilingual Bund broker – how about that? . . . German government bonds, and so there'd be a German telephone in one ear and an English telephone in the other ear.' He and Kirsten went out to lunch, and that rolled on through to dinner, and that lasted, he said, until around two or three in the morning.[12]

Farage would acknowledge that he had not made 'the slightest effort to sustain' his previous marriage. 'Clare had quite properly made a life for herself without me. At her request, I bought her a new house and she moved out with the children.'[13] He would see their young sons Sam and Tom every weekend, when he would take them fishing, or go to cricket matches.

So he simply couldn't afford time-wise or financially to become leader, which would have required him to devote yet more effort to UKIP. 'I was earning a great deal, but every penny was swallowed up by my lifestyle, children's education and, above all, politics.'[14] Farage also admitted he was 'no administrator' and that he would find it 'impossible to do all the press and public stuff which is my forte if I was also bogged down with all the internecine struggles and squabbles which beset any political party'.[15]

Instead, Farage backed Michael Holmes, a relative newcomer to the party who gave the impression he would continue to contribute generously to UKIP from his newspaper fortune. Acting leader Craig Mackinlay also stood, but he perhaps suffered from being Alan Sked's protégé. When the results were finally announced in March 1998, Mackinlay and the other contenders, Gerald Roberts and Bernard Collignon, were easily beaten. Michael Holmes appointed Mackinlay as his deputy and made Nigel Farage the new UKIP chairman. The prime task he was given by Holmes was to pick over the carcass of Goldsmith's party, and recruit Referendum candidates who had performed well in 1997.

Farage claims 160 candidates came over, though the true figure is probably around a hundred. Those brought in personally by Farage included Jeffrey Titford, a wealthy undertaker from Frinton-on-Sea in Essex, who had got almost 5,000 votes in Harwich at the election – or 9.2 per cent – the Referendum Party's best result. Farage and Holmes wooed Titford over lunch at Simpson's in the Strand. Another Farage recruit was Damian Hockney, a publisher of fashion magazines who would soon revamp UKIP campaign literature, and adopted the Referendum Party's purple and yellow colours.

Other switchers who would play a significant role in the party in future years included Mike Nattrass, Jim Carver and Richard North, who'd defected from UKIP to the Referendum Party just before the 1997 election and now returned. (Having just contested the Wirral South by-election on 27 February 1997 for UKIP, North stood for Goldsmith's party in Derbyshire in the May general election and so fought two Westminster elections for two different parties in just sixty-three days, which may be a record.)

Cleverly, Farage used the courting of Referendum Party candidates as a chance to revisit UKIP's abstentionist policy whereby any elected MEPs would not take their seats – a policy which Goldsmith never adopted (after all, he already participated in the Parliament as a French MEP). Long before the leadership result was known, Farage had written to UKIP's newsletter saying, 'The recent announcement that the Euro-elections will be contested under proportional representation presents us with a real chance of getting MEPs elected . . . Perhaps the most important reason for this change [scrapping the abstentionist policy] is that it is the only way we can unite anti-federalists in this country. Never again must we go to the ballot box, as in May 1997, with more than one moderate anti-EU party to vote for.'[16]

One of the delicious ironies of this story is that it would be the new pro-EU Blair government, determined to adopt a more positive approach to European integration, which would give UKIP their most important break.

Labour proposed that from 1999 the European elections be conducted under proportional representation (PR). The idea had been floating around for years – indeed, the Callaghan Labour government had tried to introduce PR for the first direct elections to the European Parliament in 1979, only to be blocked by the Commons. By the 1990s, however, most other EU states used PR to elect their MEPs, and the 1997 Amsterdam Treaty had committed member states to greater uniformity in how MEPs were elected. Labour decided that groups of British MEPs would be elected for constituencies covering large regions of the UK, and that those elected would broadly reflect the proportion of votes each party gained in each region. Until now UKIP had always opposed proportional representation. That was now quietly forgotten.

The advent of PR for the 1999 European elections in Britain, which made such a crucial difference to the Farage and UKIP stories, almost didn't happen, however. It's one of those behind-the-scenes dramas of the early New Labour government that is barely mentioned in Tony Blair's own memoirs, and doesn't feature at all in the autobiography of Jack Straw, the home secretary responsible for the legislation, who was a long-standing opponent of PR.

In his diaries, the then Liberal Democrat leader Paddy Ashdown explains in detail the toing and froing which took place to ensure Labour kept its manifesto pledge. In opposition, Blair had secretly promised Ashdown that he would bring the Lib Dems into government (with a long-term aim of party merger) even if Labour got a majority, but when Labour's majority was a whopping 179, that commitment was quickly cast aside. Ashdown fought to ensure that as a kind of consolation prize he at least got Blair to stick to his public pledge of PR for the European elections in 1999. And PR, of course, has long been dear to the heart of every Liberal or Liberal Democrat.

Labour's proposed closed regional list system easily got through the Commons, but was voted down six times by the House of Lords, who didn't like the way it gave party officials a lot of say in who was elected. Initially, Jack Straw announced the government wouldn't force through the PR legislation, which it could do by invoking the 1911 and 1949 Parliament Acts, allowing the Commons to override the Lords if a measure has featured in the governing party's manifesto. Ashdown pleaded with Blair that their parties' relationship and his own future as Lib Dem leader depended on the measure getting through. Tony Blair's press secretary, Alastair Campbell, wrote in his diary after one Lords defeat: 'Paddy was back on to [Blair], saying the Lib-Lab game was dead if he could not get PR for the European elections. He was in a real panic.'[17]

Blair, perhaps feeling guilty about dropping his other secret pledge to Ashdown, overrode Straw's decision, and the Parliament Acts were invoked for only the fifth time since 1911. The timetable was tight, with the PR legislation enacted just four months before polling day. 'A huge relief,' Ashdown wrote in his diary. 'I . . . will be able to say that I have presided over the first ever nationwide PR elections. Excellent news.'[18]

Yet neither the Liberal Democrats, nor the European cause espoused by Ashdown and Blair, were the real long-term beneficiaries. As one UKIP historian would observe:

> The Labour government's commitment to PR, part of its 'mod-
> ernisation' agenda, was the saviour of UKIP. There would have
> been no UK Independence Party after June 1999 if this measure
> had not been passed: we desperately wanted real electoral suc-
> cess, in the form of elected candidates, after six years fighting,
> unheard, in the wilderness. Failure at those elections would
> probably have led to disillusionment and dissolution.[19]

Jack Straw's fear was that PR was bound to help minor parties and
fringe parties. 'I wasn't always right,' he says in retrospect, 'but I
was certainly right on that.'[20]

Without Ashdown's pressure on Blair, and Blair's personal intervention, and without PR for the 1999 European election, Nigel
Farage might have remained an obscure City metals trader, though
quite possibly much wealthier. And history might have taken a very
different course.

The new PR system involved voters being given ranked lists of
candidates for each party, and used the D'Hondt system which was
very complicated to master. It meant that in a typical region with
eight MEPs, the threshold to get someone elected would be around
just 12.5 per cent of the total vote. In a bigger region, with ten
MEPs, the threshold might be as low as 9 per cent.

That was not beyond possibility for UKIP, and the party's hopes
were given a big boost in 1998 by a by-election for the European
Parliament, conducted under the traditional first-past-the-post
method, in the seat of Yorkshire South. UKIP's candidate Peter
Davies (father of the future Conservative MP Philip Davies) got 11.6
per cent, far better than the party had ever achieved in any previous parliamentary election. If that vote was reflected at the 1999
European poll, then UKIP should start getting MEPs. The result
was especially encouraging given that UKIP had never made much
effort in the North of England, and had no existing base in South
Yorkshire. This was an early sign that UKIP might flourish in run-
down working-class areas way beyond southern England.

UKIP's annual conference in 1998 finally agreed to drop Sked's
abstentionist policy, and announced that if the party got any MEPs,

they would now participate in the European Parliament (whose work is roughly split between three weeks in Brussels every month, and a week in Strasbourg in France). Nikki Sinclaire, later a prominent figure in UKIP's sagas, but then a student who occasionally worked for the party, recalls she went along to the conference opposed to the proposal, but 'I was persuaded, mainly by the force of Nigel's arguments'.[21]

The UK was divided into twelve areas under the new PR system – one each for Scotland, Wales and Northern Ireland, and nine English regions, matching the government's official regional areas. For Farage the new South East England constituency was the logical one to go for. Geographically, it formed a huge crescent round the western and southern boundary of Greater London, running from Oxfordshire and Buckinghamshire down to Hampshire and eastwards across to Kent – comprising more than sixty Westminster seats. This was where a large chunk – perhaps 35–40 per cent – of UKIP members lived. Farage saw himself as a man of Kent and had already fought three elections in the region. And picking the biggest of the new Euro-seats, with eleven MEPs, should allow Farage to get elected with less than 8 per cent of the total.

But his young friend and rival Craig Mackinlay had his eyes on the South East, too, and had just as strong a claim to be 'local'. Mackinlay, who was born and raised in Kent, had fought Gillingham in both the 1992 and 1997 elections; he lived in the Medway area, with his accountancy practice (with Farage a client) based in the old naval town of Chatham. And having been acting leader of UKIP for almost nine months, Mackinlay was well known among party members. UKIP's two brightest young Turks were up against each other.

On a personal basis, a seat in the European Parliament was a prize worth having. The salary was the same as paid to a member of the House of Commons – £47,008 in 1999 – but, compared with Westminster MPs, a British Member of the European Parliament enjoyed a much bigger budget to employ staff, and was also the beneficiary of numerous untaxed allowances for which no account needed to be given. Quite who would gain from these benefits – the person or the party – would be a bone of contention within UKIP for decades.

Hustings were held at the Abbey Centre in Westminster for the South East candidates, before a postal ballot of all UKIP's members in the region in which they had to rank contenders in order of preference. The votes were counted in December 1998, at UKIP's headquarters (which had moved to a bigger office that Tony Scholefield owned further up Regent Street, at number 189, opposite Hamleys toyshop). The count involved a complicated scheme whereby contenders got twelve points for a first place, eleven for a second, and so on. Craig Mackinlay was 'on tenterhooks' throughout, according to one of the counters, 'pacing up and down with a calculator. He kept looking over my shoulder to see how Nigel's points were adding up, so I took pity on him and pretended I was having trouble with the multiplication and would he check it for me? You've never seen a calculator whipped out so fast!' Farage was much more relaxed, and missed most of the count.

In the end Farage came top, with Mackinlay second. The figures were never released, but Mackinlay says it came down to just twelve votes between them. Contenders had been allowed, though, to apply for more than one region, and it turned out that Mackinlay topped the poll in the Greater London region, so he chose to contest that area instead of standing as number two to Farage in the South East. (Elsewhere, UKIP's list for the South West included, in bottom place, a 27-year-old Cornish fruit farmer, George Eustice. In 2020, Boris Johnson appointed him Secretary of State for the Environment, Food and Rural Affairs.)

The year 1999 promised to be a big one for UKIP, at a time of historic change in the European Union. At the start of January, eleven member states, including Germany, France, Italy and Spain, established the new single currency, the euro. But before UKIP could mount its campaign for the spring 1999 election to the European Parliament, the party fell prey to a major attempt by one of its more extreme rivals to destabilise and besmirch it. And UKIP's lead candidate made what was at best a serious error of judgement, one which has dogged his reputation ever since.

6

PICTURE OF A
COMPROMISING THREESOME

The Bavarian town of Herzogenaurach, about 14 miles north-west of Nuremburg, is best known for the extraordinary local rivalry between its two world-famous local sportswear firms – Adidas and Puma – separately established by two brothers after the war in one of the ultimate examples of sibling rivalry. In March 2020, a 50-year-old Englishman was elected as a member of Herzogenaurach's town council. Or, rather, he had been English until just six weeks before the elections, when he took German citizenship. His name was Mark Deavin.

Like Nigel Farage, Deavin married a German woman. Since 2009 he has taught in the linguistics and literary science department of the University of Bayreuth, about an hour north of Herzogenaurach, where he gives courses on international relations and white-collar crime. He'd quietly moved to Germany around 2000, thereby escaping the bitter political controversy he'd caused back in England, when his politics were very different – an episode which embroiled Nigel Farage in what he later called 'the worst mistake of my political life'.[1]

Deavin was brought up in Birmingham, in a household dominated by extreme right-wing politics. 'I grew up in a family of nationalists,' he says. 'It was stuffed down my throat from a young age.'[2] His father was an active member of the racist and often violent National Front. Deavin read law and history at Leeds University before moving to the London School of Economics (LSE) to do a PhD, briefly under another supervisor, but then with Alan Sked, who had just founded UKIP. Deavin's doctorate, on Harold Macmillan's European policy in the early 1960s and attempts to get Britain to join the Common Market, was due to be turned into a book – what Sked forecast as 'one of the great publishing events of 1995'.[3] 'Deavin was a very brilliant PhD student,' Sked says. 'One of the great disappointments of my life is that his thesis was never published.'[4]

The two men became good friends. Deavin, who was rather geeky looking and bespectacled in those days, not only shared Sked's enthusiasm for European history and politics, but also his hostility towards the European Union. So Sked recruited him to UKIP. 'I brought him into the party because he was a brilliant researcher,' he says, and in 1995 Sked even proposed to put Deavin in charge of a new UKIP research department and, according to Nigel Farage, to pay him £3,000 a year.[5] Deavin also spent almost two years on the UKIP National Executive, though he rarely attended.

Yet, astonishingly, Mark Deavin was leading a double life. While working for Sked and active in UKIP, he was also very close to Nick Griffin, a Cambridge-educated former member of the National Front who in 1993 had joined the British National Party (BNP) and become editor of its magazine *Spearhead*. By the mid-1990s the BNP had emerged as the main force on the extreme right of British politics, a successor to racist and neo-Nazi groups such as the League of Empire Loyalists and the National Front. The BNP's first leader, John Tyndall, had previously been a strong neo-Nazi who had founded the National Socialist Movement in Britain and been jailed for running a paramilitary political force. In 1999, Griffin would challenge and depose Tyndall, and he led the BNP for the next fifteen years, including five years as an MEP.

So close were Deavin and Griffin that just before the 1997 general election the pair worked on a pamphlet, *Who are the MIND BENDERS? The people who rule Britain through control of the mass media*. This maintained there was a Jewish conspiracy to control the media in Britain which involved Jews such as Jeremy Isaacs, Charles and Maurice Saatchi, Michael Grade and Alan Yentob. It also claimed Rupert Murdoch is part-Jewish through his mother (for which there is no evidence). The pamphlet asked whether these Jews had 'A power greater than government?' It was based on a similar publication written by a notorious white supremacist, William Pierce of the National Alliance, a neo-Nazi group in the United States.

Remarkably, Deavin was also involved with the National Alliance. In 1996, without anyone in UKIP appearing to notice, he became associate editor of its magazine *National Vanguard*, having written a glowing profile of the Norwegian writer and Nazi sympathiser Knut Hamsun (who died in 1952). In 1996 and 1997, Deavin spent several months working for the Alliance in its offices in West Virginia. It seems astonishing that Deavin managed to maintain two different personas simultaneously – as a friend of Alan Sked, and UKIP NEC member, and as a close confidant of the leading BNP member Nick Griffin – while also occupying a third role as adviser to William Pierce and his neo-Nazi group in the US. And all that while pursuing a respectable and successful academic career in Britain. Juggling these commitments would surely not have been possible in the subsequent era of social media when Deavin's activities and divided loyalties would quickly have been exposed.

In addition, Deavin wrote a book, *The Grand Plan: The Origins of Non-White Immigration*, which further advanced the idea of a Jewish conspiracy. He asserted that 'The mass immigration of non-Europeans into every White country on earth' had been brought about by 'a homogeneous transatlantic political and financial elite to destroy the national identities and create a raceless new world order'. And, he further claimed: 'These concerns were Jewish in origin . . . the promotion of World Government can also be seen to be in line with traditional Jewish messianic thinking.'[6]

Rumours about Mark Deavin did gradually begin to circulate within UKIP and beyond. Then in 1997, Deavin's secret association with Griffin was exposed by Roger Cook in an edition of his famous ITV programme *The Cook Report*. Several weeks before the general election, the producers had secretly filmed Deavin having dinner with Griffin, and with what the pair were led to believe were emissaries from Jean-Marie Le Pen's Front National party in France (in reality an undercover team from *The Cook Report*). 'Nick is essentially the leader in waiting of the BNP,' Deavin tells the supposed French sympathisers. 'What we need from you is experience, knowledge and financial [sic].'[7] Deavin also tells the undercover researchers that if Blair became prime minister (as he soon did, of course): 'The BNP will be the official opposition in the inner cities, in working-class areas. The UKIP will be the opposition in the shires, the county areas, the middle-class opposition. That party is a serious opposition to us in middle England, but, if we had the resources, we could tear it to pieces.'[8]

Mark Deavin and Nick Griffin saw themselves as part of a 'modernising' group within the BNP, who were planning to take control from John Tyndall and the old guard. They wanted to forge alliances with other British nationalist groups on the right, including UKIP – but only if UKIP started to campaign against immigration (Sked, an ex-Liberal who still saw himself as a 'liberal', never wanted to touch immigration as an issue). Deavin and Griffin were inspired by the experience of the Front National, and had been influenced by a recent book by the BBC correspondent Jonathan Marcus which explained how Jean-Marie Le Pen had brought together many strands of far-right French politics and campaigned strongly against immigration to gain 15 per cent of the vote in the 1995 presidential election. Marcus's book, says Deavin, became something of a 'blueprint' for the BNP modernisers in their quest for a more broad-based anti-immigration movement.[9]

When, just after the 1997 general election, producers on *The Cook Report* revealed to Sked on camera that Deavin was working secretly with Nick Griffin, the UKIP leader (as he still was) looked visibly shocked: 'It's shattering,' Sked said, 'because it's not only a political betrayal, but it's an academic betrayal; it's a personal betrayal. I was his academic supervisor. I was writing references to get him jobs in universities. I tried to get him a British Academy fellowship. I was trying to get him into my own department at the London School of Economics practically. I cannot think how I could have been more bitterly betrayed on any level.'[10]

Sked immediately expelled Mark Deavin from the party, but kept news of his identity to himself, as part of an agreement not to spoil the impact of *The Cook Report* before it was transmitted on Tuesday 17 June 1997. UKIP colleagues were told only that a far-right infiltrator who had been at the centre of the party had been thrown out.

This was all happening at the same time as the UKIP civil war being waged between Sked and his critics following the general election, which led to Sked's expulsion of Nigel Farage, Michael Holmes and David Lott. In a letter Sked warned UKIP members that he had expelled a BNP infiltrator who was about to be unmasked by *The Cook Report*. He then linked the mole with 'anyone who invites you to meetings not approved by Regent Street', i.e. Farage, Holmes and Lott.[11] And once the trio had been expelled, Sked wrote again to update UKIP members, saying: 'The infiltrator . . . has been removed from any association with the party. So, too, have certain others who were intent on bringing it into disrepute by working outside the national executive to form a new body open to Communists and the Radical Right' – a reference to the proposed 'New Alliance' with former candidates from the Referendum Party.[12]

Shortly after his expulsion, Farage says, he received a call from Mark Deavin. Farage claims he had already heard by this stage that Deavin was the individual who'd been expelled as an infiltrator, and says he'd long suspected he had BNP links. According to Farage, Deavin now told him 'he had valuable information about Sked which might help me in the battle'.[13] Farage then made the extraordinary decision to meet Mark Deavin at his office in the City, and took him out to lunch in a pub restaurant in St Katharine's Dock near Tower Bridge.

Eighteen months later, Farage would very precisely date the lunch as 17 June 1997, only hours before *The Cook Report* was broadcast. Mark Deavin says he actually met Farage significantly *after* the ITV programme, days or even weeks later.

After their lunch, having left the pub, and while out on the pavement, Deavin and Farage fell into a short conversation with another BNP figure, the notorious Tony Lecomber – known as 'The Bomber' because of his recent violent past which included several serious criminal convictions. Among these was a three-year jail sentence in 1986 for possession of bombs and grenades, and another three years in 1991 for stabbing a Jewish teacher who had tried to remove a BNP sticker at an underground station. As the three men spoke, somebody photographed them from nearby.

Around the time of the Farage lunch – whether before or after is not clear – Deavin wrote an article for *Spearhead* in which he viciously attacked his old friend Alan Sked. He claimed that in 1997 Sked had been so worried that Farage might do well in Salisbury, and even win the seat – and therefore outshine him – that Sked had fed 'dirt' on Farage to the local press, 'in particular the allegation that Farage's father had been a member of the National Front during the 1970s'.[14] (Sked has often made this allegation. Despite enquiries by this author and other journalists, no evidence has emerged that Guy Farage was in the National Front, and he denies it.)

It would be many months before the photo, and the fact of the Farage–Deavin–Lecomber encounter, actually seeped out, and even then knowledge seems initially to have been limited to people in UKIP and the BNP.

When questioned by the UKIP NEC in February 1999, Nigel Farage said he thought the photo with Deavin and Lecomber might have been taken at a 'garden party' before Deavin was expelled. The UKIP NEC chose not to pursue the matter. Then, on Saturday 5 June 1999, five days before the European elections, Andrew Pierce exposed the meeting in a substantial story in *The Times*. A copy of the photo had been 'passed anonymously' to the paper, Pierce wrote, though strangely *The Times* did not print it. The paper revealed that Farage had been 'rebuked' by Michael Holmes, the businessman who succeeded Alan Sked as leader. The timing of the story was obviously designed to do maximum damage to UKIP's election chances.

'I have no recollection of ever meeting Tony Lecomber,' Farage insisted. 'I do not know him. I am at a mystery to explain how he got in the photograph. I have been stitched up.'[15] By now Farage had dropped the 'garden party' explanation and said the photo was taken when Mark Deavin visited his office and they went out to lunch. Farage said he had 'no idea' that the photo was being taken, and he claimed that Deavin had told him about the anti-Semitic pamphlet he had written. 'I told him he was making a grave error of judgement.

I have never spoken to him since then.' 'It was short-sighted,' said Michael Holmes. 'Like many of us, people are naive.'[16]

Three days later, just two days before polling, Alan Sked took his revenge on the party he'd founded, and the man who had helped topple him, with a feature article in *The Times* under the heading, 'I would advise people voting on Thursday to help the Tory revival'. Sked cited the Deavin photo among his reasons:

> Nigel Farage has been in contact with political extremists in the British National Party, including one who has written an anti-Semitic tract and one who has served two prison terms, one for stabbing a Jewish gentleman . . . I believe that it is now impossible to support UKIP in Thursday's elections. If people have to vote, they should instead vote for the Conservative Party.[17]

UKIP immediately issued a press release saying that Sked's article contained allegations against Nigel Farage which were 'highly defamatory and wholly untrue'.[18] Two weeks after the election, with financial assistance from UKIP, Farage sued *The Times* in his capacity as party chairman. His affidavit gave the exact date of the lunch as 17 June 1997, which, if true, meant it was only hours before *The Cook Report* was broadcast. It stated:

> The true position regarding Mark Deavin was that I briefly met Mr Deavin, at his request, on 17 June 1997, and had lunch with him at a restaurant . . . The background to my meeting with Mr Deavin on 17 June 1997 was that Mr Deavin had been expelled from the UKIP in May 1997 when it was discovered that he had links with the BNP. When Mr Deavin telephoned me in June requesting a meeting I agreed to meet him as I had been shocked by his defection to the BNP and wanted to find out why he had left the UKIP. I also thought that Mr Deavin might be able to provide me with information that could assist me in my own dispute with Dr Sked, due to Mr Deavin's close association with Dr Sked . . .
>
> I have no recollection of ever meeting or speaking to Mr Lecomber in my life. I only became aware of his existence when I

was shown a copy of the photograph in November 1998. I can only surmise that Mr Lecomber was planted outside the restaurant or that the photograph has been doctored to add Mr Lecomber at a later stage.[19]

Speaking to the author in 2020, Mark Deavin gives a rather different account. He says that, following his expulsion from UKIP, and 'a week, or perhaps two weeks after the broadcast', he wrote to Sked, Farage and several other senior UKIP figures trying to explain his belief in the need for an alliance among British nationalists, and his view that 'UKIP couldn't ignore the immigration issue'. As a result of that letter, Deavin says, Farage rang him in Birmingham where he was staying with his girlfriend. 'We had a conversation on the phone, and he expressed interest in meeting me. He expressed sympathy with the sentiments in the letter, and the need for a broader-based right-wing alliance with immigration as a major issue.'[20]

Mark Deavin says Farage would have known by then that he was working with Nick Griffin, though at that stage Griffin may not have meant much to Farage, as he was not yet BNP leader and the public ogre he subsequently became. But when they chatted in Farage's office, and later over lunch, Deavin says he felt Farage wasn't interested in a Le Pen-style broad-based anti-immigration movement. 'He paid lip service to it,' he recalls. 'I don't think he displayed any desire to work with the BNP. It became clear to me that his main aim was to get information about Alan Sked that he could probably use, information that would support his position in the power struggle that was going on.'[21] So while Deavin says Farage was wrong in his affidavit about the date of their encounter, and who initiated it, he agrees that Farage's motive seems primarily to have been to gather material against Alan Sked.

Farage's account is still puzzling. First, because until *The Cook Report* was broadcast – on the evening of his Deavin lunch (according to Farage) – no UKIP officials or NEC members, apart from Sked himself, had been told the identity of the infiltrator who had been expelled, yet Farage says he had been 'shocked by his defection to the BNP'. If Farage knew before the lunch that Deavin had been expelled as a BNP mole, his explanation sits uneasily with his long-standing insistence that UKIP should never have anything to do with the BNP – to the extent that former members were officially barred from UKIP membership. Farage was taking a big risk by meeting Deavin, especially where they could be seen in public.

In his memoirs, Farage claims he had heard a rumour long before they met that Deavin was involved with the BNP, but that when he raised this with Sked, the UKIP leader dismissed the idea as 'all nonsense' and 'tittle-tattle'. Farage also claims he was told by someone from *The Cook Report* in April 1997 that Deavin was a BNP activist.[22] All this makes his decision to have lunch with Deavin – an active member of a rival, very racist party – all the more surprising.

Second, instead of Farage's vague recollection from the February 1999 NEC that they may have met at a 'garden party' early in 1997, his summer 1999 affidavit not only relates how the meeting arose, and that they had lunch together, but also a precise date. Why couldn't Farage remember any of these details when questioned by the NEC three months before?

Third, if Deavin requested the meeting, as Farage suggested in his affidavit, why did Farage not explain why Deavin had asked to meet him?

In his 2010 memoir, *Fighting Bull*, Farage says Deavin had offered him 'valuable information' on Sked. The 1999 affidavit, however, just said he 'thought that Mr Deavin might be able to provide me with information that could assist me in my own dispute with Dr Sked'.[23] According to his 2010 account, Deavin told Farage that it had never been his plan to 'betray' UKIP, but that he had been the recent victim of a mugging, and had 'found solace and support' in the BNP. 'Now he wanted to make it up to me.' When they met at the restaurant, Farage says, 'Deavin remained apologetic and conciliatory but had no new intelligence to convey'.[24]

It was only later, according to Farage, that he found he had been photographed outside the pub, not just with Deavin, but that 'one of the people hanging around us' and also in the picture, was Tony 'The Bomber' Lecomber. 'I had been right royally stitched up,' he says.[25]

Mark Deavin said in 2020 that he didn't know they were being photographed and has no idea who took the picture or why. He had arranged for Lecomber to be in the vicinity, he says, because, 'despite his shady past', Lecomber was part of Nick Griffin's 'more democratic' moderniser group, and Deavin wanted to show Farage that he wasn't operating alone. Deavin can't recall for certain, but he suspects that he warned Farage that Lecomber might be outside by saying something to the effect that he had asked a BNP associate to come and pick him up. 'I briefly introduced him [Lecomber] as being a colleague who was also interested in the things I had talked about in the letter [written earlier to Farage].' The conversation was 'just passing', he says. 'There was nothing in detail. It was in the hope, in the possibility of things coming out of the meeting. The idea was to plant seeds without too much pressure.'[26]

Nick Griffin, who helped depose John Tyndall as BNP leader in 1999, disputes some of Deavin's account. It was simply an attempt to set Farage up, Griffin maintains, and Deavin was certainly in on the plot. Griffin says that Deavin told him Farage was a rising star within UKIP, at a time when the party might become strong rivals to the BNP on the nationalist and Eurosceptic right. Once Deavin and Farage had agreed to meet, Griffin says he and Deavin arranged for Lecomber to turn up, knowing that his violent reputation might be hugely damaging to Farage – Lecomber being 'the crazed bomber'. And they also arranged for a photographer to capture the meeting. 'The photo was partly and primarily to give Farage problems,' Griffin claims. 'It was a dirty trick from beginning to end.'[27] The photo was then released more than a year later, in the run-up to the 1999 European election in the hope it would be picked up in the main-stream press. It duly was, albeit very slowly.

Over time, Farage's own explanation of why he met Deavin has gradually evolved. First, it was perhaps a chance encounter at a garden party; then a meeting to discuss Deavin's departure from UKIP; next the possibility of getting valuable information about Sked; and finally, in his memoirs, the offer of such information. The accounts don't entirely contradict each other, but the differences do suggest Farage has not been open with the truth.

On the more serious charge – that Farage met Deavin to forge some kind of alliance with the racist BNP and its would-be leader Nick Griffin – the evidence is thin. True, Mark Deavin says Farage expressed interest in some kind of accommodation when Farage phoned to arrange the meeting, but his subsequent 'lip service' to the idea of an anti-immigration alliance (according to Deavin) suggests it was merely a hook to get Deavin to see him.

Nonetheless, whatever his motive, it does seem Farage was set up by someone in the BNP – probably Griffin, as he says, along with Lecomber – and that the photograph was taken to damage UKIP and one of its rising stars amid the ongoing rivalry between the two parties.

Farage's legal action against *The Times* was quickly settled out of court, and he later revealed that the go-between had been *The Times*'s assistant editor Michael Gove. 'He did me a massive favour,' Farage told the *Sunday Times* in 2015. 'I was out of my depth and he brokered a solution with me and the editor, and he didn't have to do that. I have been very grateful to him ever since.'[28] In a short (twenty-line) article in July 1999, *The Times* merely made a minor clarification to the Sked article, saying that rather than being in contact with political extremists, Farage had 'briefly met a former UKIP member who had defected to the BNP, at that individual's request, to discuss his defection'.[29] This was perhaps enough for Farage to save face and to spare him from more costly litigation. However, when the UKIP leader Michael Holmes told the party conference that autumn that *The Times* had issued an 'apology' for the 'scurrilous' article by Sked, the newspaper's legal manager wrote to Farage to tell him they had not apologised, and he insisted that Sked's article had not been 'scurrilous'.[30] Nonetheless, in his memoirs Farage repeated the false claim that *The Times* printed 'an apology'.[31]

In his article for the BNP magazine *Spearhead*, written around the time of his lunch with Farage, Deavin explained how he wanted Farage and others in UKIP to defect to the BNP. Many UKIP members, Deavin wrote, were convinced that 'the time had come for closer cooperation with patriots from other political parties'. Deavin lauded Nigel Farage as a more nationalist figure who was willing to take up 'politically incorrect' issues such as immigration and law and order, which Deavin said Sked had always avoided. 'UKIP has no political future,' Deavin wrote. 'Whether Nigel Farage and his supporters will recognise this fact and follow me over to the BNP is still not clear. It is more likely that they will try to oust Sked, take control of UKIP and reposition it on the right.'[32]

Mark Deavin didn't disappear from Britain immediately. Later in 1997, the notorious historian and Holocaust-denier David Irving planned to publish Deavin's book *Macmillan's Hidden Agenda*. The book never came out (though remarkably it was still advertised on Amazon more than twenty years later). And in 1998 Deavin was still writing articles for *Spearhead* under his own name. He had no further dealings with Farage, he says, though when Nick Griffin was elected as an MEP in 2009 he says the BNP leader phoned him and tried to recruit him to his staff.

Today, living in southern Germany, Mark Deavin appears to be a very changed man. 'Those are things from the past that I deeply regret,' he says. 'I'm pretty ashamed of a lot of this stuff. It's certainly a sordid history. It was a very sad time, to be honest. It's difficult for me rationally to explain my behaviour.' He now sees the European Union as a 'force for good' and nationalism as 'a primitive force that can only be destructive'.[33]

While his old UKIP and BNP friends eagerly awaited Brexit Day in January 2020, Deavin hoped it would never happen, and feared it might ruin his new political career. As an Englishman, following Brexit, he wouldn't have been allowed to stand for his town council in Bavaria, and he only just managed to organise the paperwork to change nationality at the very last minute.

And from being involved with UKIP and also two organisations on the extreme racist and anti-Semitic right, Deavin's modern-day politics could hardly be more different. In the 2020 elections for Herzogenaurach council he stood for the Green Party. Sporting a beard these days, and dressed more casually than in his UKIP/BNP period, he seems to be a popular local figure. Deavin got more votes in the 2020 local election than all but three of his party's thirty candidates. He says colleagues on the council and at the University of Bayreuth do know of his extreme right-wing past.

The truth of the whole Mark Deavin episode, and why Nigel Farage met him, may never be established conclusively. Understandably, the affair has often been exploited by Farage's enemies over the years – by Alan Sked, Farage's critics in UKIP, by the BNP, and of course by people on the left. The Deavin story burst out in public at the worst possible time for Nigel Farage, as it was clearly designed to. As party chairman, campaign manager and a lead candidate, Farage was in the final throes of the make-or-break Euro-elections. If UKIP didn't get people elected this time, he told colleagues, the party's future looked 'bleak'.[34]

It was a hectic, chaotic and nail-biting campaign, according to the UKIP organiser in Oxfordshire, Peter Gardner. The day before Royal Mail was due to send out UKIP's election addresses for the South East region, only four of the party's eleven candidates had completed their nomination forms. The printers wanted money up front – money the South East party didn't yet have; there was a problem over the £ logo to go next to the party name on ballot papers; and serious tensions arose between leader Michael Holmes and his colleagues. Farage was 'depressed by the lack of press coverage', says Peter Gardner, and the party was downhearted that the BBC and other broadcasters seemed to give a lot more coverage to a new pro-EU Conservative breakaway party led by former Tory MEP John Stevens than it did to them.

Farage's campaign in the South East was run from a tiny office in a car components warehouse in Redhill, Surrey, lent to them by UKIP member Roy Walters, where Farage and UKIP activists had to find whatever space they could amid the boxes and shelves of motor supplies for Walters' business.

Nigel Farage still had time for the considerate touch, however. Nikki Sinclaire, the young UKIP activist and occasional office worker, went along to a Farage rally at the Royal Dockyard in Chatham. Only five weeks earlier she'd suffered the horror of being raped late at night on a quiet street in the East End, and Sinclaire had told several of her UKIP colleagues about the attack. At the end of the Chatham rally, she relates:

Nigel Farage came up to me and asked if I was all right. He was very sympathetic, angry on my behalf, and asked was there anything he could do. He seemed perfectly sincere and I was very pleasantly surprised. He seemed so kind. I'd known him since 1997, but I hadn't necessarily thought of him as that sort of person. He'd seemed like a bit of a joke, in his pinstripe suit that reminded me of Arthur Daley.[35]

UKIP's campaign literature tried to exploit the idea that established politicians benefited personally from the European 'gravy train', and stressed how any MEPs they got elected would resist such temptations. 'Unlike the other parties, The UK Independence Party will not join this gravy train,' one leaflet declared. 'Our MEPs will be pledged to taking only those expenses to which they have verifiable claims.'[36] Two leaflets for the South East region where Farage was lead candidate, even showed a cartoon of a 'gravy train' with one carriage marked 'crony class'. In one case the cartoon was headed: 'LET'S STOP PAYING FOR THE GRAVY TRAIN – POLITICIANS LOVE IT.' Beneath, was a Q and A which included this exchange:

Q: So you'll be on that gravy train soon, ripping us all off like the others – putting your expenses in your pension funds, working 12 weeks of the year for a fat salary, paying your girlfriends and dentists to be 'researchers and secretaries'?

A: No way. The gravy train is an outrage, and it's probably worse than all of us even think. The EU is institutionally corrupt. UKIP Euro MPs will only take legitimate personal expenses and make a substantial donation to a fund for victims of the European Union. All expenses will be receipted and will be open to annual public inspection . . . We have a clear stand against the current expenses outrage – still going on – and will not play that game ever.[37]

Earlier in the year, Michael Holmes had made an even stronger commitment. In a letter to the *Daily Telegraph*, he promised, 'All UKIP candidates have agreed to retain only a proportion of their MEP salary sufficient to live on, and contribute the rest to campaign funds to continue the fight for Britain's independence.'[38]

With three weeks to go before polling, Farage was already so exhausted by the campaign that his regional committee 'virtually ordered him to rest, at least for a day. He went to a cricket match, but still took his mobile phone.'[39]

Farage's morale took further blows with the Deavin story in *The Times* and Alan Sked's subsequent article in the same paper urging readers to vote Conservative, for which the former leader was then asked to do interviews by broadcasters. So when at last UKIP was getting the media coverage activists craved, it was so depressing that it was the last kind of coverage they wanted. 'Farage's customary confidence and optimism was dented,' Gardner writes, though it came as a bit of a relief that *The Times* only printed their article, not the photo itself. The *News of the World*, after a threat from Farage's lawyers, dropped a follow-up item, but the story was picked up by the *Daily Express* and *Evening Standard*.[40]

The Times coverage was a sign that UKIP was starting to matter, that people were starting to worry about them, but that was little consolation to Farage and his colleagues at the time. According to David Lott, the articles were a serious distraction for Farage. Lott wrote in his diary, two days before polling, that Farage 'had no thought for anything else and became unapproachable. He plans to fight it tooth and nail through [solicitors] Carter-Ruck. He shot off up to London and spent the day working on it. Some of us feel that he is right to sue *The Times* but he should delay things until after the election.'[41] Lott relates gossip that, in the West Midlands, Labour distributed copies of Sked's article in areas with lots of Black and Asian voters.

To coincide with the rest of the EU, the results were announced on the Sunday night, three days after polling. Farage, David Lott and his team met for dinner at the Wessex Hotel in Winchester before moving to the local Guildhall where South East votes were being

counted. They began to worry about 'black holes' in the campaign –
towns where UKIP had put in very little work, but as the votes
mounted Farage was confident. 'Would Nigel be the only success?'
David Lott wrote in his diary:

> As we were waiting for our result . . . we were electrified by the
> news that Michael [Holmes] was elected in the [South West].
> The cheer raised the roof. Our result followed . . . and then to
> everyone's delight we got an outsider in for the Eastern Region –
> Jeffrey Titford. THREE! No one can ignore us now.[42]

UKIP got 144,514 votes in the South East – or 9.7 per cent – and
Farage was elected eighth of the region's eleven MEPs, while in
eleventh place came Caroline Lucas, the first ever Green MEP.
Nationally, UKIP had come fourth with 6.5 per cent of the vote,
ahead of the Greens. It's hard to say, though, if the Mark Deavin
story harmed UKIP's performance, and prevented the party narrowly getting MEPs in three other regions where the margins
were tight – the North West, Yorkshire and Humberside – and in
London, where Craig Mackinlay was about 2 per cent short of the
threshold.

It was still a good result for UKIP. The Liberal Democrats are
poor campaigners when not fighting single constituencies, and
UKIP may have picked up some of their 'protest vote', despite the
two parties' very different views on Europe. The election also saw
Labour beaten by the Conservatives, whose young new Eurosceptic
leader William Hague had run a campaign against joining the single
currency. After the efforts of the Referendum Party and UKIP in
1997, Europe was showing signs of becoming an election issue, and
the Conservative delegation to the European Parliament included
its first Eurosceptics – Roger Helmer, Chris Heaton-Harris and
Dan Hannan.

In Winchester, UKIP supporters jeered when the newly elected
Labour MEP, Peter Skinner, made his speech and denounced that
night's shift to the right, which extended to other EU states as well
as Britain. 'He was howled down by UKIP,' Lott wrote. 'He then

lost it when UKIP was shouting "Off, Off, Off," yelling, "We are going to get you." With that he stalked off the stage!'

Afterwards, Lott says, the Farage team moved to the bar at the Winchester Guildhall where the barman 'disappeared for about 45 minutes so we all helped ourselves liberally. Perhaps he is a supporter.'[43]

Nigel Farage was suddenly in demand, at last, for broadcast interviews, but he and his supporters were furious when James Naughtie of BBC Radio 4 suggested on air that he must be pleased that the leader of the Front National in France, Jean-Marie Le Pen, had been re-elected. 'God these people who take our licence fee are sick,' David Lott wrote afterwards:

> Nigel handles it all so calmly and well. He is a natural with the media. How they hate to see an interloper enter the political scene and stir up their murky pond. I think he was enjoying himself with the adrenalin flowing. He is already starting the debate on Europe and is a fine advocate. He will defuse these attempts to paint us as extremists with charm and style. No one will do it better.

In later years, Farage would often claim that his first-ever live TV interview was at 1.30 a.m. that night with Phil Hornby of the ITV regional station Meridian (though actually the interview was pre-recorded).

'Next week,' Hornby suggested, 'you'll be off on Eurostar to the European Parliament, and you'll find a never-ending round of invitations – to lunches, dinners, champagne receptions. Do you think you'll become corrupted by the lifestyle?'

'No,' Nigel Farage responded with a grin. 'I've always lived like that.'[44]

7

BREAKING AND ENTERING

Shortly before midnight on 2 October 1999, a 61-year-old braved the Saturday night drunks and revellers of London's West End and entered his premises at 189 Regent Street, a block called Triumph House. He was accompanied by a locksmith. The pair took the lift to the fourth floor and proceeded to change the locks on the offices of the UK Independence Party.

Tony Scholefield then fixed a notice to the door explaining that he had informed the Metropolitan Police about what he was doing, and that he had acted in his capacity as secretary of the UKIP. Scholefield then faxed both the leader of the party, Michael Holmes, and its chairman, Nigel Farage, to demand that:

> you immediately confirm to me that you and persons authorised by you or known to you will not visit the office without prior notice to me, will not cause the office staff to stop faithfully carrying out such reasonable orders I give them, take away or interfere with the data base or any other records or property of the party.

Farage ignored Scholefield's fax. The next morning, the new MEP ordered a second locksmith to go to Regent Street and make sure the locks were changed again. Less than four months after UKIP's eye-catching successes in the European elections, the party was beset by a second internal war. UKIP was split between the leadership faction, with Holmes effectively based in Wiltshire, and a rebel group around Scholefield still based in London.

The election of three Members of the European Parliament had raised the stakes considerably in the tangled internal politics of UKIP. On European results night, even UKIP figures themselves probably didn't appreciate the enormous leap they had just taken, and the potential for internal rancour. How did their triumph unravel so fast?

Nigel Farage, Michael Holmes and Jeffrey Titford would be the first of sixty-six people over the next twenty years to be elected either as MEPs for UKIP and/or its successor, the Brexit Party. The letters MEP after their names gave each of the three men a new authority and status with the media. They'd now have plenty of staff at their disposal, all paid for from European Union funds – this in an era when MEPs were lavished more than ever with tens of thousands of pounds in allowances and extra payments on top of their basic salaries, most of it untaxed. Above all, the European Parliament would provide a new public platform. 'We're here because only by coming here can we get publicity back at home,' Farage explained to a French Green MEP on his first trip to Strasbourg. 'I've got very mixed feelings about being here. I think the procedure of the Parliament, the voting system, the whole thing is a farce frankly.'[1]

Now it was time for a reckoning.

Just seven weeks before the 1999 European election, UKIP leader Michael Holmes had written to all his candidates telling them to sign a witnessed declaration about their finances in the event of becoming MEPs. UKIP candidates had to pledge to use 'all allowances generated as a result of my membership of the European Parliament' as the UKIP NEC 'directed' them to, so long as this was in line with EU rules. And candidates also had to swear they'd pay any surpluses they made in expenses, beyond what they needed for their work as MEPs, to a UKIP trust fund for '*inter alia* the assistance and/or defence of victims of European Union regulations'. Third, budding UKIP MEPs had to agree that if elected they would provide the NEC with a 'quarterly detailed account' of what reimbursement and allowances they had received from the European Parliament, and how they had spent that money.[2]

The front page of UKIP's manifesto for the 1999 elections announced that 'all UKIP candidates have given written undertakings which prevent them benefiting personally from their expenses and allowances as MEPs'. And while the letter from Holmes had made them pledge to supply regular accounts to the NEC, the manifesto went further. These expense accounts would be made 'available publicly', the party promised voters.[3]

Nigel Farage flew out to Strasbourg in July from London City Airport with the other two UKIP MEPs and their partners. Farage was carrying a straw boater as he boarded the plane. The group was accompanied by the ITV reporter Phil Hornby, who then filmed Farage and his colleagues holding a 'celebration dinner' in one of Strasbourg's top restaurants. Later on the trip, Hornby asked: 'Is there something, Nigel Farage, a touch hypocritical about you flying out on these free flights and enjoying the restaurants and so on of the Parliament here, and enjoying the gravy train, so-called, life of an MEP? How do you square that circle?' Nigel Farage reminded Hornby of what UKIP had said 'right through' the 1999 campaign:

> We said we are not going on the gravy train; that we are the only people who are intending, annually, to publish so that the public can inspect them, our expense accounts, our allowance accounts, and the excess that we get – the excess that we are forced to take – particularly on travelling allowances, we are going to be putting into a trust fund and that money will be used to help victims of the European Union in our country. So I do reject the allegation that we're on the gravy train and there's certainly no chance of the three of us going native.[4]

In 1999, when Farage and his colleagues first went to Brussels (and once a month to Strasbourg), they benefited from a wide range of allowances:

– €3,262 (£2,113) per month 'general expenditure allowance' for office costs;

- €2,037 (£1,319) maximum annual 'travel allowance' for journeys other than those between the Parliament buildings and the constituency;
- 'subsistence allowance' of €231 (£149) per day when attending parliamentary meetings;
- €9,408 (£6,095) maximum per month 'secretarial assistance allowance'.[5]

At that time, these allowances would have been worth very roughly about £135,000 a year, assuming Farage attended the Parliament four days in every week that it met. This was on top of his basic salary of £47,008.

In addition, MEPs could also claim a 'flat-rate travel allowance' of €0.76 (49p) per kilometre for the first 400 kilometres and €0.38 (24p) thereafter, for travel between their constituencies and the two Parliament buildings. Alternatively, the European Parliament would pay MEPs the cost of a business-class airfare from their constituency to Brussels or Strasbourg and back, whether or not they actually travelled business class. If they went economy instead, the MEPs made a huge profit on every trip. This personal benefit was deemed to be tax-free.

An independent TV company, Mosaic Films, made a documentary about Farage's early weeks in the Parliament. In one scene he tries to take the cameraman into the office where MEPs claim their regular allowances. 'You've got to have a look inside here,' he says to camera. 'This is really the feeding ground . . . Come on in.' But Farage and the film crew are barred, and two officials briefly try to cover the lens. Farage speaks to camera:

That's very telling, isn't it? That the European Parliament talks about openness; it talks about honesty, but in there, there is a feeding frenzy going on in there – MEPs collecting vast allowances, most of them in cash, receipts not needed, and in this wonderful open Parliament you're not allowed to go in there with a camera to witness what's going on.[6]

Farage is then filmed going back into the office, but soon re-emerges clutching a cheque and several banknotes in high denominations. 'Everyone's a winner with Europe,' he declares, brandishing his money:

> There you are — what they didn't want you to see in the offices — the loot . . . I'm not saying that all of this is wrong, but I am saying that on travel expenses, you should have to produce receipts and I think it's absolutely monstrous that people are being paid money, way in excess of their genuine travelling requirements. Now that [holding the money] represents four working days and one jour-ney — we're talking about £1,900 . . . I worked it out — because so much of what you get is after tax — that if you used the secretarial allowances to pay your wife, on top of all the other games that you can play, I reckon this job in sterling terms is worth about £250,000 a year — that's what you'd need to earn working for Goldman Sachs or someone like that.

Turning to a Danish MEP on camera, Farage asks: 'How many people in the Parliament use these travel expenses for their move-ments and how many put it straight in their pockets?' 'I think the great majority,' the Danish MEP replies with a grin. 'Big pockets. It's part of our political structure. We do that.'[7] Farage also takes the crew into a garage full of new Mercedes cars used to ferry MEPs round Strasbourg and Brussels on request.

However, little came of UKIP's promise of openness for its MEPs' expenses and allowances. Within five months the NEC was complaining that both Farage and Michael Holmes had failed to produce the required accounts.[8] In the *Guardian*, Nicholas Watt reported: 'Fellow MEPs are watching in amusement as the patri-otic trio [Farage, Holmes and Titford] spend their daily allowances down to the last euro on smart hotels and restaurants, leaving barely any money for their promised "fighting fund" to take Britain out of Europe.' Watt revealed that the three MEPs had been staying at the Sofitel in Strasbourg where a single room then cost £130 a night, plus £10 for 'a sumptuous breakfast'. That came close to the

MEPs' flat-rate daily allowance of about £145. 'We are new boys,' said Farage, explaining that their hotel had been booked for them by the European Parliament. 'We will be looking for more reasonable accommodation so that money can be ploughed back into our campaign fund.'[9]

Nonetheless, a brief, half-hearted attempt was actually made to fulfil the front-page pledge from UKIP's 1999 manifesto to allocate surpluses acquired by the party's MEPs to help 'victims of European Union regulations'. The self-styled Metric Martyrs were a couple of Sunderland shopkeepers, one of whom was prosecuted by the local council for selling bananas in pounds and ounces and refusing to comply with two European directives that trading throughout the EU now had to be conducted in kilos and grams.

When Farage and his colleague Jeffrey Titford announced that they had contributed £11,500 from their excess travel allowances to the martyrs' fund, they were told by the Parliament that it was against the rules. Any excess could only be used by them personally, and they would face legal action unless they reimbursed the European Parliament the £11,500. 'We are at war with the Parliament over travel expenses,' said Farage.[10] In reality, had the MEPs taken the money, then quietly made personal donations for similar sums to the fund, or indeed to UKIP, the Parliament could not and would not have complained. But that would have lost them the publicity. The martyrs' organiser Neil Herron has always claimed he never received the £11,500 anyway.

Twenty-one years later, on the day he left the Parliament, Nigel Farage said he had been 'utterly bewildered' on his first day in Strasbourg. 'So there's three complete unknowns from a party not many people had heard of,' Farage related in typical self-deprecatory fashion.[11]

When MEPs came to vote, Farage says, he was again 'bewildered', so he folded his arms and 'refused to take part' because he didn't have a clue what the vote was about. He was nervous; he felt a bit out of his depth and may even have been a little daunted by the famous names and faces around him. 'This chamber twenty years ago was full of former prime ministers from European countries,' he said. 'There were really some very senior political figures here, because this is rather like the House of Lords.'

The 1999–2004 Parliament contained the former French socialist PM Michel Rocard and two future presidents, Nicolas Sarkozy and François Hollande, along with the former Portuguese PM and president Mario Soares, and two giants of Northern Irish politics, Ian Paisley and John Hume. MEPs in 1999 also included the grandsons of Charles de Gaulle, Harold Macmillan, and even the granddaughter of Benito Mussolini. Nor was it long since the former French president Valéry Giscard d'Estaing had been an MEP, along with the last crown prince of Austria-Hungary, Otto von Habsburg (who was a German MEP until 1999). 'On a personal level I had doubts,' Farage admitted. 'Was I really up to this? Was I good enough to do this? . . . And I really got off to a slow start – didn't try and rush anything, didn't run before I could walk.' It was a rare glimpse of how Farage can often be troubled by self-doubt, and fears that he might not be able to deliver.

These were 'quite nervous beginnings', Farage later confessed, but he and his colleagues also thought it was a 'real pioneering adventure'.[12] Thanks to PR, a new party had emerged onto the political stage that questioned the whole existence of the European Union and Britain's involvement.

Nigel Farage's maiden speech in the Strasbourg Parliament, in July 1999, was very dull – on an incident in Belgium where animal products had been contaminated by dioxins – and it was utterly untypical of his speeches in later years. The new UKIP MEP looked nervous as he read carefully from notes, with none of the bombast and confidence for which he would later become famous across the Continent and beyond. The European Commission was 'launching once again into frenzied legislative action', he told fellow MEPs. 'This is damaging British interests.'[13]

Farage did skilfully manage to finish on time, however, having been shocked to learn on the day he arrived that there was usually a ninety-second or two-minute time limit on speeches by backbenchers (roughly 200 or 300 words). And ordinary MEPs were only allowed to deliver twenty-eight speeches a year, though that was never a problem for Farage, who only spoke forty times in the whole 1999 Parliament – just over an hour of speech in five years. Remarkably, twelve of those speeches were on fishing policy – reflecting, in part, his own hobby. Indeed, Farage was elected to the Fisheries Committee but famously only ever attended one meeting.

Despite his pedestrian first effort, within a few months Farage was into his stride in the debating chamber. In his fourth speech, that autumn, he told MEPs: 'It is about time that my own country recognised that our interests are best served by not being a member of this club . . . While the UK has obeyed EU law to the letter, other countries are running a cart and horse through the rule-book. The "level playing field" is about as level as the decks of the *Titanic* after it hit the iceberg!'[14]

UKIP used their MEPs' parliamentary allowances to assemble a small pool of about ten professional staff. Under the rules, these people were meant to work for MEPs on their parliamentary duties. In reality, they spent nearly all their time on party political activities for UKIP, and were largely based in their MEPs' regional constituencies in southern England. UKIP was breaking the rules of the European Parliament, but nobody seemed to care much. Most other parties – British and European – bent the rules to some extent. As with many scandals in the European Union, the authorities were reluctant to investigate as it would upset too many people and might damage the whole European project. They would turn a blind eye, so long as the rules weren't flouted too obviously.

Within the politics of the European Parliament it is vital for any small party to team up with parties from other countries to form a recognised multi-national group. The Parliament will then supply extra staff and funding for the group; give its leader and spokespeople enhanced speaking rights; and group members get other perks such as places on foreign delegations. UKIP duly joined a new group called the Europe of Democracies and Diversities – the EDD – formed in 1999 under the leadership of Jens-Peter Bonde, a left-leaning Eurosceptic from Denmark who had a reputation as a master of fiddling the EU allowances system. Bonde had first been elected an MEP back in 1979 for the People's Movement Against the EEC, which wanted Denmark to leave the Union, though he later switched to the June Movement, which urged reform rather than withdrawal and had got three MEPs in 1999. The seventeen members of the new EDD group also included six MEPs from the Hunting, Fishing, Nature and Traditions group from France, which was a sort of Gallic version of the Countryside Alliance in Britain. The group worked astonishingly well, even though UKIP wanted to leave the EU, and Jens-Peter Bonde said working for withdrawal made no sense. 'We could not find a compromise between those two positions before every speech,' Bonde said before his death in 2021. 'So Nigel made his speeches; I made my speeches, and they were very different.'[15] Yet the Parliament's rules stipulated that parties in such groups had to have 'political affinity', which plainly wasn't the case here.

Among the EDD's first employees was Richard North, who in 1997 had very briefly switched from UKIP to the Referendum Party and then back again. North had been investigating the work of the European Union for years, and was writing a substantial history of the EU with the iconoclastic journalist Christopher Booker, one of the founders of *Private Eye*. In reality North says he wasn't really working for the EDD at all. 'My work was 100 per cent UKIP,' he admits. 'In terms of the rules, I was in breach of contract.'[16] North claims he wrote most of Farage's early speeches.

Yet apart from speeches in Strasbourg and the regular votes there, Farage took virtually no part in other parliamentary proceedings, having calculated that UKIP MEPs' time was better spent in Britain, 'using EU money and spurious prestige to tell everyone the truth about this vast, hugely expensive Hall of Mirrors'.[17] And, of course, Farage still had a business to run back in the City of London. Richard North says:

> Farage would swan into his office. He would be in France with his phone bill paid for by the European Parliament, and he'd be on the phone all the time to England organising the party. He'd turn up, vote, and make his speeches, and then piss off. Farage was not in the least interested in the proceedings of the European

Parliament. He would piss me off no end. He might just as well be in his office at home.[18]

North's fascination with the European Union and Euroscepticism stemmed from his personal interests in food, agriculture and the environment, which is why so many of Farage's interventions in the 1999 Parliament were on these issues. North also recalls trying to interest Farage in an EU scandal building up over a third-country fishing deal:

> The EU was trying to ravage a developing country's fishing waters. I arranged a number of meetings for him. Farage was hopeless. He wouldn't show up, or he would turn up in a grumpy mood. He wasn't a team player. He was totally out of his bloody depth. Intelligent people – he was scared of them. He has an inferiority complex about education and highly qualified people.[19]

Three weeks a month MEPs are in Brussels attending committees and group meetings, then the Parliament shifts to Strasbourg for a week, for a gathering of the whole Parliament – the plenary session. As UKIP MEPs played very little part in committees, the four-day trip to Strasbourg was the big event each month, often the only event. Sometimes, Farage and his colleagues didn't bother with the weeks in Brussels at all (though financially it was in their interests, of course).

'He treated Strasbourg as one long booze-up,' North recalls. For UKIP MEPs and their staff, visits to the French city would always involve a big dinner late in the evening on the Tuesday/Wednesday night at a smart restaurant such as À La Tête de Lard (literally the Pig's Head).

> We weren't getting to the restaurant till nine or ten. We wouldn't be clearing out till midnight. He'd then go pissing off to a bar and drinking till three o'clock in the morning and sometimes not even go to bed. It was thoroughly irresponsible. There would then be several appointments in the morning that he'd miss. He

came in tenish, elevenish, worse for wear, having been drinking all night.[20]

Meanwhile, the UKIP leader Michael Holmes bewildered and upset many party colleagues with his maiden speech in Strasbourg in July 1999. In an apparent volte-face, and to general astonishment, he demanded increased powers for MEPs. 'I am calling for true democracy,' Holmes announced, 'and for the elected representatives to have much more authority over the programme and policies of this institution.'[21]

His words were greeted with mock delight and applause by MEPs from pro-EU parties, but increased powers for the Parliament were not UKIP policy. This was heresy. Had Holmes gone native already? This suspicion was only fuelled seven weeks later when he turned up to a UKIP NEC meeting wearing his official European Parliament badge on his lapel. 'We just looked at one another in embarrassed astonishment,' the deputy leader Craig Mackinlay recalled. 'None of us knew quite what to say.'[22] Yet UKIP would be quite happy for the European Parliament to subsidise many of its activities.

Rather than an atmosphere of triumph and celebration following the European elections, UKIP instead degenerated into squabbles over Holmes's leadership. His behaviour became increasingly erratic: Holmes seemed to think people were laughing at him or plotting against him, as indeed some were. Colleagues felt, in turn, that Holmes, the wealthy former free-sheet publisher, hadn't delivered the financial contribution they'd expected when he stood for leader two years before. Things came to a head at the September 1999 NEC. When Holmes started by complaining of leaks from the National Executive, Craig Mackinlay suggested he was exaggerating. Holmes then pulled an envelope out of his pocket and fired it across the table towards his deputy. It contained a letter of dismissal. Mackinlay duly left the meeting, and when party secretary Tony Scholefield – landlord of UKIP's London office – told Holmes he was committing suicide for UKIP, he received the same treatment.

So the NEC, by nine votes to eight, voted no confidence in Holmes. Farage, still party chairman, voted for the leader, as did their fellow MEP Jeffrey Titford. The pair were concerned about Holmes's behaviour but also 'terrified' that his demise would cause 'such mess' within UKIP so soon after their election success. 'No one in the party believed that we supported him,' Farage admits.[23] Indeed, Farage had been manoeuvring against Holmes the previous February – well before the European elections – when he wrote to Holmes urging him to resign.

It was now such an embarrassing moment for the party that a compromise was struck. Michael Holmes would be allowed to carry on as leader until the annual conference a month later, on the understanding that he would then step down and not stand for re-election. The NEC would step down as well, but in the meantime Mackinlay and Scholefield, still licking their wounds, got their jobs back. All NEC members then signed a handwritten agreement to this effect, a document that looks like something drawn up by seventeenth-century pirates.

The two-day UKIP conference was held at the start of October at the National Motorcycle Museum, just off the M42 near Birmingham. It resembled two rival gangs of Hell's Angels heading for a motorway pile-up. Some of the beleaguered leader's supporters turned up on the Friday wearing 'I SUPPORT HOLMES' badges. About 800 people attended on the first day, but Holmes cleverly bided his time, knowing that most of them would return home that evening, while he had quietly encouraged his supporters to remain for the second day.

On the Saturday, Holmes seized his chance, turning the conference into an Extraordinary General Meeting (EGM), and tried to renege on the NEC resignation deal of the previous month by appealing to UKIP activists. The remaining members then voted no confidence in the NEC by 273 votes to 52 and backed Holmes by a vote of 236 to just 35. Farage, the party chairman, says he was one of those who abstained. 'Publicly I kept my head down. This was partly a politician's self-interest, partly a recognition that self-interest and the interests of the party were, in this instance, one and the same. Unity was paramount.'

Farage says that Holmes could not carry on as leader and admits that he was in 'daily – often hourly' – contact with the 'rebels', but explains: 'I could not declare for them without forcing every member of the party into one camp or another. UKIP must go on unified.'[24]

Coup or counter-coup, UKIP was in chaos.

During the conference in Birmingham, Tony Scholefield had a tip from someone close to Farage that he might try to remove the membership database from the Regent Street headquarters – hence Scholefield made a dash from Birmingham to Triumph House.

Thus resulted one of the great episodes of high farce that pepper the history of the UK Independence Party. What exactly happened that weekend, what role Farage played and why, was hugely disputed at the time, and eventually led to a police investigation in which Farage seems to have been interviewed. He wasn't charged with anything, and it would have been an interesting case for the lawyers. Farage could claim he, not Scholefield, was the more senior representative of UKIP, the tenants of Triumph House; yet Tony Scholefield would have argued the party had given him specific responsibility for Triumph House (also his premises).

What is not disputed is that Scholefield had the locks changed. Nor is it disputed that the following day, Sunday, Farage took counter-measures. Here is his own account, from *Fighting Bull*, published a decade later:

> My first fear was that the party's database might be abused, in which case members would be betrayed and would never vote for UKIP again. Back in London the following morning, I sent someone round to Regent Street to secure the computers and filing-cabinets. Tony Scholefield had already been there, using his authority as party secretary, to have the locks changed. As party chairman, I outranked him. I had the doors forced and the locks changed again, and all the sensitive files shifted down to Salisbury [Holmes's MEP office] where Holmes guarded them.[25]

By his own admission, Farage ordered the operation to enter Triumph House and remove the UKIP material. Farage's version implies he was not physically in Regent Street itself and that 'someone' else actually carried out the raid. That 'someone' was Rob McWhirter, who worked in his spare time on technical matters for UKIP head office, and ran the party website. McWhirter explained years later that 'the point – agreed in writing by Holmes and Farage – was to safeguard the membership database until HQ was sorted out'.

When Farage got to Regent Street, says McWhirter, he told McWhirter to order a taxi and take the most vital material – three computer units and the UKIP cheque books – home to McWhirter's flat in Guildford. At six o'clock the following morning McWhirter was involved in a follow-up operation 'where everything else was loaded into a van', which meant that when Tony Scholefield came in on the Monday morning he found the UKIP office stripped bare.[26]

For the next four months, UKIP operated as two parties – the Holmes faction from Salisbury, the anti-Holmes group led by the NEC majority from Regent Street. But while Farage and Holmes may have thought that they now had sole access to the database containing UKIP members' details, it wasn't quite that simple, and members started getting communications from both 'head offices'.

Nikki Sinclaire, later to become a notable MEP, had taken a year away from university to work for UKIP full time. Indeed, at one point she was shortlisted to become an assistant to Farage in his new role as an MEP. 'You know he can be quite a difficult person to get on with,' the interview panel warned her. 'How would you deal with that?' Sinclaire replied that she'd 'insist on having an inflatable Nigel Farage doll to keep in a cupboard, so that when he frustrated me I could punch it'. The panel 'burst out laughing', but she didn't get the job. Instead, Sinclaire had gone to work in the Regent Street office.

Sinclaire, who sensed skulduggery, admits she pre-empted the Farage and Holmes raid on the membership database. 'Fortunately, I had the foresight to make a copy, both digitally and paper documents. This enabled us to re-establish the Head Office in Regent Street.'[27]

As part of this internal civil war, Craig Mackinlay froze the bank account controlled by Michael Holmes. Holmes in turn issued writs against the National Executive Committee and went to a judge in chambers to try and get an emergency injunction against the NEC. Holmes dropped the case and another Extraordinary General Meeting was called for January 2000 to resolve matters.

Nigel Farage was still chairman of the party, and his manoeuvrings throughout this extraordinary series of events were the subject of much speculation. Yes, he'd backed Holmes at the September NEC, and removed the UKIP database and other records from the party HQ in Regent Street. But to this day Michael Holmes distrusts and despises Farage for the way he then turned against him.

'After much heart searching I have now come to the conclusion that I cannot support you any further,' Farage wrote directly to Holmes a week before Christmas. 'I call upon you to resign the leadership: if you cannot or will not listen to my request I shall go public to all the members informing them of my decision.'[28]

Methodist Central Hall in Westminster has become a historic meeting place since it was opened in 1912. It's been a frequent venue for political meetings and rallies over the past century, and in 1946 the building even hosted the very first meeting of the United Nations General Assembly. The UKIP EGM, attended by 900 activists in January 2000, was one of the famous hall's less peaceful and edifying occasions. Yet the platform from which so many illustrious names had spoken – among them Mahatma Gandhi, Winston Churchill, Martin Luther King and Mikhail Gorbachev – was where Nigel Farage that day came of age politically, and secured his personal grip on the UK Independence Party.

It was a noisy, uncontrollable gathering, where passions were extremely heated, and one UKIP member even suffered a heart attack. 'The crowd roared and wept and shook fists and sheaves of papers,' Farage said ten years later. 'Every speaker was shouted down. I have never, before or since, attended a meeting so constantly close to eruption into violence.'[29]

At one point Farage responded to accusations that a supporter of Michael Holmes had tried to persuade the BBC that Farage should be replaced as a guest on the *Question Time* programme with Holmes himself. This would have been the first ever appearance on the programme by a representative of UKIP, and recognition of the party's new status after the European elections. But amid the confusion, the BBC withdrew the invitation and a media opportunity was lost. 'I am not just angry, I am disgusted,' Farage told UKIP members.[30]

Even though Farage was officially chairman, the broadcaster Norris McWhirter (a very distant relation of Rob) was asked to chair the EGM, as a respected neutral figure. But McWhirter lost control amid the continuous uproar – members shouting, in tears, leaving in anger and despair.

At this, Nigel Farage dashed from the back of the hall, leaped onto the stage and cried, 'No! No! Enough! Stop!' And he took the microphone.[31]

Somehow it worked. The conference gradually calmed, came together and Michael Holmes was ordered to step down.

It was a highly symbolic moment, and one that went down in UKIP folklore. Farage would later claim that both the meeting and the entire party were minutes from disintegration.[32] It was an act of authority, or, as Farage claims, 'desperation'. Farage was highly popular with members, and easily the party's best public performer. It wasn't just that so many knew him first-hand; after years of touring the branches, Farage understood UKIP activists better than anyone else. Yet ordinary members never really knew where Farage stood on the question of Holmes's leadership, but perhaps his duty as chairman was to hold things together. The reality was that for the second time in two and a half years he'd aided the downfall of a UKIP leader. He had shown he was the one figure who could maintain a semblance of unity, yet curiously he wasn't yet interested in taking the top job himself.

'I think that I really might have won that one,' Farage later said of the subsequent leadership election. Yet instead he backed Jeffrey Titford. 'Now was a time for healing, and Jeffrey was emollient where I was abrasive.'[33]

For now he would remain king-maker and king-breaker, rather than take the battered spoils himself. Perhaps he thought, like Shakespeare's Henry IV, that 'uneasy lies the head that wears the crown'.

8

SLAYER OF KINGS

On a blasted heath, a nobleman on horseback encounters three hags circling a cauldron.

'Hail', 'Hail', 'Hail', the witches shriek as they bow before their visitor. 'Ruler of Men', 'Ravisher of Women', 'Slayer of Kings'.

The nobleman rolls his eyes dismissively. 'Why have you lured me here, you loathsome drabs?'

'One day . . .' 'Oh, glorious day!' 'One day . . .'

'Yes?' he enquires.

'You shall be King!'

'Really?' responds the delighted duke, played by a 28-year-old comedian who was himself destined for glory.

'History here I come!' he cries.

So ended the first episode in 1983 of the classic BBC series *Blackadder*, a parody of Shakespeare, which starred and was co-written by the young Rowan Atkinson.[1]

The new millennium had opened with the second regicide in UKIP's own War of the Roses. The leading contender for the vacant throne was Rodney Atkinson. Atkinson was relatively new to the UK Independence Party, having been among those who switched from the Referendum Party, for whom he was one of the few candidates in 1997 to keep their deposit. He'd been an active, eccentric figure in Eurosceptic circles for years, and built up a substantial following for his output of articles and books, and actions such as laying treason charges against the then foreign secretary Douglas Hurd over Maastricht. Atkinson had worked as a university lecturer in his time; as a City economist; and as a businessman in the

North East, but would always have the tag of being an older brother of Rowan Atkinson, the star of *Blackadder*. Where Rowan dealt in comedy, Rodney would say, he dealt in tragedy.

Atkinson quickly caught the attention of two influential *Sunday Telegraph* journalists who were sympathetic to UKIP – the paper's economics editor Bill Jamieson and columnist Christopher Booker. In March 2000, they wrote to the UKIP NEC arguing that they had staked their 'journalistic credibility on our support for the party'; they threatened that such backing might be withdrawn if the leadership went the wrong way – and by that they meant into the hands of Rodney Atkinson. It was 'vital', the *Sunday Telegraph* men argued:

> that the Party should choose someone whose analysis of the nature and failings of the European Union is based on a serious, up-to-date understanding of how and why the EU is developing in the way it is; and not some wider conspiracy theory which, however compelling to a minority of members, cannot be shared by the vast majority.
>
> We believe at least one of the candidates for the leadership falls into this latter category, Mr Rodney Atkinson. It is our personal concern that any leader holding such views might try to take the party in directions where it would be impossible for us to follow, as we would sadly have to make clear.[2]

Their letter would play an intriguing and significant role in the contest ahead, another episode in this plot drenched in *Blackadder*-style scheming and bad blood.

Atkinson had argued in a book written with Norris McWhirter that the European Union was being developed along the lines of a socialist, bureaucratic model first drawn up by the Nazis, who also advocated a single currency throughout the Continent.[3] So despite losing both world wars, the authors argued, German imperialism was reasserting itself, and 'continental fascism' was developing 'in the structures and policies of the European Union'. Atkinson also took Booker and Jamieson's reference to 'conspiracy theory' as an attack on his warnings about the Bilderberg Group, the secretive, regular gatherings of world leaders and leading businessmen, whose members, Atkinson had pointed out, included Conrad Black, who at that time happened to be proprietor of the *Sunday Telegraph*.[4]

The Booker/Jamieson letter was then posted out to the entire UKIP membership by a man called Greg Lance-Watkins, a Eurosceptic who had played a curious role in UKIP politics almost from the start. A former book dealer who lives in Chepstow, Watkins has always supported UKIP's goal of withdrawal from the European Union, but never belonged to the party. Watkins only met Nigel Farage on one occasion – when the MEP visited his old school – but says that for several years he gave Farage advice by phone:

> In 1997, more or less onwards, I was in fairly close contact with Nigel. We used to speak fairly often and then, when he started get-ting a profile on television and the like, he would not infrequently phone me on his way to the venue, saying 'What are they going to ask me? What do you think my answer to this or that should be?' And then at sort of one o'clock in the morning he'd phone me back and we'd do a debrief on what did he get right and what did he get wrong, so that he'd play the game better next time. I saw him as vaguely dodgy right from the beginning, because I could see that he was out for himself more than he was out for anything else, but I thought that this is potentially the Great White Hope.[5]

In later years, once he fell out with Farage, Greg Lance-Watkins took a mischievous delight in using social media to needle him (and from 2008 to about 2017 published a prolific, revelatory blog called *UKIP-vs-EUKIP*).

Watkins says that just after the Booker/Jamieson letter went to the NEC, he mysteriously received three separate and complete versions of the UKIP database of members and addresses. One of these unso-licited packages, he says, consisted of 'envelopes with the address-list labels on them, and stamps'. They were accompanied by thousands of copies of the Booker/Jamieson letter, together with a cash donation for Watkins to pay to print a message of his own. So Watkins sent the envelopes to every single UKIP member, each containing a copy of Booker and Jamieson's denunciation of Rodney Atkinson and his own leaflet arguing why members shouldn't vote for him.

The Regent Street raid, of course, had potentially involved a serious breach of UKIP data security. The two rival head offices which existed for several months both had copies of the membership database, which might easily have been duplicated further in the party turmoil. Greg Lance-Watkins says he has a strong idea who sent him the package of stamped addressed envelopes, but he won't name them. He doesn't suggest Nigel Farage posted him the package personally, 'but I think there was complicity with Farage. Farage as usual will never put his signature to anything . . . It was fairly obvious, shall we say, that they were Faragistas within the party. They weren't trying to get Farage in at that stage, but they wanted a safe pair of hands.'[6] The likely beneficiary was Atkinson's main rival, the former Essex undertaker and MEP Jeffrey Titford.

Watkins also claims he was later visited by police asking if he had abused the party database, and told them: 'I had no idea who sent me these things or even that it was from the UKIP database. I was delighted however to pass on the letter. Mr Atkinson was not a fit captain for my lifeboat, whereas Jeffrey [Titford] was a safe pair of hands to have on the tiller.'[7]

Among the puzzling aspects of this tale, however, is why the unknown person who sent Watkins the package of Booker/Jamieson letters, envelopes and stamps couldn't simply have posted out the mailing themselves.

Farage's man Jeffrey Titford was duly elected as UKIP's third leader in April 2000. But he won by a very tight margin – just fifteen votes of the 4,107 ballots cast (after votes for other contenders, including Mike Nattrass, Bryan Smalley and Craig Mackinlay, were redistributed).

As Farage himself observed, had he stood for the job he probably would have won. That became obvious a few weeks earlier when he easily topped the ballot for UKIP's new National Executive Committee, with 886 first-preference votes, compared to 653 for Atkinson and only 239 for Titford, his two nearest rivals in the poll. The NEC voting figures suggested that in the subsequent leadership vote, most Farage supporters preferred Titford to Atkinson.

It was such a narrow victory for Titford that had eight members voted the other way, then Atkinson would have become leader. Nigel Farage was accused of 'dirty tricks' by Atkinson, who strongly suspected him of at least encouraging Jamieson and Booker to write their letter – and Farage was close to Booker at that time. In his memoirs, Farage would describe the release of their letter as 'timely'.[8]

Rodney Atkinson was offered no role by the new leader, Jeffrey Titford. He resigned from the party and took about 200 other people with him. They included the outgoing leader Michael Holmes; Peter Davies, the candidate in the 1998 Yorkshire South European Parliament by-election; and several others who had played quite senior roles in the party. 'UKIP Condemned to the Far Right' was the heading on the joint resignation letter written by several of the quitters, who pointed out that both Titford and Mike Nattrass, the Birmingham businessman whom Titford appointed in place of Farage, had once been members of the strongly right-wing and nationalist New Britain Party:

> We are convinced that this election result condemns UKIP to the far right. Mr Titford was supported by Nigel Farage. Nigel Farage may have a strident speaking style, which UKIP's more aggressive members seem to admire, but his actions politically have been disastrous for UKIP. He has been instrumental in deposing UKIP's past leaders and attacks potential leaders. As UKIP party chairman, his inaction and poor judgement allowed the extended leadership crisis, a lack of proper party procedures, bad decision making, a continuing lethargy within UKIP, and botched attempts at high-level defections to UKIP.
>
> While Mr Farage holds important positions within UKIP, his well publicised links to the British National Party will keep sabotaging the efforts of other UKIP members.[9]

Even before he lost the leadership election, Atkinson alleged to the Metropolitan Police that Nigel Farage had stolen the membership database from Regent Street headquarters. The police assigned a detective to the case, who interviewed several people, besides Greg

Lance-Watkins. But the enquiries didn't proceed very quickly since the detective had 'many other investigations to make' which he judged to be 'more important', according to the new UKIP party secretary Bryan Smalley.

After Atkinson's resignation from the party, Smalley recommended to the new leader Jeffrey Titford and his chairman Mike Nattrass that they ask the police to drop the case and say they did 'not wish to press charges even if an offence was found to have been committed'. Smalley argued that Rodney Atkinson, who had now set up a rival political group, 'appears to be acting out of malice'.[10] Smalley also felt 'it would look bad for a UKIP MEP to be charged with theft'.[11] Rodney Atkinson, though he was no longer in UKIP, pressed the police to carry on. They officially did so, but without much obvious activity.

It's clear, from his own account, that Nigel Farage masterminded the Regent Street break-in and removal of key material. But the Crown Prosecution Service would have struggled to persuade a jury to convict him of burglary or theft since he could argue that it was simply an internal political dispute and that he had the right, as the then UKIP chairman, to break back into the party's own offices. Farage would have been on more difficult ground under data protection law, however, if it could have been shown that he supplied Greg Lance-Watkins with a database of members.

The Regent Street raid would not be forgotten, especially when taken in conjunction with other incidents that year which caused senior UKIP colleagues to question Farage's honesty and integrity.

Back in February 2000, a by-election was prompted in Romsey in Hampshire, part of Farage's European constituency, caused by the death of the sitting Conservative MP, Michael Colvin and his wife, in a fire at their home. Romsey was the seat which Alan Sked had fought in 1997, and was next to Salisbury, which Farage contested. But Romsey posed a real dilemma for UKIP at a time when the party was still in chaos and desperately short of cash. Farage thought UKIP must join the contest, and appears to have tricked his reluctant NEC colleagues into standing a candidate.

According to an email written at the time by Hugh Meechan,

a retired barrister and NEC member (and who died only a few months later), Farage told the National Executive that 'there had been a meeting the previous evening and that he had been chosen as the candidate, but that he did not want the fact publicised until after the funerals'.[12] Meechan pointed out to the NEC that the UKIP constitution said that a local branch could only select a by-election candidate in consultation with the National Executive:

> I then stated that if the constituency association has chosen Nigel we would look like a bunch of idiots if we refused to ratify their choice. He remained silent, and on the basis that he had told us the constituency had chosen him, I proposed that we ratify their choice. The motion was passed. Now I find out that the 'meeting' in question had been that of the South Eastern Committee NOT the Romsey constituency party. Nigel has applied for selection and will be considered along with any other hopefuls. Why did he not tell us the truth, or perhaps I should say more charitably, why did he not disabuse us?[13]

Meechan's account was broadly corroborated by Rodney Atkinson, who later cited Farage's behaviour over Romsey as one of the reasons for leaving the party shortly afterwards. 'The NEC's decision to agree to fight the by-election was based on [Farage's] misinformation,' Atkinson wrote. In turn, the NEC then persuaded the Romsey branch that the by-election was worth fighting.[14]

In reality, the Romsey branch of UKIP hadn't chosen Nigel Farage at all, and when they did meet to pick their by-election candidate a few days later, Farage wasn't among the contenders. He seems to have withdrawn from the process. Perhaps it was because Romsey was Michael Holmes territory – he lived in the New Forest nearby, and still enjoyed strong support in the area – and Holmes was known to think Farage was a devious man who had betrayed him and was largely responsible for his leadership demise.

Instead, the Romsey branch chose Garry Rankin-Moore, a former local Liberal Democrat councillor who was unhappy with his party's pro-EU stance and had defected to UKIP only recently. Indeed, he was such a recent convert that it emerged during the by-election campaign that Rankin-Moore was still taking the Lib Dem whip on the council.

Farage may not have been a candidate, but he did address at least four public meetings in Romsey, on four different nights. It was the 'best by-election opportunity UKIP has ever had', he said, while his friend David Lott described it as an opportunity as big as the 1998 European by-election in Yorkshire South. 'That, too, took place in the shadow of an internal dispute,' Lott wrote. 'If we do well, it really can be, "Westminster Here We Come."'[15]

Farage and Lott had badly misjudged Romsey. UKIP got just 2.3 per cent of the vote, significantly less than Alan Sked three years before. So it was probably just as well Farage didn't stand himself, and possibly a mistake for UKIP to stand at all.

Before long, Nigel Farage also upset some NEC colleagues with serious problems over the TV film he had spent four months making with Mosaic – the documentary in which Farage was seen clutching a handful of cash outside the office which handles MEPs' allowances and expenses. The half-hour film, *The Enemy Within: Desperately Seeking EUtopia*, was one of a series of twenty programmes the BBC had commissioned to show different aspects of the European Union. In the end the BBC chose to broadcast only eight of the programmes on mainstream television. And Farage's documentary – despite being a lively, provocative watch – wasn't among them.

Farage was furious and suspected the BBC of political bias. Mosaic producers were also upset, and wondered if the BBC had cold feet because no other programmes in their series reflected the view of just one political party, even though the Farage programme was probably more than balanced by numerous pro-EU voices in the other nineteen episodes. Moreover, *The Enemy Within* was shown on leading channels in several other EU countries.

As a simple courtesy, Mosaic had provided Farage with a cassette of the programme. Working from his MEP's office in Redhill, Farage then arranged for copies to be made on hundreds of VHS tapes and put in special boxes. The boxed tapes were then offered to UKIP members for £5 each, and a leaflet sent out with subscription renewals proclaimed:

The Video the BBC doesn't want you to see!

Having spent £000o's of your and everyone else's licence fee money making a film showing Jeffrey, Nigel and the UKIP 'gang' going about their European Parliament 'labours' the Brussels Broadcasting Conspiracy decided you were not mature enough to see it.

But YOU can get it for just £5 (incl. pp) . . . (Cheques payable to 'UKIP South east')

On the weekend of 26/27 August 2000, a man entered Nigel Farage's constituency office in Redhill. He claimed to be a UKIP member from Portsmouth, and asked if he could buy one of the videos. Once the transaction was complete, the visitor identified himself as an undercover official from Surrey Council's Trading Standards Office and said that Farage was breaking copyright law. 'I had had no idea that I was breaking the law,' Farage writes in his memoirs. 'I merely thought that it was the same as taping an instalment of a favourite television programme for a friend . . . A long, expensive and wearisome battle with the authorities ensued. In the end, it was accepted that I had acted in ignorance and had made no profit so no further action was taken.'[16]

Only the real story was a lot more complicated than that, and Farage was far from the innocent victim of an oversight. Indeed, what ostensibly seems a small episode involving a few hundred pirated videotapes reveals quite a lot about Nigel Farage's modus operandi as a politician, and led to the angry resignation of a senior UKIP official.

Curiously, at a UKIP NEC meeting in May 2000, Farage had tried to pass a motion that any National Executive member who fell foul of the law should have their legal expenses paid by the party. 'Nigel couldn't get majority support,' party secretary Bryan Smalley wrote later, 'and lost his temper and stormed out of the meeting. I wondered why this was so important to Nigel.'[17]

It's not clear whether those exchanges had anything to do with what then happened over the Mosaic tapes; more likely they arose from the police inquiry into the Regent Street break-in. Then, at some point that spring or summer, Farage approached Mosaic, according to the managing director Adam Alexander, and asked him about 'the rights situation' over the *Enemy Within* programme. But, Alexander said, he 'never intimated that he wanted to duplicate the film and sell it'.[18] On 31 July, Alexander faxed Farage 'to confirm that Mosaic Films has the right to distribute and sell videos of this programme throughout the world'.[19]

Bryan Smalley, a former Royal Navy commander, then heard of Farage's intention to sell boxed videos of the Mosaic film, under a clever scheme whereby the tapes themselves would be 'given away at no charge', while the special boxes containing them would cost £5 each. 'I realised,' Smalley wrote later, 'that this was an attempt to circumvent the law.'[20]

In early August, when Mosaic heard what Farage was up to, they contacted him and warned him not to sell any videos without a distribution agreement. Around the same time, Bryan Smalley sent a memo to UKIP colleagues saying he would have nothing to do with the sale of 'pirated' videos. Jeffrey Titford responded to Smalley with a fax saying: 'Nigel has permission to reproduce the video; this was given by Mosaic who made the programme. I have seen this letter.'[21]

That 'permission' letter doesn't seem to have been seen by anyone else, if it existed in the first place. Mosaic said it never gave Farage any such permission. Indeed, the next day, having heard that the MEP was still selling tapes, Adam Alexander faxed Farage a stiff letter, warning him:

> You are in breach of the Trade Marks Act and the Video Recordings Act. I must insist you send all copies of the programme you have to my office forthwith. Failure to do so will make you liable to prosecution. The tapes will be seized and destroyed . . .
>
> Please send the tapes to our Gloucestershire address to reach me no later than Wednesday 30 August.
>
> Furthermore you shall be liable for all expenses incurred by Mosaic in protecting our property and all monies received by you for sales should be remitted to us forthwith.[22]

By now Surrey Trading Standards Office had got involved, hence the visit by an undercover officer claiming to be a UKIP member from Portsmouth.

Farage failed to meet the 30 August deadline for coughing up the tapes, and two days later his office received another visit from a trading standards officer who found several tapes that had clearly not been sent to Mosaic.

Yet almost three weeks later, UKIP head office was still advertising the tapes in its subscription reminders. 'This would have been in contravention of instructions given by me,' Farage assured Mosaic, 'and would appear to be yet another attempt to provoke a reaction, for political purposes, sponsored by enemies within UKIP.' Farage agreed to pay Mosaic £293.75.[23]

Bryan Smalley, an experienced politician, was so fed up with the way Farage had behaved over the videotapes, and the way in which Jeffrey Titford and his chairman, Mike Nattrass, sided with Farage, that he stepped down as UKIP secretary and from the NEC. 'My main purpose in resigning is because I do not associate with organisations which deliberately operate outside the law,' he wrote in his resignation letter. 'Nigel Farage has no regard for the truth or law. Unfortunately he has the support of the leader and the chairman.'[24]

Yet even after Smalley's departure, the dispute rumbled on. A few days later, Farage told the South East executive committee of UKIP that he did indeed have a permission letter from Mosaic, but that he couldn't show it to them because he had left it at home. Smalley subsequently confirmed with Mosaic that they had still not granted such permission.

In his resignation letter, Smalley said six or seven NEC members were trying 'to settle old scores' or had their own agendas, adding:

> The most dangerous threat is Nigel Farage because he has an organised band of followers who work as a group which is seeking to control UKIP from outside the NEC. This is particularly worrying because Nigel was closely involved in the downfall of Alan Sked and Michael Holmes. He will displace Jeffrey Titford if he is given the chance.[25]

The 'Farage cabal', Smalley alleged, ignored London headquarters and the party's NEC and simply operated on their own. One of Farage's allies drew £500 a month from UKIP in expenses, he claimed, while another had his £900 phone bill reimbursed without NEC approval. These may seem relatively small sums, but UKIP's turnover was still tiny. And Smalley claimed that two Farage allies were allowed to attend NEC meetings and participate as members even though they had never been appointed to the National Executive. The 'Farage cabal' had placed a membership recruitment ad in national newspapers without monitoring the result and, Smalley complained, with no evidence that anyone had ever responded:

> They are now trying to raise £10,000 to repeat the exercise. It is no wonder the party is in such a desperate financial state because this group spend money without any consideration of where it is to come from or what it achieves. I estimate that, with the help of the EDD [the Europe of Democracies and Diversities group], we are spending about a quarter of a million pounds a year on salaries . . . With money coming from the MEPs as promised by candidates before the European election, we should be building up a fund to fight the next general election. Instead, we are frittering it away on salaries of people, some of whom we never see; who do not report to anyone; who have been put in place without the authority of the NEC, and who have no clear targets.[26]

'UKIP will not survive if Nigel Farage is allowed to impose his dishonest and impetuous will on the Party,' Smalley concluded. 'He is an excellent speaker. His activities should be confined to what he is good at.'[27] Smalley's letter incidentally provides more evidence of UKIP's cavalier approach to using funds from its international grouping in the European Parliament – the EDD – to pay for UKIP activity in Britain, contrary to the parliamentary rules.

Farage argued that Smalley simply had it in for him, having learned that he had told local members at a branch meeting in Stockport that Farage had 'stolen' the database from the Regent Street HQ. When Farage warned the UKIP treasurer John De Roeck that he might sue for defamation, Smalley backed down. 'I fully accept that I have no evidence that Nigel stole the database,' Smalley wrote, and added:

> I would like to kill the idea that I have set out to have a quarrel with Nigel . . . However, I would like him to start carrying out his duties honestly and legally and to stop running UKIP as though he owned it . . . I understand that he has stated that he might wish to take me to court on a charge of slander or some similar calumny . . . I, personally, would be very happy to explain my actions and bring substantiating evidence to court.[28]

Bryan Smalley, unlike most senior figures in UKIP, had experience of pulling the levers of real political power. He'd joined UKIP from the Conservatives, and had spent fifteen years on East Hertfordshire district council, including spells as council leader and chairing major committees, and had also served twelve years on the county council. Smalley now wrote to his former NEC colleagues complaining of what he alleged was a campaign of 'vilification' by Farage, and worse:

> I would level the charge of political ineptitude at Nigel. There is no doubt that when he speaks on a public platform he is successful in recruiting new party members, but all his other dishonest and impulsive antics, lose us members. It is therefore anybody's guess whether he is an asset or a liability to the party. I had hoped that one day he might realise his deficiencies and behave in a more mature way. My political experience tells me that it takes more than one man to make a political party . . .
>
> I have no qualms about Nigel taking me to court. I have enough evidence to defend myself and much more about Nigel which would only cause him and the party embarrassment. In fact, it would be more than embarrassing. So he should stop his posturing.

Smalley ended by claiming that Farage had been interviewed by the Metropolitan Police the previous week – presumably about Regent

Street and the database – before urging his former NEC colleagues to 'prevail on Nigel to behave responsibly'.[29]

Nigel Farage's spats with NEC colleagues – over the Regent Street raid; the Booker/Jamieson mailing; the Romsey by-election; and the Mosaic tapes – attracted little media interest beyond *Private Eye*. UKIP was still too small and insignificant to gain much notice from journalists. But Nigel Farage was busy gaining attention for himself.

Farage's row with Michael Holmes the previous year over which of them should appear on the BBC's *Question Time* – only for the BBC to decide neither – didn't halt his broadcasting career. Farage made his first appearance on the show in November 2000, in a broadcast from Leeds which also included the Labour education secretary David Blunkett and the Conservative Tim Yeo. It was quite an achievement for Farage. Not one of UKIP's first four leaders – including Alan Sked, Michael Holmes and Jeffrey Titford – would ever appear on *Question Time*.

An analysis on Wikipedia shows that since that first appearance in 2000, Farage has appeared on *Question Time* more frequently than anyone else in politics, at the rate of almost twice a year (with four appearances in 2010 and 2013). Over the whole four decades that the programme has been broadcast, only eight politicians have appeared more often than Farage, none of them a Eurosceptic.

Nigel Farage was a gift for *Question Time* producers, and producers of its radio equivalent *Any Questions?* – articulate, quick on his feet, controversial, funny, self-deprecating and often outrageous, and he represented a view that was slowly gaining ground among the British public, if not yet with the political class – that Britain should leave the European Union.

Farage is not only a natural broadcaster, but an eager one, too. Phil Hornby, the ITV reporter who did Farage's first interview on the night of his election as an MEP, says that often over the years Farage would drive huge distances to perform in front of a camera, even if it was only for a short, recorded sound bite.

Hornby also recalls that 'one of the first things Farage told me when I first met him was that he wanted to be a talk radio host'.[30] And in his early days as an MEP, Farage would be a regular guest of the highly argumentative TalkSport presenter Mike Dickin, who died in 2006. Farage once admitted that as a young man he would often ring phone-in programmes on stations such as LBC in London.

Headline-grabbing opportunities were high on Nigel Farage's agenda as the political temperature hotted up through 2000, in anticipation of Tony Blair calling an election the following year. Luring Tory MPs to defect to UKIP was an obvious priority, and although he was no longer chairman, Farage still saw this as his role. He didn't handle things well to start with, and the gentle, top-secret diplomacy required to charm nervous potential defectors took second place to Farage's hunger for a headline.

One rumoured defector was John Wilkinson; another was Teresa Gorman. They had both been among the nine rebels who'd lost the Conservative whip through their opposition to the Maastricht Treaty (though it was later restored). In January 2000, Farage announced on the BBC *Today* programme that a high-profile Conservative MP would soon defect to UKIP. He was booked to have lunch with Gorman that very day, and she was 'furious and embarrassed'.[31] She cancelled the lunch and quickly announced she had 'absolutely no plans' to apply to the UK Independence Party.[32]

Nonetheless, Farage told the press he was still in negotiations, and confident that at last one Conservative MP or peer would soon switch to his party: 'I think things will happen over the next couple of weeks. I think that because there is a large element now in the Conservative Party who are very unhappy with [William] Hague's policy of being in Europe and not run by Europe.'[33] But nobody took the risky leap.

Farage himself then became the target of a different kind of wooing operation. Patrick Nicholls, Conservative MP for Teignbridge in Devon, though not a Maastricht rebel, was an established Eurosceptic. In 1997 his majority had been reduced to just 281. He was worried that if UKIP ran a candidate against him in the next election he could lose the seat, so wanted them to step aside. He was friendly with Mark Daniel, UKIP's media officer, who arranged a drink with Nigel Farage at the East India Club, one of Farage's favourite haunts. For UKIP to stand down, Farage told him, Nicholls would need to sign 'a pledge that he would vote against every measure which increased the powers of Brussels'. Nicholls then whipped from his pocket a list of other vulnerable Conservatives seeking a similar deal. It was in his own handwriting, but had clearly been supplied by the Conservative whips. 'Farage scanned it,' says Daniel:

> He pointed and hooted, pointed and barked, pointed and whooped, all the time sadly shaking his head . . . Many of those named had made impressive statements about resisting integration, particularly around election time. All, however, had voted when in power for its furtherance. The Tory offer was rejected out of hand.[34]

Farage relates that 'even Patrick had to admit rather shamefacedly that the whole proposed deal was based on a fiction. He looked very sad as he left.'[35] In the end UKIP stood against Nicholls, and he lost to the Lib Dems, though their majority was significantly larger than the UKIP vote.

The Kundan Indian restaurant in Westminster was the scene of another such attempt, this time by Conor Burns, Conservative candidate for Eastleigh, the seat Farage fought in the 1994 by-election. Burns tried to convince Farage that UKIP should not run against him, stressing his Eurosceptic credentials and boasting of close ties with Margaret Thatcher. He, too, was rebuffed.

Things took a more serious turn at the start of 2001 when it was publicly revealed that UKIP had tried to extract money from the Conservatives in return for standing down in certain seats. Farage was quoted as saying: 'They want us to call the dogs off. For the UKIP to convince its constituency associations and candidates to stand down will only be possible if there is something in it for us.'[36]

It emerged that two Scottish Eurosceptic peers had hatched a plot while out stalking deer on the Highland moors the previous September. Lord (Jamie) Neidpath (now the Earl of Wemyss), was already a UKIP supporter, while Lord (Malcolm) Pearson of Rannoch was still a Conservative, but would later defect to UKIP (and briefly serve as leader). Their idea was that UKIP would help up to thirty Tory Eurosceptics retain their seats in return for financial support.

Malcolm Pearson rang Farage, whom he already knew through the Bruges Group, and with Jeffrey Titford's blessing the two men met. Pearson then pulled out the very same list produced before by Patrick Nicholls. It contained prominent Eurosceptic names such as Iain Duncan Smith, Oliver Letwin, Michael Spicer and David Heathcoat-Amory. Pearson offered to let Farage amend the list, so he whittled it down considerably:

Malcolm thought, however, that the [Conservative] leadership might still be interested. I was asked what the price would be. I replied, laughing and fully aware that even the Tories could not muster such sums nor explain a sudden deficit of this size in their fighting fund. 'Well, a million pounds would be a good start.'[37]

The Conservatives had been reduced to just 165 seats in the 1997 Blair landslide, and the party was in despair. The Referendum Party vote that year and UKIP's performance in the European election two years later made them fear further damage from the right. Yet the Conservative Party had never been more hostile to EU membership. The party of John Major, Douglas Hurd, Ken Clarke and Michael Heseltine had suddenly been replaced by much more Eurosceptic figures in the top ranks – not just William Hague in those days, but Michael Howard, Peter Lilley, John Redwood and Iain Duncan Smith. So a pact may have made some sense.

It was dangerous territory, though, for both parties. It was barely three years since the Conservatives had suffered the cash-for-questions scandal, and the new legislation on party donations and election expenditure introduced by Labour in 2000 would have made any such deal difficult to conceal, or for both parties to remain within the laws on spending limits.

The story then leaked, apparently because Patrick Nicholls gossiped about the proposed deal to a fellow Tory MP, Nicholas Soames. And William Hague immediately squashed the plans. 'It was not a formal bargain,' UKIP peer Lord Neidpath said at the time:

Would it not be nice to have £1m to £2m if UKIP candidates stood down where Eurosceptic MPs were standing? UKIP is a loose-limbed, uncentralised organisation, but we thought we could pull it off . . . The worry is that if all the potential get-out-of-Europe Tory MPs lose their seats because UKIP stands, then that will be a huge set-back for Euroscepticism . . . The leadership might then go to Kenneth Clarke, or even Michael Portillo . . . It was very unfortunate. The whole thing started to be portrayed as if we were blackmailing the Conservative Party. That was not the case.[38]

Rather than secure secret funding from the Conservatives, Farage went one better. He managed to persuade the long-standing Eurosceptic multi-millionaire and Tory donor, Paul Sykes, to switch his backing to UKIP. But Sykes forced UKIP to pay a big political price. The blunt Yorkshire businessman promised generous support, providing UKIP modified its main policy from being one of straight withdrawal from the EU, to holding a referendum first. Sykes would end up giving UKIP more than £800,000 at the subsequent election – enough to pay for 20 million leaflets and a series of press advertisements – though activists were deeply unhappy. They felt Farage had allowed Sykes to buy a policy many of them didn't like, without consulting the membership, and were upset that the NEC hadn't tried to stop him. In the end, UKIP policy was left extremely confused. A new member of the NEC at that time, Lawrie Boxall, wrote years later about how Farage always kept the committee as far away as possible from UKIP donors, and insisted on conducting all negotiations himself. 'I quickly learned that these decisions were taken by others and presented to the NEC as *faits accomplis* . . . In those days there was still much goodwill towards [Nigel Farage], and we were usually prepared to give him the benefit of the doubt.'[39]

Farage, meanwhile, had left it very late to decide where he would stand at the forthcoming election, which Tony Blair was expected to call in the spring or autumn of 2001. He took his time weighing up where he'd have the best chance in his South East region, among seats where UKIP had done best in the 1999 European vote.

Bexhill-on-Sea is an old-fashioned English seaside resort, said to be the model for Walmington-on-Sea in Farage's favourite TV sitcom *Dad's Army*. It was at the heart of the East Sussex seat of Bexhill and Battle, where UKIP achieved a healthy 14.5 per cent in 1999.

The sitting Conservative MP Charles Wardle, a former immigration minister, had announced he was retiring, but Wardle had then lost the whip for persistently asking awkward questions about the business dealings in Russia of his successor as candidate, Greg Barker. Wardle reflected the concerns of several local Tory activists who refused to campaign for Barker and considered running an independent candidate instead. Farage spied an opportunity.

There was one problem, though. UKIP already had a candidate in Bexhill – Barry Jones, a furniture maker and writer who lived in the seat and had been busy campaigning for several months. On hearing of the row between Wardle and Barker, Jones had actually phoned Nigel Farage to seek advice on whether to approach Wardle to see if he might back Jones's campaign. That was a fatal error. On hearing from Jones of Wardle's disaffection, Farage had decided he rather fancied fighting Bexhill and Battle himself.

Only days before the close of nominations, Farage convinced the UKIP committee in Bexhill and Battle that he should be their standard-bearer instead. Barry Jones had no option but to step aside. He was 'extremely disappointed', he told the local paper.[40] Farage then contacted Wardle – though the two men had never met – and invited him to a speaker meeting he was due to address in Bexhill Old Town the next night. Wardle was impressed with Farage's performance. 'He was brief and to the point,' Wardle says. 'He can self-edit in a speech. He wasn't pompous. He answered questions, and I mean he *answered* questions. I thought, "This guy is talking stuff which will strike chords here."' Wardle was still very much a political animal and keen to get involved in the election in some capacity. 'I could smell the election in the air. I was pissed off with the Conservatives.'[41] Wardle talked to his local Tory allies, and most agreed to back Farage.

A week later, just four weeks before polling day, Farage publicly announced he was now the candidate, and that Bexhill and Battle 'could be made into a very high profile campaign' for UKIP.[42] Barry Jones got the consolation prize of being UKIP candidate for next-door Eastbourne, and would be remarkably sanguine about what happened. 'Politics is a dirty business,' he says. 'I'm not bitter about it.' After the election, Jones says, he got a letter from UKIP leader Jeffrey Titford saying what had happened was underhand, and that the principle of levering out an established candidate – in the way Jones had been – wasn't really on.

At Farage's campaign launch, his dozen or so supporters – mainly the self-styled local group Tories Voting UKIP – were outnumbered by around twenty Greg Barker campaigners. The Barker team carried placards and shouted 'Judas' or 'traitor' every time a local Tory defector was introduced. These included not just Wardle but the outgoing chairman of the local Conservative Association and the chairman of the Conservative Club. One female Barker supporter got into a fracas with an elderly man who was wearing a purple UKIP rosette. 'He tried to push me over and called me a silly old cow,' she complained to a reporter. 'I did not try to push her over,' the old man retorted, 'And you *are* a silly old cow.' 'This campaign is going to be fun,' said Farage as he watched the row.[43] 'We had a hoot of a time,' says Charles Wardle.[44]

As well as supposedly being home to Captain Mainwaring of *Dad's Army*, Bexhill also had the second highest proportion of pensioners of any seat in Britain – 34 per cent.

Farage quickly set up an office in the town and, as a stunt to emphasise opposition to Britain joining the euro, paid his £500 election deposit in pound coins. Charles Wardle never joined UKIP, but he and his wife backed Farage at three campaign events, while Farage toured the area in a decorated double-decker bus – until it was sabotaged when someone put sugar into the petrol tank. Much of the seat was natural UKIP territory, Wardle says, 'full of people from places in south London like Orpington who'd come down to retire'.[45] Farage, of course, was born in the Orpington constituency.

Farage got 3,474 votes in Bexhill and Battle, a higher percentage vote – 7.8 per cent – than any other UKIP candidate in the country. (The next best, with 6.1 per cent, was his accountant and old friend

Craig Mackinlay, who fought Totnes in Devon.) Farage was UKIP's best-performing candidate for the second successive election – in seats a hundred miles apart. He was helped by Wardle and local Tory defectors, but it was also a tribute to Farage's personality and electioneering skills. Even so, Farage's vote was less than the support in 1997 for UKIP and the Referendum Party combined.

Nationally, it was a sorry picture. UKIP had been handed a gift by the disappearance of James Goldsmith's party yet gained fewer than half the votes which the Referendum Party harvested in 1997. UKIP squandered their inheritance and, as Robert Ford and Matthew Goodwin have observed, did notably badly in seats where Goldsmith's party had done well. Of the Referendum Party's best ten constituencies in 1997, UKIP lost their deposit in eight.[46]

The Conservatives barely dented Tony Blair's huge majority – down from 179 to 167 – but the Tories had become significantly more Eurosceptic under William Hague, whose claim on the Tuesday before polling day that voters had '48 hours to Save the £', inevitably struck a chord with voters who might have backed UKIP. In reality, by 2001, there was little prospect that the Labour government would actually scrap sterling and join the euro. Although Tony Blair supported the idea, his chancellor Gordon Brown had effectively blocked the policy by insisting that the British economy had to pass five tests before the country could join the single currency. Two years later, the Treasury announced, amid great fanfare, that most of these tests had not yet been met. The issue never really arose again.

'They were very, very difficult days,' Nigel Farage would say of the 2001 general election. 'Blair's political honeymoon was very long and extensive. The Conservative Party appeared to be very Eurosceptic and adopted the pound.'

Nigel Farage would later claim he saw the 2001 campaign as a 'good dress rehearsal' for whatever came later. 'Get the party on the bloody ballot paper. Get people standing. Get stuff going through doors. Start to build, dare I say it, *the brand*.'[47]

9

KILROY WAS HERE

In 2002, a middle-aged couple received an invitation 'completely out of the blue', to lunch at Shepherd's, the smart restaurant in Marsham Street, Westminster, which is a discreet location for high-level intrigue and a favourite spot for politicians, journalists and lobbyists.[1]

Neil and Christine Hamilton had become something of a celebrity team. Neil Hamilton had been brought down as a Conservative MP in 1997 over the notorious cash-for-questions affair when he was accused of taking bribes to ask parliamentary questions on behalf of the former Harrods owner Mohamed Al-Fayed, an accusation Hamilton has always denied. Famously, he then lost his Tatton seat to the anti-sleaze candidate Martin Bell, and made the mistake of suing Fayed for libel. Hamilton lost the case and, unable to pay legal bills of many hundreds of thousands of pounds, he and his wife Christine sought to reinvent themselves, and replenish their finances, by becoming television personalities who would do almost anything if the fee was high enough. Louis Theroux's engaging 2001 documentary, *When Louis Met the Hamiltons*, portrayed the couple sympathetically – indeed, almost as victims. Christine, a former assistant to a Conservative MP, even took part in the first series of the ITV reality show *I'm a Celebrity . . . Get Me Out Of Here!* and came third, having survived in the 'jungle' until the penultimate day. By the time of the Shepherd's lunch invitation, she had become a much bigger name than her husband, and a lot more popular.

'It was the usual Farage lunch,' Neil Hamilton recalls, 'four bottles, lots of laughs', and it lasted most of the afternoon. The UKIP MEP wanted to pop a question: would they be willing to stand for

UKIP in the next European elections, due in 2004? Farage and his party were hoping to expand considerably their three-strong delegation to the Brussels Parliament. It was made clear that the Hamiltons could choose whatever region they liked, and they'd have a very good chance of being elected.

After UKIP's dismal result at the 2001 Westminster election, Jeffrey Titford had stood down as leader and the party had staged its third leadership contest in four years. Nigel Farage, still only thirty-seven, again resolved not to go for the top position. Richard North, his speech writer in the European Parliament, recalls him explaining that if he did become leader he would only have the job for a few years, and then be left with nothing:

> The way Farage worked, he always liked a frontman to be in the lead. That way he could get more done working behind the scenes, than by stepping into a leadership role. He liked weak compliant people around him. He lets other people take the flak while he does his own work in the dark.[2]

Once more, as under Holmes and Titford (and to some extent Sked), Nigel Farage carried on operating as if he was UKIP leader anyway. Following their own drubbing at the polls, the Conservatives had replaced William Hague with a hardline Maastricht rebel, Iain Duncan Smith, though he proved to be the most ineffectual leader the party has had in modern times. But the move looked like posing a huge threat to UKIP and, according to Richard North, Farage took it upon himself to initiate more of his 'work in the dark' by a clandestine attempt to broker a merger between the two parties.

Farage confirms in his memoirs that 'one wing' of the Conservative Party 'continued to flirt with us. They wanted to know my price for bringing the Eurosceptic strays back into their fold. My answer was "a commitment to a referendum on continued membership of the European Union".' Note how Farage talks about 'my price' and 'my answer'.[3] Nothing about what other UKIP figures thought, yet here he was apparently negotiating on closing down the party and merging it with another.

A referendum on EU membership wouldn't have been a problem for Iain Duncan Smith personally. But pledging an In-Out referendum on EU membership in 2001 or 2002 would have caused a huge split within the Conservative Party at a time when the vast majority of Tory MPs still favoured Britain's continued membership of the EU. And according to Richard North, the Conservatives thought Farage was too volatile to be trusted.

UKIP's new leader was Roger Knapman, a successful surveyor and businessman in his late fifties, who'd spent ten years as Conservative MP for Stroud, and the final year of the Major regime as a government whip, even though he'd rebelled many times on Maastricht and other European matters. Knapman initially had two opponents, but both withdrew, and he was elected unopposed.

Knapman had only run for leader, Farage has said, 'after a great deal of coercion and special pleading from me and others'.[4] And just as with Sked, Holmes and Titford, the relationship would soon turn sour. Knapman, a rather grey figure, found it hard to understand why broadcasters always interviewed Farage and never him. It was because he never had anything interesting to say, one UKIP press officer bravely told him.

Knapman had appointed Farage's close ally David Lott as the new party chairman and kept Farage in charge of a new European Elections Committee, with the aim of finding an attractive list of candidates for the next European contest in 2004, when Knapman stated he hoped to achieve ten MEPs.

Hence Farage's long lunch at Shepherd's with the Hamiltons.

'Are you sure?' Neil Hamilton responded when Farage asked if he'd like to stand. Hamilton pointed out that he was still bankrupt following the 1999 libel case. More important, his reputation had yet to recover from the cash-for-questions scandal – he more than any other MP had come to personify 1990s Conservative 'sleaze'. 'He wasn't bothered about that at all,' Hamilton recalls. Farage took the view that with an insurgent party the important thing was making people aware of your existence. Almost any publicity was worthwhile if it helped get the party noticed, particularly if

it involved names who meant something to the public, and could
generate headlines in the popular press.

Christine was adamant that Neil shouldn't go back into the fray,
and she certainly didn't want to stand herself – politics was too
nasty, she thought: 'I said over my dead body. No way – ever.'[5] In
any case, there was no evidence that UKIP could make much difference. 'Nobody thought we could change the course of history,'
says Neil Hamilton. 'It was a tantalising offer in a way. I could have
had whatever seat I wanted.' But the answer was no.

Partly in gratitude for their fine lunch, Neil Hamilton thought the
couple should at least join the party, so unbeknown to Christine he
signed them both up, and Hamilton was among a growing number of
former MPs to join UKIP. Yet for the next nine years the Hamiltons
remained fairly inactive.

Farage was confident that after the next 2004 elections the UKIP
delegation to Europe would be much larger, and he spent considerable time trying to fix who the new UKIP MEPs would be. It was
partly through these efforts that he fell out with Richard North,
who wanted to stand for UKIP in his home region of Yorkshire and
the Humber.

Farage had grown exasperated at how much time North was
spending working with Christopher Booker on their huge tome
about the EU, *The Great Deception*, published in 2003, as well as
helping with Booker's weekly column in the *Sunday Telegraph*. North
was also lobbying to set up a think tank on what we would now call
'post-Brexit Britain'. He concluded that Farage wasn't interested in
ideas, that he was anti-intellectual, and 'that all he wanted was to
sabotage my book by keeping me busy'.[6]

North can be a difficult character, and Farage wasn't the only
person in UKIP unhappy with his work. Things came to a head in the
summer of 2003 when North says Farage flew to Brussels to persuade
the EDD leader, the Danish Eurosceptic Jens-Peter Bonde, and the
group administrator Clo Van Grunderbeek, to sack North (the EDD
group was officially North's employer). 'The first thing I knew was
when Clo rang me up and said, "I've been told to fire you." Farage
didn't have the guts to do it to my face.'[7] North resigned instead.

Richard North believes that Farage sabotaged his attempts to become a UKIP MEP for Yorkshire and the Humber, helping instead a good friend, City economist Godfrey Bloom, who had got to know Farage as a member of the Farage's Foragers which toured Great War battlefields.

Roger Knapman, like Farage, was also on the prowl for star names and talent, and not just to become MEPs. On a Mediterranean cruise in 2003, Knapman and his wife happened to meet Dick Morris, who had worked for twenty years as Bill Clinton's main strategist and pollster, and had worked on all Clinton's victories, as well as successful campaigns for many other US politicians, mostly Democrats. Morris, who was still reeling from a sex scandal, offered to help UKIP – for a large fee. Another recruit, also not cheap, was the publicist Max Clifford, a former Labour supporter who was then at the height of his powers bringing juicy exposés and kiss-and-tell stories to the tabloid press (a decade before his own conviction for indecent assault).

Then, only weeks before the 2004 elections, came the biggest recruit of all.

For almost seventeen years, Robert Kilroy-Silk had enjoyed one of the best-paid jobs in television, as presenter of *Kilroy*, a daytime show which got audiences of around a million people, four days a week. Kilroy-Silk, widely known as 'Kilroy', was the Piers Morgan of his day, and one of the most recognised and popular broadcasters in Britain. Handsome, loud-mouthed and charismatic, neither working class nor middle class, he also suffered ridicule for his extraordinary orange tan. His programme involved a seventy-strong studio audience debating controversial issues – often social and domestic topics – and lifted the lid on the seedy world of outlandish sexual habits, crime and family feuds.

Kilroy-Silk could rightly claim that he'd acquired a greater understanding of public opinion, and the way ordinary people feel emotionally, than most politicians. But the BBC had grown increasingly concerned in recent years about Kilroy's disparaging, and often racist, remarks about different nationalities and racial groups – the Germans, the French, Spaniards, Pakistanis and also Black youths in Britain. In

April 2003, just after the US and British invasion of Iraq, Kilroy-Silk had written a column for the *Sunday Express* which went almost unnoticed at the time. Arabs should go down on their 'hands and knees and thank God', he said, 'for the munificence of the United States'.

> What do they think we feel about them? That we adore them for the way they murdered more than 3,000 civilians on September 11 and then danced in the hot, dusty streets to celebrate the murders? . . . That we admire them for being suicide-bombers, limb amputators, women-repressors?[8]

Then, through an extraordinary blunder at the *Sunday Express*, Kilroy-Silk's column was accidentally reprinted at the start of 2004. This time Kilroy's remarks were noticed, and they caused uproar among several Muslim groups, who protested to the BBC. The Corporation felt it had no option but to sack the presenter from his £600,000 a year job.

Now unemployed, and staying at his holiday home in southern Spain, Kilroy-Silk happened to be invited over to lunch by the Earl of Bradford, a hereditary peer who lived nearby. Richard Bradford, who had been active in UKIP for several years, had stood for Stafford in 2001 (one of the few candidates to keep his deposit) and had been picked to stand again in the West Midlands for the imminent European contest. The party had heard that Kilroy's wife Jan was a UKIP voter, and surmised that her husband might be one, too. Why not stand for UKIP? Bradford asked Kilroy-Silk, suggesting that it would be possible to put him top of the party list in almost any English region he chose.

Politics was nothing new to Robert Kilroy-Silk. Now almost sixty-two, he'd been a lecturer in the subject at Liverpool University, then a Labour MP for twelve years, initially as a left-wing socialist who said Labour should fight a class war and impose its values on society. Like most left-wingers of his generation, he was Eurosceptic long before the term was invented. Kilroy-Silk campaigned for a No vote in the 1975 referendum, and regularly defied the Labour whips on European issues in Parliament.

He fancied the idea of standing. In fact, he more than fancied it. And taking up campaigning for a few weeks could fill the sudden big hole in his life. 'I didn't want to get elected,' he said later. 'And then all hell broke loose. It just literally took off.'[9]

The Earl of Bradford rang Nigel Farage to tell him about Kilroy and how keen he was. Farage made some enquiries and arranged to meet Kilroy-Silk at his London home. Then, uncharacteristically, he forgot to turn up.

Deeply apologetic, Farage suggested they meet instead at the East India Club – in the smoking room – and they held a second get-together at Kilroy-Silk's grand Georgian country house at Little Chalfont in Buckinghamshire. 'As we spoke,' Farage would write, 'he repeated my best phrases to himself.' That indicated an enthusiasm to learn, Farage felt.[10] 'I did not know whether he was capable of being a team-player. In fact, I very much doubted it, but I was in no doubt that the short-term gain was well worth the possible long-term pain.'[11]

Understandably, the UKIP leader Roger Knapman feared Kilroy would be too much of a loose cannon. Would the short-term publicity coup really be worth the inevitable trouble later on? Kilroy-Silk might be charming with ordinary people, and might be a superb TV performer, but he also had a reputation for being temperamental, for being an extreme egotist.

The former leader Jeffrey Titford, who was stepping down as an MEP, was worried Kilroy-Silk was 'a man with his own agendas, and I did not see how we could control him if he decided to pursue them . . . I was certain that he was using us to his own ends.'[12] Richard North later remarked that nobody warned Farage that Kilroy-Silk could not be 'manipulated' in the way Farage had manipulated others in the past. 'But there was no one who dared to warn him. He just ploughed on, and the general attitude was: "Farage has taken some almighty risks in the past, and they've paid off. We'll trust him on this one too."'[13]

Knapman met Kilroy-Silk, and the pair didn't get on, but Farage says Knapman left him with the 'final decision' on whether to go ahead with him.[14]

Farage threw the dice. UKIP needed the tabloid attention which the former daytime TV star would undoubtedly bring. 'If anyone stood to lose from having Kilroy on board, it was surely I,' Farage explained. 'He was a fine speaker and a master of the media. I might have a few fans, but he would command the worship of thousands.'[15]

But where should Kilroy stand? Farage decided the East Midlands was best, but top spot in that region was already occupied by Derek Clark, a retired teacher. Farage says Clark didn't mind having his arm twisted, and immediately offered to step down a rung on the UKIP list. This was generous, since even with Kilroy-Silk's following it was doubtful whether UKIP would harvest enough extra votes to secure two MEPs in the East Midlands. Farage's aide Steve Harris told Clark not to worry, and that Kilroy would boost the UKIP vote so much that Clark would glide in on the TV star's coat-tails.

It was also a selfless move by Farage. Robert Kilroy-Silk was famous throughout politics as the man who, in 1974, as he travelled down to Westminster for his first day as a new Labour MP, had brazenly told a TV reporter on the train that he wanted to be prime minister within fifteen years. Since the fall of Alan Sked, Farage could probably have seized the leadership job at any time he wanted: he would easily have overcome Michael Holmes in 1998, Jeffrey Titford in 2000, or Roger Knapman in 2002. Farage was still, without question, the most popular person within the party, as the poll for the UKIP NEC elections in 2003 had shown. He again came top by a long chalk – for his third NEC election in a row – with 2,156 votes, almost 300 ahead of his nearest rival. In later times Nigel Farage earned a reputation for squashing any rivals who threatened his leadership, but in welcoming Kilroy to the UKIP in 2004 he was imperilling any ambitions he harboured.

Farage's strategy seemed to work. European campaigns are seen as deadly dull by most of the media. Here suddenly was a story for journalists to latch onto and have some fun. Robert Kilroy-Silk was probably the biggest name ever to contest the Euro elections in Britain. His arrival brought UKIP publicity on a scale it had never known before. And Kilroy-Silk also presented one of the party's election broadcasts, in which Farage made two short contributions which just underlined that his new colleague was the more relaxed and natural broadcaster. Nigel Farage even ceded his place on an election edition of *Question Time* to UKIP's new star, an extraordinarily generous gesture. 'I stood aside,' Farage explained, 'because I believed there would be a lot more people who would watch Kilroy on *Question Time* than myself. He appeals to lots of people who wouldn't necessarily vote UKIP.'[16]

On the street, Kilroy-Silk was an even better campaigner than Farage, and enjoyed instant recognition among old and young – beckoning people to come over and chat, shaking hands, patting them on the back, hugging and kissing old ladies, cuddling younger ones and pecking them on the cheek, signing autographs, posing for some of the early selfies, and colourfully enumerating the iniquities of the European Union, and the perils of immigration. To many of the public, Kilroy was a regular companion in their sitting rooms. Now here he was for real, keen to press the flesh and win their votes. Kilroy knew how to make people smile and laugh; he knew how to craft a good sound bite to keep reporters happy; above all, he knew how to make politics fun. It was a rare skill which Nigel Farage shares (and later Boris Johnson, too). But Kilroy wouldn't spend long on the street – Farage noticed how, after an hour of oozing charm and making eye contact with the public, the TV presenter needed a rest.

In some ways, Robert Kilroy-Silk was an early, British version of Donald Trump, another television creation, tanned, arrogant and boastful. He would be 'surprised' if he was not elected, he said, 'because that means I have read everything wrong, and I am usually very astute politically'.[17] 'In a matter of days,' says one history of the 2004 contest, 'the UKIP/Kilroy-Silk combination had become *the* phenomenon of the elections.'[18]

But the campaign wasn't all happy hugs and handshakes. Four days before polling, Kilroy-Silk managed to open up the leadership issue by giving too frank a response when pressed about his ambitions by *The Sunday Programme* on ITV: 'You are right to ask those questions, and I would be foolish and I would be lying if [I said] they have not been raised with me by people in the party – both Westminster and the leadership – and I have not given some thought to them. Of course I have, but it is really, honestly, one step at a time.'[19]

Compared with 1999, UKIP had a lot more coverage from broadcasters, and Farage established a good rapport with the BBC executive whose job it was to advise producers and reporters on the rough proportions of time to which each political party was entitled. There was also better coverage in the newspapers, especially the tabloids, thanks to Max Clifford; and the *Sun* was especially positive about UKIP in the final days.

UKIP was much better organised than in any previous election – with a national campaign HQ in Bramshott in Hampshire; eight regional call centres; and ads on 1,800 billboards, with a simple logo devised by Dick Morris, which just said NO, with the letter 'O' in the form of the EU's own ring of twelve stars. UKIP membership had soared over the previous three years – from 8,500 to 24,000. And the party unveiled a drip-drip of celebrity endorsements: actors Joan Collins and Edward Fox; racing driver Stirling Moss; TV astronomer Patrick Moore; and cricketer Geoff Boycott. Indeed, 2004 was probably the best-run campaign in UKIP history, before or since.

It was also well financed. UKIP outspent both Labour and the Liberal Democrats, thanks to more generous funding from Paul Sykes, and also a new donor whom Farage had found, retired book-maker Alan Bown. Local UKIP branches were also told to transfer all their funds to regional bank accounts to help the Euro effort – 'strip the branches' was Farage's motto.[20]

The 2004 Euro election was also the first time that UKIP made a big issue of curbing immigration, which was a strong feature of Kilroy-Silk's election broadcast. Ten new member states had just joined the European Union, most of them former communist countries, in what was the biggest ever expansion of the EU. In theory, 73 million new people now had the right to work and live in Britain. Only weeks before the election, the immigration minister Beverley Hughes had been forced to resign over a scandal about fraudulent visa applications from two other East European states who were due to join the EU later – Romania and Bulgaria. One UKIP leaflet had the headline 'IMMIGRATION SET TO SOAR' over a cartoon of East Europeans flooding through the 'Channel funnel'. After the accession of the ten new states on 1 May 2004, the headline became 'IMMIGRATION SOARS'.

The headlines proved to be true. Within weeks, TV news bulletins were reporting on the coachloads of Poles who were coming to Britain to work and set up home. Government officials had estimated that only between 5,000 and 13,000 people a year would come from the accession countries, and the UK was one of just three EU states – along with Ireland and Sweden – which chose not to adopt 'transitional arrangements', an option that allowed EU members to limit migration from accession states for seven years.

Around 850,000 EU citizens moved to Britain between 2004 and 2011, two thirds of them from Poland. They soon built new communities in towns such as Crewe and Peterborough, complete with lots of Polish shops and pubs, and the reliable, hard-working 'Polish plumber' or builder who would take any task became a feature of modern life. Most of the East Europeans were in the 18–34 bracket, and many didn't intend to stay in Britain permanently. The idea was to support their families by sending money back to Poland, to build up their savings before returning home themselves. The Blair government's decision to reject transitional arrangements had a far-reaching effect on the economy – such immigration provided a significant boost to growth and jobs – though often the jobs they took were poorly paid and insecure. And the political ramifications were huge.

Many Labour MPs and ministers had been privately very worried about growing immigration, and yet others welcomed the prospect. Some in the Blair government were encouraged by a report which suggested that foreign-born people in the UK contributed ten per cent more to Treasury revenues than they took out. Andrew Neather, an adviser to both Downing Street and the Home Office, later said he felt that Labour people thought mass immigration would 'make the UK truly multicultural', and he had 'the clear sense that the policy was intended . . . to rub the right's nose in diversity'.[21] Some Labour people no doubt hoped the new EU arrivals would eventually supply the party with a new pool of voters.

Crucially, the famous '13,000 a year' forecast was based on the assumption that each of the existing 15 EU states would adopt an open-door policy rather than seven-year transitional controls – not least Germany which would have been the obvious destination for many Poles and other East Europeans, rather than Britain. In the event, the UK ended up taking most of the East European migration which might otherwise have been spread throughout all the West European EU states. The Blair government's decision not to adopt transitional controls was probably the single most important event in the rise of UKIP, and on the road to Brexit.

As one poll ahead of the 2004 Euro election showed UKIP might secure 18 per cent of the vote, the Tories struggled to respond. Their new Eurosceptic leader Michael Howard (who'd taken over after Tory MPs deposed Duncan Smith the previous year) at one point described UKIP's policy of withdrawing from the EU as 'extremist', though Howard would vote for Brexit twelve years later.[22]

A leaked Conservative briefing paper advised candidates to dismiss UKIP as 'cranks and political gadflies', and to stress their links with the extreme right.[23] It was a foolish move. The leak – probably deliberate by the Tories themselves – generated one of the biggest media stories of the campaign. This only drew attention to UKIP, and many voters attracted to the party were disaffected Tories whom Howard needed to win back. 'If sixteen per cent of the life-forms in this paddock are gadflies,' Farage responded, 'there must be a great deal of manure around.'[24] The name stuck. *Cranks and Gadflies* was the title of an early history of UKIP, and as before in politics, what started as an insult was soon borne with pride. Farage turned UKIP MEPs' monthly dinners into the Gadfly Club, complete with a gadfly tie, and himself as president (a post he still proudly cites in *Who's Who*).

Just as he had in 1999 and 2001, Alan Sked tried to wreck UKIP's prospects, and delivered strong attacks in the Sunday press two weeks running. In the *Sunday Telegraph*, Sked quoted at length the resignation letter of Richard North, when he was pushed out by Farage the previous summer:

I am not and was not prepared to be a 'bag-carrier'. Nor would I 'fetch and carry' for Farage, or write his letters, or be available to pour him into a taxi when he was so blind drunk that he could no longer stand, or cover for him when he failed to turn up for morning appointments because he had been out on the tiles all night long. I am almost old enough to be his father, but I am not in the business of being his nanny.[25]

Alan Sked repeated in the *Sunday Telegraph* his old allegation about Farage saying 'the nig-nogs will never vote for us', and then publicly revealed a story of Farage taking NEC members to a sleazy 'Mayfair strip-club'. And in the *Mail on Sunday*, Richard North related a similar story about Farage taking half a dozen people to a seedy bar after a UKIP Christmas party in Strasbourg:

It was a normal bar at the front. Behind was where the mugs were shepherded in for the strippers. The girls were wearing practically nothing. We stayed three or four hours until about 4am. Nigel was with two beauties, stuck in their warm embraces. The champagne was 132 euros a bottle. It was the only thing on offer. I didn't want to be there. It seemed like a ridiculous amount to pay for a drink.[26]

Furthermore, North revealed that Farage's fondness for drinking even led to him missing the Parliament's vote on the EU budget in 2001: 'This was the most important vote of the year but he turned up after the vote at about lunchtime. The night before, we had been with him until midnight. Then he headed off declaring his intentions to drink some more.'

While Farage again strongly denied Sked's 'nig-nogs' allegation, he declined to comment on the stories about the strip club and his excessive drinking.[27] Such reports weren't good for Farage or UKIP, but the fact that two Sunday papers wanted to carry such damaging material was another sign that the party was making an impact.

But Farage and his party got themselves into trouble when he gave an extraordinary statement about a spate of letter bombs which had been sent to politicians and EU officials around Europe. Farage reminded people of his past warnings that if the EU denied its citizens democracy then it would end in violence. 'We have spent ten years warning that the route the EU has chosen for itself, to swallow up nation states without giving the people of Europe the final say, was destined to end in civil unrest and violence. We can only hope that the EU comes to its senses and listens to the people.'[28]

Frank Maloney, the boxing promoter who had been chosen as UKIP's candidate for Mayor of London, announced: 'I do not support the comments made by one of my party's MEPs; it is not the view of UKIP that these attacks are justified or that we support them in any way.'[29] In fact, it seems the bombs were the work of Sardinian anarchists.

Then Maloney himself caused more outrage against UKIP when he said he wouldn't be campaigning in Camden, because there were 'too many gays' in the borough. 'I don't have a problem with gays, what I have a problem with is them openly flaunting their sexuality,' he said.[30] Farage tried to brush off Maloney's remarks: 'Frank's not a career politician. He's the chirpy chap that he is. He's an honest bloke who doesn't try to put a spin on things.'[31] (Eleven years later, to huge applause, Farage would introduce Maloney to the UKIP spring conference in Margate. Yet now, Frank had become 'Kellie', and Maloney explained she was undergoing gender reassignment.)

Maloney performed badly in London – with just 6.2 per cent of the vote – but UKIP did better in elections for the Greater London Assembly where the PR list system secured two members, including the magazine publisher Damian Hockney, who'd pulled out of the leadership contest against Knapman. And the nationwide European results, announced two days later, were a huge breakthrough. The party came third with 2,650,768 votes – 16.1 per cent – and surprisingly pushed the Liberal Democrats into fourth. UKIP now had twelve MEPs, compared with just three in 1999, and representation in every region of England except the North East.

The figures suggested that Robert Kilroy-Silk deserved much of the credit, even though he'd only been with UKIP for two months (he was never an actual member). The East Midlands, where he was elected, was suddenly the party's strongest region, with UKIP ahead of Labour on 26.1 per cent of the vote, almost three and a half times the party's support in the area in 1999. In most English regions, UKIP roughly doubled its vote. Four areas elected two UKIP MEPs, and Derek Clark's sacrifice proved worthwhile as he became the party's second MEP in the East Midlands.

But Nigel Farage deserved credit, too. Had he not backed Kilroy-Silk's candidature, and reassured his anxious UKIP colleagues, the party would have fared significantly worse. Nobody has managed to quantify the 'Kilroy-Silk effect' in 2004, but, at a guess, he may have been worth 750,000 extra votes and four or five extra seats. Not since former Conservative Enoch Powell urged people to vote Labour in the February 1974 election had someone who wasn't a party leader had such an impact on a British nationwide contest.

UKIP's delegation to Brussels and Strasbourg was now four times its previous size. That meant four times the income, much of which effectively went to the party, and four times the staff, most of whom effectively worked for UKIP. But Nigel Farage's efforts to improve the quality of the UKIP team had been dismally unsuccessful. Of UKIP's twelve MEPs in 2004 – all men – two would go to jail for offences of dishonesty (in one case parliamentary expenses fraud); Derek Clark would be forced to repay the Parliament £31,800 for unjustified staff costs; a fourth UKIP MEP retired early, and three others ended up resigning from the party or were expelled.

At the South East region election count in Didcot, the wife of the number two on the UKIP list, Ashley Mote, burst into tears on hearing of her husband's election. They weren't tears of joy. Two days later it emerged in the press that Mote was about to go on trial on ten charges of benefit fraud to the tune of £67,000. Given that Farage ran the South East region of UKIP as a personal fiefdom, he must take responsibility for this oversight. He was furious, since he knew nothing about the case, and Mote had been placed second on the UKIP's list in the region, while Farage's good friend David Lott, placed third, failed to get elected.

Then, on the first day the new Parliament met in Strasbourg, Farage's battlefield foraging chum Godfrey Bloom caused a stir throughout the building by joining the Parliament's Women's Rights Committee, so as to promote 'men's rights', he said. Bloom then declared that 'no self-respecting small businessman with a brain in the right place would ever employ a lady of child-bearing age'. He came from Yorkshire, he explained, where women were expected to have their husbands' tea on the table by 6 p.m., and then Bloom delivered his notorious remark: that he wanted a say on women's issues because 'I quite simply feel that they don't clean behind the fridge'.[32]

Farage described Bloom's intervention 'as what used to be called "bamming", or teasing the easily teased', a practice which Farage knew all about from his days at Dulwich.[33] Bloom's regular remarks – whether jokey or serious – would prove to be a growing embarrassment when Farage had gone out of his way to ensure Bloom was elected an MEP, at the expense of Richard North. Nevertheless, their relationship grew stronger with the weekly trips to Europe. Bloom and Farage would often spend evenings out drinking, and eventually they shared a flat in Brussels.

UKIP's most immediate problem was Robert Kilroy-Silk, who was asked after his election what he hoped to achieve in the Brussels Parliament. 'Wreck it!' was his blunt reply.[34] In the end he did more to wreck his party, and lasted just seven months as a UKIP MEP.

Farage was initially very welcoming to Kilroy. He told the producer of *The Man Behind the Tan*, a BBC documentary about Kilroy-Silk's early days as an MEP:

> Apart from Tony Blair, I can't think of another British politician that's as easily recognised in the street as Kilroy – that's what they call him, Kilroy. They all know who he is. And he's spent 18 years, not just on the television, but actually reaching into their homes and talking to them about family issues and things that really affect them. So he's made a massive difference and I think he isn't finished yet.[35]

But the tensions were obvious. Even before he was elected, Kilroy-Silk had once signed himself as 'UKIP Leader *de facto*' in a visitors' book. 'No,' Kilroy replied when the filmmakers asked if he wanted to be leader of UKIP as a whole. All that concerned him was 'ensuring we can govern ourselves . . . and I don't need to be the leader of any political party to do that'.[36] That stance didn't last long.

Roger Knapman may have been a lacklustre, uninspiring figure as leader, but he soon made clear that he wasn't going to stand down, not least because he didn't want Kilroy-Silk taking over. After all, he had just presided over the most successful campaign in UKIP's history. He planned to serve out his full four-year term to 2006. So Kilroy-Silk sought, behind Knapman's back, to find some kind of consolation, or compromise. How about if he and Farage split the role in a *de facto* way – Farage would run the party in Brussels, while Kilroy-Silk would effectively look after the show back in Britain? Farage must have 'gulped and gawped' at this suggestion, says Richard North. 'In Brussels and Strasbourg he spends his entire time on the phone to Britain. The British end is his patch, his power-base, his home ground. He hates the European end. The monster of his creation was threatening to get out of hand.'[37]

It was clear, however, that the major UKIP benefactor Paul Sykes wanted Kilroy to replace Knapman. 'Sykes wanted to take over the party and establish a headquarters in London,' Kilroy-Silk claimed later. 'He was going to spend a lot of money. He was talking *millions*. But only if I became leader.'[38]

Farage, however, has always denied suggestions that he had previously promised Kilroy-Silk that he could lead the party, though he confesses he may have made noises in that direction:

> It is the conjuror's and the con-man's first principle. Let people deceive themselves . . . Kilroy assumed that he would stroll into the leadership. I nodded and assured him, quite truthfully, that, with a little work and patience, he might well do so. Since he always talked at you, not to you, and never listened, I doubt that he heard the qualification.[39]

Slowly, Farage realised UKIP had a major problem. 'We had a mini-Mosley on our hands,' he later recalled, referring to the historic

British fascist leader Sir Oswald Mosley.[40] In an interview with David Frost that autumn, Kilroy-Silk admitted: 'I would like to be leader of UKIP. I would regard it as a privilege and an honour . . . I've been told by every senior member of the party that they would like me to be leader.'[41] Kilroy later admitted his previous denials had been a lie:

> Yeah, yeah. It's the one thing I said that I shouldn't have said at the time. I was trying to be helpful to the party and it was the wrong thing to do. I should have told the truth . . . The members have to decide whether they want to take charge of their party. For three months, now four, I kept quiet about what I regarded as irresponsibility, political irresponsibility bordering on criminality.[42]

At times, Kilroy-Silk also seemed in two minds about whether he really could lead UKIP, and had particular concern about the party's finances. 'There were a lot of things about money, which I didn't want to know about and I didn't want to be a part of . . . I thought I've got to lead it and change it, or I couldn't belong to it.'[43]

Not only did he think Roger Knapman was 'incompetent' and 'absent' as leader, but he also claims to have been horrified with the politics of some of his fellow UKIP MEPs, and even more by some of their parliamentary allies from other EU countries. Apart from his views towards other racial and national groups, Kilroy-Silk had been a notably liberal politician in the past. 'I might have moved to the right but all my principles are still liberal socialist,' Kilroy said years later. 'I'm not homophobic. I'm not racist. I'm not xenophobic. I believe in a woman's right to choose, and in feminism. I'm against the death penalty, all those kind of things.' And the problem wasn't just with some of the racist and socially conservative foreign MEPs with whom UKIP teamed up in Europe; he heard similar views from members of the party back home. 'I didn't know those kinds of opinions and attitudes still existed . . . From that moment, I wanted out. I handled it really, really badly. I find all that thing totally embarrassing. It was the worst moment of my life.'[44]

It was like 1999 again for UKIP, only a lot worse, and a lot more public. The party had enjoyed success in the European elections, only to engage in months of bitter struggle over who should lead them forward. Long-standing party activists grew increasingly hostile to an abrasive newcomer who'd only been with them for a few weeks. Farage, the man who had championed Kilroy-Silk against the doubters, and promoted him, quickly sensed the mood and turned against the arriviste. Farage's ally David Lott – the former squadron leader who'd toured English market towns in the converted horse-box – personally visited Kilroy-Silk and appealed to him to postpone any leadership challenge until the end of Knapman's term in 2006, but Kilroy declined. He also rejected offers to become deputy leader; or UKIP's candidate in the 2004 Hartlepool by-election; or to run UKIP's campaign for the next general election.

Kilroy's departure from UKIP was ragged and acrimonious. Initially, he resigned the UKIP whip in the European Parliament – no great hardship to either side – though Kilroy-Silk still said he was aiming to become UKIP leader. He even declared he would be leader by Christmas, and unsuccessfully pressed for an Extraordinary General Meeting to try to topple Roger Knapman.

In part, he blamed Farage for his demise. 'Nigel wasn't known, and I was this celebrity. Don't judge Nigel by what he is now,' Kilroy-Silk said in 2019, 'because he hadn't become what he is now. And he was pissed off.'[45]

In January 2005, however, Kilroy-Silk announced his departure from UKIP, though technically he had never actually joined. A few weeks later he confirmed he and several others, including Damian Hockney, were forming a new party called Veritas – Latin for 'truth' – though critics soon dubbed it 'Vanitas'. Kilroy-Silk launched it as 'the straight-talking party' at a bad-tempered press conference in the East Midlands. He promised to fight a substantial number of seats at the forthcoming general election, which was bound to threaten UKIP's hopes of doing better than in 2001.

'Sadly, he went completely crackers and started to believe his own publicity,' Farage said years later. 'And he didn't have the ability to laugh at himself, which is never a good thing in any walk of life.'[46] In his memoirs, however, Nigel Farage still maintained that inviting Robert Kilroy-Silk into the party had been worthwhile:

The long squabble unquestionably tarnished the UKIP brand, but it also made millions of people aware of us and of our cause. There is, I must confess, an irrepressible streak of vulgarity in me – perhaps there must be in any trader. If taking on Kilroy was the equivalent of installing glitter balls and painting the gallery shocking pink in order to sell a product in which I believed, so be it.

Farage would also compare it to Winston Churchill's view of alcohol: 'We took more out of Kilroy than Kilroy took out of us.'[47] But it's hard to believe he felt that way at the time.

Farage again left it rather late to decide where he would stand at the next general election, which Tony Blair was expected to call in May 2005. What has never been revealed before is that while Robert Kilroy-Silk was increasingly throwing his weight around, Farage had again been doing his 'work in the dark' making efforts to stand not for UKIP, but as a Conservative.

In October 2004 the Tory MP for Tunbridge Wells in Kent, Archie Norman, announced he wouldn't fight the seat at the next election. Norman, a former boss of Asda supermarkets, had been elected in 1997 with high expectations, but by 2004 the prospect of high ministerial office looked remote.

That autumn a county councillor in Surrey, Helyn Clack, who was chairman of her local Conservative association, got a message from a local friend who had worked with Farage on the London Metal Exchange. The friend explained that Farage wanted secretly to meet Clack.

Through this intermediary, Clack invited Farage to her home in Horley, along with her local Conservative MP, Sir Paul Beresford, a New Zealander who'd been a junior minister in the Major government and was then part of a small team which helped train people to become Tory candidates.

Farage turned up by car with the mutual acquaintance late one afternoon just as it was getting dark. 'He came dressed as a country squire,' Clack recalls, 'tweed jacket and yellow corduroys – because we live in the country, I suppose. We didn't really expect him to be like that. We expected a City gent.'[48]

Beresford recalls that the intermediary asked if he and Clack should withdraw and just leave Farage and the Tory MP together. Best not, said Beresford. He didn't trust Farage and wanted to have witnesses, though he didn't say that. Helyn Clack's husband also heard the ensuing conversation.

Farage pretty soon made clear, according to both Clack and Beresford, that he wanted to stand as a Conservative in a safe seat in the area. How should he go about it? Clack recalls Farage specifically mentioning Tunbridge Wells, while Beresford thinks that seat probably came up, but isn't sure. Beresford has never been a fan of Farage, so was pretty lukewarm about the idea, and explained that it wouldn't be simple to get selected. Candidates couldn't just be imposed from on high:

> I said: 'You've got to leave UKIP, join the Conservative Party, apply for the candidates' list, do a weekend assessment course, and pass that, and then apply for a seat.' I was not helping him at all. I was just laying out the ordinary procedure. The thought of him as a candidate was absolute anathema to me.[49]

The meeting lasted the best part of an hour. Clack had been friendlier than Beresford, who wanted to do his best to stop Farage. 'I thought he went away looking smugger than he ought to look,' Beresford recalls.

Nothing came of the meeting. Shortly afterwards, the Conservatives in Tunbridge Wells chose a very different candidate, the future Cabinet minister Greg Clark. Farage gave the BBC a rather different version of the secret gathering a couple of years later:

> There was a pretty strong approach made to me about a very safe seat that had come up, more or less at the last minute . . . Having given up my career and so much for this cause – I could not put my shoulder behind a party that believed in almost the opposite even though, on a personal level, it would have been very cosy and very nice.[50]

In other words, Farage claimed the Conservatives had approached him, rather than the other way round. In *Fighting Bull*, Farage features what seems to be the same event quite prominently:

> I was approached by a Tory Knight of the Shires and asked to attend a meeting at a private house. There, with a mutual guarantee of confidentiality, I was told that Michael Howard would look very favourably upon my application for the candidacy in the safe seat of Tunbridge Wells at the forthcoming general election . . . Archie Norman was standing down, and this was my sort of seat. It was close to my home. There were lots of business people, lots of fishing people here.

Farage relates that the 'Tory Knight' suggested he would have to modify his stance on Europe: all his talk of withdrawing from the EU was impractical, but the Conservatives were a broad church, and the party could really use him. 'I drained the whisky, which was far too good to be wasted . . . and brought the meeting to a mildly uncomfortable close.'[51]

Beresford and Clack insist Farage approached them. There are similarities with the dispute over whether it was Farage who approached the BNP activist Mark Deavin in 1997 or the other way round, with Farage using his memoirs in both cases to insist it wasn't he who made the first move. And in both episodes, even if one accepts Farage's version of events, he never satisfactorily explains *why* he went to each meeting. We already know he had been involved with many clandestine meetings with Tory MPs in the past, but this was usually to get them to defect to UKIP. In this instance, why go out of his way to see a Conservative MP who was not known to be sympathetic to his politics?

Farage eventually decided on a seat to fight, for UKIP – South Thanet in Kent. The constituency was at the south-eastern tip of his Euro constituency, overlooking the English Channel, and largely based on the seaside town of Ramsgate, and the resort of Broadstairs where Charles Dickens had lived. It looked promising, for in the 2004 European elections UKIP had got 27.2 per cent of the vote in the wider Thanet council area.

Like Bexhill and Battle, South Thanet also had a disaffected Conservative ex-MP, the former Cabinet minister Jonathan Aitken who'd lost the seat to Labour in 1997, just a few weeks before he was jailed for perjury. Aitken was a long-standing Eurosceptic, who during the 1980s had helped organise a group of about forty Eurosceptic Tory MPs in Parliament – the original Conservative European Research Group. Indeed, earlier in 2004, the local UKIP branch had even approached Aitken about fighting his old seat again. He was cautious at first, not wanting 'to piss in my own back yard where I'd been MP for twenty years', but soon warmed to the idea and was confident he could bring over many local Tories. Nigel Farage encouraged him to stand, but UKIP's latest national chairman, Petrina Holdsworth, a barrister, was hostile.[52] She felt that the offences for which Aitken had been jailed were serious, and 'clearly reflected on his lack of probity', and that he would have 'undermined' the party both nationally and in Thanet.[53]

The Thanet UKIP newsletter reported in November 2004 that:

> The NEC of the Party has turned down Jonathan Aitken in his application for interview as a potential General Election Candidate. As we had to find a candidate to represent the constituency your branch committee advertised the vacant position of PPC on the party website. At the deadline for applications only one candidate had applied. Nigel Farage, MEP has applied for the vacant position.[54]

Farage had been persuaded to stand by the UKIP branch chairman Martyn Heale, a local businessman who often worked door-to-door. Heale had thought about running himself, but chose instead to act as Farage's agent. He had a problem. In the late 1970s, Heale had been a member of the extreme-right National Front before spending twenty years as a Conservative. Farage has a habit of employing people with difficulties in their past, and Heale became a significant friend and ally, both in 2005 and beyond, despite Heale's NF history often being hurled against the MEP. Farage also has a habit of ignoring UKIP rules when it suits him.

Strictly speaking, Heale's former membership of the National Front – even if it was twenty years before – should have disqualified him from joining UKIP and certainly from holding office. Farage himself had even told a press conference during the European campaign in May 2004, that 'new UKIP members must now sign a pledge to say they were not, nor had been, members of extremist organisations', and he would frequently make similar claims over the years.[55] What's more, UKIP branch officers were required to sign a declaration which included the words: 'I declare that I am not, and have never been, a member of any anti-democratic organisation, or any organisation advocating racist, violent or criminal activity.'[56]

Jonathan Aitken never joined UKIP, but struck up a good relationship with Farage and offered his expertise. He gave advice on the Thanet area, and also wrote a couple of speeches for Farage – one on immigration, another on public spending. UKIP and Farage might also have benefited nationally from Aitken's long experience of politics, government and journalism, as well as his wealthy business contacts. 'I would have been a useful catch for UKIP by being a sensible manager for a rising political party,' says Aitken. But Aitken's offer wasn't taken up, which may be just as well since he and Farage would probably have fallen out before long.

In a way, the South Thanet constituency symbolised the evolving demographics of UKIP support. The party's early base was more around Sussex and Surrey – retired colonels in blazers, enjoying a G&T after a round of golf – and especially strong in middle-class retirement communities along the south coast – the so-called 'costa geriatrica'. South Thanet had its genteel parts, too – Broadstairs, and the ancient Cinque Port of Sandwich, now inland – but its biggest community, the port of Ramsgate, was far from prosperous. Indeed, when Jonathan Aitken first visited Ramsgate in the early 1970s and toured the council estates and tower blocks, he couldn't believe it was a Conservative seat. It was a very working-class area, where many inhabitants had moved from the North. Aitken recalls his predecessor as MP telling him not to worry, and that it was dominated by natural Tories – 'retired landlords, retired bookmakers, retired criminals, and retired prostitutes'.[57]

Alan Bown was one of Aitken's typical locals, a wealthy retired bookmaker who'd joined UKIP after Farage happened to put a leaflet through his letterbox while campaigning in Margate five years before. Having sold his chain of betting shops to Coral for £5 million, he'd become a big UKIP donor. Bown provided premises for a campaign HQ in Ramsgate and also gave £200,000 to UKIP's effort nationally (which led to a big court case, when it emerged that, under the new 2000 election laws, Bown's donations were 'impermissible' as he had failed, for that one year, to put himself on the voting register).

In 2005, for once, the Farage campaign touch deserted him, and he doesn't even mention the contest in *Fighting Bull*. The defending Labour MP, Stephen Ladyman, was impressed at how 'energetic' Farage was – 'he worked very, very hard' – but the 2,079 votes he got were barely 5 per cent, worse than either Salisbury in 1997 or Bexhill and Battle in 2001.[58] But Farage's campaign probably ensured the Conservatives didn't win South Thanet back, and Ladyman held on by 664, a third of the number who had voted for UKIP.

Nationally, a pattern was emerging. As in 2001, when it came to general elections, UKIP failed to emulate their success in the previous European contest. UKIP's vote rose from 1.5 to 2.2 per cent between 2001 and 2005, but it was disappointing compared with the election of twelve MEPs. One consolation was that Veritas, which fielded only sixty-five candidates, was reduced to 0.1 per cent. True, Robert Kilroy-Silk got a slightly higher percentage in Erewash in Derbyshire than Farage managed in Kent – but Veritas was effectively dead.

A growing worry for Farage and UKIP, however, was the progress of the extreme right-wing British National Party under its young leader Nick Griffin. They fought far fewer seats than UKIP, but actually managed more votes per candidate.

THE AWKWARD SQUAD

'Do you think homosexuality is a sin?' Robert Kilroy-Silk was seen asking in the BBC documentary about his early days in the European Parliament.

'Yes,' replied a Polish MEP, 'but I have a whole respect for the persons of homosexuals and I know a lot of them.'[1] The MEP was a member of the League of Polish Families, a party belonging to the very first parliamentary delegation from one of the EU's ten new accession states. And the League had quickly joined the same international group as UKIP.

Nigel Farage had landed two new leadership roles when he returned to the European Parliament as a re-elected MEP in 2004. Surprisingly, despite now having become an MEP himself, Roger Knapman appointed Farage as leader of UKIP's delegation to Europe. With four times as many MEPs as before, the party now packed a lot more punch in Strasbourg and Brussels, and Eurosceptics had done well elsewhere, too: across the now twenty-five EU states there were roughly twice as many MEPs as before who were broadly critical of the European Union. That made one of Farage's first tasks as group leader – putting together a new international grouping – slightly easier.

Farage and his old Danish friend Jens-Peter Bonde became joint presidents of the new Independence/Democracy group which initially had thirty-seven MEPs. This gave him much smarter offices in Brussels and Strasbourg, and more staff. And the BBC documentary showed Kilroy-Silk ribbing Farage that as a group leader he got a car to ferry him around (a perk which Farage himself had denounced in a similar documentary five years before). Independence/ Democracy – often called IND/DEM – was the sixth largest group in the Parliament and could boast the combined votes of more than 5 million people across Europe.

Farage had jumped into bed with some embarrassing allies, however. One was George Karatzaferis of the Popular Orthodox Rally from Greece, who in 2001 had publicly asked why Jews at the Twin Towers in New York did not 'come to work on 9/11', implying they had been warned of the attack.[2] Karatzaferis also asked the Greek prime minister whether he had a daughter who had 'secretly married a Jew', and he challenged the Israeli ambassador to debate 'the Holocaust, the Auschwitz and Dachau myth'.[3]

The League of Polish Families was also tainted by anti-Semitism. When it was founded in 2001, the League had declared itself to be the successor to the pre-war National Democracy Party, an anti-Semitic group which had a policy of excluding Jews from economic and social life, and ultimately of forcing them to leave Poland. A leading founder of the League of Polish Families had been the late Ryszard Bender, a history professor who served several terms in the Polish parliament. In 2000, Bender had caused an outcry when he told a radio station: 'Auschwitz was not a death camp, it was a labour camp ... Jews, Gypsies and others were annihilated there through hard labour. Actually, labour was not always hard and not always were they annihilated.' The following year, 2001, Bender opposed the commemoration of a pogrom in the town of Jedwabne, in which 340 Jews were murdered in 1941, most of them burned to death in a locked barn.[4]

In *Fighting Bull*, Nigel Farage proudly and amusingly relates how he repelled the advances of Alessandra Mussolini, the actress, model and granddaughter of the Italian dictator, who had just been elected to the European Parliament for the first time.

We sat there over coffee and she flung back that lovely hair and fixed me with those lovely eyes. She covered my hand with hers and she said, 'Nigel, I am so lonely ...'

'*Yes!*' cheered the adolescent Farage who lurks always at the back of my cranium.

'I'm all on my own,' she purred. 'I want so much to be with you . . .'

What she meant, of course, was that she was fed up with being a *'non-inscrit'* member and would like to be accepted into our group. I had to explain that her policies were, um . . . slightly irreconcilable with ours and that it would not be possible until she too became a libertarian.[5]

Yet unlike the League of Polish Families, Mussolini and her Social Alternative party claimed to be feminist, and in favour of gay rights and abortion. The real problem with admitting Mussolini, of course, was that someone with her name would have been so controversial back in Britain, at a time when UKIP was trying to distance itself from the neo-fascist British National Party (BNP), and avoid jibes about being the 'BNP in blazers'. What's more, Farage already had Italian allies in the Independence/Democracy group's motley crew of misfits – four MEPs from the Lega Nord, the populist party based in northern Italy, and they would probably have vetoed Mussolini as a member.

The Lega Nord contingent included the party's leader Umberto Bossi who had once been given a one-year suspended jail sentence for incitement to violence for saying: 'We must hunt down these rascals [neo-fascists], and if they take votes from us, then let's comb the area house by house, because we kicked the fascists out of here once before after the war.'[6] Another Lega Nord MEP was Mario Borghezio, who would be convicted in 2005 for setting fire to the wooden pallets of migrants sleeping under a railway bridge in Turin. In later years, Borghezio extended his notoriety by praising the Serbian leader and war criminal Ratko Mladić, and in 2011 for lauding several of the views of Anders Behring Breivik who carried out three terrorist attacks in Norway, including the one on a Norwegian young socialists' summer camp where sixty-nine people died. A third member of the Lega Nord team, Matteo Salvini, would become almost as controversial many years later when he served for a year as deputy prime minister of Italy.

Now that UKIP was the lead partner in a much bigger group,

Farage was determined they should spend a lot more time being awkward and become a thorn in the flesh of the EU establishment. 'It was really only in my second term, from 2004 onwards, that I really felt I can stand up and take this place on,' Farage later explained. Gone were the self-doubt, the feelings of inadequacy and bewilderment of 1999. With 162 new members from the ten accession states, plus scores of first-time MEPs from existing EU countries, the whole Parliament was very different in 2004. Farage was no longer a junior MEP; he was now an experienced old hand, who had been elected twice and enjoyed the backing of a substantial band of supporters.

The Eurosceptic's newfound aggression came at a time when Parliament as a whole was beginning to flex its muscle, as the new president of the European Commission found to his cost. José Manuel Barroso, the social democrat former prime minister of Portugal, was charged with recruiting a team of commissioners to form the EU's equivalent of the Cabinet. But he hit trouble when his Italian nominee for a post could not satisfy one of the Parliament's scrutiny committees over his ultra-conservative views, both on homosexuality and women. The president was forced to rejig his plans and the process dragged on for months.

Barroso got even deeper into a quagmire over his proposal that a French politician, Jacques Barrot, should be one of the vice-presidents of the Commission, and commissioner for transport. Normally such appointments are a formality. Not this time. The co-leader of the new Eurosceptic IND/DEM group was on Barrot's case. Someone in Farage's team did a Google search and discovered that, only four years earlier, Barrot had been convicted in France of embezzling £2 million of public money. The offence had occurred in the early 1980s when the funds were diverted to Barrot's then party, the Centre of Social Democrats. He got an eight-month suspended prison sentence, but this was immediately quashed because of a presidential amnesty on political funding issued by President Chirac in 1995 (who was himself later convicted of corruptly diverting public funds). So Jacques Barrot (who died in 2014) had no criminal record. UKIP's discovery pointed up not just a surprising choice by Barroso, but also the failure of any other political group in Europe, or indeed the press, to uncover his history. Even if there was technically no criminal conviction, it raised questions about Barrot's probity and character.

Farage couldn't believe his luck, though perhaps the leader of UKIP was not the best person to draw attention to politicians diverting public money for party political purposes (which was pretty much UKIP's stated policy). In November 2004, only minutes before the Parliament was due to approve Barroso's new Commission, Farage rose in the Strasbourg chamber for what was his first speech as a group leader. Speaking in front of a full audience, he cut to the chase, revealing how in 2000 Barrot had received his eight-month suspended jail sentence for the embezzlement case, and Farage also claimed – incorrectly – that Barrot had been 'banned from holding public office for two years'.

One by one, Farage then attacked several other members of the Commission team, which Barroso had boasted was of 'high quality':

From Hungary, we have Mr Kovacs. He'll take on taxation. For many years, a Communist apparatchik. A friend of Mr Kadar, the dictator there, and an outspoken opponent of the values that we hold dear in the West. [applause] His new empire will produce taxation policy and he'll look after the customs union, from Cork across to Vilnius. Are the EPP [European People's Party] and British Conservatives really going to vote for that?

From Estonia we have Mr Kallas, for twenty years a Soviet party apparatchik until his newly acquired taste for capitalism got him into some trouble. Though, to be fair, he was acquitted of abuse and fraud, but convicted for providing false information. And he's going to be in charge of the anti-fraud drive!

'I mean, you couldn't make it up!' Farage added, using one of his favourite phrases, and he was met by some applause.

The Farage list also included the new British commissioner, the former Labour minister Peter Mandelson. He was 'twice removed from the British government, yet to be fair, he's one of the more competent ones,' said Farage. The Dutchwoman Neelie Kroes had been 'accused of lying' to the Parliament, Farage pointed out, by Paul van Buitenen, a former EU official who'd just been elected a Dutch MEP (having brought down the Commission of Jacques Santer with corruption allegations). 'Ask yourself a question,' Farage thundered on:

> Would you buy a used car from this Commission? I mean, the answer simply must be 'No!' But even if they were competent, and even if this was a 'high quality' Commission – and sorry, Mr Barroso, but I don't think it is – we would still vote 'No' . . .
>
> It is the Commission that is the embodiment of all that is worst in this European Union; it is the Commission that is the government of Europe and is not directly accountable to anybody.[7]

'It was like a bomb going off,' Farage would claim years later. 'People were screaming and shouting.'[8] A less theatrical account was given by the Eurosceptic Conservative MEP Daniel Hannan, who said a French party ally of Jacques Barrot, Jacques Toubon, 'rushed up and down the aisle, apparently looking for someone to punch'.[9] Farage recalls Toubon shouting, 'Cessez, M. Le Président, cessez!'[10]

Farage had made a serious error about Siim Kallas, who was proposed as the new anti-fraud commissioner. And UKIP compounded that mistake with a press release which had the heading 'Conviction Politics: Anti-Fraud Commissioner has criminal record'.[11] Yet Kallas hadn't actually been convicted of providing false information. It was another four months, though, before these serious errors were acknowledged through another press release, which stated: 'UKIP now accepts that Mr Kallas was not in fact convicted of any offence.' The party apologised to Kallas 'for any distress caused' and said it had relied 'on an erroneous newspaper article'. Strangely, the press release didn't mention Nigel Farage, even though he had first made the allegation, and it disappeared from the UKIP website a few days after it was posted.[12] Farage did meet Kallas, and expressed his regret, though 'apologies is too big a word', says a former Kallas aide.[13]

Farage had, however, broadly been right about Barrot. He *had* received a suspended eight-month prison sentence, but under the terms of Chirac's amnesty in 1995 it was illegal to mention details of the sentence publicly in France, and Strasbourg of course, is in France. This absurd law only fuelled the outcry among many MEPs. Then Barrot's lawyer threatened Farage with legal action, arguing that the French law trumped Farage's parliamentary privilege. Remarkably, even some British media outlets that reported this row chose to comply with this French law and did not mention the detail of Barrot's penalty.

Leaders of other groups in the Parliament, of left and right, leaped to Jacques Barrot's defence, and the French Green MEP Daniel Cohn-Bendit (one of the student protest leaders in 1968) suggested many French parties had such problems. The Spanish president of the Parliament, Josep Borrell (since 2019, the EU foreign minister), warned Farage of the possible legal consequences of what he'd said about Barrot, and urged him to have his comments expunged from the record of proceedings. Farage accused Borrell of a 'veiled threat':

> I believed that it was a function of parliaments – even though I'm not particularly a fan of this one . . . that you were able to speak freely, to make statements, and to ask questions. I thought that was what parliaments were all about . . . If it's proved that what I said is wrong, if it's proved that my research is flawed, then of course, in those circumstances, I would withdraw the remarks and apologise wholeheartedly.[14]

He didn't withdraw or say sorry, but his revelations were too late to stop MEPs approving Barrot and the new Commission, with a 66 per cent vote in favour.

Barrot was still unhappy and told Farage to 'take back what he said, so that everything can be fully clarified, so that parliament can be sure of the truth'.[15] But the story was pretty much true, and the UKIP MEP held firm. For a day or two, there was speculation that Farage might even be arrested for breaking French law, but he only revelled in the possibility and the publicity. In reality, that was never likely since the law applied only to French officials, and the Parliament building was regarded as extra-territorial and outside French jurisdiction.

It was quite a coup for Farage, the first time he had made an impact in Strasbourg or Brussels. And it got good coverage in the British media. It later emerged that Barrot hadn't told José Manuel Barroso about his conviction or the amnesty, and Barroso's spokeswoman publicly revealed her boss's unhappiness that he was only informed about it on the day of the vote. The Socialist group was angry that Barrot hadn't disclosed his quashed conviction in hearings with MEPs, and demanded an urgent meeting with Barroso. The leader of the Liberal centre grouping in the Parliament, British Lib Dem MEP Graham Watson, who had called the UKIP MEPs 'football hooligans' over Farage's intervention, later suggested that Barrot should resign.

Fresh from his publicity coup over Jacques Barrot, Farage kept up the pressure, demanding in Brussels a fortnight later that Barroso come and explain how the Frenchman came to be appointed.[16]

Farage was on a roll. Then, early in 2005, around the time that the British press had embarrassed Labour over holiday hospitality received by Tony Blair and the Scottish First Minister Jack McConnell, the UKIP delegation received an extraordinary tip-off. Someone had written a letter stating that the Commission president José Manuel Barroso had enjoyed summer hospitality from the Greek shipping tycoon Spiros Latsis. This was potential dynamite.

Farage went on the attack, but didn't raise the Barroso–Latsis point straight away. Instead he sent out a letter to Barroso, and all the other EU commissioners, asking what hospitality they had accepted since their appointment. His letter caused huge anxiety, almost panic, within the Commission, especially in Barroso's office. The fear was that Farage was on to something big. One by one, the commissioners refused to answer his query.

Derk Jan Eppink, a Dutch former journalist who was then an adviser to Siim Kallas, the anti-fraud commissioner whom Farage had erroneously attacked, was both curious and worried. He decided to drop in on an old Belgian friend, Herman Verheirstraeten, who worked as secretary-general of the UKIP delegation. 'So why did

Nigel Farage send out his letter to all the commissioners?' Eppink tried to ask nonchalantly. Verheirstraeten pulled the tip-off letter from his drawer. He wouldn't let Eppink read it, but eventually told him about Barroso accepting summer hospitality from Latsis. 'From where we're sitting,' the Dutchman recalls Verheirstraeten saying, 'it looks like we've got the president by the balls. In fact, we've got the entire Commission by the balls. You think Farage is stupid. But who's looking stupid now?'

Farage 'might look like a comic-book figure', Eppink writes in his memoirs, 'but he had stolen a march on the Brussels bureaucrats he despised so much'.[17] Before long the German newspaper *Die Welt* publicly revealed that Barroso and his wife had been guests of Latsis – an old university chum – on a week-long cruise on the magnate's luxury yacht the previous summer. *Die Welt* estimated the benefit to be €20,000, though Barroso said that was a gross overestimate.

The benefits received by the new trade commissioner from Britain, Peter Mandelson, took longer to emerge. Initially it was revealed that Mandelson had enjoyed five days' hospitality in the Caribbean on the way to an EU engagement in Guyana, though he wouldn't identify his host at first. *Die Welt* then learned that it was a lobbyist called Peter Brown, who entertained Mandelson on the island of Saint Barthélemy, and that part of his stay was spent at a cocktail party given by Paul Allen, the co-founder and major share-holder of Microsoft, on his luxury yacht *Octopus*, moored offshore. Mandelson denied, however, that he'd spoken to Allen at the party (which seems rather impolite for a guest).

This all mattered because, not surprisingly, businessmen as wealthy as these had interests which involved the EU. Spiro Latsis had received a €10 million European Union grant for his shipyards, while another of his firms was bidding to build a motorway which would be funded in part by the EU.

Farage, ever the thorn in the Commission's side, persuaded 10 per cent of all MEPs to sign a petition to force a debate in the European Parliament (though both the conservative group, the EPP, and the Socialists refused to sign up). But José Manuel Barroso insisted that it was purely his own business with whom he took holidays, and accused

Farage of making a 'malicious allegation'. Barroso claimed not to think, however, that the UKIP group leader bore him 'a personal grudge':

> He merely finds it very strange that someone should receive an invitation to spend some days on a yacht. I must admit that I know of no one who would be brave enough to invite him aboard a yacht for a single day. I well understand his difficulty. [Laughter and applause] . . . This type of attack reflects a populist undercurrent which resorts to manipulation by oversimplifying important and complex matters, an undercurrent opposed to the Europe we are engaged in building.[18]

'Because most MEPs still regarded [Farage] as the European anti-christ, 589 of them, out of a total of 731, were willing to back Barroso and this team,' writes Derk Jan Eppink, the adviser to Siim Kallas. 'The President had survived, but with a badly tarnished image. And Farage had made a name for himself.'[19]

Barroso's embarrassment was especially acute because Farage's hospitality crusade came at a very sensitive time. Only four days later, the French were due to vote in a referendum on the new EU Constitution. It was designed to replace all the existing EU treaties with a single text, to streamline and further integrate decision-making. Qualified majority voting – the complicated system whereby various day-to-day decisions of the Council of Ministers didn't require unanimity – would be extended to most areas apart from the most sensitive topics (such as foreign policy and taxation) where each state would still have a veto. Most controversial, and symbolic, was the plan to create two new EU posts – president of the European Council, and a new EU minister for foreign affairs.

To Europhiles these reforms were a logical step on the road to 'ever closer union', a necessary way to strengthen the EU and make proceedings simpler after the admission of ten new countries. To Eurosceptics, the Constitution was yet more proof that the EU was really a political project, and another step on the road towards their ultimate nightmare, the European super-state which Margaret Thatcher warned of in her famous Bruges speech.

But the Constitution had to be ratified in each EU state, in many cases through a referendum, including in Britain where Tony Blair had promised one. The French referendum, in May 2005, would be crucial, but the No side in France, led by former socialist prime minister Laurent Fabius, was short of funds. Farage asked fellow Eurosceptic MEPs to dig into some of the €50,000 a year information allowance which each of them received – money which was meant to be devoted to promoting the work of MEPs and understanding of the European Union: €200,000 was raised in all.

A week before the vote, Farage was among the speakers at a 'No' rally in Paris, where several thousand Parisians were buoyed by five successive polls which showed No ahead. Unusually, Farage spoke from a script, simply because his O-level French wasn't good enough for his normal off-the-cuff oration. Seven days later, the French rejected the Constitution by almost 55 per cent to 45 per cent. Three days after that, the Dutch voted even more decisively against it, by more than 61 per cent to 39 per cent. The EU Constitution now looked dead, and five other states, including Britain, announced their referendums were cancelled. Farage likes to tell a story of how he was in the press bar of the European Parliament in Brussels on the night of the Dutch vote, celebrating with friends, and confident that they had blocked further centralisation within the EU. Then a German socialist MEP, Jo Leinen, one of the politicians who'd help draft the Constitution, walked by.

> I sort of half-jokingly said 'Will you join us for a glass of champagne to celebrate this outbreak of democracy?' And he looked at me and he said, 'You may have your little party; you may think this is a victory, but we have 50 different ways to win.' And it kind of just all drained from me, and I realised how fanatical these people were . . . That for me was the moment that I went from being not just a believer that the UK was a square peg in a round hole, and that we should leave – that was the moment I became an outright opponent of the whole European Union . . . I just realised that this place had the most enormous power and it wasn't prepared to surrender it.[20]

In 2007, many of the integrationist measures which were contained in the defeated Constitution resurfaced when EU leaders agreed the new Lisbon Treaty. The treaty came into force in 2009, by which time it was a well-established target of Eurosceptic wrath.

Many members of the European Parliament were very familiar, of course, with the practice for which Jacques Barrot had been briefly convicted – diverting public funds for party purposes. The European Parliament has long been a source of substantial funds for parties across Europe to pay for staff, accommodation and campaigning activity back in their home countries. Indeed, most of the political parties in the Parliament – left, right, or centre – have been guilty of this over the years.

In raising the case against Jacques Barrot, Farage had run the risk that one of UKIP's many enemies in Brussels, Strasbourg or Britain would start looking into their affairs. UKIP MEPs, not least Farage, almost wallowed in their ability to divert EU funds to the political purposes of their party. In my research for this book, no UKIP figure has ever tried to argue it didn't happen.

UKIP MEPs did make some effort to keep their faces clean. Not long after the 2004 European election, they unanimously agreed new rules for themselves. Roger Knapman later explained how the group decided 'that we would not go on "junkets" to other countries and secondly that we would not employ our wives. This was to prevent us getting dragged into the comfortable EU world that leads down the path to "going native".'[21] The rules about employing wives followed some disquiet at Westminster over the extraordinary number of British MPs – roughly a third – who employed members of their families, and the famous 'Betsygate' affair of 2003 when it emerged that the Conservative leader Iain Duncan Smith employed his wife Betsy on his Westminster payroll, though he successfully refuted accusations that she did virtually no work.[22] Speaking just after Betsygate, Farage publicly opposed parliamentarians employing their spouses. 'The reason we need to have MEPs' interests laid out in front of us,' he told the *Sunday Times*, 'is because the public no longer trusts us.'[23] Addressing fellow UKIP MEPs, Farage was wholeheartedly in favour of the new rule, and group members were keen not to be seen to be enriching their families at EU expense.

Before the 2004–9 Parliament was over, however, one UKIP MEP, Derek Clark, was obliged to repay £31,000 to the Parliament, and in 2009 another, Tom Wise, was jailed for two years for frauds in relation to European Parliament expenses. Wise had siphoned off £30,000 in expenses which were meant to go to employing a member of his staff. Wise changed his plea to guilty on the morning Nigel Farage was due to give evidence in court against him, though previously Farage had shown some sympathy for Wise, and told Daniel Foggo of the *Sunday Telegraph*, who exposed the scandal, that the MEP had committed a simple, silly error by making himself a 'paying agent' for his own staff (which was against the rules). Farage had also argued that Wise had not tried to gain personally.[24] Years later Farage himself would be obliged to pay back tens of thousands of pounds for misused parliamentary grants.

Gawain Towler, a former Conservative adviser and candidate who had joined Farage as his European press spokesman in 2005, remembers how his boss had 'a huge capacity for synthesising complicated information and turning it into something for ordinary people'. Towler, who'd previously edited a satirical magazine in Brussels called *The Sprout*, established a good rapport with journalists, who came to trust he would pretty much tell them the truth. 'Working with Farage was a great joy,' Towler says. 'He'd give great copy and come up with the immediate sound bite. He never needed a second take. We didn't get much coverage, so there's no way he'd say, "No, I'm busy." If your boss is committed it does make your life easier.'[25]

As co-president of the international grouping, as well as leader of the UKIP delegation, Farage spent much more time in Europe after 2004 than he had during his previous five-year term, and his profile was considerably higher. When the UK took over the rotating presidency of the European Council in the second half of 2005, just after Labour won its third term, Tony Blair visited the Parliament, both at the start of the British presidency and then again at the end. That December, EU leaders agreed a new six-year budget package which would see Britain give up much of the budget rebate negotiated by

Margaret Thatcher twenty years before, while extra funds were assigned to poorer East European states which had joined in the recent enlargement. Farage laid into Blair in the Parliament chamber:

> Why should British taxpayers pay for new sewers in Budapest, for a new underground system in Warsaw, when our own public services are crumbling in London? ['Hear hear!', probably beyond the UKIP group]. Why should we pay a penny-piece into an organisation whose accounts have not been signed off by the auditors for the last eleven years in a row? This Budget deal is game, set and match to President Chirac – no cheese-eating surrender monkey he. Unlike you, he stands up for the French national interest, not some bizarre notion of Europe. And he has outclassed and outplayed you at every turn. Your only real achievement is that Britain is now isolated, alienated, we are completely alone within the European Union [cries of 'You are alone'] which is why, which is why . . .

At which point the President of the Parliament tried to cut Farage off. 'Hang on a second,' Farage objected. 'Everyone else gets an extra minute, Mr President. I'm asking for ten seconds.' And he got them. 'Which is why, Prime Minister, I urge you, it's often been said that you wanted to be the permanent president of Europe. Please stay on for a further six months. Six more months of the British presidency, and they'll kick us out. Thank you.'

Blair, sitting in his shirtsleeves amid a crowd of dark suits, grinned and laughed, and shook his head and turned to José Manuel Barroso and laughed some more. 'Yeah well,' he said to his audience. 'Thank you very much, all of you,' he added sarcastically, before starting his response. He began slowly, before he unleashed his pent-up anger, gesticulating in Farage's direction:

> In my experience in politics, there are three groups of people. There's first of all the reactionaries. And let me just tell you sir [pointing to Farage], and your colleagues: You sit with our country's flag [still pointing]. You do not represent our country's

interests [wide applause] . . . This is the year 2005, not 1945. We're not fighting each other any more. These are our partners; they're our colleagues, and our future lies in Europe. And when, when you and your colleagues say: 'What do we get in return for what we contribute to enlargement?' I'll tell you what we get: we get a Europe that is unified after years of dictatorship in the East. We get economic development in countries who we have championed. We get a future reform that allows us once and for all to put an end to discussion about rebates, Common Agricultural Policy, and get a proper reform budget for Europe. That's what we get if we . . . seize that opportunity.[26]

Two of the most formidable communicators of early twenty-first-century British politics had met head-on, and both were on top form. The whole nature of Nigel Farage's contributions in the European Parliament had changed radically. During his first parliament, 1999 to 2004, his speeches had often focused on narrow areas of policy. Now he was much more pugnacious. His speeches were designed not just for fellow MEPs, but to grab headlines for a much wider audience outside, and he was increasingly successful at this. Using blunt and simple sentences, often rhetorical questions, with few adjectives or adverbs, Farage spoke the kind of English which was easy for other Europeans to understand.

And the advent of the internet video platform YouTube, which was launched in May 2005, would in time give Farage a huge new audience and fame way beyond Britain, Strasbourg or Brussels. The strict time limits on contributions, even for a group leader like Farage, actually helped in a way as they forced him to speak in punchy, pithy sound bites, which were ideal for television coverage and for the new world that was opening up – politics through social media: Twitter, Facebook, YouTube and other online outlets.

The Farage–Blair encounter hid the fact, though, that back in Britain things had got much worse for UKIP after the 2005 general election. The party didn't even bother to fight the Cheadle by-election a few weeks later, which allowed Veritas one dying gasp in which they got less than one per cent.

And when a by-election was called in Bromley and Chislehurst the following spring, as a result of the death of Conservative MP Eric Forth, it was almost home territory for Nigel Farage – only a couple of miles from where he'd lived all his life. Yet UKIP seems to have been undecided about fighting it.

The party had been taking a hammering in the polls (perhaps because of the arrival of David Cameron as Conservative leader), and according to one account Farage suggested to the Tories that UKIP could step aside. His condition was that the Tories pick as their candidate the Eurosceptic MEP for London, Syed Kamall, who was on the Conservatives' final shortlist of three. When Farage's colleague Gerard Batten heard of the plan, he was furious, and threatened that if Farage didn't stand then he would do so instead.

So Farage did contest the seat, and spent £65,000 doing so. He campaigned in an open-topped vintage Alvis adorned with UKIP's purple and yellow colours, hoping to attract those more right-wing and traditional Conservative voters who were put off by the Tories' rapid move to the centre ground under 'moderniser' Cameron. In a radio interview only a few weeks before, the new Tory leader had dismissed UKIP as 'just a sort of a bunch . . . of fruitcakes, and loonies and closet racists, mostly'. Cameron later admitted his remarks had been a mistake, as they risked alienating voters 'we were trying to win back', and they also drew attention to UKIP at a time when the party was lagging badly behind.[27] Farage threatened to sue and hit back:

> Let him tell us anything that we have said that could be construed as remotely racist, otherwise we demand an apology . . . I don't mind him calling us loonies – I don't mind him calling us fruitcakes. We are big enough and ugly enough and we have a sense of humour . . . But what you cannot do in the 21st century is to lob about accusations of racism.[28]

At UKIP conferences thereafter one would often find a stall selling or giving away fruit cake, and for better or worse UKIP was stuck with Cameron's jibe ever after. In 2014, an edition of the TV panel show

Have I Got News for You?, on which Farage was a guest, played a round called 'Fruit Cake or Loony?', which he handled remarkably well.[29]

In Bromley, however, Farage would receive quiet help from an unlikely quarter – the Liberal Democrats. The Lib Dems' canny strategist Lord (Chris) Rennard knew that as the main challengers for the seat, the Lib Dems needed not just to boost their own support, but reduce the Conservative vote. 'We advised canvassers who found Tories possibly reluctant to vote Tory but unwilling to vote Lib Dem, to back Farage instead,' says Rennard, who mischievously points out that in such cases his party promoted the UKIP contender as a 'local candidate'. 'I reckoned that we needed Farage to get 10 per cent for us to win Bromley.'[30]

Farage fell short of that, though there were positives. His 8 per cent of the vote was the highest he'd achieved in five attempts at becoming an MP, and he pushed Labour's candidate, twenty-seven-year old Rachel Reeves, into fourth place, when she'd come second at the general election only the year before. But, as Rennard had calculated, Farage's 8 per cent meant the seat stayed Conservative.

In the summer of 2006, Roger Knapman's four-year term came to an end, and the leadership was up for grabs again. 'It made the choice for me very easy,' Farage would say later. 'I was then over forty. I'd done every other job in UKIP. Becoming leader of UKIP when it was less than one per cent in the opinion polls and off the radar, well it was a good time to buy stock. Taking over at that time, I simply couldn't lose.'[31]

Farage faced three opponents, none of whom was a substantial UKIP figure, and his two main rivals were fairly new arrivals from the Conservatives. His main challenger, Richard Suchorzewski, UKIP's leader in Wales, was the openly 'anti-Farage' contender. Derisively nicknamed 'Suck-a-horse-ski' by Farage, Suchorzewski had been a City banker but had since returned to Wales where he was born, and joined UKIP only in 2004. David Campbell Bannerman, recently appointed UKIP chairman by Roger Knapman, was distantly related to the Liberal prime minister of Edwardian times, Sir Henry Campbell-Bannerman. He had switched from the Tories only in 2002.

The figures show Farage won fairly comfortably:

Nigel Farage	3,229	44.0%
Richard Suchorzewski	1,782	23.5%
David Campbell Bannerman	1,443	19.0%
David Noakes	851	11.2%

While Farage now had a hat-trick of leadership roles, he had not pulled off as substantial a victory as one might have expected given his past successes in NEC contests. He'd got well under 50 per cent of the vote, against three unexciting rivals. It was a sign of how, by now, the lustre seemed to be coming off Nigel Farage's reputation among some UKIP members. Many in the party feared that their MEPs had been corrupted by their high salaries and astonishing expense allowances, and had grown too fond of the high life of champagne on tap and gourmet dinners in French and Belgian restaurants. Nobody epitomised this more than Nigel Farage. Not all UKIP members saw themselves as libertarians in the way Farage did: many were elderly, and socially very conservative. Indeed, Richard Suchorzewski had stood on a ticket of 'Transparency, Integrity and Equality', and on the ethical and Christian principles on which he'd based his life. It was a platform clearly directed against one man.

Alan Sked and Richard North had already told stories of Farage's drunkenness and of his consuming champagne in lap-dancing clubs in London and Strasbourg. At the start of 2006, the *News of the World* had run the first of many tabloid exposés which would afflict Farage over the coming years. The front-page headline was 'EURO MP CHEATS ON HIS WIFE WITH A WOMAN' – note how Farage was still not well-enough known to be named in the headline. The report claimed the UKIP MEP had picked up a young blonde from Latvia, Liga Howells, in a pub in Biggin Hill, less than two miles from his family home, and returned with her to her house.

Howells, a former reporter for Latvian TV, who was half-German and half-Swedish, claimed they had made love seven times. 'He had very good stamina,' she said. They reportedly had a bath together and oral sex with ice cubes. 'He has a very good body for a man his age,' she added. 'He was quite well-endowed too.' But it was well into the night, she claimed, before Farage revealed he was married.

'It wasn't after the first time we had sex that he told me,' she said. 'It was after quite a few times. Afterwards he fell asleep and kept me awake because he was snoring like a horse.' And Howells further related:

> He also liked to call me 'Miss'. It was 'Yes Miss' or 'No Miss' when we were in bed. I found this very odd. It was like he needed for me to dominate him. He enjoyed being controlled. I found it all a bit weird . . . He asked me to smack him. He went, 'Smack me, Miss.' I have never, ever heard anything like this in my whole life. He did ask me to humiliate him. It is beyond belief some of the things he asked me to do. And I wasn't prepared to do what he asked me.

The paper even included a dreadful pun about how Farage wanted Liga Howells to be 'MaaSTRICHT' with him. She said that later Kirsten Farage found her number on Nigel's phone and called her. 'She was completely quiet on the other end. It freaked me out.' Nigel Farage admitted to the *News of the World* that he was in the 'dog house' for staying up all night with the Latvian. 'I made a huge error of judgement going back with her.' But 'I didn't have a sexual relationship with her,' he insisted. 'That's her fantasy.'[32]

Liga Howells's account should be treated with scepticism, and much of it sounds embellished. 'Given the amount I had drunk on the night in question,' Farage wrote in his 2010 autobiography, it was 'a physical impossibility' that they had sex seven times. 'Liga wasn't screwed. I was. It did get me into fearful trouble with Kirsten. She did not find Lothario Nigel after a hard night's drinking credible, but she was furious at me for being so bloody stupid and inconsiderate as to pass out three miles from home.'[33]

Years later, it emerged in the *News of the World* phone-hacking trial against former editors Andy Coulson and Rebekah Brooks, that both Farage and Liga Howells had their mobile phone voicemails intercepted by Glenn Mulcaire, the private investigator who pleaded guilty to carrying out hacking for the paper. Farage was among dozens of victims who successfully sued the *News of the World*'s parent company News International.

And Greg Lance-Watkins, who worked closely with Farage at this time (though later became a fierce public critic) has suggested the story was largely concocted by Howells. He claimed to have spoken to Farage earlier on the day in question:

> It was clear from my conversations on the Friday that the silly man was far too drunk to have made any intelligent choices and by the evening he was far too drunk to have performed in any manner as claimed by Liga Howells! Kirsten did confirm that he had phoned her to come and collect him from the pub but she refused – partly in annoyance but far more consequentially as she could not leave the babies at home in bed and swan off to act as taxi to a drunk some distance from home! The state in which Farage was on the [Saturday] confirmed that he would have been completely incapable sexually the night before and gave the lie to the whole story that Liga had concocted to sell![34]

But Kirsten Farage was understandably angry – not just about her husband's encounter with Howells, but the humiliating front-page story. Not long afterwards, Nigel Farage gave his wife a job on his staff in the European Parliament. One theory is that this was to placate her with extra income of around £30,000 a year, but also to make Kirsten feel that she could keep a close eye on him, though she worked mainly from home. Her work included co-ordinating Farage's diary, and looking after his emails (which, according to her and colleagues, he didn't know how to write).

But brazenly, his decision to employ Kirsten came only months after all the UKIP MEPs had decided to ban themselves from employing spouses from European Parliament funds, a policy which Nigel Farage himself had publicly advocated. Farage didn't tell his colleagues about Kirsten's appointment, and was storing up huge trouble for himself, creating yet another stick with which his critics could beat him.

MYSTERY OF THE
OLD BETTING SHOP

Nigel Farage had always appreciated that UKIP needed money. The party would never thwart the established big boys of British politics without substantial funding, preferably on the scale which Labour received from the trades unions, or the Conservatives obtained from big business. UKIP had a handful of wealthy donors, but needed to become more efficient at squeezing funds from its thousands of members, and also the millions of people who were sympathetic to UKIP's aims, but not yet committed enough to join the party.

In February 2003, more than three years before Farage became leader, the UKIP NEC set up a call centre at its then headquarters in Broadwick Street in London's Soho, with a professional staff who sold both membership subscriptions and also solicited donations. The centre had access to the database of existing and lapsed UKIP members – and of people who'd expressed sympathy with the party and its aims in the past. It had also assembled the contact details of more than 200,000 people who'd signed various Eurosceptic petitions over the years. The telesales staff had the incentive of being paid 8.5 per cent commission on successful transactions.

Soon afterwards, Nigel Farage was offered a former shop in Kent to operate free of charge as a second UKIP call centre. The proposal came from Alan Bown, the retired bookmaker and big UKIP donor from Margate. Bown offered the party one of his old betting shops in Ashford, at a crossroads on Beaver Road, in a working-class area not far from the station. The 1,200 square foot premises, which already had thirty phone lines, opened in October 2003, when the *Kentish Express* reported that UKIP's venture had created ten new jobs, with 'another 20 staff expected to be working in town on their campaign for the European elections next June'.[1] Farage and Bown celebrated with drinks at a 'grand opening' with Tim Brinton, the former Tory MP for Gravesend who'd just defected to UKIP.

The outside of the building was painted in the party's garish purple and yellow colours, with UKIP posters in the window, and the premises were later pictured in the party's *Independence* magazine. Inside, the ground floor looked like any other office, with desks, phones and computer terminals for both a daytime and evening shift to make calls for almost twelve hours a day, from 9.30 a.m. to 9 p.m. 'Without the use of professional telesales at Ashford we would still be a small party,' Nigel Farage was later quoted as saying. 'Now we are a medium-sized party and, if we keep pushing, we will become a big party.'[2] The phone bank was staffed mainly by students, supplied by a firm specially set up by Alan Bown for the purpose. Ashford was also used for phone canvassing during election campaigns, and for handling calls to the party's freephone number. The operation recruited new supporters through ads in right-leaning national papers – the *Mail*, *Express*, *Telegraph* and *Sun*. Headed 'The Truth About the European Union', the ads urged people to fill in a printed coupon and post it to the Ashford address to obtain a UKIP video and brochure, or to call the freephone number.

In May 2003, the UKIP NEC acknowledged Nigel Farage's enthusiasm for telesales by putting him in charge of both call centres, and they agreed to his request that the commission be doubled to 17 per cent. These decisions proved to be a huge error. There was an obvious conflict between UKIP's needs as a national party, and those of Farage as a South East MEP. That September the UKIP Finance Committee identified the problem that 'The South East operation has, by default, a goal to maximise revenues for the South East European election fund which is in conflict with the needs of maintaining a properly financed Central Office function. These roles should be separated and Nigel Farage should concentrate on the South East operation only.'[3]

The Ashford call centre would be the cause of acrimonious arguments within UKIP which dragged on for more than a decade, amid allegations that Farage had misused its proceeds. Farage would be accused of channelling to his own South East region – and hence to his campaign for re-election to the European Parliament – tens of thousands of pounds raised from members and supporters across the country which should have gone to UKIP head office to finance activity nationwide, or been spread across every region which had promising chances of electoral success.

The problem became more acute when the Soho call centre was closed down. It had proved to be uneconomic because of high wage and running costs, as well as staff incompetence. Before long, Ashford's work stirred up bitter divisions within the party, both among senior figures, but also between ordinary activists and the UKIP high command.

The Ashford telesales team offered UKIP supporters discounted membership rates if they joined for three years or five years. The understanding with the NEC had long been that if a new member was signed up at a local level, then the local area would retain the first year's membership fee, while the income for the subsequent four years should all go to head office to pay for the cost of servicing that membership – sending out newsletters and so on – and to contribute to UKIP work nationally. Farage and the South East almost immediately seemed to overlook that, and were accused of keeping many membership fees entirely for their region. And when the Ashford centre began venturing beyond the boundaries of the South East to recruit members and raise donations in other regions – in the South West, Scotland or wherever – Farage and the South East were accused of keeping those membership fees as well.

Farage's own patch had always been UKIP's strongest region internally, and around this time probably about 30 per cent of all members lived in the South East area outside London. By trawling for new recruits and donations nationwide, the Ashford call centre was effectively getting UKIP supporters in the rest of the country to subsidise Farage's re-election – and campaigns for a second or third MEP in the South East – at the expense of other regions. This didn't really make tactical sense. Farage's re-election in the South East was pretty much assured, and in 2003 one would have expected the party nationally to have spread their resources more evenly, with perhaps an extra effort in the six English regions where they didn't yet have an MEP. It was foolish to concentrate on just one region.

An early report, in September 2003, by a team comprising the party treasurer John De Roeck, former treasurer Craig Mackinlay and former national secretary Tony Scholefield was critical of how Farage had operated. 'Should regions solicit long-term membership with no remittance to Central Office,' the document warned, 'the party is being asked to finance membership maintenance for up to five years with no cash.'[4]

A few days later, De Roeck wrote to his colleague, the UKIP secretary Derek Clark, to complain that 'the Ashford office is in clear breach of party rules at this time by withholding moneys due to the Central Office'. De Roeck also wrote of 'complaints from members that the Ashford office has been storing bulk membership applications, possibly one hundred for membership and renewals during the last four weeks, and not supplying these to Head Office for processing in order to avoid paying moneys to the Central Office'.[5] Nigel Farage's response to the allegations and concerns by senior colleagues about Ashford is that the NEC 'were too stupid to understand its potential, so I underwrote the entire financial risk personally. It was a great success. Those idiotic NEC members you refer to were manipulated up by those who wanted to hurt UKIP. I tried to professionalise and commercialise the party – not an easy job with low grade NEC members.'

John De Roeck now estimates that about half the funds spent by the South East region for the 2004 European campaign should in fact have gone to the rest of the country. 'Nigel was benefiting himself by pulling funds towards his region,' De Roeck says, 'because as a candidate he personally benefited by money going to his region and not to Head Office. It's like the director of a company boosting his sales figures, so as to get higher commission.'[6]

At an NEC meeting only a few weeks after De Roeck's complaint to Derek Clark, Farage tried to get rid of him as UKIP treasurer.

De Roeck survived, but left the party a few months later, and in 2005 joined Robert Kilroy-Silk's Veritas party.

The former UKIP chairman Petrina Holdsworth recalled how Farage and the NEC had agreed 'that a certain amount would be paid by Ashford into the central funds every time a new member was recruited. It was that payment into the UKIP funds that I was not happy was being adhered to.'[7] Another NEC member, Linda Guest, is reported in the minutes as saying she 'felt that the NEC had not been told the truth about Ashford'.[8]

Richard Suchorzewski, the main challenger to Nigel Farage in the 2006 leadership election, said during the campaign that a 'cloud still overhangs the Ashford call centre and various aspects of UKIP accounts'.[9] Suchorzewski had only been elected to the UKIP NEC that same year, and spent much of his early days trying to understand the finances of Ashford. 'What I found on the NEC was a nest of vipers,' Suchorzewski said in 2013.[10] As a member of the National Executive he was legally responsible and financially liable (along with every other NEC member) for UKIP's financial affairs, and therefore obliged to get to the bottom of everything.

'Nigel was the brain behind it,' Suchorzewski said later. 'Nigel said it was the greatest fund-raising operation UKIP had ever adopted.' But Suchorzewski found that in 2005 just over 10 per cent of the money collected had gone to the central party. When he and colleagues asked what had happened to the remaining 90 per cent they were 'stonewalled', he said.

> We never got to the bottom of it. We were the governing body. There should be no secrets. We were personally liable. We weren't given the figures – just told it was a successful fund-raising operation. Nigel doesn't take criticism very well. He would just walk out in a fit of temper. People of talent and ability would be purged. If you make a criticism you are condemned. His supporters would then spread rumours that you were in the BNP. Had I been elected [as leader], the cupboard would have been opened, with skeletons inside. He was afraid of what I would reveal.[11]

Ashford's operation seemed to be exceedingly complicated, perhaps deliberately so. Not only was it officially part of Nigel Farage's South East region of UKIP, but day-to-day operations were run by Alan Bown's company, Ashford Employment Ltd.

There were also widespread complaints from UKIP activists that commission-hungry Ashford callers were too pushy in requesting membership renewals and soliciting money; their methods were 'too American', they said.[12] 'We have lost potential members from telesales,' one activist wrote on a chat site. 'Members have been cultivating local supporters only to find that telesales have called these supporters and by being too aggressive have totally turned them off. Potential members declare that they will now never join.'[13] 'In the Eastern region we are sick to death of the Ashford call centre,' another activist wrote, adding:

> it was trying to take money from our region, but we never saw any accounts as to where the money finished up . . . In the South Essex branch we have asked our members and supporters to ignore any calls from Ashford and . . . if they give us the money direct, there is nothing dedicated for commission.[14]

In October 2005, three officials from the UKIP branch in Chichester, which was probably the strongest in the country, met Farage and other senior party figures to air their grievances about Ashford, which were mainly about the off-putting, aggressive style of the telesales callers. Farage defended the call centre ferociously. It had been 'an absolute lifeline', he said. It had taken nine years for UKIP to get to 9,500 members, and they had now 'doubled the size of the party because of the call centre'. He cited one branch, the Isle of Wight, which suddenly found it had 150 new members 'thanks to the activities of the call centre'. And in areas where UKIP had no branch structure, 'we [the call centre] are often the only contact the members have'.[15]

Farage even asserted that Ashford had brought in £400,000. It was a rash claim, which made the operation look far more successful than it was, and it naturally aroused people's suspicions about what had happened to all the money. The £400,000 was clearly a gross sum over several years, since financial statements showed that for one year, 2005, Ashford had an income of £163,919, but also outgoings of £138,380, so the net profit was just £25,539. Of this, £17,881 had gone into UKIP election funds. By January 2006, Ashford was making a net loss.[16]

In 2005, the then leader Roger Knapman announced that Ashford had been brought back under control of the national party. In the spring of 2006 it was closed down altogether by the chairman David Campbell Bannerman.

'Towards the end of the Ashford call centre's life the costs had become too high,' Campbell Bannerman said in 2007, explaining that 85 per cent of the income was taken up by staff wages, office costs and other expenditure. 'This proportion I considered unacceptable as chairman, and actioned the closure of that facility, and the move to more volunteer-driven call centres around the UK.'[17]

Campbell Bannerman says it was his decision to close it down. 'It wasn't a scandal,' he said. 'It was a call centre. It didn't endear me to Nigel. There were so many accusations being thrown around. We were kind of running the party for the benefit of the call centre. Nigel didn't like me closing Ashford down, but I said we couldn't afford it. He saw it as a way of building up the party.'[18]

But Farage would continue to defend the operation. In 2007 he said:

All the money raised by Ashford can be seen in the accounts for the south-east unit – no money has disappeared . . . The Ashford call centre was something that I opened up. It doubled the party's membership and it made a very substantial profit. It's the single most successful thing UKIP has ever done . . . The NEC did not want to have any responsibility or risk for Ashford because we had run call centres in the past at a substantial loss . . . We ran call centres in London and they lost £5,000 to £6,000 every month. I said: 'This is ludicrous, let's do this professionally.' The NEC refused to take responsibility for it.[19]

The problem seems to have been that the call centre only worked well in the early months, in 2003 and early 2004, according to Doug Denny, the treasurer of the South East committee, who was then a Farage ally:

> Ashford was a spectacular success when it was set up in those few months before the European election; and increased the membership dramatically over a very short period; *and* collected huge amounts of money which went into the campaign which is what it was set up for. It *was* a success, and a brilliant one – for a while. But I saw it would become a millstone around UKIP's neck afterwards.[20]

Not long after the closure of Ashford, Farage set up a new South East call centre in Ramsgate, run by his former election agent Martyn Heale. The then UKIP treasurer Bruce Lawson told UKIP's annual business meeting in 2007 that it 'had been started without his knowledge or approval' and that 'he had not been able to get the financial information he was asking for' about its work. When Lawson proposed a motion that Ramsgate be closed down, several Farage supporters leaped to its defence, and Lawson was defeated.[21]

For years afterwards, however, there would be suspicions about a black hole of more than £200,000 in the Ashford finances. Critics pointed to a mystery £211,267 in unspecified 'other costs' in the South East accounts for the year 2004.[22]

Several leading figures in UKIP raised questions about Ashford over the years, and tried to investigate, but without much success. These included Damian Hockney (UKIP GLA Member, 2004–5); Martin Haslam (deputy treasurer, 2006–8); Linda Guest (NEC, 2005–7); Ian Gillman (NEC, 2003–5); Geoffrey Collier (chairman of the Chichester branch); Geoffrey Kingscott (UKIP secretary); and Tony Ellwood, an accountant who worked for the MEP Derek Clark and was a UKIP official in the East Midlands.

'We tried to find out answers but the shutters were always put up,' Ellwood told Channel 4 in 2013. 'You were ridiculed if you asked those questions, because no one wanted to know. We were perceived as troublemakers, but we were just trying to protect the innocent in the party.'[23] Whenever these people asked for accounts they were stonewalled. NEC members who queried the situation were met with an aggressive response by Farage and his allies. Delroy Young recalled that when a female NEC member tried to ask Farage about Ashford and MEPs' expenses, he said, 'Shut up you, stupid woman!' 'He went berserk,' said Young. 'I said "Who do you think you are? . . . She has a right to be asking these questions."'[24] Young also recalled that when Linda Guest proposed to an NEC meeting that Richard Suchorzewski be asked to examine UKIP's finances, since he had a financial background, 'there were shouts from Nigel Farage's crowd telling her to sit down'.[25]

Ian Gillman from Northamptonshire, who'd been a UKIP parliamentary candidate, resigned from the NEC in 2005. He was 'no longer prepared to collude with the shoddy behaviour that is beneath the standards of integrity that can reasonably be expected of such a body', Gillman wrote in his resignation statement. 'Back-stabbing is very counter-productive, yet all too prevalent. Foul, abusive and unnecessarily aggressive emails and speech appear to win the day; integrity is sneered at; respect absent,' Gillman wrote.[26]

Gillman's concerns over the two years he'd spent on the NEC weren't just about Ashford, but the other financial ventures as well: a UKIP lottery and a wine club, both of which had failed and for which there was little by way of paperwork or accounts. And when Gillman persistently tried to get to the bottom of things, he was denounced as a troublemaker. 'Quite a lot of us were asking questions for a number of years and thwarted at every turn,' Gillman said in 2013. One meeting, due to end at 6 p.m., he says,

> went on with terrible rows until 9 p.m. in the evening, and those rows would pertain to the Ashford Call Centre . . . demanding to know where the money had gone . . . It was just that money was being raised on quite a grand scale, and where was it going? . . . It was singularly unpleasant:

shouting, swearing and the most abusive language to one's fellow man.

Gillman says he suffered similar intimidation on the UKIP East Midlands regional committee, and had to endure an hour and twenty minutes of 'threats and abuse' at one regional meeting. 'I was given three clear threats of being taken outside and beaten up . . . I was subjected to a level of viciousness that shocked me.'[27]

Tony Ellwood, the East Midlands UKIP regional official who worked for the MEP Derek Clark, faced even worse. Ellwood says that in 2007 he was asked by UKIP general secretary Geoffrey Kingscott to carry out an investigation into one of the national party's bank accounts. 'Large cash withdrawals were being made from this account. He [Kingscott] wanted to know where it was going – into another bank account, or into a black hole? When people found out I was trying to reconcile the accounts, I was accused of trying to conceal some of the bank statements, but I never managed to complete the accounts as I never saw all the bank statements. Of the ones I did see, there were large cash withdrawals.'

Ellwood says, however, that when he returned from holiday in South America the office where he'd been working in Nottingham had been raided by two senior UKIP figures and all his work destroyed, including the computer hard drive which contained the details of his investigation. 'UKIP was my life,' he says, 'but it got to the stage where there were too many dubious dealings, too many unanswered financial questions.' Ellwood says he lost his job and was expelled from the party. 'I tried to renew my membership, and head office told me I'd been blacklisted and wouldn't be able to renew. Anyone who tried to investigate financial irregularities in UKIP got purged.'[28]

At almost twenty years' distance, with very little paperwork, and memories fuzzy and fading, it's hard to establish the truth of what happened over Ashford. What's striking is the utter chaos and disorganisation inside UKIP at that time, with an ever-changing cast of senior officials, tensions between the regions and the national

headquarters and internal feuding and rivalries. The finances of the
Ashford call centre were especially complicated in that the national
party had passed responsibility to Farage and the South East region,
but then much of the work was farmed out to Alan Bown's company. There was nervousness, too, about regulatory matters such
as data protection, and reporting to the Electoral Commission. But
it was hard to reconcile Farage's claims of success for Ashford –
£400,000 raised – with the lack of apparent income, and with the
fact that 'the single most successful thing UKIP has ever done' was
closed down.

Nigel Farage and his allies made things worse by their apparent determination to be secretive and defensive about Ashford's
finances. The more that senior figures tried to probe, the more
Farage got angry that anyone should question his project, and his
integrity, loyalty and competence. And the more he clammed up.
At one NEC meeting, the minutes say Farage explained he was
not circulating accounts for Ashford 'because these may leak'.[29]
Another excuse was that the work was carried out by Bown's firm,
Ashford Employment Ltd, which was a private company and UKIP
had no right to their records. Yet the very fact that Farage failed to
be transparent only aroused the suspicions of his critics, some of
whom pressed harder, and saw Ashford as a prime example of his
autocratic style. It would become a familiar pattern over the years.

In fairness, Farage hadn't originally intended that Ashford be
solely an operation within his own South East region. NEC minutes
show he initially argued it should be a project for national benefit,
but the NEC rejected the idea because that would have meant bear-
ing any losses nationally, too.[30]

In 2006, the UKIP treasurer Bruce Lawson threatened to resign
over another aspect of the party's chaotic finances, when he discovered that five donations in 2005, totalling £118,000, including money
from Alan Bown and Roger Knapman, had been registered with the
Electoral Commission without ever going through the party books
or bank accounts. 'These five cheques were not banked in any of the
four Royal Bank of Scotland accounts,' he wrote to Nigel Farage. 'I
have been badly misled.' The conclusion seemed to be that someone

had been operating a secret UKIP account, which Lawson had not been told about. 'I will not be associated with this sort of behaviour,' Lawson told Farage.[31] In 2007, Lawson did resign as UKIP treasurer, saying he was 'unhappy with the style of leadership and financial management of the party'.[32] Bruce Lawson later worked with other disaffected UKIP members to set up United Kingdom First, which was initially declared to be an internal grouping. But when some of their members, including Lawson, were expelled from UKIP in 2009, they became a rival party, though it didn't last long.

In the end, Ian Gillman, the former policeman, resigned his UKIP membership as well – 'in disappointment, with deep human emotion', and also joined Lawson in United Kingdom First. 'To ask about Ashford,' he reflected later, 'was to sign your own death penalty in UKIP.'[33]

As for the corner shop in Beaver Road, Ashford, for almost a decade the premises have been occupied by the Figjam Tattoo Studio. The business advertises itself online as 'cover-up specialists'.

I2

GAME, SET AND MATCH TO FARAGE

Within a month of Nigel Farage being declared leader of the UK Independence Party in the autumn of 2006, his main opponent Richard Suchorzewski had resigned from the party. 'Nothing . . . prepared me for the scurrilous behaviour, defamatory comments and downright dishonesty of some of Nigel Farage's and David Bannerman's staff,' Suchorzewski wrote in his resignation letter:

> I was accused of having associations with the BNP – even when those scoundrels knew that my grandfather was murdered by the Nazis in a concentration camp and my great-grandfather was discovered hanged by them from a lamp-post near his home by my 14-year-old father . . .
>
> I stood for leader knowing full well that it was a challenge I was unlikely to win. Farage had control of a number of advantages that if abused would guarantee him success. Knowing this, I was more than surprised that he allowed his cronies, supporters and certain staff to openly and reprehensibly lie and rubbish a loyal UKIP member, with elected duties, who devoted the last two years of his life, full-time, unpaid, to help UKIP progress.

Indeed, Suchorzewski had a signed statement from one UKIP member in which she said that during a hustings meeting in Exeter in Devon that July, one of Farage's closest aides had approached her and told her 'that Richard Suchorzewski had lied about his background/career and was a BNP supporter'.[1]

Suchorzewski's resignation statement continued:

Even now in 'victory' Farage appears determined not to change his ways, and because of this I cannot support this party under his leadership any longer.

Reluctantly, I am left with no honourable action open to me other than leave, as I am not prepared to give my good name, reputation and integrity in support of Farage and many in his clique.

Suchorzewski said he'd been accused of being homosexual, and of running up £4 million of debt in one of his businesses. He claimed that 'Farage colluded with, and thus endorsed the scurrilous behaviour'.[2]

Nigel Farage's first spell as UKIP leader, from 2006 to 2009, was a very unhappy and rancorous time for the party. He was constantly in dispute with colleagues on the National Executive Committee. Many were forced out. Others resigned. Several of his critics would be accused of being infiltrators from the British National Party. The UKIP team in the European Parliament was beset by arrests, investigations and accusations of fraud and corruption.

These were years when UKIP should have thrived and gone from strength to strength. The European Union had abandoned its plans to establish a Constitution for itself, but instead agreed the 2007 Treaty of Lisbon which introduced almost all the same integrationist measures as the Constitution – a red rag to the Eurosceptic cause. Public concern was also growing about vastly higher immigration from the new eastern European member states than the Blair government had forecast. Meanwhile, the Conservatives had moved to the centre under David Cameron – the self-styled 'heir to Blair' – who posed with huskies in the Arctic to show his concern about climate change, and who supposedly said we should 'hug-a-hoodie'.

Well before Nigel Farage became UKIP leader, the public had become disillusioned with the political class over the Iraq War and continuing hostilities in Iraq and Afghanistan. Since 9/11 and the 7/7 bombings in London in 2005, there had been serious concerns about Islamist terrorism in Britain and the growing Muslim population. The 2008 financial crisis which beset the new Gordon Brown government knocked public confidence still further, followed by the

2009 scandal over MPs' expenses. Yet Farage had very little success in exploiting this disillusionment in electoral terms and making UKIP a major party of protest.

A troublesome, anti-EU rival had entered the fray. Nick Griffin, the modernising leader of the BNP, was fast tapping into political disaffection and growing Islamopobia, and making real inroads, particularly among white working-class communities in London's East End and the North of England. He had been convicted of inciting racial hatred in 1998, but having since studied the success of Jean-Marie Le Pen and others on the far right in Europe, he had shifted his own focus and the party's emphasis from biological racism and Holocaust denial to the 'cultural incompatibility' of different ethnic groups. Griffin's brand of populist nationalism was soon reaping electoral dividends.

In contrast, UKIP's performance in parliamentary by-elections in Farage's first three years was dismal. After Tony Blair stood down in Sedgefield, County Durham, in 2007, they got just 1.9 per cent, and came only sixth, whereas the BNP came fourth with 8.9 per cent, more than four times as many votes as UKIP. In the summer of 2008, UKIP then got 2.2 per cent in Crewe and Nantwich, followed by 2.4 per cent in Henley-on-Thames a few weeks later (when Boris Johnson left to become Mayor of London), and the BNP again surpassed them, with 3.6 per cent. For UKIP to be outgunned by the BNP in northern Sedgefield was perhaps understandable when at that time UKIP's appeal was broadly southern and middle class, whereas the BNP was more of a northern working-class party. But Henley? You would expect UKIP to beat the BNP there.

It was a similar story in local elections, where the BNP got almost twice as many votes per candidate as UKIP over the three local election days of 2006, 2007 and 2008. During that period, UKIP picked up just six council seats, whereas the BNP got 58.[3] In the 2008 London Assembly elections, the BNP won almost three times as many votes as UKIP, and caused quite a storm by getting its first elected member of the assembly, while UKIP lost its two seats.

The BNP's rise under Nick Griffin cast a huge cloud over UKIP activities in the late noughties. Farage was being urged by colleagues to respond, as he told the academics Robert Ford and Matthew Goodwin:

> There were lots of people saying to me at that time, 'You've got to do a deal with them.' I even had Tory MEPs saying to me, 'Nigel, you've got to do a deal with these people.' We were being beaten by them regularly, in local elections. So there was huge pressure on me. 'We should do a deal.' I always said it was completely unthinkable, unconscionable, and I'm not doing it. They're authoritarian, we're libertarian. I believe in free trade and globalism and they believe . . . a list as long as your arm. [Nick] Griffin and I were fucking poles apart really on virtually all aspects of policy.[4]

Farage accused the BNP of being 'authoritarian', yet numerous critics within UKIP would use the same word about him. And the UKIP leader would use the threat of the BNP, and the real possibility of infiltration by Nick Griffin's supporters, as a prime way to eliminate his internal critics. Richard Suchorzewski was not the first or last to fall victim to such accusations (though not all Farage's targets were entirely innocent of such links).

By 2008, Farage had four leading critics in the higher ranks of his party, three of whom sat on the UKIP National Executive Committee. The fourth was UKIP's deputy treasurer Martin Haslam. All four men had long been asking serious questions about UKIP's financial affairs, and particularly the highly controversial Ashford call centre, and what had happened to the proceeds. They were also concerned about the issue of UKIP MEPs' expenses and allowances. Another growing controversy was Nigel's Farage's involvement in selection processes for UKIP candidates for the next European elections. They formed a group intent on holding Farage to account.

By far the most controversial of the set was David Abbott. A Winchester GP who was also a committed Christian, he had been a UKIP candidate in a couple of elections before joining the NEC in 2006. But in 2007 the *Daily Telegraph* revealed that while working in the USA several years before, Abbott had given two donations of $100 to the Friends of BNP, and met the BNP leader Nick Griffin in the US at a meeting of a white supremacist group. The *Telegraph* also revealed that when Abbott returned to Britain he had gone to the annual dinner of the BNP fund-raising group, the Trafalgar Club, which was attended by Griffin. Abbott claimed these actions were simply naivety on his part. He said he did 'not know who the BNP were' while living in America. 'I am absolutely not a racist. I didn't realise at the time any contact with the BNP tarred you with a certain brush.'[5]

In 2008, Abbott was joined on the NEC by Eric Edmond, a mathematician who had been an academic at Liverpool University, before spending four years with the Bank of England. He now spent his retirement in Somerset participating in Eurosceptic politics, partly through his own website and a blog. A much younger member of the rebel group was Delroy 'Del' Young, a businessman from Leicestershire who had been chairman of the UKIP Independence Youth organisation, and was notable for being one of the few Black people active in the party. Martin Haslam, UKIP's deputy treasurer, and the most heavyweight Farage critic outside the NEC, was a prosperous accountant who ran a successful practice in Burgess Hill in West Sussex.

In the summer of 2008, the four-strong rebel cabal – Abbott, Edmond, Young and Haslam – was joined by a fifth UKIP member who had grown increasingly unhappy about the way Farage ran his party and the secrecy over its finances. He was a high-profile critic but one with substantial baggage.

Christopher Mottram, known to one and all as 'Buster', had achieved fame in the 1970s as an international tennis star. He was the British number one for many years, and at his peak in 1978, and again in 1983, he was ranked number fifteen in the world. Mottram rarely shone in grand slam tournaments, but he did represent England for eight seasons in the Davis Cup, and played in the 1978 final when Britain lost to the USA. However, Mottram's tennis career was blighted by his occasional public support for the racist National Front, though later he almost became a Conservative

MP (and in 1983 came second to David Amess in the selection for Basildon in Essex).

Mottram had joined UKIP at the start of 2007, and did so, it seems, with Nigel Farage's blessing. Mottram says he had lunch with Farage at the Hurlingham Club, the exclusive west London private members' sports and social club, after an introduction by the former Conservative MP Piers Merchant (who was now active in UKIP). They were mutual fans at first.

At around the time Mottram joined the party, Farage wrote to MPs of all parties telling them that UKIP had not yet picked any candidates for the next general election (due by June 2010). He gave them a stark warning. They had until 30 June 2007 to sign the public Better-Off-Out pledge – a non-UKIP venture – or face a possible UKIP challenger.

Mottram was soon serving a few aces. He repeated the same threat as Farage, but made it sound more menacing, with or without the leader's support is not clear. In March 2007 the *Western Morning News* reported a complaint by the recently elected MP for Torridge and West Devon, Geoffrey Cox (later appointed Attorney General by Theresa May) that UKIP was 'trying to cheat the ballot box' through an 'utterly sickening, nasty tactic'. Cox revealed that Mottram had sent him an email saying that if he signed up to the pledge to leave the EU, then 'of course' he 'would not have to face any UKIP candidate in the general election', and he would also get campaign help from local UKIP activists.

'On the other hand,' Mottram threatened, if Cox was to 'oppose our position on Europe [he] would be specifically targeted by our supporters.' It was an astonishingly clumsy move by Mottram, who claimed to be working 'on behalf of Mr Farage'.[6]

When approached by the *Western Morning News*, Farage said he had not expressly ordered contact to be made with MPs in the region, but did support the effort in principle. Farage also defended Mottram being a UKIP member, despite his past support for a racist party. 'Buster was in the National Front in the 1970s,' he said, 'but Buster has joined us from the Conservative Party . . . It was a youthful indiscretion of 30 years ago. Having come through a mainstream party, we can live with that – but we don't want hordes of them. He's a brand new member. He's only been with us for a few weeks . . . We have absolutely made it 100 per cent clear that nobody who has been in the BNP will be either a candidate at any level or a branch secretary.'[7] That didn't square, of course, with Farage employing Martyn Heale, another former National Front member from the 1970s, as his agent in South Thanet.

The Hurlingham guest book would make interesting reading, for around the same time Farage was defending him, Buster Mottram was also hobnobbing with the BNP leader Nick Griffin. Mottram caused quite a stir in the club's refined environs by taking Griffin to lunch there, too. Mottram had been introduced to Griffin through a wealthy Sussex landowner named Andrew Moffat, a UKIP member who seems to have operated during this period as a BNP mole inside Farage's party, co-ordinating people he thought might be sympathetic to the BNP. (Having belonged to the National Front in the late 1970s, Moffat was UKIP candidate in 2005, and later stood for the BNP in 2010.)

Griffin, whether for strategic reasons or just to cause trouble, suggested to Mottram the idea of an electoral pact between the two parties. 'We felt it extremely unlikely that Farage would accept it,' says Griffin, 'but believed that his rejection of it would upset some of their people . . .'[8] (The same idea had been quickly dismissed in 2003, when Farage said there were 'absolutely no circumstances' in which UKIP would consider it.)[9] Mottram agreed to promote the idea again.

Martin Haslam, a member of the rebel cabal, was also a friend of the BNP mole Andrew Moffat, and it seems to have been through Moffat that Haslam became friends with Buster Mottram, too. He says they found common ground over concerns about UKIP's finances and Farage's style of leadership. A friendly game of tennis between the pair, and conversation afterwards, would have major repercussions for the party.

Both Haslam and Mottram later stated that on the afternoon of Tuesday 2 September 2008, they met for a game at the All England Tennis Club in Wimbledon, though Haslam says it was more like a 'coaching session' for him. 'Playing singles tennis is always tiring,' he would write, 'but playing for an hour and a quarter against one of the all-time greats is both physically and mentally exhausting, particularly as that was the first time I had played Buster.'

According to Haslam, Mottram mentioned before the match that he had been talking to the press about the concerns they shared regarding UKIP MEPs' expenses. 'After I came off after the game,' says Haslam, 'I was having a cup of tea and Buster came into the room to say that James Macintyre from the *Independent* was on the phone and wanted to talk to me. James Macintyre and I then discussed the question of MEPs' expenditure and the problems in the party and so on regarding this subject, and this subject alone.' Haslam would later assert that when Macintyre tried to ask about other things, such as gossip about Farage and his press officer Annabelle Fuller, he replied that he couldn't comment as 'it's not my sphere of influence'.

Three days later, on the eve of the UKIP conference in Bournemouth, Haslam says Nigel Farage confronted him face to face about talking to Macintyre (though the published article was fairly innocuous). 'He tore me off a strip for speaking to the press without his permission; he started off very aggressively asking me what the hell I was doing . . .' Haslam said: 'Nothing, Nigel.' The accountant says the argument was over in five minutes. 'He said: "Ah well, we will forget all about it." We then shook hands and that was that.'[10] Or so he thought.

In the meantime, Buster Mottram had sent an email to a UKIP official who advised MPs on their expenses, and this then achieved wider circulation. In his message, Mottram expressed several of the concerns he shared with Martin Haslam and the other senior rebels:

I, as a member of UKIP, want to be reassured that our MEPs are behaving with integrity. Seeing is believing. You can imagine my shock and disappointment to discover that Nigel Farage has employed his wife. Whilst this of course is totally above board it looks appalling and reeks of opportunism . . . We should be whiter than white, and set the example . . . No amount of spin can change the undeniable – appalling Welsh Assembly results, a disastrous London mayoral campaign and assembly results, a derisory vote in Crewe and Nantwich and then Henley. Some sort of confidence has to be restored in UKIP . . .

Mottram added that he wanted to outline at the next NEC meeting a 'white knight' solution, promising new financial backers for UKIP. 'The NEC should then take up the budgets with these individuals, groups etc whose money, time and help will be invaluable in returning at least some MEPs rather than facing probable desecration.'[11]

Del Young, who sat on the National Executive, tried to secure a chance for Mottram to address the NEC. He wrote to Paul Nuttall, a 31-year-old Scouser who had just been appointed UKIP chairman by Farage. This suggestion seems to have been rejected by the UKIP high command.

Around the same time, according to Haslam, Nigel Farage rang him to announce he had changed his mind and to say he no longer had any confidence in him as deputy treasurer. He wanted Haslam's resignation. Haslam felt he was being treated unfairly by Farage, and appealed to the UKIP NEC to be allowed to keep his job. It was agreed that he would be given a hearing at the next meeting. Haslam decided to take Buster Mottram as a witness to what he'd said during the phone call with James Macintyre.

Here was a lucky chance. Having failed to get a hearing before the NEC over his concerns about UKIP and his 'white knight' proposal, Mottram was now going to meet the NEC as Haslam's witness.

Martin Haslam and Buster Mottram duly presented themselves at 1 p.m. on Monday 3 November at the Farmers Club, the watering hole of country gents situated next to the National Liberal Club in Whitehall, where the NEC was due to meet. Enough mud would soon be flying to fill even the most commodious of farmyards. Sitting together on one side of the boardroom were the three NEC members of the rebel cabal. The NEC wouldn't let Haslam speak at first, but eventually relented and the deputy treasurer duly explained his version of events.

Haslam went on to detail the many financial and personal

contributions he had made to UKIP's work over the years: how he'd paid £10,000 towards the wages of a new party treasurer; how he'd offered to pay some of Farage's driving expenses, and paid £2,000 towards Paul Nuttall's travel costs. He reminded the NEC that he'd paid for a fund-raising dinner at the House of Lords; and worked for free on both UKIP's national accounts and those for Farage's own South East region.

Then came one of several extraordinary moments that afternoon. On the matter of Haslam's alleged offence – his phone conversation with James Macintyre – Nigel Farage shamelessly told the NEC that he had deliberately sought to catch Haslam out. The UKIP leader informed his colleagues that he had actually suggested to the *Independent* journalist that he ought to contact Haslam, because he saw it as a clever test of the deputy treasurer's loyalty. According to David Abbott, the UKIP leader admitted to the NEC that 'he had known the day before that the reporter was going to phone. But instead of alerting his colleague, he had waited to see if the call would be reported to him. It was a trap.'[12]

That is corroborated by Abbott's rebel colleague Eric Edmond, who recalled that Farage 'brazenly admitted he had set up an *Independent* journalist to entrap Martin to "test his loyalty"'.[13]

After Martin Haslam spoke, Buster Mottram was allowed to take the floor in his friend's defence. But once he'd finished explaining what Haslam had said on the phone at Wimbledon, Mottram launched into his critique of Farage's leadership. It was wrong, Mottram said, that Farage employed his wife on a large EU salary contrary to UKIP policy, and wrong that UKIP MEPs didn't contribute to party finances, as had been promised.

The mood of the committee rapidly began to deteriorate, and efforts were made to silence Mottram. According to the formal NEC minutes, a motion was passed, 'That Buster Mottram be asked to leave', which went through by 8 votes to 3 (the rebels rebelling). 'Buster Mottram then refused to leave,' the minutes record, 'and proposed a deal be made with the BNP.'

But that brief, factual account on the official record fails to capture the mayhem unfolding that afternoon. With breathtaking audacity Mottram had seized his chance to hijack the agenda and urge a pact with the British National Party, whereby the parties would divide up the country between them. In making his pitch, Mottram declared that he was in touch with BNP leader Nick Griffin who backed the idea.

Buster Mottram was 'waving a bit of paper around like Neville Chamberlain', recalled Paul Nuttall. 'I have this piece of paper, it's a deal, and Mr Griffin has OK'd it.'[14] Immediately after the NEC meeting, Nuttall would email UKIP branch chairmen with this account:

> Mr Mottram was told that he had no right to speak at the meeting but insisted that he had something else important to say. A truce with the BNP was Buster Mottram's intention, whereby the BNP would contest the North of England and we would contest the South in the European elections next year. He said that Nick Griffin had agreed to this.[15]

Another contemporary source, Farage supporter Douglas Denny, says Mottram waved what he said was a cheque in front of Nuttall and Farage – 'money for UKIP which was available – all we had to do was accept'. But Farage told him 'in no uncertain terms he can keep his money, we didn't want it and, if he wished, could stick it'.[16] 'It was true high drama,' says former chairman David Campbell Bannerman:

> It was out-of-the blue. It was done with great dramatic effect. The four on the NEC were slapping down papers. It was the first time there was a very clear agenda of working with the BNP, and we didn't want to know. There was utter pandemonium. It was farcical, completely disrupted the proceedings.[17]

Electorally, there might have been a case for a UKIP–BNP pact at that time, for Mottram was addressing the NEC only four months after the BNP had humiliated UKIP in the Henley by-election. Politically, however, the idea was toxic both outside and within UKIP.

Writing two days later, Mottram said that he put his plan to the NEC 'at the behest of some potential donors. It was simply an idea for discussion given UKIP's recent poor electoral results. It is complete nonsense to suggest that this was some sort of BNP plot to destabilise the party!'[18]

But according to Nuttall's account, Mottram poured fuel on the fire by declaring: 'The deal could not work if Nigel Farage remained leader of UKIP. Accordingly, branch chairmen were being contacted with a view to calling an EGM to remove Nigel Farage.'[19]

The uproar seems to have gone on for at least half an hour. David Abbott said he felt 'physically insecure' amid the violent shouting and threats.[20]

Finally, with the former tennis player refusing to quit the court, the police were called in. Accounts of what ensued vary. The leadership version was that Buster Mottram had to be escorted off the premises by police officers; he said he left of his own accord just as the police turned up. This was backed up by Eric Edmond who later said: 'The police arrived as Mottram was leaving. Mottram was therefore not ejected by the police.'[21]

The NEC minutes simply record: 'The police were called and Buster Mottram left, together with David Abbott, Eric Edmond and Martin Haslam.'[22]

Whether he left the meeting of his own accord or not, Buster Mottram's behaviour that afternoon provided Nigel Farage with a gift, which enabled him to pounce and purge most of his NEC critics. Farage would later claim that he had deliberately flushed out those sympathetic to the BNP, provoking their exit. He maintained that Abbott and Edmond voiced support for the pact with Griffin, though both deny it. 'They were the angry old men of *old* UKIP who thought UKIP were doomed,' Farage said.

> I said to them, 'Well, we can have a vote around the table to expel you or you can just leave.' They left. That was it. It was a very important moment for us, a very, *very* important moment . . . I played a good hand of cards that day . . . because I knew I could

smoke out those from within who felt that way. That was a big moment. We had faced them down.[23]

Farage goaded Abbott, as he often had in NEC meetings, over his past dealings with the BNP – his jibes often in response to probing questions on party finances. But if Abbott and Edmond deny voicing support for the pact, why, then, did they leave? Eric Edmond wrote afterwards that the problem was Farage's admission as to how he had tricked Martin Haslam:

> I said to Farage his action was despicable and I would not continue to stay in a meeting with someone who behaved as badly as he had. David [Abbott] echoed my comments and it is scarcely surprising that Martin also left with us given he had been so betrayed by someone to whom he had given so much of his loyalty and his money . . . Why were David Abbott and Martin Haslam, both honest, decent, honourable men who have worked and donated funds for years to UKIP, made the targets of such dirty tricks? Who will be next?[24]

David Abbott later gave similar reasons for leaving: 'This sneaky, untrusting treatment of a kind, honest man so incensed me . . . I could not sit at the same table as a man who demanded trust but could not trust others, who did not recognise as valuable anyone who didn't totally agree with him on every single issue.'[25]

With Del Young the only rebel left in the meeting, the NEC then made a series of important decisions. They voted 12–0 to reject the idea of any association with the BNP, and decided 11–0 'that Mr Mottram be immediately expelled from the party for his association with an extremist organisation, namely the BNP'. And the post of deputy treasurer, held by Martin Haslam, was abolished by nine votes to one, whereupon Delroy Young left the meeting in protest at the eradication of Haslam's job, which meant all five rebels had now left the room. There was a brief pause from the slaughter when Douglas Denny proposed that the NEC should thank Martin Haslam for his work. Everyone supported that, except Nigel Farage who abstained.[26]

The executions continued. The NEC considered a complaint that had been formally tabled against Eric Edmond by David Campbell Bannerman, who accused him of being 'disruptive' at past NEC meetings. The retired economist was no longer there to defend himself, and the original proposal that he be suspended from the NEC was now upgraded to outright expulsion. David Abbott was not present either to defend himself against a long-standing charge that he had breached confidentiality and brought the NEC 'into disrepute'. Abbott, the Winchester doctor, was expelled 9–0. Nearly all Farage's critics had been purged in the space of just a few minutes. Buster Mottram had badly blundered. It was game, set and match to Nigel Farage.

He was quick to take advantage, immediately telling the BBC there had been an attempt 'over many months' to infiltrate UKIP and try to 'demoralise' members into believing the party had no future without a deal with the BNP. 'I was pleased for Mr Mottram to come and say this,' Farage said, 'because it finally got this agenda out in the open.'[27] 'We had worked out who those people were, that had infiltrated UKIP. We were on the verge of getting rid of them, and they began to panic so they thought they would play their trump card.'[28] Farage's words – that he was 'pleased' for Mottram to say what he did – suggest he may have encouraged him to speak so as to denounce his enemies.

However, Paul Nuttall's email to branch chairmen, written immediately after the event, gives a slightly different account to Farage on the reasons for the afternoon purge.

Buster Mottram was expelled from UKIP after being removed from the meeting by uniformed police officers.

Further to this, the NEC voted to remove Eric Edmond and David Abbott as NEC members. They have both publicly opposed NEC decisions time and again and have made the NEC dysfunctional. The post of deputy treasurer was removed and Martin Haslam thanked for his past efforts.

The NEC will now act as a united body to get us ready to fight the big campaign next year.[29]

Nuttall said Edmond and Abbott were expelled for opposing NEC decisions and making the body 'dysfunctional', whereas Farage strongly suggested they were expelled for their links to the BNP.

Both of them, though, saw it as a triumph. 'That was one of the pivotal moments in UKIP's history actually,' Paul Nuttall later said, 'because we then had an NEC for the first time in many, many years where we were all a cohesive group, and could start to get the party ready for the 2009 European elections.'[30] Any 'suggestion that UKIP was linked to the extremist BNP had been expunged,' Nuttall adds. 'On that day, Nigel Farage had showed both resolve and political acumen, which in many ways paved the way for the future mainstream success of the party.'[31]

All the other rebels – Abbott, Edmond, Haslam and Young – were condemned by association with Mottram, tarred with the same brush as far-right extremists. 'You have been naive in bringing Mr Mottram to the meeting,' NEC member Douglas Denny told Martin Haslam afterwards in an email of apparent sympathy:

> The offer made by Mr Mottram was so ludicrous in concept, so politically inept and crass, that I find myself even now unable to comprehend that anyone in their right mind would think it possible that anyone in a UKIP NEC meeting would be so daft as to even think of considering it . . . It was sheer lunacy . . . Your friend Mr Mottram may have tried to help you but actually made things infinitely worse. It was a bad decision to bring him along.[32]

It was natural for people to suspect the rebels of being in on Mottram's plan to hijack the meeting, suspicions fuelled by the fact that they sat together, by their failure to condemn Mottram, or to encourage him to leave the room, and then most of them left at the same time as he did. According to Douglas Denny, the trio also failed to voice dissent when Mottram claimed they were his 'friends'. It was 'inconceivable', Denny said, that Haslam, Edmond and Abbott did not know of Mottram's 'mission'.[33]

The four men expelled by Farage (together with Del Young) had certainly been acting in concert as critics of his leadership, and indeed they had met for tea and scones at Wimbledon a few weeks before the showdown NEC meeting. 'Buster wanted us to get into bed with his friends in the BNP,' says Eric Edmond. 'And I didn't want to have anything to do with it; neither did Delroy Young. Buster had something on David Abbott, as he had made donations in the USA linked to the BNP. I tried to explain to Mottram that it wouldn't fly, and we were quite clear – that was Delroy and I.' Haslam and Abbott were more neutral, Edmond recalls.[34]

How much were they linked with the BNP? Mottram had supported the National Front, and by his own admission was in contact with Nick Griffin.

David Abbott claimed after the meeting to have spoken against Mottram's BNP pact. In one of his posts, Abbott also said he was used to Nigel Farage using the 'BNP' accusation against him. During NEC meetings, he said, 'If I asked a question about the accounts, Farage would merely chant "BNP, BNP, BNP".'[35] Yet Farage had known about Abbott's BNP connections for four years, and supported his candidature for Winchester in 2005. But Abbott couldn't escape the fact that he had twice given money to the BNP, and attended at least two meetings at which Nick Griffin was present.

'Belittling, mocking, ignoring NEC members who ask questions or demand answers is not the British way of doing things,' Abbott complained. And he revealed that when Farage appointed Paul Nuttall as UKIP chairman, it was announced before some NEC members were told. Farage claimed to have rung round the NEC for their approval, but Abbott said he hadn't phoned Eric Edmond, Del Young or himself. According to Abbott, when Eric Edmond asked Farage at the next NEC meeting whom he had phoned, 'Nigel replied "obviously not you", and everyone else stared at the table in embarrassment.'[36]

A few weeks after the fateful NEC meeting, Martin Haslam, too, met Nick Griffin when he was one of several dozen guests at a right-wing dinner at a country house near Haslam's home in West Sussex, to which both UKIP and Conservative supporters had been invited and at which Andrew Moffat was also present.

But not all the rebel group of Farage critics had BNP links. Eric

Edmond was tarred by Farage with the 'extremist' brush, and yet there is no evidence he had links to the BNP or other groups on the extreme right. He accused Farage and the NEC of expelling him on 'trumped-up charges' and behaving in a 'fascist style'.[37] Del Young, who became an isolated voice against Farage on the NEC, was unlikely, as a Black person, to be sympathetic to Nick Griffin and his racist party. He was eventually drummed out of UKIP in 2009.

In defence of Farage, his former chairman David Campbell Bannerman, who has mixed views about him, says the rebels 'operated as a bloc. They just worked away at it. It was pretty unpleasant. They were a terrible element. It wasn't for the best interests of the party. It was NEC after NEC for four or five months. Either they hated Farage, or they had another agenda.'[38] Campbell Bannerman says he and others couldn't understand what was driving the rebels' 'energy'; they assumed some outside force was at work.

Buster Mottram claimed two days after the event that the NEC 'exceeded its powers in purporting to expel me', denying him his basic rights and giving him no chance to defend himself. The BNP issue was an 'excuse', he said. The 'real reason' for his expulsion

> was my continued demand for the disclosure of MEPs' expenses, and demands for transparency with regard to the use of these expenses by MEPs. My criticism of Mr Farage, who broke an undertaking not to employ any of his family members by employing his wife, sealed my fate.[39]

The Farmers Club NEC meeting would evoke historic Nazi comparisons, by both sides. The blogger Greg Lance-Watkins, by then an arch-critic of Farage, described it as his 'Reichstag fire moment', while Douglas Denny – then a strong Farage loyalist – compared Mottram's appearance at the NEC with the occasion in 1941 when Hitler's deputy Rudolf Hess suddenly turned up in Scotland seeking peace talks with the Duke of Hamilton.[40]

Farage continued to face criticism within UKIP over his autocratic style of leadership. In the run-up to the 2009 European elections, his habit of intervening in selection processes for candidates became the source of much tension and resentment. One case in particular upset many people. In 2007, Farage had recruited as UKIP treasurer Marta Andreasen, a former chief accountant with the European Commission, whom he now wanted to stand for UKIP in the European elections. Andreasen had garnered considerable coverage in the media throughout Europe when she was sacked in 2002 after she publicly highlighted faults in the EU accounting system which exposed the institution to fraud.

Farage pulled out all the stops to ensure Andreasen was picked as his number two on the UKIP list for the South East region for the Euro contest. The only problem was that Andreasen's selection broke several UKIP rules. Among these were that she wasn't resident in Britain (and mainly lived in Barcelona); she wasn't on the electoral register in Britain; nor was she even a paid-up member of UKIP, despite holding high office in the party. What's more, Andreasen told people that she didn't believe in withdrawal from the EU, only that it should be reformed.

Lynnda Robson, an adviser to the UKIP MEP Gerard Batten, who had also tried to become a candidate, complained to the NEC, only to have her complaint dismissed. As so often happened when Farage went out of his way to recruit star names, the Andreasen story would later end in tears.

Another disputed selection involved Robin Page, the presenter of the BBC TV series *One Man and his Dog*, who was also a farmer in Cambridgeshire. Page had stood for the Referendum Party in 1997, then for UKIP in a couple of Westminster elections. Page was popular with many of the public, as shown by the fact that he topped the poll in membership elections for the council of the National Trust. Page said he was persuaded to stand for UKIP in the 2009 European elections, but for health and other reasons he had 'special dispensation' to submit his forms beyond the deadline. When he did so, he was astonished to find that UKIP officials told him his application was too late. Page appealed to Farage who said he'd do his best to help, but said 'it'll be up to the political committee'. Farage came back a few days later to say, 'The political committee won't accept your late documents. I'm really sorry.' Page later discovered that the political committee was, in effect, Farage himself. 'It runs at his whim with no obvious agenda or minutes,' he wrote:

> It seems that Nigel Farage has managed to obtain almost complete centralised power of UKIP. Other late nominations were apparently accepted, some people heading MEP lists have been forced out to be replaced by others and three members of UKIP's National Executive Council [sic] were expelled for criticising the leader ... The party's own policies – such as opposition to GM crops – have been reversed without the membership knowing, including me. Stories from Brussels suggest that UKIP's MEPs have come to love the high life of gravy and status. The party created to fight centralised government, sleaze and corruption has become a mirror image of the body it professes to loathe. The grassroots of UKIP are good people, but their party has been stolen from them by their executive; and with David Cameron seemingly afraid to say the word 'Europe', they have nowhere to go – unless lured by the false smile of the BNP.

Page accused the party of having a 'leadership cult'. Farage, he wrote, was a 'Blair-like, ex-public school leader', who ran UKIP as his own personal party.[41] His formal resignation letter to the UKIP chairman Paul Nuttall was even stronger: 'I want to belong to a party free of sleaze, greed and corruption (in the true meaning of the word). UKIP is clearly no longer such a party. I want a party that is transparent, accountable and above all honest, and in my view UKIP fails on all three counts. The party that was against centralised government, the EU and troughing-it – has become a parody of itself.'[42]

Disaster loomed in the run-up to the 2009 European elections, as many UKIP activists feared the party would lose most of their remaining seats in Europe (following the awkward departures of MEPs Tom Wise, Ashley Mote and Robert Kilroy-Silk). A trouncing by the BNP looked quite likely. The commentator Iain Dale observed that 'most political pundits think 2004 was a high watermark for

Half dressed: Farage's mother, Barbara (née Stevens), posing for a *Calendar Girls* style calendar in 2008, when she was in her late sixties. It was one of several such calendars she organised to raise funds for charity. (© Simon Hildrew)

Well dressed: Nigel Farage gets his smart dress sense from his father, Guy, who had a reputation as the best-dressed man in the City of London, where he spent five decades as a stockbroker. Guy is seen here in 2016, when he was eighty. (© Kent and Sharpshooters Yeomanry Museum)

Schoolboy Nigel in the woods at Dulwich College, the private school he attended as a boy and where, even in his early days, he courted controversy. (© Patrick Neylan)

Dulwich under-13½ second XI cricket team, 1977. Farage is third from left in front row. (Ian Oakley Smith)

Farage's brother Andrew, who is two years younger than him, and was a partner in their metal trading business, Farage Futures. (Louis Quail/In Pictures via Getty Images)

Farage (second from right) campaigning in the 1993 by-election in Newbury for Alan Sked (standing in door), the then leader of the Anti-Federalist League (which became UKIP later that year). Another future UKIP leader, Gerard Batten, is on the far left. (Sked archive, LSE)

Farage at the count in Salisbury in May 1997 where he kept his deposit after getting 5.7 per cent, the best UKIP performance in Britain. He was helped by Sir James Goldsmith's decision that his Referendum Party should not contest the seat, since the sitting Tory MP Robert Key – a former aide to Ted Heath – had backed a referendum. (© Salisbury Museum)

The notorious photo of Farage (middle) meeting Mark Deavin (right) and Tony 'The Bomber' Lecomber (left) in the spring of 1997. Deavin had been expelled from UKIP over his links with Nick Griffin of the BNP. Lecomber had twice been jailed – for possessing bombs, and for stabbing a Jewish teacher. Farage said he had no idea who Lecomber was, and Griffin later said the Lecomber encounter was set up to embarrass Farage and UKIP.

Farage welcomed the former Labour MP and daytime TV host Robert Kilroy-Silk into UKIP ahead of the 2004 European elections, but the relationship was bound to fail. (Alamy)

Farage meets the Queen and Prince Philip at a palace reception for MPs and MEPs in 2007. (Getty Images, Anwar Hussein Collection/ROTA/FilmMagic)

Nigel Farage escapes from the wreckage of the two-seater plane in which he was flying after it crashed on general election day in 2010. Had Farage been killed – and he came within inches of death – then Brexit might never have happened. (Hyde News & Pictures Ltd)

Farage got the better of Liberal Democrat leader and deputy PM Nick Clegg in their two broadcast debates ahead of the 2014 Euro elections. The debates established Farage as a serious player in British politics and UKIP then topped the poll with 24 seats and 26.6% of the vote.

(Ian West – WPA Pool/Getty Images)

Farage's second wife Kirsten, whom he married in 1999. For years she was a paid member of Farage's staff as an MEP and ran his office, despite a UKIP pledge that the party's MEPs would not employ their spouses. (Alamy)

Laure Ferrari, whom Farage met while she was working as a waitress in Strasbourg, is thought to be the real love of his life. Ferrari stood for a French Eurosceptic party in the 2014 European elections, later ran UKIP's Pan-European research group, the Initiative for Direct Democracy in Europe, and became Farage's partner after he split up with Kirsten in 2017. (Jean-Christophe Verhaegen/AFP via Getty Images)

Annabelle Fuller, now called Trixy Sanderson. When Nikki Sinclaire exposed their long-standing affair in the European Parliament in 2014, both Fuller and Farage denied it, but Fuller later confirmed it publicly. (Antonio Olmos/ Eyevine)

Alexandra 'Alex' Phillips has been very close to Farage for almost a decade, though she always denies it has ever been a sexual relationship. Phillips' attempts to become a UKIP member of the Welsh Assembly were thwarted by Neil Hamilton, but Farage helped ensure she became a Brexit Party MEP in 2019, and they are now fellow presenters at GB News. (Getty, Simon James/GC Images)

The controversial businessman Arron Banks first teamed up with Farage when he donated £100,000 to UKIP in 2014. Banks later formed Leave.EU, the campaign through which most UKIP activists fought the 2016 referendum, but the relationship cooled when Banks was shown to have close ties to Russia. (Matt Cardy/Getty Images)

It was a major coup when the Conservative MP Douglas Carswell defected to UKIP in 2014 and won a by-election in Clacton. Once again, Farage would soon fall out with a senior figure he had encouraged to join UKIP.
(Justin Tallis/AFP via Getty Images)

At the 2015 UKIP conference, signing a tattoo of himself on the arm of admirer Kerrie Webb.
(Ian Forsyth/Getty Images)

It was all smiles when Farage launched the 2015 UKIP manifesto with its main author Suzanne Evans. Within weeks, the two fell out and Farage thwarted Evans's hopes of succeeding him as leader.
(Carl Court/Getty Images)

Nigel Farage lost South Thanet by 2,812 votes in 2015 – defeated by his former friend, accountant and UKIP rival Craig Mackinlay (second right), who'd once been acting leader of UKIP. Farage never stood for Parliament again.
(Carl Court/Getty Images)

Within half an hour of losing South Thanet, Farage announced his resignation as UKIP leader, even though the Conservatives had just gained a majority and an EU referendum was now likely.
(Niklas Halle'n/AFP via Getty Images)

UKIP and they will be lucky to be left with enough MEPs to fill a telephone box in June'. Farage told Dale: 'If we win fewer than ten seats, that's a failure and I will resign . . . Quite clearly, if we do badly, then I've tried my hardest, and that's that. It will be time for someone else to do it.'[43]

Nigel Farage's first three years in office had been extremely difficult. If anything, the party had gone backwards. 'Those were the days when nothing was going right,' says Clive Page, UKIP's former head of press. 'Yet that was when Farage was at his absolute best. He worked his socks off; he charmed everybody; he never got angry; never seemed to get depressed. The problem was the lack of money and resources.'[44]

A month before the Euro elections, three polls had UKIP on an average of barely 7 per cent.

But then, suddenly, Nigel Farage and his party were offered the most extraordinary lifeline, and by one of the great ironies with which this story is peppered, it came from the most unlikely of issues. Expenses. Parliamentary expenses, at that.

On 8 May 2009, twenty-seven days before polling day, the *Daily Telegraph* broke the story based on a stolen computer disc which the paper had bought, but which was about to be made public anyway under a Freedom of Information request. The disc contained details of expense claims for all 650 MPs. Then night after night after night for several weeks the *Telegraph* published drip, drip, drip details of the astonishing and often absurd claims which MPs had been making – tens of thousands of pounds in many cases – for furniture for their second homes, for decoration, for gardening, for food and, famously, claims to clean a moat and to buy a duck-house. Several MPs would go to jail for claims which were fraudulent, and dozens were sacked by their parties from standing at the next election.

The public was outraged by the details which came out – indeed, more than ten years later British politicians are still tainted by it. Voters took against all the established parties at Westminster – Conservative, Labour, Liberal Democrats and others – to the benefit of parties who had no Westminster representation.

Yet only a fortnight before polling day, Farage made an unguarded admission during a debate at the Foreign Press Association with the Labour MP Denis MacShane (who would subsequently be jailed over his own Westminster expense claims). MacShane asked Farage how much, aside from his salary, he had received in expenses and allowances in the ten years since becoming an MEP in 1999. 'It is a vast sum,' Farage admitted. 'I don't know what the total amount is but – oh lor – it must be pushing £2 million.' MacShane was amazed. 'Is it too late to become an MEP?' he asked light-heartedly. Farage explained that he hadn't pocketed that amount, but had used this 'very large sum of European taxpayers' money' for the 'best of causes', to help promote UKIP's message of withdrawal from the EU.[45]

Later, seizing the initiative in the European campaign and exploiting the public outcry, Farage pledged UKIP to complete transparency: 'From the moment any UKIP members get elected, all elected MEPs will provide a clear and traceable quarterly statement of their expense accounts,' he said.[46] Yet no such pledge by Farage or UKIP would have been necessary had he and the party actually fulfilled very similar promises which they made in the European elections of 1999 and 2004, but were quickly forgotten.

Voters didn't seem to know – or care – that two of the UKIP MEPs elected in 2004 had got into serious trouble for financial dishonesty. Ashley Mote had been jailed for nine months in 2007 for benefit fraud committed before he was elected (and in 2015 he would be jailed again for £500,000 in fraudulent claims made as an MEP). And only eleven days before the *Telegraph* broke its story on MPs' expenses, Tom Wise first appeared in court charged with using more than £30,000 of his Brussels Parliament secretarial allowance to buy a car, fine wines and other luxuries, and to pay off his credit cards. Six months later, just before Farage was due to give evidence against him in court, Wise changed his plea to guilty and received a two-year jail sentence.

What's more, despite the high ideals of the 1999 European election, when UKIP promised its MEPs would devote their surplus allowances to worthy causes, UKIP MEPs had clearly enjoyed lavish lifestyles in Brussels and Strasbourg. And the party broke the rules by blatantly employing staff who were meant to work on European Parliament activity, as if they were party employees, working on UKIP politics and campaigns in Britain. People deemed to be advisers and assistants to MEPs were often, in effect, UKIP party organisers in each MEP's region. The MEPs' regional offices were *de facto* regional offices for UKIP. The mainstream parties did the same, of course, but not quite so brazenly.

Quite apart from the expenses issue, UKIP also benefited from the decision by broadcasters that, unlike 2004, the party should have three TV election broadcasts, on a par with the other main parties. This was due entirely to UKIP's strong showing in 2004, since other considerations – polling support, votes in local elections, or votes for Westminster elections – would have given them just one broadcast. Election broadcasts aren't important in themselves, since most voters probably ignore them, but the relative distribution of broadcasts is always a big factor for news producers in deciding how much coverage to give each party in their bulletins. So this time UKIP got considerable time on the news, and broadcasters were glad to have Nigel Farage as a very available, highly articulate voice who could give an alternative view on Europe.

Astonishingly, Farage emerged with what could be presented as a great triumph. UKIP actually came second in the Euro elections, well behind the Conservatives, but almost one per cent ahead of Labour, the governing party. It was historic – the first time a minor party had ever got into the top two in any nationwide British election. UKIP's 16.0 per cent of the vote was slightly up on its 15.6 per cent in 2004, and the party ended up with thirteen seats (the same as Labour), one more than before. Each European election had seen UKIP make progress: after coming fourth in 1999 with three seats, and third in 2004 with twelve. Meanwhile, their arch-rivals the BNP had scored just 6 per cent, though they did well enough to get their first two MEPs, including leader Nick Griffin.

Even more heartening for Farage must have been the performance of the UKIP breakaway, the UK First Party, which stood in just three English regions but whose lists contained many of his critics – Robin Page, Bruce Lawson, Petrina Holdsworth and Ian Gillman.

UK First got just 0.5 per cent of the national vote and were never heard from again.

It was UKIP who gained most from the public's disgust over MPs' expenses. Polls at the start of the European campaign suggested about 80 per cent of voters planned to vote Conservative, Labour or Lib Dem. On polling day the big three managed to get just 57 per cent.

For once, there was something to be gained from having no MPs.

13

CRASHING TO EARTH

By the autumn of 2009, the pressure was just too great. When UKIP assembled for its annual autumn conference in Southport on Merseyside, Nigel Farage made a big announcement. At the next general election he had decided to fight Buckingham, the seat where John Bercow was the sitting MP. 'I do think it is very important that UKIP gets a voice in Westminster,' he told UKIP activists. But, he explained, 'I have come to the conclusion that I may just have bitten off more than I can chew. I think I am better to the party doing fewer jobs better.' And, he said, 'It is just desperately hard to be leader of a group of people there [Europe] and to be leader of a domestic political party here.' So, after three years in the job, he would stand down as UKIP leader, and an election would be held for his successor. But he would remain leader of the UKIP delegation in the European Parliament, and co-leader of its international group.[1]

'I'd bought this stock at a tuppence,' he said years later, using an analogy from his years in the City, 'and like Poseidon shares it had gone to one hundred and twenty eight quid. I thought for the first time in my life, I'm going to get out on top.'[2]

Many colleagues didn't see it that way at all. Nor was Buckingham the real reason. 'Buckingham was *a* reason,' he said subsequently. 'I was free! I was out!'[3]

Farage in 2009 felt underappreciated by his party. Any politician would have had to have been superhuman to keep the UKIP show on the road. For three years Farage had coped with the demands of leading three different, and very fractious, arms of the same Eurosceptic movement – UKIP in Britain; the UKIP delegation to

Brussels and Strasbourg; and the wider international group within the European Parliament, now reconstituted as the Europe of Freedom and Democracy group (EFD). UKIP may have performed an astonishing recovery in the 2009 European elections, but for more than a year Farage had faced an onslaught of pressures from all sides. Within UKIP itself, he'd suffered complaints about his autocratic style, regular questions about the party's mysterious finances and a string of high-level and bile-charged resignations. UKIP's wider European group was still full of troublesome characters, while it was hard to hold it together amid accusations that many of its MEPs were racist, and when all of UKIP's foreign partners really wanted to reform the EU not leave it. Nor can life have been easy for Farage at home. His marriage to Kirsten had produced two young daughters, yet as he grew more famous the tabloids were keener to probe rumours of extra-marital affairs.

Farage did have some achievements. He'd fought off the serious challenge from the dark knight of the BNP (though Nick Griffin's party now had two MEPs). And on Farage's watch, UKIP had started developing polices beyond the EU question, though he took little interest in this work. The party moved in to occupy some of the right-wing policy ground which the Conservatives had vacated under David Cameron, arguing for the return of grammar schools; more spending on defence; a 50,000 annual limit on immigration; a flat rate of income tax of 31 per cent; and opposition to more wind farms.

Buckingham was a strange choice, however. Just three months before, John Bercow had become Speaker of the House of Commons, elected overwhelmingly with the support of Labour MPs, and only a handful of MPs from Bercow's own party. Bercow had previously been seen as on the right of the Conservatives, before a rapid move to the left in recent years, influenced – some thought – by his high-profile wife Sally who was a Labour Party member, and there had long been rumours that he, too, might join Labour. Labour had already had two successive Speakers – Betty Boothroyd and Michael Martin – so it was thought to be the turn of a Conservative MP when Martin announced his resignation in 2009. Labour MPs suddenly realised they could use their party's Commons majority to upset their opponents by electing a Speaker who had become deeply unpopular with many in the Tory ranks.[4]

Of course, Farage and Bercow were similar in many ways. Neither was comfortable in traditional Conservative politics; both achieved political prominence through non-traditional routes; both have a ferocious temper; both can be ruthless; both are 'Marmite' figures, loved by some, detested by others; and both crave the limelight.

It is also a long-standing convention (not always kept) that the main political parties don't stand against Mr (or Madam) Speaker in general elections, and that he or she stands purely as 'Mr Speaker'. So the contest in Buckingham was expected to be confined to Bercow and various minor parties and insignificant independents. Farage perceived, however, that there were good pickings to be had among Tory supporters who were dismayed by Bercow's move to the left, and felt they no longer had a sympathetic MP. And there was a second factor in Farage's thinking.

British politics was still suffering from the MPs' expenses scandal. Even though he was Commons Speaker, Bercow, too, was tainted by the affair. He was among scores of MPs who had flipped their homes – changed the designation between his constituency and London homes as to which was his main residence, possibly to avoid paying capital gains tax. Bercow had done this not once, but twice, and also claimed £1,000 in expenses from the Commons to employ an accountant to complete his tax returns. When this was exposed, Bercow did agree to pay HMRC £6,508, though he was never in real trouble with the taxman or the Commons authorities. Yet within a few weeks of his election as Speaker, Bercow came under fire again when it was revealed that he planned to spend £20,000 from public funds refurbishing his official residence inside the Palace of Westminster.

Buckingham was part of Farage's South East of England European seat, at the very opposite end of the geographic crescent which curved all the way round from South Thanet, which he'd fought in 2005. Farage should have been fairly familiar with the politics of Buckingham, but seems to have misjudged just how different a seat it was. (Tellingly, unlike South Thanet, where people would vote

3–2 in the 2016 referendum to leave the EU, Buckingham would vote narrowly for Remain.)

For much of the twentieth century Buckingham was a marginal seat, and once had the crooked publisher Robert Maxwell as its Labour MP. Since 1983, when the constituency lost Bletchley and the growing Milton Keynes, it has been a solid Conservative rural seat covering the Vale of Aylesbury. Scores of villages surround the medieval market town of Buckingham itself. The seat includes the prime minister's country home, Chequers; Waddesdon Manor, country estate of the wealthy Rothschild family; and also South Pavilion, an eighteenth-century house at Wotton Underwood which was once owned by Sir John Gielgud, and had just been bought for £4 million by Tony and Cherie Blair.

In 2005, John Bercow's 27,748 votes were the highest total for any Conservative candidate in Britain (though Kensington and Chelsea had a higher percentage), and Bercow boasted a formidable majority of 18,129.

So Buckingham may just have been an excuse for Farage to quit the leadership, though that may not have been an entirely personal decision. UKIP's biggest donors weren't happy at the way things had gone under his regime. One malcontent was Stuart Wheeler, the Eurosceptic former Conservative donor who'd given UKIP £100,000 earlier in 2009 and was immediately expelled by the Tories. It's thought Wheeler said he would give the party much more, but only if Farage stepped down.

Five candidates stood to succeed him. The favourite was Lord (Malcolm) Pearson of Rannoch, an insurance businessman, who'd been made a Conservative life peer by Margaret Thatcher. Pearson, educated at Eton and a member of the men-only White's Club, seemed to epitomise the Tory establishment which many UKIP members despised. Indeed, his full title was Lord Rannoch of Bridge of Gaur in the District of Perth and Kinross, evoking Scottish castles and grouse moors, and Pearson made no secret of his love of deerstalking. He had been expelled from the Tories, however, in 2004 for backing UKIP, and says he tried to persuade Farage not to stand down. Three of the other contenders – Gerard Batten, Mike

Nattrass and Nikki Sinclaire – were UKIP MEPs. While most out-going party leaders in politics tend to steer clear of the election for their successor, Farage intervened in a big way. During an interview with the BBC's *Daily Politics* programme, he said that of the five con-tenders 'only one of them is a serious, credible candidate and that's Lord Pearson, who has had major achievements in his life in business and politics too . . . If Lord Pearson gets that job and I'm leading the party in the European Parliament, then I would argue that UKIP is stronger and will be for several years . . . If it's not Lord Pearson, things will be tricky. But I think it will be Lord Pearson. He is head and shoulders above the others.'[5]

Gerard Batten, the former British Telecom salesman who'd been one of the founders of UKIP back in 1993 (and would become leader almost a decade later), was furious. 'Nigel's remarks,' he said, 'are an attempt to unduly influence the campaign and an insult to the other candidates and our members . . . He has created an unnec-essary problem for the new leader, if that is someone other than Lord Pearson, by saying that they are not a serious, credible leader in advance. I regard myself as a very serious and credible candi-date. A lot of UKIP members share that view.'[6] Arguably, Farage had breached party rules which stated that candidates and their supporters should conduct campaigning activities in a friendly and constructive manner.

Of the almost 10,000 members who voted, Pearson beat Batten by almost two to one: 4,743 votes to 2,571 (with Sinclaire and Nattrass well behind). But the new leader later admitted that he'd taken the job on an understanding that he would step aside and let Farage return if he wanted to. He also stood on a platform of 'Country before Party', a hint that if he were elected UKIP wouldn't stand against Tories who agreed with UKIP's policy of leaving the EU.

The day after Pearson's victory was declared, *The Times* revealed that shortly after the European elections Pearson held secret talks with the Conservative leader in the House of Lords, Tom Strathclyde, over a possible pact. Astonishingly, this might have led to UKIP not standing any candidates at the coming general election. Years later, Pearson described the secret meeting in detail:

Tom, an old friend, was enthusiastic. 'This is just what we need,' he said. 'I'm having a one-to-one with David [Cameron] for an hour on Thursday. I'll pass this on and come back to you.' Silence ensued. Unluckily for Tom I bumped into him at the peers' entrance the following Monday. He walked straight past me. I said, 'Thomas, I'm speaking to you, what happened on Thursday?' He turned half round and said, 'It's all too bloody awful. I can't talk to you,' and off he went.[7]

The Pearson–Strathclyde plan was simple: UKIP would withdraw from the election if David Cameron gave a written pledge to hold a referendum on Britain's membership of the EU. When the story broke in The Times, Pearson confirmed it and explained that he'd gone to see Strathclyde at the behest of Nigel Farage, taking with him another former Conservative peer, David Willoughby de Broke. It was really a gathering of Tory aristocratic mates. No party has disputed that the meeting took place.

News of the proposed pact infuriated two of the defeated leadership contenders, Nikki Sinclaire and Gerard Batten. It was 'a betrayal of the members', Batten said. He predicted 'a wave of resignations' and said Pearson would probably have come bottom of the poll had members known about the deal. Sinclaire, who'd risen from lowly office assistant to leadership candidate, blamed Nigel Farage. 'I do not see what legitimacy Nigel had to make such a deal. A lot of members feel very cheated.'[8]

Meanwhile in Buckingham, there were similarities with Bexhill in 2001 and South Thanet in 2005. UKIP already had a candidate in place in the seat, who'd been canvassing and campaigning there for two or three years. Dave Fowler, a local plumber, remembers being approached by Farage's adviser Steve Harris, but he readily agreed when Harris asked him to step aside. When Fowler subsequently met Farage at the UKIP conference in Southport 'Nigel walked out and shook me by the hand and said, "Dave, thanks very much. If you'd have said 'No', I wouldn't have stood."'[9] Over coffee, Farage asked Fowler to be his election agent.

Clearly, Farage's hope was that he would be the main alternative to John Bercow, and would attract not only UKIP's usual supporters, but also people who normally voted Conservative, Labour or Liberal Democrat who felt irritated that they weren't able to vote for their normal parties; people who felt disgusted by the expenses' scandal, as well as those who didn't like Bercow personally, or thought he was simply a bad constituency MP. In short, he was hoping for a kind of protest coalition which would attract voters beyond UKIP's normal Eurosceptic base.

What Farage and his colleagues in Buckingham hadn't foreseen was the arrival on the battlefield of an alternative Conservative who says he stood deliberately to try to split the anti-Bercow vote and stop Farage. John Stevens was a wealthy former foreign exchange and bond trader in the City who had been an MEP himself, a Conservative for the Thames Valley seat between 1989 and 1999. He'd then left the Conservatives and founded the short-lived Pro-Euro Conservative Party, before a spell in the Liberal Democrats.

Around six months before the election, Stevens had obtained opinion-polling conducted by a local Conservative grandee, which suggested Farage might win the seat because of the expenses scandal. It was that polling, Stevens says, which prompted him to join the contest:

> It was drawn to my attention that Farage could get into Parliament because the Speaker had a whole lot of weaknesses – that's why I ran basically. But he didn't take my chances seriously. My impression was he believed another candidate's participation might help him win the seat. Completely wrong. All the evidence we had suggested that only another candidate, who could draw some of the poison against Bercow away from Farage, was the only way to stop him. There was a significant anti-Bercow vote, and the trick was to ensure that it didn't all go to Farage.[10]

Farage faced another complication when Patrick Phillips, a member of the local Conservative association who'd been high sheriff of Buckinghamshire, announced he was throwing his hat into the ring, too. Phillips was also a Eurosceptic, and stood because he and other Conservatives felt disenfranchised, he said, by the Bercow situation. 'Patrick was an admirer of Nigel's UKIP position,' his widow Jocelyn explains, 'but he disapproved of him muscling in to our Bercow problem.'

One day Farage rang Phillips to say he was attending an evening meeting in a neighbouring village. Could he drop by, around tea-time? Phillips agreed, having guessed why Farage wanted to call. Jocelyn Phillips baked a cake in anticipation; her husband lit a fire. 'Nigel duly arrived with two assistants and parked himself comfortably by the fire,' Jocelyn Phillips recalls. 'We offered tea to everyone, but Nigel confessed that he could do with something stronger, so his tea-time drink was a large gin-and-tonic!' But Patrick Phillips wouldn't be budged; he was determined to stand.[11]

In 2010, Nigel Farage was nothing like as famous with the British public as he would soon become. UKIP was still quite a minor party; leaving the EU was still a fringe cause; and broadcasters were still reluctant to give UKIP and Farage much airtime. His public profile received a huge boost in February 2010, however, with a speech in the European Parliament. Three months earlier EU leaders had met to choose the new post created by the Lisbon Treaty, the first ever president of the European Council, the gathering of EU heads of government which sets the Union's strategic direction. There was talk of the job going to a big name, such as Tony Blair, but in the end leaders compromised with the Belgian prime minister, Herman Van Rompuy, a rather grey man who had been PM for less than a year, having been a banker and university professor in his past life. Van Rompuy would take charge of the Council when the EU was still in turmoil following the banking crisis and the great recession, and when a crisis in Greek government debt threatened the future of the single currency.

When Van Rompuy came to address the European Parliament for the first time, Farage grabbed his chance and spoke as co-leader of the EFD group. 'I don't want to be rude,' Farage began before letting rip, and being just that:

But you know, really, you have the charisma of a damp rag and the appearance of a low-grade bank clerk, and the question that I want to ask. [jeers] The question that I want to ask – that we're all going to ask – is: 'Who are you?' I'd never heard of you. Nobody in Europe had ever heard of you. I would like to ask you, President: 'Who voted for you? And what mechanism . . .' – Oh, I know democracy's not popular with you lot – 'And what mechanism do the peoples of Europe have to remove you?'

The chamber was sparsely attended at that point, but Farage's words were met with an outburst of boos, and the president of the Parliament, Jerzy Buzek, tried to indicate that Farage should tone his words down. The UKIP MEP ignored him, and pressed on:

Is this European democracy? Well, I sense though that you're competent and capable and dangerous, and I have no doubt that it's your intention to be the quiet assassin of European democracy and of the European nation states. You appear to have a loathing for the very concept of the existence of nation states. Perhaps that's because you come from Belgium which, of course, is pretty much a non-country.

Herman Van Rompuy looked away, and scratched his nose as Farage continued:

But since you took over, we've seen Greece reduced to nothing more than a protectorate. Sir, you have no legitimacy in this job at all, and I can say with confidence that I can speak on behalf of the majority of the British people in saying: we don't know you; we don't want you, and the sooner you're put out to grass the better.[12]

Farage had struck a chord, and not just with Eurosceptics. Like Farage, few people in Europe had ever heard of Van Rompuy, and to many he did indeed seem a dull, uninspiring choice for such a high-powered and pioneering job. Yet the rude and personal nature of Farage's attack did not go down well with some, especially bank clerks and Belgians. Farage didn't care: he had got the publicity he craved. His ninety-second speech was widely broadcast round Europe, and got millions of hits on YouTube.

Farage had already been reprimanded three months before, for calling Van Rompuy and the new EU foreign minister, Baroness (Cathy) Ashton from Britain, 'political pygmies'. Now Van Rompuy's successor as Belgian prime minister, Yves Leterme, demanded a public apology for Farage's 'slander', while Martin Schulz, leader of the Socialist group, called on him to resign as an MEP. Buzek asked Farage to come to see him the following week. 'He has been summoned to the headmaster's office,' a UKIP spokesman said, 'and expects a spanking.'[13]

'The only people I am going to apologise to are bank clerks the world over,' Farage said. 'If I have offended them I am very sorry indeed . . . I am not going to apologise if I have sparked off a debate on vital issues such as who governs the EU and are they democratically accountable. That's a good thing to have done.'[14] Jerzy Buzek said Farage had 'insulted the dignity' of the new Council president and fined him ten days' worth of his daily parliamentary allowances, or €3,000.

Farage had become a big beast within the European Parliament, deeply unpopular with most MEPs, but a formidable operator and performer.

Every MEP is allocated a fixed seat, and MEPs and groups who sat in close proximity to Farage, such as the British Conservatives, were irritated, according to Derk Jan Eppink, 'that whenever Farage got up to deliver his next series of polemical one-liners, they provided his background decor! They decided that the only thing they could do to prevent this was to leave the chamber before the UKIP president started to speak! . . . the idea was that Farage should appear isolated, to give the impression that his views didn't count.' Eppink, who by now had become a Dutch MEP, and a member of the Conservative reform group in Strasbourg, says, 'our group president, who sat next to Farage during the debates, was told on no account to laugh during his speeches – which I knew from personal experience was not always easy'.[15] Eppink points out that during the famous Van

Rompuy speech, the Conservative group leader, Timothy Kirkhope, who was sitting next to Farage, 'put his hands over his face so that he wouldn't be recognised in the television footage'.[16]

Farage's higher public profile, in Europe and Britain, and his audacious challenge to Bercow, were accompanied by the publication of his first memoirs, *Fighting Bull*. It was an easy read, with a chatty, breezy style in keeping with Farage, though some passages were very clearly the words of Mark Daniel, his ghost writer. Daniel was a novelist who in 2005 had also published *Cranks and Gadflies*, the first history of UKIP, which had been very sympathetic to Farage.[17]

The *Sunday Times* columnist Camilla Long, a descendant of the Dukes of Newcastle, has a reputation for raunchy journalism and 'hatchet-job' profiles, and went to interview Farage at the Westminster office of the European Parliament.

Long made no secret of her distaste for Farage. 'I am quite relieved that Nigel Farage has only one testicle,' her profile began. 'Tearing around with a loudhailer on his campaign to oust John Bercow,' she wrote, 'working "100-hour weeks", inhaling whole packs of Rothmans and chuffing down hundreds and hundreds of pints, I dread to think what he would be like with . . . two.'

'At 45,' Long added, 'he has the complexion of a used teabag . . . . Farage is pretty odious: a shifty saloon-bar lizard.' She asked about his affairs; she asked about his drinking. 'People that know me well,' Farage claimed, raising his voice, 'would tell you that they've hardly ever seen me pissed. And I'm rather proud of that.' And he didn't worry about being an alcoholic like Guy, his father. 'I can pack it up for a week and it's not a problem. It's how we're made. My father was made in the way it took him over and it wrecked him. But I'm lucky. I'm one of those people who can take it or leave it.'[18]

But there was one personal question Camilla Long hadn't posed. The UKIP press officer Gawain Towler wrote a blog on the day of publication in which he claimed Long had rung him up after the interview. 'Look Gawain,' she reportedly said, 'I am really sorry to ask you this, but the editors have told me to . . . They want me to ask which one of his balls was removed after his cancer.'

The question was pretty impertinent, Towler told Long, but he reluctantly agreed to ask it. Farage was 'unusually for him, somewhat put out, but after saying that he thought it a cheap shot he then recovered his normal poise. "Tell her if she is so bloody interested that she can come over and check herself."'[19]

Camilla Long's account was more colourful. Farage was in 'high spirits' in the pub, she wrote, having just made a speech to a UKIP conference. Over the convivial din, she claimed, Farage shouted: 'Tell her to come and find out, ha-ha-ha.' His offer wasn't taken up.[20] (If Long had read *Fighting Bull* carefully she would have known it was his left testicle.)

Farage may seem publicly to have a tough skin, but he can be much more sensitive than people realise. He found Long's question deeply hurtful. He complained that if a woman politician had a mastectomy because of cancer, no journalist would dream of asking her which breast had been removed. It was a fair point.

Farage believed the *Sunday Times* editor John Witherow was behind the 'which ball?' question, yet only a month later Farage consented to what turned out to be an insightful and very funny campaign profile in the same paper. The author was the late travel and food writer A. A. Gill – Adrian Gill – a recovering alcoholic who also had a reputation for being acerbic:

> Farage is hearty, hale and seedy, in a blue checked suit and electric blue tie. He's a man whose character has been formed by a thousand snug bars. He has that confidence that is the by-product of an enormous amount of alcohol and laughs often and loudly.
>
> He also has breath that could club a baby seal to death. Even across his desk, every time something strikes him as funny there is a draught like Carnarvon opening a pharaoh's tomb. The first rule of standing for parliament is: a toothbrush is not just for Christmas.
>
> His office is a shop front selling a range of amazingly naff UKIP memorabilia. I'm particularly drawn, and then repelled, by a motley motel dressing gown with pound signs on the cuff – just the thing for entertaining the Moldovan escort before reporting her to the Home Office. And a tie, with a crank and a fly on it, because Michael Howard called UKIP a bunch of cranks and gadflies. 'I'm lifetime president,' Farage guffaws . . .

I ask him if we can go out and do a bit of canvassing. He trav-
els mob-handed, firing up a Rothmans, scattering the mobility
scooters. We stand outside Boots. 'Very small, Buckingham,' he
says. 'Not many people around,' implying that he usually attracts
crowds. There are only 12,000 inhabitants and everyone is at
home. An elderly woman approaches and asks if he's got a moral
core. 'Yes,' he says emphatically. 'We've got a very large Christian
group,' making it sound like a penis.

'Good,' she says. 'What are you going to do with the Church
of England?'

'First thing,' he bellows, 'we should get rid of the Archbishop
of Canterbury. When he said sharia law was not just necessary
but inevitable, I thought: no, he's got to go.'[21]

Farage's campaign in Buckingham began with high hopes. Ladbrokes
quoted him at 4–1 when he announced he would be a candidate, and
Tim Montgomerie, editor of the activist website conservativehome.
com, said he'd be 'tempted to vote UKIP' if he lived in Buckingham.
'It would be one way of getting a Speaker who wasn't the choice of
Brown's Labour MPs.'[22]

Farage had begun canvassing in the snows of January 2010, and
UKIP put huge resources into the seat. Once again, Farage's contest
was deemed to be the party's prime target. The campaign opened its
headquarters in a small modern shopping precinct near the centre of
the town, where Farage would sit beneath a large poster of Winston
Churchill. Every few hours, he would venture out for an hour or
two door-to-door, accompanied by what one sketch writer called
'a posse of henchmen . . . like a scene from *Foyle's War*'.[23] The aides
would go ahead to identify potential supporters who might be worth
a chat with Farage. Every now and then he would take a break for a
cigarette. And there were regular pub stops, too.

Indeed, early on Farage had promised to drink a pint in every
pub in the constituency, which was quite a challenge given there
must have been roughly eighty of them across the whole seat. In the
months before the election, Farage would visit the seat at weekends,
and his unofficial agent Dave Fowler would recce three or four pubs

in advance to make sure they were happy to be a Farage campaign stop:

> He never wanted to go in cold, and I'd been there before and took a few notes and got the landlords' names, so he could go in and say: 'Hello Dave, hello Sheila. I understand you come from the Midlands,' and it worked very well, and we visited loads and loads of pubs. He always used to say 'Every pub's a parliament.' He does care a lot about people. He'd sit and talk to ordinary people and try to advise them about their problems. He was always well-received – always. If there was a nice beer on he'd have one, or quite often a half. But never more than two pints, and if he was driving he wouldn't have any at all.[24]

John Bercow didn't approve. 'I accept that sadly some now see politics as a bit of a lark,' he remarked. 'But Buckingham deserves better than being treated as a glorified pub crawl or media event.'[25]

For much of the campaign, Farage seemed confident of victory – that Buckingham would give UKIP a 'bridgehead' at Westminster, in the same way that he and his two colleagues had made a break-through into the European Parliament eleven years before.

UKIP hopes were boosted by the advent of immigration as a serious campaign issue. The Liberal Democrat leader Nick Clegg argued the numbers couldn't be controlled, while the prime minister Gordon Brown was forced to apologise after he was famously overheard describing Gillian Duffy, a pensioner he met in Rochdale, as 'bigoted' after she complained to him about rising immigration. And when travellers set up an unofficial encampment outside the village of Nash, near Buckingham, over the Easter weekend, Farage seized on the incident as another illustration of the problems of EU membership: 'We have an open door to 10 million Romany gypsies in Eastern Europe,' he told a Nash voter:

> To my mind, it's mad. What's happening in Nash could be a microcosm of what's to come . . . There should be time-restricted work permits for overseas workers, and no automatic right to

settle and plug into the social security system. Clegg offering amnesty is crazy . . . Too much of our country has been given away to Brussels, where 75 per cent of our laws are made. We need a referendum. I suggest you vote for me.[26]

A. A. Gill seems to have spent only a day in Buckingham, and John Bercow proved elusive, but the writer quickly spotted what Farage and his allies had overlooked – that actually Bercow was a diligent and popular constituency MP. A local farm labourer who'd been a Labour councillor and town mayor told Gill how Bercow would respond to constituents by return of post. 'He's a really good bloke,' the Labour man said.[27] Farage may have assumed that because Bercow could be bumptious and arrogant, and shifted politically from right-wing Conservative to the fringes of Labour, that he'd be an easy target. He'd miscalculated. Over the years Bercow had acquired a reputation for turning up and being seen at every event, and had a certain charm.

Farage managed to work his own charisma on Buckingham voters, touring pubs and housing estates. Dave Fowler recalls how they visited one pub and found two 'Tory' women who made loud, disparaging remarks and asked what Farage was doing there. But he turned on the charm. 'Within about half an hour,' says Fowler, 'they were linking arms with him and having a laugh.'[28]

UKIP spent lavishly on Farage's campaign leaflets, including a twelve-page full-colour brochure published ahead of the official campaigning period. 'By toppling the Speaker,' the front cover declared, 'you will cause a political earthquake in British politics . . .' Immigration featured prominently, with the headline 'Let's Take Back Control', a full six years before Dominic Cummings and the Vote Leave campaign famously made that phrase their own in the 2016 EU referendum. 'We must take back control of our borders from the EU,' the pamphlet declared, though only one other page mentioned Europe. Other populist policies Farage pressed included the retention and creation of grammar schools (in a county which, unusually, still has selective state education); and opposition to the HS2 rail project which was planned to run through the middle of the constituency.

Farage was dogged throughout by John Stevens, whose campaign had become more than just an anti-Farage effort; he now seemed to be trying to win. He was assisted by Mark Seddon, a former editor of the left-wing *Tribune* newspaper who'd stood for Labour in Buckingham in 2001. He recalls how they organised for Bercow to be followed by 'Flipper the dolphin' to remind voters of Bercow's house-flipping, while they tailed Farage with 'U-kipper', a character dressed as an orange kipper. It may have seemed an odd move to try to help Bercow by publicly attacking him, but there was a compli-cated logic to it, if Stevens could seriously split the anti-Bercow vote.

Inevitably, as his party's star name, Farage's commitments were divided and he still campaigned for candidates in other seats. He was also a frequent media performer, especially now both the BBC and the commercial channels had agreed to give UKIP more airtime than in 2005. Buckingham had the advantage of being better placed geographically for trips to other seats or London TV studios than South Thanet, which is hard to get to by road or rail.

On polling day, Thursday 6 May, Farage rose early and went to Hinton-in-the-Hedges airfield, about four miles west of the constit-uency, where UKIP aides had arranged a photo-opportunity. There he rendezvoused with Justin Adams, a pilot who had just flown in from Winchester in a blue Wilga 35A plane. Not so much an air-craft, Farage said later, 'rather like a tractor, actually, with wings'.[29]

The idea was that the plane would pull a UKIP banner, with the party's £ logo and the slogan VOTE FOR YOUR COUNTRY – VOTE UKIP and fly low over Buckingham and the surrounding area. UKIP had invited the press to witness the scene, but the only person to turn up was Neil Hall, a local agency photographer.

For some reason – maybe just boyish Biggin Hill enthusiasm – Farage wanted to fly as a passenger, even though people would not be able to spot him from the ground. The idea was that he would receive text messages from UKIP colleagues in various locations, advising where the banner could be seen to the best effect. Yet it's hard to see why Farage himself had to undertake this task; though he had flown twice before with Justin Adams, he had found the experience very unpleasant.

The publicity benefits were likely to be limited, however. On polling day broadcasters are banned by law from covering any campaigning before the close of poll, while the chances of newspapers or websites showing photos of the flight were not great. In the event, many media outlets would end up covering it well before people had stopped voting.

'I just hope the plane doesn't blow up and crash,' Farage had joked to the handful of people at the airfield, puffing on a cigarette, laughing for the camera, waiting for take-off.[30] Farage squeezed himself on board wearing his typical pin-striped suit, a purple and yellow UKIP rosette attached to his lapel.

You can't just attach a big banner to the back of an aircraft. Rather, the plane has to take off, achieve some height and then swoop down low in a deep dive with a grapple hook dangling beneath it, and pick up a wire stretched between two poles about ten feet off the ground, and which is in turn attached to the banner. Often the pick-up operation requires several goes.

This time it took five attempts. The first and second time the hook failed to pluck up the wire between the poles, and the pilot had to soar back up and loop round again. After the second attempt, the pilot wondered if the wire was actually stretched between the poles and he got Farage to text his press man Duncan Barkes on the ground to check. The wire was in place, ready to be collected.

The fifth dive seemed successful. 'We've picked up,' Justin Adams announced but then, as he looked back, he saw all was not well. 'This is an emergency,' Farage would recall Adams shouting. 'Real trouble.' 'Why?' Farage asked. 'Banner's wrapped around the tail and rudder!' the pilot replied.[31] Farage knew at once that meant a crash-landing.

Adams grappled to keep control of the aircraft with the banner impeding its rear. 'The pilot found that the control column was being pulled forward with a force that required both hands to resist,' an official report found later.[32] Adams kept the plane level at about 300 feet and with nowhere to land straight ahead, decided to do a circuit and find somewhere suitable.

'Oh fuck!' cried Farage. 'I was pretty much certain we were going to die,' he said later. 'I could not see how anything as flimsy as that plane could crash into the ground at seventy or eighty mph and leave mere organic tissue fit to function.'

'With all options gone, I was suddenly very calm,' he would recall. 'Like a Great War subaltern, I just hoped not that I would escape the inevitable but that it would be quick.'[33] He thought about his past life, he later said, and 'relationships that had gone wrong and that had gone right'.[34] He estimated the ordeal in the air lasted about five minutes.

Lurching from side to side because of the flapping banner, the plane descended rapidly towards the airfield. It flew over a group of houses and cleared a hedge, but Adams struggled to keep the nose up. The banner was first to hit the turf, then the plane nose-dived into the ground with an almighty force. Farage says he closed his eyes just before impact, not expecting to see anything ever again. He felt a series of hard blows to his body as the aircraft took the full impact, and the engine fell apart.

'He was coming around to do another run,' an eyewitness said, 'and then it fell out of the sky, and flipped over on its front. It was all over in a couple of seconds. I really thought they had both died.'[35]

But no. 'That astounding awareness of not being dead takes a few seconds to sink in,' Farage related. He was upside down, his head only a few inches above the ground. 'Nigel, you all right?' Justin Adams asked. Farage couldn't respond properly because he found it difficult to breathe. He soon felt pain in his ribs, his back, his knees and calves, but was relieved to find he could still move his legs and toes.

The pilot mentioned 'fuel' and Farage suddenly felt liquid seeping over his body. 'For the first time, terror kicked in,' he said later. 'Now, upside down, bound and impotent, I was going to be burned to death – my worst terror from my worst nightmares.' He felt helpless to get out. There was blood across his face.

Meanwhile, the agency photographer, Neil Hall, had jumped into his car with Duncan Barkes and sped across the airfield:

There were bits of engine far away and it looked crumpled, and we were going very very tentatively because we didn't quite know what we were going to see. We feared the worst. When we got there I saw his legs, and the pilot's legs dangling out. I thought 'Oh God!' For a moment you don't know what you're seeing – it might be a dead body. And I heard sort of, 'Get me out, get me out!' I had a few words about whether it was the right thing to do, in case we did more damage if somebody's got a fractured vertebrae, but he seemed very animated.[36]

'Nigel, are you all right?' Barkes asked.

'No, I'm scared. I'm scared. I'm scared. Just get me out of this fucking thing.'

Neil Hall says it was 'strange' to see what a 'traumatic incident can do to a person who is naturally so confident. He was telling me – a stranger – that he was just so scared.'

Barkes undid Farage's buckle. He'd been joined by Alfred Thomas, an elderly local in a woolly hat, who had seen the crash while out cycling. They gently lifted Farage from the debris and got him to his feet before going round to help the pilot, whose foot was trapped. Adams couldn't be freed until the fire brigade arrived.

Gingerly, Neil Hall had taken a few shots. 'There's a view that it's quite a heartless thing to do to take pictures of that situation,' he says. 'Duncan asked me to stop, and Nigel said: "It's okay. Let him take his pictures."' Hall doesn't think Farage was hoping to milk the publicity. 'He was just relieved to be alive.'

Farage staggered off across long grass a few dozen yards from the plane and took out his packet of cigarettes. He asked Barkes to light one. Barkes was reluctant because of the aviation fuel, but did as he was asked. Farage took a few drags but they only made him feel much worse.

'My suit trousers were glued with blood to my thighs and knees. My upper lip was bleeding. My breastbone and the surrounding area hurt like hell. Expanding the chest was agonising, as I was starved of oxygen. My lungs seemed full of treacle but I could not cough.'[37]

Farage's mother, Barbara Stevens, later related how she heard the news in a call from Nigel's brother, Andrew. 'He said, "Mother, please do not look at the television. There are some terrible things about Nigel." And I did look at the television, and I saw my son as a crumpled mess in that plane. How he survived it, I do not know.'[38]

An ambulance arrived, but Farage wanted to sink into unconsciousness. The ambulance men kept asking questions to keep him awake. What was his name? How old was he? Farage gave them a V-sign and was angry at the way they tried to stop him dropping off. But the bumpy ride across the airfield, and then the journey into Banbury, kept him conscious anyway, and a stretcher bore him into A&E at the Horton Hospital. Farage's lip was stitched up; he was given a CAT scan, and told he need not worry: there seemed to be no serious danger. The local UKIP candidate visited him, only for Farage to insist he would be fine. Go away, he urged him, and 'Get out the Vote.'[39]

UKIP had hoped the photo-shoot might get some extra publicity, and within an hour or two they had more coverage than they could ever have wished for. Neil Hall's exclusive shots had suddenly enlivened election day – which is normally quiet for the media until the polls close at 10 p.m. His sequence of pictures quickly appeared on social media, on TV and on the front pages of the evening papers: Farage hanging folded upside-down in the wreckage; Farage red-faced and shocked as he is helped out by Thomas and Barkes; Farage steadying himself against one of the plane wheels; Farage looking dazed as he stumbles away through the long grass. Farage would later suggest Hall had done well out of the crash, but he had merely earned his day rate; the profits went to his agency.

The doctors told Farage he had a punctured lung, two chipped vertebrae, a fractured sternum and several fractured ribs. He'd have to go to the John Radcliffe Hospital, 30 miles away in Oxford, for more examinations.

Farage's press man Gawain Towler turned up on the Friday morning with all the newspapers, and he was shocked to see the extent of the awful pictures. But Towler was just as concerned that day with preventing an even more embarrassing picture being taken if he didn't take swift action, of which more later.

Farage was still in hospital when the Buckingham result was declared at lunchtime on the Friday. The top four candidates fared as follows:

John Bercow (The Speaker)	22,860	(47.3%)
John Stevens (Ind)	10,331	(21.4%)
Nigel Farage (UKIP)	8,401	(17.4%)
Patrick Phillips (Ind)	2,394	(5.0%)
Majority	12,529	(25.9%)

Farage was represented at the count by his agent, and it was a huge disappointment to have been pushed into third place by John Stevens (who sent flowers to his injured opponent). Without Patrick Phillips, the Eurosceptic Conservative independent who kept his deposit, Farage might just have come second.

He later said it had been a serious mistake to challenge John Bercow. 'I have never been anywhere and met a more popular local MP,' Farage admitted. 'He worked very hard in a way most MPs wouldn't.'[40] He also wrongly assumed that David Cameron wouldn't come out in support of Bercow. When he did, it deterred many wavering Conservatives from defecting, and meant Bercow could print pictures of Cameron on his Tory-blue election leaflets. 'Pre-Cameron, he was very nervous,' Farage observed, 'post-Cameron he was very relaxed.'[41] And Farage reckoned without John Stevens's well-resourced campaign – his glossy leaflets, compared with UKIP's lower-grade literature, 'looked like *Vogue* next to *Private Eye*', Farage later remarked.[42]

'It was a right stitch-up,' says Farage's agent Dave Fowler. 'Bercow and Stevens were mates and they got together to make sure he didn't get in. Stevens sent out nine leaflets each with a second-class stamp on, to every house in the area – about 40,000 houses. Yet each candidate was only allowed to spend forty grand.' When Fowler stood in for Farage when the result was announced, he says Stevens was behind him. 'I happened to look round and Bercow winked at him.'[43]

Nonetheless, Buckingham was UKIP's best result in 2010 – the third time Nigel Farage had achieved that feat (after Salisbury in 1997 and Bexhill in 2001) and he had almost twice the percentage of the next highest UKIP performer (9.5 per cent in Boston and

Skegness). Nationally the party got 3.1 per cent, compared with 2.2 per cent in 2005. It was the highest ever figure for a Eurosceptic party in a general election, well up on what Jimmy Goldsmith and his millions had achieved with the Referendum Party thirteen years before. Having fought 558 of the 632 seats in Great Britain, the experts said this 'represented the largest minor party challenge ever to be mounted, and generated the largest share of the vote ever won by a minor party'.[44]

Farage left hospital two days later, on the Saturday morning, went home to Downe, and the following day he even posed for another press photo supping a pint in the George and Dragon. But he was still in pain, and he has never recovered fully from his back injuries. Farage was not able to play golf again, or do strenuous physical work. He would tire a lot more easily, and nights out drinking in Brussels or Strasbourg would largely be a thing of the past.

The plane crash suddenly aged him, he said, physically and mentally. He reassessed things philosophically, and vowed never again to get obsessed with trivialities, and to concentrate instead on what mattered. And he did to some extent. He would devote more time to leisure pursuits – cricket, fishing, a quiet evening at home – to spending time with his family, including his young daughters, by now aged ten and four. 'I am, I think, soberer, more reflective,' he wrote in the updated paperback version of his memoirs (suitably renamed *Flying Free*). 'Good God, I might even be growing up a bit.'[45]

'I've considered myself, ever since that moment, very, very lucky to be alive,' he said in 2015. 'And if before that crash, in politics I was unafraid to take on the Establishment, since that day I've been fearless.'[46]

The pilot Justin Adams, meanwhile, had been cut out of the wreckage and taken to hospital in Coventry. 'We've both had a miraculous escape,' Farage said.[47] For the third time in his life, Farage had avoided death.

The story ended in tragedy, however. The official air accident report, published six months later, didn't blame the pilot, but Adams couldn't work while awaiting the outcome and his mental health was badly affected. Insurers refused to pay for repairs to his plane until the Civil Aviation Authority (CAA) investigation was completed. His business collapsed, as did his marriage. He blamed Nigel Farage for his plight and felt he'd lost a chance to sell his story to the press, having been advised not to do so. Over a period of three days, Adams made persistent threats to both Farage and the CAA investigator Martin James. He had a gun, he told them, and could 'shoot to kill'.

In the spring of 2011 Adams was prosecuted in Oxford on five charges of threatening to kill, and Farage was a prime prosecution witness. Thom Airs, who reported the trial for the *Oxford Mail*, remembers Farage as 'quite theatrical' in court.

> He thumped the lectern to get his point across. He was a natural public speaker compared to most people who go into a witness-box and are overawed by it. I have a strong recollection of him being very forthright, booming and quite demonstrative. I'm not sure it went down well with the jury . . . He almost overdid the theatrics – it was bombastic – just a bit at odds with the more considered evidence heard previously.[48]

Farage told jurors how, a few days after the official report had absolved the pilot, he'd phoned Adams at his home. 'He was really, really angry,' Farage told the court. 'He started saying: "You sold your story to the *Sunday Telegraph*. You've done nothing for me. UKIP has done nothing for me. I'm going to sell my story."' Out of concern for Adams, Farage said he drove to Oxfordshire to see him at his home, and they went for lunch at a village pub. They were accompanied by a psychiatric nurse who decided to come along after Adams had told him on the phone that he planned to kill Farage.[49]

Over lunch, Adams had continued to be belligerent. 'I used to be in special forces and no one's safe. Do you understand me?' Farage said Adams remarked. Then later, when Adams seemed more calm and rational, he reportedly told Farage: 'I was going to kill you today, but I've decided not to, but I can't preclude it from happening in the future.' The court also heard how the pilot had warned

Farage's secretary that he was buying a gun, and would give him a week to issue a joint press release giving Adams's side of the story 'or else'. Farage explained to the jury that he was often prey to 'all sorts of crackpots and threats', and usually ignored them. This case was 'different' because it was 'specific'.[50]

Justin Adams also rang the police to say he had a weapon and enough ammunition to kill Farage, the crash investigator and himself.[51] 'I've lost my wife, my house, my child,' Adams said in the recorded call. 'I've only got eight bullets, but I only need four.'[52]

Adams was found guilty. Having already spent six months in custody, he was given a two-year community order instead of a prison sentence. The pilot's threats had been a 'cry for help', the judge decided, 'as well as an expression of anger and resentment' while suffering 'a depressive order' and drinking to excess.[53] It wasn't reported at the time, but Farage had written a letter to the judge to urge him to be lenient with Adams.

It was a very sad story.

In 2013, Justin Adams was found dead at his home. He had committed suicide.

He was forty-eight.

I 4

NIGEL'S BACK

By his own admission Malcolm Pearson was not a good leader of UKIP. Astonishingly, in several seats on the 2010 election, such as Wells, Somerton and Frome, and Taunton Deane, all in Somerset, he urged people to vote Conservative even though his own party had candidates standing. Pearson even campaigned for the Tory nominee in a couple of seats where UKIP didn't field a candidate, which infuriated local activists. A few days before polling, a *Sunday Times* reporter secretly made a recording of Pearson in which he explained how to get round the law on declaring donations; he described some UKIP members as 'neanderthals'; and he said Stuart Agnew was 'one of our only really sane MEPs'.[1] In a TV interview Pearson had admitted he didn't know every detail of the party's manifesto. It was no surprise when, in August 2010, Pearson announced he was stepping down after less than a year in the job. 'I have learnt that I am not much good at party politics, which I do not enjoy,' he candidly admitted.[2]

Everyone assumed that Nigel Farage would now return. It's often said in life that you should never go back to your old job, but Farage had noted how Alex Salmond had shown in Scotland that a comeback can occasionally be more successful that the first performance. Salmond had stood down from the SNP leadership in 2000, only to return in 2004 and to take his party into government three years later as Scottish first minister.

Surprisingly perhaps, the first politician to send Farage a get-well message after his plane crash had been David Cameron. Both the sons of stockbrokers, the two had seen a fair bit of each other over the years, having become elected politicians around the same time. They first met on the BBC South politics programme in 2001, the year Cameron was elected an Oxfordshire MP; then appeared together on *Any Questions?* the following year, and Farage was also a guest when Cameron made his debut on BBC's *Question Time*. 'We spent much of the evening on the roof smoking cigarettes,' Farage once said, 'all of them mine.'[3] Four summers later, by chance, their families ended up as next-door holiday neighbours in the north Cornwall resort of Mother Ivey's Bay, though Cameron declined Farage's invitation for a pint in the local pub.

David Cameron and the Conservatives replaced Labour as the biggest party in Parliament, but they were twenty seats short of a Commons majority. After five days of fraught negotiations, Gordon Brown stood down as prime minister and Cameron formed a Coalition with Nick Clegg and the fifty-seven Liberal Democrat MPs, creating the first British Coalition since 1945.

It was a historic moment. For sixty-five years the Lib Dems, and their predecessors the Liberal Party, had been the traditional 'party of protest' for anyone disillusioned with the Conservatives or Labour, and they had recorded many historic by-election victories in the process (not least Orpington, the Farages' home seat, in 1962). For its first eighteen years of existence, UKIP had to compete with the Lib Dems for the protest vote. This was no longer so – it was arguably as important in UKIP's history as the advent of proportional representation in European elections eleven years before.

Suddenly the Lib Dems were now part of the establishment. Before long, Nick Clegg and his colleagues made themselves very unpopular with their activists and voters by supporting Conservative austerity measures, and by reneging on their pledge to oppose university tuition fees. UKIP's policies, especially on Europe, may have been the polar opposite to those of Nick Clegg's party, but the public didn't always see it like that. It often surprised journalists in by-elections to meet voters who said they couldn't make their minds up between the Lib Dems and UKIP. If Nick Clegg had stayed out of office in 2010 this story might be very different. Polls showed that the 23 per cent vote share which Clegg and his party recorded at the

2010 general election had collapsed to 10 per cent by the end of 2010, and the Lib Dem vote has never really recovered since.

These promising prospects for UKIP weren't very apparent back in 2010, however. Progress on achieving withdrawal from the EU, or even a referendum, looked bleak, since the pro-European Liberal Democrats effectively had a veto on any Eurosceptic moves which the Conservatives might make (though, in fact, the Lib Dems' manifesto in 2010 had advocated an In-Out referendum on the next occasion there was a 'fundamental change' in the relationship between Britain and the EU).

Nor was it certain that Farage wanted to lead UKIP again. Months after the plane crash, his back often caused him serious pain. And although he'd purged most of his internal critics from the UKIP NEC, the job of leader would still involve huge pressure from all sides. David Cameron had had a point – though Farage could never admit it. UKIP did contain quite a few 'fruitcakes, loonies and closet racists'.

Among the early candidates to declare for the leadership was the monetarist economist Tim Congdon, a well-known pundit on TV and radio, who during John Major's government in the mid-'90s had been one of the 'wise men' economic advisers to the Treasury. Congdon suggests it was a sign of just how much Farage 'vacillated' over whether to stand that he travelled to the economist's home in Gloucestershire that summer to discuss what he might do with the party. Congdon told Farage that while he agreed with UKIP MEPs participating in the European Parliament, he was unhappy with the way they seemed to enjoy life in Brussels and Strasbourg too much. 'I represented the segment of the party who wanted the indulgence to stop.'[4]

Farage finally confirmed he was a candidate in his speech at the UKIP conference in Torquay in early September. He'd only made up his mind at the last minute, he said – chatting to colleagues over drinks the night before, then finally deciding over breakfast. 'What would you like me to do?' he teased the audience. 'Would you like me to run?'[5] They cheered, of course, and shouted 'Yes'.[6]

'I'm far from perfect,' he told the BBC, 'but I do think I'm able, through the media, to deliver a good, simple, understandable message.'[7] And a Farage press release pointed out that the video clip of his Van Rompuy speech had just passed 1.5 million hits online. Yet Farage would soon suggest his attack on Van Rompuy was partly to blame for his poor performance in Buckingham. 'Alas, the speech upset the middle-class shire Tories. Any charm offensive which I might have essayed was doomed.'[8]

Farage's other main opponent was David Campbell Bannerman, now an MEP, who had faced Farage in 2006 and come third. His main gripe about Farage's previous period as leader was that he seemed almost completely uninterested in policy. Campbell Bannerman believed that this partly explained UKIP's repeated failure to translate advances in European elections into success at the subsequent general election. It was fine in Euro contests for UKIP to be considered a one-policy party – withdrawal from the EU – but in general elections Campbell Bannerman wanted policies across the board. He had written much of UKIP's 2010 manifesto, though Farage never expressed any enthusiasm for it:

> To me, a political party is policies . . . Nigel was never interested in policy; he was always unhappy with it. I felt he was more interested in UKIP being a 'pressure party' – where it brings pressure on the Conservative Party to do the right thing. And I think that was more the game of some of his backers, such as Stuart Wheeler.[9]

And at the UKIP conference, Campbell Bannerman told activists that the party had to 'grow up' and become more professional:

> If I am fortunate and honoured to serve this party as the next Leader, then mark my words: the lazy days of UKIP are over! The days of us only being accountable to ourselves for what we say, rather than what we do, will be numbered. I believe a new UKIP must be a party of action, not of talk. Not a party of navel gazers or those who think their role is to compete with [the Conservative MEP] Dan Hannan for YouTube hits![10]

Campbell Bannerman gained a clever advantage over his rival by travelling down to West Sussex to visit the man who was then arguably UKIP's most famous member. Sir Patrick Moore had achieved fame and celebrity as an amateur astronomer and eccentric boffin who wore a monocle and had presented the long-running BBC television programme *The Sky at Night* since its inception in 1957.

Moore had strong right-wing views. He was fiercely anti-immigration and anti-EU and very conservative on social issues. Having belonged to the far-right New Britain Party, he joined UKIP in around 1997 and was an occasional visitor to annual conferences. Campbell Bannerman persuaded a prominent UKIP member from Dorset, Douglas Denny, who visited the astronomer twice a week, to take him to meet Moore at his home in Selsey on the coast. Then after a long conversation, and to Denny's surprise, the visitor asked Moore if he would support him for the UKIP leadership. Moore agreed to, so Campbell Bannerman then asked if he would sign his nomination form there and then. Moore signed on the spot. 'Patrick was . . . so generous he agreed straight away without even thinking about it,' Denny wrote a couple of years later.[11]

When Nigel Farage heard of Moore's support for his opponent, Denny says, he 'went instantly into apoplectic meltdown' and challenged Denny as to 'how dare I go and get Patrick to sign DCBs papers? He was hopping mad at DCB getting in first and asking, and his not doing it.'[12]

Farage duly despatched one of his staff, Ray Finch, down to West Sussex to plead with the 87-year-old Moore to change his mind, claiming that he had already promised to support Farage. Douglas Denny doesn't believe he'd given any such pledge. Moore initially refused, says Denny, 'saying he had given a promise and once a promise was given he would not contemplate changing it. This whole distasteful event put Patrick in an invidious position: he was of the "old school" . . . Patrick felt trapped and Finch persisted.'[13]

In the end, Finch persuaded Moore to make a compromise endorsement of Farage, so that publicly he appeared to be backing both contenders. Doug Denny says that when he went to see Sir Patrick a few hours later, he was 'incensed', felt 'used' and wanted to resign from the party. Denny persuaded him not to, but Moore never again gave an 'endorsement' to anyone. Denny had been one of Nigel Farage's biggest supporters within UKIP, a guaranteed vote during his years on the NEC, but the Patrick Moore incident is part of the reason why he turned against him. 'This was a despicable thing of Farage to do,' he says. 'That incident (out of many I witnessed) illustrates very well what a totally self-centred, narcissistic, egotistical person Farage is . . . I have despised him for this incident more than any of his other outrageous acts in the fifteen years or so that I knew him.'[14]

On Bonfire Night 2010, Nigel Farage won back the leadership easily:

Nigel Farage	6,085	60.5%
Tim Congdon	2,037	20.3%
David Campbell Bannerman	1,404	14.0%
Winston McKenzie	530	5.3%

Farage had one and a half times as many votes as his three opponents combined. 'That was the end of David Campbell Bannerman,' says Clive Page who observes that Farage would not have welcomed the critical nature of his campaign. A few months later, Campbell Bannerman returned to the Conservatives.

One of Tim Congdon's main disagreements with Farage had been over the question of creating a pan-European party (PEP), which leaders of the European Union were then encouraging as a move towards further political integration within Europe. This was a step beyond the temporary international groupings to which UKIP and Farage belonged in the European Parliament. PEPs, in contrast, were envisaged as full political parties, operating well beyond the European Parliament, and crossing the EU's internal state borders. The idea had initially been mooted in the 1992 Maastricht Treaty which added a new article 138a to the Treaty of Rome, as follows: 'Political parties at European level are important as a factor for integration within the Union. They contribute to forming a European awareness and to expressing the political will of the citizens of the Union.' Now, almost twenty years after Maastricht, some EU leaders were arguing that in the European elections of 2014, voters should have two ballot papers – one on which people voted, as usual, for a party from their own country; and another on which they would have a choice between all the pan-European parties that were established. This was seen as a step towards a day when parties which were purely national would be excluded altogether from elections to the European Parliament.

Given the vehement hatred of the Maastricht Treaty expressed by UKIP and Farage over the years, and their rejection of anything that smacked of a more federal Europe, it seems astonishing that they should entertain such an idea, but Farage was all in favour. Tim Congdon reflected the views of many UKIP members in his adamant opposition to joining any PEP. Most UKIP MEPs sided with Farage; a few, including Gerard Batten, backed Congdon.

So *why* was Farage in favour of such a blatantly federalist initiative? Money. The 1997 Treaty of Amsterdam had allowed such parties to be funded from the EU budget. And the European Union was also willing to fund think tanks – or Euro-foundations – affiliated to any PEP. Substantial sums were on offer – more than ten million euros a year to be shared between all the PEPs and their think tanks. Several other parties had already established PEPs and taken advantage of these generous subsidies. Congdon calculated that a PEP roughly based on UKIP's new grouping in the European Parliament – the EFD – might bring in almost a million euros a year (of which UKIP's share might be around €400,000). But UKIP and its fellow parties would be restricted in what they could do with the money – they couldn't use it to promote UKIP within Britain, for example, or to campaign for a referendum on EU membership.

At the UKIP conference in 2010, Congdon had argued that UKIP should roundly reject the idea, and he reckons support for his case was so strong they didn't bother to take a formal vote. Many UKIP members already thought their MEPs had 'gone native' and joined the EU 'gravy train' which the party had so strongly denounced in 1999 and subsequent Euro elections. They were horrified at the stories of expense abuses, high living, their MEPs' failure to channel their profits into the party and the way that Farage and others put their spouses on the parliamentary payroll. And Congdon was strongly influenced in his outlook by talking to Roger Knapman, who, since becoming an MEP in 2004, had grown increasing worried about the behaviour of Farage and his colleagues. The PEP controversy led to 'a bitter and rancorous debate in the party generally', Congdon says, 'but relations between myself and Nigel were never particularly strained'.[15]

Farage pointed out that the dispute had echoes of 1998 when UKIP had decided to ditch its 'Sinn Fein' position of boycotting the European Parliament, and instead exploit the EU resources on offer, to further its cause. Now, Farage argued, 'by creating and joining the right party, we potentially have access to huge sums and we will be the only party to use this money AGAINST the European project. This will be particularly helpful when we have a United Kingdom referendum because this taxpayers' money can be used for this purpose.' And Farage argued that if the EU went ahead with the two ballot papers proposal in the next elections in 2014 (it didn't), it was vital for UKIP to ensure that voters across the EU had a Eurosceptic pan-European party as one of their choices.

Farage then made it personal. 'I am asking you,' he pleaded with activists, 'as you have in the past, to back my political judgement and to vote "Yes".'[16]

But they didn't. In a poll in the summer of 2011, UKIP members rejected the PEP proposal by more than two to one – 5,161 votes to 2,535. It would be the only occasion in almost ten years as official UKIP leader, or twenty years as effective leader, that Nigel Farage was rebuffed by the party's rank and file.

Another of Farage's earliest challenges in this second term as leader came from Nikki Sinclaire, the first-ever transgender British parliamentarian, who'd been elected a UKIP MEP for the West Midlands in 2009. Having failed to beat Pearson for the leadership that year, she had contemplated pitting herself against Farage in 2010, and even drove to Torquay and parked a brightly coloured van outside the conference centre to promote her candidacy. But Sinclaire was disqualified because the previous winter the NEC had expelled her from the party, and she had then stood in the 2010 general election in opposition to an official UKIP candidate.

She had been kicked out following her public attack on Farage's decision to form UKIP's new international group in the European Parliament – the Europe of Freedom and Democracy (EFD). As a trans woman and a lesbian, Sinclaire was outraged to find that Farage had teamed up again with Lega Nord – the Northern League – from Italy. Lega Nord had been expelled from the predecessor group back in 2006 after one of the party's government ministers wore a T-shirt showing one of the controversial Danish cartoons depicting the Prophet Mohammad.

In 2009 Farage had been willing to get back together with Lega Nord, even though the notorious Mario Borghezio was still an MEP, and some leading Lega Nord members had in the past been extremely hostile to gays and lesbians. In 2007, the Lega deputy mayor of Treviso, Giancarlo Gentilini, had declared: 'I will immediately give orders to my forces so that they can carry out an ethnic cleansing of faggots . . . Here in Treviso there is no chance for faggots or the like.'[17] Yet Lega Nord had gained some respectability from now being part of the Italian governing coalition under Silvio Berlusconi.

Other members of the EFD included two MEPs from the Danish People's Party, one of whom, Morten Messerschmidt, had been forced to resign from the Danish Parliament in 2007 after he was spotted in a bar in Copenhagen making Nazi salutes and singing Nazi songs. Sinclaire didn't just object to UKIP's new European bedfellows for their unsavoury views, but also because they were out of kilter with the party on the big political question. Unlike UKIP, all the other parties in the EFD believed in reforming the EU; none believed in withdrawal.

Nikki Sinclaire believes she had also antagonised Farage by showing him and other UKIP MEPs how European parliamentary allowances should be used properly – by employing lots of staff and carrying out research which was directly related to their duties. Many people in UKIP also suspected that Sinclaire was behind a blog called Junius which began in 2008, an extensive operation which often attacked Farage and the leadership, not least over MEPs' allowances and expenses. The blog included dozens of postings every month, as well as the texts of leaked documents. Junius's identity has never been proved, though its author or authors were clearly close to Sinclaire. Curiously, when Sinclaire published her memoirs, *Never Give Up*, in 2013, the imprint was Junius Press, a firm which doesn't seem to have published any other books.[18]

One of the themes which bound David Cameron and Nick Clegg's Coalition together was constitutional reform. In response to the outcry over the MPs' expenses scandal, and the growing view that politicians were out of touch, the Coalition agreed to give the public an occasional say on what was discussed in the Commons. When Sinclaire read the 2010 Coalition Agreement she spotted the pledge, which stemmed from the Conservatives' manifesto, that 'any petition that secures 100,000 signatures' would be eligible for 'formal debate in Parliament'.[19] Sinclaire seized the moment, and in July 2010 launched a petition to hold a referendum on EU membership. Using experience she'd gained working on petitions in California, she took her colourful camper van to more than fifty towns, mainly in her own Euro constituency, the West Midlands. Many UKIP members supported her campaign, including MEPs Mike Nattrass and Trevor Colman, both of whom had also left the international EFD grouping. But Sinclaire couldn't get support from Farage, which was hardly surprising given their mutual animosity. Farage 'refused to sign on several occasions', Sinclaire says, and she claims that his Brussels office even sent a letter to a British voter saying 'such petitions were a waste of time'.[20]

Farage's former adviser in Brussels, Richard North, says the UKIP leader had never really believed in the referendum route towards leaving the EU. He preferred the parliamentary road, North explains, first by using the European Parliament to build up a base of MEPs, later to attract defections among Westminster MPs, and ultimately to split the Tories, with a breakaway Conservative group joining up with a UKIP rump, to get a sufficient majority in the Commons to vote for withdrawal. Sinclaire's assistant Gary

Cartwright says Farage offered her money for her list of petitioners, but she declined.[21]

By the summer of 2011 Sinclaire had secured well over 100,000 names and delivered her petition to Downing Street, where Nattrass and Colman joined her on the doorstep, along with Labour MPs Kate Hoey and Kelvin Hopkins, and the deputy leader of the Democratic Unionists, MP Nigel Dodds.

Petitions rarely make any impact on British politics, but Nikki Sinclaire's proved to be a significant milestone on the road towards Brexit. In line with the new constitutional policy, the Commons Backbench Business Committee granted a full-day debate in late October. David Cameron could have ignored the occasion, of course, and not bothered to whip his MPs, but the danger was that Labour might have abstained and the motion would have slipped through with the backing of Tory Eurosceptics. Parliament would then have been seen – officially at least – to back an EU referendum. Instead, Cameron chose to confront the issue head-on by whipping Conservative MPs against a referendum, and he even got the date of the debate changed to allow himself and the foreign secretary William Hague to attend and speak. Cameron's decisions may have been a serious mistake.

'In the end, we won,' Cameron relates in his memoirs, 'but eighty-one Conservative MPs rebelled.' More than a quarter of his parliamentary party had defied the government whips, despite their strenuous efforts. At the time it was the largest ever backbench revolt over Europe by Tory MPs. 'My tactics may have been cack-handed on this occasion,' Cameron added:

> but I believed that preventing the government from being under-mined by a badly timed and dangerously drafted motion was in the national interest.
>
> In the event there was little doubt that the 'PM versus party' narrative was as bad as, if not worse than, a landslide defeat on an insignificant Thursday motion. As Commons victories go, it was as pyrrhic as they get. And it showed the extent to which the ground was moving beneath us.[22]

It was a historic moment for Eurosceptics, a huge step in establishing support among elected politicians. 'Outside on College Green, broadcast journalists were interviewing all the usual suspects,' wrote Nikki Sinclaire:

> I was exultant, feeling that we'd created history. But I was astonished to see Nigel Farage, of all people, ranting to a TV reporter about how remarkable an indication of public feeling this was . . . So I pushed myself alongside him and in firm but softly spoken tones pointed out that since he had previously refused to sign he might wish to do so now. I shoved the paperwork into his hands and with a camera pointed at him, he scrawled his name.[23]

The debate and vote were good news for Nigel Farage and UKIP, but in his refusal to support Sinclaire's petition at an earlier stage he had missed a golden opportunity to claim some credit for a historic vote. The UKIP leader can't have enjoyed being embarrassed by Sinclaire in front of a television audience, exposed as something of a hypocrite, and publicly forced to sign at the very last minute. Things had changed markedly from the time, twelve years before, when Sinclaire was a young UKIP activist and Nigel Farage had shown genuine sympathy over the appalling rape she suffered. In subsequent years relations between the two would get progressively worse, with dramatic consequences.

Sinclaire had been one of UKIP's first two women MEPs, and Farage had quickly fallen out with both of them. After disappointing local election results in 2011, Marta Andreasen, the former European Commission whistleblower, called on Farage to resign, even though he had initially fixed her up with a UKIP seat. Farage publicly retaliated, saying that Andreasen didn't know what she was talking about, whereupon his MEP threatened to sue him.

Andreasen had a fair point about UKIP's election performance. It took Farage and his party a surprisingly long time to take advantage of the rapidly changing politics of the early 2010s, and to replace the Liberal Democrats as the main party of protest. In the five parliamentary by-elections held in England in the two years after the 2010 election, UKIP's results continued to be unremarkable:

13 Jan 2011	Oldham East & Saddleworth	5.8%	4th
3 March 2011	Barnsley Central	12.2%	2nd
5 May 2011	Leicester South	2.9%	4th
15 Dec 2011	Feltham & Heston	5.5%	4th
29 March 2012	Bradford West	3.3%	5th

The average vote was just under 6 per cent – scarcely better than UKIP had performed in the run-up to the 2010 election – and only 4.4 per cent if you exclude the exceptional result in Barnsley (the first time UKIP came second in a Westminster contest). Then, suddenly, in November 2012, the party began to take off, in six by-elections held on two separate days:

15 Nov 2012	Manchester Central	4.5%	4th
	Corby	14.3%	3rd
	Cardiff South	6.1%	5th
29 Nov 2012	Rotherham	21.7%	2nd
	Middlesbrough	11.8%	2nd
	Croydon North	5.7%	3rd

The 14.3 per cent in Corby broke the record set in Barnsley, and then, a fortnight later, UKIP came second again, in Rotherham, with a remarkable 21.7 per cent. The vote in Rotherham had been boosted by anger that the local Labour council had taken three foster children away from a couple's care, because they were UKIP supporters.

The UK Independence Party was starting to profit from rising anxiety about two developments which increasingly dominated EU politics. First, the Greek debt crisis, which was spreading to other southern European states; and second, the crisis of illegal migration across the Mediterranean and through southern Europe on a huge scale following the Arab Spring. And while UKIP was finally exploiting the dramatic fall in popularity of the Liberal Democrats, equally significant was a collapse in support for the British National Party.

The BNP had never really recovered from the highly controversial performance by Nick Griffin on BBC *Question Time* in the autumn of 2009, which attracted more than 8 million viewers who saw him fare badly. He had none of Farage's charm as a broadcaster, or his ability to use humour and sometimes to laugh at himself, and the programme exposed many of the BNP's extreme policies. Griffin's party actually did slightly better than UKIP in 2010, measured in terms of votes per seat contested, but the BNP fell rapidly in the polls thereafter and tore itself apart through bitter internal warfare which eventually led to Griffin's expulsion. The BNP was never again the force it had been in the mid-noughties. Nigel Farage would later declare that seeing off the BNP was one of his greatest achievements, but it hadn't been easy. 'I destroyed the British National Party,' he told *Russia Today* in 2016.

UKIP's electoral success, especially in winning over BNP voters in the north, was partly thanks to a deliberate strategy drawn up by its latest deputy leader, the Liverpudlian Paul Nuttall. UKIP campaigns now focused more on immigration and rather less on Europe, though the two issues were closely linked because of the EU's Freedom of Movement policy which made it much harder for British governments to control immigration numbers (or meet the Conservatives' stated target of getting net immigration below 100,000). Until around 1998 the migration flows in and out of Britain had roughly balanced each other out. Now, immigration into Britain was at record levels – over 600,000 a year – about a third of whom came from the EU, and since 2004 the annual *net* immigration figure – allowing for departures – hovered at around 250,000.

The more UKIP was successful, the more Farage and his colleagues came under media scrutiny. Despite the promise made in 2009 that MEPs would regularly publish their expense claims online – following similar pledges in 1999 and 2004 – there was limited progress. British politics had entered a new era of openness and transparency, with Westminster MPs suddenly finding that minute details of their expense claims, including receipts for tiny items such as bottles of milk, were published online. But for the European Parliament it was still up to the individual MEPs, and Farage lagged behind his colleagues. Most other MEPs from the South East had published their claims, but strangely Farage's statements ceased in June 2010. The details had not been put online, Farage's spokeswoman Annabelle Fuller told a local newspaper group in March 2012, because the receipts had been 'lost somewhere in transportation' between his office and his accountant. He also continued to employ his wife Kirsten, though he insisted, 'There is "no feathering of nests" in the Farage household, I can assure you.'[25]

Farage knew that real progress outside European elections meant overcoming the first-past-the-post voting system, which would be extremely difficult. Hence UKIP support for a Yes vote in the May 2011 referendum – initiated by the Lib Dem side of the Coalition – on introducing the Alternative Vote, a proposal defeated by a margin of more than two to one. Farage had also been studying closely how the Liberal Democrats had made progress before 2010, and how insurgents elsewhere made breakthroughs. 'First-past-the-post is devilishly hard,' he told a Conservative activist website:

> And for us to win two things have to happen. First we have to do what the Reform Party of Canada did and that is to win a by-election. Second we have to win clusters of district and county council seats. The Lib Dems built up from about a dozen seats in Parliament to about 60 by building up local centres of excellence.[26]

The strategy had first been tried in the Norwich North by-election in 2009 when UKIP polled a creditable 11.8 per cent after a campaign in which activists were told to concentrate on promoting the candidate, and to stress immigration as an issue. But the Reform Party of Canada's by-election success had been back in 1989, and the party had benefited from its support being concentrated almost entirely in the west of Canada, while UKIP's support was more evenly spread across England and Wales. Whereas UKIP's early base had been in southern England, after 2011 the party was suddenly making inroads in predominantly white, working-class seats of old heavy industries, such as Barnsley, Rotherham and Middlesbrough.

By late 2012, while both major parties were worried by UKIP, David Cameron felt especially under the cosh. He knew he was losing not just voters to Farage's party, but Tory members, activists and donors, while the case for EU withdrawal was gaining ground among his MPs, and even some of his Cabinet.

15

BLOOMBERG AND BLOOM

Early on Wednesday 23 January 2013, Nigel Farage arrived at UKIP's office in Mayfair to welcome some breakfast guests. The prime minister's motorcade, meanwhile, was snaking its way through the rush-hour traffic to the headquarters of the Bloomberg Media Group in the City of London. Farage had invited a group of journalists to watch the broadcast of a hotly anticipated event. David Cameron was about to deliver what was probably the most important speech of his six-year premiership – what became known as his Bloomberg speech.

Despite the power of his office, the prime minister was in a bind. Under the Coalition's new law, the next general election could not take place until May 2015, and until then his partners, the Liberal Democrats, effectively had a veto on European policy. All Cameron could do was make promises about what the Conservatives would deliver if they won a majority in 2015. That morning at Bloomberg he made a pledge which, he later claimed, he'd thought more about than any other decision of his time in government.

> Simply asking the British people to carry on accepting a European settlement over which they have had little choice is a path to ensuring that when the question is finally put – and at some stage it will have to be – it is much more likely that the British people will reject the EU. That is why I am in favour of a referendum. I believe in confronting this issue – shaping it, leading the debate. Not simply hoping a difficult situation will go away . . .

His party's next manifesto, Cameron vowed, would include a promise that the next outright Conservative government would broker a
new and improved deal between the UK and the EU, which would
be based around membership of the single market:

> And when we have negotiated that new settlement, we will give
> the British people a referendum with a very simple in or out choice.
> To stay in the EU on these new terms; or come out altogether.
>
> It will be an in-out referendum.
>
> Legislation will be drafted before the next election. And if a
> Conservative government is elected we will introduce the enab-
> ling legislation immediately and pass it by the end of that year.
> And we will complete this negotiation and hold this referendum
> within the first half of the next parliament.
>
> It is time for the British people to have their say. It is time to
> settle this European question in British politics.[1]

Cameron's pledge was a high-stakes strategy, opposed by his friend
and chancellor George Osborne, who feared it could be a massive
own goal. It had been well trailed in advance. Nigel Farage, beam-
ing and in jolly spirits, provided his breakfast guests with a running
commentary as they crowded round UKIP's TV. Even before
Cameron delivered his historic words, he tried to scotch suggestions
that the PM had got one over UKIP. 'Frankly, the genie is out of the
bottle,' he told reporters. 'Once the "out" word has been mentioned,
it is going to be very difficult for the Prime Minister, or [Labour
leader] Ed Miliband, or anybody else, to put it back in.'[2]

In his memoirs David Cameron denies that he was driven 'predominantly by electoral considerations', and that he was 'spooked'
into making the speech 'by the rise of the UK Independence Party':

> UKIP's role in the formulation of the referendum pledge tends to
> be overstated . . . I started seriously mulling over the possibility
> of a referendum in January 2012. At that point UKIP was still a
> small force. Polling showed it regularly on less than 5 per cent,
> and it was less popular than the Lib Dems.

Yet I did see the attraction of UKIP to Tory voters as an indi-
cation of public feeling. And I also thought that if UKIP came
first in the May 2014 EU parliamentary elections (when they
would receive a higher profile and were more likely to perform
well) the pressure to pledge a referendum would be too great to
resist . . . That was undoubtedly an additional incentive to move
before being forced to do so.[3]

Almost immediately, there would be an electoral test of whether
the Bloomberg pledge would halt UKIP's momentum. At the start
of February, the former Liberal Democrat Cabinet minister Chris
Huhne had to resign his seat after suddenly pleading guilty to per-
verting the course of justice over a speeding case from 2003, in
which he'd persuaded his wife to claim she'd been driving their
car so she could take his penalty points. It meant another English
by-election, this time in Eastleigh in Hampshire, the first seat Nigel
Farage had ever fought, in the 1994 by-election. 'The idea of standing again has its romance,' Farage said, but he wanted to concentrate
on the local elections in May.

Nonetheless, UKIP fought one of the best campaigns in its
history, with an impressive candidate in Diane James, a 53-year-
old former Conservative from Surrey. James was articulate and
engaging and could easily have passed as a Tory minister. But she
wasn't Farage's ideal choice, it seems. His press officer Annabelle
Fuller, who was very close to him, warned colleagues by email: 'I
understand from the man who knows best we've been lumbered
with an utter bitch who is Marta Mk 2', a clear reference to the
UKIP MEP Marta Andreasen who had fallen out badly with Farage
(and would soon defect to the Conservatives).[4] Farage had warned
Fuller that it would be difficult to overturn Diane James's selection, however, since she got 90 per cent of the vote when the local
party picked her.

Again UKIP went big on immigration, with EU membership
being blamed. Most of the media were slow to notice the party's
steadily rising figures in the polls, and journalists didn't take the
contest seriously until the final few days when it suddenly looked

to be a three-way fight between the Lib Dems, who ran the local council, the Tories and UKIP.

The result was astonishing, in two ways. First, despite their national unpopularity, the Liberal Democrats retained the seat with a majority of 1,771. But even more startling, only a month after Cameron's historic referendum pledge, UKIP, and not the Conservatives, came second. They gained 27.8 per cent of the vote, 6 per cent more than in any previous Westminster election, and the nearest UKIP had yet come to winning a Commons seat. The Conservative candidate was a thousand votes behind. Polls suggested that UKIP more than doubled its support during the three-and-a-half-week-long campaign, steadily eating into the Tory vote. UKIP were up against the formidable local machine of the Liberal Democrats, who'd built up their resources over almost two decades since the 1994 by-election. The Lib Dems had been quick to call the contest, and many observers reckoned that, had the campaign lasted a few more days, UKIP would have won instead.

The result also suggested that David Cameron's Bloomberg speech had no effect on stemming growing support for Nigel Farage's party. Far from quenching the thirst of Eurosceptics, it had only given added impetus to those demanding the UK get out of Europe.

Ten weeks later, for the first time, UKIP made a real impact in the local elections, which were largely confined to the shire councils. The haul of 147 councillors was tiny compared to the total number of 2,374 seats up for grabs. Much more important, UKIP got 19.9 per cent of the overall vote, and psephologists projected UKIP's performance as being the equivalent of 22 per cent in a general election. This was serious progress for a party which, as Cameron points out in his memoirs, had been on about 5 per cent only sixteen months before. And on the same day, UKIP came second in the South Shields by-election in the North East. 'I can't believe it,' Farage said as he toured Westminster TV studios, and enjoyed a pint in the nearby Marquis of Granby. It was more than he 'dreamt possible', he said:

I've had so many disappointments. I thought I was the patron saint of lost causes . . . This is a real sea-change in British politics . . .

It's a fascinating day for British politics. Something has changed here. I know that everyone would like to say that it's just a little short-term, stamp your feet protest – it isn't. There's something really fundamental that has happened here . . . Give us a by-election in a marginal seat and we will win it.[5]

The gloom in Downing Street deepened with internal advice to David Cameron saying the same – that UKIP would probably win a by-election by the end of the parliament, and come first in the 2014 European contest, exactly the threat which the Bloomberg pledge had been intended to see off. But the Mayor of London, Boris Johnson, urged Cameron and other Conservatives not to panic about UKIP's sudden success. It suggested Conservative values were 'broadly popular', and Farage had always struck him as a 'rather engaging geezer', Johnson said. 'We Tories look at him – with his pint and cigar and sense of humour – and we instinctively recognise someone who is fundamentally indistinguishable from us.'[6] The admiration was mutual. 'Boris is obviously a fascinating character,' said Farage. 'One thinks that his instincts are closer to ours than they are to Mr Cameron's.'[7] Years later, Farage would claim to have 'been a Boris-sceptic for years': having observed Johnson reporting from Brussels in the 1990s, he was never convinced by his apparent Euroscepticism. 'I honestly, genuinely don't think that he ever really believed in these things.'[8]

The 2013 local elections – the first time UKIP had taken such elections seriously – also provided the party with their first ward-by-ward guide as to where their strength lay on the ground. The answer was much of eastern England, where immigration from the EU was making a sizeable impact. UKIP was now the second biggest party, and therefore the official opposition, on three shire councils – in Kent (where it won 17 seats); Lincolnshire (16) and Norfolk (15). The party had done especially well in the Boston and Skegness constituency in Lincolnshire, an area which had seen large numbers of migrants from eastern Europe; and the seats of North and South Thanet in far east Kent, where people often witnessed immigration – legal and illegal – across the Strait of Dover.

The ward-by-ward picture was a huge step in Farage's new strategy of trying to emulate the Lib Dems in building support from the grassroots. But despite the electoral advance, many of UKIP's new councillors were shocked and slightly embarrassed to win, having only stood on the assumption that they wouldn't, and quite a few would go on to have poor attendance records, and quickly resign their seats, or defect to other parties. For Farage, however, the results were a huge boost.

When UKIP held its annual conference in September 2013, at the Methodist Central Hall in Westminster, there was high excitement and a sense that they had finally made a breakthrough. After its recent progress, UKIP should aim to come first in the European elections the following May, Farage declared: 'Let's make May 22nd our referendum on EU membership. Let us send an earthquake through Westminster. Let us stand up and say: Give us our country back!'

Two weeks later, Iain Dale placed Farage second in his annual list of the 'Top 100 most influential Right-wingers' (up from seventeenth place in 2012) only behind David Cameron. He was just ahead of Theresa May and Boris Johnson.

Yet, in truth, his speech to his annual conference was far from vintage Farage: he seemed to be sweating under the lights and not his usual ebullient self. He may perhaps have been distracted by a film on Channel 4 the night before about his time at Dulwich College, and extracts from the letter from the teacher Chloe Deakin containing comments by colleagues that Farage was a 'racist' and a 'fascist'. When I tried to doorstep Farage outside the hall, he got very angry and called me 'despicable'.

That lunchtime came further bad news. Farage's Brussels flatmate and old drinking pal Godfrey Bloom had agreed to address a champagne reception on the subject of 'women in politics'. Champagne and feminism seemed a risky mix, given Bloom's reputation, and so I went along to see if he would say anything newsworthy. Only a few weeks before, Bloom had caused a major outcry with an attack on Britain's foreign aid budget, when he said it was stupid to give a billion pounds a month to 'Bongo-bongo land'.

At some point in the reception a woman said something like 'None of us clean behind the fridge', a jibe at the controversy Bloom had caused in 2004 when he first went to the European Parliament.

Bloom then heckled 'Well, you're all sluts' – clearly meant as a joke, though an unwise one given his previous record. And the audience laughed. Before long, however, sensing the dangers, Annabelle Fuller sidled over to Bloom and gently eased him out of the gathering. I followed them, and out on the street Bloom was asked by Sky reporter Darren McCaffrey about the 'sluts' remark. Bloom tried to explain, while Fuller suggested McCaffrey was perhaps getting mixed up between the word 'slut' and 'slag'. 'You sad little man,' Bloom chided McCaffrey as the reporter persisted.

I then asked Bloom about a different matter – the UKIP conference programme. The front cover was a collage of hundreds of tiny photos, including many of the people elected as UKIP councillors the previous May. It was hard to spot any who weren't white.

'Mr Bloom,' I asked, 'what do you make of the front cover of the conference brochure with no Black faces on it?'

'What a racist comment is that!' Bloom replied with apparent anger. 'How dare you. That's an appalling thing to say. You're picking people out for the colour of their skin. You disgust me. Get out of my way.'

It was hard to tell if Bloom's anger was genuine, or just an act to rebuff my questions. I followed him down the street.

'You are an appalling man,' Bloom said. 'You, sir, are a racist!'

'Why am I a racist for saying there aren't any Black people?' I asked. With that, Bloom grabbed the programme from my hands.

'You've checked out the colour of people's faces,' he said with high indignation, and then he rapped me over the head with the brochure, before dropping it on the ground.

'Disgraceful! Disgraceful!' he added, before Annabelle Fuller shuffled him away into a taxi.

Within minutes, the incident was being broadcast repeatedly on the BBC and Sky news channels. When Nigel Farage got to hear of it, he was furious. 'Hitting Michael Crick over the head? Tempting!' he joked. 'I can understand that. I wouldn't do it.' As for Bloom's remark about 'sluts'? 'It sounds appalling. It sounds wholly and highly inappropriate. Clearly it was his attempt at a joke . . . It sounds very, very stupid indeed . . . I don't run the discipline of the party. The party chairman does but, you know, there comes a point when people do cross too far over a line.'[9]

Having seen the television coverage, Farage was even angrier. UKIP had put huge effort and expense into organising its annual conference, and over recent months Farage had gone to great lengths to rid his party of anyone who might be perceived as sexist, racist or otherwise embarrassing. Bloom 'dynamited months and months of hard work', one Farage adviser says.

That afternoon Farage held a crisis meeting with his chairman Steve Crowther, a retired former journalist from Devon always known for his loyalty to the leader. They decided Bloom should be suspended from his post, and have the whip withdrawn as a UKIP MEP, before facing a disciplinary enquiry. Later that afternoon Farage returned to the conference hall to explain the decision, unable to hide his rage over Bloom's behaviour:

> I've had very sharp words with him about it. There is no media coverage of this conference, it's gone, it's dead, it's all about Godfrey hitting a journalist and using an unpleasant four-letter word. We can't put up with it and . . . we cannot have any one individual – however fun or flamboyant or entertaining or amusing they are – we cannot have any one individual destroying UKIP's national conference, and that is what he's done today.[10]

It was a highly symbolic – Nigel Farage's Falstaff moment. 'I know thee not old man', as the newly crowned Henry V told his old drinking and whoring friend Sir John Falstaff in Henry IV, Part 2. 'Presume not that I am the thing I was.' Now Farage disowned his bar companion in the wider interests of showing decisive leadership. Farage had fallen out with numerous colleagues in the past, but never before had he discarded someone so close – Godfrey Bloom, in fact, was probably his nearest male friend in UKIP. The next day, a calmer Farage said Bloom's recent remarks had been part of his 'mid-1960s army officers' mess sense of humour. It doesn't translate well into modern Britain. But I honestly don't think there was any malice in what he said.'[11]

At the time, Godfrey Bloom didn't seem that bothered. He claimed he'd only discovered he'd been sacked as a UKIP MEP when he saw his friend on TV the following morning. 'Nigel told me via television this was happening,' Bloom explained a few weeks later. 'Fair enough. That's what he wants to do. He's the leader. I'm fired.'[12]

The disciplinary hearing never happened. Four days later, Bloom announced he wouldn't seek to get the parliamentary whip back, as he had 'felt for some time now that the "New UKIP" is not really right for me'.[13] Bloom later said he thought of resigning before, having become increasingly worried by UKIP's stance on immigration. His father-in-law, he told people, had been a Polish immigrant.

Of the thirteen UKIP MEPs elected in 2009, five had now gone: Nikki Sinclaire, expelled from UKIP in 2010; David Campbell Bannerman, who rejoined the Conservatives; Marta Andreasen, who joined the Tories in February 2013 after Cameron's Bloomberg speech; Mike Nattrass, who left in September 2013; and now Bloom. Campbell Bannerman, Sinclaire and Nattrass were all past leadership candidates.

To lose five MEPs out of thirteen was unfortunate, and even worse than the 2004–9 Parliament when the attrition rate was four from twelve. On the plus side, Farage had gained Roger Helmer, an MEP who defected from the Conservatives.

A year after quitting the party, in 2014, Bloom went full blast with his criticism of Farage, in an interview with Andrew Neil on the BBC:

I know you chaps seem to buy this 'Good old Nigel in the pub with the pint' image, but believe me, he's nothing like that. He's a very ruthless operator, and even a hint of criticism from anybody, and you have your membership card chopped up, and that's how it's been for some years . . . The party was rebranded with a new constitution five years ago. It was rebranded Nigel Farage's UKIP, or the Purple Army, and that's how it is . . . It's a very autocratic organisation, and there's no room for criticism.[14]

It's a sad story. He and Farage continued as flatmates, and Bloom claimed they had a pint together and were still friends, but it wasn't really true. The two chums, brought together by their shared passion for military history, and who enjoyed much good food and drink in each other's company, drifted apart. 'There are two Nigel Farages really,' Bloom says:

The Nigel Farage pre-2010 when it was fun; it was a bit laddish – drinks, dinners, lunches. Nigel what you saw is what you got – a beery, smoking, bonhomie dude. After 2010, Nigel became totally introverted, and to an extent it stopped being fun. The plane crash had a big impact, I believe. He became more difficult to deal with. Half of us left because he became a bit of a bully and was no longer fun to work with. Babies went out with the bathwater. UKIP became politically correct. You couldn't discuss non-EU immigration. If you didn't toe the party line completely, your branch was closed down. Nigel went to the Stalin School of Management. Post-2010, there was no democracy in the party at all. I was pressing for each region to elect a member of the NEC. 'No, that's not good,' he said. 'I can't control it.' Some regions felt they were not being represented, and being used just to distribute leaflets . . . Mood swings, depressions, anti-social behaviour all came after the 2010 crash. Somebody might make an observation at a meeting, and he'd say: 'Well you would say that, cos you're a wanker!' You don't treat people like that if you expect loyalty. He wouldn't do that before the crash. We were all having fun then.

Bloom recalls the inscription 'To my best friend in UKIP' in a copy of Farage's 2010 memoirs, and how the UKIP leader would regularly stay with the Blooms at their home in East Yorkshire. Now? 'I haven't spoken to him for years', Bloom says. 'Nigel had been looking for the opportunity to get rid of me for years. He sees that if somebody else in UKIP is getting popularity and on TV, it was taking away from him. Which is why nobody of any stature came out of UKIP.'[15]

In the meantime, Nigel Farage faced problems with yet another maverick whose UKIP career he had initiated and encouraged, and who also had quite a profile of their own.

It took a long time for Christine and Neil Hamilton to respond to Nigel Farage's overtures over lunch at Shepherd's in 2002. Nine years, in fact. Instead, they rebuilt their bank balances by developing their careers as media celebrities, with appearances on TV light entertainment shows, and at the Edinburgh fringe festival. Neil twice won *Ready Steady Cook*, while Christine even appeared in pantomime. Apart from the occasional speaking engagement or trip to by-elections, politics took a back seat.

But in 2011, again at Farage's invitation, Neil Hamilton spoke at the UKIP conference in Eastbourne. No one seemed to care about the cash-for-questions scandal, or perhaps they'd forgotten. It was a sign of Hamilton's popularity that during a brief BBC interview in Eastbourne, he was interrupted three times by well-wishers who wanted to shake his hand. When Hamilton put his name forward for election to the National Executive, Farage seconded him. He topped the poll with 61 per cent of the vote, well beyond his rivals. Farage said he was 'very pleased', adding that Hamilton's 'experience and wisdom' would 'contribute significantly' to the party.[16]

Neil Hamilton says it was while sitting on the UKIP NEC that he first noticed Farage's ability to fall out with people. 'He would arrive late for meetings, ignore the agenda, say something abusive about the NEC, attack them for not doing enough, talk about how he was working himself to the bone, and say we should all be raising more money.'[17]

Hamilton approached Farage about standing at the coming European elections, the suggestion the UKIP leader had made at lunch almost a decade before. The trouble was that Nigel Farage had really been directing his then overtures towards Christine Hamilton, whom he regarded as potentially a much more attractive catch for his party, less tainted by the cash-for-questions affair. And in trying to woo Christine, Farage had to keep Neil sweet. But although Christine usually accompanied her husband to political engagements, she always made it clear that she would never be a frontline politician.

Hamilton says Farage professed to back him being a European candidate, but somehow he didn't get through the process which whittled applicants down to 100 names. 'I remember it as clear as today,' Hamilton recalls:

> Steve Crowther rang up and said: 'We're going to announce the list tomorrow.' 'Jolly good,' I said. Then there was a pause. 'And you're not on it.' And I said: 'But if you look at my record, my speaking abilities and so on, why am I not on it?' He didn't give a reason. It was clear that Farage didn't want me on his list of 100. It was perfectly clear Farage didn't want me competing for the limelight.[18]

Neil Hamilton's omission caused a big row on the National Executive. And Hamilton was a much more formidable adversary than many of those whom Farage had squashed in the past. As an MP for fourteen years, and a whip and junior minister for four, Hamilton was probably the most experienced politician UKIP had ever had (and perhaps the only UKIP member ever to have sat in the EU Council of Ministers). To placate Hamilton and his allies, Farage suggested that he be made deputy chairman of UKIP, and employed full time as director of the party's 2014 European campaign. Farage knew that Hamilton had quite a following – perhaps only second to himself among activists – and it would only cause problems if the row festered. Yet Farage's fear was that if Hamilton was a candidate the UKIP campaign would be dominated by historic brown envelopes, and Hamilton's feud with Mohamed Al-Fayed would be dredged up again by the press. And, indeed, it would have been.

Hamilton claims, however, that Farage's decision was purely personal. 'He has to be the bride at every wedding, the corpse at every funeral, the baby at every christening,' he says, quoting Alice Roosevelt Longworth's comment on her presidential father Teddy Roosevelt:

It was perfectly clear that he is a sociopathic narcissist with a mes-
siah complex. He has to be the centre of attention at all times and
has to be able to impose his will. Anybody who might disagree
or who needed their arms twisting is not wanted on the voyage,
if they are of an intractable disposition.[19]

Not surprisingly, Neil Hamilton's new job as UKIP campaign director did not work out. Problems first surfaced publicly at the party
spring conference in Torquay in 2014, less than three months before
the hotly anticipated European vote. Farage was asked at a press
conference whether Hamilton was an embarrassment to UKIP given
the cash-for-questions affair. Hamilton was standing at the back of
the room and so heard when a much-irritated Farage was then asked
whether he saw Hamilton being the 'new face' of the new UKIP. 'No,
he's the backroom boy. He's the campaign manager,' Farage replied.[20]

'I nearly went into orbit,' says Hamilton. A quick-thinking BBC
reporter got an immediate interview with him outside the room,
where Hamilton calmly explained he was sometimes 'front of house',
having, for example, done three public meetings the previous week:
'That doesn't sound like a back room.' Back in the press conference,
when Farage was told about Hamilton's quick response, the UKIP
leader grew even more irritated. 'He's not a candidate. I've answered
that already, thank you.' Farage tried to solicit another question, but
reporters pressed him. 'This is really very boring,' an angry Farage
replied. 'He's not a candidate – that's the point I'm making . . . He's
not a candidate. End. You're obsessed with it, but I'm bored with it,
and I'm not answering any more questions on that subject.'[21]

The incident would only have confirmed Farage's fears that
Hamilton and his past would embarrass the party, just at the
moment they planned to top the poll in the European elections.
And he was further upset the following day when Hamilton gave
an interview to the *Observer* in which he was asked about a pledge
by the Yorkshire multi-millionaire Paul Sykes to fund the European
campaign. Neil Hamilton couldn't hide his concern that Sykes had
yet to cough up any funds. 'So far we haven't seen the colour of his
money,' Hamilton remarked. 'This spending needs to be committed.

Obviously it would have been much easier if the money were in UKIP's bank account and I could plan sensibly for the campaign far enough in advance . . . It's been a big problem for us in fundraising and elsewhere, as people say, "You don't need my money, because Sykes has signed a big cheque."[22]

Paul Sykes was furious. He contacted Farage and threatened to withdraw funding altogether, and Hamilton admits his throwaway 'colour of his money' remark had been foolish. Farage sacked him as campaign director, which came as something of a relief since Hamilton hadn't found it easy working with the UKIP leader.

'Farage is a chaotic influence on any campaign,' Hamilton recalls.

He would do things without telling me. I came to realise that Nigel and organisation don't go together. He is a dynamic force and has the capacity to get publicity for himself, but never able to put a team together to capitalise on 'dynamic Nigel'. All he wanted was his acolytes providing him with the essentials. A security team like he was Vladimir Putin, to make him look important.

He would ring out-of-the-blue at eight o'clock in the morning without even saying 'It's Nigel.' Then: 'What the hell are you doing?' And he'd go on about some rumour that was completely false.

So I was finding it increasingly impossible to do the job. He was actually a toxic influence at getting anything done. He meddled in minutiae. You couldn't communicate with him by email because he dealt with everybody on his phone. He never read emails. This was a revelation to me.

He spends the whole day on the phone. There's no record of who he spoke to or what was decided. There's no structure.[23]

Neil and Christine Hamilton believe Farage deliberately avoids using email or writing letters so there's no paper trail and things can be denied or disavowed. Hamilton recalls how Farage never used a laptop on a train, or worked on the computers in the UKIP HQ in Brook's Mews in Mayfair. It was a pretty 'low-grade set-up', he recalls. The building was in poor condition and UKIP had to share corridors with workmen while they were drilling away and creating noise and dust. Farage had designated one room as a 'bedroom', not to sleep or for sexual shenanigans, but so that he could smoke.

Despite being sacked as campaign director, Hamilton remained in post as UKIP deputy chairman and for once Farage was constrained because the former Tory MP had significant support among the party rank-and-file, and on the increasingly vocal NEC. 'That was always his Achilles heel,' Hamilton says.[24]

Hamilton wasn't giving up the fight. Having been blocked from becoming an MEP, he would seek selection as a Westminster candidate instead, which was theoretically in the gift of the local parties.

His first choice was Boston and Skegness, where UKIP had several councillors, and which was one of the party's top targets for 2015. Hamilton visited the Lincolnshire seat several times, did lots of canvassing, quite a few events and interviews with the local media, and would probably have been picked by the local branch. But Steve Crowther, working on behalf of Farage, again put a stop to it. Hamilton claims he got a promise from Farage, however, that he wouldn't be stopped for the next seat.

That was South Basildon and East Thurrock in Essex, another strong UKIP prospect. In October 2014 the original candidate, local UKIP councillor Kerry Smith, was sacked by party HQ because, it's thought, of racist and homophobic remarks he'd made in the past. That left the way open for Hamilton. But only hours before the local party was due to meet, and looked set to pick Hamilton, the process was interrupted by UKIP's new communications director Paul Lambert, a former BBC producer, known to everyone as 'Gobby' because of his past habit of shouting loud questions to ministers in Downing Street. Lambert rang me and then emailed a copy of a letter UKIP headquarters had that afternoon sent to Hamilton raising various queries about his expenses. It was an obvious attempt to destroy Hamilton's chances in Essex that night.

Suddenly and simultaneously, Farage had also decided that Kerry Smith was now acceptable after all, and he was placed on the Basildon shortlist at the last moment.[25] Neil Hamilton denied the expenses allegations, but by the time he got to Basildon he saw which way the wind was blowing and felt he had no choice but to stand aside in favour of Smith.

'It was an example of Farage's complete unscrupulousness,' says Hamilton. 'Having first got rid of Kerry Smith as an embarrassment to the party, he then exhumes Kerry Smith as a way to stop me.'[26]

Smith didn't last long. Three days after his second selection, the *Mail on Sunday* published details of many offensive remarks he'd made in the past, including the phrase 'fucking disgusting old poofters'.[27] Smith, too, was forced to stand down.

At the next UKIP NEC meeting Hamilton says he exploded at Farage and at Andrew Reid, the latest party treasurer. Reid was a wealthy lawyer and part-time judge from Mill Hill in north London who bred and trained racehorses in his spare time, and let part of his offices in Mayfair for UKIP to use as their headquarters (and which he'd previously let to Boris Johnson for his campaign for London mayor). One of several characters in this story who hovered between the Conservatives and UKIP, Reid had become a close adviser to Farage, and clearly enjoyed his reputation as a behind-the-scenes fixer.

'I was absolutely furious,' says Hamilton, 'and did my speech standing up and let rip at him [Reid] and Farage. I made clear what had been done to me, and the absolute perfidy practised by Farage. By this stage UKIP had become very fractious. Nobody had behaved like this towards Farage before. Nothing more happened over the expenses allegations. They were completely untrue.'[28]

The feud between Farage and Hamilton was typical of so many of the UKIP leader's battles in the past, and illustrated so many of his ruthless ways of operating. But it also illustrated a growing discipline in Farage, a determination that as the party tried to make further electoral breakthroughs, and ahead of a possible EU referendum, he had to be single-minded and ruthless. The UKIP high command had to prevent the media being distracted by eye-catching mavericks such as Bloom and Hamilton.

Bloom might now be out of the picture, but Neil Hamilton was by no means finished. He would remain a headache for Nigel Farage – not just politically, but personally too.

16

A WEAKNESS FOR WOMEN

There were only about forty-five MEPs in the chamber when it happened.

On 12 March 2014, European parliamentarians were in Strasbourg to hear the president of the Commission, José Manuel Barroso, discuss the European Council meeting due the following week. He was followed by short speeches from leaders of each of the main parliamentary groups, including Farage on behalf of the EFD.

'The European dream is crumbling, absolutely crumbling,' Farage told MEPs. Over the previous five years the EU had made two big mistakes, he said – extending the Eurozone to Mediterranean countries and extending the free movement of people to those from eastern and southern Europe. 'The electors are going to have a chance in seventy-two days' time to give their verdict,' he concluded. 'I suspect the next European Parliament will be very much more exciting than this one has been this morning.'

More exciting? He'd spoken too soon.

Nikki Sinclaire, who'd been elected for UKIP in 2009, but became an independent MEP a year later, then signalled she wanted to ask Farage what's called a 'blue card' question. Procedurally, Farage had to give his consent, which he did, though he would surely never have done so had he known what was about to hit him:

Mr Farage, with unemployment still a problem across Europe, and indeed the UK, does Mr Farage think it's a fair use of tax-payers' money – namely his secretarial allowance – not only to

employ his wife, Kirsten, but his former mistress Annabelle
Fuller? Is this a responsible use of taxpayers' money, Mr Farage?

Her question took just nineteen seconds, and she sat down to a
smattering of applause. The president of the Parliament Martin
Schulz asked the EFD leader if he wanted to respond. 'I do not see
any need to answer that at all,' an embarrassed Farage replied. 'Oh
my goodness,' Schulz remarked before moving on.[1]

Sinclaire had long been concerned with how UKIP MEPs used
their parliamentary allowances; indeed, her constant agitation on
the issue, and efforts to set a good example, had contributed to the
breakdown in her relations with Farage. But there may also have
been other factors behind her outburst, and having bided her time
before publicly raising the matter, creating maximum damage was
perhaps one of them. Sinclaire planned to stand in the European
elections for the We Demand a Referendum Now party which she
had established a couple of years before.

Sinclaire had shone a light on an important issue, but it was
undoubtedly an act of retaliation. Indeed, Derk Jan Eppink, the
Dutch journalist who had become a Belgian MEP, says he often stayed
in the same hotel as Sinclaire and remembers her 'deciding to take her
revenge'.[2] She had worked on the precise wording of her attack with
her adviser Gary Cartwright and a British journalist, Philip Braund,
while in a Brussels bar, the Beer Factory. They'd hit on the idea of
exploiting parliamentary privilege to get the story into the public
domain, without the risk of having to prove it in a libel court. This
was a trick Farage himself had used a few times in the past. And just
like many of Farage's utterances in the chamber, Sinclaire's words
went viral. So what lay behind Sinclaire's cold dish of revenge?

Sinclaire had been probing the issue of MEPs' allowances and
expenses when in 2012 she was rudely interrupted. She was arrested
on suspicion of fraud relating to her own parliamentary allowances.
This followed a complaint made to the Brussels authorities in 2010,
around the time she was expelled from UKIP. Sinclaire wasn't
actually charged until the summer of 2014 – four months after her
incendiary question to Farage in Strasbourg – accused of money

laundering and misconduct in public office. The allegation was that Sinclaire had wrongly claimed £3,200 of expenses for car and ferry journeys when she had actually travelled by plane. The main witness against Sinclaire, her former political assistant John Ison, claimed there had been a difficult relationship between her and Farage, and that the UKIP leader had said after the 2009 Euro election that he wished he had twelve MEPs, not thirteen. Ison admitted in court that he'd been 'a mole' for Farage inside Sinclaire's office. For several weeks between November 2009 and January 2010, he'd secretly passed 'sensitive' information to Farage about what she was doing, so as to 'protect the party', he said. No evidence was ever produced that Farage had encouraged Ison to take his allegations to the police, but Sinclaire's friends suspected he was behind her prosecution. Sinclaire was acquitted on all counts, and outside the court blamed the police for pushing a 'vanity trial' on the say-so of 'one embittered man'.[3]

In 2014, having initially declined to rebut Sinclaire's unexpected allegation about him and Fuller, Farage quickly issued a statement denying it. He accused Sinclaire of 'malicious' gossip, and of being bitter about her failure to become UKIP leader. Kirsten Farage was more circumspect about Sinclaire's claim. She and Nigel would be 'discussing it tonight', she told a reporter.[4]

Nikki Sinclaire's words in Strasbourg got huge coverage in the media, including the BBC evening news and most of the press. 'Did UKIP with your aide Nige?' asked *The Sun* in its front-page headline. The *Daily Mirror* said Farage had been 'done up like a UKIPPER', while an extra-marital dating site claimed their survey showed that more than a quarter of philandering British women would have an affair with Farage.[5]

Nikki Sinclaire was now in demand for interviews. The LBC presenter Nick Ferrari accused her of 'a low blow' and suggested to her that because of 'bad blood' between her and Farage, 'this was your way to get under the belt'.[6] The left-wing *Guardian* columnist Owen Jones came to Farage's aid by describing Sinclaire's question as 'personal, lowest common denominator, play-the-man-not-the-ball nonsense'.[7] But Sinclaire explained to the BBC that she had been exposing the hypocrisy of Nigel Farage who told all UKIP MEPs in 2004 that they could not employ their wives, and he went behind their back and employed his wife. Let's remember, each MEP gets three times the average national wage, and on top of that he has chosen to employ his spouse. I think that's pure hypocrisy.[8]

Writing for the *Daily Mail*, Sinclaire continued her attack, and called Farage a 'bullying, hypocritical, preening show pony'. When the *Mail on Sunday* political editor Simon Walters mentioned this line to Farage in an interview a few days later, Walters says Farage's 'frog eyes bulged with fury'. He scowled, leaned forward, and 'aggressively' said: 'You normally rely on people on bail for fraud charges, do you?' When Walters suggested Sinclaire's remarks had got under his 'skin', Farage with 'nostrils flaring', shot back: 'What gets under my skin is that the BBC decided it was headline TV news.'[9]

Had Farage had sex with Annabelle Fuller, Walters asked. 'I don't think we should go into the grisly details,' Farage replied.

Had he slept with her? Walters pressed him.

'No.'

Had he kissed her?

'No. When you work in a tight team, I understand why people might get the wrong idea.'[10]

Farage maintained that stance a month later when he fulfilled an agreement to appear on *Have I Got News For You?*.

He clearly knew he would be pilloried on the show, and when the issue came up of Maria Miller resigning from Cabinet that week over her expenses claims, Farage seized the initiative with fellow panellist Ian Hislop: 'I think it's absolutely disgusting, all these elected politicians using all these expenses to better themselves. Disgraceful, isn't it, Ian?'

'It is absolutely disgraceful, Mr Kettle,' said Hislop, to loud laughter.

The presenter, actor Stephen Mangan, then reminded the audience that in 2009 Farage had claimed to have made £2 million from EU allowances and expenses, which prompted loud boos.

Farage tried to defend himself by pointing out that his £2 million claim had been brought to public attention by the Labour MP Denis MacShane, who later faced expenses problems of his own.

'Yes, but he's in jail,' Hislop shot back, 'but you're not.'

'I had noticed that,' Farage replied.

'As a tax-funded MEP,' Stephen Mangan continued, 'Nigel Farage is an equal opportunities employer. Some of our money has gone to his wife, and some to his mistress.'

Amid the audience laughter, a grinning Farage interjected: 'Um, I think that is "allegedly", don't you? . . . I think you ought to say "allegedly", quite honestly.'

'I mean,' said Ian Hislop with typical mock outrage, 'that sort of allegation is pretty distressing,' and then added with a smirk: 'Is it true?'

'No, afraid not,' said Farage.

'Not true at all?' pressed Hislop.

'Not true at all,' Farage repeated.

'Any of the good bits?' Hislop asked.

'I'll tell you afterwards,' a grinning Farage replied.

At that point – as Farage must have anticipated – Mangan cut to the video of Sinclaire's question, drawing attention to a translator in the bottom corner of the screen who couldn't hide her astonishment as the MEP delivered her allegation.[11]

Nigel Farage had handled his appearance brilliantly. Instead of losing his temper – as he often does – he was astonishingly composed and relaxed. He smiled, and grinned, and laughed, and succeeded in reducing all the allegations about expenses and Annabelle Fuller to one big joke. Few other politicians could have pulled it off. Few others would have dared to appear in the first place.

Yet Nigel Farage had been having sexual dalliances in Europe ever since he was first elected to Brussels and Strasbourg back in 1999, according to Richard North. 'Anything in a skirt he would be after,' he says. 'So he had a string of girlfriends. He had a squeeze in the office, a little French girl, definitely.' And North says that when Kirsten grew suspicious at one point, she came over to Strasbourg to make enquiries. 'She then went round the office asking, "Is he

having an affair?" It put us in an impossible position. "Um, er . . ."
It was very, very difficult,' North says:

> He'd shag anything that let him. He had an intern who he
> employed because he was shagging her. He'd not talk about it. But
> it was that obvious when he was snogging her in the office. The
> first girl was quite useful to us – a French speaker. These were
> very sought-after positions – there were lots of students from
> Strasbourg University applying. It was so naff and distracting:
> we were there to work.[12]

A former colleague from his days in the City recalls that Farage 'has a
penchant for the Rubens-esque woman, amply bottomed. We always
said he would choose [actress] Hattie Jacques over Kate Moss, which
always made us giggle.'

Farage's behaviour in employing Kirsten on his payroll for almost
a decade rankled with many of the party's MEPs – and published
declarations showed that Kirsten was paid between £25,000 and
£30,000 a year. Mike Nattrass, who left UKIP in 2013, was especially upset: 'We were told wives could not be on the payroll. My
wife Joyce was at the Parliament helping me, and was earning nothing. Then we found out Nigel was paying his wife. That pissed me
off, and yet Joyce came to every meeting.'[13]

There is no dispute, though, that Kirsten worked hard on her husband's behalf, and at all hours. 'I sit at my computer in my nightie,'
Kirsten once said, 'and I am very dutiful.' Nigel was pretty hopeless
with mobile phones and computers, she explained when questioned
by a journalist just ten weeks after Sinclaire's infamous question. 'He
has a steam-powered telephone; he can send and receive texts, and
that's it. If I sit him down, and there is something for him to read,
he can scroll up and down. He has learned that, but that is pretty
much it. He honestly doesn't know how to [use a computer] and he
has missed the boat. I don't think he ever will now.'[14]

Nigel Farage first met Kirsten Mehr when he went to Frankfurt
in 1996 seeking business for his firm. She was two years younger,
the daughter of an interior designer, and came from Hamburg. In his

2010 memoirs, Farage described Kirsten as 'a stunning government bond broker whose brisk efficiency at first sight belied her aethereal appearance. She could have stepped into a pre-Raphaelite painting and no questions asked.'[15] The relationship blossomed when Kirsten moved to London the following year to work as a translator for a German bank. By this time, Farage had left his first wife Clare (and Kirsten successfully sued the *Daily Mail* in 2014 for suggesting it began as an adulterous relationship). Their daughters, Victoria, born in 2000, and Isabelle, born in 2005, were brought up bilingual.

Kirsten and Nigel married in November 1999, but people who met Farage around that time were left with the impression that he thought the marriage might not last. Richard North also thought it could never last, since there was too much antagonism between the couple, and he once heard them having a screaming match in his office. 'The Germans were still "the Hun" in his mind. He told me once how he went over to meet her family, and it was not a success.' And while Nigel enjoyed high living, Kirsten appreciated simpler pleasures. One summer, says North, Kirsten booked a campsite in Germany for the family, and North was invited, too. 'We were living in caravans, which Farage absolutely hated.'[16] After that, Kirsten took the girls caravanning round Europe without their father.

In an interview in 2010, on the day England lost 4–1 to Germany in the World Cup, Kirsten revealed that she'd hung a German flag over the garden fence of their home near Downe. 'It winds Nigel up quite a bit,' she said:

> I do take the mickey when we win and, because that is usually what happens, Nigel doesn't get much chance to come back at me. The best he can manage is that silly old song, 'Two World Wars and One World Cup' . . . I have brainwashed the girls into shouting 'Come on Germany!' So for the time being they will be supporting Germany, though I am not sure how interested they will be in the match.[17]

Kirsten said Nigel was hurt by accusations he was racist, and denied it was true. 'If he was a racist I wouldn't be with him. I don't think he has got a nasty bone in his body; he is not a bully; he likes things done properly.'

She naturally worried about Nigel's 'very hectic' lifestyle. 'He doesn't get a lot of sleep,' she once said. 'He doesn't get a lot of rest; he lives on adrenaline a lot; he doesn't eat regular meals – now I'm beginning to sound like his mother – and he smokes and he drinks too much.'[18]

Kirsten mainly worked from the family home, though might occasionally visit the UKIP headquarters or accompany her husband on a trip. At UKIP conferences, she sometimes sat in the audience, largely unrecognised, or she would run Farage's personal MEP's stand in the conference foyer which was meant to promote his work in the European Parliament. She also handled much of his correspondence. At the Conservative conference in 2013, on a day when Farage had gatecrashed the Tory gathering by addressing a few fringe meetings, Boris Johnson revealed to a rally that he had once received a letter from Kirsten inviting him to speak to the UKIP conference. Kirsten's letter was 'really heart-warming', the future prime minister said, and he described her as the 'brains' and 'power behind the throne', before making a strong political point.

> I was very flattered and amused. My instinctive reaction was to say 'Yes', but then I thought 'No, no, no, no.' This is the moment to lash myself to the mast and resist the siren song of Kirsten . . . With a general election less than two years away, there is only one relevant fact: there is a risk the party she supports would deprive [people] of the chance to have a vote in a EU referendum because they would help put [Labour leader Ed] Miliband back in power. My message to the charming Mrs Farage . . . is don't vote for UKIP, don't even think about it, because we will see this country sleepwalk into a Labour government.[19]

Being his wife had its difficulties, but allegations of being his mistress were even worse. After Nikki Sinclaire's bombshell in Strasbourg about her and Nigel Farage, Annabelle Fuller said she 'had been continually hounded by the press with these false allegations since 2006', with journalists outside her home:

> It's a shame that as a woman I am considered fair game for accusations of alleged affairs. It's hard enough being a woman in politics without having to justify why I am employed. It is safe to say that this would not have happened if I was a man. Surely this is something that Nikki Sinclaire should have considered.[20]

Yet the accusations were true, of course.

The daughter of a property developer, Fuller attended a private school before getting a master's degree in international relations. In 2004, aged just twenty-three, she joined the UKIP team in Brussels as a researcher. She found Farage 'polite and cool' when she first met him in her second week in the job. 'Looking back, I don't recall an immediate spark of attraction on either side. To me, he was just another middle-aged man in a suit.' After work, when UKIP staff went for a drink in bars near the Parliament buildings, Farage would sometimes join them. She gradually found herself attracted to him as he held court with his younger audience. 'He was fun, with a wicked sense of humour,' she would later say. 'He had the best jokes and easily the most interesting political stories. I loved listening to him. I was captivated by his worldliness.'[21]

The relationship developed slowly. Initially, over several months, Fuller regarded Farage – seventeen years her senior – as a father figure, and she became something of an adviser. 'He took me into his confidence about work and party matters, and would often ask for my advice. I was young but I was bright and I was eager to get stuck in,' she said.[22] Fuller helped with speeches, on amendments to EU legislation and working out how UKIP MEPs should vote. Gradually Farage would confide in his young companion more and more – not just about political issues, but personal matters, too. 'He told me the marriage was not a real one,' Fuller said later, and that it was a marriage 'in name only'.[23]

When Farage stood in South Thanet in the 2005 election, Fuller went to help as a campaign volunteer. Farage stayed at a hotel in

Broadstairs and one evening, after a day pounding the streets, he invited his campaign team out for a late dinner. By the end of the meal, the party was down to Farage, Fuller and one other person.

> Nigel offered us a sofa bed to sleep on because there were no taxis, but I was the only one to take up the offer . . . I knew what would happen if I stayed and I wanted it to. When we got upstairs I took one look at the room and said, 'But there's no sofa bed,' and we both just laughed.

The next day Farage asked if she regretted it. 'I said No, and he said neither did he, and that my arse had looked amazing in the moonlight.' Farage told Fuller that their relationship had to remain secret, and that if people found out they would make her life hell. 'I was already committed. I knew what we had was very special. I was in love. I was happy.'

Before long, Annabelle Fuller and Nigel Farage were regularly seen dining together in restaurants and bars around Brussels and Strasbourg, or at his favourite London restaurant, Boisdale in Belgravia. So much for it being secret. Colleagues in UKIP, staff in the EU cities and people in the media had quickly worked out what was going on. They were a 'proper couple', Fuller says: she acted like a wife, arranging aspects of his domestic life as well as his professional activities. When Farage visited Brussels he would stay at her flat in the Maalbeek district, where he kept several sets of clothes and shoes. Farage wasn't easy to live with – he had a habit of leaving wet towels on the floor, though he was almost obsessive about polishing his shoes. Although Fuller was almost a generation younger, she felt like 'Nigel's mother' at times. She reminded him that drinking just tea with his breakfast kippers was unhealthy, and that he should drink plenty of water, too. 'I defended him. I would always take a bullet for him.'[24]

Whenever Farage had to return to England, Fuller was desolate. She found it hard to cope with the fact that Farage couldn't even ring her because he was home with his family. But Fuller says that Kirsten knew of the relationship because somebody in UKIP told her. When Fuller rang Farage at home for work purposes, Kirsten might hang up the phone, or pass it to Nigel and say in a frosty tone, 'It's *her*.' Fuller grew ever more unhappy about her role as Farage's clandestine lover. She wanted a normal life and a proper relationship. Growing more and more depressed, she began to self-harm, and deliberately cut herself. 'When I told Nigel, he was devastated and blamed himself.'[25]

Mike Nattrass loves telling people how he presented Farage with a bottle of 7 Up in 2006, on the morning after the *News of the World* claimed his MEP colleague had had sex seven times with the Latvian TV journalist Liga Howells. He says the relationship with Annabelle Fuller, who had briefly been on Nattrass's staff in Brussels, was an 'open secret' within UKIP. 'She used to go strutting about saying, "I will be the next Mrs Farage." Nigel has got a reputation for women anyway. She was caught sitting on his knee a number of times in the office.'[26]

In 2006, Fuller moved back to London to work at UKIP headquarters. The relationship continued, but things remained difficult. Farage insisted his family had to be his priority, and especially his two young daughters, by then aged six and one. But towards the end of that year, they decided to end it. 'Over the last few weeks I too have realised that for us to be together properly is just so difficult,' Farage told Fuller in a handwritten farewell letter, which she kept. The letter suggests a sensitive, vulnerable side to Farage which contrasts with his image to the outside world. When they were together, 'we are so happy and content', he wrote.

> *I wonder whether I am capable of this job without you. I will miss you horribly and painfully and the love that we have shared. I will still think about you and worry about you. Promise me that you will look after yourself. If you take too much alcohol it ruins you and I have watched with admiration as you have cut right back. Be happy, you deserve it. I only wish that I had been free for you.*
> *With all my heart and body*
> *Love Nigel X*[27]

It was the first time, Fuller says, that Farage revealed his feelings for her so openly. It was agony for both of them, but the parting was only temporary. Barely twelve months later they were back together, and the relationship continued on and off for almost another decade. Fuller didn't make much effort to hide the affair.

The party's former regional organiser in the North West, Gregg Beaman, once related how, at a UKIP conference in Morecambe in 2008, two senior figures asked him to pass on to the UKIP national chairman their concerns that 'Annabelle Fuller had spent the Saturday evening texting Nigel Farage, quite suggestively and quite openly, about what she wanted to do with him when he came to the North West the following day'.[28]

In 2008, Fuller revealed she'd received night-time phone calls from someone who accused her of being a 'whore'. For a while she left her job with UKIP and began working for military charities before establishing her own public relations firm, Athena PR, all of which still involved operating around Westminster and round the political world. Her website quoted Farage testifying to Fuller's ability to 'resolve problems which may arise'.[29] She rejoined Farage's employment in 2010, and helped run his leadership campaign, though it was hard to distinguish between what was work for Farage as an MEP; work for Farage as party leader; and what was direct work for UKIP. A lot of her job involved handling the press and broadcasters, which she did very ably. But she also acted as an adviser to Farage, drafting speeches and articles and helping him with strategic thinking. Between 2010 and 2012, Fuller says, the relationship was strictly professional – no sex – but then, only months before Nikki Sinclaire's intervention early in 2014, the couple became lovers again.

A UKIP spokesman dismissed Sinclaire's remarks in the European Parliament as 'beneath contempt' and accused her of abusing her parliamentary position to make them. 'Sinclaire has been saying the same thing to anyone who would listen since 2006. Regarding Miss Fuller, Mr Farage has been asked about this before and the answer has always been, "No, it is false."'[30] Fuller kept up those denials a couple of years later when interviewed by the *Daily Mail* (having changed her name to Trixy Sanderson). 'I did not have an affair with Nigel Farage,' she said. 'I go for hunky army types, which Nigel is not. He's a nice person but he's just not my type: he doesn't have muscles.'[31]

In 2017 Fuller finally admitted the allegations were true when she told her story to the *Mail on Sunday*. The denials had been lies. 'Right from the beginning, lying about the affair was a strategy we decided on,' she said:

> We had many conversations about it . . . He told me I had to keep quiet. I said to him: 'Do you have any idea how painful it is for me?' and he would say 'Yes'.
>
> Nigel and I both knew we had to keep quiet to save Brexit. We are both liars and hypocrites but the reason I had to lie throughout the years was that I didn't want UKIP or the cause we were fighting for to be damaged.
>
> He said, 'They will use anything they can to stop this, they will use anything they can to stop me. We are going up against the Establishment here. They will come after you.'[32]

Even after the exposure by Nikki Sinclaire, the pair still saw each other from time to time, though they had to be even more careful, to maintain the deception. Fuller felt she was being used. And only three months after they'd been outed in Strasbourg, and the day after the European results, she was humiliated when she turned up to a big UKIP celebration party at the InterContinental Hotel in Westminster, an event also attended by one or two other women linked with Farage, together with the man himself. Kirsten spent some time manning the door.

Fuller had helped out on the Euro campaign, but while she was talking over drinks to Farage's former aide Ray Finch, who'd just been elected an MEP, one of Farage's security men came up and asked her to leave. Kirsten Farage is then said to have screamed at her, 'I will have security drag you out by your hair if you don't leave.' Fuller recalled a few days later:

I was escorted out in front of colleagues and friends I had known for years, and I knew outside there were a load of TV cameras and journalists. I was humiliated. I knew it had nothing to do with Nigel, and I called him up and he said, 'What the hell's going on?' He then comes along, he hugged me and I was in floods of tears – the floodgates opened like they had never opened.[33]

Fuller retreated to the pub next door, the Feathers, but Kirsten was soon in pursuit. 'Someone said, "Can you leave this pub please, because Kirsten's coming soon." I said, "She can go fuck herself!" quite loudly, so she would have heard. Kirsten then pretended to cry and left. I don't know what she was having a go at me for. All his other girlfriends were there.'[34] Fuller returned to her home in north London feeling 'ashamed, useless and alone'.[35] That night, she slit her wrists, burned her arm several times with a cigarette end and took an overdose. Thanks to quick work by two friends, she was taken to hospital.

That was just one of four suicide attempts, caused in part by her very public relationship with Farage. For all that time she had to share him not just with his wife Kirsten but also other women. Some were just quick dalliances, but two other women in particular were probably as close to Farage as Fuller was – Laure Ferrari, a Frenchwoman he met in Strasbourg, and a UKIP press officer, Alexandra – or Alex – Phillips.

His great friend Godfrey Bloom put it bluntly around the time he left UKIP in 2013: he is 'partial to crumpet', he said. 'We all have our foibles and our weaknesses – mine is real ale – I've never been partial to crumpet. Nigel's is women. It's not something he ever denied.'[36] In most political biographies, the subject's affairs and extra-marital relationships would play only a small role and be regarded as irrelevant to the main narrative. But, as we shall see, in Farage's case they are important to the story of his career, and his party's history – both as his close advisers in several cases, and prime targets for his adversaries. 'UKIP is hinged on Nigel's very complicated personal life,' a former member of staff told *The Times* the day after the Nikki Sinclaire question. 'There are skeletons in his closet. Nigel is dragging Highgate Cemetery behind him.'[37]

In an interview in 2010 with the Belgian magazine *Up Front*, Farage even appeared to boast about the number of women he had got pregnant in the past. Speaking against the idea that women should be allowed to have front-line roles in the armed forces, Farage said: 'Maybe it's because I've got so many women pregnant over the years that I have a different view.'[38]

Godfrey Bloom says it was he who first came across Laure Ferrari in a restaurant in Strasbourg around 2007. Ferrari, from Épinal in north-east France, studied English at Strasbourg University and first got involved in politics while supporting the No side in the French referendum in 2005 which rejected the proposed European Constitution. 'I said to myself: the EU is going behind the backs of European citizens here. I was always a bit of a rebel,' Ferrari once said.[39] She was in her mid-twenties when she met Bloom, and working as a waitress in the restaurant.

'One evening,' says Bloom, 'I was there and spoke to her in my awful French, and she advised me not to bother speaking French to someone who spoke good English.'[40] The pair got chatting and Ferrari explained that during the day she ran a fashion shop called Urban Flavor. But business wasn't going too well, so in the evenings she helped a friend who owned the restaurant. Laure Ferrari soon revealed her sympathies for Eurosceptic politics, and she and Bloom became good friends. 'I think the relationship was rather more platonic than Godfrey would have wished,' says one former UKIP official. Bloom then introduced her to Farage, who arranged for Ferrari to get a job on the staff of the Independence/Democracy group, and after 2009 she ended up doing PR for the British section of Ind/Dem's successor, the Europe of Freedom and Democracy group. 'Everyone says that I am Nigel Farage's parliamentary assistant,' she once complained, 'but this is not true! I was head of public relations.'[41] Ferrari had just the fiery energy her name suggests. 'She is a driving force,' says Godfrey Bloom. 'She can make things happen. You can wind her up and she will get it done.'[42]

Dark-haired and petite, Ferrari was always elegantly dressed, or 'chic'. 'She is amazing; she is so much fun; she's intelligent; she's cute,' says one of Farage's other close female friends. 'She's like a little Audrey Hepburn-style character, just warm and charming.'[43] Before long Farage and Ferrari were lovers, though they always denied it, and she and Annabelle Fuller came to loathe each other. Ferrari got more and more involved in politics, and in 2014 even stood for the European Parliament as a candidate for a new party called Debout la République (Republic Arise). The party was Eurosceptic but with very different politics to the Front National of Marine Le Pen and her father Jean-Marie, and Ferrari claimed to have demonstrated against the Front when Le Pen senior was the main challenger to Jacques Chirac in the 2002 French presidential election. 'Some of their ideas, like those regarding the death penalty and immigration, disgust me,' she said.[44]

The third major relationship was with Alexandra Phillips, though she has always denied it was sexual. Again, Phillips was significantly younger than Farage, and a year or two younger than Fuller and Ferrari. After reading English and philosophy at Durham University, she met Farage in 2007 when she was a journalism student at Cardiff University. For that year's elections to the Welsh Assembly, Farage had talked the socialite baronet Sir Dai Llewellyn, a notorious drinker and womaniser, into standing as the UKIP candidate in Cardiff North. Farage and Llewellyn campaigned further afield, too, and for a placement she was doing with ITV in Cardiff, Phillips persuaded them to let her film as they travelled round South Wales in a classic Cadillac DeVille which Llewellyn had borrowed from Nathan Gill, a UKIP activist from North Wales.

'I sat on the front seat, and trained my camera onto them in the back where they were swigging champagne straight from the bottle, smoking copious amounts of cigarettes, and having a really good time actually! I was made to feel very welcome. It wasn't long before the champagne bottle was passed to me.' Phillips spent several days with the UKIP team, as Llewellyn toured about yelling at voters with a megaphone, and roundly enjoying themselves in what one might call a party on the move. 'There were lots of pints and shots of boozing, laughs, smoking cigarettes. It was great material,' she says.[45] 'Immediately I was captivated by Nigel,' she wrote years later, 'a larger-than-life character with magnetism almost impossible to ignore.'[46]

Phillips spent a lot of time with Farage again in 2009 during the Euro elections when UKIP was trying to win its first Welsh seat (and succeeded) and she was now working for BBC Wales. But she hated what she felt was 'overt snobbery' about Euroscepticism in the BBC. 'I remember people in the [Cardiff] newsroom saying UKIP were Nazis and fascists, and yet it was clear there was a conversation to be had about the EU.'[47] She decided politics was the life for her, became a freelance journalist and started writing speeches for UKIP MEPs and press releases for the party's flamboyant, dandyish head of press Gawain Towler. In 2013, Phillips joined UKIP full time as part of the press team at a time when Farage was developing a public image as the man with the pint. It wasn't a deliberate ploy, Phillips says – and came about because for a while UKIP's London base was in the European Parliament offices at 32 Smith Square (the old Conservative HQ building), but the EU banned them from doing anything on the premises to do with domestic politics. So for media interviews, UKIP would often retreat just round the corner to the famous Marquis of Granby pub – known as 'MoG'.

Phillips and Farage saw a lot of each other and became very close. Many people assumed they were having an affair, and Phillips's body language certainly gave that impression. 'I adore Nigel,' Phillips says, though she has long insisted their relationship was merely platonic. It's irrelevant really. What matters is that people *thought* they were lovers, and that would play an important part in the Farage story.

In explaining things, Alex Phillips says she always got on very well with Farage's wife. 'We were really good friends and I love Kirsten to bits,' she says. 'She is an amazing woman.' They sometimes had lunch together, and when Phillips went on holiday to India, her cat Murdoch (named after Rupert) was looked after by Kirsten and the girls for a fortnight.[48] Phillips would often spend time at the Farages' home as well, and even arranged for her parents to bring down some of her childhood horsey books for their youngest daughter Isabelle.

Phillips says she and Kirsten discussed the fact that rumours were spreading about her and Nigel, and she says that Kirsten advised her, 'Just ignore it, forget it, Alex. Don't get involved in those silly games.' But Phillips says she wouldn't be surprised if Kirsten had texted UKIP friends and colleagues about having concerns.[49] She says the rumours were got up by people in the party who didn't like her and resented her closeness to Farage. Yet I recall that such stories were also put about, and believed, by people who weren't hostile to Phillips.

'Nigel's relationship with women is very different to men,' says Roger Bird, an Oxford graduate who briefly served as the national general secretary of UKIP in 2014. 'With women, he can confide in them his deepest secrets and take astonishing risks on the basis of the shortest possible acquaintance. With men it is very diffi-cult. There's a public school type of bonhomie, but also a sort of awkwardness.'[50]

Bird recalls how in 2011 he and his then wife Serra went on a trip to Brussels for UKIP members. The jaunt had been organ-ised by Kirsten Farage, and used a scheme whereby the European Parliament subsidises such visits to introduce people to EU institu-tions (UKIP were frequent users of the scheme). Farage and Serra Bird ended up talking late into the night in a bar after the UKIP leader had consumed many bottles of Belgian lager and several glasses of red wine. Kirsten Farage kept her eye on her husband, though nothing sexual was ever likely to result. What Roger Bird found astonishing was just how much the drunken Farage confided in a woman he'd never met before, and how willing he was to unload everything about his chaotic private life.

> And the things I managed to find out from her later were aston-ishing, and I wouldn't tell those things to anybody. Examples were to do with his first wife, and the people he was 'seeing' in Brussels. And he referred to one woman as the 'love of his life'. I later checked up on what he'd said, and discovered this was probably Laure Ferrari.[51]

Psychologists say people often like confiding their most dangerous secrets to strangers because it's easier; they won't cause offence, and they will probably never see the stranger again. For Farage, it also seemed to show an inner loneliness and unhappiness, as well as an astonishing recklessness for a figure who by then was quite well known both in Britain and Europe.

Nikki Sinclaire's intervention in Strasbourg came not long after Annabelle Fuller had resumed their relationship. She got the devastating news in a text from a friend. 'I had a massive panic attack. "My fucking life's over," I said. For years he'd always said: "They're going to come after you because it's easier than going for me."'

Fuller rang Farage, and then she got a call from Alex Phillips, who was then working as UKIP's head of media:

> Nigel said the party will pay for a taxi, and it picked up Alexandra on the way and drove us to my parents' home – we were friends at that point. He was just saying, 'Here, have some money to go to your parents' house. Just deal with it yourself.' . . .
>
> Then my enemies gathered and said: 'We know how you are unhappy. We know Nigel's not supporting you.' They offered me money to fuck off. Nigel didn't try to keep me. He just wanted me out of the way. For the next few months, friends and colleagues would not speak to me.[52]

Annabelle Fuller believes that Farage had relationships with her, Laure Ferrari and Alex Phillips 'in parallel' (indeed, there was also a spell, from 2010 to 2014, when Fuller, Ferrari and Kirsten were all being paid from EU funds). She compares life in UKIP, and being part of the female circle around Farage, to what it must have been like under the Plantagenet kings in the England of the Middle Ages. 'Only he has a better track record in Europe,' she jokes.

> He's ruthless, always lying. He is the most ruthless person you've ever met in your life. The way he can manipulate and use people, then he's done with them, and he can cast them out and have nothing more to do with them. I've never known lying come so easily to someone. Women are there as playthings, to be used and cast aside, but he will never treat them seriously because in his

eyes they are not as good as men. He will not give a shit about you, if something you've done has a negative effect. At one moment I'm being thanked; the next I'm an embarrassment.

He must have no conscience. I've known him cry once – over me actually. It's almost like he's taken a hit to the frontal lobe. When I broke up with him, a friend said he was shit-faced in Brussels saying he couldn't live without me.[53]

Fuller says that in the early years Farage did once ask her to marry him, but that she didn't want to break up his family. Remarkably, around 2010, when she returned to help Farage's second leadership campaign, she and Kirsten were reconciled and were quite close professionally. 'She worked out that I had ended it with him,' says Fuller, 'and she and I worked together quite happily. During the campaign I was having to keep a look-out to see if a new mistress was on the scene, and report back to his wife. And yet it was very awkward because obviously he was still cracking on to me.'[54]

An insight into the relationship between Farage and his women is given in a book called *UKIP Exposed*, published by Jay Beecher, who was once an assistant to UKIP's former party director and by-election organiser, Lisa Duffy. Part of Beecher's book is based on a secretly recorded conversation he had with Duffy in which she claimed that immediately after Farage's plane crash in 2010 she had to 'juggle' the women who wanted to visit Farage in hospital – his wife Kirsten, Fuller and, he says, a 'red haired woman named "Fi-fi" (presumably Laure Ferrari)'. 'Lisa had to make sure that the visiting schedule was handled in such a way that neither [sic] of them bumped in to each other so as to avoid any unwanted drama.'[55]

Only Duffy's schedule didn't quite go according to plan. When Gawain Towler got to the hospital he found Kirsten Farage, Annabelle Fuller and Laure Ferrari all there at once, amid a pretty frosty atmosphere. What's more, one or two freelance photographers were trying to wheedle their way into the hospital ward to get a photo of Farage in bed with his injuries. Towler knew it would make a pretty sensational picture for the tabloids if they were caught on camera together. Fortunately, the snappers were kept at bay.

Later, in 2013, Fuller joined the campaign effort in the Eastleigh by-election where she worked closely with Lisa Duffy, who ran the UKIP campaign. Fuller was an important figure in the Eastleigh team, though she was handicapped by having her leg in plaster following a skiing accident. At one point, Duffy sacked her from the campaign only for Nigel Farage to intervene and insist that she be taken back. According to Jay Beecher:

> Lisa told me that Mrs Farage was 'furious'. She called Lisa and, with a raised voice, asked her why she had taken Annabelle back. At that moment Lisa finally snapped. She told Kirsten that she was overworked and overburdened on the campaign and that she had endless other problems to worry about [rather] than be embroiled in petty dramas. Kirsten lowered her tone, offered to come down and help, and the matter was brushed aside.[56]

Yet according to Fuller, Kirsten Farage actually enlisted her help on one occasion when she'd got so fed up with Nigel that she decided to up sticks with their daughters and leave. It was an 'awful situation', Fuller says. 'I had to tell Nigel that Kirsten had told me she was taking the children off to Germany – she had spoken to their headmaster and they were off. I had to tell Nigel she was going to remove the children and he was not going to see them again.' So how did Farage react? 'He just made some phone calls,' she says, but believes Farage suspected 'that somehow I was involved in it'.[57]

As UKIP and Farage became more successful after 2013, the strains became too great. Kirsten knew all about her husband's relationship with Laure Ferrari, the 'love of his life', and how he would see her whenever he went to Brussels or Strasbourg several times a month. She must have been hurt, angry and resentful, but still lived with him and worked for him. It seems that Kirsten thought the Frenchwoman was simply trying to build her political career on his, while avoiding all the responsibilities and work she carried out both at home, as the mother of their children, and as his paid assistant. She also tried to maintain good relations with Farage's two sons, Sam and Tom, from his first marriage, and treat them almost as her own, though Kirsten never found members of the Farage family easy to get on with. By the mid-2010s she no longer had any love for or loyalty towards Nigel; she could no longer trust him; sometimes she no longer had any feelings for him at all.

But Kirsten didn't want a separation or a divorce, for the sake of their two school-age daughters. He was 'a good man', Kirsten said. 'There is not much time for a family life, but we watch him on the telly when we want to see him.'[58]

TOP OF THE POLL

Nikki Sinclaire's revelations in the European Parliament seemed to do nothing to stop the growing momentum of the UK Independence Party. A sharply contrasting attempt to halt UKIP's rise came from the Liberal Democrat leader Nick Clegg, who by the spring of 2014 had been deputy prime minister to David Cameron for almost four years. His Liberal Democrats were bobbing along on around 10 per cent in the polls, 2 or 3 per cent behind UKIP. They looked set for heavy losses in the local and European elections, the last big test before the general election due in May 2015. Clegg decided on a dramatic gesture to revive his party's fortunes. He challenged Nigel Farage to take part in two TV debates on Britain's future relationship with Europe – himself versus Farage, without anyone from Conservative or Labour.

The two leaders were polar opposites on Europe, but Clegg would later interview Farage for a podcast and admit 'we have a lot in common', and he couldn't hide his sneaking respect for the UKIP man.[1] Both attended elite London day schools; both were new boys in the European Parliament in 1999; both had European wives; and both were first-class communicators. Where Clegg saw himself as a 'radical Liberal', Farage sometimes called himself a nineteenth-century 'Manchester Liberal'. And in bringing his party onto the main stage of British politics, Farage admitted how he modelled many of his tactics on the Liberals and Liberal Democrats.

Agreeing to such a debate was a risk. Two poor performances might easily have brought UKIP's progress to an abrupt halt, and Clegg had earned a reputation as a formidable debater during the TV encounters with Gordon Brown and David Cameron in the 2010 general election, when his relaxed and well-argued performance in the first debate briefly saw him and his party topping the opinion polls – what was dubbed as Clegg-mania.

But Farage accepted the challenge at once. They'd take part in two broadcast debates in front of live audiences. The first would be chaired by Nick Ferrari on LBC radio on 26 March 2014; the second by the less aggressive David Dimbleby on BBC2 seven days later, using a similar format to the 2010 election debates. The events were another sign that British politics was moving towards UKIP's agenda. 'I've battled on for 20 years,' said Farage.

> I've been laughed at, ridiculed, attacked. But at no point in the 15 years that I've now been an MEP have we ever had a full national debate about the merits or demerits of EU membership . . . Therefore, when the deputy PM says he wants to go public and have a debate with me on this issue, I have absolutely no choice . . . I've got to say yes, because we need to have a national debate on what I think is the most important issue this country has faced for hundreds of years.[2]

The decision by established broadcasters to hold such debates so near to the European and local elections in May coincided with a historic announcement by the broadcasting regulator Ofcom, which decided for the first time that UKIP must be given equal status in TV coverage to the three traditional parties. These were major breakthroughs. UKIP was now officially the fourth party in British politics.

The LBC debate was also broadcast on TV. The most striking line was Farage's claim that the EU had 'blood on its hands' over its handling of Russian aggression towards Ukraine, and had pursued an 'imperialist, expansionist agenda'. Clegg's main sound bite was: 'I want us to be Great Britain not Little England', to which Farage responded, 'I'm British, I believe the best people to govern Britain are the British people themselves.' Inevitably, Clegg went for Farage over the employment of his wife. Few people had 'worked the hours and had so little fun' as he had over the past few years, Farage replied (no doubt to some disbelief on the 'fun' aspect). He needed someone to help manage his life when he got home at midnight every night. And when Clegg claimed that only 7 per cent of British legislation related to the EU, Farage claimed that 75 per cent of UK laws were made in Brussels. Farage taunted Clegg that he'd never run his own company or had a proper job. 'He and I were actually elected as Euro-MPs on the same day on 1999,' Clegg fired back. 'I left the European Parliament after five years. He still remains a Euro-politician.'[3]

The Times sketch writer Ann Treneman said: 'Well I think that, on the whole, Farage was the winner. Sorry but that's the verdict. He didn't fall over.'[4] A quick poll by YouGov suggested Farage won comfortably – by 57 to 36 per cent.

Farage had turned up at the first debate feeling sweaty, straight from a drinking session at the Westminster Arms near the Houses of Parliament. Before the second debate, he prepared himself more carefully. He went without alcohol for several days; went for early morning walks on the North Downs; and took early morning swims. It paid off. Even the *Guardian* thought that in the second encounter Farage 'triumphed', after Clegg had been 'more emotional but over-scripted'.[5] Clegg accused Farage of wanting to take Britain back to a bygone age: 'I don't believe in the dishonesty in saying to the British people that you can turn the clock back. What next? Are you going to say we should return to the gold standard or a pre-decimal currency, or maybe get W. G. Grace to open the batting for England again? This is the 21st century, it is not the 19th century.' Outside the EU we would have a 'sort of Billy No Mates Britain – well it will be worse than that, it will be Billy No Jobs Britain, a Billy No Influence Britain.'

Farage claimed immigration had produced a 14 per cent fall in real wages since 2007, and he accused Clegg of lying about the EU. He urged voters to join his 'People's Army':

Let's take back control of our country. Let's control our borders and have a proper immigration policy. Let's stop giving away £55m a day as a membership fee to a club that we don't need to be

a part of. I would urge people: come and join the people's army.
Let's topple the establishment who have led us to this mess.[6]

That passage showed again, incidentally, that the slogan 'take back
control' wasn't simply dreamed up by Dominic Cummings in 2016.
An instant poll suggested Farage had beaten Clegg by 69 per cent to
31 per cent, more than two to one.

A month later, however, in May 2014, Farage endured a much
more difficult encounter, on LBC radio, with the abrasive presenter James O'Brien. It was probably the most difficult broadcast
interview Farage has ever done, and gave a considerable boost to
O'Brien's reputation and career.

O'Brien asked early on about Alan Sked's allegations that Farage
had been racist, and also raised his notorious lunch with the BNP
man Mark Deavin in 1997. 'In politics, you know, all sorts of disappointments happen to people, and they throw mud,' Farage said of
Sked. On Deavin, he wanted to find out what on earth had 'made
somebody change their point of view', when he defected from UKIP
to the BNP; 'Nothing more than that. I haven't spoken to him since.'
Which was rather different from his earlier claims that he had been
seeking material about Sked. O'Brien quizzed Farage on his controversial right-wing allies in Europe – including Mario Borghezio
and Francesco Speroni of Lega Nord from Italy. Farage countered
that UKIP refused to sit with Marine Le Pen's Front National from
France, or the nationalist Freedom Party from Austria. 'We are not
a party that wants to be linked to the far right. But I promise you,
if you look at the associations *everybody* has to form in the European
Parliament, a degree of compromise is needed.'[7]

It was a highly combative interview. Farage was frequently interrupted, and O'Brien spoke almost as much as his guest. He threw
at Farage the case of John Lyndon Sullivan, a recent UKIP council
candidate in Gloucestershire who'd tweeted only the previous
month: 'I rather often wonder if we shot one "poofter" . . . whether
the next 99 would decide that on balance, that they weren't after
all? We might then conclude that it's not a matter of genetics, but
rather more a matter of education.'[8] He was asked about a UKIP

small business spokesman, who was just found to have employed seven illegal immigrants; and a recent story in *Private Eye* alleging that Farage's medical bills had been paid by a businessman.

With this, the exchanges got very heated:

NF: I'm not having libel thrown at me on . . .

JO'B: Aren't you?

NF: . . . live on the radio?

JO'B: Are you taking legal action against *Private Eye*?

NF: My medical bills have not been paid by *anybody*, all right? Other than, other than *partly* by myself – more than I could afford – and the rest by an insurer.

JO'B: OK, so will you be taking legal action against *Private Eye*?

NF: I may do. I'm, at the moment – it may surprise you to know – I'm busy running an election campaign, so I'll think about that afterwards.

JO'B: OK, too busy to know who's standing on the council in Gloucestershire under your own banner?

NF: I *lead* a political party!

JO'B: OK, so . . .

NF: I don't *run* the day-to-day management of it, but make sure we stick to our principles and we've *done* that, and . . .

And so it went on. O'Brien mentioned recent remarks by Farage that he had felt 'discomfort at listening to foreign languages' on a train home from Charing Cross. (Farage's actual words, to reporters at the UKIP spring conference in Torquay, had been: 'It wasn't until after we got past Grove Park [eight miles from Charing Cross] that I could actually hear English being audibly spoken in the carriage. Does that make me feel slightly awkward? Yes.')[9]

I made the point that I got on a train, and went for several stops and there were a lot of people around me and no one spoke English, and I thought: 'You know, this is –' I didn't say, I didn't *object* to it. I felt *slightly* uncomfortable. I think actually, isn't that the problem? Isn't this, of all the countries in Europe, the most *accepting*, the most *tolerant* . . . ?

Then O'Brien asked about another recent Farage story, that he had said he wouldn't be comfortable living next door to Romanians. 'I didn't say that,' Farage replied: 'I was asked: "If a group of Romanian men moved in next door to you, would you be concerned?"'

'What about if a group of German children did?' O'Brien replied, a clear reference to Farage's family. 'What's the difference?'

'The difference, and you know what the difference is . . .'

'No, I honestly don't,' said O'Brien, before Farage quickly moved on to people trafficking and immigration in general.

The interview was scheduled to last twenty minutes, and at around eighteen minutes O'Brien tried to ask Farage about his expenses as an MEP. At that point the studio door opened and in walked Patrick O'Flynn. O'Brien explained on air that O'Flynn was UKIP's director of communications, and former political commentator on the *Daily Express*. It was a highly unusual move for a political aide to interrupt his boss's live interview, especially in a way that listeners could hear. 'I'm sorry, we had an agreement about timing,' O'Flynn said. 'You've massively . . .'

Farage looked irritated by O'Flynn's sudden intervention. 'Hang on, hang on,' he said, gesturing for O'Flynn to shut up. Farage then explained that there are no expenses in the European Parliament, only allowances, and that he'd kept by the rules.

Despite this and other challenges, the 2014 European elections did deliver the extraordinary UKIP breakthrough that Farage – and, privately, Downing Street – had forecast. The party topped the polls with 24 seats, compared with 20 for Labour and 19 for the Conservatives. UKIP got 26.6 per cent of the vote; Labour 24.4 per cent and the Tories 23.1 per cent. It was the first time in British electoral history that all the traditional parties had been beaten by an outsider – not a third party, but the fourth party. The Liberal Democrats were reduced to just one MEP. In the local elections, held under the first-past-the-post voting system on the same day, UKIP got 17 per cent and picked up 163 council seats.

It was a historic moment – 'the most extraordinary result that has been seen in British politics for 100 years,' said Farage, 'and I am proud to have led them to that . . . It is now not beyond the bounds of possibility that we hold the balance of power in another hung parliament.' And an In-Out referendum was becoming an even more realistic prospect, too. Nick Clegg had been right to stand up to UKIP, said the Liberal Democrat MP Tim Farron but, he warned that 'Britain is drifting to the exit door of the European Union'.[10]

Across Europe other Eurosceptic parties made significant progress, too. In Brussels and Strasbourg, the international grouping which UKIP belonged to was reconstituted, and the controversial right-wing Lega Nord group replaced by seventeen MEPs from the Five Star Movement, which had suddenly taken Italian politics by storm, having come third in the 2013 general election. Led by a comedian, Beppe Grillo, and a web strategist, Gianroberto Casaleggio, the movement was based on the internet and claimed a 'direct' role for its supporters through online communications and regular votes on policy. So, whereas UKIP's 2009–14 grouping had been called the Europe of Freedom and Democracy, the word 'direct' was added and the new alliance called the Europe of Freedom and *Direct* Democracy (EFDD), with Farage and the Five Star MEP David Borrelli as co-presidents.

It was hard to place the Five Star Movement politically since it was Eurosceptic and concerned about immigration, but also supported stronger public services and environmental measures. Beppe Grillo was quite a fan of Farage, and often praised him in his blog. After the pair had lunch in an Indian restaurant in Brussels, Grillo said Farage was not a racist, and 'not the way he is described, just as I am not the fascist and Nazi the Italian papers describe me as'. The UKIP leader had 'a sense of humour and sense of irony', he added.[11] Grillo was also reassured to learn that Farage hadn't been a banker, but a metals trader. The alliance with Farage was highly controversial, however, and only approved after he made a video appeal to Five Star members. They voted 78–22 to back the deal which became known as 'Grillage people' in Brussels. Over the next few years, the Five Star Movement came to have a big influence on Farage.

However, Farage only secured the numbers for their new EFDD grouping by luring away a member of Marine Le Pen's Front National (FN) group, Joëlle Bergeron – even though, seven months earlier, Farage had said anti-Semitism was 'still deeply embedded' in Bergeron's party.[12] Le Pen was furious, especially as she hadn't recruited enough MEPs from enough states to form her own grouping. 'Nigel Farage has formed a group with an unstable woman elected on an FN platform and an unpredictable Beppe Grillo,' she complained. 'I will tell Mr Farage that illicitly acquired goods never benefit you in the end.'[13] Once again, for someone who professed not to believe in European unity, Farage had shown himself a master of building international alliances.

Back in Britain, meanwhile, the great prize of a Westminster seat, which had long eluded Farage and his colleagues, now looked tantalisingly within reach after the Euro elections. The big breakthrough might come just two weeks later when a by-election was due to be held in Newark in Nottinghamshire, due to the resignation of the Conservative MP Patrick Mercer over a cash-for-lobbying scandal. The seat looked promising, especially since it was an astonishing twenty-five years since a Conservative government had won any seat they had defended in a by-election, and UKIP expectations ran high.[14]

Normally an insurgent party would plough all its people and resources into a promising by-election, but UKIP was handicapped because the first three weeks of the campaign overlapped with fighting the local and European contests. The Conservative effort, in contrast, seemed to have no limits on money or personnel. The party co-chairmen Andrew Feldman and Grant Shapps rashly piled everything they could into the battle to defeat UKIP. Professional Conservative agents were sent to Newark from regional offices and constituencies all over the country, and put up in hotels at party expense, while the whips press-ganged more than a hundred Tory MPs and ministers up from London. It was a sign of David Cameron's deep concern about UKIP's growing strength that he visited the seat four times (including once with Boris Johnson). In the past it had been pretty rare for a prime minister to visit a by-election campaign even once (the six PMs from Home to Major never campaigned in by-elections at all).[15]

The result was deeply disappointing for Farage as the Tories won easily with a majority of 7,403 – or 45.0 per cent to UKIP's 25.9 per cent. At the count, Farage cried foul, and suggested the Conservatives must have breached the rules which legally limit any party to spending £100,000 in Westminster by-elections. 'Given the number of paid professional people from the Conservative Party here,' he told me, 'it is difficult to believe that their returns are going to come in below the figure [£100,000] . . . It seems to me the scale of campaign they've fought here, it is so vast.' A subsequent investigation by Channel 4 in 2016 showed the Tories spent at least £6,600 beyond the legal cap in Newark and the Electoral Commission fined the party £20,000 for making a misleading declaration. Newark was a blow to UKIP's ambitions. Farage had always known it would be hard to win any by-election from a standing start. He became more convinced than ever that the best chance of penetrating the seat of power would be to persuade existing MPs to defect. Farage had been quietly working away at this for years, and Stuart Wheeler had helped him with a series of dinners and lunches to woo Eurosceptic Tories. Some MPs had seemed on the point of defecting, but then someone would leak the name, the Tory whips would bring their pressures into play and the target would be frightened off.

On 24 July 2014, that began to change. And this time Farage hadn't carried out the seduction.

The UKIP leader had been invited to lunch at the London flat of his predecessor Lord Pearson, in West Square in Kennington, south London, not far from the Imperial War Museum. There was one other guest – Douglas Carswell, who since 2005 had been Conservative MP for Clacton in Essex.

Carswell was a Eurosceptic; indeed, many of his views were so close to those of UKIP that the party hadn't opposed him in 2010, though he'd never met Farage before. He'd spent years, however, studying the UKIP leader's character, and the effect Farage was having on public opinion. This analysis had been carried out with two Conservative Eurosceptic friends: Dan Hannan, the Tory MEP elected to Brussels the same year as Farage; and the Kent MP Mark Reckless. Carswell and Hannan had been close for years; having shared a London flat in their twenties, they were now godparents to each other's daughters. Despite having the same big aims as UKIP, the three Conservatives were anxious about the party's huge success in the European elections.

Carswell had planned the Kennington encounter carefully. He'd discussed his intentions with Malcolm Pearson during a walk in St James's Park, where the former UKIP leader advised that if he was going to talk to Farage then 'you need a witness' – hence the lunch at Pearson's home.

Over the informal meal in Pearson's kitchen, Carswell gave Farage the big news: he wanted to join UKIP, but only on certain conditions. First, Carswell wanted to resign his seat, and then contest it for his new party in a by-election – something he'd always said that defecting MPs should do. He was also insistent he would become a UKIP candidate automatically – he didn't want any fuss about going before a selection committee; UKIP would have to cough up the £100,000 it would cost to fight the campaign; and the party would have to find a job for him if Carswell lost the seat. What's more, everything had to be kept totally secret until they went public. The UKIP leader readily agreed. A close friend of Farage later said Carswell was promised 'a considerable sum of money from UKIP' should he lose the by-election.[16]

Five weeks later, on a quiet news day at the end of August, UKIP summoned journalists to the headquarters of the Institution of Civil Engineers at 1 Great George Street, opposite the Treasury (a favourite venue for party announcements, and also for filming political dramas). As the press arrived, UKIP staff were unusually cagey about what was going on. A big new UKIP donor was one theory. Or a big-name endorsement? Or was Farage perhaps about to stand down, at the peak of his success?

Suddenly Farage marched in, followed by the unmistakable figure of Douglas Carswell, with his gawky limbs and prominent jaw.

Farage immediately ceded the floor to Carswell: 'Good morning,' said Carswell. Then, with a nervous smile, he got straight to the point:

'I'm today leaving the Conservative Party and joining UKIP.' Having delivered this hammer blow to David Cameron, Carswell wasn't done with surprises. He then made a speech which was remarkably unlike UKIP in tone. He was joining the party, the MP said, 'not because I'm a Conservative who hankers after the past'. He welcomed the advance of feminism and rights for disabled people. 'What was once political correctness gone mad,' Carswell said, 'we now recognise as just straight-forward good manners . . . UKIP is not an angry backlash against the modern world.' More important, he declared,

> I am not against immigration. The one thing more ugly than nativism, is angry nativism . . . We must welcome those who want to come here to contribute. We need those skills and drive. There's hardly a hospital, a GPs' surgery, a London bus, a super-market, which would run without that skill and drive. We should speak with pride and *real respect* about first-generation Britons.

Then came the second big development. It wasn't enough simply to leave the Tories and join UKIP, Carswell explained: 'As someone who's always answered directly to the independent-minded people of Essex, there's only one honourable thing for me to do: I must seek permission from my boss – the people of Clacton. I will now resign from Parliament and stand for UKIP in the by-election that must now follow.'[17]

The new recruit was under no obligation to resign his seat, of course. Most MPs who switch parties don't spark by-elections, and some who have done so in the past have lost them. But Carswell had always argued this was the right thing to do. 'Principle in politics is more important than the career of an individual MP,' he said. 'Even when that MP happens to be me.'[18]

'No wonder Farage's grin seemed even wider than usual that August morning,' Owen Bennett wrote in *Following Farage*, his 2015 account of Farage and UKIP.[19] Yet in a telling moment, Douglas Carswell also joked about his rebellious past as a Conservative. 'It's nice to have a leader with whom I agree,' he told the reporters. 'It is early days though,' Farage joshed back, prophetically.[20]

There was one small problem with this. Just as with Bexley and Battle in 2001 and Buckingham in 2010, UKIP already had a parliamentary candidate in Clacton. Roger Lord had no intention of stepping aside, and said so in numerous interviews. Lord was quickly squashed by UKIP; so he quit the party and urged his supporters to vote Lib Dem.

Carswell's decision to defect to UKIP wasn't just a personal matter. Since 2012 he and his friend Dan Hannan had been discreetly holding meetings at Tate Britain to discuss Eurosceptic strategy. Hannan had suggested the Tate on the grounds that few journalists or people in politics would have the 'aesthetic taste' to be in the gallery on a weekday afternoon, and so it proved. 'One of the ideas we toyed with at the Tate,' he wrote later, 'was that some of us should switch to UKIP. Perhaps one after the other.'[21]

Douglas Carswell's defection, he later admitted, was part of a deliberate attempt to detoxify the UKIP brand – hence some of his stark and very non-UKIP remarks in his defection speech at the Institution of Civil Engineers. He and Daniel Hannan had long worried about how difficult it would be to achieve more than 50 per cent of the vote in David Cameron's proposed EU referendum, when the main withdrawal party – UKIP – and its polarising leader were disliked and distrusted by most of the population. They'd studied the polls closely. 'The more that Nigel Farage's profile and UKIP's poll ratings grew,' Carswell wrote later, 'the more that support for Leave seemed to shrink.' UKIP's high-profile recruit was struck by the 'Farage Paradox', which had been publicly identified by the left-leaning commentator Sunder Katwala, the day after Farage's triumph over Nick Clegg in their second TV debate:

Last year, there was an average lead for 'out' over 'in' of sixteen points: 48 per cent to 32 per cent. Since then, Nigel Farage has rarely been off the television, but the trend is now neck and neck. After Farage won the first [Clegg] debate, the *Sunday Times/ YouGov* poll had a six-point lead for 'in', the biggest lead for the pro-EU case for two years. The polls will continue to fluctuate, but the rise of UKIP has certainly put 'in' back on level terms.

There is no doubt that Nigel Farage resonates very effectively for the one in four who are certain that Britain should leave . . . Yet the UKIP mood music can be a turn-off for softer Eurosceptics and 'don't knows' who are not uncomfortable with the society they live in, and risks turning those who were 'leaning more out than in' back into reluctant Europeans.[22]

By 2014, both Carswell and Hannan had lost faith in David Cameron's Bloomberg speech, and suspected he wasn't really committed to a fundamental renegotiation of Britain's relationship with the EU. Cameron would do the minimum required to win 50 per cent in a referendum, they felt, and thereby thwart his Eurosceptic critics. 'Farage, it seemed to us, was going to help him do it,' Carswell recollects. And after UKIP's extraordinary success in the 2014 European elections, Carswell feared that:

Euroscepticism now had as its highest-profile spokesman a man that was inadvertently pushing the swing voters over towards Cameron. It was crystal-clear to us that if the referendum became a Cameron v. Farage contest, we would lose. And Downing Street knew it, and was manoeuvring to make it happen.[23]

Or, as Douglas Carswell told the journalist Tim Shipman later: 'We understood that there was going to become a symbiotic alliance between the Remainers in Downing Street, and the purple Faragists.'[24] So in the spring and summer of 2014, with the knowledge and support of Dan Hannan, Carswell had begun secret negotiations with Malcolm Pearson about defecting to UKIP. His aim was to give the Leave cause a more popular and less populist image – less strident, and more positive about life outside the EU – to turn UKIP into an asset during a referendum campaign, not a liability. 'What, we wondered, if some of us were to join UKIP? What if we were to speak up for a softer, more sensible sort of Euroscepticism?'[25] Carswell felt that nostalgia for a white, middle-class Britain of the 1950s was not the way to secure EU membership. 'We wanted to put men in their trench,' he subsequently explained, 'and to do that, we had to go over the top, and we talked about a very different type of UKIP. We tried to decontaminate the brand.'[26]

Carswell's new party couldn't have stopped him causing a by-election even if they'd tried. It was a gamble, of course, but his seat, Clacton, had long been highly Eurosceptic, and the prize would be spectacular. Only three months before, the political scientist Matthew Goodwin had said that Clacton was the most 'UKIP-friendly' seat in the entire country. Farage suggested Carswell's defection would be the first of several. 'We have talked to Tory and Labour MPs over the course of the last six months who very, very strongly support everything UKIP is trying to do,' he said, but he knew the number would depend on what happened in the Essex sea-side resort. 'This by-election is going to be a High Noon moment.'[27]

The Conservatives again pumped huge resources into the fight. Channel 4 later found 361 room-nights at local hotels that weren't declared on the party's expense return, and the Electoral Commission later fined the Conservatives £15,000 for failing to report its spending properly.

Farage needn't have worried. Carswell romped home with a majority of 12,404 – 59.7 per cent compared with 24.6 per cent for the Tory contender. The Conservative–UKIP swing was a whopping 44 per cent, the second greatest swing in a Westminster contest since 1945, when such statistics were first calculated.

Although Douglas Carswell wasn't a natural campaigner – he didn't warm to meeting voters in the way Farage does – his vote in Clacton partly reflected his local reputation. He now carried new authority as UKIP's first elected Member of Parliament. That made him UKIP leader in the Commons, alongside the party's existing, overall leader outside. And his acceptance speech at the count showed how much he now planned to remould UKIP in his direction:

> To my new party, I offer these thoughts. Humility when we win, modesty when we are proved right. If we speak with passion, let it always be tempered with compassion. We must be a party for all Britain, and all Britons, first and second generation as much as every other. Our strength must lie in our breadth.[28]

'Nigel was utterly pissed off at that speech,' one of his aides revealed later. 'I was standing next to him.'[29] 'The journalists on the balcony,' Owen Bennett recalled, 'looked at each other and began wondering: was Carswell already trying to remake the party in his own image? Would this message of inclusiveness play well with the UKIP faithful? Was this a leadership challenge?'[30]

A challenge for Farage, certainly. Carswell knew full well what he was doing. 'The political capital I had with my new party following my by-election win,' he later explained, 'I started to spend.' And the new UKIP MP would return to the themes of his defection and victory speeches in subsequent press articles. UKIP should be an upbeat, optimistic and inclusive party for change, he argued. 'Not every Kipper entirely agreed with me, but my audience was the 99.9 per cent of voters who weren't UKIP members. I was determined that they should not be repelled by UKIP in the coming referendum.'[31]

Carswell even contacted Sunder Katwala, who ran the think tank British Future, and arranged to give a speech on 'Why Enoch Powell was wrong about immigration'. Powell, of course, was one of Nigel Farage's great heroes, the legendary politician whom he'd met at school, and later ferried to Newbury in the 1993 by-election. 'Why be subtle?' Carswell would write. 'I wanted to challenge people's assumptions about UKIP while I had their attention . . . I accepted every TV or radio interview – facing endless questions that began with "But the leader of your party says . . ." I took every opportunity to sound reasonable. Not everyone in my new party appreciated it.'[32]

Perhaps not since the Trotskyist Militant tendency entered the Labour Party in the 1970s and '80s and caused such huge disruption had anyone so successfully burrowed their way into a British political party. And while Farage had warned for years about infiltration of UKIP by the BNP and fascists who wanted to drag the party to the right, here was someone who had plotted and calculated with fellow Conservatives as to how one of them might join UKIP so as to help soften and moderate the party's image.

Where Nigel Farage had increasingly campaigned against immigration, Carswell followed what he said in his defection speech with what he said on doorsteps. When Clacton voters told him there were too many foreigners in Britain, he told them bluntly that they were 'wrong to blame immigrants for the problems they associate with immigration'. It was perfectly rational for people to want to come to the UK, Carswell argued, and immigrants made a positive contribution to the economy, and the NHS and other public services.[33]

Farage wasn't happy: yet another star catch was veering out of control. Farage travelled to Clacton to revel in the by-election result, yet even before the polls had closed he'd already distracted people from Carswell's historic victory with an interview for the magazine *Newsweek Europe* in which he said that immigrants who had HIV should be barred from entering Britain. 'UKIP want to control the quantity and quality of people who come,' Farage said. 'That Latvian murderer shouldn't have been allowed here,' he protested, in reference to an immigrant who'd recently killed a 14-year-old girl, having been convicted of a previous murder in Latvia. So, the interviewer Robert Chalmers suggested, 'quality' meant people without a homicide conviction? 'Yes,' Farage replied. 'And people who do not have HIV, to be frank. That's a good start. And people with a skill.'[34]

If you were looking for issues to divide Farage and Carswell, you couldn't have chosen better than immigration and HIV. Carswell's father, Wilson, was a distinguished specialist in AIDS and HIV who'd first come across the disease in Uganda in the 1980s. Indeed, the Carswell family had been expelled from the country because Dr Carswell refused to remain silent about the extent of the epidemic, and horrifically the family's cook and gardener were bludgeoned to death in the Carswell home by thugs employed by the Ugandan authorities, to ensure the family got the message. 'Twenty-something years on,' Carswell wrote, 'even if flush with success from a landslide by-election win the day before, HIV was still a sensitive subject with me.'[35]

When Farage agreed to speak to the *Today* programme that morning, it was inevitable he would be asked about his comments to *Newsweek Europe*. Rather than close the discussion down, Farage was only too happy to elaborate his views on migrants and HIV:

We want people to come who have got trades and skills, but we don't want people who have got criminal records – and we can't afford people with life-threatening diseases . . . I do not think people with life-threatening diseases should be treated by our National Health Service and that is an absolute essential condition for working out a proper immigration policy. We have leading cancer experts in Britain saying the burden now of treating overseas people is leading to huge shortages in the system.[36]

'Mr Farage has stooped to a new level of ignorance. He should be truly ashamed,' said the chief executive of the HIV/AIDS charity the Terrence Higgins Trust, who was angry that Farage had linked AIDS victims with murderers.[37] Carswell believes Farage was deliberately muscling in on his by-election success, and as the two men did a victory walkabout along Clacton High Street, HIV immigrants were what most reporters and broadcasters wanted to ask about.

'Your father was a pioneer,' Nick Watt of the *Guardian* shouted. 'Your father was a pioneer, Mr Carswell. Your father was a pioneer!' While Carswell carefully avoided the questions and journalistic heckling, Farage happily engaged, and mentioned tuberculosis as another life-threatening disease which might exclude people from entering the UK.[38]

'It was not something that had come up during the by-election,' Douglas Carswell later recalled:

It is my opinion that Nigel said what he said to put himself back in the spotlight. Not content with being the leader of a party that had just won its first seat in Parliament, he had in my view to make himself the absolute centre of attention, even if it meant negative attention.

It was a pattern of behaviour that Carswell says he saw 'repeatedly'.[39] There was another pattern, too. Robert Kilroy-Silk, Marta Andreasen, Godfrey Bloom, Neil Hamilton . . . and now Douglas Carswell – successful, well-known names whom Nigel Farage had actively encouraged to join the party; and all people with whom he fell out.

Despite their public differences, Nigel Farage made sure to be in the Commons when Carswell was sworn in as UKIP's first elected MP three days after the historic result. Farage didn't have to sit in the public gallery, but enjoyed a ringside seat down below on the green benches set aside for MPs' families and friends – the nearest he has ever got to sitting in the House. The place had been found for him by an old Dulwich contemporary, the Conservative MP Philip Hollobone, who was himself often mentioned as a possible defector (though he never became one). Only two MPs seemed to acknowledge Farage's presence – the Leader of the House William Hague, who reportedly gave him 'an icy stare', and the Chief Whip Michael Gove, who 'caught Farage's eye and slowly tipped his head'. After swearing his oath of allegiance to the Crown, and a few minutes in the chamber, Carswell joined Farage in a Commons café. 'Right,' Farage said in a poke at David Cameron, 'let's order some fruit cake.'[40] He was still pretty oblivious as to Douglas Carswell's true plans for his party (in which there would be little room for 'fruitcakes', 'loonies' or 'closet racists').

Yet for all the celebratory joshing, the Commons swearing-in ceremony also marked a monumental Farage blunder – a missed opportunity on an epic scale, which might have rocked both major parties. Behind Carswell in taking the oath came Liz McInnes, the new Labour MP for Heywood and Middleton in Lancashire, who'd been elected in another by-election on the same day as Clacton. But only just. For McInnes's majority was a mere 617 over UKIP. Labour had deliberately rushed the by-election to thwart the insurgent 'Kippers' – as they were increasingly known – and the trick had worked. UKIP had decided to divide its forces roughly 50-50, encouraging northern activists to help in the Lancashire seat, and southern supporters to go to Essex. In reality, many UKIP people in the North ignored the Lancashire battle and travelled to Essex because they thought Clacton was the place to take part in history.

Nigel Farage had lowered expectations a few weeks before when he said the northern seat was 'too big a mountain to climb in that short space of time', and a poll by Lord Ashcroft three days before voting suggested UKIP was 19 per cent behind Labour. The UKIP organiser on the ground, Paul Oakden, didn't believe that. That wasn't the response they were getting locally and Oakden felt that with more resources UKIP could win. 'Ignore the Ashcroft poll!' Oakden shouted down the phone to party colleagues in Clacton, begging them to divert people to the North. 'The problem,' said UKIP deputy leader Paul Nuttall, who was helping Oakden, 'was that all of the resources and people who had ever run a by-election were sitting in an office in Clacton. Douglas was demanding every resource under the sun. We were given the scraps. The team came in, set up the office, but then buggered off.' 'Douglas was at that point very influential,' Oakden later told the academics Matthew Goodwin and Caitlin Milazzo. 'So he got the resources. He was obsessed with being the first MP. Everything else was secondary.'[41]

Labour's campaign repeatedly accused UKIP of wanting to privatise the NHS, and cited past statements by Nuttall, Carswell and Farage which suggested that the Health Service should depend much less on funding by the state. 'I think we are going to have to move to an insurance-based system of healthcare,' a film revealed Farage saying at a meeting in Sussex only two years before. 'Frankly, I would feel more comfortable that my money would return value if I was able to do that through the market place of an insurance company, than just us trustingly giving a hundred billion a year to central government and expecting them to organise the healthcare service from cradle to grave for us.'[42] That statement would be hurled against Farage and his party again and again.

UKIP lost Heywood and Middleton by just 2.2 per cent, on a swing of 18 per cent. Indeed, the by-election was arguably UKIP's most impressive ever performance in a Westminster contest (given that Clacton involved a sitting MP). Yet it had long been plain that Carswell would easily retain the Essex seat – two polls the day after his defection had him around 60 per cent of the vote there. What's more, during the campaign Farage had actually spoken publicly of parking UKIP's tanks on 'Labour's lawn' in the North. Had the party switched more of its Clacton people, money and resources to Heywood and Middleton, the party might have pulled off a historic double triumph and delivered a resounding declaration that they threatened Labour in the North as much as the Conservatives in the South.

Farage must have realised he'd made a huge error in not changing tack when his press officer Clive Page rang him from the count in Lancashire to say UKIP were behind, but that it might go to a recount. 'Oh Christ,' he recalls Farage's response. 'We had that won,' Page says. 'The leadership of UKIP made a disastrous decision politically.'[43] To have beaten both the Conservatives and Labour simultaneously would have sent the established parties a terrifying message, since no insurgent party in living memory – not even the Liberals or Lib Dems – has toppled the big two in separate by-elections on the same day. Some analysts believe that had Labour lost Heywood and Middleton – normally a safe Labour seat – then Ed Miliband would have been forced out as party leader.

And victory in Heywood and Middleton wouldn't just have scared Labour; it would have changed the balance of forces within UKIP by making Carswell's victory look much less of a personal achievement.

Farage had uttered his remarks about tanks on 'Labour's lawn' a fortnight before the two by-elections, at the UKIP annual conference, held in the grandstand at Doncaster racecourse in South Yorkshire. It was a deliberately provocative venue, since Ed Miliband was a Doncaster MP, and the event took place amid a heady atmosphere. The first day, Friday, was very busy, but some journalists decided the Saturday agenda was too dull to stay for. So they went home, or switched to the Conservative conference which was due to start in Birmingham. How wrong we were.

Late morning on the Saturday, a car arrived at Doncaster racecourse and a man was smuggled through a back entrance, without anybody noticing. A few minutes later Nigel Farage stepped onto the stage and announced, 'I would like you please to give a warm welcome to somebody who is not a member of our party. He's a Member of Parliament for the Conservative Party . . . Would you please give a warm welcome to Mark Reckless.' 'Today, I am leaving the Conservative Party,' he announced as members spontaneously rose to their feet, 'and joining UKIP.'

'U-kip! U-kip! U-kip! U-kip! . . .' a loud chant erupted from the ranks, like a football crowd.[44]

Like Carswell, Reckless promised to stand down as an MP and fight a by-election, in his constituency of Rochester and Strood. Frankly, he didn't have much option – it would have looked cowardly and unprincipled not to follow Carswell's example. But Rochester and Strood was a much less certain prospect than Clacton. Demographically, the Kent seat was near enough to London to contain many commuters, whereas Clacton was more isolated from the metropolis.

Reckless's announcement sent tremors through the Conservative party conference just as David Cameron arrived in Birmingham. Conservative bigwigs were close to panic, and since Carswell's departure they'd been on 'defector watch'. David Cameron says he had 'despatched [Chief Whip] Michael Gove to see every suspect, instructing him to get them to promise, preferably in writing, that they were not going to cross the floor. They all reassured him.'[45] Yet those giving reassurances had included Mark Reckless not long before his announcement. Each defection, the Conservatives feared, would encourage more, and every UKIP success would reassure wavering MPs that they need not fear rejection by their constituents. Much greater haemorrhaging was also taking place at lower levels. While two MPs had defected, dozens of councillors had switched as well, along with thousands of Tory activists and millions of Conservative voters. It was no secret that many constituency officials in Tory seats had voted for Nigel Farage and his party in the European elections that May. It was a sign of how worried Cameron was about UKIP that in his closing speech in Birmingham he took the gamble of mentioning UKIP and its leader by name, warning voters that they risked a Labour government. 'If you vote UKIP – that is really a vote for Labour,' said Cameron, looking ahead to the general election. 'On the 7th of May you could go to bed with Nigel Farage, and wake up with Ed Miliband.'[46]

That evening UKIP rattled Cameron's cage again, with another eye-catching coup. Earlier in the day it had been reported that an obscure but wealthy businessman called Arron Banks was giving UKIP £100,000, which was not an exceptionally large sum. When the former Conservative leader William Hague was asked about Banks's gift on the *Today* programme, he said he had 'never heard of' Banks. 'So I'm not gonna get too upset by that.'[47]

Within hours, UKIP invited reporters to Arron Banks's country house, Old Down, near Bristol, for what was billed as another big announcement. Many journalists thought it might mean another defection.

Banks had become very rich by selling personal insurance through his call centres and websites, and had bought Old Down from the musician Mike Oldfield six years before. Until quite recently he had been a Conservative donor, having stood for the Tories as a council candidate when he was only twenty-one. On the well-kept lawn of Old Down, with a vista looking down to the Severn, Nigel Farage introduced his new donor to the press. Banks explained that having heard Hague's remark on the radio, he would now increase his pledge to UKIP tenfold, to £1 million.

Hague is a shrewd politician, but his throwaway comment on *Today* must go down as one of the most foolish things he has ever said, and one he must now regret, given that by 2014, after four years as foreign secretary, his past Euroscepticism had turned into support for continuing British membership of the European Union. And Banks's £1 million donation was just the start, for someone who would soon become one of the biggest and most influential donors in British political history.

Arron Banks is not grey, media-shy or instinctively cautious like many businessmen but, like Nigel Farage, is someone who loves causing mischief. He is highly intelligent, and has the demeanour of a cheeky-chappy wide boy, with an almost permanent grin on his face. He rarely holds back in what he says, and nor does he seem to care what people think. And he was plainly thrilled to invite cameras and well-known broadcasters to Old Down, where he readily swapped numbers with the political reporters. The media attention became as much of a drug to Banks as it was to Farage, and the two men quickly became very close.

Arron Banks's gift was desperately needed by UKIP as they struggled to match the Conservatives' spending in their bid to stop Reckless in Rochester and Strood. Cameron and the party high command devised a clever wheeze – asking local voters to help choose their candidate. At an estimated cost of £100,000, the party sent out details of two possible contenders together with a ballot paper and pre-paid return envelopes. In reality, it was a ploy to give extra publicity to the local party and its candidate. Because the 'primary' was conducted before the by-election was officially called, the expenditure didn't count towards the Conservatives' spending total.

Strangely, the voters of Rochester and Strood were not given much choice in the Conservatives' primary – just two contenders – Kelly Tolhurst and Anna Firth – who looked fairly similar and were both middle-aged, somewhat uninspiring councillors from Kent. The primary process began with Cameron holding a public meeting in the seat with both contenders, and he also sent a letter to every voter with the accusation that 'Nigel Farage and Mark Reckless want to turn this election into a national media circus.'[48] It was an odd jibe given that prime ministers don't normally turn up with their two possible candidates, or write to every voter just before the start of a by-election campaign, and Cameron visited four more times once the contest was officially under way

Subsequently Channel 4 found that the party spent almost £57,000 – more than half the expense limit – on accommodation for professional staff alone, and the party must have spent several hundred thousand pounds in all, way outside the law.[49] In 2016 the Electoral Commission fined the Conservatives £10,000 for serious breaches on their expense return (on top of £35,000 for similar offences in Newark and Clacton).

The fact that Conservative HQ was so cavalier – reckless, one might say – with the expenses rules in Rochester and Strood – showed how worried the party was about UKIP's progress that year, given it was only six months before a general election. UKIP's work in Rochester was run by polling expert Chris Bruni-Lowe. He'd defected from the Tories with Carswell and overseen his battle in Clacton, where he'd used a database of voters for the first time in a UKIP campaign. But the party on the ground still lacked the organisational experience of their rivals. Although UKIP canvassed the Rochester seat twice over, many of their canvass returns proved to be pretty useless, as there was no common notation system. Bruni-Lowe noticed that on one canvass sheet everyone had been marked down as 'L'. 'Why is everybody in this street Labour?' he wanted to know. 'That is impossible.' 'They are not Labour,' an activist replied. '"L" means we leafleted them.'[50]

Nigel Farage grew increasingly exasperated with Douglas Carswell and his friend Mark Reckless. As the Conservatives in Rochester and Strood now focused on immigration, he wanted to do the same, fearing the Tories might outflank UKIP on what they claimed was their issue. 'Douglas said no,' Reckless reportedly told Farage when the UKIP leader demanded they go big on immigration. 'We need to do the wholly local stuff.' 'If you do not do immigration you will lose,' Farage shot back, and eventually changes were made.[51] And Cameron's repeated visits were meanwhile exploited as a gift by Chris Bruni-Lowe. 'It made classifying Kelly Tolhurst as David Cameron's candidate so much easier,' he said afterwards, because it helped squeeze working-class Labour voters towards UKIP. 'We just tied absolutely everything to Cameron.'[52]

Nigel Farage got so tense and worried about the Rochester outcome that he even attributed an ulcer to the stress of the campaign. On polling day he planned to arrive at 3 p.m., but went down early instead and began making calls to cajole UKIP staff and MEPs who weren't there to help. 'You'd better get here,' he warned. Farage then spent the autumn evening knocking on doors to get out the vote. 'I don't think I will ever forget Nigel in those last hours,' one activist said afterwards. 'It was pitch black. He was completely alone, marching up and down the roads. He was obsessed with getting out the vote. He knew we had taken a major gamble.'[53]

That gamble paid off, as Mark Reckless won with a 2,920 majority – a margin of 7.3 per cent. The result prompted immediate speculation that UKIP might win at least a dozen seats at the election due in May 2015, and many of their targets, like Carswell and Reckless's constituencies, were around the Thames estuary.

Indeed, if they could win twelve seats – Farage even spoke of forty – then who knew what might happen? They might even hold the balance of power in a hung parliament. That was the hope.

18

THE BATTLE OF THANET

In August 2014, two days before Douglas Carswell's dramatic defection to the UK Independence Party, it was announced that Farage would fight South Thanet again, at the election which by law would be held in May 2015. It was one of the target seats identified by UKIP's new polling expert Chris Bruni-Lowe.

This sent the Conservative Party into a great flurry of worry and activity, which only intensified with the two UKIP by-election victories. Neither Douglas Carswell nor Mark Reckless were charismatic politicians or sparkling communicators, but the prospect of having Nigel Farage leading a bunch of UKIP MPs on the green benches of the Palace of Westminster sent shivers through the Conservatives.

The sitting MP for South Thanet, Laura Sandys, had announced she was giving up politics, and earlier that summer the Conservatives there chose as her successor a man who couldn't have been more different from her politically. Where Sandys was a strong supporter of British membership of the European Union, the new standard-bearer was an emphatic and long-standing Eurosceptic. The local party thought he was just the man to see off any threat from the UK Independence Party.

That candidate was a 47-year-old accountant from Chatham. His name was Craig Mackinlay.

Mackinlay had, of course, two decades before, enjoyed a substantial career in UKIP himself. He was the party's founding treasurer and, in the eight months between Alan Sked's resignation in August 1997 and the election of Michael Holmes the following March, he had been the acting leader of UKIP. He'd then spent two years as Holmes's deputy; and had also stood for UKIP six times in general and European elections. In the late 1990s he and Nigel Farage had been the future of the party – personable, enthusiastic and good communicators. As so often happens in politics, they were friends but also rivals.

In the summer of 2005, however, Mackinlay defected to the Conservatives. UKIP was going nowhere, he felt, and he had grown increasingly exasperated by the constant infighting on the UKIP NEC, and by Nigel Farage's domination of the party (even though he was not yet leader). Mackinlay became a magistrate, was elected to Medway Council, and in 2012 stood unsuccessfully for the new post of police and crime commissioner for Kent.

All was set for a good old scrap between former pals. The Battle of South Thanet in 2015 would prove to be one of the great constituency contests of modern times, with repercussions which lasted years.

The Conservatives resolved they had to stop Farage at all costs. That would mean the kind of campaign only ever seen in by-elections. And the 2014 campaigns in Clacton, and in Rochester and Strood provided something of a model. The seat would be flooded with party staff, and leaflets, and money. Once more, the legal expense limit would be ignored.

Farage seems to have given little thought to standing anywhere other than South Thanet. He'd fought the seat before; he had friends in the area; he could say he was born in Kent, and Thanet was, of course, part of his European seat. Out with Sandys went the Conservatives' incumbency advantage, and with Labour still in play, Farage could hope to split his opponents 50-50 and come through the middle.

But in many ways South Thanet was not a sensible choice. A noted Eurosceptic like Mackinlay would attract more of the anti-EU vote than the Europhile Laura Sandys. And geographically South Thanet might seriously impair his ability to lead the national campaign. The seat was at the far tip of south-east England, with poor road and rail links, and on the way to nowhere else in Britain. All party leaders have the dilemma of dividing time between the national campaign and their own seats, but they usually have the advantage of incumbency. Farage was the face of his party, in massive demand by the media, and there were few suitable replacements. Remarkably, while Farage had been UKIP leader for more than eight years, this was the first time he had led his party into a general election.

Fortunately for them, UKIP's organisation in Thanet had made progress since Farage last stood in 2005. The party had won seven of the eight wards in the two Thanet seats in the 2013 Kent county council elections, then taken 46 per cent of the vote across the Thanet district in the 2014 European poll – the best in the South East region – and only five other council areas in Britain did better for UKIP.

The local Conservatives appointed as their agent Nathan Gray, who was only twenty-five and highly inexperienced, but in reality the campaign would be run by Marion Little from Central Office, a formidable election organiser over many decades who had been heavily involved in the three 2014 by-elections. Little made regular visits to the constituency, and then from the end of March effectively became the full-time organiser of the South Thanet campaign. As the election approached, the seat was visited by other party staff from London, as well as two special advisers to Theresa May, then Home Secretary – Nick Timothy and Stephen Parkinson. Many of these visitors stayed at the Royal Harbour, an attractive boutique hotel on the Ramsgate seafront. By polling day, the Tories had racked up bills at the Royal Harbour of nearly £15,000, almost the whole of the legal expenses limit of £15,016 (much lower than the £100,000 cap in by-elections). And from the end of March 2015, Mackinlay was also provided with a full-time professional press adviser. None those staff costs or accommodation bills would appear on Craig Mackinlay's expenses return.

Yet UKIP also managed to make its spending go an awfully long way. Someone who worked on the campaign told the journalist Owen Bennett that the party had 'twenty-five public meetings, we did about twenty direct mailings, we must have done about forty different leaflets, we had about thirty ad trucks down there, we had every billboard in the constituency . . .'[1] UKIP was careful, however, not to provide accommodation for activists and staff in the Thanet area, but in neighbouring seats. One volunteer recalls how the party put him up in a hotel in Canterbury, about 18 miles away, 'and it went on the expenses of the UKIP candidate in Canterbury'.

This was Nigel Farage's seventh attempt at becoming an MP, but only the first time he had a serious chance of winning. There was a sense of 'now or never'. Foolishly, when Farage published his second set of memoirs, *The Purple Revolution*, early in 2015, he wrote:

> It is frankly just not credible for me to continue to lead the party without a Westminster seat. What credibility would UKIP have in the Commons if others had to enunciate party policy in Parliament and the party leader was only allowed in as a guest? Was I supposed to brief UKIP policy from the Westminster Arms? No – if I fail to win South Thanet, it is curtains for me. I will have to step down.[2]

The book was serialised in the *Daily Telegraph* only eight weeks before polling day, and the paper gave the 'curtains' line a prominent headline. It was an 'all-or-nothing gamble', the paper said.[3] Farage may not have really meant what he'd written, but the quote – almost a pledge – acted as a rallying cry to Farage's enemies, and especially the Conservatives. If they could only defeat Farage in South Thanet, then he would quit as leader and UKIP would be considerably weaker. 'It was the wrong decision,' said Douglas Carswell.[4] It also gave outside activists from all three rival parties – the Conservatives, Labour and Lib Dems – an extra reason to go and campaign in Thanet. And Farage increasingly found the other parties ganging up on him, not through any deliberate agreement, but tacitly.

During the Blair/Brown governments – from 1997 to 2010 – South Thanet had actually been a Labour seat, though always marginal. Labour also had the advantage that their candidate, Will Scobie, was local and had been chosen a year before Mackinlay or Farage. At the end of March 2015, a poll in the *Independent* suggested the three parties were all within 1 per cent of each other, but a fortnight later YouGov showed Labour falling behind, suggesting it was really a two-horse race between the Tories and UKIP. Although Labour had a full-time agent in Thanet, the party's national HQ never identified the seat as a prime target worthy of extra resources and big-name visits.

Will Scobie was astonished that Farage didn't follow up his selection as UKIP's candidate in August 2014 with an early blitz of the constituency and regular appearances. Between August and Christmas, Farage barely visited the seat. He had too many other diversions – the by-elections in Clacton and Rochester, UKIP's internal politics and his responsibilities in the European Parliament. It gave Craig Mackinlay plenty of time to gain ground. By the start of 2015, Farage was going through one of his regular bouts of despondency. 'I sit here at the start of the year,' he told Matthew Goodwin and Caitlin Milazzo, 'and I'm not looking forward to any of it. I don't think I am going to enjoy it like I did last year. The sheer time pressures on me are becoming almost impossible. And I understand that Thanet is going to be very, very difficult.'[5]

Despite their success in council elections, the local UKIP branch was not a bundle of energy and enthusiasm. Many of its members were elderly pensioners. The branch chairman Martyn Heale, who'd run Farage's 2005 campaign, again played a role, though it was inevitable that journalists raked up his past as an organiser for the National Front. And growing criticisms that UKIP was racist were fuelled by a BBC fly-on-the-wall documentary in February 2015, *Meet the Ukippers*. It was broadcast just ten weeks before polling day, based on filming with UKIP activists in South Thanet at the end of 2014. A local UKIP councillor, Rozanne Duncan, was filmed talking to a UKIP press officer. Casually filing her nails, Duncan remarked that she wasn't racist. 'The only people I do have problems with,' she added, 'are negroes':

> And I don't know why. I don't know whether there's something in my psyche, or whether it's karma from a previous life, but I really do have a problem with people with negroid features. I really do. A friend of mine said 'What would you do if I invited you to dinner and I put you next to [one]?' And I said, 'I wouldn't be there.' I simply wouldn't.[6]

Duncan was expelled from UKIP as soon as the programme makers alerted the party to her remarks, but that didn't defuse the damage. '*Meet the Ukippers* has really fucked us up in that seat,' admitted Chris Bruni-Lowe, who effectively ran Farage's campaign.[7]

Only a few weeks later came further local embarrassment when Janice Atkinson, who'd been elected a UKIP MEP in 2014, and was candidate for Folkestone and Hythe, another nearby target seat, was forced to step down. *The Sun* had exposed a member of Atkinson's staff as having inflated a large bill for a UKIP women's lunch held in Margate the previous month.

At times, the South Thanet contest got heated and nasty. The seat became the focus not just of activists from other parties, but people from anti-racist and left-wing organisations such as Hope Not Hate; UKIP – Beyond Diversity; and a local group which emerged called Thanet Stand Up to UKIP. In late March, Farage had described UKIP – Beyond Diversity as 'scum' and accused them of frightening his daughters – then aged fourteen and nine – when they burst in on him and his family while they were having Sunday lunch at the Queens Head in Downe, the village near his home. A group of protestors – including migrants, gays, disabled people and HIV activists – clad in fancy dress, staged what they called a 'cabaret of diversity' in the pub. When Farage decided to leave, they blocked his car. One protestor even jumped on the bonnet. 'I hope these "demonstrators" are proud of themselves,' he said. 'My children were so scared by their behaviour that they ran away to hide.'[8]

After the election, UKIP admitted they put a man into the group Thanet Stand Up to UKIP to report back on its plans. The *Guardian* linked the man to Farage's security team and claimed he had encouraged members of the campaign to deface UKIP placards and heckle Farage at public meetings.

By now the polling expert Chris Bruni-Lowe, who had defected from the Conservatives with Douglas Carswell, had quickly become one of Farage's closest confidants. 'Chris always had Nigel's ear,' said another aide, 'and his relationship with Nigel grew and grew to the point where he became his number one political and strategy adviser.'

Another aide whom Farage brought down from London was Raheem Kassam, aged just twenty-eight. He, too, had been a Conservative, and from 2014 had worked for the new London bureau of the right-wing American website Breitbart News Network, becoming a disciple of Breitbart's energetic US editor Steve Bannon, long before most people in America – let alone Britain – had ever heard of Bannon. Farage had earlier – in 2012 – made friends with Bannon who'd spotted the UKIP MEP's potential as a right-wing disruptor. Kassam quickly made his mark on the Thanet campaign, bringing a new aggression to it and telling people he was Farage's 'chief-of-staff', though it's not clear that Farage actually called him that. Bruni-Lowe and Kassam shared an office at the UKIP HQ in Mayfair, became close friends and would refer to Farage as 'Boss Man'.[9] But the sudden huge influence of the young pair on Farage also caused deep resentment among more established UKIP colleagues, and gave a harder style to the party, which became less friendly towards the media.

Alex Phillips suddenly found herself and her strategy pushed aside. She believed that UKIP had to soften its image and push beyond its core 15 per cent base.

It was this really testosterone-driven, angry, aggressive sort of domineering presence down in Thanet that wanted to wrest control of everything, and I remember being extremely devastated because I'd spent two years working hundred-hour weeks helping build the party up to a position of respectability where it had got about 25 per cent of the vote share in the European elections. Within a matter of weeks I'd been very deliberately isolated and the whole strategy and messaging completely changed . . . For them to secure their position and influence over Nigel, it was imperative that they kept me isolated.[10]

'Our aims are quite simple,' Chris Bruni-Lowe told *The Spectator* in March 2015: 'Get Nigel elected in South Thanet, win a good number of seats, and then come second in more than 100 northern constituencies.'[11] In the event that UKIP held the balance of power,

Farage explained in *The Purple Revolution* that, unlike Nick Clegg in 2010, he wouldn't join a Cameron Coalition: 'I have no desire to sit around a Cabinet table in No. 10, no desire to have a ministerial title and absolutely no desire to swap the chance to get Britain out of the EU for some grandee position in government.' Instead he expected to do a three-way deal with the Conservatives and the Democratic Unionists from Northern Ireland, but only so long as it involved an In-Out EU referendum by the end of 2015.[12]

Bruni-Lowe and Farage's analysis was that at the subsequent election, in 2020, Labour would collapse in the North of England, much as it had already done in Scotland, and that UKIP would reap the rewards (which was remarkably prescient given what happened in 2019 in what by then had become known as the 'Red Wall' seats). The fact that Farage's two main advisers lived in South Thanet for much of the election showed how much the party depended on success there.

Whether around the country or in South Thanet, Farage basked in public recognition and adulation. For most people, almost all senior politicians are anonymous and unrecognisable figures, not the sort of characters they want to meet. By 2015, however, Farage had become a rare exception, something of a political 'rock star' like the London mayor Boris Johnson. At times the response was almost as good as Johnson's.

Farage had become a TV celebrity. He was in regular demand for the Sunday politics shows, and rarely turned down an invitation. He now appeared on BBC *Question Time* more often than any other leading politician, around twice a year (and four times in 2013). It was partly because Farage was such a charismatic and articulate performer. 'He's a highly intelligent man,' the Liberal Democrat peer Shirley Williams said on one *Question Time* she did with Farage. 'He's also great fun to have a drink with.'[13] Many on the left of politics, and even people within radio and television, complained that in giving Farage so much airtime, the broadcasters had helped create UKIP as a political force, and were generating anti-EU sentiment (a view expressed by the BBC presenter Samira Ahmed in 2021). But Farage reflected a significant and growing body of Eurosceptic opinion within the British public, which the broadcasters had a duty to reflect. Moreover, the BNP's Nick Griffin had shown with his *Question Time* appearance in 2009 that TV coverage doesn't always make one more popular.

Just before Christmas 2014, Channel 4 had transmitted *Steph and Dom Meet Nigel Farage*, filmed the previous summer when the UKIP leader visited the middle-class couple Steph and Dom Parker who starred in the channel's *Gogglebox* series and lived in a large Lutyens manor house near Sandwich, in the South Thanet seat. 'I don't think I know anybody in politics as poor as we are,' Farage lamented. 'We live in a small semi-detached cottage in the country, and I can barely afford to live there. We don't drive flash cars. We don't have expensive holidays. We haven't done for ten years.' More significant was that Farage also claimed that his wife Kirsten, who had long worked for him in the European Parliament, was no longer paid 'by the public sector', but by 'the party'.[14]

Since the 2014 election, the European Parliament had banned MEPs from employing spouses, but the Parliament website now showed that Kirsten worked as an assistant to a new UKIP MEP from the South East, Ray Finch. After the broadcast, UKIP confirmed Kirsten was being paid £800 a month to help Finch. A spokesman told the *Independent* that Farage had not misled the programme, as at the time of the filming his wife was indeed being paid by the party and he was unaware that she had made the arrangement with Mr Finch.[15] Since Finch was himself a former employee of Farage, and still a close ally, it looked like an attempt to get round the Parliament's ban on employing spouses.

The programme with the *Gogglebox* couple had been part of an attempt by Alex Phillips to 'push' Farage 'down a sort of soft media avenue'. Another example was a comic video ad which Farage did for Paddy Power for the September 2014 Ryder Cup golf tournament between Europe and the USA, filmed at Westerham golf course near his home.[16] On the street, passing drivers would often shout or toot their horns. Members of the public would ask for autographs, and his aides carried a ready supply of placards for him to sign, in the hope people would put them in their windows, thereby showing neighbours they weren't ashamed to vote UKIP. Though he wasn't as touchy-feely as Robert Kilroy-Silk, he readily exchanged hugs and kisses and flirted outrageously. One woman in Ramsgate passed Farage her phone to speak to her husband. 'Hi Melvyn,' he cheekily announced, 'I'm rather busy with your wife at the moment.'[17]

As Farage walked the streets, and went door-to-door in the Kent seat, an aide carried his lighted cigarette, ready for regular fag breaks. He loved talking politics with voters, listening to their gripes about the established parties, and about the major issues, trying to reassure them that he and UKIP were different. But Farage also had a major weakness in campaigning. He had no interest in constituents' complaints about local issues, and would sometimes moan to aides about having to listen to grievances about housing, or litter, or noisy neighbours, or dog mess on the grass. Indeed, it's striking how leaflets from Farage's Westminster campaigns make very little of local problems. UKIP's then director of communications, Paul 'Gobby' Lambert (who had recently joined the party from the BBC), later recalled an exasperated Farage asking whether MPs really had to put up with all this stuff. Yes, they did, Lambert told him emphatically. These 'bread and butter' issues were what mattered to many constituents – his potential voters – and MPs had to spend much of their lives, Lambert bluntly explained, listening to such problems and trying to resolve them. Lambert got the impression that Farage suddenly found the idea of becoming an MP a lot less attractive.[18]

Farage also had a huge personal problem of his own.

Late one evening in early April, with the election now in full swing, UKIP's head of media Alex Phillips visited the Farages at their home near Downe. Kirsten went to bed and it seems she then came down and found her husband on the sitting room sofa with Phillips. She seems to have concluded that rumours she had heard – that Phillips and her husband were having an affair – must be true.

According to Paul Lambert (who died in 2020), Kirsten immediately texted him and a couple of other UKIP colleagues to express her anger. Lambert's account was that Kirsten demanded that within twenty-four hours Phillips be banished from working with her husband, otherwise she would leave him and not hesitate to explain the reasons to the press. Phillips was exiled to London for the rest of the campaign and replaced at Farage's side by a former journalist, Sarah White. Political reporters were puzzled and couldn't understand why Phillips had suddenly gone, when they'd always found her so helpful.

Alex Phillips agrees there was a problem, but reiterates that she never had an affair with Farage. When she went to Downe that evening, she says, only Kirsten and the girls were there to start with, and Nigel had yet to return home. She cooked the family one of her favourite dishes, a buttered chicken curry, and while she was there Kirsten raised the rumours about Phillips and her husband having a relationship. Phillips insisted the gossip was untrue and merely the work of her enemies within UKIP trying to undermine her. Farage eventually came home and they had the curry, she says. Kirsten went to bed while she and Nigel sat up watching the campaign coverage on TV. Phillips then says her parents called to take her back to her home in London, and Kirsten came down to answer the door.

> It was the next day that Nigel phoned me and said, 'Look, Kirsten is starting to get alarmed' and I was like 'well, you know where this is coming from, there's a very easy way of sorting this out, you know: hold the people accountable who are doing this' and that's kind of the last I heard of it, really.[19]

If Nigel Farage was canoodling with Alex Phillips in his sitting room while his wife was upstairs, then it was astonishingly reckless, especially during a general election campaign. Kirsten's anger and his relationship with Phillips were two more troubles for Farage to worry about amid the already enormous pressures. The Farages' marriage never really recovered; nor did Kirsten's friendship with Alex Phillips. It was the last straw.

In one way, Phillips was glad to be free from any involvement in Farage's constituency campaign. 'I got the impression Thanet was run a bit like a frat house,' she says:

Some of the things that I heard were going on deeply alarmed me – *deeply* alarmed me – especially with some of the men down in Thanet – and I'm not including Nigel in this, let's make that very clear – but certainly with some of the male staff in Thanet . . . There was use of young female volunteers, girls who were basically sixth-form age, and I think that some people in positions of power down there were using the 'Oh yes, we'll get you to the count,' and 'Yeah, yeah, you can get to meet Nigel,' to essentially coerce young women to do things. I was very, very alarmed at some of the things I found out, and believed were going on, and I raised these issues directly. Obviously I raised them confidentially, but it got back to the people I was concerned about, that I was raising these issues . . . and then I think that was it: vengeance was sought.

The Alex Phillips story was far from over, however.

At one point Farage had been favourite to win South Thanet, but after a poll in early April suggested he was no longer front-runner, he appealed to UKIP activists all over the country. 'I know a lot of you are fighting your own campaigns locally,' he told supporters on Facebook, 'but if you could spare just one or two days, I'd really appreciate the support.'[20] It did not endear him to candidates in other target seats.

The big problem was that UKIP still hadn't learned how to campaign in Westminster elections. The party's success in European contests stemmed from making an impact at a national level, and Farage was brilliant at doing that. Winning seats in the House of Commons requires a totally different style of electioneering – identifying your likely voters one by one, building up records of support, and then a huge effort to ensure those people vote, preferably by post, or at polling stations. This was what the main political parties had done for decades, building up canvass returns which often stretched back over many elections. Farage's party had scores of activists who'd been involved in such granular campaigns for other parties, and yet UKIP didn't adopt such methods in the 2015 general election. UKIP's main activity in South Thanet – and elsewhere – was very old-fashioned: make a lot of noise, with plenty of purple placards, balloons and leaflets; hold public meetings where the audience was overwhelmingly committed; and visit lots of pubs.

In some ways, Craig Mackinlay's campaign was just as badly organised. Compared with other marginal seats, local Tories had made contact with very few voters, hence the decision by Conservative headquarters in London to send down experienced election organiser Marion Little to run the campaign. From the start of 2015, Conservative HQ pumped huge sums of money into Thanet, and Little seemed to have no concern about sticking to the legal expenditure limits, including the omission of her own party salary from the Tories' local spending return, as well as costs for other wages for imported staff and their hotel accommodation.

Four years later, in one of the most important election spending trials of modern times, a jury convicted Marion Little of 'two very serious offences'. The judge gave her a suspended prison sentence, but said she would have gone to jail had her husband not been 'gravely ill' with cancer. Little had been 'carried away', the judge said, 'by her conviction that the defeat of Nigel Farage was an over-whelmingly important political objective'.[21]

By 23 April – with two weeks to go – Farage seemed to think things were back on track. A Survation poll, commissioned by local UKIP donor Alan Bown, suggested he was nine points ahead of Mackinlay, while the Tory candidate had also been embarrassed by the revelations that he owned a website which encouraged Hungarians to come to Britain for work. Newly buoyant, Farage and his team celebrated St George's Day with a late-night dinner at an Italian restaurant in Ramsgate, with Farage dressed in an apron based on a St George's flag. Just before midnight, after many glasses of red wine and a plate of seafood, 'the well-wined UKIP leader stood on a chair . . . to bellow out a rendition of *New York, New York,*' reported Rowena Mason of the *Guardian*, who was lucky enough to be invited along to what she called a 'virtual victory party':

A little unsteady on his feet, the UKIP leader then rounded off the night with *The Wild Rover* outside on the pavement, as aides persuaded him that moving on to a nightclub or revisiting his teenage days of skinny-dipping were not sensible for a party leader two weeks before the most important election of his life.

'We're bloody winning, aren't we?' Farage had excitedly asked his agent during his seafood dinner. 'We haven't seen him like this for months,' an aide said.[22]

And Farage still had the national campaign to lead, of course. Following his remarks about immigrants with HIV after the Clacton victory, he had continued to make eye-catching and controversial remarks on policy. In March 2015, in an interview with the former chairman of the Equality and Human Rights Commission Trevor Phillips, Farage suggested that many race discrimination laws could be repealed. 'The situation that we now have,' he said, 'where an employer is not allowed to choose between a British-born person and somebody from Poland, is a ludicrous state of affairs.'

Would UKIP have laws against discrimination on the grounds of race or colour, Phillips asked. 'No,' Farage replied. 'We as a party are colour-blind.' While concern about race discrimination 'would probably have been valid' forty years ago, it was no longer the case. Attacked on Twitter by all three main party leaders – David Cameron, Ed Miliband and Nick Clegg – Farage pointed out that it was Gordon Brown who once advocated 'British Jobs for British Workers'.[23] Four days later, he revealed that he personally thought children of new immigrants should not immediately be allowed to go to British state schools, and that immigrants should only be permitted to bring their dependants into the country after they had been in Britain for a set period.[24]

In 2010, the three main party leaders had held TV debates for the first time in history. In 2015, David Cameron did all he could to avoid a similar confrontation with Ed Miliband and Nick Clegg. Instead, it was agreed that ITV would run a debate with seven parties – the big three leaders, plus UKIP, the Greens, the SNP and Plaid Cymru. It took place on 2 April at Media City in Salford and lasted two hours. It was Farage's only chance to take on David Cameron, though in the end there was little engagement between the two. The authors of the Nuffield election study observed, 'With the exception of the Greens, who wanted to try to present themselves as "anti-UKIP", almost everyone had decided that they would largely try to ignore Nigel Farage.'[25] Farage tried to look as distinctive as possible from the others – they were very much 'the same', he said more than once – and by daring to say things that none of the others would.

His most notable contribution came in response to a question about how each leader would fund the NHS. Initially, Farage said nothing remarkable but then returned to the issue of 'health tourism' and the NHS treating immigrants with HIV.

OK, here's a fact, and I'm sure that other people will be mortified that I dare to talk about it. There are 7,000 diagnoses in this country every year for people who are HIV-positive, which is not a good place for any of them to be, I know. But 60 per cent of them are not British nationals.

You can come into Britain from anywhere in the world and get diagnosed with HIV and get the retroviral drugs that cost up to £25,000 per year, per patient. I know there are some horrible things happening in many parts of the world, but what we need to do is to put the National Health Service there for British people and families, who, in many cases, have paid into the system for decades.[26]

'This kind of scare-mongering – scare-mongering rhetoric – is dangerous,' Leanne Wood of Plaid Cymru immediately responded. 'It's a fact,' Farage interrupted. 'It's a fact. It's a fact.' 'It's dangerous,' Wood continued, to loud applause from the studio audience. 'It divides communities and it creates stigma to people who are ill, and I think you ought be ashamed of yourself.'

'I'm sorry, but we've got to put our own people first,' Farage responded. 'Would you, Leanne, open it up to 17,000 people, 27,000 people? The question is how do we fund the NHS, and if up to two billion pounds a year is being lost on health tourism, surely that is a very real problem?'

'When somebody is diagnosed with a dreadful illness,' the first minister of Scotland, Nicola Sturgeon, remarked, 'my instinct is to view them as a human being, not consider what country they come from.'[27]

Nigel Farage's comments dominated social media and headlines the next day. That was intended, for they had been far from spontaneous. They were part of a deliberate tactic to fire up UKIP's core vote, and he and his advisers had discussed the idea several times and rehearsed the intervention in the practice session beforehand. Farage was encouraged by the positive letters and emails he'd received from members of the public following his remarks after the Clacton victory six months before. Originally for the debate, Farage planned instead to mention immigrants being treated for tuberculosis, until he was told that the cost of treating HIV patients was far greater. But at least one of his advisers, it seems, was against the idea. After the debate, in the so-called spin room in Salford, Kassam told journalists it was part of a strategy of 'shock and awe', or perhaps, 'shock and awful'.[28]

Douglas Carswell was furious. He'd not been warned about the move, and feared it would backfire. 'There's a powerful point to be made about health tourism,' he said. 'But would you say the same about people with leukaemia? . . . Why invite people who want to think the worst of you to have an excuse to think badly of you? It was awful.'[29]

The week before, Sky News had hosted an event at their headquarters in west London, entitled *The Battle for Number Ten*, in which David Cameron and Ed Miliband were individually interviewed by Jeremy Paxman, and also questioned separately by the studio audience. Clegg and the minor party leaders hadn't been invited, but Farage's team arranged for him to turn up as a commentator in the spin room where journalists observed the event. It was probably not a great idea, since Farage was suddenly confronted by three young Black people who had been at Sky for a programme to encourage the younger generation to vote. One woman complained to Farage that 'every day' someone in UKIP was accused of 'a racist slur or homophobic slur', and that Farage always dismissed the problem as a 'couple' of people. 'Racism is not gone,' she went on. 'It's alive and clear. I was born in Barnsley. We used to have our house egged on a daily basis . . .'

Farage did not handle the confrontation well. The woman spoke at length, but Farage kept interrupting her with put-down comments such as, 'Is this a question or a speech?' and 'If we can't have a conversation . . .', and 'I have no doubt your economic skills are brilliant . . .' Owen Bennett, who got to know Farage well at that time, later said it was:

> the first time I had seen Farage be sarcastic and dismissive to a voter who was pressing him. The young woman was being a bit aggressive, and certainly wouldn't cut Farage any slack, but was her behaviour any different to when the UKIP leader accused . . . Herman Van Rompuy of having 'all the charisma of a damp rag and the appearance of a low-grade bank clerk'?[30]

The other TV event involving Farage was the so-called 'Challengers' debate on the BBC, chaired by David Dimbleby. This occasion was confined to the five main party leaders who weren't in government, so no David Cameron or Nick Clegg. When Farage got a hostile reaction from the live audience, he questioned whether the BBC had composed it fairly. It was a 'remarkable audience', Farage complained. 'Even by the left-wing standards of the BBC, I mean this lot's pretty left-wing, believe me.' Dimbleby quickly slapped him down, explaining that they had been chosen not by the BBC but an independent polling company. At that, the audience cheered and applauded. 'The real audience is sitting at home actually,' Farage went on, to further jeers, before saying that open-door immigration had contributed to the housing crisis. 'You're worried every problem is caused by immigrants,' Nicola Sturgeon told Farage – to more applause.[31]

People observed that Nigel Farage looked tired and unwell at campaign appearances. And no wonder. He was still dogged by health problems from the 2010 plane crash; his spinal injury had got worse, causing him 'horrible' pain and making it impossible to lift his arms more than 45 degrees. Twice a week he visited the private

London Bridge Hospital for treatment, and he'd been prescribed strong sleeping pills and muscle relaxants. Having firmly denied at the start of the campaign that he was 'unwell', a fortnight before polling day Farage revealed his problems to the *Daily Telegraph*:

> I was getting increasingly terrible pain in my shoulder, my back and so I was suffering from neuralgic pain . . . I was not ill, but I was in a lot of pain, and neuralgic pain is horrible. It is nerves. I would move my arm and it would go. I was really having a bad time . . . It is something I have got to live with, and I have got to pace myself. I think I am going to have medical treatment for the rest of my life.[32]

The first few weeks of Farage's national campaign had been a shambles. He'd failed to appear at an event he'd scheduled with people campaigning against the proposed HS2 railway, claiming the weather as an excuse. He also didn't turn up at a pub in Grimsby where the landlord had brewed a special beer in his honour, though he misspelled it as 'Fraage Ale'. Farage had been doing an interview with the young TV star Joey Essex, with whom he was so impressed that they then had lunch instead of him visiting the pub with the special ale and meeting supporters. UKIP claimed the visit was cancelled because of a protest outside. 'Where is Nigel Farage?' one Fleet Street reporter tweeted. 'He should be in this pub in Grimsby.' It was a sign of how things were that he even managed to upset Chris Hope of the *Telegraph*, who has often been the reporter he goes to if he wants to make an announcement. 'So,' Hope tweeted, 'Nigel Farage preferred to have lunch with a celebrity called Joey Essex than have a beer with supporters in a pub in Grimsby. Rubbish.'

The 2015 election was the first in which the media treated Farage almost as if he were one of the main party leaders, and several print and broadcast reporters were assigned to him for the whole campaign. But Team Farage seemed to concentrate instead on activities which kept him at arm's length. Farage and UKIP were 'wasting an opportunity with this general election', Chris Hope reported on the *Telegraph*'s rolling blog:

The party is lucky to have teams from Sky News, BBC and ITV News following Mr Farage around the country. Yet his aides keep organising controlled media opportunities, which only serve to keep Mr Farage away from real people . . .

If UKIP is an insurgent political force, then it has to start behaving like it in media terms. This will mean letting Mr Farage behave like an insurgent leader and take on his critics directly – and even debate with them in the street. But UKIP don't seem to want to do that.[33]

Polling day didn't start well for Farage. The *Daily Mail* published parts of a best man's speech which Farage had made back in 2001 at the wedding of his younger bother Andrew. The marriage took place just four months after a young man had been found dead in the swimming pool at the home of the gay TV star Michael Barrymore, after a drug-fuelled party. 'As far as the smokers here are concerned, it's been a good news, bad news story,' Farage said of his brother's wedding reception:

Because the bad news was, we weren't allowed to smoke until the coffee was served, but the good news folks, for those of you who are smokers, is we were far better off here than if we'd been at Michael Barrymore's house. Because there they removed all the ashtrays on the basis that now they chuck all the fags in the pool.[34]

A video recording shows Farage's highly tasteless and homophobic joke was met with laughter and applause (though the singer Rod Stewart, who was also present, looked uncomfortable). The video was given to the *Mail* by a guest at the wedding who said they wanted the nation to see it. 'He claims not to be homophobic,' the guest said, 'but why tell a joke about throwing fags in a pool at his brother's wedding?' 'It was a best man's speech for Christ's sake,' Farage replied. 'If you look at the whole video I told a whole series of jokes . . . There was absolutely no malice intended in it at all. That particular joke was one doing the rounds quite widely at the time.'[35]

Farage later said he knew by lunchtime on polling day that he would lose. 'I could see the wards in Broadstairs with 80 per cent turnouts, with people queuing for [an] inordinate amount of time to vote. I talked to lots of them down in the street and they just said: "Look, Nigel, we love you but we can't have Nicola Sturgeon running the country."'[36] Far from UKIP holding the balance of power, as they'd hoped, the fear among many voters was they might help Labour run the country with the SNP.

The South Thanet result was expected overnight, but was severely delayed because of problems getting the different tallies of votes to match. Farage spent most of the night in a hotel near the count in Margate, and emerged at 9 a.m. on the Friday. Would he still stand down as UKIP leader if he lost South Thanet? Chris Hope asked him. 'Are you calling me a liar?' Farage replied. 'I have never ever broken my word before so I am very unlikely to start now.'[37] Farage was surrounded by a media scrum as he entered the Margate Winter Gardens. 'We've lost by about seventeen hundred votes,' Chris Bruni-Lowe told journalists.

The outcome was finally announced at 10.32 a.m.:

Craig Mackinlay (Con)	18,838	38.1%
Nigel Farage (UKIP)	16,026	32.4%
Will Scobie (Lab)	11,740	23.8%
Eight others	2,797	5.6%
Conservative majority	2,812	

It must have been agony for Farage. His old chum Craig Mackinlay was now an MP, and he wasn't. On the platform, Farage and Mackinlay were standing either side of the comedian Al Murray, who had stood as the 'Pub Landlord' candidate. In a scene broadcast many times in the coming years, Murray feigned astonishment at the result, while Mackinlay rubbed his hands in glee (in reality both knew the precise result well in advance). Farage 'seemed to shrink before my eyes,' wrote Owen Bennett:

This man who, for two years, I had seen winning applause and admiration in town halls across the country, who had persuaded two Tory MPs to risk their careers and join the party, who had survived a plane crash, a car crash and cancer with a devil-may-care attitude, suddenly seemed very small, very vulnerable. And very lonely.[38]

Suffering the jeers and cheers of his opponents' supporters, Farage had to listen to Craig Mackinlay's acceptance speech, and the cruel taunts of a man who had held several high offices in Farage's party: 'People here have shown that there is no need for Nigel Farage and there is no need for UKIP.' Farage then replied: 'Five years ago on election day I was in intensive care after an aeroplane crash, so compared with that, this feels pretty damn good.' And he concluded: 'On a personal level, I feel an enormous weight has been lifted from my shoulders, and I have never felt happier. Thank you.'[39] With that, Farage walked off stage without bothering to hear the other contenders, and was followed by a huge media entourage. 'It was very rude,' says Will Scobie. 'He'd turned up very late, saw he'd lost, and didn't even stay to listen to the other candidates.' The video record suggests Farage never congratulated Mackinlay, or shook his hand.

Scobie thinks Farage had suffered from an on-off local campaign, in which he would work intensely in South Thanet for a week, then vanish for several days to fulfil his duties as party leader round the country.

The most interesting thing is that when Farage was down here he seemed unstoppable, and there wasn't much we could do about it. Everyone wanted to talk to him. And people wanted to talk *about* him on the doorstep. Then he'd leave for a week, and UKIP went quiet, so we got the chance to get our message across, and the Tories had a chance to get their message across. So he was only a part-time candidate, which made it impossible for him to work against claims that he'd only be a part-time MP. That room – of him leaving for long spells – gave a chance for the Tories to come back. Because UKIP kept losing momentum they were never far enough ahead to make up for their organisational disadvantages. If Farage had been around for the whole campaign, I think he might have won.[40]

There's an alternative view, held by Farage's close adviser Alex Phillips, who believes he spent *too much* time in Thanet, at the expense of his national responsibilities. She argues that if Farage had switched his efforts to activities elsewhere, he would have generated more national media coverage, and that in turn would have converted and enthused many more voters in Thanet than by approaching them house by house. Phillips says she'd taken 'great pains' to devise an extensive 'grid' of national engagements for Farage, most of which was jettisoned.

> It was basically thrown in the bin and I was told 'We're staying in Thanet, he's not leaving Thanet, he's just going to knock on every single door.' And the journalists were phoning me saying 'Where is he? What's he doing?' and I was like, 'I don't know, he's in Thanet, you'll have to speak to Raheem, that's where they are.' And just having people come to me all the time complaining about a lack of access, complaining about Raheem's approach and attitude to them.[41]

For a couple of years after the election, people close to Nigel Farage would make an extraordinary claim about the South Thanet campaign – that it had been sabotaged by Douglas Carswell. The essential allegation was eventually published in *The Bad Boys of Brexit*, the memoir of UKIP's major new donor Arron Banks.

Banks had built his insurance business by amassing data about his millions of customers, utilising the latest developments in communicating through social media. So he was something of an expert in handling data. In his book, Banks claims that Carswell was one of just three people who had access to sensitive UKIP data showing party support, house by house and street by street, in the party's target seats, including South Thanet. 'Farage was surprised and concerned,' Banks says, 'to find that Tory activists were targeting the exact same individuals in South Thanet' and subjecting these voters to a 'push-polling' operation in which people were asked loaded questions about the UKIP leader. 'How did they come to be so well informed?' Banks asked.[42]

> We may never know. Long after polling day, however, my own forensic post-mortem examination of South Thanet revealed something quite remarkable: Carswell was routinely downloading the data and sending it to an anonymous computer server.
>
> He did so on six separate occasions. While there were files on every target seat in the country, curiously, only the information about South Thanet was shared. Quite where the information went once it left our offices, nobody knows, but I can make an educated guess: the Tories. This private data could have made it much easier for the Tories to target floating voters in the constituency.[43]

It is an astonishing allegation, to which Douglas Carswell responds: 'The claim that I accessed data and passed it on in this way is untrue. Perhaps the real offence I committed in the eyes of some in UKIP was that I won my seat – not just once, but twice. I'm not sure some ever forgave me for that.'[44]

Nonetheless, even without their leader being elected, UKIP had achieved something remarkable in historic terms. They were now Britain's third party, having polled 3,881,099 votes – more than four times the tally of 2010. This was one in eight of all those who voted, almost half as much as Labour, and more than the combined vote of the Liberal Democrats and the SNP (who had sixty-four seats between them). It was easily the best ever performance in modern history by any party outside the main three. Yet UKIP had won precious little for that support – just one seat, Clacton – which Douglas Carswell retained with a much-shrunken majority. Fellow defector Mark Reckless was defeated in Rochester and Strood, and UKIP failed in all of their other prime targets.

The party had fought all 573 constituencies in England and Wales (and two thirds of the fifty-nine in Scotland) and come second in

120, in some cases with token candidates who ran no real campaign. And the party had another impact. The election chroniclers Philip Cowley and Dennis Kavanagh concluded that 'UKIP took their votes disproportionately from the Conservatives, but because of the geographical distribution of those votes, they disproportionately hurt Labour in terms of seats'.

In their book about the 2015 election, they quoted one Labour MP in the immediate aftermath as warning: 'This is an existential crisis for the Labour Party. UKIP could "SNP" us in England, if they just hold their nerve. If we don't get this right, there won't be a Labour Party in 2020.'[45]

Another political analyst, Matthew Goodwin, who has written several books about UKIP and the far right, argues that if Farage had adopted a more populist, anti-austerity economic policy in 2015, then UKIP might have won another 5 per cent of the vote. That could have given them a dozen or more seats, and maybe even enough to hold the balance of power. Two years later, Goodwin argues, the Labour Party under Jeremy Corbyn would show how an economic policy of reversing cuts, huge public investment, and taxing the rich, could have substantial appeal. But Farage never seized that opportunity.[46]

Farage in the aftermath of 2015 was faced with a paradox. His personal defeat meant he was morally obliged to resign as UKIP leader, and yet his party had just won a resounding number of votes, and its long-standing political goal had suddenly become tantalisingly close.

QUITS OR DOUBLE?

'Botany Bay Hotel, now!' barked the UKIP spin doctor 'Gobby' Lambert in his rough London voice as Farage and the media scrum scurried out of the Margate Winter Gardens.

The pack of reporters and cameramen quickly jumped into their cars to make the ten-minute drive to a scenic spot high above the beach where the North Sea merges into the English Channel. Unusually, this Botany Bay gets its name from Australia rather than the other way round, because people caught smuggling there were often transported Down Under. On a sward of grass over-looking neighbouring white cliffs and high above the waves, barely thirty-five minutes after the result had been announced at the South Thanet count, Nigel Farage made another speech. He was carrying out the famous pledge he'd first made in his book *The Purple Revolution*:

> Now, I said as this campaign went on that if I didn't win I would stand down as leader of UKIP, and I know that you in the media are used to party leaders making endless promises that they don't actually keep, but I'm a man of my word. I don't break my word, so I shall be writing to the UKIP National Executive in a few minutes saying that I am standing down as leader of UKIP. I will recommend that *pro tem* they put in place as acting leader Suzanne Evans, who I think has emerged from this campaign as an absolute tower of strength within UKIP. She works in London, she's based in the London office, and I think that's the right way for us to go.[1]

His words sounded conclusive. He wasn't like other leaders who endlessly broke their promises – 'I don't break my word,' he'd emphasised, yet it seemed odd for Farage to set such store by a promise, when so many of his past pledges had meant so little. He seemed to be anointing Suzanne Evans as his chosen successor – 'the right way for us to go'. He then, however, sowed huge doubt:

> I haven't had a fortnight's holiday since October 1993. I intend to take the summer off, enjoy myself a little bit, not do very much politics at all, and there will be a leadership election for the next leader of UKIP in September, and I will consider over the course of this summer whether to put my name forward to do that job again.
>
> One thing I'm absolutely certain of is there are opportunities coming up electorally – I look at the Welsh Assembly elections next year, the Scottish Parliament, the year after the London Assembly elections, goodness knows what by-elections may come, and I think those four million people out there are pretty loyal . . . and I think the next chapter of UKIP has begun.[2]

Something was strangely missing from Farage's list of forthcoming public votes, for during the short journey from the Margate Winter Gardens, at 10.50 a.m. – unnoticed perhaps by Farage – a hugely symbolic moment had occurred. David Cameron had secured his 323rd MP in the Commons, which meant the Conservatives now had enough to govern on their own, without a coalition, without support from the much-depleted Liberal Democrats or anyone else. That would mean that Cameron – if he was to keep *his* promise – was now obliged to hold an In–Out referendum on Britain's membership of the European Union. Surprisingly, Farage seemed not to have spotted this, and said nothing of the coming plebiscite in his Botany Bay announcement.

Nor does the likely referendum seem to have occurred to him later that afternoon, when he gave a joint interview to a group of journalists in a social club in Ramsgate. He was too old to go back to metal trading he said, but he might deploy his skills for sensing trends in public opinion. 'There are commentators who present radio shows,' he mused. 'I am going to rethink my life.' And he was even nicer about Suzanne Evans – 'a highly competent woman whom I am recommending to the party', though he also suggested Douglas Carswell might try to be his successor. 'I'm an honourable man,' Farage added. 'I keep my promises. I said I would go if I lost. What's done is done. I'm relieved.'[3]

Suzanne Evans says Farage rang her at UKIP headquarters in Mayfair just before the Botany Bay speech to warn her he was about to appoint her as acting leader. 'What are you doing that for?' she recalls asking. 'You have just got four million votes. You've just got the first UKIP MP elected. You don't need to resign. You've done well.' Farage replied that he had said he'd resign and so he must do so. And he was fed up with several senior colleagues, he told Evans.[4] She was very nervous, and also wary, since her appointment would have to be ratified by the UKIP NEC the following Monday.

Evans had been up all night watching the election results and doing media interviews. She told Farage that she would now go home to get some sleep before taking over. She recalls the UKIP leader asking why she was going home. 'You're on the doorstep of Claridge's. Go and book yourself into a room.' Evans recalls protesting that she couldn't do that. 'Yes you can,' Farage reportedly said. 'You're the leader of UKIP now. You can do anything you like.'

'No I can't, it's a complete waste of money,' Evans protested.

'The party will pay,' said Farage.

'I'm not spending our members' money on that,' Evans says she replied.

Despite Farage's warm words about Evans and Carswell, the Botany Bay speech would quickly cause deep divisions within UKIP – a divide which was never really healed, in fact. Some thought Farage's original promise had been foolish, and that he'd also been wrong to announce he was sticking to it. Others, conversely, thought it was the right decision, and he was wrong to sow doubts about whether he would cease being leader.

That weekend UKIP headquarters was bombarded with emails from members insisting that Farage should stay. Much of the email traffic was the result of an effort organised by a senior UKIP official, David Soutter, who'd been in charge of candidates. Soutter caught up with Farage just after he'd finished outside the Botany Bay Hotel. 'Nigel, what have you done?' he recalls asking. 'I promised,' Farage replied.[5] 'You've won four million votes, for God's sake,' Soutter pleaded. 'You should see this as a victory!'[6]

Soutter began organising. As head of candidates he was well placed to contact every one of the 624 people who'd stood for UKIP in the election to urge them to support Farage. 'It is vital that Nigel stays at the helm,' Soutter wrote, 'and I know you will all support this call to him to carry on the fight. Please email with messages of support today. This is the most important thing you can do today.'[7]

Farage and Soutter would meet again, by chance, the next day, at the seventieth anniversary service for VE Day at Westminster Abbey, and later amid the commemorations on Horse Guards Parade. Soutter was struck by the numbers – including Chelsea Pensioners, policemen and ordinary members of the public – who came to wish Farage well and wanted their picture taken with him. 'He was mobbed by a huge crowd of people, who pushed the barriers aside,' Soutter recalls. 'I said, "If you resign you'll regret it, and for the rest of your life."'[8]

Paul Nuttall, the UKIP deputy leader, was especially upset by what Farage had said at Botany Bay. Not only had Farage not bothered to consult him about the resignation announcement, but he had only warned him minutes beforehand. 'It made me look a fool,' he later said. 'I was angry.'[9] Nuttall was especially furious when he heard Farage appoint Suzanne Evans as acting leader, even though Nuttall was his official number two. And Nuttall had been a senior figure within the party for almost a decade, having served as chairman for two years, before five years as Farage's deputy, and he had been an MEP since 2009. Suzanne Evans, in contrast, had been a member of UKIP for just two years. There was also a significant difference between the two apparent front-runners – more so than in any previous leadership contest. While Evans was a middle-class southerner who had only left the Conservatives two years before, Nuttall was a working-class Liverpudlian who epitomised UKIP's drive to break into Labour heartlands in the North.

Nuttall quickly got to work, and threatened that unless it was made clear that Evans wouldn't stand in the leadership election, then he would get the NEC to block her as interim leader. Nuttall also said Farage promised to back him, not Evans, in the election.

Suzanne Evans, meanwhile, spent most of the Saturday working out what to do now she was supposedly in charge. She had little idea what was going on. Then suddenly on the Sunday morning she got a call from the party secretary Matt Richardson to say she must sign some 'paperwork' to pledge she wouldn't stand for leader in September.

'This was out of the blue,' Evans recalls. '"Why would I sign that?" I said.' Richardson explained that if she was interim leader she would have an unfair advantage as a candidate. Evans went to consult Farage at his home in Kent. She outlined her plans for the party, which included a major fund-raising effort, and resources for councillors in Thanet where UKIP had just taken control of the council. 'I also said that it's obvious that now the Conservatives have a majority and David Cameron will call a referendum, we need to start talking to big-name Brexiteers in other parties to get the campaign going so that we can leave,' she recalls. 'Unbeknown to me, that was the line that totally sealed my doom.'[10]

Evans explained she was a 'team-worker' and believed in building a 'united front', but Farage didn't seem impressed. 'Nigel went "Yeah, yeah, um, um," and put his tongue in his cheek. "I'm gonna have to come back, aren't I? I was at the VE Day commemorations, in Westminster Abbey, and you know, I got a bigger cheer than the veterans."'

'We were having a lovely conversation about me being interim leader,' says Evans, 'and it wasn't until I mentioned the referendum that it all went wrong. He wanted to be the figurehead for the referendum campaign. Brexit was his baby.'[11]

Much more important than the weekend politicking behind the scenes – the pressures from ordinary members and from Nuttall – was that the big implications of the new political situation had finally dawned on Farage. Even though the Conservative majority was small – just twelve – there was no way that David Cameron could now avoid holding a referendum during the new Parliament,

at some time before 2020, and probably by the end of 2017, as the
Tory manifesto had promised.

'The real clincher was this,' Farage explained later. 'I'd spent all
these years looking like the Patron Saint of Lost Causes but now we
had finally got the referendum. I felt that to walk away now, when this
great battle was upon us, was just not the right thing to do.' What's
more, Farage quickly realised that before the plebiscite itself there
would be another mighty battle among British Eurosceptics to lead
the campaign to leave the EU – between traditional forces, such as
Conservative backbenchers, and the more radical groups like UKIP.
As Farage saw Tory Eurosceptics limbering up for the fight over that
weekend, he felt, in the words of Matthew Goodwin and Caitlin
Milazzo, 'like the striker who had been substituted, forced to sit on
the bench for the remainder of the game. And it was hard to watch.'[12]
Farage feared that if he didn't change his mind, he would be replaced
as leader by one of the two former Conservatives he had identified
at Botany Bay – Douglas Carswell or Suzanne Evans. Yet both were
very late arrivals to his party, people who didn't share his outlook,
and in Carswell's case took a very liberal view of immigration.

When Farage and Carswell spoke on the Monday morning before
the UKIP NEC, the re-elected Carswell could not hide his relief
that Farage had apparently stood down. 'Douglas was very keen
that I was going,' Farage said, 'and that I would not be playing a
role in the referendum debate . . . Two or three people in the upper
echelons [of UKIP] were trying to prevent me from coming back.
They would sideline us in the referendum and give up on our core
message.'[13] Chris Bruni-Lowe, who had worked closely with both
men, put it more colourfully when he later related Farage's response
after Carswell asked if he planned to return: '"Well, I've not really
given it much thought, but I probably will now there's going to be a
referendum." And Carswell says, "You cannot do that, you're toxic.
You'll damage the cause." And Nigel thought, "Well, fuck this."'[14]

Douglas Carswell had already come under growing suspicion
among those close to Farage during the South Thanet campaign, as
they became more and more convinced that he had leaked sensitive
UKIP data about local voters to the Conservatives.

Later on the Monday morning, when Nigel Farage walked into the UKIP NEC at the party headquarters in Brook's Mews in Mayfair, he was blunt. 'If you want me to go,' he said, 'then I will go.' No, said NEC members, we need you. We need you to lead the referendum campaign. And David Soutter produced a huge pile of letters from UKIP candidates and members who'd written into headquarters insisting that their leader must stay. Tim Aker, who had been the candidate in Thurrock, and came close to winning, pointed out that he'd got 15,718. But only 718 of those votes, he said, were due to himself. Farage was responsible for the other 15,000. Farage looked round at his colleagues. 'It became apparent at that moment,' he says, 'that coming back was the only option.'[15]

The question, then, was whether Farage would return immediately, or go through an election process which would give him time to rest before he was no doubt re-elected that autumn. The NEC decided that party chairman Steve Crowther should become acting leader, and they would ask Suzanne Evans to switch from being interim leader to chairman in Crowther's place. The National Executive voted for this without seeking Evans's approval – since she wasn't on the NEC. She says the UKIP treasurer Andrew Reid offered her 'lots of money' to take the job (as a party employee). 'I said "No." It was just surreal. So Farage un-resigned.'[16]

Farage's decision to stay on was reinforced by his differences with Douglas Carswell, in particular over a new bone of contention thrown up by the election results. The pair found themselves at odds over Short Money, the state funding which opposition parties get to help them organise their parliamentary business, and to which UKIP was now entitled. Named after Edward Short, the Labour minister who introduced the system in 1975, the subsidy is seen as a way to offset the advantage which government parties get from having the civil service machine at their command. The formula for calculating the funding involves a combination of the number of MPs a party has and its total vote at the previous election. That should have entitled UKIP to around £670,000 in 2015 – and more than £3.3 million over a five-year Parliament. UKIP was in particular difficulty because it had already made spending decisions on the assumption that Short

Money would rescue them after the election, and people who'd resigned from the European payroll to help the election effort had been promised party jobs afterwards. 'We were all depending on that money,' one of them explains.

The problem was that the linkman for obtaining such funds was UKIP's sole MP, Douglas Carswell, who had long said he was opposed to any state funding of political parties. While the NEC was meeting, Carswell had emailed the UKIP party secretary Matt Richardson saying he thought UKIP should only take £350,000 in Short Money (just over half the amount UKIP could have claimed). Farage was immediately suspicious. 'I've got a horrible feeling about all of this and where I think this is going,' he reportedly told close colleagues at UKIP HQ. 'I think we're being infiltrated.' And maybe Farage had a point, given Carswell's subsequent revelations that his purpose in defecting to UKIP had been to drag the party in a different direction ahead of the EU referendum.

Carswell's email to Richardson reinforced Farage's resolve. Paul Nuttall later told how Farage thought that coming back was the only way to stop the suspected infiltration going any further. 'Gentlemen, I fear we're being hijacked,' Farage told his colleagues. 'Reload!'[17]

Farage's two main advisers, Raheem Kassam and Chris Bruni-Lowe, visited Carswell at the Commons that evening to urge him to think again, but were less than diplomatic in their approach. The prospect of receiving around two thirds of a million pounds a year was an 'absurdity', Carswell said, for a parliamentary party of just one MP. Farage's advisers suggested that Carswell could use the money to employ fifteen members of staff. 'I am not a US senator. I don't need 15 staff. UKIP is supposed to be different,' Carswell told the BBC.[18] 'Naturally, I turned down most of it . . . I knew I could not justify spending that sort of money on my parliamentary office.'[19] Yet this was no benefit to the Treasury, since what Carswell failed to take for UKIP would simply be reallocated to other opposition parties, mostly to Labour.

As Carswell explained his position publicly, he also suggested that Farage was wrong to take his job back – which wasn't surprising given Carswell's concerns about the image and tone of Out forces in the expected EU referendum. 'Knowing how difficult it is to lead a party makes me admire Nigel Farage all the more,' Carswell wrote in *The Times*. 'On his watch, UKIP has done extraordinarily well . . . Yet even leaders need to take a break. Nigel needs to take a break now.' Carswell continued:

> At times, UKIP has failed to strike the right tone. By all means we should highlight the problem of health tourism. But we need to admit that using the example of HIV patients to make the point was ill-advised. UKIP has been at its most persuasive when we have been most optimistic. Anger is never a great way to motivate people – at least not for very long.[20]

And Carswell joined his ally Suzanne Evans in urging that the Leave forces in the referendum should be a cross-party united front.

> Rather than focusing on the 13 per cent of people who voted UKIP at the last election, the Out campaign needs to find ways of winning the argument among the 87 per cent of people who did not. Strident Euroscepticism won't do it.
>
> The clue is in the name. UKIP was founded to make the UK independent of the EU. That's what brought us into politics. We mustn't get distracted. We mustn't confuse ends and means. We should be prepared to work with people across the spectrum who want ultimate power to reside with people answerable to the rest of us rather than Eurocrats. There are many decent Green, SNP, Labour, Lib Dem and Conservative voters who share this aim. Are we going to work with them or talk over them? Are we going to play our part in a positive coalition, making the case for a better future or are we going to drown out messages other than our own?[21]

A third senior figure, Patrick O'Flynn, who was now UKIP economics spokesman as well as being an MEP, and was a close ally of Suzanne Evans, joined the attack. In an interview for *The Times*, O'Flynn went further, and described Farage as 'snarling, thin-skinned and aggressive'. UKIP was in danger of looking like an 'absolutist monarchy or a personality cult', the MEP said, and he denounced a 'Tea Party, ultra-aggressive American influence' within UKIP, which was clearly a reference to Farage adviser Raheem Kassam and UKIP party secretary Matt Richardson, both of whom had strong American links.

The Conservative MEP Dan Hannan recalls Nigel Farage's long-standing media adviser Gawain Towler as saying: 'Every single UKIP MEP recognises the truth of what Patrick has just said. Something bizarre has happened.' Indeed, Hannan believes that the years roughly between 2014 and 2017 saw a Farage who in temperament, his associations and a harder, more abrasive politics, was very different from the man he had known for so long in the European Parliament (and would recognise again after 2017). 'For whatever reason, there [were] a couple of years, when not only his character but his whole approach to politics changed. And it was a very, very striking thing.' Hannan suspects it may have been related to the 2010 plane crash, and the fact that Farage was taking painkillers, at a time when he was still drinking heavily. 'Booze and painkillers are often quite a bad mixture,' he suggests. This new Farage had a dramatic effect on the whole politics of Euroscepticism after the 2015 general election, Hannan argues.[22]

Carswell, Evans and O'Flynn were increasingly identified as a modernising, more centrist group within the party. Farage's allies accused them of trying to mount a coup.

Others joined the attacks on Farage. He was 'clearly now an extremely tired and stressed man', said his old drinking buddy Godfrey Bloom. 'Time for him to move over, one might think. One of the problems that UKIP have had now for several years is that any criticism – constructive criticism of the policy or the leadership – has got you sacked. You do not criticise the leadership and stay in office. You are out of the door at the speed of light.'[23]

The UKIP donor Stuart Wheeler, who'd made his fortune from spread-betting and also funded the Tories in the past, said that while he was a 'huge admirer' of Farage, he thought he must be 'naturally exhausted' and suffering pain because of his injuries. He didn't think Farage 'should have resumed the leadership the way he did, and I don't like the way it happened,' he said.

I don't actually think he's the right person to be leading UKIP now. His methods of speaking and everything were fantastically good, but up to this point. He's a bit divisive and aggressive – which is just what we needed – but when it comes to the Out campaign, the people who voted UKIP in the general election would almost all vote to leave the EU anyway. So the battle will not be for their votes, the battle will be for the people who really haven't made up their minds. And I think a softer approach, sort of rather quieter approach, is probably what's going to be needed.[24]

In *The Spectator* a week later, Wheeler extended his argument, pointing out that while Farage had won 32.4 per cent of the vote in South Thanet, UKIP candidates standing for the local council across the same seat won 36 per cent. Farage was 'in his way, an absolutely outstanding orator,' Wheeler wrote, 'whether on TV or radio, or at public meetings. He speaks with great clarity, he is highly intelligent, articulate, well-informed and quick on his feet, and that is the main reason why the party has become such a force in British politics.' But that oratory was no longer suitable, Wheeler said, for the forthcoming fight over the EU:

> To win the referendum we must have 50 per cent rather than 12.5 per cent, or even 32.4 per cent, and we need a quiet, well-reasoned approach to convince the waverers, in a battle which will be more important to this country even than any general election. We have to get over to the undecided voter that everyone will be better off, in fact far better off, outside the EU.[25]

O'Flynn's very personal attack on his 'snarling, thin-skinned' leader must have especially angered Farage given that he had gone out of his way to get the former *Express* reporter chosen as a European candidate for UKIP only the year before. Realising he'd made a huge error, O'Flynn quickly went to see Farage in the European Parliament, said he'd got things 'horribly wrong' and offered to step down as economics spokesman. His resignation was accepted. 'That takes a big-hearted honest man to do it,' Farage said, 'and we all respect him for it.' UKIP MEPs 'burst into applause' when O'Flynn addressed them and admitted his error. 'They could see an honest human being, who was prepared to admit they'd made a mistake,' Farage said, 'and there's too little of that in politics these days . . . I respect him hugely for the way he's handled this today . . . No longer do I bear any anger about what he said.'[26] Farage showed surprising magnanimity and good humour about the O'Flynn episode, perhaps because he knew that by going too far and having to say sorry so publicly he had put the moderniser group on the defensive, whereas a week earlier they seemed to have the leadership of the party within their grasp.

Within the space of just a few days, Farage had outmanoeuvred the small band of moderniser critics. Thereafter, Douglas Carswell, Suzanne Evans and Patrick O'Flynn would never again play a major role in UKIP.

But there was one adversary whom Farage would not vanquish quite so easily.

Despite being thwarted by Farage in his attempt to become a UKIP MEP in the 2014 elections, and despite being blocked from becoming a Westminster candidate in 2015, Neil Hamilton was not one to give up. He now had his sights on Wales. And while David Cameron and his team were busy preparing the ground for the In–Out referendum, UKIP was about to get heavily embroiled in yet more bitter internal warfare, this time in the principality.

Nigel Farage had stated in his Botany Bay remarks that one of UKIP's next big electoral hurdles would be the elections for the Welsh Assembly in 2016. In the early years of UKIP, Wales had always been pretty barren territory, but the party's sudden spurt in popularity in the early 2010s was greater in Wales than almost any other part of Britain. And the assembly's system of proportional representation promised rich pickings. While forty of the Assembly's sixty seats are elected by a traditional first-past-the-post process, the remaining twenty are elected under a top-up procedure in each of five Welsh regions, so that the overall distribution of assembly members (AMs) better reflects the party vote in each area. The odds were that whoever was placed top of the UKIP list in each region would almost certainly get elected as an AM, and possibly one or two of the runners-up as well. And these were jobs worth having, with a guaranteed salary for five years, as well as office expenses and staff.

It was also in Wales that Nigel Farage and the UKIP high command spotted an opportunity for Mark Reckless. Farage didn't feel the same hostility towards Reckless as he did towards his friend Douglas Carswell, and he felt bad that Reckless had taken the risk of defecting from the Tories, but then lost his seat in the 2015 election less than six months later. The trouble was that UKIP's rules stated that you had to be resident in Wales or work there to qualify as a candidate for the party. In the summer of 2015, the NEC was asked to change those regulations. Neil Hamilton went along with the amendment, though didn't really appreciate the reason behind it. Then he suddenly realised there might be an opportunity for him, too. Though he now lived in Wiltshire, and had been an MP for an English seat, he'd actually been born in Wales; he grew up there and went to Aberystwyth University. 'Over my dead body,' Christine Hamilton recalls saying when her husband came home and announced his intentions. 'You are not going back into politics. I will divorce you.'[27] But Christine relented. Neil Hamilton relates how his wife joked that for Farage he was 'like a turd that kept coming back'.[28] It's an interesting example of the value of persistence in politics.

Yet ordinary UKIP members in Wales were understandably wary about candidates parachuting in from England, or being imposed upon them. Hamilton's popularity with grassroots members everywhere was probably enough to overcome that, but it might prove a problem for Reckless, who had no Welsh connections, and also for another senior UKIP figure who now entered the fray. Alex Phillips had moved to Wales after the 2015 election – following the difficult incident which aroused Kirsten Farage's anxieties about Phillips's friendship with her husband. She became a UKIP press officer in Cardiff, where she'd been to university, and joined the payroll of the Welsh UKIP MEP Nathan Gill. Encouraged by Gill, her plan was also to stand for the Assembly in 2016.

So, for almost a year after the 2015 general election, at a time when UKIP nationally should have been concentrating on the EU referendum, much of the NEC's time was taken up with vicious wrangling over who should be allowed to stand in elections to a body which represented less than 5 per cent of the UK population.

Under the official UKIP selection process, applicants for regional list seats in Wales were first due to be 'sifted' by party officials, and then chosen and listed in order by the leader of UKIP in Wales, who happened to be Nathan Gill. This was a slightly odd situation since Gill – who had been chosen as Welsh leader by Farage, and was a loyal ally – hoped to become an AM himself. When Gill conducted this process, he excluded both Hamilton and Reckless, but included Alex Phillips and put her top of the list in South Wales Central (Cardiff and the surrounding area). Gill had overplayed his hand. Had he just excluded either Reckless or Hamilton, his line-up might have been approved. But NEC members weren't willing to see purged from the Welsh lists two high-profile men whom they felt had been badly done by in their different ways, or to accept a woman whom many of them barely knew and whom they felt was only being placed in a prime position because of her close association with Farage. 'Their view was that enough was enough,' says Hamilton. 'They thought I had been unfairly treated and that I deserved my place.'[29] NEC member Piers Wauchope, a barrister from Kent, recalls that Farage got very angry when the NEC refused to comply with his wishes. He'd previously told colleagues that Alex Phillips would be 'the face of the election in Wales'. So a new selection system was introduced, a more democratic process, whereby UKIP members in Wales would vote on who should be the party's candidates.

Piers Wauchope says that until 2015 Nigel Farage hadn't actually had serious problems with the National Executive, and they had almost always complied with his wishes – a view shared, funnily enough, by Alex Phillips. But as the NEC became less compliant, Farage began telling colleagues that UKIP needed to be a 'modern party', and he cited as an example the Five Star Movement, which had just emerged as a significant force in Italy. It didn't escape the notice of NEC members that the Five Star Movement was largely controlled by its leader and didn't bother with structures such as a national committee.[30]

Alex Phillips feels she was the victim of an NEC that was suddenly flexing its muscles for the first time in many years, and because she was seen as 'Nigel's right-hand woman'. 'So it's like tit for tat, "Let's get rid of Alex." And most of these people sitting on the NEC at the time, you wouldn't let them babysit your dog. They were straight out of the asylum, a lot of them.'[31]

Things turned very nasty. An anonymous individual got hold of the address list for all 2,000 or so UKIP members in Wales, and posted each of them a leaflet attacking Neil Hamilton. 'Are we going to allow other people to come and walk into an elected seat on the back of all of our hard work?' the leaflet asked. 'Just because they have the only name you have heard of, yet have never laid a finger in Wales, they are trying to get elected on the back of years of your efforts.' The leaflet was clearly directed against Neil Hamilton, for it reproduced a *Guardian* front-page story from 1996, which was headlined 'A liar and a cheat' over a large picture of Hamilton. This was from the time when, on the eve of going to court, Hamilton abandoned a libel case against the *Guardian*.

The second article, from the BBC website in 1999, was headlined 'Hamilton "took £30,000 bribe"', and was based on the opening speech by Mohamed Al-Fayed's QC in Hamilton's 1999 libel trial against Fayed, the owner of Harrods. 'We should have no association with Neil Cash-for-questions Hamilton,' the anonymous leaflet declared. 'He will taint us all, and make us all look like the rest of the political class.'[32] The letter had been posted from south-east Wales, using stamps – first class – rather than a franking machine, presumably to make the sender difficult to trace. The venture must have cost at least £1,000.

The move was similar to another underhand operation in the UKIP leadership election in 2000, when Greg Lance-Watkins was sent the entire membership list – by someone close to Nigel Farage, he said – and Lance-Watkins then posted out material denigrating the leadership contender Rodney Atkinson.

'The distribution of this leaflet is not only a breach of our campaigning rules, but was distributed with the aid of a UKIP database that could only have come from a source within the party,' UKIP members were told in an email from Piers Wauchope, who was returning officer for the Wales selection. 'I cannot have the election derailed by the criminal activity of a person or persons within the party.' Wauchope then gave Hamilton a right to reply, in which the former minister told Welsh UKIP members that the Inland Revenue had subsequently 'dismissed these allegations as lies' after forensic accountants had examined his finances for the period 1987–97. 'I know the vast majority of you will be shocked by the viciousness of this personal attack.'[33]

It got worse. Around the same time as the anonymous leaflet, five NEC members wrote to the UKIP national chairman Steve Crowther to complain that Alex Phillips 'has injudiciously made derogatory remarks in public about the Welsh . . . this is exposing the party to an unacceptable risk of bringing it into disrepute and damaging our campaign in Wales . . .'[34] The five NEC members urged Crowther to ask Phillips to stand down as a candidate, and copies were sent to every NEC member. Neither Crowther nor Phillips complied.

Remarkably, the following day Kirsten Farage joined the dispute, on the side of Alex Phillips, with a strongly worded reply which was sent to the whole NEC:

Dear All

How you can even begin to imagine that this letter, which is based on information about a drunken conversation at conference, is not going to brand Alex a racist for life I honestly don't know.

Looking at the signatories I know for a fact that some of you have been guilty of lurching drunkenly around meetings or conferences behaving inappropriately and making ill-thought out comments.

Clearly some of you have taken against Alex personally – I am not her biggest fan either – but this is unprofessional and plain wrong. You are about to ruin a young woman's career.

Best wishes.

Kirsten[35]

This was the only time, according to Piers Wauchope, who sat on the National Executive for seven years, that Kirsten Farage got involved in its business. Given the circumstances, it was a very generous act, though a more cynical interpretation may be that Kirsten was keen for Phillips to get elected in Wales so as to keep her away from London and her husband.

Neil Hamilton was chosen by Welsh members as UKIP's lead candidate in Mid and West Wales, while Mark Reckless was placed top of the party's list for South Wales East, which pretty much ensured they would both be elected AMs. But Alex Phillips was much less well-known to UKIP members in Wales, and only came second on the UKIP list for South Wales Central (the weakest of the five regions for UKIP). Being second on the list meant Phillips probably wouldn't make it to the Assembly.

Nigel Farage couldn't hide his anger with the UKIP NEC. 'Many of its current crop are among the lowest grade of people I have ever met,' he later said in a column he wrote for the Breitbart website. 'I have been fought at every step of the way by total amateurs who come to London once a month with sandwiches in their rucksacks, to attend NEC meetings that normally last seven hours.'[36]

Farage then removed Neil Hamilton as deputy chairman of UKIP, arguing that fighting for a Welsh seat would limit his ability to campaign in the EU referendum. 'I am pleased to have Nigel's good wishes for my candidature for the Welsh Assembly' was Hamilton's tongue-in-cheek reply. 'If successful in May, I look forward to reciprocating in full measure the support he has given me in so many ways in recent years.'[37]

The bickering over Phillips's candidacy was not over. Before the public election in May 2016, an attempt was made to depose Gareth Bennett, the man who'd beaten her to come top of UKIP's list in South Wales Central, which would have allowed Alex Phillips to take his top position. In an interview with Martin Shipton of the *Western Mail*, Bennett had complained about rubbish being left on the street among the new immigrant communities in Cardiff. 'Some of the ethnicities that have moved in – possibly the eastern Europeans – they just don't have any awareness of the hygiene problem that is being caused at times.'[38] Amid a public outcry, Bennett accused Phillips, in her capacity as UKIP head of media in Wales, of deliberately setting him up by arranging the interview with a journalist who was known to be hostile to UKIP. Sixteen UKIP candidates signed a petition calling for Bennett to stand down.

'I think it was stitched up between Shipton and Alex Phillips to get me deselected as a candidate,' says Bennett. 'I assumed I'd be deselected.'[39]

But the UKIP NEC snubbed Farage and his allies for a second time and backed Gareth Bennett. Phillips immediately announced she was pulling out as a candidate for the Welsh elections. 'I've given it a lot of thought and have decided party politics is not for me,' she said. 'It's a personal decision – I don't want to take on a partisan role.'[40]

Neil Hamilton and Mark Reckless were duly elected to the assembly, along with Gareth Bennett, and all served their full terms until 2021. But when the new group of seven UKIP AMs met after the 2016 results, Neil Hamilton managed to get his revenge. By four votes to three, Hamilton deposed Nathan Gill as leader of the UKIP group in the assembly, even though Farage had said that Hamilton would be unsuitable for the job. Afterwards Farage told LBC he was 'not particularly in favour of Mr Hamilton's return to the front line, aged nearly 70 . . . I think it is difficult to return to frontline politics after a 20-year gap when you are getting on a bit in years.'[41] 'Hamilton's record,' he also said, 'would attract negative publicity and seriously upset nearly all of UKIP's donors.'[42]

Farage also took a swipe at Douglas Carswell for supporting Hamilton on the UKIP NEC, saying 'the man who has campaigned on a new, radical, cleaned-up form of politics has put back into public office one of the most discredited political figures of modern times'. It was very different from the Nigel Farage who, back in 2002, had encouraged Hamilton to stand for UKIP in elections.

'I'm the only man who's been beaten by Farage,' Hamilton boasts, 'and then beaten him.' It was also a sign that despite UKIP's electoral surge in the run-up to 2015, and the advent of an EU referendum, Nigel Farage was losing his grip on his party.

20

A DESIGNATION MATTER

Striving to slay a few dragons in Wales was nothing to the fight UKIP's St George had on his hands back in London. Much more significant and every bit as toxic was the vicious struggle to take command of what became known as the 'Leave' forces, ready to do battle in the coming national vote on Europe. As Suzanne Evans and Stuart Wheeler had made clear, many of the squabbles within UKIP weren't really about the party or who should lead it, but a much wider and more important battle over the organisation of the Brexit side in the coming national plebiscite on Europe.

'Who leads the "out" campaign in the referendum' was the issue. 'Who's the hero?' Farage told Owen Bennett. 'There's a high priest of Euroscepticism who thinks quoting large amounts of Shakespeare will help connect with people,' Farage said. 'The posh boys are going to talk about trade when you've got an open goal with immigration and should use that.'[1] By 'high priest of Euroscepticism', Farage undoubtedly meant Daniel Hannan with whom he'd enjoyed a rivalry ever since they'd first been elected MEPs together back in 1999. Despite persistent overtures, Hannan had always declined to join UKIP, though he'd persuaded his friend Douglas Carswell to do so, of course.

But now another of Carswell's friends was to enter the fray – a man who had been adviser to the Eurosceptic Cabinet minister Michael Gove in the early years of the Coalition, before Downing Street insisted he be sacked. More sorcerer than priest, his name was Dominic Cummings. Almost immediately after the 2015 election Cummings convened a cross-party 'exploratory committee' of MPs to help set up a professional No campaign. Carswell was among the seven MPs involved, along with three Tory MPs and three from Labour. When *The Sun*'s political editor Tom Newton Dunn suggested it was a 'humiliating snub' that Farage had not been invited to take part, Cummings responded on his blog:

> It is not a 'humiliating snub' to Farage. The group is a group of MPs. By definition Farage could not be on the group. I am sure that the NO campaign will want to work constructively with Farage and that he will think the same. Anything else would be pointlessly destructive. A successful NO campaign will require people with profoundly different views to co-operate in persuading people to vote NO to Cameron's deal.[2]

Cummings had been recruited by Matthew Elliott, the strategist who had led the fight against the Alternative Vote in the 2011 referendum, and later founded and ran the Eurosceptic campaign Business for Britain. But Elliott was limited in how far he could go with Business for Britain since the group was committed to first allowing Cameron to try to reform Britain's relationship with the EU, rather than adopting a position of withdrawal, come what may.

In June 2015, Matthew Elliott happened to meet Nigel Farage as fellow members of a party of two dozen or so mainly businessmen, on a three-day cruise to Guernsey on the liner *Queen Elizabeth*. It was organised by a secretive Conservative fund-raising group, the Midlands Industrial Council. Farage was accompanied by his polling expert Chris Bruni-Lowe, and when Elliott told the assembled guests about his plans for the EU referendum campaign, Bruni-Lowe urged him to get Farage involved. 'If you don't do that, and you let Nigel out into the wild, then you lose control,' Bruni-Lowe reportedly warned Elliott.[3]

When they reached Guernsey, Farage and Bruni-Lowe went for a lunchtime pint in St Peter Port. Enjoying their drink outside, they spotted Elliott and beckoned him to join them. The meeting didn't go well. 'You should leave it to the experts,' Elliott reportedly told the UKIP pair, by which Elliott presumably meant campaigners like him. Elliott feared that if the anti-EU campaign dwelt too much on immigration it would be accused of xenophobia and racism and, like Douglas Carswell and Dan Hannan, he felt that Farage was too divisive a figure to win over voters who were undecided. Farage and Bruni-Lowe were upset. They thought that Elliott lacked any strategy, and were dismayed that he had no plans to focus on immigration, or to allocate a role for Farage. The *Sunday Times* journalist Tim Shipman reports that afterwards Farage turned to his colleague and declared: 'Shit, we've got a problem. We need to get Banks going as quickly as possible.'[4]

Back on board ship, Farage quickly phoned the new and deep-pocketed UKIP donor Arron Banks. 'We're going to lose this referendum unless we do something,' Banks records Farage saying in his diary of this period. 'I listened carefully to what Nigel had to say, and knew immediately that I wanted to help.'[5]

Banks had already approached Farage soon after the 2015 general election to offer more financial support to UKIP. Farage was so enraged by events immediately after the election, and especially the row with Carswell and what he saw as an 'attempted coup', that he urged Banks to devote his resources not to UKIP, but to building a wider campaign for the referendum. Farage was 'now deeply mistrustful of the Tories and elements within his own party', Banks writes. 'He asked me to consider running it. I said yes immediately.'

Farage had a 'clear vision', Banks says, for the role to be played by him, and also wanted to include Banks's friend, business partner and general sidekick Andy Wigmore, known as 'Wiggy'. While some people speculated that the EU referendum might not take place for a couple of years, Farage was convinced that David Cameron would want to be quick, to clear the decks for other activities in the rest of a Parliament in which he now had a majority. Banks explains that Farage's orders were plain. 'Our brief was to do what even he could not: be as provocative as required to keep immigration at the top of the agenda.'[6]

Immigration from the rest of EU remained contentious and now shot to the top of the political agenda due to the mounting pressure of migrants escaping from strife and economic collapse in Africa and Asia. By the summer of 2015, this had become an increasingly intractable problem for the European Union. After the turmoil over Greece and the Eurozone, it was the EU's second great crisis in five years. Night after night, TV viewers saw dramatic and often harrowing pictures of migrants crossing the Mediterranean in overcrowded and often unseaworthy boats and rubber dinghies, frequently launched from Libya, which was still in the throes of civil war. Thousands died on the journey. Then on 2 September 2015 the world was shocked by pictures of a three-year-old Syrian boy, Alan Kurdi. His body had been washed up on a Turkish beach after the inflatable boat in which his family had been hoping to get to Greece capsized.

Just over a million people entered the European Union in the course of 2015, a fourfold increase on the year before. Italy and Greece, where most of the migrants landed, couldn't cope. On 4 September, Angela Merkel dramatically announced that Germany was opening its borders to migrants crowded into neighbouring states. That may only have encouraged many more people to try their luck, and pay criminal people-traffickers thousands of dollars to get them into the EU. Some of these migrants made their way to Britain, often hidden in the backs of lorries. At the time, there seemed no way for the EU or the UK to stop the influx of migrants. Despite the Conservatives' pledge in 2010 to bring levels of net migration down to the 'tens of thousands', the figure actually peaked in 2015 at more than 300,000. It was not an auspicious time for David Cameron to hold a referendum in which the EU's open borders between most member states, and its Freedom of Movement policy, were bound to feature heavily.

Nigel Farage, Arron Banks, UKIP and their allies might be small in number, but they had Banks's wealth behind them, and the advantage of agility and speed. On 21 June 2015 Banks announced in the *Sunday Telegraph* that he and a group of businessmen had raised £7 million towards a target of £20 million to organise a campaign provisionally called 'No Thanks – We're Going Global' which they planned to launch in September. The business backers included Richard Tice, a friend of Banks who had made his millions from investing in property. Banks told the *Sunday Telegraph* that the business group would have nothing to do with politicians, including Conservatives and UKIP. 'This is too important for politicians to be taking the lead,' Banks said. 'It has got to be business, and the wider public.' And surprisingly, Banks seemed to concur with the concerns of Douglas Carswell, Dan Hannan, Stuart Wheeler and others when he told the paper, 'Nigel is not the right person to lead the campaign. He does not reach out to everybody.'[7]

Nonetheless, at the start of July, Banks and Andy Wigmore took Farage off on a much-needed holiday, though it was only for five days. Banks shares Farage's passion for fishing, and they travelled to Belize in the Caribbean, where Wigmore has joint citizenship. He also served as trade and press attaché at the Belize High Commission in London, and represented the country in trap shooting at the 2014 Commonwealth Games.

'I'm clear how we can help win the referendum,' Banks would record in his diary before they departed for Central America, 'by acting as the provisional wing of the Brexit campaign, doing and saying the things that, as leader of Britain's third largest political party, Nigel can't.' Banks had been known as a rule-breaker ever since being expelled from boarding school for, among other things, selling lead stolen from the roofs of the school buildings.

'Let's shake this up,' Banks now told Farage. 'The more out-rageous we are, the more attention we'll get; the more attention we get, the more outrageous we'll be.' Farage 'looked a little unconvinced by this strategy', Banks related. 'Only time will tell if you and Wigmore are geniuses or complete idiots,' he apparently replied.[8] He and Wigmore enjoyed a 'complicated relationship' with Farage, Banks also explained:

> We're like loyal guard dogs that are more than a little feral and unpredictable when off the lead. He loves us and we love him, but occasionally we bite him on the backside and he responds with a sharp kick.

We can tell how much trouble we're in by the number of missed calls we get from him on our mobiles. If it's one, he's happy; two, something's up; three or more means we're in the soup and it's best to lie low until he's returned to room temperature.[9]

'At the time,' Wigmore told Tim Shipman, 'Farage was considered a has-been, not to be taken seriously. Because the media wanted to airbrush Nigel out, the only way we could do it was to be as outrageous as possible . . . We had to play the press like Trump has, like the string of a lute.'[10] Farage soon found the game irresistible and threw himself into it, too. Every act of Farage or Banks's 'outrage' would be played out on Twitter and Facebook, and Wigmore and Banks could carefully note what worked and what didn't, and respond accordingly. In each case it wasn't just the initial outrage that was generated, but further noise when Banks or Farage refused to apologise. Often statements would be taken down from the internet and then reinstated, sometimes more than once, simply to provoke even more of a reaction. It all generated publicity and it was all free.

Farage and his new friends were influenced by the growing momentum in America of the campaign to get the New York businessman and TV host Donald Trump elected to the White House. Banks and Wigmore had been following the Trump campaign on social media, and in the summer of 2015 went to see leading members of Team Trump in New York where they learned how their man attracted attention through noisy acts and outrageous statements on the internet. Wigmore explains:

We actually were monitoring Trump, and he started sending out all these crazy messages, just to get attention. This was brilliant for Arron – he loved this – so we started sending out some of the most outrageously provocative tweets, and they were all immigration-led, so when it comes to the bad stuff, we totally took the Trump rule-book and tried to apply it here, and we quickly discovered it worked. And we got more and more fearless, we would talk about who particularly we were going to pick on, whether that was an individual politician, or a party or a subject . . . It was literally 'Who shall we pick on today?' Now this was war.[11]

At this stage Arron Banks was probably Farage's closest political ally, and unusually one of the few people in politics to have become a close personal friend. And Farage had become hugely dependent on Banks for political funding. 'You know what, Nigel, I'm gonna put in as much money as it takes,' Andy Wigmore recalls Banks telling the UKIP leader.[12]

As soon as Farage arrived in Belize, Banks recorded, he was 'up at the crack of dawn, itching to get out on a boat. His ability to get by on a few hours' sleep, even after his usual heavy nights, never ceases to amaze.' The holiday involved lots of fishing, lots of drinking and lots of good food, and getting around in small boats and light planes, all at Arron Banks's expense. After lunch on the Sunday with the Conservative peer Lord (Michael) Ashcroft (who has strong business ties to Belize), Banks, Wigmore and Farage spent the afternoon in a 'dodgy bar' where Farage ended up 'paralytic' before suddenly remembering that he'd agreed to write an article for the *Daily Telegraph*. 'He grabbed his phone and stumbled outside,' Banks records. 'It looked bad, but just a few minutes later, I could hear him, cool, calm and collected, dictating flowing prose on the fly. He was as lucid and precise as if his belly were full of nothing but lemonade. God knows how he does it.'[13]

Back in England, from his home and offices just north of Bristol, Banks set to work on his referendum campaign. Initially, Farage and Chris Bruni-Lowe didn't plan to confront what they saw as 'establishment' Eurosceptics, but hoped to chivvy them along towards adopting more aggressive positions, and to find a major role for the UKIP leader. 'Nigel and I effectively got Banks to set this up in order to give Nigel a voice,' Bruni-Lowe would relate, 'because it became clear when we sat down with Matthew Elliott that he didn't want to touch Nigel with a barge pole.'[14]

Banks wanted to get ahead of his Eurosceptic rivals. 'I want to set a pace that blows their minds,' he wrote.[15] He and Richard Tice launched a second group with the bizarre name The Know (on the assumption that the referendum would involve a Yes-No choice). Banks aimed high, very high. He even tried to poach Lynton Crosby, the Australian election strategist credited with numerous victories for Conservative candidates in both Australia and Britain. Banks had heard Crosby didn't like the EU and offered him £2 million to work for him. Crosby considered the offer for a couple of days, but eventually thought it would be disloyal to work against David Cameron whom he'd helped get re-elected in 2015. Instead, Banks hired a Washington political consultant, Gerry Gunster, who specialised in referendum campaigns, which are common in US states.

By July it was clear that two distinct and increasingly hostile camps had formed among British Eurosceptics. When Arron Banks and Richard Tice held an attempted peace meeting with Matthew Elliott and Dominic Cummings at Banks's Mayfair club, 5 Hertford Street, the split only got worse. Banks told Elliott and Cummings that Eurosceptic MPs didn't know what they were doing, that they were Tories controlled by Downing Street, and that he was going to establish the organisation which under the referendum process would achieve official 'designation' as the main anti-EU campaign. What's more, it was crazy waiting to see how David Cameron's reform talks got on before establishing an organisation (especially now that the EU had made clear such reform could not involve changing its treaties, and was therefore likely to be limited). Cummings would recall Banks telling them: 'I've got more money than any of you and I'm much more clued-up than any of you, so it's really a question for you guys of, do you want to be part of what we're doing, or not?'[16]

In response, Elliott and Cummings warned Banks that he and Tice didn't understand politics. Very well, Banks replied, let's see how it works out. 'In life, you get people who are so clever they're stupid,' Banks would say. 'Dominic Cummings certainly falls into that category.'[17] 'I thought he was supposed to be some kind of mad genius,' Banks wrote in his diary a month later. 'So far, not seen any evidence of either madness or genius. He's just boring.'[18]

But relations between the two camps had not yet broken down completely. That summer, Arron Banks had texted Dominic

Cummings and offered him £200,000 to defect from Elliott to his team, with a £200,000 bonus if the referendum was won. Cummings even met Banks for coffee, though he ultimately refused. Banks would later claim he was merely trying to 'destabilise' his rivals, and 'show power'.[19]

And Richard Tice also tried to lure Boris Johnson to their side, despite the London mayor not yet having declared which way he would go in the referendum. 'We would be thrilled to have the support and leadership skills of Boris,' Tice told the *Daily Express*, adding that he would be 'a Churchillian figure in the fight to save our country'.[20] Farage had long declared that Johnson was the one senior Conservative he admired.

Although Arron Banks had given more than a million pounds to UKIP over the previous twelve months, he never joined the party and had a marked contempt for it as an organisation. 'The party's a shambles,' he wrote. 'I'd kick half of them out if I had my way, starting with that Tory turncoat Douglas Carswell . . . He's been nothing but a pain in the backside.'[21]

During the summer and autumn of 2015, Arron Banks had several advantages – lots of money; an existing call centre in Bristol with 200 staff recruited for his insurance ventures; and a growing database of supporters for what was quickly becoming known as Brexit – British exit from the EU. Banks had even signed up the left-wing railway workers' union, the RMT, and the group Trade Unionists Against the EU, to whom he gave £25,000. Banks was inspired in part by the way in which Barack Obama had used 'big data' and social media to win the elections of 2008 and 2012. So he enlisted a mysterious American research group which specialised in big data and voter psychology. Cambridge Analytica was run by a British Etonian called Alexander Nix, and had Steve Bannon on its board.

Both Banks and Farage were also hugely influenced at this time by the activities of the Five Star Movement, Farage's new Italian allies in the EFDD group in the European Parliament, led by his friend and admirer Beppe Grillo. In January 2015, Farage had travelled with his adviser Raheem Kassam, and Banks's business colleague

Liz Bilney to Milan – or 'Milano' as Farage called it, having often visited the northern Italian city for his past business activities. They turned up at the offices of Casaleggio Associati in a wealthy district in the centre of Milan. There they met Gianroberto Casaleggio, Five Star's co-founder, and the brains behind Italy's new digital populist party. Casaleggio, who would die a year later, looked like a refugee from the 1960s, with long, curly, bedraggled hair, flat cap and John Lennon glasses, the total opposite of the smart suits, cufflinks and polished brogues of Nigel Farage.

For a man who couldn't cope with a computer and had to get his wife to write his emails, it was an epiphany moment. The Grillo/Casaleggio invention was a party which supposedly practised 'direct democracy', where members were recruited online and voted for policy digitally; they applied to become candidates through the internet and ran campaigns through well-made video ads on social media. Farage was fascinated and immediately converted. 'If I was starting UKIP today,' he said, 'would I spend 20 years speaking to people in village halls, or would I base it on the Grillo model? I know exactly what I would do.'[22]

Farage and Banks also noticed how the Five Star Movement had 'a tightly controlled central structure', in Banks's revealing words, 'almost a dictatorship at the centre . . . If you have a tightly controlled structure, then the crazies can't take over.'[23] The 'controlled central structure' was partly exercised through the impact of Beppe Grillo's blog, edited by Casaleggio. That trip to Milan would influence Farage and Banks hugely as they geared up for the coming referendum, and more long term, they worked out how, in Banks's phrase, Farage could 'subtly delink' from UKIP and build a new movement along the lines of Grillo's Five Star.[24] They had seen the future, and thought it worked.

In October 2015, the businessman Derek Wall of the Midlands Industrial Council (who'd organised the *Queen Elizabeth* cruise party) had a long meeting with Farage at Boisdale, Farage's regular restaurant near Victoria station, to try to bring the sides together. Wall and Farage invited the two leaders Matthew Elliott and Arron Banks to see them separately, but when Elliott turned up he told them that there was no way he could ever work with Banks. Farage then asked, according to Tim Shipman: 'If God himself came from heaven and smote down the British people and said, "I will deliver Leave if you work with Arron Banks," would you work with Arron Banks?' 'No,' Elliott replied. 'We had a couple of hours of Banks and we had a couple of hours of Elliott,' Farage said later. 'And it was absolutely clear from that minute that Elliott and Cummings were not prepared to work with anybody. This was going to be their show and their game.'[25]

The most distinctive aspect of the Banks/Farage pitch was that immigration should be at the heart of the Leave campaign, and Gerry Gunster's polls suggested that was the issue voters cared about most. Elliott, Cummings and the Vote Leave side argued that a big emphasis on immigration would only deter the block of around 30 per cent of voters who were still undecided and up for grabs. It also worried Farage and Banks when Dominic Cummings later said there was a 'strong democratic case' for holding a second referendum once the first had been won, and the terms of Brexit had been agreed.[26]

In September 2015, a small spoke was put into the wheels of Arron Banks's operation when the government accepted advice from the Electoral Commission that instead of the referendum ballot involving a straight Yes-No question, voters should be asked whether they wanted to 'Remain' in the EU, or to 'Leave'. According to one source in Banks's team, 'They were furious as they'd spent tens if not hundreds of thousands of pounds with this branding and merchandise with "The Know" on.' 'The Know' was ditched, and the organisation became the rather more comprehensible 'Leave.EU'.

Relations between Farage and Banks weren't always easy. In early September 2015, Farage travelled all the way to Banks's office, overlooking a Premier Inn on a business estate near Bristol, only to find Banks had forgotten the engagement. 'In walks Nigel,' says one witness, 'and then it's sort of this weird rockstar moment – he got a standing ovation and he was waiting for Arron. He was quite pissed off – he'd come all the way to Bristol and Arron had just completely forgotten he was going to be there.' But Farage couldn't complain too much, as he had become so dependent on Banks financially and for advice. 'Nigel ends up waiting there, sat there twiddling his thumbs for about two and a half, three hours. So he was kind of privately huffing and chuffing, but then as soon as Arron came in it was as if nothing had happened.'

Meanwhile, Banks's London offices, in Great Smith Street, Westminster, also became the offices of Nigel Farage and UKIP, and known internally as 'Fort Farage'. 'Fort Farage was really like a locker room,' says one of the staff. 'The guys would have fist-fights; they would do practical jokes and horrible things. Everybody there was a big personality, even the sort of juniors were very full on and none of them were scared to tell each other what they thought – they'd shout and swear at each other.'

Meanwhile, David Cameron was on a charm offensive, clocking up thousands of miles touring the capitals of Europe in a desperate bid to win concessions on immigration, and secure what might pass as a credible renegotiation. On his success or failure, the prospects of the pro-Europeans hung.

While the prime minister was focused on trying to get a brake on freedom of movement, Britain's Eurosceptics were busy battling each other to win designation as the official 'out' campaign.

Under the Political Parties, Elections and Referendums Act of 2000 (PPERA), the Electoral Commission was assigned the power to decide which organisation should be the official 'designated' campaign for each side in any British referendum. The Commission's decision would involve a selection process – much like applying for a job. Designation was a crucial stage in the referendum battle – indeed, it was compared to the way in which America holds a two-stage process in its presidential elections – first with primary contests within each party, followed by the general election between the party nominees. Designation would confer all sorts of advantages – a higher spending limit of up to £7 million; the free distribution of information to voters; official campaign broadcasts; and £600,000 of state funding to cover certain costs. Groups other than the designated campaign would be restricted to a spending cap of just £700,000, though there was no limit to the number of such secondary campaigns.

A week before the 2016 referendum, Farage and Labour MP Kate Hoey tried to emulate Kate Winslet and Leonardo DiCaprio during a Fishing For Leave event on the Thames. (Jeff Spicer/Getty Images)

Farage alienated several of his Conservative allies early in 2016 by inviting the controversial socialist politician George Galloway to speak at a Leave event in Westminster.

(London pix/Alamy)

Unveiling the notorious 'Breaking Point' poster which many critics denounced as 'racist'. It was all the more controversial because it was unveiled only ninety minutes before the murder of Labour MP Jo Cox. (Mark Thomas/Alamy)

Remainers countered the Breaking Point event (see Breaking Point van in background) with their own anti-Farage poster van.

Despite their political differences, Farage and the then European Commission president Jean-Claude Juncker had very good relations, helped by sitting at adjacent desks in the European Parliament. Astonishingly, this greeting came only five days after the 2016 referendum.

(2E6MP23: Eric Vidal: Reuters)

Farage caricatured along with the other main Brexit leaders Michael Gove and Boris Johnson at a Remain event during the 2016 referendum. (Trevor Mogg/Alamy)

The new elected leader of UKIP, Diane James, appears to grimace as Farage tries to congratulate and kiss her at the party conference in Bournemouth in September 2016. James lasted just eighteen days in office. (Daniel Leal-Olivia/AFP via Getty Images)

Farage backs Donald Trump at a presidential campaign rally in Jackson, Mississippi in August 2016, the start of an important friendship. (Jonathan Backman: Getty Images)

Three days after Donald Trump's victory in the 2016 election, Farage visited the president-elect at Trump Tower in New York, along with Gerry Gunster (left), Arron Banks (second left), Andy Wigmore (second right) and Raheem Kassam (far right). (© Andy Wigmore)

Farage in Berlin at a campaign event during the German federal elections in 2017 with Beatrix von Storch, deputy leader of the anti-immigration far-right Alternative für Deutschland party, the AFD.
(Odd Andersen/AFP via Getty Images)

The Nigel Farage condom (unused), produced by UKIP youth group Young Independence. (M. Crick)

Farage is the victim of a milkshake attack in Newcastle while campaigning as Brexit Party leader during the 2019 European elections.
(Ian Forsyth/Getty Images)

With most of the twenty-nine newly elected Brexit Party MEPs in May 2019, after pushing the Conservatives into fifth place (with less than 9 per cent of the vote) and forcing Theresa May's resignation as prime minister. (TAPDND: Dominic Lipinski/PA Images)

For a while in 2019 Farage and his Brexit Party seemed to be the deciding force in British politics. This Remain rally in July 2019 showed Farage pulling the strings of puppets Boris Johnson and Jeremy Hunt, the main Conservative leadership contenders.

Back in Strasbourg in July 2019, this time with Richard Tice and Ann Widdecombe. The Brexit Party group was the biggest in the European Parliament, but only stayed until the UK left the EU seven months later. (© Stuart Mitchell)

'I am ready!' Farage tried to put pressure on Boris Johnson and his new government by unveiling scores of candidates who were ready to stand against the Conservatives in the election expected at the end of 2019. (© Stuart Mitchell)

During the 2019 general election with the Zimbabwe-born British boxer Derek Chisora, a Brexit Party supporter with whom Farage struck up a good friendship. (Reuters/Hannah McKay)

Farage celebrates at a Leave Means Leave party and rally in Parliament Square on 31 January 2020, the day that the UK formally left the European Union. (Leon Neal/Getty Imgaes)

Campaigning in Arizona in October 2020 in support of Trump on his failed re-election campaign. (Chip Somodevilla/Getty Images)

Fishing is one of Farage's favourite pastimes. Even when politics was most busy, he would sometimes go sea-fishing for several hours in the middle of the night. Farage now has a house on the Kent coast which has given him regular first-hand experience of asylum seekers arriving on English shores.

(© Stuart Mitchell)

In 2020 Farage began reporting on video about the growing numbers of migrants crossing the English Channel in small boats, an interest he kept up after he joined GB News as a full-time presenter. (DMGT)

Vote Leave, as the Elliott/Cummings group now called itself, was officially launched on 8 October 2015, with a cross-party group of MPs, and several wealthy businessmen, including Stuart Wheeler and the Labour donor John Mills. Their slogan, they announced, would be 'Take Control' which was soon modified to 'Take Back Control', and Dominic Cummings later claimed credit for the simple phrase which would be attributed to playing a decisive role in shifting opinion.[27] The HBO and Channel 4 drama *Brexit: The Uncivil War*, in which Cummings was played by Benedict Cumberbatch, showed him inventing the slogan in a great moment of creative genius. (As we have seen, though, UKIP widely used the slogans 'take back control' and 'let's take back control' during the 2010 general election and the 2014 European elections, when the phrases featured all over the party's literature.)

But the rivalry between the two Leave camps continued for months, and Arron Banks's antics became increasingly absurd. Just before Christmas an astonishing story emerged in which both sides accused the other of spying on them. Banks sent a bizarre email to Elliott, in which he suggested that he should be careful about surveillance. 'I have a personal investigator on my tail,' Banks told Elliott. 'You might want to watch out – I have a business that specialises in personal security and counter-intelligence.'[28] Elliott took the email as a threat, and gave its contents to the *Mail on Sunday*.[29] He also alleged that Banks had put 'operatives' on *his* tail.

In the end, Arron Banks and Nigel Farage did not apply directly for their Leave.EU organisation to get official designation. It was a wise move since Leave.EU was almost entirely associated with UKIP, and unlike Vote Leave, it could show no breadth of support with other parties. Shrewdly, they teamed up instead with another Leave organisation, Grassroots Out, known as GO, which was formed in January 2016 by the Conservative MP Peter Bone and several other leading politicians who were disillusioned with Vote Leave. These included Bone's Tory MP ally Tom Pursglove; the Labour MP Kate Hoey; Sammy Wilson of the Democratic Unionists; and Nigel Farage. A month later, GO, UKIP and Leave. EU all joined a wider consortium known as Go Movement Ltd, which involved eighteen different political entities, including unions and parties on the left. And it was this body which formally applied for designation. The complicated series of manoeuvres was an attempt to show the Electoral Commission a range of support which went well beyond UKIP and Arron Banks. GO organised a series of major rallies where Farage spoke alongside senior Conservative politicians such as David Davis, Liam Fox and Bill Cash, as well as Kate Hoey and Sammy Wilson, all to demonstrate its cross-party nature. The diverse politicians would cement their new cross-party relationship over supper and drinks afterwards – sometimes in a good restaurant, or at least once in a branch of McDonald's.

In reality, Arron Banks and Nigel Farage were always the main driving forces behind Grassroots Out. Banks was not only one of the major donors, he also provided GO with accommodation in Millbank Tower in Westminster, right next to the offices of his own organisation Leave.EU. They seemed to have learned some of their tactics from groups on the left. GO, in effect, was a Leave.EU front organisation, and the distinctions between Leave.EU, Grassroots Out and GO Movement Ltd were often pretty blurred.

The Conservative MEP Dan Hannan was involved in trying to broker peace between the two warring Leave groups. Despite Farage's disparaging remarks about him being a 'high priest' and quoting Shakespeare, Hannan says he always got on well with the UKIP leader, and credits him with doing more than anyone to achieve the referendum in the first place. Hannan joined Matthew Elliott and Dominic Cummings in another effort to bring the two sides together ahead of the expected set-piece television debates:

> Nigel's position was either I have to be the leader, and the sole representative in the TV debates and so on, or I'm gonna do my own thing. And we said 'Look, if you become leader, we will lose. And we can show you that this isn't some weird personal thing. We can show you the data. We've spent a lot of time looking at this.' 'Ah you make figures prove whatever you want,' he said.

Hannan, Elliott and Cummings offered that instead Farage could be the equivalent of Labour's working-class deputy leader John Prescott during the leadership of Tony Blair. It would be Farage's job to rally and energise the Leave 'base', the most fervent anti-EU voters. Most UKIP activists would have been horrified, Hannan believes, had they seen how Farage behaved in some of the negotiation meetings:

> If he couldn't lead it, he was gonna run his own thing. And even if that meant we lost – I don't think that really gave him much pause for thought. I suspect he never thought we could win. And therefore his objective was to make sure UKIP, and he personally, came out of it well.[30]

There were several more attempts to bring Leave.EU and Vote Leave together, but the venom between the two groups made that impossible. In early February, Banks sent a letter to every MP saying that Elliott and Cummings were 'two of the nastiest individuals I have ever had the misfortune to meet', and that he 'wouldn't put them in charge of the local sweet shop'.[31] Even more damaging to Leave unity was an interview which Banks gave to Lucy Fisher of *The Times* around the same time. 'The enemy for us is not the "in" campaign – they're laughable – the enemy is our own side,' Banks told Fisher. 'Our job is to defeat the enemy and move on.' Elliott was 'more interested in winning a peerage than the referendum,' Banks said. 'He wants to be Lord Elliott of Loserville.' Douglas Carswell, whom Banks had previously described as 'borderline autistic', was now merely 'slightly dysfunctional'. And Banks even hit out at David Cameron over his severely disabled young son, Ivan, who had died seven years before: 'Anyone who can use their disabled child as a prop to show that they're human,' Banks said, 'is in my mind a dreadful person.'[32] Such remarks did much to alienate Conservatives at a time when Banks and GO Movement Ltd needed to show the Electoral Commission that they were a harmonious, cross-party coalition. Matthew Elliott copied the interview and distributed it to every MP. Peter Bone angrily told Banks that his interview had lost GO the backing of thirty MPs.

Banks also revealed to Lucy Fisher that he planned to sue Matthew Elliott and Dominic Cummings for defamation, and was instructing libel lawyers Mishcon de Reya. Fisher described how Banks then slapped the 'back of one hand in the palm of the other' and cried 'Bosh!'.

And so, only eight days before GO Movement Ltd submitted its designation application, Arron Banks served a writ (technically a claim) on Matthew Elliott. 'I decided to sue the bugger,' Banks wrote in his diary, 'or at least scare him a bit – to teach him a lesson about responsibility.' What's more, Banks sent along an undercover cameraman to film the moment when the writ was served on Elliott, supposedly as evidence that he had received it. 'The resulting footage is quite entertaining,' he boasted:

> Out comes Elliott for a cigarette, perching on a bench outside the office. As he puffs away, no doubt dreaming of the day he will ascend to greatness as Lord Elliott of Loserville, he is approached by a seemingly innocuous gentleman brandishing a document and asking if he's Matthew Elliott. He immediately looks suspicious and tries to demur. Then it all gets a bit Monty Python as the question is repeated, and Matthew actually denies being himself. Finally, our man says: 'I have information that you are indeed Matthew Elliott,' explaining that he has instructions to deliver the envelope. Elliott can't really refuse and the last image is of him with palm outstretched, looking apprehensive and bewildered.
>
> That should shake him up a bit.[33]

Banks seemed to enjoy acting like a Mafia boss who puts the frighteners on an unco-operative nightclub owner.

Over a short spell, roughly eighteen months, Nigel Farage had acquired a whole new entourage. Alongside Banks and Wigmore, Farage's advisers Chris Bruni-Lowe and Raheem Kassam represented a much more aggressive, masculine, devil-may-care style, akin to that of Donald Trump and Steve Bannon. There were few women around Farage any more. Annabelle Fuller was gone; Alex

Phillips had abandoned politics after her troubles in Wales; and Farage was effectively estranged from his wife Kirsten. It was a very laddish atmosphere – men who enjoyed hard-drinking, often smoked, used blunt and sometimes sexist language, didn't care about causing offence and had adopted outrage as a political tactic.

Into this group, in January 2016, arrived a young man from an aristocratic background who quickly became known within UKIP and Leave.EU as 'Posh George'. George Cottrell's grandfather was Yorkshire landowner Lord Manton, while his uncle, Lord Hesketh, had once owned a Formula One team, and served as a minister in the Thatcher and Major governments before defecting to UKIP years later. Cottrell's mother Fiona was an equally colourful character and had posed fully naked (except for a pink necklace) over eleven pages of *Penthouse* magazine as their pet-of-the-month in 1973. Fiona was later wooed by Prince Charles, though the story goes that Charles was slow in the process, and when he finally rang her to arrange a date she thought it was a prank. She already had a date, she told him, with Mark Cottrell (whom she later married).

Farage employed George Cottrell as his personal assistant and fixer, but also as a serious fund-raiser for UKIP, to exploit his contacts among wealthy aristocrats and successful businessmen and arrange 'face-time' for them with Farage. Posh George was just twenty-two, well-dressed, blond and tubby, and he fitted in as a drinker and smoker who enjoyed the high life. He was remarkably self-confident for a such a young man. He'd never been to university but instead worked for several banks and seems to have learned an extraordinary amount about banking and the mysteries of offshore finance and tax avoidance. Cottrell moved into Farage's glass office at UKIP's headquarters in Mayfair, where he installed, he later revealed, 'my Berry Bros wine collection stashed in the cabinet'.[34] Farage quickly became something of a father figure to Posh George.

Farage himself enjoys the odd bet on the horses, or on politics, but it didn't take long for him to notice that his new protégé had a serious and costly gambling addiction. Cottrell had been placing bets since the age of twelve, and was now playing for very high stakes. By the time he joined UKIP, Cottrell later said, his gambling 'was out

of control. I'd saunter to the William Hill round the corner with a
Harvey Nichols bag with fifty grand in it, to have a bet on the 2.05
at Lingfield on a horse I knew nothing about. I was neglecting work,
friends, family, girlfriends. It was all-consuming.'[35]

Cottrell's fund-raising efforts can't have been easy while the
civil war between the two Leave groups still raged. Arron Banks's
interview with *The Times* made relations between the warring Leave
factions far worse, of course. His hostility towards the Elliott/
Cummings operation could easily have scuppered the whole Brexit
cause. 'It was an absolute bloody nightmare,' says Dan Hannan.
Wealthy businessmen who wanted to help fund the Leave campaign
couldn't understand why the camps didn't just get round a table
and sort out their differences, and weren't willing to give a penny
until that was done. It wasn't a problem for Leave.EU, which had
Banks's money, but it meant Vote Leave couldn't take advantage of
the 'peacetime' period, before the official referendum campaign
started, when people could spend without limit. So for many
months, Hannan explains, the Remain camp 'were able to spend
money in peacetime without getting within the £7 million cap, and
we didn't have a penny because of this stupid wrecking operation'.[36]

The tensions surfaced again when UKIP held a couple of regional
'spring' conference events in February 2016. The UKIP deputy
chairman Suzanne Evans had joined the main board of Vote Leave
while Douglas Carswell was on its campaign board. At the West
Midlands gathering at Wolverhampton racecourse, Evans helped
run a Vote Leave stand in the foyer. Later, as she was listening inside
the hall, her phone rang out loud and she quickly killed it. She then
saw that the caller was Nigel Farage. Evans recorded in her diary:

This must be the first time he's called me in at least six months!
Nine minutes later I call him back. He's in a foul mood and
doesn't waste any time:
  'The whole party is backing GO yet you're still promoting Vote
Leave. It's incompatible with your position of deputy chairman.'
  'Why? What's wrong with campaigning with all the Brexit cam-
paigns? Not all our MEPs have dismissed Vote Leave . . . Our MP is

backing Vote Leave, so are our peers and 75 per cent of our councillors,' I retort. 'Our members want everyone to work together!'

'All but one MEP,' he snarls, referring of course to Patrick [O'Flynn]. 'And our peers are all now with GO. It's the only cross-party campaign, the only one campaigning, and it's the one we all have to get behind.'

I can't recall his exact next words, but they were not complimentary about Vote Leave, shocked me, and I asked: 'Are you saying that if Vote Leave get official designation, UKIP won't back them?'

His reply was utterly unambiguous: 'Of course we won't! They don't want to leave! They'll stuff us with a second referendum. There's no way I can back them.'

'Nigel, our members really won't stand for that. UKIP's fought for a referendum for decades, and when we get the chance we won't be part of the official campaign? You simply can't do this, it's madness!'

He hung up.[37]

'It was the last call I ever got from him,' Suzanne Evans says. Four days later, Farage sacked her as deputy chairman of the party, but that only emboldened her.

The following weekend, alongside Douglas Carswell, Evans addressed a Vote Leave fringe meeting at UKIP's Welsh spring conference in Llandudno. Inadvertently, the meeting coincided with a Grassroots Out event at precisely the same time inside the conference. At her sparsely attended Vote Leave meeting, Suzanne Evans quoted a report published by the think tank British Future called *How (not) to talk about Europe*. This analysis, Evans explained, showed that:

the two least trusted voices on Europe are Tony Blair – which isn't surprising – and also Nigel Farage. You might not like it but that is what the book says . . . They say really, even if you love Nigel Farage and you love UKIP, it's best not mention it unless somebody else mentions it instead.[38]

And Evans argued that immigration wasn't much help as a campaign issue, since polls also suggested that people who felt strongly about it were already committed to voting for Leave. Evans was wrong, Farage replied afterwards. Polling data gathered by Chris Bruni-Lowe, he claimed, showed that immigration and security matters were the most important issues for voters in contemplating how they would vote. 'As far as [Evans] saying that, well, she's an ordinary member of UKIP,' Farage pointedly told reporters. 'She can say what she likes. I couldn't care less.' Asked why Douglas Carswell hadn't spoken at the Welsh conference, Farage replied: 'Who? . . . Oh, I remember, I met him once.'[39]

But Farage clearly did care. When sacking Evans as deputy chairman the previous week, he seemed to have forgotten that she was also UKIP's welfare spokesman. Four days later she was stripped of that job, too. Farage had now sacked Evans from three different posts in less than ten months, and her punishment wouldn't stop there.

Meanwhile, David Cameron's nine-month tour of the other twenty-seven capitals of the European Union trying to renegotiate Britain's relationship was reaching the end of the road. A deal was finally reached in February 2016 which had four main features.

First, on immigration, it was agreed that all EU states would be able to apply an 'emergency brake' if they faced 'exceptional' levels of inward migration from the EU. For a seven-year period, a country would be allowed to restrict welfare benefits to people who had arrived from the EU, though benefits would have to rise to reach parity with home nationals after four years. And there were also adjustments on access to child benefit. And there were measures to make it easier for states to deport migrants from other EU states.

Second was a proposed 'red card' system, which was designed to enforce the EU's commitment to subsidiarity. This would mean that if any country had support from fifteen other states, they could refer rules passed by the European Parliament back to the Parliament for further changes.

Third, Britain would now be exempt from the symbolic aspiration from the 1957 Treaty of Rome to 'ever-closer union'.

And fourth, the deal gave assurances that, in the future, states outside the Eurozone, such as the UK, would be protected from measures which favoured Eurozone members, such as having to make financial contributions.

Fundamentally, though, the Europeans had not budged on freedom of movement.

David Cameron immediately announced that he would campaign for Remain in the forthcoming referendum, and the date was set for 23 June 2016, while the deadline to apply for designation was 31 March. And, following the precedent of the previous such vote in 1975, ministers would be free to join either side. Any hopes Cameron had of gaining a quick advantage were dashed, however, when his close friend Michael Gove came out against the deal just before it was signed and declared he would help lead the Leave forces. He was followed by five other Cabinet members, and all six aligned with the Elliott/Cummings Vote Leave project. A few days later, after much speculation and much agonising, Boris Johnson made the historic announcement that he, too, would support Leave.

In the meantime, Arron Banks urged Leave supporters to bombard the Electoral Commission to show the breadth of support for Grassroots Out getting designation. It was perhaps an 'outrage' too far, for the Commission's servers couldn't cope with the 7,500 emails which people sent in, and the Commission told Banks that in any case they would ignore direct representations from the public.

On the crucial issue of which of the rival Leave groups could show 'breadth' of support, Matthew Elliott and Vote Leave had one big advantage in having Douglas Carswell on board – what Elliott describes as 'the UKIP bloc in the House of Commons' – true, of course, because UKIP had only one MP.[40] Vote Leave also had the UKIP MEP Patrick O'Flynn, so Arron Banks made a huge effort to counter these rebels by mounting a show of UKIP unity. He invited all the party's other MEPs, and the whole National Executive, to his country house overlooking the Severn. Some were put up there overnight; others in expensive hotels nearby, and every one of them found a welcoming bottle of champagne in their room. Banks also treated them to a grand dinner, with plenty of alcohol, and then gave them a tour of the nearby Leave.EU offices next day. The visit worked. Although the MEPs and the UKIP NEC paid a formal visit to Vote Leave, they almost unanimously backed Banks's GO Movement Ltd – Patrick O'Flynn, Douglas Carswell and Suzanne Evans were the only major exceptions.

But Banks and Farage pushed their efforts to show widespread backing too far. At a rally held by GO at the Queen Elizabeth II Centre in Westminster in late February, an unidentified special speaker was promised, somebody who'd been recruited by Farage. A few nights earlier, Farage had appeared on Russia Today, the TV channel run by the Russian government. The programme's host was George Galloway, the former Labour MP who was now leader of the far-left Respect Party. Farage reckoned that having Galloway on board would be a huge asset in Labour areas, and also places with large Muslim populations (the pro-Palestinian Galloway had been an MP for two strongly Muslim seats). But many in the audience at the QEII rally were disgusted when they saw Galloway arrive on stage, and several walked out – they felt, among other things, that Galloway had been too sympathetic to the Iraqi dictator Saddam Hussein. Other speakers on the platform thought they'd been ambushed. Several Conservatives subsequently refused to have any-thing more to do with Grassroots Out.

Farage and the Grassroots Out campaign handed in their 222-page application a day early, accompanied outside the Electoral Commission by a Labour GO bus, a Leave.EU truck, and fifty or so activists, together with GO T-shirts, hoodies and flags. They carried into the building ten boxes with messages of support. 'The designation document was a bloody masterpiece,' Farage boasted. 'Eighteen separately identifiable political organisations including the New Communist Party of Great Britain.'[41] Vote Leave, meanwhile, were in some chaos, and with only hours to go suddenly realised that nobody had read the Electoral Commission's criteria, or explained in their application how they complied with them. The Elliott/ Cummings organisation submitted their forms only twenty minutes before the Commission's deadline.

In the end, nobody was surprised that the Electoral Commission chose Vote Leave, since the organisation had a much more distinguished list of big names, including six Cabinet ministers as well as London mayor Boris Johnson. Vote Leave could also boast other prominent supporters from the Conservatives and Labour, as well as UKIP. Despite this, the designation process was far from clear cut, and the Commission's official scorecard showed Vote Leave won by only 49 points to 45. For all their outrageous antics, Nigel Farage and Arron Banks had come astonishingly close, and Farage came within a whisker of becoming the leader of the official Leave campaign. Indeed, he might well have done so had Arron Banks never spoken to Lucy Fisher of *The Times*, and had Farage never spoken to George Galloway.

Several Vote Leave figures believe the referendum would have been lost had Farage and Banks won the designation. Not only would the UKIP pair have made a lot more TV appearances, they argue, and thereby put off wavering voters, but their leadership of the official campaign would have deterred many senior Conservatives, especially Boris Johnson, from playing major roles.

Farage formally congratulated Vote Leave on Twitter, but Arron Banks was 'stunned' and very despondent. 'He talked about going and downing a whole bottle of whisky, and he was in a pretty bad place for a few days', according to the ghostwriter of his diary, Isabel Oakeshott.[42] Banks announced he would go to court and seek a judicial review. Senior UKIP figures thought this unwise. 'Both me and Nigel have told him to back off,' party chairman Steve Crowther told a colleague.

Crowther then explained the businessman's highly cynical thinking. 'Arron reckons a court case would postpone the referendum until October and then we'd have the benefit of a further migrant flood over the summer.'[43]

Farage, in contrast, told Banks he wasn't too worried about not getting the official designation. The cause for which he'd been fighting all his political life was about to be put to the people.

INDEPENDENCE DAY

Farage had been quite anxious about how he would have run the designated campaign if he'd been put in charge. What's more, he felt that not being tied to the official Leave effort gave him a lot more freedom to do and say what he wanted. Under the rules, Grassroots Out, Leave.EU and all the other organisations in favour of leaving the European Union would still be allowed to campaign up to a spending limit of £700,000 each, and UKIP as a party could spent up to £4 million. There was also the consolation that the campaign fought by Leave.EU had forced Vote Leave to raise their game and start publicly campaigning at a much earlier stage.

Farage began the referendum campaign with a stunt in which he, Diane James and UKIP's London mayoral candidate Peter Whittle walked to Downing Street and returned one of the millions of booklets the government was sending out to every voter explaining why they should vote Remain, at a cost of £9.3 million. 'The government has chosen to spend nearly ten million pounds of *our* money to tell us what we should think and how we should vote,' Farage told the TV cameras. 'I don't believe that's within the rules. Even the Electoral Commission have said it's not within the *spirit* of the rules.'[1]

Ahead of the designation announcement, one of the leading Vote Leave ministers, the Leader of the House of Commons, Chris Grayling, tried to ensure that Nigel Farage and Arron Banks behaved themselves during the campaign and all the leavers now worked in harmony. He invited Farage to his home in Surrey, then a few days later drove down to Bristol to see Arron Banks. The meeting did not go well.

Grayling 'drearily recited the Vote Leave mantra', Banks later wrote, 'no talking about immigration'. Grayling spent two and a half hours with him, according to Banks, and towards the end urged him to make sure that Farage toned down his comments, and not say anything along the lines of his past remarks about migrants with HIV. When Banks reacted badly, Grayling left, though Banks claims in his diary that the exchanges went like this:

'How dare you come to my office and tell me "Oh, you've got to control Nigel?!"'

'I just wasted my whole last three hours, didn't I?' he asked, looking greyer than ever.

'Yeah, pretty much!' I replied brightly. 'There's your car.' I gestured at the vehicle, like I was swatting away a fly. 'There you go, get out.'

So I basically told him to fuck off.

Texted Nigel straight away to tell him what had happened, informing him that I'd sent Grayling away 'with a flea in his ear'.

At least we now have confirmation – as if there has ever been any doubt – that they plan to airbrush Nigel out of this referendum campaign.[2]

It might have been better had Grayling approached Farage to control Banks, not the other way round. Only three days after the minister's trip down the M4, Grayling and Farage shared a platform at a Grassroots Out rally in Stoke-on-Trent, the first time Farage had collaborated with any Cabinet minister. Banks was also at the rally, but in no mood to make up after their row in Bristol, and when Grayling tried to shake his hand, Banks turned his back on him. 'Why do you have to be so aggressive,' Farage later asked Banks. 'Nigel, I'm being aggressive on your behalf,' Banks says he replied. 'These guys are just out to shaft us.'[3]

By the end of April, Farage was feeling surprisingly downhearted – not just about the prospects of success, but he often felt bruised by the constant personal attacks. Banks records in his diary how, late one night, he received 'a very miserable text from Nigel saying he was "at the end of the road"'. Banks wrote: 'I'm worried about him. I know he doesn't mean it but the pressure of the past year is taking its toll. He gets such a battering in the media and while he's very resilient, the constant accusations of being a "racist" do get to him sometimes.'[4]

Despite the bad blood between the two Leave camps, Farage did try to set up some joint campaign events with Boris Johnson, who was now the effective leader of Vote Leave. Among his ideas was a big rally at the Albert Hall where he, Johnson and Kate Hoey would be the main guests. Alternatively, he and Johnson might spend several days on a joint bus tour. Farage later claimed the two men spoke 'every Sunday' on the phone, to try to co-ordinate their messages and activities. One day, Farage suggested that in a display of unity, hoping to dominate the agenda for 48 hours, they should converge – in Andover, say – for a big event, in their vehicles – Johnson in Vote Leave's famous red coach and Farage on UKIP's purple and yellow open-top bus, known as the 'Flying Aubergine'. According to Farage, Johnson was enthusiastic. 'He said it'll be like the Russians and the Americans meeting on the Elbe [in 1945],' he later recalled. But Dominic Cummings and Matthew Elliott blocked the idea, he says.[5]

Elliott says the joint Farage–Johnson bus tour was never a possibility, and the other events never occurred either.[6] Instead, Farage spent much of the ten-week campaign travelling round in the Flying Aubergine as the sole attraction. Johnson and Farage were not once seen together, which may have been just as well as it might have exposed their differences. Nigel Farage did not like Vote Leave's notorious claim that leaving the European Union would mean another £350 million a week for the NHS – a figure which every analyst said was a gross exaggeration. When journalists asked him about it, Farage said he didn't agree with the figure. 'I begged them to change it,' he claimed. 'I spoke to Gove. He said: "It's all a bit late for that."' It was by now painted on the Vote Leave bus and removing it would have been a big story. Farage also claimed to have raised it with Johnson.[7]

As promised, Nigel Farage, Arron Banks and their Leave.EU

operation placed great emphasis on immigration and the argument that it could only be controlled by withdrawing from the EU and its free movement regime. At the end of April, in the Emmanuel Centre in Westminster, opposite the Home Office, Farage raised the temperature by warning about possible Turkish membership of the EU, and he reminded people of the sexual attacks by young migrants at the recent New Year's Eve celebrations near Cologne railway station in Germany:

> We saw mass, open, sexual molestation of hundreds of women appearing in public. And frankly, if we're prepared to accept, or if Germany and Sweden are prepared to accept, unlimited numbers of young males from countries and cultures where women are at best, second-class citizens, then frankly what do you expect? . . . And I do not want one of those men who were outside Cologne train station to have one of these [holds up a passport] in a few short years and to be able to come to our country . . .
>
> And now Mrs Merkel has decided that Turkey must become a member of the European Union by 2025 at the latest. So if you vote to remain, ladies and gentlemen, you're voting to go into a political union with Turkey. You are voting to go into a free-travel area with 77 million people and rising fast in Turkey . . . I used to worry that we were living in an increasingly German-dominated Europe, but from what I can see it might become a Turkish-dominated Europe . . . We have to, in this campaign, make people understand that EU membership and uncontrolled immigration are synonymous with each other.[8]

Then, two and a half weeks before polling day, just as postal voters were starting to cast their ballots, Farage raised the stakes by telling the *Sunday Telegraph* that possible attacks on women by migrants were the 'nuclear bomb' of the referendum contest. 'There are some very big cultural issues,' Farage said. He accused the prime minister of being 'Dishonest Dave' for not keeping his pledges to cut immigration and to renegotiate Britain's terms of membership. This

was 'outright blatant scaremongering' by Farage, said the pro-Brexit
energy minister Andrea Leadsom. 'I wouldn't support suggesting if
you vote to remain you'd be raped. Obviously that is just an outrageous thing to say.' Michael Gove, too, disowned Farage's remarks.[9]

Such was the high-octane background to what was expected to be
Farage's big personal moment in the 2016 campaign. Two days later
he was due to appear in an event on ITV alongside David Cameron.
The Vote Leave camp had reassured themselves that winning the
designation would exclude Nigel Farage from the major set-piece
TV events. They were wrong. What they hadn't reckoned with
was a strange alliance of interests between David Cameron and
Nigel Farage which saw them participate in the same television
broadcast. The prime minister and his advisers were always very
conscious about the long term, and the need to bring the Tories
together again after the referendum, and they were determined that
at no point should Cameron be seen to go head-to-head with other
senior Conservatives, such as his Cabinet colleague and close friend
Michael Gove, or Boris Johnson, who had just stepped down as
London mayor and was expected to join the government before long.
Cameron's communications director Craig Oliver explained in his
memoirs how he made the case to Cameron for doing a programme
with Farage. 'He's the unacceptable face of Leave to millions – let's
put him in the centre of the frame.'[10]

ITV bosses weren't bothered about the fact that Farage wasn't
the choice of the official Vote Leave side. There were no rules that
said they had to confine their set-piece broadcasts to representatives
of the designated campaigns. Indeed, the ITV men had told Farage
they wanted him in a debate when they met him for lunch as long
ago as the previous June, at the Betjeman Arms on St Pancras station. As a commercial network, their prime concern was audience
figures, and Cameron versus Farage was a 'box-office' attraction. So
ITV planned from early on that their big head-to-head event would
involve the leaders of the two biggest right-of-centre parties, though
it was never a debate, in fact, and never really head-to-head. Vote
Leave complained that ITV was working at the behest of Farage,
and at one point threatened to pull out of its bigger referendum

debate later on if they were not allowed to nominate who should face Cameron. The threat was never likely to succeed.

On 11 May, six weeks before polling, Craig Oliver, who was on secondment to the official Remain organisation, Britain Stronger In, phoned ITV to explain that Cameron had agreed to face Farage. He urged ITV to announce it publicly on their news bulletins, which they did almost immediately, so that Vote Leave couldn't easily stop it. Vote Leave accused ITV of letting Downing Street choose who should oppose Cameron, which was a fair point. Very late that night Dominic Cummings sent political journalists an email which was extraordinary even by his standards: 'ITV is led by people like [political editor] Robert Peston who campaigned for Britain to join the euro,' Cummings wrote (though it wasn't true about Peston). 'ITV has lied to us in private while secretly stitching up a deal with Cameron to stop Boris Johnson or Michael Gove debating the issues properly. ITV has effectively joined the official In campaign and there will be consequences for its future – the people in No 10 won't be there for long.'[11] The threat of 'consequences' sounded ominous, but what Vote Leave really feared was that the BBC might set up a second Cameron–Farage event.

ITV's encounter, entitled *Cameron & Farage LIVE*, took place on Tuesday 7 June, and the Conservative leader turned up at the new ITV studios in Olympic Park in his official grey car. Farage, in contrast, travelled there on the top of the Flying Aubergine, UKIP's purple bus, which had a large picture of Farage on the outside and a well-stocked drinks cabinet inside. The latter might well have been needed en route to the ITV studios when the bus almost had a nasty accident under a low bridge. The driver had to reverse and take another route.

Farage was accompanied by half a dozen male aides, including Arron Banks and Andy Wigmore, the two main architects of his strategy of pushing the immigration issue. As Banks said, they looked 'like something out of *Reservoir Dogs*'.[12]

Speaking off the cuff is Nigel Farage's normal style, but before the ITV event he prepared thoroughly. The former Conservative Cabinet minister David Davis was among those who joined Farage for an all-day rehearsal – bringing the experience of having debated against Cameron in the 2005 Tory leadership contest. He was joined by the Labour MP Kate Hoey, and Mark Reckless, Gawain Towler and Chris Bruni-Lowe.

In fact, Farage and Cameron were never seen together on screen. Indeed, they weren't meant even to meet at the studios. Banks reports that Farage was 'very tense all day, pacing up and down chain smoking', and just before going on air, he nipped outside for a final cigarette. But when Farage and his aides returned to the studio they ran into Cameron and his team coming the other way. 'His flunkeys looked horrified,' says Banks. 'They'd specifically told ITV they didn't want any backstage encounters and now they couldn't avoid us. Trapped in a narrow corridor, Cameron tried to hide his dismay behind a rubbery mask of good cheer as Farage greeted him with a mischievous "Hello, Prime Minister!"' Andy Wigmore took a picture of the 'super-awkward moment' on his iPhone, and quickly tweeted it.[13]

First, Farage fielded questions for twenty-five minutes from the 200-strong audience; then, after a commercial break, David Cameron did likewise. And the hour was dominated by the issues of immigration and race, as Farage may have hoped.

Earlier that day, addressing the Commons home affairs committee, the Archbishop of Canterbury, Justin Welby, had been asked about Farage's recent remarks that staying in the European Union could 'lead to sexual attacks such as the ones we saw in Cologne'. Welby seemed to agree with the suggestion by the committee chairman Keith Vaz that such comments were 'racist'. 'I think that is an inexcusable pandering to people's worries, and prejudices. That's giving legitimisation to racism, which I've seen in parishes in which I've served, and has led to attacks on people in those parishes, and we cannot legitimise that . . . That is accentuating fear for political gain, and that is absolutely inexcusable.' So would Welby 'utterly condemn' Farage's comments? 'Without hesitation,' Welby responded gravely, 'without hesitation.'[14]

Cameron's team was confident that the publicity given to Farage's recent remarks about Cologne and immigration would only help

Remain win support from people who hadn't made up their minds. Farage had a difficult time from the ITV audience. One young Black woman attacked him over Cologne. 'Just calm down there, a little bit,' Farage told her tetchily. 'I'm used to being demonised.' Another Black woman angrily accused Farage of 'scaremongering and inflammatory comments'. Was he not embarrassed, she asked, that Justin Welby had accused him of 'legitimising racism'?

Tim Shipman writes in his masterful account of the Brexit saga, *All Out War*, that David Cameron was ready to attack Farage very hard if he had said anything outrageous, along the lines, say, of his HIV comments in the 2015 TV election debate. 'We thought Farage would totally go for the PM and say lots of horrible things', in which case, he was 'really prepared to lay into Farage', says one of Cameron's aides:

> He was prepared to go on and say, 'This guy's really unpleasant. I've listened to this guy for several years now, and I just want to get something off my chest: he calls Chinese people chinks, he calls gay people fags, and this is not British; it's not who we are and it's not right. It's divisive and it's wrong and we should have no part in it. It's not the Britain I love.' He was going to totally go for it, but the moment never came.[15]

At the same time, some of the audience accused David Cameron of failing to meet his targets on immigration, partly because Britain was limited by European Union rules on freedom of movement. 'The right thing to do,' Cameron concluded, 'the British thing to do, is to fight for a Great Britain inside a European Union and don't take the Nigel Farage 'Little England' option.'[16] As so often with highly anticipated TV encounters, the verdict was that neither man delivered a knock-out blow.

The BBC, in contrast, planned to televise the *Great Debate*, a two-hour programme from Wembley on the eve of poll, 22 June, in a format involving three big-name politicians on each side – six in all. And that raised the obvious possibility that Nigel Farage might be one of the three on the Leave side. On 22 May the BBC announced, however, that the Leave line-up for their debate would instead be Boris Johnson, the Labour MP Gisela Stuart and Andrea Leadsom, all from Vote Leave.

Now it was Farage's turn to feel aggrieved. 'This calls for war,' Arron Banks wrote, and he launched his assault by publicising the personal phone numbers and email addresses of 'everyone involved in this Establishment stitch-up'. His hit list included the BBC director-general Tony Hall and the head of political programmes Robbie Gibb, as well as several Vote Leave figures – Matthew Elliott, Dominic Cummings, Douglas Carswell and the organisation's main press officer. Banks left it to Andy Wigmore to post their contact details on Facebook.

It caused havoc. Tony Hall and Robbie Gibb were bombarded with calls and voicemails, and texts accusing them of being the 'BIASED BRUSSELS CORPORATION'. 'I can't do my job; I just can't,' Gibb complained to Wigmore as he rang to protest.[17] Gibb had to ask the BBC to supply him with a new phone, and it was a foolish move by Banks and Wigmore, since Gibb was a long-standing Eurosceptic who for several years had argued within the Corporation that UKIP and other anti-EU voices deserved more airtime and should be taken more seriously. The UKIP leader personally liked Gibb, and complained to Wigmore that he'd 'gone too far'. 'What next?' an angry Farage reportedly asked him and Banks. 'Are you going to adopt ISIS tactics and blow up Television Centre? Throw bricks through their windows?'[18]

'Having thrown the grenade,' Banks wrote, 'I was thoroughly enjoying the explosion. But Nigel was furious. He told us there was "no upside" to our mischief and complained about having to run around cleaning up our mess.'[19]

Dominic Cummings would later argue that Vote Leave's recruitment of Boris Johnson was crucial to the campaign's success, partly as a big-name, popular counterweight to Nigel Farage. 'Without Boris,' Cummings wrote in his blog in 2017:

Farage would have been a much more prominent face on TV during the crucial final weeks, probably *the* most prominent face.

(We had to use Boris as leverage with the BBC to keep Farage off, and even then they nearly screwed us, as ITV did.) It is extremely plausible that this would have lost us over 600,000 vital middle-class votes.[20]

Instead, Farage spent most of the two-month campaign touring England and Wales in the Flying Aubergine, visiting predominantly working-class towns and cities in northern England, the Midlands and Wales, where the UKIP and Leave.EU message was likely to strike a chord with people who felt 'left out'. Playing the famous theme tune from *The Great Escape*, the bus would roll up in communities where Farage held open-air events and rallies. These were often well covered on regional TV and local radio, but he received relatively little coverage nationally, though after each event Farage's team put out a video on social media.

Perhaps the most memorable set of images of the entire contest was from a Leave.EU event involving both Nigel Farage and Arron Banks. To highlight the gains they foresaw to the fishing industry if Britain left the EU's Common Fisheries Policy, they hired a luxury cruiser on the Thames and sailed from Tower Bridge to the Palace of Westminster: Arron Banks had arranged and paid for several dozen fishermen to help form a small armada with their boats – from tiny fishing smacks to substantial trawlers. 'This is not a booze cruise,' said Farage, who wore a blue blazer with brass buttons, looking vaguely like a sea captain. 'We've got to be sensible and well-behaved,' he warned his crew.[21]

Some hope. It was a fine day, and the predominantly UKIP party on board couldn't help but enjoy a few drinks from the downstairs bar. Since the exercise had been well publicised in advance, Remain supporters had ample chance to retaliate with a bigger armada of pro-EU boats. Those on the Thames included the singer Charlotte Church and Boris Johnson's pro-Remain sister Rachel; while a small dinghy bobbed about carrying the family of the Labour MP Jo Cox. 'We literally almost ran them over,' recalls Gawain Towler.[22]

As the Leave.EU boats approached Westminster a much larger vessel drew up alongside playing very noisy music. On board was the rock star Sir Bob Geldof, in cream cap and sunglasses, who had brought an effective PA system. He flicked V-signs, and mouthed 'wanker' at Farage with accompanying lewd hand gestures, all captured by the TV cameras. Passengers on the Geldof boat seemed to have drunk even more than the Farage–Banks crew. 'You're a fraud, Nigel Farage,' Geldof bellowed. 'You are no fishermen's friend . . . Stop lying. This election is too important.'[23] Geldof blasted through his megaphone the fact that, while a member of the fisheries committee in the European Parliament, Farage had only attended one meeting in forty-three – which seemed a bit complicated for political banter on the high Thames. The fishermen accused Geldof of being dismissive of their concerns.[24] 'Fancy Bob Geldof coming to laugh at poor people,' Farage protested to me.

Another highlight was the sight of Farage and the Eurosceptic Labour MP Kate Hoey together on the prow of their boat, pretending to look lovingly into each other's eyes, in the style of Leonardo DiCaprio and Kate Winslet in *Titanic*. It was all glorious material for sketch writers and TV news reporters – and one of the best campaign events I have ever witnessed.

Farage was not amused, however. 'Don't react, don't react', Banks heard him responding to Geldof's jibes, as he tried to calm everyone down. 'He was a crap pop star and he's not even British as far as I understand. He's from the Irish Republic; he hasn't got a say in the matter,' Farage said, though perhaps he had forgotten that his first wife was Irish. 'Nigel is not short of courage, but today the Nelson touch distinctly failed him,' Banks wrote. 'Sometimes, his response to the latest broadside from the Good Ship Geldof was to rush down below. It was only the ciggies that stopped him losing it totally today.'[25] The other Leave.EU leaders had reacted in very different ways to the enemy flotilla. To Banks, Geldof's appearance just added to the fun and colour of the day; Farage seemed anxious that he'd been upstaged, and that their cause might have been damaged. It was hilariously funny, yet raised serious issues, and Geldof's appearance gave the stunt far more attention than the organisers dared imagine. 'We thought we were just gonna get page 10 of the *Daily Mail*,' says Gawain Towler.[26]

Despite their long-standing claims that Farage would go overboard on immigration, Vote Leave soon focused heavily on immigration, too, and began advocating an Australian-style points system for immigrants, which had long been UKIP policy. Many of Vote Leave's ads, sent to millions of individuals on Facebook, were also about immigration, and Boris Johnson and Michael Gove both warned of the vast influx of migrants who might arrive if Turkey was allowed to join the European Union.

In theory, immigration should have become rather less of an issue. For during the campaign the European Union struck a deal which hugely reduced the numbers of arrivals from Syria through Turkey, and the Turkish government agreed to house the refugees instead, helped by billions of euros in EU grants. The numbers of immigrants arriving in Europe would fall dramatically, though there was no sign of this by polling day.

Banks and Farage were much more brazen than Vote Leave, however, about what they saw as the dangers of the EU's porous frontiers. On 13 June, with just ten days to go, Arron Banks decided that for the rest of the campaign immigration should be the *sole* issue for Leave.EU. The day before, in Orlando, Florida, an Islamist with an assault rifle had killed forty-nine people in a gay night club. 'We weren't ashamed to use it to remind voters of the dangers posed by open borders,' Banks says. So the campaign posted an ad online saying 'Islamist extremism is a real threat to our way of life. Act now before we see an Orlando-style atrocity'. Andy Wigmore then tweeted: 'Freedom of movement for Kalashnikovs in Europe helps terrorists. Vote for greater security on June 23. Vote Leave.' Nigel Farage 'thought it was a step too far', Banks wrote, 'but the truth is, he doesn't like being upstaged. He wants to be the one delivering shock and awe.'[27]

Three days later, on Thursday 16 June, Farage turned up in Smith Square, Westminster, and unveiled an advertising van which would instantly go down as one of the most notorious posters in British political history. The headline 'BREAKING POINT' was imposed on a colour picture of a long column of hundreds of what looked like mainly Asian refugees and migrants, almost entirely young men. The picture had been taken on the border between Croatia and Slovenia the year before, not long after Angela Merkel had announced that Germany's borders were open to migrants who had arrived in southern Europe in high numbers.

Dave Prentis, the leader of the trade union Unison, immediately reported the poster to the police as a 'blatant attempt to incite racial hatred and breach UK race laws'. Others compared it to similar pictures used by the Nazis. Boris Johnson said it was 'not our campaign' and 'not my politics'.[28] The playwright Bonnie Greer tweeted the image alongside a quote from the Nazi leader Hermann Goering: 'All you have to do is tell them they are being attacked . . . Works the same way in any country.'[29] The Vote Leave camp were furious, says Matthew Elliott:

> The last thing you want in the final furlong of the campaign is to have a shout or a scream towards your core vote, because you just turn off the swing voters you're trying to attract . . . It just felt like Nigel Farage was waving and saying: 'Look I'm over here, remember me? Give me some coverage on TV.' It felt incompetent.[30]

Not surprisingly given his worries about 'Islamism' immediately after the Orlando attack, Farage had been 'jittery' about the 'Breaking Point' poster, according to Arron Banks, who advised him to hold his nerve. But then disaster struck.

Ninety minutes after Breaking Point went up, the Labour MP Jo Cox, a keen Remain supporter, was murdered by an extreme white supremacist, Thomas Mair, in her West Yorkshire constituency. The poster would thereafter be cited by Remainers and others as the worst example of the hateful and nasty politics which had spread during the referendum contest and perhaps incited Mair. Arron Banks and his colleagues suspended Leave.EU's campaigning and issued a statement expressing shock and sympathy. The next day Nigel Farage laid flowers on the memorial to Jo Cox which had sprung up in Parliament Square, but he feared Remain 'would push this for all it is worth'. According to Banks, Farage 'veered between saying it won't make much difference to the outcome and being very despondent and saying we have lost momentum just when things were going in our direction'.[31]

Chris Grayling, prompted by Dominic Cummings, went the next day to see Farage at a pub near the UKIP leader's home in Kent, and urged him not to run any more such ads. Farage agreed to concentrate on sovereignty instead.

When Farage was invited onto the BBC *Today* programme four days later, on the Monday morning, Arron Banks and Andy Wigmore encouraged him to say the Breaking Point poster had been a 'mistake' – that it was intended as 'an attack on the system', not on those fleeing their countries – but Farage continued to defend it. 'I didn't invent that picture,' he told *Today*. 'The picture was real, the picture was on the front pages of all our national press last year.'[32]

Farage is always extremely upset when people accuse him of racism, and was especially distressed at the way some people used the Breaking Point poster somehow to implicate him indirectly in Jo Cox's death. He tried to answer this in a speech in Gateshead on the Monday night, three days before polling day:

> There are one or two in the Remain camp . . . some of their speakers, who have tried to say that the motives of that man [Thomas Mair] were somehow whipped up or inspired by a Leave campaign that had fought on a nasty, negative and hateful agenda.
>
> I want to say: that man, who had his own mental health issues, that man acted in isolation. What that man did was an act of barbarism and every one of us who will go out to vote to leave condemns utterly what he did.[33]

In the final few days, Farage seemed convinced that Leave was heading for defeat, though a private poll commissioned by Arron Banks, of 10,000 people, suggested otherwise. 'Nigel is on edge, and I'm not surprised,' Banks wrote on the eve of poll. 'He's been building up to this moment for the last twenty-five years of his life. He thinks the Jo Cox murder has cost us the Referendum.'[34]

On polling day, 23 June, Banks organised what Farage calls a PFL – a 'Proper Fucking Lunch' or 'Proper Farage Lunch' – at his favourite Italian restaurant, Zafferano, in Belgravia. There, Banks gave him a signed copy of Ernest Hemingway's *For Whom the Bell Tolls* which he'd found in an antiquarian bookshop the night before. 'He was so preoccupied I don't think he really took it in.' They were joined by Andy Wigmore, Chris Bruni-Lowe and 22-year-old George Cottrell — Posh George — who had been working unpaid since January as Farage's aide-de-camp. 'We spent most of the time talking about what would happen if we lost,' Cottrell later said, 'and Arron said I was a pessimist and that we would win. But Nigel was pretty brooding throughout.' The despondent Farage kept repeating: 'We're going to lose . . . I can feel it in my waters.'[35] Chris Bruni-Lowe agreed with him. 'Nigel was a wreck,' another colleague recalls. 'He must have smoked 200–300 cigarettes that day, one after the other. In his office, it was really mellow. It felt like a wake. I think there was only one or two of us in the office that thought we'd actually won this.'

That evening Banks had organised a big party above Leave.EU's offices in Millbank Tower. He contacted Farage beforehand to boost his spirits and told him a second poll of another 10,000 again showed Leave would win narrowly. But Farage was also speaking to contacts in the City. They'd been doing their own polling which suggested a narrow win for Remain.

So when a Sky News journalist spoke to Farage around 9.40 p.m., he remained pessimistic and gave them a statement which Sky broadcast immediately after the polls closed at 10 p.m. 'It's been an extraordinary referendum campaign,' Farage said, 'turnout looks to be exceptionally high and [it] looks like Remain will edge it.'[36] His words went right around the world and cheered the Remain camp hugely. 'What are you doing?' a perplexed Steve Bannon says he rang Farage and protested. 'Don't concede — we've got this.'[37]

Farage was still gloomy when he came out of the lifts at the top of Millbank Tower, entered the party and looked around. He immediately complained to Banks about the number of journalists present, and Banks got so annoyed that he had to leave for a spell to calm down. When he returned, Farage was in the midst of a media scrum. 'Nigel was being jostled by photographers and reporters, and people were shoving, shouting and being knocked over,' Banks records. 'My strop over, I tried to take some of the pressure off him by giving some interviews myself.'[38]

George Cottrell, as ever a heavy gambler, had quickly seen his chance to exploit the widespread assumption that Leave had lost. 'At 10 p.m., I couldn't believe I was still getting 9–1 [for Leave],' he said later.[39]

Then, after midnight, came the first results – from the North East. Newcastle, expected to be strongly Remain, saw them win by fewer than 2,000 votes. Sunderland next door then voted Leave much more heavily than psephologists had forecast. 'The atmosphere at our party underwent a dramatic change,' says Banks. 'Now the mood was electric: there was all to play for! With every new area that voted Out, or voted to Remain by the narrowest of margins, our whoops and cheers grew louder.'[40]

George Cottrell, meanwhile, was still sitting in the Leave. EU campaign office and, now working the markets, was doing extremely well. 'I was tracking all the major stock indices, the dollar and pound currency markets. When it got to 3 a.m., I was getting my managers out of bed to get me another 50 grand on here, another 50 grand there, to short sterling. I just couldn't help myself.'[41]

Farage, having got things embarrassingly wrong with Sky News, had to be careful not to be silly again. Only at around 3.45 a.m., as dawn was about to break after one of the shortest nights of the year, did Farage tweet, 'I now dare to dream that the dawn is coming up on an independent United Kingdom.'[42] He then told the party:

If the predictions now are right, this will be a victory for real people, a victory for ordinary people, a victory for decent people. We have fought against the multinationals; we've fought against the big merchant banks; we've fought against big politics; we've fought against lies, corruption and deceit. And today, honesty, decency and belief in nation, I think now, *is* going to win. We'll have done it without having to fight, without a single bullet being fired; we'll have done it by damned hard work on the ground.

He was surrounded by numerous UKIP colleagues, but the only one he mentioned by name – with a hand on his shoulder – was 'my friend Mr Banks here'. Farage finished with the words: 'Let June the 23rd go down in our history as our Independence Day', and he raised his arms aloft like a conquering hero.[43]

The drunken, victorious revellers then retired to Chris Bruni-Lowe's flat nearby. George Cottrell had not just the Brexit victory to celebrate, he'd also made a six-figure sum with the bookies and on the markets.

Around 7.20 that morning, Farage appeared before the TV cameras on College Green outside Parliament. An hour later David Cameron resigned as prime minister, and Farage went to a celebration breakfast – with kippers, of course – given by the Barclay brothers at their hotel, the Ritz. George Cottrell, though, was still gambling. He put most of his overnight winnings 'on some horse . . . I was a compulsive, habitual, addicted gambler.'[44]

In the final tally, Leave won by 17,410,742 votes to 16,141,241 – by almost 1.3 million votes – or 51.89 per cent to 48.11 per cent. Both major parties were in turmoil, and there were new doubts about whether Scotland or Northern Ireland could stay much longer in the United Kingdom, since both countries had voted Remain. Reeling from the shock, the Remain establishment struggled to make sense of how they had misjudged the mood in much of England, and failed to connect with so many disaffected voters outside the metropolis.

Ever since, there has been debate about who most deserved credit for achieving the Brexit vote. Most focus was on the Vote Leave strategist Dominic Cummings, especially after he was given the central role in the HBO/Channel 4 drama written by James Graham, *Brexit: The Uncivil War*, and later spent a turbulent year as Boris Johnson's chief-of-staff in Downing Street.

Without Nigel Farage, however, and pressure from the gradual growth of UKIP over its first twenty years, then the party's much more rapid rise after 2012, David Cameron would never have promised the referendum in the first place, or carried it out after the Conservatives got a majority in 2015.

Some of his detractors in the Vote Leave team suspect, however, that Farage didn't really want Leave to win the referendum, and cite his forecast of defeat as the polls closed as evidence of this. The theory goes that Farage didn't want to give up the comfortable Brussels lifestyle, which had brought him a substantial status and income over the previous seventeen years. But Farage's prediction may in part have been a reflection of his general gloom and pessimism, after so many years of having his hopes dashed in Westminster elections. Arron Banks's account may be exaggerated and embellished, and may not be a true contemporaneous diary, but the constant references to Farage's despondency – together with his phenomenal workrate during the campaign – do strongly suggest he genuinely wanted Leave to win. Matthew Elliott thinks a 'bitterness towards the end of the campaign' explained Farage's forecast:

> This was meant to be his moment. He had, in his view, secured the referendum, built up the Brexit movement over 25 years, why wasn't he the one doing the debates, why wasn't he the one accepting the prize? There was a bitterness there and I actually think that's why he came out . . . at 10pm on referendum day with his prediction that Leave had lost.[45]

The other big question is whether having two main camps on the Leave side actually helped, despite the poisonous blood between them. 'I remember at the time thinking this is a disaster. It looks ridiculous that the two Leave factions are fighting,' says Alex Phillips.

> In retrospect, it is the most genius thing that ever happened – that's what won the referendum, having these two entities. If it was just the Tory-controlled Vote Leave entity, the Faragistes wouldn't have gone out and voted; they wouldn't have even turned up at the polling station. Leave would not have won as a Tory vehicle. If it had been a Leave.EU entity it wouldn't have won because it would have become, 'Gosh, all these people who like Farage and Banks and a pint, are the people voting Leave and we're middle-class professionals who might be sympathetic to

Euroscepticism.' Having the two entities was not just increasing the spread of appeal but actually being against each other was an extremely, in the end, potent device because it enabled people to say 'Oh yes, I'm for Brexit but I don't like Leave.EU, I'm a Vote Leaver' with that sort of respectability, or 'Yes, I'm for Brexit but I'm not a Tory voter.' And I think in the end actually it was the thing that won it.[46]

Matthew Elliott, who suffered so much from Arron Banks, agrees that having two separate strands of Euroscepticism may have helped win over undecided voters whose hearts said they should vote Leave, but were concerned about the economic impact. 'One characteristic of those voters was that they didn't want to feel like they were voting for Farage by voting Leave. So actually having Farage parked in a different camp and not being part of Vote Leave was crucial because they could feel they were voting for Boris Johnson.'[47] If Arron Banks hadn't established Leave.EU then Elliott says Vote Leave would have felt obliged to give Farage some major role on their ship.

Dominic Cummings disagrees. He thinks that the overall effect of Nigel Farage and Leave.EU was to diminish the Leave vote by about 6 per cent. He later claimed:

Farage put off millions of (middle class in particular) voters who wanted to leave the EU but who were very clear in market research that a major obstacle to voting Leave was 'I don't want to vote for Farage, I'm not like that'. He also put off many prominent business people from supporting us. Over and over they would say, 'I agree with you the EU is a disaster and we should get out, but I just cannot be on the same side as a guy who makes comments about people with HIV.'[48]

Three years later, a BBC presenter asked him whether he would still produce the Breaking Point poster. No, Farage replied, because immigration was no longer 'the burning issue of the time'.[49]

Yet for years afterwards Nigel Farage would publicly claim the poster 'transformed European politics' and helped win the referendum. 'I'm very sorry for the timing of that poster,' he told *Newsnight* four weeks after the result. 'I'm sorry for the way in which it was used. I'm *not* sorry for showing the truth, but perhaps unwittingly, it did in the end get the debate back for the last few days onto the one thing that people out there really, really do care about.'[50]

The earthquake long forecast by Nigel Farage had struck.

TRUMP THAT

It's one of the best jokes Bob Monkhouse ever delivered – short, simple and self-deprecating: 'They laughed when I said I wanted to be a comedian. Well, they're not laughing now.'

And when Nigel Farage returned to the European Parliament five days after the EU referendum, he delivered a variation on Monkhouse's famous lines: 'Mr President, isn't it funny? When I came here seventeen years ago and said that I wanted to lead a campaign to get Britain to leave the European Union, you all laughed at me. Well, I have to say, you're not laughing now, are you?'

Understandably, Farage's speech was not well received, and he was met with 'protests and catcalls', the record says, when he told MEPs that 'virtually none of you have ever done a proper job in your lives, or worked in business, or worked in trade, or indeed ever created a job'.[1] The Liberal leader in the Parliament, Guy Verhofstadt, compared Farage's Breaking Point poster with Nazi propaganda and said: 'Finally, we are going to get rid of the biggest waste in the budget of the Union that we have paid for seventeen years. Your salary.'

A week later, Farage announced he was stepping down as leader of UKIP – for the second time (or perhaps third, given his three-day resignation in 2015). He suddenly had time on his hands, but wisely turned down an invitation to appear on the TV show *I'm A Celebrity . . . Get Me Out of Here!* even though, according to Arron Banks, he claimed to have been offered 'a monster sum' – supposedly £250,000.[2]

The result of the referendum had made headlines around the

world, but aroused particular interest in the United States where politics was dominated by another insurgent campaign trying to topple the establishment. Much to the astonishment of many political analysts, Donald Trump had become a strong contender in the 2016 presidential election, and was about to be formally confirmed as the Republican candidate at the party's convention in Cleveland, Ohio.

Farage, Arron Banks and several friends decided they had to be there.

Farage had been interested in US politics ever since his days in the City when his trading firm was part of the American investment bank Drexel Burnham Lambert, and more especially after 1994 when Farage Futures worked under the umbrella of the US firm Refco. 'I've been a regular, monthly commuter for over 30 years,' he told a magazine in 2021. 'I've spent a significant amount of my time in the States, not just in the big cities but also in the industrial heartlands, where they were using various kinds of industrial metals.'[3] He developed a 'strong affinity' for America and its 'can-do attitude'.[4]

But Farage's interest grew in the summer of 2012 when he was invited to the United States by the man who'd just taken over as boss of the American right-wing website Breitbart News Network, following the death of its founder Andrew Breitbart. His host was Steve Bannon, a 58-year-old Virginian who'd filled several roles in his adult life – naval officer, banker, Hollywood producer and now standard-bearer of what had become known as the 'alt-right', or alternative right. Over several days in New York and Washington, Bannon introduced Farage to various conservative contacts, including the staff of Jeff Sessions, a Republican senator from Alabama. During a later trip to New York in 2014, Farage got a message that Donald Trump would like to see him. 'The person that approached me from the Trump organisation said, "He's been watching your speeches in the European Parliament."'[5] It proved impossible, though, to arrange a meeting.

After the 2015 election, Farage began writing a weekly column for Breitbart News, whose London bureau had been run by Raheem Kassam, his chief adviser at that time, and Kassam went to watch the early stages of the Trump presidential campaign. Farage recalls him reporting: 'I can see something happening on the ground, just like it was with you in 2012, 2013 when Ukip were bubbling away . . . No one in New York is noticing; the media don't get this . . . I've seen the audiences at these meetings and something's going on.' And Farage got feedback that the Trump team liked what he and UKIP were doing in the run-up to the EU referendum.[6]

In February 2015, Farage was invited to speak at the Conservative Political Action Conference (CPAC) held just outside Washington DC, the annual gathering which attracted the most diehard members of the American right. And for his US audience Farage showed a distinctly harder tone than he seemed to display back home.

On Fox News the night before, Farage had warned that British mosques were being infiltrated by criminal hate preachers, and he then told a drinks reception: 'We have a fifth column living within our communities, a fifth column that hates us and wants to destroy us, and if we are going to win this great battle – for our liberty, for our democracy, for our civilisation and our culture – we are going to have to start standing up for our Judeo-Christian values.'

By the time Farage spoke to CPAC itself, most delegates seemed to have drifted off to parties and fringe events, so it was a meagre audience. But he was prescient in his advice:

> I think the Republican Party needs to get the kind of people voting for it that were voting for it 30 years ago . . . Do you remember the Reagan Democrats? These were people who worked hard . . . who aspired and wanted to get on, and I don't think at the moment the Republican Party is actually attracting those kind of people.[7]

'I'm American UKIP,' said Jeff Duncan, a congressman from South Carolina who was impressed with what Farage said, although in the winter of 2015 the UKIP leader was still unknown to most American conservatives. As the Trump campaign gained momentum, however, people began comparing the two men over their hardline stance on immigration, though Farage was slow to become a fully paid-up Trump supporter. The presidential candidate's policy of banning all Muslims from travelling to America was a 'somewhat knee-jerk reaction', he said, and 'perhaps for him a political mistake too far'. But Trump was someone who 'keeps pushing the boundaries of debate and that can be a healthy thing in politics'.[8] Rather like Nigel Farage himself.

During a debate held by the *Daily Express* in the midst of the EU referendum, the Labour MP Chuka Umunna had pressed Farage on whether, if he was an American, he'd vote for Trump or the likely Democrat nominee Hillary Clinton. 'I would never vote for Hillary. I think she's a crook,' he quickly shot back, 'and she'll get found out. I worked for the company at the time of Whitewater-gate and let me tell you I saw . . .' but Farage was then brushed aside by other voices. He quickly seemed to realise the legal implications of what he'd said, and stressed with a smile: 'I only said I *think* she's a crook. I didn't say she definitely was one.' He might 'abstain' in the US election, Farage added, saying he 'didn't think in office [Trump] will be anything like as extreme as we fear'.[9]

But what did Farage mean by 'I worked for the company at the time of Whitewater-gate?' In 1994, when President Clinton and his wife were under intense investigation over the Whitewater affair stemming from the couple's time in Arkansas politics, the *New York Times* published an extraordinary revelation. In the period 1978–9 Hillary Clinton had traded cattle futures and, astonishingly her $1,000 investment was turned into $100,000 in just ten months. Questions were asked as to whether this quick hundredfold profit was, in fact, a cover for bribery, and Hillary was less than frank in giving a full explanation. The broker for these transactions was the wonderfully named Robert L. 'Red' Bone of Refco (who died in 2012), the firm which oversaw Farage's business – hence his monthly trips to the US.

By the time of the referendum result, when Farage and his party set off for the Republican convention in Cleveland, Ohio, he had become something of a hero among American conservatives. The Trump campaign saw Brexit as evidence that a political establishment could be beaten. In the end, Arron Banks couldn't go to Ohio; he collapsed with high blood pressure, so Farage flew out with

Andy Wigmore, Richard Tice, George Cottrell and the journalist Isabel Oakeshott, who was helping to write Banks's book, *The Bad Boys of Brexit*.

In Cleveland, Farage suddenly found himself to be an even bigger celebrity among Republican activists than he was back home. They wanted his autograph, and to talk about how he'd won the Brexit vote. 'I was amazed by his profile in America,' says Isabel Oakeshott. 'He was stopped everywhere he went. He was an absolute magnet for women of a certain age – they kept coming up to him, desperate to have their photo taken. Naturally, he loved the attention, and would always oblige. "If only they were 20 years younger," he said.'[10] At the same time, Farage had a string of invitations from politicians to come and speak in their states.

Late one evening, in an Italian restaurant, Andy Wigmore was approached by someone saying that Donald Trump was seeking Farage's endorsement. Then a group arrived at the restaurant which included Roger Stone, the notorious dandyish fixer who was a long-standing friend of Trump. Stone had a long conversation with Farage, Banks says, and seemed to be sizing him up. Farage's spokesman later said that the meeting in the Cleveland restaurant was 'purely by chance'.[11]

Stone had first achieved notoriety at the age of twenty, when working on Richard Nixon's 1972 re-election campaign, and quickly earned a reputation – spread partly by himself – as a 'black arts' dirty trickster. He later worked for numerous other senior Republicans, including Ronald Reagan, Bob Dole and George W. Bush, while at the same time operating as a Washington lobbyist for Donald Trump. Stone was also the author of several books which made extraordinary allegations about past presidents – including that Lyndon Johnson was involved in a plot to murder John F. Kennedy, and that Richard Nixon had a long-standing relationship with a woman from Hong Kong who may have been a Chinese spy. Farage met Roger Stone only days before he became embroiled in controversy over the publication by WikiLeaks of emails which were embarrassing to Hillary Clinton, a focus of the subsequent official Mueller inquiry on Russian interference in the 2016 election.

Also present at the Farage–Stone meeting was the alt-right Texan broadcaster Alex Jones, who is famous for his internet radio station InfoWars, and was also loosely linked in the WikiLeaks affair. Jones has promoted numerous bizarre conspiracy theories, including the suggestion that the Bush administration was behind the 9/11 attacks; and that Barack Obama was really born in Kenya, not Hawaii (and therefore disqualified from being president) – the so-called 'birther' theory, of which Donald Trump had been an early adherent. Farage already knew Jones, having done several radio interviews on his show, dating back to 2009. Recordings of these broadcasts show that Farage rarely challenged Jones about his outlandish ideas, and sometimes contributed conspiracy suggestions of his own.

In Cleveland during this period, Roger Stone was actually co-operating with a camera crew who were following him around to make the documentary film *Get Me Roger Stone*, which was released in 2017. Yet, for once, it seems Farage was not so keen to be caught on camera. One of those making the film, Daniel DiMauro, subsequently told the British journalist Carole Cadwalladr that when they went with Stone to the restaurant, 'Farage's people were: "No, no, no! You can't film. You can't film." It was weird. Jones and Stone were totally open to it. But Farage was "No way." He didn't want any record of it. We didn't know what to make of it.' Another member of the film team told Cadwalladr: 'It was the first time that Alex Jones, Roger Stone and Nigel Farage met face to face. We'd had a wire on Roger everywhere we went, but when we turned up to meet Farage and his guy, he [Farage's aide] was absolutely adamant.'[12]

What's interesting is that Cadwalladr's two filmmakers recalled the encounter with Stone as not 'by chance' – as Farage's spokesman said – but a pre-arranged meeting (one calls it a dinner). And even Arron Banks (who wasn't in Cleveland, though Isabel Oakeshott was) suggests Stone turned up to see Farage by arrangement with Andy Wigmore, but they just 'had a long conversation in a corner of the restaurant which ended inconclusively'. Banks and Oakeshott make no mention, however, of Alex Jones.[13]

Within days of their late-night meeting in Cleveland, the flamboyant Stone became embroiled in one of the great American political scandals of modern times. The controversial WikiLeaks website released 20,000 emails which had been hacked from the higher ranks of the Democratic Party. Twelve days later, Stone received an email from a right-wing colleague, the author Jerome Corsi, alerting Stone that WikiLeaks would soon release more emails damaging to Hillary Clinton. WikiLeaks was still run by the Australian Julian Assange, who had been granted asylum by the Ecuadorian government, and for four years had been confined to their embassy in London, to avoid extradition to Sweden on suspicion of rape, and to America to face espionage charges.

'Word is friend in embassy plans 2 more dumps,' Jerome Corsi wrote to Stone. 'One shortly after I'm back. 2nd in Oct. Impact planned to be very damaging.'[14] Two days after receiving Corsi's email, Stone went on Alex Jones's InfoWars show and claimed that Assange had 'devastating' information and 'proof of wrong-doing' in the Clinton Foundation, the family's charitable organisation. 'I think he is going to furnish it for the American people.'[15]

Exactly what the nature of Nigel Farage's relationships were, not just with Stone, Jones and Corsi but also with Julian Assange himself, would later come under scrutiny from the US special counsel Robert Mueller in his investigation of Russian interference in the presidential contest.

On the final day of the Republican convention, Farage watched Donald Trump's acceptance speech. 'If I'm honest it wasn't that good,' he said later. 'It was a bit rambling. I wasn't massively impressed.'[16] That night, Farage and Andy Wigmore were in a bar in Cleveland when a group of about twenty people suddenly arrived, some of whom worked for Phil Bryant, a radical conservative who had just started his second term as governor of Mississippi, and was one of Trump's most fervent Republican supporters. 'Oh, Governor Phil Bryant just loves you, Nigel!' one of his team reportedly told Farage. 'He watches all your videos.' And so Bryant's chief aide invited Farage and his colleagues to come down to Mississippi a few weeks later and help the Republican campaign. Bryant had followed the Brexit contest closely, and claims to have told his wife, on hearing the result, 'That was Trump's first victory.'[17] Farage readily accepted the invitation, though wasn't sure it would ever happen.

On the return flight from Cleveland there occurred one of those episodes which shows that Nigel Farage's life is never dull or without incident, though for one young man it was deadly serious and frightening. Earlier, on the outward journey, Farage's aide George Cottrell – Posh George – had been briefly detained by customs officers at Chicago airport, but the UKIP party assumed it was merely a routine check. At the start of the return journey, when they arrived at Cleveland airport they had been surprised when security staff went through everyone's luggage and checked every item extremely thoroughly, flicking through magazines, for instance, page by page. Having flown to Chicago's O'Hare Airport, where the party was booked on a connecting flight to London, they were all kept on a bridge in the sweltering heat. Suddenly Posh George was arrested by eight agents of the Internal Revenue Service (IRS) and led away in handcuffs. Nobody could understand why. 'We didn't know what to do,' says Isabel Oakeshott. 'Nigel was quite paternal towards George and was deeply troubled. He has sons of almost that age, and didn't feel right just abandoning him. He was very uncomfortable.'[18] The party flew back to London without him.

Cottrell had been caught in an elaborate sting operation by the IRS which had been initiated two years before, in 2014, well before he joined Farage and UKIP. Posh George now faced twenty-one serious charges which included attempted extortion, money laundering, blackmail and fraud, most of which carried a maximum penalty of twenty years each.

The IRS team had found Cottrell operating on the so-called dark web – a dangerous world frequented by criminals, paedophiles and terrorists – advertising 'money laundering consultation services', to set up offshore bank accounts to help clients disguise their profits and evade taxes. Cottrell's intention was not just to levy a generous fee but, he later admitted, to steal his clients' money.

In March 2014, Cottrell was contacted by undercover agents posing as drug-traffickers who wanted him to launder between $50,000 and $150,000 a month through offshore bank accounts, but

Cottrell then blackmailed the 'drug traffickers', threatening to shop them to the authorities if they refused to pay him $80,000 in bitcoin.

To blackmail what Cottrell thought were high-level criminals seems an astonishingly foolhardy thing to do. But Farage's 22-year-old aide was consumed by his voracious addiction to gambling. Over the years he had amassed huge debts – much of them owed to other criminals.

Cottrell was refused bail on the grounds that he might abscond, and later extradited to Phoenix, Arizona, where he faced the prospect of many more years behind bars.

Not surprisingly, Cottrell's lawyers did a plea bargain with the prosecution, whereby he pleaded guilty to one charge of wire fraud and the other twenty charges were dropped. Prosecutors urged the trial judge to treat Cottrell with leniency because he had been willing to provide 'additional information about his role in the offence and how he became involved'.[19] Nor was there any evidence that Cottrell had actually carried out any money-laundering. So his prison sentence was limited to just eight months – nearly all of which he'd already served – and a fine of $30,000. He was released in March 2017 and deported back to Britain. Nigel Farage, who can show great sympathy for people who have serious personal problems, decided to re-employ Cottrell and help his rehabilitation.

Meanwhile, a month after Cottrell's shock arrest in Chicago, in late August 2016, Farage, Banks and the gang flew back to the US, and to Jackson, the state capital of Mississippi. They arrived much the worse for wear after a long journey mostly spent drinking, and were immediately whisked away in Governor Bryant's blacked-out car for dinner at his Greek revival-style mansion.

Farage regaled Phil Bryant and his guests with tales from the Brexit campaign, and afterwards, once the ladies retired, the governor took Farage and the other men into his 'man cave', a converted garage furnished with motorbikes, old Chevvies and a bar stocked with Southern tobacco. And there the full truth started to emerge. Wigmore and Banks had vaguely warned Farage a couple of weeks before that he might be asked to address a fund-raising event for Donald Trump, in the candidate's presence, the following evening. Banks and Wigmore had trodden carefully as they knew Farage was 'risk averse' and feared he would either reject the idea or agree but then change his mind.

But now, in Bryant's 'cave', one vague speaking engagement seemed to be turning into rather more. The governor asked if, as well as the fund-raiser in Jackson the following evening, Farage would afterwards deliver a second address at a big rally at the Coliseum basketball stadium in the city, ahead of a speech by Trump himself. Farage didn't take the suggestion very seriously, and assumed it was no more than talk.

Next morning Farage was interviewed on *The J. T. Show* on SuperTalk Mississippi radio. He spoke at length to the well-known local presenter J. T. Williamson about the similarities between the Trump campaign and the Brexit triumph. 'If you vote for Mrs Clinton – Hillary – then nothing will change,' he told his host. 'She represents the very politics that we've just broken, through the Brexit vote back in the United Kingdom. She represents that politics of the big multi-nationals, the big banks on Wall Street, the self-interest of the large corporates ... The parallels between the people that voted Brexit, and the people that could beat Clinton in a few weeks' time here in America are uncanny.'[20]

That evening, when Bryant and his UKIP guests were clutching their drinks at the reception before the fund-raising dinner, Donald Trump suddenly appeared. 'Where's Nigel?' he asked. Greeting Farage with a great bear hug, he congratulated him on Brexit. Trump was then so pleased with Farage's short speech at the dinner, that aides confirmed Bryant's invitation to speak at the rally which was due to follow.

Farage was worried. He'd been sort of bounced into things. Addressing a private dinner was one thing; speaking to a large public rally was a very different proposition. It was 'ten minutes' notice', Farage would recall. 'I'm slightly in panic. Trump comes over and says, "Thank you for agreeing to do this." I was in a state. They said, "Donald's going to introduce you."'[21]

Nigel Farage gets surprisingly anxious about speaking before large crowds, and this was worse because it was unfamiliar territory. His biggest concern was what to say. He knew that as a foreigner he could not really endorse Trump. And until then, at least privately, Farage had reservations about Trump's candidacy. So cleverly he would turn things round.

By that stage, late summer 2016, Trump was struggling in the polls, and only a few days earlier, to create new impetus, he had appointed Steve Bannon as chief executive of the campaign. Remarkably, it seems that Bannon claimed some of the credit for the Brexit vote in Britain, having established the Breitbart bureau in London two years before. The American journalist Michael Wolff quotes Bannon as saying, 'Farage will tell you . . . that Breitbart was the difference.'[22] It sounds like mere flattery by Farage.

Bannon and his colleagues hoped the association with Brexit would give Trump an extra boost, mainly by enthusing his most avid supporters. So during his address at the Coliseum, Trump described Brexit as a bid for independence and claimed his own election would lead to 'American independence'. Farage had stood up against the European Union 'against all odds', Trump declared:

> This is a great honour for me. I am going right now to invite onto the stage, the man behind Brexit, and a man who led brilliantly the United Kingdom Independence Party in this fight, and won despite all odds, despite horrible name-calling, despite so many obstacles. Ladies and Gentlemen, Mr Nigel Farage.

Most of the crowd were probably still puzzled as to who this smartly dressed Englishman was. 'I come to you from the United Kingdom with a message of hope and a message of optimism,' Farage began. 'On the day of the vote itself . . . they put us ten points behind,' he told his American audience. Brexit had been 'for the little people, for the real people,' he said:

> We reached those people who have never voted in their lives but believed by going out and voting for Brexit they could take back control of their country, take back control of their borders and get back their pride and self-respect [cheers]. Now the big card the Prime Minister decided to play in the Referendum is he got

a foreign visitor to come to London to talk to us. Yes, we were visited by one Barack Obama [long boos] and he talked down to us. He treated us as if we were nothing – one of the oldest functioning democracies in the world, and here he was telling us to vote Remain. So I, having criticised and condemned his behaviour, I could not possibly tell you how you should vote in this election. But, but . . .

Not everyone appreciated the note of irony in Farage's voice, and a chant of 'Trump, Trump Trump!' erupted from the floor. 'I get it, I get it, I get it,' Farage replied. 'I'm hearing you,' he said, as he drank in the moment, enjoyed his tease, and played his audience like Yehudi Menuhin on a Stradivarius:

But I will say this, if I was an American citizen, I wouldn't vote for Hillary Clinton if you paid me. [cheers] In fact, I wouldn't vote for Hillary Clinton if *she* paid me [cheers] . . . I think that you have a fantastic opportunity here with this campaign. You can go out. You can beat the pollsters. You can beat the commentators. You can beat Washington. [cheers] . . . And remember, anything is possible if enough decent people are prepared to stand up against the Establishment. Thank you. [cheers][23]

'Wow!' exclaimed Trump. 'Thank you, Nigel. What a job, what a job he did, against all odds.' Privately, Trump told Farage he would be his 'friend for life'.[24] It had been an extremely rare example – possibly unique – of a senior British politician speaking on the same campaign platform as a major nominee for the US presidency.

'When you can get ten thousand Mississippians in one room, and they were all drinking the Kool-Aid, licking the jar,' Governor Bryant later said, using an unfortunate metaphor. 'They were fired [up]. This man had spoken their language. They understood what he was talking about . . . He touched that nerve . . . Is there anything wrong with being proud of your country and hoping that it would be great?'[25] The crowd had applauded and cheered Farage, though the response wasn't quite of 'Kool-Aid' proportions.

Presidential candidates do hundreds of rallies in the course of a campaign, and the event in Jackson might have been long forgotten had it not been for Hillary Clinton's angry response. The next day, in Reno, Nevada, she delivered one of the strongest and most significant speeches of her campaign. Clinton had planned to speak about her ideas for business, but instead delivered a scorching attack on Trump and his politics, with a strong denunciation of the way, she said, that the Republican Party had been taken over by the alt-right. It was a speech that had been building up inside Clinton for months, and Farage happened to appear with Trump just before the moment her fury erupted. 'Just yesterday,' she said:

> one of Britain's most prominent right-wing leaders, a man named Nigel Farage, who stoked anti-immigrant sentiments to win the referendum to have Britain leave the European Union, campaigned with Donald Trump in Mississippi. Farage has called for a bar on the children of *legal* immigrants from public schools and health services: has said women are – and I quote – 'worth less than men'; and supports scrapping laws that prevent employers from discriminating based on race. That's who Donald Trump wants by his side when he is addressing an audience of American voters.[26]

Farage had indeed said in 2015 that the children of immigrants should not immediately be admitted to state schools, and argued that the race discrimination laws were no longer necessary and could be repealed. But her claim that Farage had said women were 'worth less than men' seems to have been unfair. It was probably based on remarks in 2014 when Farage referred to the specific example of a woman in the City who had a client base, and took time off to have children, as being 'worth far less to her employer when she comes back because that client base won't be stuck as rigidly to her portfolio'.[27]

Hillary Clinton also accused Farage of being part of a 'rising tide of hardline, right-wing nationalism', the 'grand godfather' of which, she said, was the Russian president Vladimir Putin.

And she denounced Farage for appearing on 'Russian propaganda programmes'.[28]

Farage, Banks and Andy Wigmore were at Atlanta airport when they suddenly saw Clinton on the big screen in the bar where they were enjoying their drinks. 'Did she just call you a white supremacist?' Banks reportedly asked. 'Fuck, she really is having a proper go at me!' Farage responded with incredulity. 'Whether we like it or not,' Banks wrote, 'we were now guerrilla fighters in the Trump insurgency – not a bad gig for a trio of Brexit revolutionaries with plenty of rounds still left in the tank, really!'[29]

Until his visit to Mississippi, Farage was not quite 100 per cent committed to Donald Trump – it was more a case of being anti-Clinton – but from that point he became a loyal supporter. He loved playing a part in a presidential campaign – publicly lauded by one contender, denounced by the other – and was chuffed to have become seemingly so close to the man who might be the next US president and told him he would be his 'friend for life'. He was just as delighted that Clinton had hit back so quickly, so personally and so directly. 'It is clear Hillary Clinton absolutely hates me, and I'm pleased about that,' Farage boasted.[30] Egged on by Arron Banks and Andy Wigmore, it had all started as a bit of a laugh to take a bit part in American politics. 'It is fairly astonishing that I should be a political football in the US presidential election,' he said, clearly basking in the limelight. Farage's mother Barbara later told how she rang him to ask what 'on earth' was happening. 'Mother,' he replied. 'He could be the next President of the United States.'[31] It made a return to the American campaign 'irresistible'.[32]

Suddenly, Nigel Farage had become a minor celebrity in America, at least among people keen on politics. From then on, he became a regular performer on American television and radio, commenting on politics in the USA, Britain, Europe and the rest of the world, and always gave broadcasters great value. He had become not just part of the Trump campaign, but was now closely connected to a new network of individuals – several of them conspiracy theorists of highly dubious veracity – who would be the focus of the investigations into Russian electoral interference for the next three years.

Six days after the Mississippi rally, Farage did a seventeen-minute interview with Alex Jones on InfoWars in which he seemed to have adopted the language of the alt-right. Some of his new American friends constantly decried a globalist 'empire' of big business, bankers and establishment politicians – a 'New World Order' in which the Hungarian-American – and Jewish – businessman George Soros often featured as a powerful and demonic figure – which prompted accusations of anti-Semitism. But this 'New World Order' was now on the defensive, they argued, because of the Brexit vote, the success of Trump and other developments. Billing his guest as 'a major historical figure', Jones asked: 'How is the empire going to strike back?' 'The empire is bewildered,' Nigel Farage replied:

> The empire is befuddled . . . The empire doesn't get Brexit . . . After Brexit, they're in trouble. And I have to say that these American elections – this could be a result, globally, far bigger even than Brexit. If America, as the leader of the western world, once again becomes the leader of the free world, well then I think, basically, we will have done away with the globalists.[33]

Fox News and its owner Rupert Murdoch were also big supporters of Donald Trump, and Fox invited Farage to America to be a guest commentator for the second presidential TV debate, which was due to be held in St Louis, Missouri, in early October. Trump was already trailing Clinton badly, but then, only two days before the encounter, things got much worse for him when the *Washington Post* released a previously untransmitted video of Trump in 2005, caught on a live microphone, telling how he seduced married women: 'I just start kissing them. It's like a magnet. Just kiss. I don't even wait. And when you're a star, they let you do it,' Trump had said, before uttering the infamous words: 'Grab 'em by the pussy. You can do anything.'[34]

'Convincing Nigel not to board the first flight to Heathrow was no easy task,' Arron Banks relates. He was due on Fox in a few hours, but how could he possibly defend or explain what Trump had said? He might do himself huge damage. Andy Wigmore tried to come up with all sorts of suitable lines, most of them absurd. So how does Trump get out of this one, the Fox presenter asked. Farage replied:

> If I were Trump going into this tomorrow, I would say: 'Hands up. I behaved in a very alpha male boorish way. I apologise, but hey, let's talk about the real issues . . .' At least there's an honesty about Trump. Whether you like it or not, he is what he is. And do you know what? He's not running to be Pope. He's running to be President of the USA. A human being. Every human being is flawed, and if his flaws are all out there, and if the public have suspicions that we haven't heard all of Hillary's, in a week's time this may not look as bad as it does this morning.[35]

That night, during the TV debate, Donald Trump didn't actually heed Farage's advice – apologising is not his nature. Instead, he did an extraordinary thing. Rather than just stand by their lecterns, the two contenders were allowed to walk round the stage, and sometimes when Clinton was speaking Trump walked up behind her and watched over her in a highly aggressive manner. Farage had been enlisted as a Trump supporter to talk to the media in the spin room afterwards, to give a favourable view on what had just happened. 'I think he was like a big silverback gorilla prowling the studios,' Farage told Sky News in a tone that suggested admiration for Trump's tactics:

> I don't think he did it in a particularly aggressive way. I think that what you saw tonight was the way he is, and he took control. He dominated Hillary Clinton – she was very much on the back-foot all evening . . . He came into this evening absolutely needing a good performance after a horrendous 48 hours, and an embarrassing, cringe-makingly embarrassing, 48 hours. It was real backs-to-the-wall stuff. He's come out of this very well. He'll be leaving here a happy man tonight.[36]

Farage was right. The so-called 'grab a pussy' video didn't cause

Trump anything like the damage analysts had expected at the time, and which had caused traditional Republicans to panic. 'Senators, congressmen, supporters, they were all running for the hills, disavowing Trump,' Farage said years later. 'He virtually at that moment became an independent candidate . . . with nobody prepared to defend him . . . He knows that at the absolutely low point of [20]16, I didn't run away.'[37]

Donald Trump recovered, of course, and would indeed be grateful that Farage came to his aid at a time when many prominent Republicans disappeared for a while. For the remaining four weeks of the 2016 campaign, Trump would often refer to his imminent victory as 'Brexit plus'. In North Carolina, on the eve of poll, he even said, 'I think it's gonna be Brexit plus, plus, plus.'[38]

After losing to Donald Trump – though she won the popular vote – Hillary Clinton included Nigel Farage among those she blamed, and she accused her adversaries of using the tactics which had been used by the Brexit campaign. 'Brexit should have been a bigger alarm than it was,' she said. 'It was some of the same people working for Trump, advocating for him. They thought, "Hey, we've got this figured out, just tell a really horrible lie over and over again, keep people off balance and make them think that this will, if not make their lives better, make them feel better."' When Clinton's memoirs were published in 2017, she said Farage had come to the US 'to campaign for Trump and spent half of his remarks insulting me in a very personal way and talking about Trump as the alpha male, the silverback gorilla. Think of those images and what that says about what's acceptable and what's not.'[39] Referring in a BBC interview to Farage specifically, she said: 'The Big Lie is a very potent tool.'[40] That only gave Farage another chance to attack Clinton. 'Absolutely. I'm a terrible person; I'm an unacceptable human being, as she said. I'm only sorry she didn't call me deplorable – I would have enjoyed that,' he joked in a sympathetic interview with Fox News. 'What she's doing here is . . . acting as the high priestess of the globalist movement . . . She's making a sad sorry spectacle of herself . . . She's deep in denial. I just think she ought to recognise she lost. It's over. Move on.'[41]

A week before Clinton's defeat, Farage had been given the Lifetime Achievement award at the annual *Spectator* awards in London for what the magazine called 'the greatest democratic coup in living memory'. The award was presented by George Osborne, who'd just been sacked by the new prime minister Theresa May, and who had been a key Remain figure. 'My good man, just keep holding that for a moment,' Farage jokingly instructed the ex-chancellor, as he got him to hold his award while he made his acceptance speech.

In front of Theresa May, and much of the British political establishment, Farage claimed that he was 'booked on the first flight out, next Wednesday morning, to Washington, where I'll be joining Donald Trump's team in the White House'. That prompted jeers. 'Oh, come on!' Farage cried:

> Cheer up! He's gonna be the next leader of the western world, what's the matter with you? But that's, of course, the attitude that you all took towards Brexit – it could never happen; it was irreverent [sic]. My achievement has been to take an issue that was considered to be completely wrong, perhaps even immoral, and help to turn it into a mainstream view in British politics . . . And British politics will never be the same again – just that I won't be there, and I'm very pleased about that, and so are you.[42]

A week later, on the day Americans voted, Farage was teased by Robert Peston on the ITV programme *The Agenda* about whether he'd spoken to Trump about a job in his administration if he were to be elected. Farage ignored the question at first.

'I think that's a "Yes",' Peston prodded. 'No, no, no,' Farage eventually replied. Then he added with a playful smile: 'If he did offer me a job, I would quite like to be his ambassador to the European Union. I think I would do that job very well.'[43]

FRIENDS OF VLADIMIR

Nigel Farage, Arron Banks and the team watched the US results in Millbank Tower in Westminster, having started the evening at a book launch held by their Caribbean holiday-friend Lord Ashcroft. They carried on drinking through the night before Farage set off for the United States the next morning. That Saturday, the self-styled Bad Boys of Brexit gathered in New York, where they were told to get to Trump Tower for 1 p.m. prompt. On arrival, they found the place besieged by protestors, but wheedled their way in with the help of a friendly policeman. First Farage had a one-to-one meeting with his old ally Steve Bannon, then he, Banks, Andy Wigmore, Gerry Gunster and Raheem Kassam were invited upstairs, to the office of Donald Trump's senior adviser, Kellyanne Conway. After much chatter she asked, 'Shall we go and see the President-elect?'

It took several lifts to reach the golden doors outside Trump's top-floor apartment. Farage rang the bell, and the door opened to reveal the man himself. 'There he is!' said the president-elect as he moved to greet his special guest. 'We were both roaring with laughter,' Farage said afterwards. 'We were two people who had been through quite an ordeal. But suddenly, you know, we'd won.'[1]

'Nigel,' Trump asked, 'do you think Brexit was bigger, or was my election bigger?' Trump's victory was 'Brexit plus, plus, plus', Farage replied diplomatically. And Trump spoke encouragingly about a free trade deal with the UK.[2]

Among other topics they discussed, according to Banks, were wind farms: Trump thought they looked unsightly from his Scottish golf course. 'The world was wanting to ring him,' Farage said later, 'and we had an hour with him, a fascinating conversation . . . I've never disclosed any of that conversation . . . Trump kept saying Brexit was what began the whole thing, so normally we follow every trend that comes from America – appalling junk food, unwatchable telly – and for once America followed us.'[3]

Was there anything else he should consider? Trump asked as the group was about to leave, whereupon Raheem Kassam suggested to the new president he should return the bust of Winston Churchill to the Oval Office. 'Yes, I love that,' said Trump, and he asked Kellyanne Conway to follow up the suggestion (and the bust was duly returned).[4]

Then Andy Wigmore asked if he could take a picture. Trump posed with Farage in front of the golden doors; then for a group shot with Banks, Kassam, Farage, Wigmore and Gunster. Wigmore quickly tweeted the Trump–Farage picture and, even though it was now past midnight back in Britain, it went viral.

'Fuck,' said Farage as the photo appeared on American TV news. 'I think the PM is going to hate me even more now.' In fact, Theresa May had spoken to Trump by phone two days before, when she'd suggested the possibility of the new president coming to Britain on a state visit, so when he met Farage and his party he couldn't hide his excitement at the prospect of meeting the Queen. On hearing of the Farage trip, however, a Downing Street aide snidely remarked, 'I think the UK brings enough to the special relationship for it to be special without Nigel Farage.'[5]

Farage was, as Arron Banks pointed out, 'the first British politician to meet the new leader of the free world – and much like Brexit, it was going down like a cup of cold sick with the British establishment. You have to laugh!'[6]

When he got back to London Farage says he sent a message to the Foreign Office asking if they'd like to talk to him about his conversation with Trump. 'But I heard nothing. No attempt to engage whatsoever,' says a man who for the second time in just a few months felt shunned by the political establishment. 'I am greeted by negative comments coming out of Downing Street. The dislike of me, UKIP, and the referendum result is more important to them than what

could be good for our country . . . I am in a good position, with the
President-elect's support, to help. The world has changed and it's
time that Downing Street did too.'[7]

The Foreign Office say they have no record of any such message
from Farage, and the then British ambassador to the USA, Sir Kim
Darroch, says he was never told of any offer to brief them. But if
Farage did send a message, Darroch is not surprised that the government ignored it: 'They would have thought Farage would have used it
for his own ends, and to set himself up as a kind of one-man embassy.'[8]

A few days later, in his capacity as a diplomat for Belize, Andy
Wigmore met an even more famous head of state at Buckingham
Palace in an event for the Commonwealth. He was firmly told not
to say anything to the Queen about the visit to Trump, or the photo.
But the Queen caught up with Wigmore, according to Banks, and
asked if he'd had a 'good weekend'. Wigmore told her what had
happened.

Ten days later, Donald Trump tweeted that Farage should join
him in Washington. 'Many people would like to see Nigel Farage
represent Great Britain as their Ambassador to the United States.
He would do a great job!'[9] Farage was in Strasbourg when Andy
Wigmore woke him in his hotel room and, in disbelief, responded
with the words 'Fuck off, Andy'. Whitehall was not pleased at
this freelance diplomacy with Trump, and one government press
officer went so far as to call Wigmore 'a cunt', which in diplomatic
language presumably means they're not being very helpful. Had he
become ambassador, Farage said, 'the UK government would have
had direct, regular access – a broker in the middle – and secondly,
the best parties ever at the Embassy'.[10]

A few days afterwards, when *Telegraph* co-owner Frederick
Barclay held a party for Farage at his hotel, the Ritz, Wigmore got
an assistant to go out and buy as many boxes as possible of Ferrero
Rocher – the gold-foil covered hazelnut chocolates which became
the joke treats of diplomacy after a famous advertising campaign in
the 1990s. 'Monsieur,' the glamorous blonde in the TV commercial
told her ambassador host, 'with these Rochers you're really spoiling
us.'

'I was able to hand a plate of 200 chocolates to Farage when he arrived at the Ritz,' Banks wrote. 'It made an absolutely perfect picture, and I'm sure Downing Street were crying bloody murder when they saw it.'[11]

British ambassadors to Washington have occasionally been political appointees – such as John Freeman and Peter Jay in the 1960s and '70s – but Farage was never a serious possibility under Theresa May, even though her new foreign secretary was his fellow Brexiteer Boris Johnson, with whom Farage had generally got on well. 'There is no vacancy,' Johnson told MPs.[12] Britain had only just sent Sir Kim Darroch to Washington, though he was forced to resign in 2019 when emails were leaked showing his biting analysis of the Trump regime. (The emails would be published in the *Mail on Sunday* by Isabel Oakeshott, close friend of the Bad Boys of Brexit.)

Farage may be one of the most effective rebels of modern times, but he also likes belonging to establishment institutions, such as Dulwich College and the East India Club. He not only resented the way Whitehall so sniffily dismissed the idea of him becoming ambassador, but was also miffed that the Foreign Office didn't contact him to find out more about what Trump had said – either on this occasion or after subsequent meetings with the new president.

That resentment only intensified when Farage was turned down for a knighthood in 2017. The former UKIP leader Lord Pearson nominated him for the title, but under the rules, and since it was a political honour, approval had to be sought from UKIP's leader in the Commons. Douglas Carswell, who was no longer on speaking terms with Farage by this stage, refused to support the proposal.

Nigel Farage went back to Washington in January 2017 for Donald Trump's inauguration. The day before the big ceremony Gerry Gunster (the American referendum specialist who'd been recruited by Leave.Eu) arranged a lavish reception on the top floor of the Hay-Adams Hotel, which overlooks the White House. Laure Ferrari accompanied Farage to Washington and was his companion at the party. Arron Banks was there, Andy Wigmore, and many of their right-wing American friends such as Governor Phil Bryant, and Ted Malloch, a political academic who had spent many years teaching in England and had known Trump since the 1980s. Guests were given free hardback copies of Banks's new book *The Bad Boys of Brexit*, whose publisher, Michael Ashcroft, was among the guests, along with Isabel Oakeshott. But one face was missing from the Bad Boys' festivities. Donald Trump hadn't dropped by – somewhat to the relief of British diplomats.

During the Trump presidency Farage became a regular visitor to the United States for political conferences and media events. Whenever he visited Washington he would stay at the Trump Hotel, a few blocks from the White House, which Donald Trump himself would often drop into because he didn't like the food at his official residence. Hanging round the lobby, Farage might occasionally be invited to join the presidential dinner party.

'Every time I come to America, I'm feeling a little bit more American,' Farage told the annual CPAC gathering near Washington in February 2017. But by now he was developing much wider ambitions. He wanted to exploit the success of Brexit to go further:

> What happened in 2016 is the beginning of a great global revolution, and this will roll out across the rest of the West. We've got some very exciting elections coming up in the Netherlands, in France, in Germany, possibly even in Italy . . . Even if the challengers don't get over the line in this year, what they will do is shift the centre of gravity of the entire debate, because what is happening across Europe is people are rejecting this form of supra-national government.[13]

What did he mean by 'exciting elections'? Who did he have in mind as potentially doing well in the countries he mentioned? In Holland, where an election was barely two weeks away, the main challenger to the centre-right prime minister Mark Rutte was Geert Wilders and his Party for Freedom. The next French elections were due in May 2017, where the recently emerged young Emmanuel Macron, a strongly pro-EU centrist, was likely to face the leader of the Front National, Marine Le Pen, in the final run-off. And in Germany, the Alternative für Deutschland party – the AfD – looked like they might hold the balance of power in the elections due that autumn. All three right-wing parties are nationalist groups who've often been accused of racism and Islamophobia. Indeed, in no case had Farage ever considered them as serious partners for UKIP when it came to the regular wrangling over forming a cross-country group in the European Parliament, and it would have been damaging to UKIP in Britain had the party teamed up with any of these parties.

Jens-Peter Bonde, the co-leader of some of UKIP's previous European Parliament groupings, says that Farage had always been very reluctant to have anything to do with Marine Le Pen and her party. 'From the very first day we discussed it, the Front National, he [Nigel] was very clear that he'd never, ever work with them. He could not do that. British voters would never, ever accept that – that was his pure understanding. It was out of the question.'[14] And in 2013 Farage had said of Le Pen's party, the Front National, 'We're not going to touch them with a bargepole. Anti-Semitism is written into the DNA of that party.'[15] Yet by 2017, Farage's attitude was changing. A few weeks after CPAC, Farage met Le Pen for an LBC interview and later publicly backed her against Macron. That summer he also spoke at an AfD election event in Germany.

For the first seven months of the Trump presidency, Farage's friend Steve Bannon worked in the White House as chief strategist. When, in March 2017, Theresa May triggered the Article 50 process which set the two-year timetable for Britain leaving the EU, Farage voiced his gratitude to his American friend: 'Well done, Bannon, well done Breitbart – you've helped with this – hugely,' he said in a video, holding a pint.[16] He then elaborated in a live radio interview with Raheem Kassam, who was now back working for Breitbart:

> I think when Bannon opened up the Breitbart office in London and began to give the arguments that I was making a fair hearing, and very quickly, as Breitbart does well, started to reach a very, very big audience. I think actually on this great Brexit day I have to say a personal thank you and tribute to Steve Bannon for having the foresightedness of doing that with Breitbart, and I'm extremely grateful.[17]

Farage was over-egging it, flattering both Kassam and Bannon. Steve Bannon had an influence, but Breitbart's role in achieving Brexit was negligible.

When Bannon was sacked by Trump in August 2017, he began working on an ambitious new project – to bring together populist and nationalist parties from around the world. And the following month Bannon invited Nigel Farage to a meeting in Mobile, Alabama, to campaign for a right-wing candidate who was running for the Republican nomination for the Senate seat which had been vacated by Donald Trump's appointment of Jeff Sessions as Attorney-General. Roy Moore was a controversial figure, a birther who didn't believe in the theory of evolution and was hostile to gay people. Farage's trip to Alabama was largely out of loyalty to Bannon, and showed a rare disagreement with Donald Trump who was backing Moore's main opponent. After Moore won the Republican nomination, Farage remained loyal to him, despite the emergence of allegations that, as a young man in the 1970s, he'd sexually assaulted three women, two of whom had been girls aged fourteen and sixteen at the time. While senior Republicans were urging Moore to stand aside, Farage asked why the sexual assault claims had not been raised before. Moore had 'been in public life a long time', Farage said, 'and he has been outspoken in his views and in his positions. I think a lot of reasonable-minded people will ask "why now?"' Moore lost the election to a Democrat, and Farage later said it had been a 'last-minute decision' to back him, in response to appeals from other people. It had been 'a mistake', he admitted.[18]

Pursuing his global ambitions in Europe, Bannon teamed up with The Movement, a body founded in 2016 by a far-right Belgian politician, Mischaël Modrikamen, a friend of Farage, which had Laure Ferrari as a founding member. They envisaged that The Movement would bring together Eurosceptic parties to try and win a large block of seats at the next EU elections in 2019. Their ambitions didn't stop there. Farage and Bannon were also interested in joining right-wing leaders beyond Europe, as illustrated in a meeting between the two men which was filmed in October 2017 for a fly-on-the-wall documentary, *The Brink*.

In the film, Bannon and Farage are seen facing each other across a table at Bannon's office in Washington. 'If you're interested, what I'd like to do is set up something and I'll fund it somehow,' Bannon tells Farage. 'I think you're the perfect guy. We help knit together this populist, nationalist movement throughout the world, cos guys in Egypt are coming to me; Modi's guys in India; [Rodrigo] Duterte [the Philippines]; and we get Orbán [Hungary]; and somehow some sort of convening authority for conferences and stuff like that, so we can get ideas out. Do you think that's a worthwhile thing?' Farage is seen on camera assenting that it is a good idea, and doesn't query any of the names which Bannon suggests. 'It's a global revolt,' Bannon says. 'It's a zeitgeist. We're on the right side of history. But it's gonna need the motive power and the thing that's missing is . . . the ideas.'[19] Another populist leader mentioned in *The Brink* as a potential member of Bannon's movement was the new rising conservative politician in Brazil, Jair Bolsonaro. In footage not used in the final cut of the film, Farage discussed with Bannon a proposed meeting at the Ritz in London to try to raise funds for the movement from the hotel's wealthy co-owner Frederick Barclay.[20]

In talking of such new allies, Farage seemed to be developing a rather different kind of politics, which not only involved leaders in Europe whom he'd once condemned as extreme, but others internationally who were often illiberal and authoritarian. Rodrigo Duterte was elected president of the Philippines in 2016 after a campaign in which he'd promised 'a thousand pardons a day' to police and members of the armed forces accused of human rights abuses, and also said that at the end of his six years in office (in 2002) he would issue a presidential pardon to himself 'for multiple murders'.[21] Previously, when Duterte was mayor of Davao City, the UN accused him of supporting death squads which killed hundreds of street children and criminals. Jair Bolsonaro, who would be elected president of Brazil in 2018, was an admirer of the previous military dictatorship in his country, and of other past military regimes in South America.

At the same time, Farage, like his hero Donald Trump, had become something of a fan of the long-standing Russian leader Vladimir Putin. In 2014, in an interview for *GQ* magazine, Alastair

Campbell asked Farage which current world leader he most admired. 'As an operator, but not as a human being, I would say Putin,' Farage replied. 'The way he played the whole Syria thing. Brilliant. Not that I approve of him politically. How many journalists in jail now?'[22] A few days earlier, in his first TV debate with Nick Clegg, Farage was accused of siding with Putin over Russia's invasion of Ukraine. Not only had Farage told Clegg that the EU had 'blood on its hands' for encouraging revolution in Ukraine, but also said, 'We have given a false series of hopes to a group of people in the western Ukraine. So geed up were they that they actually toppled their own elected leader. That provoked Mr Putin . . . It has not been a thing for good in the Ukraine.'[23] Clegg said afterwards that Farage's loathing of the EU had become 'so all-consuming' that he ended up 'siding with Vladimir Putin'.[24] There were some similarities between Putin and Farage's styles of leadership, with little tolerance of dissent, and the elimination of opponents (though possibly tempted, Farage never resorted to murdering his opponents within UKIP).

Farage's critics also argued that his regular appearances on the Russian state-funded TV channel RT – formerly Russia Today – were evidence of an increasingly pro-Putin outlook. The *Guardian* calculated in 2014 that Farage had made seventeen appearances on the channel over the previous four years.[25] In the summer of 2016, he was offered his own show by RT, and they also discussed the idea of him becoming a roving reporter in the US election, though nothing came of these proposals.

The UK edition of RT, broadcast in English, started in 2014, from studios in Millbank Tower, the same building which housed the main Leave.EU offices in Westminster. He appeared several times on *Sam Delaney's News Thing*, which combined serious chat with a satirical look at the news. In an especially bizarre scene from March 2017, Farage was 'knighted' by a young girl dressed as the Queen. Farage knelt down while the girl, wearing a red robe and toy crown, gently touched him with her sword on both shoulders. 'Well, thank you,' Farage said, and Delaney announced: 'You are now *Sir* Nigel Farage. We're also making you honorary British ambassador to America, and honorary MP for South Thanet because they didn't elect you for real.'

'My mummy says you hate foreigners,' the girl suddenly blurted out. 'Did she? I don't think that's quite right,' Farage replied, trying to make light of it. 'No, no, little girl,' Delaney told her in mock admonishment. 'No, no, no, no, no, you're not supposed to say that – that's very naughty.' 'The Queen has to be non-political,' Farage added, before the closing titles rolled.[26]

Delaney was surprised that Farage didn't complain. 'There was nothing afterwards saying the kid's line was out of order – he hung around, shook hands, probably said it was funny. No hint of taking himself seriously, but I also thought, "Why don't you care?"'[27]

With the exception of George Galloway – also a regular Delaney guest – it's hard to think of any other senior British politician willing to indulge in such silliness. It showed, perhaps, what a good 'sport' Farage was; yet it also gave the impression that he wanted any publicity, no matter how demeaning.

Sam Delaney would also put serious questions to Farage. Did he feel in any way responsible, he asked, for the hostility surrounding the referendum? Farage admitted some Brexit supporters had 'hurled racist abuse at Polish people', and some Remain supporters 'sent insults and threats' through social media. 'Do I feel responsible for people saying extreme things?' he continued.

> Quite the reverse. I destroyed the British National Party. Right, we had a far-right party in this country who genuinely were anti-Jew, anti-Black, and all of those things, and I came along and I said to their voters, 'If you're holding your nose and voting for this party as a protest, don't. Come and vote for me. I'm not against anybody. I just want us to start putting British people first.' And I almost single-handedly destroyed the Far Right in British politics. That's not a bad achievement . . . If I hadn't been around, and done what I'd done, that strain of opinion would have been represented by Nick Griffin and the BNP, and would genuinely have been motivated by hate.[28]

It was one of Farage's most cogent defences of his record as UKIP leader, or *de facto* leader, for the previous twenty years, although it lacked humility. He spoke in terms of 'I . . . I . . . I' and 'vote for me', with no mention of his party or colleagues. But Farage had a point. Had UKIP collapsed around 2008; had Farage been deposed as leader at that time or resigned, then Nick Griffin and the BNP might have become far more popular and potent in British politics. Brexit might never have happened either. But these claims came on RT soon after he had begun promoting far-right parties in Europe.

Most observers saw RT as a Kremlin mouthpiece, or, at best, an attempt by Moscow to gain influence in Britain. RT has been condemned by the broadcasting regulator Ofcom for bias on controversial issues, such as the civil war in Syria and Russia's attacks on Ukraine. More recently, since the Skripal poisonings in Salisbury in 2018, almost certainly by Russian state agents, RT has achieved pariah status in British politics. Many of Farage's RT appearances survive online, but they don't show he said anything pro-Putin or pro-Russia, and nothing like his remarks in the Nick Clegg debate, or his *GQ* interview. Farage mainly used RT as another platform from which to pursue his normal anti-EU agenda, though that coincided, of course, with the interests of the Russian administration.

For the next four years Arron Banks, Farage and Leave.EU faced suspicion that their side of the Brexit campaign had taken funding from illegal sources – perhaps from the Isle of Man, or worse still, Russia. After Banks and his colleague Andy Wigmore appeared before the Commons committee on Culture, Media and Sport in 2018, the committee accused them of misleading them over the Russia meetings, and of leaving their hearing early to 'avoid scrutiny'. The committee said the pair had 'failed to satisfy' them that Banks's £8.4 million funding had 'come from sources within the UK'.[29] The MPs referred the case to the Electoral Commission, who then said it had 'reasonable grounds to suspect' that Banks was not the true source of his loans. The Commission passed the case on to the National Crime Agency (NCA).[30]

These concerns were fuelled by mystery surrounding the true extent of Arron Banks's wealth, and whether he himself was really rich enough to devote such a large sum to fighting for Brexit. While the *Sunday Times* Rich List had estimated his wealth at £250 million in 2017, Bloomberg valued it at just £25 million, and the group open-Democracy at even less than that.[31] Banks must have spent 'half his lifetime earnings' on Brexit, openDemocracy said – 'an amazingly generous amount'.[32]

Suspicions that the money might ultimately have come from Russia were encouraged by Moscow's record in recent times of funding campaigns in the West. In 2014, for example, a Russian bank with links to the Kremlin lent Marine Le Pen's Front National €11 million to help her 2017 run for the French presidency.

The NCA has greater powers than the Electoral Commission, most notably access to bank records, but after almost a year it said it had found 'no evidence that any criminal offences have been committed' by Banks or his associates, under either election or company law. It would take no further action. The NCA added that it also had no evidence that Banks and his companies received money from a third party, and the Agency was satisfied that all his funding came from businesses of which he was the 'ultimate beneficial owner'.[33]

Arron Banks then threatened to sue the Electoral Commission over what it said when it sent his case to the NCA, and the Commission had to make an embarrassing climb-down in which it agreed with the Agency that Banks and his colleagues had committed no crimes, nor taken funds from a third party.[34] Nigel Farage said the Commission had been involved in an 'establishment' effort to 'rubbish anyone prominent in the Brexit campaign'.[35]

Nonetheless, the Electoral Commission still found the Banks/Farage campaign Leave.EU guilty of several other breaches of election law, by failing to include payments which meant, according to the Commission, that Leave.EU had spent around £150,000 – more than 20 per cent over the legal limit. Leave.EU was fined £70,000 for four separate offences, reduced to £66,000 on appeal.

Now we come to the second major controversy, relating to Russia and the 2016 presidential election, and the publication by WikiLeaks in the summer and autumn of 2016 of emails which were damaging to Hillary Clinton. According to Robert Mueller, the special counsel who was appointed by the US Justice Department in 2017 to investigate Russian interference in the election, this material had been 'stolen' by 'a Russian intelligence service' (though WikiLeaks denied that).[36] After the first dump of 20,000 emails, in July 2016, the Trump campaign had high hopes that if, as expected, WikiLeaks published further documents, it could turn the election Trump's way.

Several people close to Trump were naturally keen to find out from the WikiLeaks founder and editor Julian Assange when he might publish more material, and what it might say. Two of those involved in trying to establish with Assange what his plans were – Roger Stone, the political fixer, and Ted Malloch, the UK-based academic – were on friendly terms with Nigel Farage. It was even suggested within the Trump camp that Farage himself might be a good conduit to Assange.

Since 2012, Julian Assange had taken refugee in the Ecuadorian embassy in London. Then around 11 a.m. on 9 March 2017 – four months and a day after the presidential election – Nigel Farage was involved in a development which to this day remains something of a mystery. A man called Ian Stubbings, who worked in an office nearby, happened to walk past the embassy and spotted Farage going inside. 'I thought "Hang on a moment. That looks a bit dodgy." . . . But I thought, "That's got to be worth telling," and I was the only person who'd witnessed it.'[37]

Stubbings quickly tweeted what he'd witnessed: 'Genuine scoop: just saw Nigel Farage enter the Ecuadorian embassy.' A reporter for BuzzFeed, Marie Le Conte, noticed his tweet, messaged Stubbings, and then got round to the embassy in time to see Farage leave. As Farage and another man walked to a car waiting round the corner, Le Conte asked Farage if he'd been visiting Julian Assange. He seems to have been unusually taciturn and forgetful. Le Conte's reported for BuzzFeed that Farage could not remember what he had been doing in the building, which seems an astonishing memory lapse. 'I never discuss where I go or who I see,' Farage told Le Conte.[38]

In the following months, this lack of candour by Farage only fuelled suspicion and theories about the true purpose of his visit. Had Ian Stubbings and BuzzFeed stumbled on some clever plot? Farage's visit to the embassy received considerable coverage in the

US media, even though the presidential election was long over and Donald Trump was by then firmly in the White House.

The suspicions about Farage's trip to Assange would be further stirred during a congressional inquiry eight months later. The Intelligence Committee of the House of Representatives held a closed session with Glenn Simpson, a journalist-turned-private investigator whose firm Fusion GPS had in 2016 employed the former MI6 agent Christopher Steele to compile the famous Trump Dossier, which detailed alleged past contacts which Donald Trump and his advisers had with Russia. In his testimony to the committee, Simpson briefly mentioned UKIP and Nigel Farage, and suggested that Farage may have been part of a chain linking Trump and Roger Stone to Assange and Russia. 'We started going into who Stone was and who his relationships were with,' Simpson told the committee:

> and essentially the trail led to sort of [the] international far right. And, you know, Brexit happened, and Nigel Farage became someone that we were very interested in, and I still think it's very interesting. And so I have formed my own opinions that . . . there was a somewhat unacknowledged relationship between the Trump people and the UKIP people, and that the path to WikiLeaks ran through that. And I still think that today.

Simpson went on to mention Steve Bannon being involved in the network; he said that Ted Malloch, too, was 'a significant figure in this' and also mentioned Robert Mercer, a leading shareholder in, and donor to, Breitbart News. Adam Schiff, an experienced congressman from California, who was the leading Democrat on the committee and took a keen interest in the Trump/Russia story, asked Simpson whether he was 'able to find any factual links between the Mercers and Assange or WikiLeaks or Farage'.

Simpson mentioned that Nigel Farage and Arron Banks had made 'a number of trips' to New York and the US, and then declared: 'I've been told and have not confirmed that Nigel Farage had additional trips to the Ecuadorian Embassy than the one that's been in the papers, and that he provided data to Julian Assange.'

'What kind of data?' Schiff asked.

'A thumb drive,' Simpson replied – otherwise known as a USB stick, or data stick. But Schiff had no chance to press Simpson further, as his time was up.[39]

When the committee testimony was published two months later, Farage dismissed what Simpson had said as 'conspiratorial nonsense'. And earlier, dismissing a Carole Cadwalladr article on him and Assange in the *Observer*, Farage told his radio audience:

> It would appear that I am the bagman – I'm the one running messages and exchanging information between the President of the USA and Julian Assange . . . Well, let me just tell you this is a complete lot of baloney. I have said it before, I will say it again: the reason that I met Julian Assange was because somebody at LBC organised it. And not only that, when I went to meet Julian Assange I took with me my producer from LBC. You know, if I was running some special mission for the US President, do you really think I'd have taken an LBC [producer] with me? Unless of course LBC are part of the conspiracy.[40]

The producer Farage took to the Ecuadorian embassy was Christian Mitchell, a long-standing journalist with LBC, where Farage had recently become a regular presenter. Mitchell says their visit resulted from a small incident a few days earlier when an LBC reporter was broadcasting live from outside the embassy. Someone inside had spotted the LBC logo on the reporter's microphone, came out and asked whether LBC and Nigel Farage might be interested in interviewing Assange. The visit to the embassy, says Mitchell, was to try to firm up such an interview, though they wanted to keep their visit quiet so as not to alert other outlets that Assange might be available to talk. 'I did not see any data stick pass between them,' says Christian Mitchell. 'I didn't see anything like that.'[41]

Farage and LBC, too, have always insisted that his trip to the embassy was purely journalistic. And if Trump or his allies in Washington wanted to pass material to Julian Assange, especially if it involved several meetings, as suggested by Glenn Simpson, then why do it through such a recognisable figure? It would be much simpler, surely, to find a go-between who was totally obscure?

On the other hand, during the three years he worked as a presenter with LBC, there were very few occasions when Farage made a trip to see a potential interviewee. Indeed, the guest-booking was normally done by Christian Mitchell even, as we shall see, when it came to trying to interview Donald Trump.

In his much-anticipated report, eventually published in the spring of 2019, the US special counsel Robert Mueller identified Farage's friend Ted Malloch as a go-between. Mueller said Malloch was working at the behest of Roger Stone (whom Farage met during the Republican convention in July 2016 when he seemed keen not to be seen on camera). The American political scientist Theodore Malloch, known as Ted, was mainly based in England and in the early days of the Trump presidency openly touted himself for the job as Trump's ambassador to the European Union (a job Farage had told ITV's Robert Peston that he'd like). When Malloch appeared on the BBC's *This Week* a few days after Trump became president, extolling his credentials for the Brussels posting, Farage tweeted 'Ted Malloch is the boy!'[42] Farage had met Malloch several times and even wrote the afterword to his book *Hired: An Insider's Look at the Trump Victory*, in which Malloch said that the British government should use Farage 'as a back channel to Trump'.[43]

A draft legal document prepared by Robert Mueller during his famous investigation, and which was leaked in November 2018, added to the suspicions about whether Farage played a role. Mueller quoted an email in which Roger Stone told writer Jerome Corsi, 'Get to Assange at the Ecuadorian Embassy in London and get the pending WikiLeaks emails.' Corsi forwarded the email to Farage's contact Ted Malloch in England.

When Roger Stone's intriguing email became public, Corsi admitted, 'Ted Malloch and I were in touch. Roger Stone wanted Malloch to go and see Julian Assange and I did pass the message on . . . but to my knowledge he did not. I don't think he ever saw Assange.'[44]

In June 2017, the *Guardian* reported that Nigel Farage was a 'person of interest' to Robert Mueller, partly because of his March 2017 visit to Julian Assange, but also his links to Trump and people who were close to the new president during 2016. 'Person of interest' doesn't mean that Mueller suspected Farage of wrongdoing, merely that he was seen as a possible source of information. 'One of the things the intelligence investigators have been looking at is points of contact and persons involved', a Mueller source told the *Guardian*. 'If you triangulate Russia, WikiLeaks, Assange and Trump associates, the person who comes up with the most hits is Nigel Farage. He's right in the middle of these relationships. He turns up over and over again. There's a lot of attention being paid to him.'

Jerome Corsi told the *Guardian* that FBI investigators had asked him 'about both Nigel and Ted Malloch, I can affirm that they did . . . But I'm really not going into detail because I respect the special counsel and the legal process.'[45] In June 2018, the *Washington Post* reported that two Trump sources had told the paper that 'Mueller's investigators asked about Farage's relationship to Trump associates in witness interviews this year'.[46]

In the end, however, it doesn't seem that Robert Mueller thought Farage was important enough to interview. Farage's name does crop up in the very long Mueller report, just once, in a section about Roger Stone's efforts to make contact with Julian Assange. Mueller wrote that according to testimony to the investigation by Ted Malloch, Corsi had asked Malloch to be put in touch with Assange, because Corsi wished to interview him. And according to the Mueller report:

> Malloch recalled that Corsi also suggested that individuals in the 'orbit' of UK politician Nigel Farage might be able to contact Assange and asked if Malloch knew them. Malloch told Corsi that he would think about the request but made no actual attempt to connect Corsi with Assange.[47]

Nigel Farage has always denied any involvement with either Assange or Moscow in the publication of damaging documents about Hillary

Clinton. But suspicions are understandable when he was close to several key players in the historic story. He was on good terms with both Trump and his campaign chairman Steve Bannon, and also knew three of the right-wing Americans who were heavily involved – not just Roger Stone and Ted Malloch, but the radio broadcaster Alex Jones, to whom Jerome Corsi had declared on his InfoWars channel in August 2016 that WikiLeaks was about to release 'devastating' information and 'proof of wrong-doing' in the Clinton Foundation. And there is the coincidence that, several months after Corsi's suggestion that Farage's 'orbit' be used as a conduit to Assange, he did then visit the WikiLeaks founder, though he and his producer say it was purely for journalistic reasons. And Glenn Simpson told Congress he had heard that Farage made other visits to Assange and may have given him a data stick.

With such a range of circumstantial evidence, you can see why Trump's critics and Clinton supporters might get excited, together with many journalists and conspiracy theorists. Yet neither Roger Stone nor Ted Malloch can be regarded as a reliable witness, and the Trump/Russia story would attract conspiracists from right and left. Despite several Congressional investigations and the hugely extensive Mueller report, no hard evidence has ever emerged to show Farage was involved in a plot to discredit Clinton through WikiLeaks.

In 2019, Roger Stone was convicted of seven charges – five of making false statements to Congress, along with obstruction of justice and witness tampering. He was found guilty and sentenced to forty months in prison and a $20,000 fine. President Trump initially commuted Stone's sentence to omit the prison element, and a month before he left office in 2021 he granted Stone a presidential pardon.

Another intriguing question is why Nigel Farage seemed to get so annoyed when people asked him about his visit to the Ecuadorian embassy. He misled the BuzzFeed reporter on the doorstep that day; he subsequently avoided questions about it from the investigative reporter Carole Cadwalladr; and in May 2017, two months after the visit, Farage walked out of a pre-arranged interview when Steffen Dobbert, a reporter from the German website *Die Zeit* Online, raised similar questions.

'Why did you meet with Julian Assange in the Ecuadorian embassy in London?' Dobbert asked Farage. At that point, the reporter said, Farage paused to think. 'For journalistic reasons. I will not say anything more about that. But I did it for journalistic reasons, not for political reasons.' And then a Farage spokesman interrupted to say that Dobbert's interview had been arranged to discuss trade and that Farage didn't want to talk about his connections with Assange, or about Russia. 'It has nothing to do with you. It was a private meeting,' Farage replied when Dobbert tried to press him on Assange. It all seems extraordinarily defensive. If the trip was purely innocent, why not just laugh it off, as Farage often did on other occasions? He could simply have said that he was trying to fix up an interview with Assange, and expressed dismay that the trip proved fruitless. By being so angry, Farage made it look like he had something to hide.

'I think you are a nutcase! You really are a nutcase!' Farage told Steffen Dobbert when the German went further and asked him about contacts with Russians. The reporter was 'mad' and 'away with the fairies', he said. And when Dobbert asked if UKIP and Russia shared the same agenda, Farage angrily replied: 'You know, you are the first person who has asked me if Russia supported me. Maybe you have a special German mindset. No other journalist in the world has asked these questions.' Farage's wife Kirsten was German, of course, and his two daughters half-German. 'You should be on a comedy show, not be a journalist,' Farage told Dobbert.

That seemed a bit rich for a man who, only two months before, had appeared on an RT comedy show and received a mock knighthood from a young schoolgirl.[48]

2 4

BREAKING UP

'He's dead,' a frantic Nigel Farage told Arron Banks on the phone.

'Who's dead?' asked Banks, who had no idea what his friend was talking about.

'Woolfe. He's dead.' Farage was referring to his fellow UKIP MEP Steven Woolfe.

Banks started laughing in disbelief.

'It's not fucking funny,' said Farage. 'This is serious . . . He's dead. I'm standing over him, they're taking him to hospital.'[1]

Fortunately Steven Woolfe wasn't dead, only injured, but, once more, Nigel Farage's attempts to pass on his leadership to a safe ally had come badly unstuck.

He had been UKIP leader for ten years, with a short break from 2009 to 2010, and pretty much *de facto* leader since the demise of Michael Holmes in 2000. Now was a chance to get his life back, to see more of his family, make some money and forge a whole new career. Only a few months after the Brexit referendum, Farage signed up with LBC to become one of their regular presenters. LBC had begun in 1973 as the London Broadcasting Company transmitting just within the area of the capital and was the first commercial radio station in Britain. Since 2014, LBC had been available nationwide, and was now the main talk radio competitor to the BBC stations Radio 5 Live and Radio 4, and rebranded as 'Leading Britain's Conversation'. It was agreed that Farage would present *The Nigel Farage Show* between 7 and 8 p.m. four nights a week (switched later to 6–7 p.m.), along with a two-hour show from 10 a.m. to noon on Sunday.

Farage had achieved a lifelong ambition: he had his own regular talk radio show.

Farage would later reminisce on his programme about how, as a young man, he had occasionally rung into LBC to express his views as an ordinary member of the public – 'Nigel from Orpington' presumably. And through all his time as a politician he regularly told people he would love to be a radio host. On his increasingly frequent trips to America, he enjoyed tuning in to highly opinionated radio presenters – or shock jocks, as Americans call them – sparring with callers on phone-in programmes. 'I have always had a real yearning for radio, and I look at how American radio is developing,' he told Alastair Campbell in the 2014 GQ interview. 'Potentially I would be very interested in being a shock jock, though Ofcom might be tricky,' he said. 'Some of the American stuff is appalling, wild stuff, crazy conspiracy theories.'[2] But Farage, too, had been known to dabble with the odd conspiracy theory himself.

Although his programmes were relatively short in LBC terms, the fact that Farage was performing five days a week was a heavy commitment, and would require complicated logistics to enable his live broadcasting performances to fit in with his continuing parliamentary commitments in Europe, his political engagements in Britain and what had now become regular trips to America.

Farage's experienced full-time producer Christian Mitchell – the man who accompanied him to see Julian Assange – spent each weekday thinking up topics for that night's broadcast. Late morning or lunchtime, Mitchell would ring Farage to check what subjects he preferred and what ideas he had himself. Mitchell prepared factual briefs for his presenter, and a draft forty-five-second introduction to his programme. Farage usually didn't need it – he could speak for hours off the top of his head.

LBC was increasingly employing full-time politicians as regular presenters. Others included the Tory MP Jacob Rees-Mogg, the former Lib Dem leader Nick Clegg, the former SNP leader Alex Salmond, and Boris Johnson. Nonetheless, the broadcasting regulator insisted that these shows could not simply be propaganda outlets. Each had to reflect a range of opinion, and so Mitchell would often book guests to balance Farage's strong opinions. Two regulars on Farage's shows were Tony Blair's former spin doctor Alastair Campbell and the former Labour transport secretary Andrew Adonis, both of whom were passionate Remainers. Most days Farage would arrive at LBC's office in Leicester Square an hour or so ahead of transmission.

The Nigel Farage Show first went on air on Monday 9 January 2017, and each programme opened with Donald's Trump's slow, booming introduction from the rally in Jackson, Mississippi, the previous August: 'Mr Nigel Farage.'

'He didn't need much coaching at all,' says Christian Mitchell. 'He's just got a natural gift for that.' Farage was fluent, quick on his feet, chatty, full of humour, well informed, and found it easy to speak to people from any background. 'This may make liberals' teeth grind,' wrote the former head of BBC News, Roger Mosey, in the *New Statesman*, 'but the Farage show is often an entertaining hour of radio and he is a natural broadcaster.'[3]

Most of his weekday shows comprised phone-in debates, and it was striking how fair Farage was with those who called in, even when they were fervent Remainers – and many clearly called in the hope of getting the better of the UKIP MEP. Some critics would expect a bitter argument only for the conversation to end on the best of terms. Many people – Brexiteers and Remainers – rang in again and again. 'One thing I was quite proud of,' says Mitchell, 'is that people would actually ring up, or we'd get texts or tweets to say, "Actually Nigel, I disagree with you; I don't like what you stand for, but, you know what, fair dos as to how you handled that caller."'[4]

Farage did very occasionally lose his temper, though, such as when a Remainer rang his show to complain about 'the lies' he had told during the referendum. Among these, she said, was that there would be an extra £350 million a week for the NHS.

'Hang on, I never mentioned that,' Farage interrupted. 'Never. Not once', and he grew increasingly exasperated. 'I never mentioned it once. Don't put words into my mouth that are false.' The caller then raised the Breaking Point poster.

'You do sound like a very, very sore loser,' Farage told her.

'I'm upset with the fact that people like you are given a platform.'

'I know,' said Farage sarcastically, 'isn't it dreadful? Can you imagine that someone like me, who led a party in 2014 to winning a national election – something that had not been done since 1906 by [anyone other than] the Labour or Conservative parties, should have a platform. Can you believe it? Isn't it ghastly? I'm happy for anyone to ring up, but please, please get your facts right, because that one wasn't correct.'[5]

Or Farage might tell a troublesome caller, 'We are fortunate to have your intellect.' But on the whole it was good-natured. He was at ease, quick and well informed; he'd laugh a lot, tell personal stories and be self-deprecating; and his dialogues would be peppered with favourite Farage phrases: 'You know what?', 'I'll tell you what', 'You've made your point', 'You couldn't make it up', or simply 'But hey!'

Not all Farage's discussions were frontline politics. One of his Sunday shows did an hour on mental health and depression, and Farage listened patiently and sympathetically as people phoned in, and in some cases, spoke about their mental health problems for the very first time.

Brexit dominated the news agenda, of course. Theresa May and her government grappled to secure deals with the EU on how Britain would leave, while also struggling with a small majority, and then after the 2017 election, a precarious majority which was only cobbled together with support from the strongly pro-Brexit Democratic Unionists from Northern Ireland.

The logistical problems of presenting daily shows while regularly on the move were obvious. In only his second week, Farage presented the programme from Washington DC where he'd gone for Donald Trump's inauguration. Farage's personal assistant would send Christian Mitchell copies of Farage's schedule with his engagements for the next two or three months. Mitchell would plan accordingly, and follow Farage wherever he went. Usually he would find a hotel with good WiFi and book a room to set up a studio, which required not just sound equipment but also a pop-up LBC backdrop which looked like the studio in London, since *The Nigel Farage Show* was televised live on YouTube, Facebook and Periscope. The differing locations rarely affected the broadcast quality – Farage might have been speaking from the LBC studios in Soho. Each programme was promoted vigorously on Twitter, and Mitchell encouraged Farage's press officer Dan Jukes to tweet extracts to the MEP's million-plus followers. The variety of outlets meant listening and viewing figures were hundreds of thousands each day, and with people catching up with programmes later on, the numbers grew over time.

Farage's new career as a journalist also included other outlets. He ended his regular column for Breitbart, and instead wrote columns for the *Daily Telegraph*, the *Daily Express* and the international magazine *Newsweek*, which would all be researched and drafted by one of his assistants. In America he was still a regular commentator for Fox News.

Farage couldn't stop dabbling in politics, however. He was addicted. And his inability to let go of the reins at UKIP was already adding to new drama and chaos, as the party struggled to redefine itself following the referendum.

After Farage's resignation as UKIP leader in July 2016, the party had great difficulty replacing him, and the leadership election which followed descended into extraordinary farce. For many observers, Suzanne Evans would have been the obvious replacement. Having once been a professional broadcaster, Evans was a good communicator, but had also been widely praised for the way she put UKIP's 2015 manifesto together in just a few months. Farage had anointed her as acting leader after his short-lived resignation, post-Thanet, but the two had fallen out badly in the months before the referendum, especially over Evans's support for Vote Leave rather than the Leave.EU campaign of Farage and Arron Banks. Three months before the EU vote, Evans was actually suspended from UKIP membership for six months, which would almost certainly bar her from the leadership contest which everyone expected later in the year.

Suzanne Evans's support for Vote Leave and her unfriendly public remarks about Farage weren't the official reasons for her suspension. The charges against her related to a UKIP candidate called Alan Craig who had written a blog saying that society was being crushed under pink jackboots. Evans had signed a public petition saying Craig should not be allowed to stand for UKIP, only to be told she had broken an internal UKIP rule which said members of the party should not publicly criticise other members in public.

Evans took the case to court but failed to overturn the disqualification. She had engaged a colourful young barrister named Henry Hendron, who astonishingly was simultaneously in the middle of a serious criminal trial at the Old Bailey where he was actually in the dock, having admitted supplying drugs to his gay lover who had died as a result.

Instead, the front-runner for the leadership, quietly backed by Nigel Farage, was Steven Woolfe, a Manchester-born solicitor who had been appointed UKIP economics spokesman in 2011 and became an MEP three years later. By the close of nominations, however, Woolfe's form still hadn't arrived. It turned up seventeen minutes later, and Woolfe claimed that the party computer had been unwilling to accept his submission. The NEC – which Woolfe had promised to abolish – applied a strict reading of the rules, so he was disqualified.

It seems that Woolfe's late nomination was a bit of a smokescreen; his candidature was already in serious trouble. People were asking questions about his ability to cope with pressure and there was also a problem in that, back in 2012 when he was the UKIP candidate for police and crime commissioner (PCC) in Greater Manchester, Woolfe had failed to declare an old drink-driving conviction. Under the strict rules for PCC elections any criminal offence, no matter how old, meant automatic disqualification. Moreover, Woolfe may not have been qualified to stand for UKIP leader either. He was said to have let his party membership lapse for fifteen months, between December 2014 and March 2016. He denied this, but, if true, it would have breached the rule that contenders had to have held a membership card for the previous two years.

Jay Beecher, who was campaign manager for a rival leadership candidate, Lisa Duffy, claims in his book *UKIP Exposed* that he was told by a 'senior member' of Woolfe's team that 'they had made the decision to deliberately submit his paperwork late so that he could be struck from the ballot paper with "as much dignity as possible".[6] A London activist, Paul Oakley, noted in his diary how Woolfe seemed to accept the NEC's disqualification without much complaint. 'It's almost as though he didn't really want the leadership,' Oakley recorded.[7]

The Farage camp had panicked when news of Woolfe's problems first emerged a few days before nominations closed. None of the remaining contenders – Duffy, two MEPs, Bill Etheridge and Jonathan Arnott, and Liz Jones, deputy chair of UKIP in Lambeth – were to the Faragistes' liking. Initially, it seems they considered a rather obscure alternative – Peter Jewell, the UKIP deputy treasurer, who sent out an email claiming that Farage had asked him to run. 'Steven Woolfe, it seems, cannot stand for leader and we are in a panic,' Jewell explained. 'Nigel and others have asked me to stand and hold the fort for a while. I need 50 signatures tomorrow – could you sign please?' Attached to Jewell's email was a nomination form. 'Scan it back VERY urgently,' he begged.[8] But Jewell's candidacy wasn't needed in the end.

Diane James had been mooted as a future UKIP leader ever since her outstanding performance in the Eastleigh by-election in 2013, and she became an MEP a year later. But James had strong reservations about assuming such a high-profile role, especially following in the footsteps of Farage. James is rather a reserved person and valued her privacy and family life. But only hours before the close of nominations, Farage persuaded her to stand. Around ten o'clock on the Saturday morning – twenty-six hours before the deadline – when some of her team were on a UKIP training weekend at the county cricket ground in Derby, James rang in from holiday in France to say she would join the race after all, and asked them to get the necessary fifty nominations from at least ten different branches. They met the deadline of noon the next day with fifteen minutes to spare. One theory is that James only agreed to stand so as to keep Farage in effective control, and on the understanding that she would stand down within months of being elected.[9] Members of James's team deny this.

Diane James immediately became the strong favourite, though

her campaign was pretty inactive. She declined to participate in any of UKIP's official hustings meetings held around the country for members, and instead held her own meetings. She also refused to appear on the BBC's *Daily Politics* show in a 'UKIP's Got Talent' contest, so the programme simply represented James with an empty lectern.[10] It made no difference. She won with almost twice as many votes as Lisa Duffy, her nearest rival, and made her acceptance speech at the UKIP conference in Bournemouth in September. As Farage gave her a congratulatory kiss on the cheek, James grimaced in apparent horror. 'I thought "Oh, my God,"' says Reeders Cunningham, one of her team. 'She wasn't the sort for that kind of greeting. She was more of a handshake sort of person.'[11]

Afterwards, in total contrast to Nigel Farage's style of leadership, James avoided questions from journalists. She gave only a very brief press conference and did no interviews.

Farage had looked forward to the Bournemouth gathering, confident he would get his candidate installed and feeling he would soon be free from the responsibilities of office. Farage and his friends Arron Banks and Andy Wigmore booked into a hotel in Sandbanks, the wealthy resort on a peninsula just down the coast from Bournemouth. They had come early for a brief break, and after dinner on the Thursday night the three carried on drinking on the hotel terrace, despite the noise from a wedding reception which sprawled over from the hotel next door, and in spite of a looming thunderstorm. After plenty of drinks and chat, Banks suggested a paddle in the sea. According to Wigmore, 'Nigel said, "No, no, let's go full monty. We're all chaps here; we're a bit drunk; let's go for a skinny-dip."'

'If you're sitting on a sea-front,' said Farage, 'and it's midnight, and it's a lovely evening, then a bit of skinny-dipping has always struck me as a good thing to do, and I'm very pleased that Arron joined me.'[12] Wigmore screamed in the cold water while Farage apparently started a rendition of 'Singin' in the Rain'.

Then the storm hit, with thunder and lightning, and buckets of rain. 'The water was bloody freezing,' said Wigmore. 'We couldn't get out because it's much safer in the water. So we swam up and down the beach for half an hour in a thunderstorm. It was great fun.'[13] When they returned to the beach, they couldn't find their clothes at first, then realised they were 300 yards away and, Banks says, far too wet to wear:

> So Bournemouth was treated to the spectacle of three drunken, overweight, middle aged nudists waddling up the beach in hysterics . . . Back on the terrace, the wedding party turned out to be the only people in Britain with no idea who Nigel is, allowing us to carry on our naked piss-up in peace.[14]

The problem was the group couldn't return to their hotel rooms for an hour or so because they couldn't put their soaking clothes back on, and wedding guests were still wandering about.

The next day, after a political briefing from Nigel Farage, Arron Banks left Bournemouth to go to Coventry to appear on *Any Questions* on Radio 4. On air, both the Labour MP Angela Eagle and the presenter Jonathan Dimbleby teased Banks that Farage's departure as leader might only be temporary. 'I can tell you he's not coming back,' Banks assured them. 'I can tell you he's demob happy,' he explained, before mentioning the nude late-night bathing the night before. 'So if ever a man is about to leave British politics, that's it,' Banks concluded.

'Can we just record for posterity,' interrupted a rather excited Jonathan Dimbleby, 'that you, Arron Banks and Nigel Farage last night went skinny-dipping off Bournemouth pier? Is that what you said?'

Banks confirmed the story, though claimed the skinny-dipping had been his idea, not Farage's.

'I think there should be a law against it,' Angela Eagle said, tongue-in-cheek.

'I think there is, Angela,' replied Banks.[15]

Nigel Farage rather spoilt the story later when he claimed it wasn't skinny-dipping, because he'd kept his underpants on. 'Oh, he would say that, wouldn't he?' Wigmore retorted. 'We went skinny-dipping – all of us.'[16]

But any sense of freedom and euphoria Farage may have felt must have been short-lived.

The morning after the nude dip, on the first day of the UKIP conference, Farage was further exposed when Alex Phillips suddenly made a public announcement. Six months after withdrawing as a UKIP candidate in Wales, she had decided to leave the party and join the Conservatives. Phillips had long been unhappy about the way in which the party – and Farage himself – had increasingly fallen under the influence of male newcomers who surrounded the leader – not just Arron Banks and Andy Wigmore, but also Raheem Kassam, and his new friends in America, most notably Steve Bannon.

Phillips's announcement was timed to cause UKIP the maximum embarrassment – on the day of Farage's triumphant post-referendum departure speech, and the unveiling of the party's new leader. And it can't have pleased Farage to learn that, while Phillips was still a huge fan of his, she said: 'He has a tendency at times to create rifts with people. You can fall out of favour with Nigel – and some people have learned that to their cost.'[17] Daringly, Phillips compared her membership of UKIP as like living with a bohemian boyfriend. 'I may have run away with the bad boy of the neighbourhood for a few years, and had a bloody good time, but realised I'm more suited to the boy next door. Even better, he's grown some balls and got some swagger. I've had my fun, but now I'm ready to settle down.'[18]

Alex Phillips was especially vituperative in one interview about Neil Hamilton, who had thwarted her efforts to secure election to the Welsh Assembly. On that she had allies in both Farage and his heir apparent. One of Diane James's first acts on her very first day as party leader – indeed, one of the *only* acts of her leadership – was suddenly to ditch Neil Hamilton from the conference agenda for that afternoon. It was a ruthless act, and UKIP seemed to be in the hands of another decisive character.

But no. Nigel Farage had been premature in being 'demob happy'. Diane James's striking public silence after her election continued for another two and a half weeks. Then astonishingly, just eighteen days into the job, she announced that she, too, was stepping down. She became the Lady Jane Grey of UKIP history, having served just double the short reign of the forgotten queen who briefly sat on the English throne for nine days in 1553, between Edward VI and Mary Tudor.

'It has become clear,' James said in a statement, 'that I do not have sufficient authority, nor the full support of all my MEP colleagues and party officers to implement changes I believe necessary and upon which I based my campaign.'[19] She had wanted to clip the wings of the NEC, which understandably met resistance. Moreover, she had also been verbally abused and spat at on Waterloo station, and her husband wasn't well. It later emerged that she had signed the Latin words *vi coactus* – under duress – next to her signature on the official form which UKIP had to submit to the Electoral Commission declaring herself as UKIP's new leader, which delayed the form being processed. It was clear she never wanted to be leader, and had been press-ganged into it.

Nigel Farage agreed to return once again, but only as acting leader while UKIP went through a new contest. The party press officer Gawain Towler joked: 'I have served under nine UKIP leaders, four of whom were Nigel Farage.'[20] A month later, James resigned her party membership, too, much to Farage's fury. 'This is yet another act of irrational selfishness from Diane James,' he said publicly. 'This pattern of behaviour says that she is unfit to continue as an MEP. She should do the honourable thing and resign.'[21] She didn't.

But the farce of UKIP's attempts to find a successor to Farage and James had more astonishing twists to come. First, Stephen Woolfe decided, despite his previous problems, that he would throw his hat in the ring again.

Then suddenly, on 6 October, a picture went viral on social media of Woolfe sprawled out, lying face down on a balcony in the European Parliament in Strasbourg. Minutes before, he had been involved in an argument with fellow MEP Mike Hookem in a UKIP group meeting to discuss reports that Woolfe had recently spoken to the Conservatives about jumping ship. Woolfe had suggested they settle their differences 'mano a mano' outside the room. Hookem then – according to Woolfe – delivered a blow to his face. Hookem denied any punch or slap, and said Woolfe attacked him first, but that it was only a 'slight scuffle'.[22] It was several minutes later, while MEPs were in the process of voting, that Woolfe suddenly collapsed.

'It's the one time I've seen Farage look petrified,' says the British Conservative MEP Sajjad Karim, who had just left the parliamentary chamber and saw Woolfe 'spreadeagled' on the floor. 'I saw him turn around, white as a ghost, and he said, "He's killed him." He was absolutely petrified.'[23]

Woolfe wasn't dead, fortunately. He'd had two seizures, and spent three days in hospital, but eventually recovered. However, his career did not survive. Ten days later, Woolfe announced the end of his campaign, and that he, too, was leaving the party. UKIP was in a 'death spiral', he suggested; it had 'something rotten' in it, and he didn't think UKIP was 'governable' without Farage in charge.[24] It was hard to disagree.

This extraordinary saga of events in the late summer and autumn of 2016 was unfolding at the same time as Nigel Farage was jetting back and forth to help Donald Trump in America. Now, Farage's close ally Raheem Kassam, the editor of Breitbart UK, declared himself a contender for the succession. And to help him, Farage persuaded the UKIP NEC to reduce the qualification rule from two years' membership to just twenty-eight days.

Kassam was only thirty. He had Farage's backing but was always too controversial to win. Kassam ran on a slogan of 'Make UKIP Great Again', in the style of Donald Trump's 'Make America Great Again', though MUGA was a rather less attractive acronym than MAGA. He also gained attention for the abusive and unpleasant nature of many of his past messages on social media. Kassam had a habit of simply replying 'Fuck off' to anyone who disagreed with him. And only four months earlier, during the referendum, he had tweeted, 'Can someone just like . . . tape Nicola Sturgeon's mouth shut? And her legs, so she can't reproduce.' Kassam's tweet was all the more offensive when it later emerged that Sturgeon had suffered a miscarriage five years before, though he did apologise.

Raheem Kassam withdrew from the contest just before the close of nominations. The two leading contenders were now Suzanne Evans, whose six-month suspension had now expired, and Paul

Nuttall, who had avoided the previous contest but was now clearly Farage's candidate – his fourth preferred successor in four months – and Nuttall beat Suzanne Evans easily, by a margin of more than three to one.

When a by-election was triggered in Stoke-on-Trent Central in February 2017, Nuttall came under huge pressure to stand, not least from Farage. It was a promising seat for UKIP: the party had come second in 2015 and the city had voted 69 per cent for Leave the previous summer. And the UKIP vote had held up remarkably well in national polls since the referendum – well over 10 per cent – perhaps because of growing doubts about whether the new prime minister Theresa May was truly committed to withdrawal, despite her well-known slogan 'Brexit Means Brexit'. Farage and many other Brexiteers were angry that May had not yet triggered the two-year leaving process as set out under the famous Article 50 of the Lisbon Treaty.

Labour was also in long-term decay in Stoke, and during the noughties many working-class voters had forsaken the party to elect several BNP councillors as well as an independent elected mayor. So, with expectations running high, Nuttall agreed to stand. He got off to a good start when Labour pursued a bizarre strategy of hiding their nominee, Gareth Snell, from the media, perhaps because he was no fan of Jeremy Corbyn.

Things began to go wrong for Nuttall, however, when someone leaked to me the fact that he had recently registered as a voter in the constituency at a terraced house in Oxford Street, but didn't seem to be living there. If you looked through the ground-floor windows, the property seemed to be almost empty. I spotted some window cleaners across the road, who kindly lent me a ladder to investigate upstairs! When I confronted Nuttall on camera half an hour later, he confirmed that he'd never even been to the house, let alone lived there, but would be moving in soon. 'I'll be in there, and I'll be there for the rest of the campaign,' he said in a car-crash interview. He had pretty much admitted a breach of electoral law, which requires that someone should already be living at an address when they register there as a voter. Nuttall had clearly put his name down on the electoral roll for the property to make himself look like a local candidate on official election notices. In reality, he lived on Merseyside. (The police did investigate, but dropped the case.)[25]

Journalists and rival parties began exploring Nuttall's claims about his past life, and discovered, or dug up afresh, various discrepancies. He claimed to have been a professional footballer with Tranmere Rovers, when he was merely a youth player. He admitted his claim to have lost 'close personal friends' in the 1989 Hillsborough disaster was not true, and strong doubts were raised over Nuttall's claim to have been at Hillsborough that day. It all made Nuttall a laughing-stock, especially on social media.

Snell won the election relatively easily, with a majority of 2,620 over Nuttall (or 12.4 per cent). The new UKIP leader couldn't hide his fury as I pursued him out of the count that night, and his reputation never recovered. If the party could not win a by-election in a working-class seat in Stoke-on-Trent, they probably couldn't win anywhere.

'This was an election that we really should have won,' Nigel Farage wrote immediately afterwards, saying that he had expected Nuttall to win. Nuttall had his 'full support', he said, but the campaign tactics had been wrong; UKIP should have been more radical, squeezed Tory voters into voting tactically and focused more on immigration.[26]

In fact, Stoke-on-Trent Central was still a pretty good result for UKIP in historic terms, but it marked the end of the four-year period, dating back to Eastleigh in 2013, when UKIP seriously threatened the major parties at the ballot box.

Before long the party would experience far worse results. Five weeks later, Theresa May did finally trigger the Article 50 timetable, which meant Britain would leave the EU on 29 March 2019. Two and a half weeks after that, May abandoned her previous pledges not to call an early election. She hoped to improve on the Conservatives' working majority of just seventeen in the Commons, which, given the numbers of Tory rebels of various kinds, would have made steering Brexit legislation through the Parliament very difficult. For several weeks, Conservative strategists were confident that the slow decline and reorientation of UKIP would help improve their majority. 'UKIP is fast morphing into more of a threat to Labour's traditional working class,' wrote May's adviser Chris Wilkins for a Chequers strategy meeting in February. 'In effect, a whole group of voters has been unlocked for us by last year's referendum . . .'[27]

The day after May's election announcement, Farage only added to the pressure on Paul Nuttall by telling the *Today* programme: 'He's got six weeks to prove himself, hasn't he? It's just as simple as that.'[28]

For about twenty-four hours Farage mulled over whether to fight his eighth Westminster election as a candidate. One possibility was to stand for a third time in South Thanet, especially since the Crown Prosecution Service (CPS) was actively considering election expenses offences by the Conservatives in the seat during the 2015 contest. Only five weeks earlier Farage's old colleague Craig Mackinlay, now the Tory MP, had been interviewed by police under caution.

In March, Douglas Carswell had announced his resignation from UKIP, and as soon as the election was called he said he would not contest his Clacton seat again, no doubt sensing the way the wind was blowing. Farage wrote in his *Telegraph* column that it was 'tempting' to stand himself in Clacton, 'which is now Carswell-free, and possibly the most Eurosceptic constituency in the country by demographics. It would be an easy win and a personal vindication to get into the House of Commons after all these years.' But Farage decided against fighting either seat. He'd found previous campaigns to be an exhausting and demoralising process, and felt he was unlikely ever to beat the first-past-the-post system.

Instead, Farage claimed he could make a much bigger contribution though his leadership of the Eurosceptic group in the European Parliament, 'which gives me a big media platform across the EU. I have a front-row seat where it matters most. If I compare the platform I have in Strasbourg to being a backbench MP, there is frankly no comparison.'[29]

Farage was right not to fight. The 2017 general election was catastrophic for UKIP. Unlike 2015, when the party fought almost every seat, this time they confined themselves to just 378, and there was an early sign of what was to come when they gained just one new councillor in the local elections in early May, and lost all 145 seats they were defending. 'If we use the analogy of UKIP as a racing car,' said Arron Banks in his vivid verdict, 'Nigel was a skilled driver who drove the car around the track faster and faster, knowing when to take risks, delighting the audience. The current leadership has crashed the car, at the first bend of the race, into the crowd, killing the driver and spectators.'[30]

Banks, too, thought of fighting Clacton – once Farage said he wouldn't – but it's highly unlikely that either man could have held the Essex seat, or that Farage would have achieved the 'easy win' he wrote of. On election night the Conservatives romped back there with a whopping majority of almost 16,000 – and UKIP fell behind Labour, to get just 7.6 per cent of the vote. South Thanet was even more embarrassing. UKIP came third with only 6 per cent, as Craig Mackinlay's majority rose to more than 6,000. This was despite the fact that just six days before polling the CPS announced that Mackinlay was being charged with election offences from 2015, though he was eventually acquitted in 2019. Paul Nuttall did no better in Boston and Skegness, a seat UKIP almost won in 2015. He came third with just 7.7 per cent. All this was despite it being a disastrous night overall for the Tories, too, as Jeremy Corbyn's party did better than almost anyone expected.

The broadcasters in 2017 had still treated UKIP as one of the five main parties (along with Greens), on the strength of their votes in the Euro elections of 2014 and the general election of 2015, as well as recent opinion polls, and Paul Nuttall and other UKIP people took part in some TV debates. In the first four months of 2017 UKIP had averaged around 11.5 per cent in national opinion polls, yet in the final result UKIP's share plummeted to just 1.8 per cent, their worst result since 2001. The UK Independence Party was now effectively finished as a force in British politics.

But Nigel Farage wasn't.

As he had promised, Farage now focused more on the European Parliament and the party's international grouping which he led, the Europe of Freedom and Direct Democracy (EFDD). Although Farage's attendance record was very poor (the third lowest of British

MEPs), he continued to exploit the opportunities the Parliament provided.[31]

After the 2014 elections, Farage and the UKIP NEC had formed the Alliance for Direct Democracy in Europe – ADDE. This was a pan-European party (PEP) in line with EU efforts to encourage and fund new parties to work on an EU-wide basis, beyond the Brussels and Strasbourg structures. But ADDE was set up by Farage in defiance of the internal UKIP ballot back in 2011 when members had roundly rejected the idea of establishing a PEP. ADDE was duly recognised by the European Parliament in 2015 and granted roughly €1 million in EU funds, while an associated research body, confusingly called IDDE – the Initiative for Direct Democracy in Europe – collected another half a million euros. Farage never officially held any position in ADDE or IDDE, but his fingerprints were all over the development. And his mistress Laure Ferrari was put in charge of IDDE and moved from France to set up an IDDE office in London.

The motivation behind forming ADDE and IDDE was financial, with the brazen aim of using these extra EU funds to make the case against EU membership. Not surprisingly, ADDE and IDDE soon came under close scrutiny from the authorities.

In November 2016, the leadership group of the European Parliament – known as the Bureau – declared that ADDE had misspent €500,000 of the money it had been granted. and the Bureau decided to recover €173,000, and to suspend a further €501,000 which was due to be paid. The European Parliament accused UKIP of using ADDE money to pay for national election campaigning, and specifically revealed that ADDE and IDDE had spent €321,000 on opinion polls in eight UKIP target seats before the 2015 election, including South Thanet where Farage was the candidate. 'Most of the constituencies can be identified as being essential for reaching a significant representation in the House of Commons,' the Bureau said.[32] And ahead of the EU referendum, ADDE and IDDE had conducted further polls on British voters' attitudes to the European Union. 'This is pure victimisation,' Farage complained, arguing that the decision was politically motivated. 'I am the most investigated MEP in history. Look at what the pro-EU groups were spending.'[33]

The European Parliament's decision also raised the question of whether UKIP, in making use of ADDE funds, had been in breach of British law on party funding, which bans donations from 'impermissible' sources, such as from overseas. Both ADDE and IDDE were arguably foreign entities. The Electoral Commission launched an investigation, but two years later came down in UKIP's favour. The 'evidence was insufficient', the Commission decided, to say that the purpose of ADDE's polling was to help UKIP, and there was 'no evidence that UKIP received or benefited from any of this work'.[34]

In 2019, Farage, UKIP and ADDE would receive another favourable verdict from an institution they despised even more than they hated the Electoral Commission. The European Court of Justice (ECJ) – the supreme court of the European Union – overturned the Bureau's verdict against ADDE on the grounds of 'bias'. It decided that one of the Bureau's members, an Austrian vice-president of the Parliament, Green MEP Ulrike Lunacek, had 'prejudged the issue' back in 2016 by saying in advance that 'the money must be paid back and UKIP held to account for its fraudulent manipulation of the British electorate'.[35]

The ECJ's decision was not enough to save ADDE and IDDE, however. They had closed down in 2016 as a result of the initial ruling, and UKIP made no further attempt to start a pan-European party. In May 2018, the now defunct ADDE was ordered to repay another €1.1 million to the European Parliament after an investigation into its finances for the second year of ADDE's existence – 2016. ADDE had misspent €299,270, the inquiry found, though investigators had not been able to find out what happened to the rest because ADDE failed to submit any documentation.

UKIP MEPs had been investigated many times before, but in the period after the referendum, scrutiny by the European Parliament got significantly tougher. In 2017, the Parliament decided that Farage had wrongly been paying one of his assistants, Christopher Adams, from his European Parliament staffing allowance, when Adams was really doing political work for UKIP. From January 2018, the Parliament docked half of Farage's monthly salary until he had repaid the €40,000 deemed to have been misused.

Back in the UK, the dismal 2017 election result had been swiftly followed by Paul Nuttall's resignation, plunging UKIP into yet another leadership contest. There was speculation that Farage might return to the job, and it took him three weeks to scotch the rumours. Many people had been lobbying him and urging him to return, he claimed in his *Telegraph* column, but it was 'already something of an ongoing joke about the number of times I have stood for the leadership and resigned'. With little modesty he declared that his standing down in 2016 'was bound to leave a big hole. When you are such a dominant figure, it is always going to be tough for anyone to follow. Little did I know just how dramatic this period would be.'

Then, intriguingly, he said it would be 'premature' to stand for the job, though he didn't rule out returning to 'the front line' if the Brexit process went badly. And he delivered a sharp warning to UKIP: 'If it does not sort itself out and make the changes necessary to become a professional, modern political party, and if then we find ourselves with a Brexit that falls short of the mark, another vehicle will then come along to replace it.'[36]

His words were a stark warning of what was to come, as over the next eighteen months UKIP continued to collapse amid bitter infighting, and the issue of curbing Islamic extremism, rather than Brexit, came to dominate its politics. The man elected as Paul Nuttall's replacement was a former army officer, Henry Bolton, who had emerged from nowhere. His main opponent was Anne Marie Waters, a former Labour candidate, who ran a group called Sharia Watch and was hostile to further Islamic immigration. Bolton had argued during his campaign that UKIP risked becoming the 'UK Nazi party', while all but two of the party's twenty MEPs said they would resign from UKIP if Waters won.

Superficially, Bolton appeared to be an ideal choice: he looked serious and respectable, and had a good CV, having been a policeman and served as a British diplomat. Remarkably, he had stood for the pro-EU Liberal Democrats in the 2005 election. But under close examination, several details of his record would turn out to be almost as inaccurate as Paul Nuttall's. Bolton also carried a hugely embarrassing personal life, having left his third wife to conduct a very public relationship with a model called Jo Marney, who was almost thirty years younger than him and whose political views were well to the right of Bolton's and outright racist. Marney was suddenly suspended from the party after a series of text messages emerged in which she had said that Prince Harry's then fiancée Meghan Markle was 'just a dumb little commoner' with a 'tiny brain', who would 'taint' the royal family with 'her seed' and lead the way to a 'black king'.[37] Bolton claimed they had broken off their relationship, only for them to be seen dining together at the National Liberal Club. Senior UKIP spokesmen started resigning, and in January the NEC agreed a 'no confidence' vote in Bolton almost unanimously – the one exception was Henry Bolton himself.

Privately, Farage had been frustrated by Bolton's low profile and lack of activity as leader, but nonetheless the day after the National Executive meeting he backed him publicly. It was partly, no doubt, because Farage had come to despise the NEC in recent years, but also because Bolton promised to modernise the party and reduce their role. In his *Telegraph* column, Farage suggested a parallel with the Labour leader Jeremy Corbyn, who managed to survive after most of his shadow Cabinet resigned in 2016:

> Corbyn was written off by the press, but the rank and file membership saved him. If Bolton has the courage and the vision to introduce a new constitution, and shows that he can be a strong spokesman for Britain leaving the single market, taking back its fisheries and restoring pride in the UK, he may well surprise all of his critics too.[38]

In February 2018, however, an Extraordinary General Meeting of UKIP members deposed Bolton as leader by a vote of almost two to one. He was succeeded by Gerard Batten, one of the party's original founders twenty-five years before, and no friend of Nigel Farage.

Throughout 2017 and 2018, as Theresa May and her negotiators struggled to reach a withdrawal deal with the EU and their negotiator Michel Barnier, Nigel Farage was naturally among those urging a tough line and insisting that Brexit meant not just leaving the EU, but leaving both the customs union and the single market. Like increasing numbers of Conservative MPs, led by Jacob Rees-Mogg and Steve Baker in the parliamentary European Research Group, he argued against any compromise on these principles. Leaving the EU on 29 March 2019 with No Deal, he said, might be better than a bad deal which produced Brexit In Name Only, what became known as Brino. No Deal would mean trading outside the EU on the World Trade Organisation system of tariffs until one-to-one trade deals could be negotiated.

Yet Farage hadn't always been so hardline about leaving the single market. Before and during the referendum campaign, Farage had argued that what became known as the 'Norway option' or 'Norway model' might be a possible settlement when the UK left the EU. Britain might rejoin the European Economic Area (EEA – a wider group which involved the EU and the three members of EFTA, the European Free Trade Association: Norway, Liechtenstein and Iceland). Norway, which had twice voted against EU membership in the past, has access to the single market, but little say in its implementation, and had to abide by most EU legislation and to contribute to the European Union budget. In 2013, Farage had seemed to extol Norway's situation when he said on *Question Time*:

> I have to say that everybody from David Cameron to half this panel say, 'Wouldn't it be terrible if we were like Norway and Switzerland?' Really? They're rich, they're happy; they're self-governing. And unlike the fishermen in Lincolnshire out of Boston, what the Norwegians have got is 200 miles of North Sea where all the fish in the sea are their own, and they've got a thriving fishing industry.[39]

He also appeared the same year in a film made by the Bruges Group called *The Norway Option*, which stressed the benefits to Britain rejoining the EEA as an alternative to EU membership. And during an online debate hosted by the *Daily Mirror* during the 2016 referendum, Farage sarcastically remarked: 'It would be ghastly if this country was like Norway. Can you imagine it? Rich, free, catching your own fish, and with a seat at the World Trade Organisation!'[40]

On another issue which increasingly dominated the interminable Brexit wrangling of the May administration – the idea of a second referendum – Farage also seemed to shift his ground. In 2016, he had said that if the Remain side won by a margin of two to one then that would end the matter, but if Remain won by only 52–48 'this would be unfinished business by a long way', implying that Brexit campaigners would press for a second vote.[41]

And 52–48 was exactly the ratio of the victory achieved by Leave in 2016. For months, Farage denounced the growing clamour from Remainers for a rematch, but in January 2018 he seemed to concede that a second referendum might be the only way out of the growing impasse between Britain and Brussels, and to overcome the pro-Remain majority in Parliament. 'The Cleggs, the Blairs, the Adonises', he said, would never give up, and go on whingeing and whining:

> So maybe, just maybe, I'm reaching the point of thinking that we should have a second referendum on EU membership . . . I think if we had a second referendum on EU membership, we'd kill it off for a generation. The percentage that would vote to leave next time would be very much bigger than it was last time round, and we may just finish the whole thing off, and Blair can disappear off into total obscurity.[42]

'I agree with Nigel' was Nick Clegg's witty tweet in response. Farage's UKIP colleagues and Brexiteer friends weren't pleased, and he never repeated what many of his friends must have regarded as heresy.

Farage applauded in July 2018 when first the Brexit secretary David Davis, and then the foreign secretary Boris Johnson, resigned from Theresa May's Cabinet after the 'Chequers plan' was agreed at the prime minister's country home in Buckinghamshire. The plan involved the UK having continued access to the single market; a new customs arrangement which would ensure frictionless trade;

and Britain signing up to EU regulations on environmental matters, employment and so on. Farage had never been impressed by Theresa May; he would have preferred Andrea Leadsom to have become prime minister, and at times his attacks on May became quite personal. Chequers was a 'cowardly sell-out', he said. 'She doesn't believe in Brexit,' he declared. 'She doesn't believe in Britain; she doesn't believe we're good enough to run our own affairs. I'm afraid she bears a very heavy burden of responsibility.'[43]

Newly energised, Farage announced he was now joining frontline politics again with a campaign to 're-engage the public, to restart the Brexit campaign'. He no longer trusted ministers to implement Brexit, and now felt he had to counter the growing campaign from the increasingly noisy and well-funded People's Vote movement. 'What Chequers does, it leaves us half-in, half-out. In many ways, it leaves us worse off than being a member of the Union.'[44]

Significantly, Nigel Farage's return to politics, and making the case for a full Brexit, came not with his party, UKIP, but through an organisation, Leave Means Leave, which had been set up in late 2016 by Richard Tice, the property businessman, and John Longworth, who had been ousted as director-general of the British Chambers of Commerce for publicly backing Brexit. Tice was determined that, if a second referendum were to happen, they had to get the designation this time. Leave Means Leave was seen as the vehicle for that, so it had to be as cross-party as possible.

Just two days after the Chequers Plan was effectively killed off by EU leaders at a summit in Salzburg, Leave Means Leave took to the streets, with Farage arriving by open-top bus in the small south Lancashire town of Westhoughton, followed by a rally for around 1,500 people under one of the stands at Bolton Wanderers football ground, where David Davis and the Labour MP Kate Hoey also spoke. There was little sign of UKIP there.

Leave Means Leave held dozens of big rallies over the next few months. They were well organised, noisy and extremely well attended; they were more like a combination of a pop concert and a religious fundamentalist event. Week by week, John Longworth studied Farage's speaking and campaign style closely:

He's not actually very confident. He's quite a tense person really, not at all relaxed. He is somebody with a lot of insecurities. He could get quite sharp with minions in his team. Nigel would pace up and down and practise what he was going to say. He would complain sometimes that Richard Tice had stolen his best lines, or spent too long on stage – he would say this while waiting in the wings. He was also quite a magpie. I'd listen to his speeches and suddenly hear something I'd written in the *Daily Telegraph*. I'd think up a good line for a speech and then suddenly, before you knew it, Nigel would be using it. He's a collector rather than an inventor. His evening cycle would be: first, tense and nervous; then a few bevvies; and then he could be a bit sharp. Then the speech would go well, and everything would be marvellous and 'What a great rally!'[45]

One curious aspect of Leave Means Leave is that the campaign didn't involve Arron Banks, even though its chairman Richard Tice had been close to Banks. Tice was worried that the National Crime Agency investigation into Banks might do the Leave cause huge damage. Banks had probably been Farage's closest male friend for the last three or four years. They'd fought the referendum campaign together; they'd become Donald Trump's buddies together; they'd gone on holiday together; they'd even gone skinny-dipping together; but now everything seemed to have cooled. It was odd, because Banks had often spoken publicly himself about the drawbacks of UKIP, and the need to establish either a new party, or a new organisation along the lines of the left-wing Corbynite group Momentum in the Labour Party. Farage had done just that, but without Banks.

When Farage appeared on *Piers Morgan's Life Stories* early in 2017, Arron Banks had been a guest in the audience. Banks had funded several of Farage's trips to America over the previous year, and just before the programme was broadcast it was revealed in the press that Farage was living in a rented house in Chelsea with Laure Ferrari, whom he'd taken to the Trump inauguration celebrations in Washington only a fortnight before. Farage claimed, improbably, that he and Ferrari weren't having a relationship, but that she had merely sought his help with finding somewhere to live. Ferrari had been forced to leave her previous flat in London, because the European Parliament had stopped funding IDDE, the think tank she effectively ran on behalf of UKIP.

The trip to Washington seems to have been the final straw for Kirsten Farage. Pictures of her husband and Ferrari in Washington had appeared on social media, and a few days after Farage's return to England, Kirsten issued a statement to the press saying that her husband had moved out of the family home in Kent. They had been living 'separate lives for years', she said. 'This is a situation that suits everyone and is not news to any of the people involved.'[46]

It later emerged that the rent on the Chelsea flat was being paid by Arron Banks. Channel 4 News subsequently estimated that the rent on the property was around £13,000 a month – and that Banks was also paying for further costs including furniture and fittings, council tax and utilities, and other aspects of Farage's lifestyle. He had paid for Farage's car and his driver and £5,000 a month for his security team, as well as regular flights to America for both political and business purposes. The total funding by Banks was estimated at almost £500,000.

The business side of Farage's trips to America was known internally as 'Brand Farage', a scheme by Arron Banks and their 2016 political consultant Gerry Gunster to launch Farage as a superstar in America and to exploit his political and media reputation for huge financial reward to all three of them. Little seems to have resulted from this venture, apart from trips to New York and Atlanta to meet executives from Coca-Cola.

In 2019, the president of the European Parliament, Antonio Tajani, launched an investigation into whether Banks's generosity amounted to support which Farage should have included in his declaration of interests as an MEP, and the Parliament's advisory committee accused Farage of a serious breach of the code of conduct. The seriousness of the breach, the committee said, 'would merit the highest penalty foreseen by the Parliament's Rules of Procedure'.[47] Farage maintained he 'did not receive any private money for political purposes'.[48]

But well before the European Parliament investigation, Banks's funding for Farage suddenly stopped. Farage moved back to the family home in Kent while Kirsten and his daughters moved to another village nearby. It seemed that relations between the two old friends had cooled. Farage felt he had to distance himself from the embarrassment of Banks being investigated over his links with Russia, and revelations in the *Sunday Times* by Isabel Oakeshott – who was by now Richard Tice's girlfriend – based on emails she had seen while working for Banks. These suggested that Banks's dealings with the Russians were far more extensive than previously stated. Banks and Andy Wigmore, Oakeshott wrote, were 'highly valuable – and surprisingly willing – tools' and were 'shamelessly used by the Russians'. Banks responded: 'I had two boozy lunches with the Russian ambassador and other cups of tea with him. Bite me. It's a convenient political witch-hunt, both over Brexit and Trump.'[49] Yet more of the major relationships in Nigel Farage's life seemed to have collapsed.

Now, too, would his association with the organisation which had become almost synonymous with Nigel Farage – the UK Independence Party.

2 5

THE MASSACRE OF MAY

The founder of the Brexit Party was not, at first glance, an obvious agent for change. Catherine Blaiklock had never been that political, in fact. Astonishingly, she didn't even vote in an election until she was fifty-two, in 2015, the year UKIP reached its peak in Westminster elections with 3.9 million votes. Blaiklock had joined the party the year before, having grown convinced that Britain had to leave the EU.

Her unusual early life, though, provides some clues to her later energy and insurgency. The daughter of an Antarctic explorer, she spent much of her teens in care because she had bulimia and her parents found her too 'wayward and difficult'. Her companions were 'drug dealers, and people who were there having underage sex, and car thieves'.[1] Despite her difficulties, she got into Christ Church, Oxford, then launched a highly successful career as a trader in the financial markets, and ended up working for Merrill Lynch in New York and the Far East. 'I was earning half a million a year in the late 1980s,' she says. 'By the age of twenty-eight I never needed to work again.'[2] She gave up financial trading to start a family, but later established her own businesses in property, and now also runs a guest house in a village east of Norwich.

After the referendum, however, Blaiklock channeled her energies into UKIP, and her rise was rapid. She got to have dinner with Farage one evening at Boisdale in Belgravia, then stood in Great Yarmouth in 2017 – one of UKIP's prime targets at the previous election – and became chair of the party's eastern region. She and Farage kept in touch by phone or text, and Blaiklock gave him titbits about the financial markets.

In September 2018, Farage's latest successor, Gerard Batten, made Blaiklock the party's spokesman on economics. In Birmingham, just ten days later, she delivered the main economic speech at the UKIP conference, where Farage was still a hero to many activists. The Young Independence stall was even selling, for a pound each, 'Nigel Farage condoms' with the former leader's face on the wrapper (though not the condom itself), and the words 'For when you have a hard Brexit'. (When I tweeted about this novelty, one Tory Cabinet adviser asked me to get five Farage condoms for himself.)

The night before her speech, Blaiklock attended the annual gala dinner where Farage was, as usual, the main speaker. The event also marked twenty-five years of UKIP, and Farage and Batten, as founder members, were both presented with heraldic shields.

Only this gala dinner was different. Instead of basking in adulation from inebriated activists, Farage delivered a stiff message. This would be the last time he addressed a UKIP gathering, he announced, and then warned the 150 or so people present – Batten especially – that the party faced 'total and utter marginalisation' if it became extreme and more hostile towards Islam. Batten was an admirer of the Dutch far-right leader Geert Wilders and shared his vision of a crusade against what they saw as the threat of a religion which Batten had described as a 'death cult'.[3] Suddenly, Farage found himself being heckled by some of Batten's supporters – shouting 'in a rather Butlins-like manner', Blaiklock recalls. Farage's speech received only lukewarm applause. It was a poignant, symbolic moment. Farage stomped out, just as Gerard Batten began his own speech.

Three weeks later, Catherine Blaiklock travelled to a Leave Means Leave rally in Bournemouth, with Farage and Richard Tice among the cast. The passionate atmosphere prompted her to write an article for the Brexiteer website *Independence Daily*, in which she urged UKIP to get more heavily involved in the battle to secure Brexit. She openly criticised Batten for being distracted by other issues, rather than the continuing struggle to leave the EU. 'Why do we not get involved in these Brexit events?' Blaiklock publicly asked UKIP colleagues. It was wrong, she said, to dismiss other Brexiteers as 'a pile of old Tories', and instead dwell on internal rivalries.

> There is animosity between Gerard and Nigel, and Gerard and many of the MEPs . . . but that is not the only reason. The main reason is that no one is making any effort to be part of these Brexit groups, write for them, help them, realise that we are all fighting for the same thing. Instead we are nowhere to be seen. It's a disaster. Our enemy is not other Brexit groups.

'I might get fired for this,' Blaiklock added, 'but I had to say it.'[4] A day or two later, Gerard Batten sacked her.

People couldn't accuse Batten of being indecisive or inactive, the charge often levelled against his predecessor Henry Bolton. But Farage was one of many leading UKIP figures concerned about Batten's attempts to forge links with the notorious Tommy Robinson, the former leader of the far-right street protest group the English Defence League (EDL). Robinson, real name Stephen Yaxley-Lennon, had a string of convictions, including for assault, fraud and public order offences.

In mid-November, the UKIP NEC voted 11–4 to delay a decision on whether to bar Robinson from joining UKIP, in line with party rules banning those linked to the EDL. Ignoring the clear mood of the NEC, Batten and Robinson jointly announced in an online video two days afterwards that they would both be leading a 'Brexit Betrayal March' through central London in early December. Batten then announced that he had appointed Robinson as his personal adviser on 'rape gangs and prison conditions and prison reform'.

Nigel Farage was so angry about Batten and Robinson that for the first time he publicly denounced his successor. He would now write to all members of the NEC, he said, to urge them to have a vote of no confidence in Batten so 'we get rid of him', and he would also discuss the situation with UKIP MEPs in Brussels the following week. 'We are going to have one last go at getting rid of somebody who as leader is dragging us in a shameful direction.'[5]

Batten and Robinson's pro-Brexit march would be 'full of skin-heads, tattooed to the eyeballs', Farage warned:

> They'll all be drunk before they get there. There'll be punch-ups and God knows what . . . This is how Brexit will look. It will look like a bunch of far-right football thugs and I am absolutely disgusted by it. So I've held my silence as a former party leader until now, but we now have to get rid of this bloke as leader because he is not just damaging UKIP, he's damaging Brexit. Twenty-five years of my life, to take a fringe organisation, to winning a national election, to forcing a referendum, to helping to win it – on paper, UKIP is the most successful party in history. And to see it now be dragged literally into the street, literally street-fighting – yobby, thuggy, nasty, extremist, racist – I'm heartbroken by it.[6]

It was a rather unpromising move, given Farage's own poor relations with the UKIP National Executive, where he now had very few allies. 'Nigel has done nothing for UKIP for the last two years,' Batten replied. 'Brexit is bigger than Nigel Farage's ego. If I were an NEC member, irrespective of their view of my appointment of Tommy Robinson, I wouldn't take kindly to being written to by somebody who described NEC members as very low-grade people and a swamp that needed to be drained.'[7]

Farage's colleague Arron Banks had been warning publicly for a couple of years that UKIP might be past its sell-by date, and privately Farage concurred. But it took Catherine Blaiklock – who had kept in close contact with Farage – to make the first move.

She registered an off-the-shelf company. Her first decision was the name. Having set up numerous companies in her business career, Blaiklock consulted the online Formations Company, and on a whim spent £9.99 buying Nigel Farage Party Limited, without getting his approval. Another possibility she considered was Alternatives for Britain Limited. But on 23 November 2018, coincidentally the day of Farage's outburst against Robinson, Blaiklock spent another £9.99 buying The Brexit Party Ltd, which was duly registered with

Companies House. Blaiklock was its only shareholder, its company secretary and its sole director. Its registered address was her guest house in Norfolk.

Nigel Farage knew nothing of this at the time, says Blaiklock. But barely six months later he would lead this newly registered £10-name company to one of the most stunning victories in British election history. Subsequent accounts would praise the party's rise from nowhere, as a brilliantly run campaign, employing all the latest election techniques. Yet the story of the early days of the Brexit Party is, in truth, a chronicle of indecision, mishaps and chaos. The party could so easily have fallen at the first fence.

The same day that Blaiklock registered The Brexit Party as a company, UKIP's chairman in the South West received a call which astonished him. Richard Ford had just joined the NEC and barely knew the woman who represented the party's MEPs on it, Margot Parker. She told him the deputy leader, fellow MEP Mike Hookem, was about to resign over Tommy Robinson and pressed him to act, as Farage had urged. 'I was shocked,' says Ford:

> because Mike Hookem and Gerard Batten in meetings were always the best of buddies. I was also shocked that she was ringing me and not long-serving members of the NEC. It put the wind up me, because if we went down the Tommy Robinson line then we would lose most of our members. Everything everybody had worked for so hard, could be ruined.[8]

Ford drove to London to confront Batten face to face at a party meeting at the Union Jack Club near Waterloo. Signing up Robinson, Ford warned, and marching with him would split the party and damage efforts to get Brexit done. Batten's eyes 'glazed over', Ford recalls. 'I saw that I couldn't shift his opinion. I was flogging a dead horse. I thought that I couldn't change Batten's mind.' Ford knew he would have to put down a motion of no confidence.[9]

He rang Nigel Farage, having got his number from Catherine Blaiklock. But Farage made clear he wasn't interested in becoming UKIP leader for a fifth time. It was up to the NEC to act, he argued.

'My fear was he could leave,' says Ford, 'and yet he was our biggest asset.'

Ford spent days lobbying fellow NEC members and thought he had the numbers for his motion. But when it came to the NEC meeting – back at the Union Jack Club, on Sunday 2 December – the anti-Batten forces crumbled. The minutes record that Batten couldn't hide his contempt for Farage and the UKIP delegation to Europe. 'Our current MEPs are a stagnant pool of self-interest,' Batten said. 'They disgust me.' And he later told the NEC: 'I'm sick of being attacked by Nigel Farage.'[10]

'Gerard Batten is sticking two fingers up to the NEC,' Ford told colleagues, but the leader won the vote easily.

Nigel Farage was in despair. Gerard Batten was entrenched for the foreseeable future. Two days after Ford's attempted coup, on 4 December 2018, Farage announced live on his LBC show that after twenty-six years' membership of the UK Independence Party, with almost ten years as leader, he was resigning his membership. He accused Batten of being 'obsessed with the issue of Islam. And with this figure called Tommy Robinson . . . I simply can't go on with it. I don't recognise the party as being the one that I helped to found and fought for, for all those years. I believe the brand has been now so damaged, so tarnished . . . So with very great reluctance I have, as of now, resigned my membership of UKIP.'[11]

'I have to say that I think that Nigel left the party in spirit after the Brexit Referendum in 2016,' Gerard Batten responded. 'Earlier this year he stated that he was dedicating "100 per cent of his efforts to Leave Means Leave" . . . Sadly that left 0 per cent for UKIP.' And he called on Farage to honour the pledge made by all UKIP's candidates before the 2014 Euro election to resign from the European Parliament if they ever left the party. 'It would be a sad end to his political career if he joined the ranks of those dishonourable MEPs who left UKIP but kept their seats.'[12] Farage ignored him, of course.

Catherine Blaiklock resigned her UKIP membership the following day. For the next six weeks, she worked tirelessly behind the scenes turning her registered company name into a viable political party. On 10 December, Blaiklock had paid a £150 fee and submitted an application officially to register The Brexit Party (definite article included) with the Electoral Commission, and a month later submitted a draft version of her proposed constitution. She had consulted Farage occasionally, and his press man Dan Jukes, but also had several conversations with Andrew Reid, the lawyer who had been UKIP's landlord in Mayfair for several years, and acted as a behind-the-scenes adviser to Farage.

Before Christmas, Blaiklock had sought advice from Farage, Richard Tice and Chris Bruni-Lowe on who could help with technical and media matters – a website, data protection, bank accounts and public relations. Blaiklock says Farage recommended a firm based in Brussels called Growl, run by his old friend Alex Phillips and her business partner Will Steele, which had also worked successfully for Leave Means Leave. Blaiklock met Phillips in the hotel at St Pancras station and together they drew up a proposal which would cost £6,500 a year. 'I was happy to use her,' says Blaiklock, 'as I was convinced she could do a good job.'[13]

For its first few weeks, Catherine Blaiklock was leader of the Brexit Party, though she knew it was only a temporary role. 'Nigel and I had a gentleman's agreement,' she says, 'that once we got going, he would become leader.' But none of this was public, beyond speculation and rumours. The main purpose was to create a vehicle for Farage and his allies, in the event that the government failed to meet the Brexit deadline of 29 March 2019, which might mean that Britain had to hold another set of elections to the European Parliament in May. In that case, Blaiklock says, Farage had promised that she would be a Brexit Party candidate 'near the top of the list'.[14]

Then, on 20 January 2019, Nigel Farage suddenly announced publicly that the Brexit Party had been created, and that he supported it. He did so not under the TV lights of a dramatic press conference or colourful launch event, but through an interview with David Wooding of the *Sun on Sunday*. 'This was Catherine's idea entirely,' Farage told Wooding, 'but she has done this with my full knowledge and my full support.' But it was only a provisional move, he said, and might not be necessary. Farage promised only to 're-enter the fray' of politics if the government failed to achieve Brexit by the stated deadline of 29 March 2019:

There would be a huge public backlash and without doubt the people will flock to a real pro-Brexit party in droves. Our first task would be to fight the European elections on May 23 . . . I've been campaigning to leave the EU for a quarter of a century. I believe in it with all my heart and soul and gave up the best part of my adult life for it. The Eurocrats are laughing their socks off at how they have 'screwed the Brits'. If we do not get a proper Brexit, I will be forced to do something again.[15]

Typical of Farage, the woman who'd actually set the party up was kept in the dark about his announcement until the *Sun on Sunday* presses were rolling that night. 'I got a call from Nigel at 10.30,' Blaiklock recalls. 'It was roughly: "You're gonna be in the paper tomorrow." He wasn't asking me. He was telling me.'[16]

Farage's scoop delivered to the *Sun on Sunday* was dangerously premature. The Brexit Party hadn't yet been approved by the Electoral Commission; indeed, it still barely existed beyond a company name, Catherine Blaiklock, and some dealings with Alex Phillips and her firm.

For the previous six weeks, Blaiklock had been dealing with the Electoral Commission, with emails back and forth which saw her draft constitution go through several versions. The document set out all the traditional aspects of a political party – membership, the leader, a party board, branches, annual meetings and so on – and was very similar to the structure of UKIP, which the Commission raised as a possible problem. Blaiklock was worried that if the Commission didn't approve the Brexit Party quickly then Nigel Farage might have to find another vehicle if the European elections took place in May. 'Nigel might end up going with somebody else,' Blaiklock wrote to Alex Phillips on the morning of Friday 5 February. Farage's most likely alternative, Blaiklock felt, was the Libertarian Party to which UKIP MEP Bill Etheridge had defected a few months before. Etheridge had then publicly urged Farage to lead a new party. Farage even seemed to consider a link-up with his protégé Henry Bolton who, having been ousted as UKIP leader, had formed a new Eurosceptic party called Our Nation. Blaiklock warned Phillips that she had 'total radio silence right now from the EC [Electoral Commission]' and that approval was not likely to happen until around the start of March.[17]

Then out of the blue, that afternoon, the Electoral Commission publicly announced their approval, several weeks earlier than expected. Blaiklock and her party weren't ready. 'It was just chaos, madness,' she says. 'I hadn't got anything set up. Dan Jukes was on the phone. Nigel was on the phone. I'd got an email saying we'd been approved, and Dan Jukes said, "Shit, we've got no website."'

Catherine Blaiklock quickly went online to try to set one up. Some unknown person, having no doubt heard the earlier announcement, had already bought BrexitParty.com, presumably out of mischief. Catherine Blaiklock consulted a domain website. 'And as I was online,' she says, 'BrexitParty.co.uk disappeared before my eyes.' Somebody had bought that, too. 'But I managed to grab BrexitParty.org. But then we had people grabbing all the Twitter handles and so on.'

The chaos lasted weeks. The website was channelling tens of thousands of applications for membership to Blaiklock's personal computer. Nigel Farage claimed 35,000 people signed up within forty-eight hours of the launch. The trouble was that these included 'Willie Stroker', 'Dr Wax E Lemon' and 'General Ian Bong McFuckbiscuits'.

What's more, because the new party didn't yet have an official bank account, it had to take people's donations by PayPal, which was soon a cause of great mischief to its enemies. If people donated just one penny, and then asked for their money back, the party had to pay a penalty to Paypal of ten pence, and it took up a huge amount of time. And for weeks the party failed to acknowledge people when they pledged money and support. Blaiklock says she ended up with 100,000 emails from PayPal. And at a personal level, hostile people were now bombarding the TripAdvisor site for her Norfolk guest house with fake and nasty reviews.

In exasperation at Farage and Tice's failure to make decisions, Blaiklock went to a website expert called Fox Tucker who worked above a barber's shop in Norwich. 'I had to go to my local IT guy to help run a political party,' she says, 'a man who usually runs local daycare websites.'[18] Tucker told Blaiklock that the existing arrangements were 'absolutely outrageous'. 'Fox was just overwhelmed. He nearly had a nervous breakdown. He said it needed to be data cleaned.' Another source recalls that the database was so flawed that it allowed someone to submit the entire ebook of *The Lord of the Rings* as an email address. Tucker arranged a data protection audit, which produced 'the most damning report' on the party. In their disorganisation and haste, Blaiklock and her colleagues had overlooked the need to register with the Information Commissioner's Office.[19] And yet the new party was bound to be subject to very close scrutiny by opponents.

Then Nigel Farage brought another problem. He didn't want the Brexit Party to have members. He wanted to copy what the right-wing populist Geert Wilders did in the Netherlands. His Freedom Party has no mass membership: its sole member is Wilders himself. Instead, Farage suggested, the Brexit Party should merely have 'registered supporters' who would have no democratic say in the party organisation. That, of course, was also the model used by Sir James Goldsmith for his Referendum Party in the mid-1990s.

Only six days after the Electoral Commission had approved them as a party with a membership, Blaiklock wrote back to the Commission to announce:

> We would like to amend the constitution so that we do not have members. This is to stop the EDF [EDL, presumably] and BNP members who are banned by our party. We would like to have supporters only . . . There is an issue with someone who is claiming, we believe, attempting to impersonate The Brexit Party and maybe collect money. There are five Twitter accounts, none of which we control. More seriously there is a website. I will provide more details tomorrow. We know the name of the person who has at least two names and we believe a criminal record.[20]

In the event the constitution remained unamended, though the Brexit Party never had any members, only registered supporters.

Three months later, Farage would talk of a new type of politics in which his party would 'directly liaise and have votes among our registered supporters to shape policy and shape our future direction', along the lines of the Five Star Movement in Italy. 'We will produce policy on the basis of what our supporters think ... This is going to be the most open political party you've ever seen in Britain.'[21]

That never happened. It became the leader's personal fiefdom, with no possibility of grassroots dissent. Nor did the party board set out in its constitution ever meet. So the two normal democratic mechanisms of modern British parties – to elect a new leader through a membership ballot; and a vote of no confidence to depose him or her – couldn't ever occur. More complicated still, its constitution was only meant to come into force through a ballot of the membership, which never existed, of course.

The infant Brexit Party also faced an even bigger problem: Catherine Blaiklock's history. As soon as plans for the new party went public in January, journalists began digging, and so did the anti-racist Hope Not Hate organisation. Blaiklock had made numerous controversial statements on social media in the not so distant past. Just two days after the *Sun on Sunday* article, the *Guardian* uncovered an article, by then deleted from her personal blog, in which Blaiklock suggested that poor academic achievement by Black men may have a racial basis: 'What is good for winning 100m races might not be great for passing A-level maths exams.'[22]

And in a posting which was still online, Catherine Blaiklock also expressed anxiety about meeting a Muslim woman who was wearing a full veil, and her concerns about Muslim immigration.[23] In another article, in the *Salisbury Review* in 2018, Blaiklock had said: 'I cannot talk or have a normal interaction with anyone in a burqa.'[24] In mid-February, BuzzFeed quoted a Blaiklock tweet from Christmas Day, only seven weeks before, when forty migrants were rescued from the English Channel. '40 people all from Islamic countries,' Blaiklock tweeted. 'When will 40 become 400, become 4000, become 40,000, become 4m, become 40m?'[25]

Catherine Blaiklock says that initially Nigel Farage raised no objection to these revelations. It was ironic, however, that he had just left UKIP over Gerard Batten's anti-Muslim position, only to join a party whose leader seemed to hold similar views. Blaiklock defended herself by saying: 'I have been happily married to a Jamaican man for six years, so anyone implying I am racist is revealing more about themselves than me.'[26] And her previous husband, she pointed out, had been Nepalese.

Worse was to come a few weeks later. The *Guardian* now revealed research by Hope Not Hate showing Blaiklock had posted several messages hostile to Islam on a personal Twitter account which had been deleted a few months before. 'Islam = submission – mostly to raping men it seems', read one tweet. Another said of Islam that it is 'perfectly rational to be phobic about people who want to kill you'. A third said: 'I want my country back. I want seaside donkeys on the beach and little village churches, not acid attacks, mobs and mosques.'[27]

As soon as Farage was approached by the *Guardian* about these latest revelations, both he and Gawain Towler (recruited to help the new party) rang Blaiklock and bluntly told her she had to resign at once and agree a public statement which they had drafted. 'You've got to resign; you've got to resign; sign it,' she recalls Towler saying.[28] Her remarks had been 'out-of-character' and 'unacceptable in tone and content', the statement said. 'After speaking to Nigel Farage, I realise that my comments fall well short of what is expected in any walk of life. I have accordingly tendered my resignation as party leader.'[29]

The situation had left Farage in a very difficult position, as one of his public reasons for leaving UKIP had been Gerard Batten's growing relations with Tommy Robinson. Yet Blaiklock had herself retweeted seven messages from Tommy Robinson, and forty-five tweets from a notorious and racist former BNP activist, Mark Collett, including one tweet from 2018 showing a picture of a multiracial school with the caption: 'This is a British school. This is white genocide.'[30] Once more, Farage had shown poor judgement of character. He failed to get his advisers to carry out simple background checks.

The plan had always been that Blaiklock would hand over to

Farage, but the sudden way it happened caused huge problems. Blaiklock was understandably aggrieved. She had founded the party and registered it. It was her work that had produced the constitution; she negotiated approval from the Electoral Commission; and she claims to have worked with a graphic designer to produce the distinctive logo with the words 'THE BREXIT PARTY' inside a rightwards pointing arrow within a circle, which subsequently became famous. Blaiklock had hoped to be a Brexit Party candidate in the May Euro elections, if they happened. Now, that just wasn't possible, Farage insisted.

Blaiklock still had her hand on several levers within the embryo structure. She was the sole director and company secretary of The Brexit Party Ltd; and one of the two trustees who held the only share that company had issued. Blaiklock was also the sole signature on the party's three bank accounts, and still registered with PayPal, and was the owner of the domain name. If not handled carefully, Catherine Blaiklock could bring the whole venture crashing down before it was half built, and it would probably be far too late for Farage to set up another party to fight the European elections.

Blaiklock was determined to hang onto at least some of her baby. But the party's leading figures – Farage, Andrew Reid and Richard Tice – knew they would be seriously handicapped so long as Blaiklock retained such responsibilities. Without consulting Blaiklock, and three weeks after her resignation as leader, Companies House were told on 11 April that on 28 and 29 March she had ceased to be company secretary and had been replaced by an accountant, Phillip Basey. In addition, Nigel Farage and Mick McGough were appointed as company directors. Also on 11 April Basey tried to set up 'an urgent meeting' with Blaiklock in Norwich, but she declined to attend as she was travelling to Wales. Several times that day Andrew Reid tried to phone Blaiklock, then texted her at 9.50 that evening.

The reason why it was so urgent became obvious, as the Brexit Party was formally launched the next day with great fanfare at a family engineering firm next to the M6 in Coventry. 'I do believe that we can win these European elections and that we can again start to put the fear of God into our members of Parliament in Westminster,' Farage warned. But the party wasn't just about Brexit: 'Our task and our mission is to change politics for good, to change all aspects of politics in this country.'[31] He was joined by some of his prospective candidates for the Euro elections, including Annunziata Rees-Mogg, sister of the arch-Brexiteer Conservative MP Jacob Rees-Mogg (their father, the former *Times* editor William Rees-Mogg had encouraged Farage in his early UKIP days). Outside on the street, a group of Remainers had set up a camping table to try to persuade people attending the launch that they were misguided. The new party's opponents were there, but not its founder.

Blaiklock says she was 'completely unaware' of the Coventry event 'since no one had the common courtesy to inform me'. She only found out from the press that Richard Tice had now been made chairman.[32]

Blaiklock emailed Farage, McGough and Basey to complain. All the company changes had been made without consulting her as the existing company secretary and sole director, and without the necessary board meetings, while Farage and McGough were not shareholders, so not qualified to be directors. 'I believe that the information at Companies House is incorrect,' Blaiklock wrote. 'This is a serious matter.' The appointments, she warned, 'would appear to be in direct contravention of company law and the company's Articles of Association'.[33] And as a director and trustee she asserted her right to be informed, and to approve of, the large sums of money which the party had spent in recent days.

Meanwhile, the likelihood of European elections in May was fast growing as the deadlock over how Brexit might actually be achieved continued in Whitehall and Westminster, and in Brussels and other European capitals. In late November 2018, Theresa May and EU leaders had finally reached a Withdrawal Agreement, but then the deal was three times rejected by the Commons – by 432 votes to 202 in January 2019 (when 118 Tories rebelled); by 391 to 242 in mid-March (75 Conservative rebels), and on what was meant to be the leaving day, 29 March, by 344 to 286 (with thirty-four rebels). In December, Theresa May had only just survived a 'no confidence' vote in her leadership by the parliamentary party. On 11 April 2019, the day before the Brexit Party was officially launched, EU leaders extended the deadline to 31 October. That meant the UK would almost certainly have to hold elections to the European Parliament on 23 May, unless the government could in the meantime get the Withdrawal Agreement through Parliament, which looked exceedingly unlikely.

For the Brexit Party the timetable was extremely tight, since candidate nominations closed by 25 April. Farage rang Blaiklock to ask what she wanted. 'I said: "I want to be involved,"' she recalls. 'Nigel said: "Yes, yes, yes" which proved to be a nonsense.'[34] Farage then wrote to Blaiklock, both to soothe her anger, and to deliver a stiff warning. 'I will be eternally grateful to you,' he wrote (though his letter had clearly been drafted by someone else, most likely Andrew Reid):

> and I do understand your feelings of rejection, even alienation, from the people at the centre of the Brexit Party. The truth of it is that your social media messages are so serious that they would sink our campaign, and everyone is scared of that. There is no conspiracy against you, these are the things that you said and have to take responsibility for.[35]

Farage made no attempt to explain or justify the apparently irregular changes in the company, and in the meantime Blaiklock hadn't been the only one forced to stand down. A fortnight after her fall, the *Guardian* uncovered several past Facebook comments by Farage's friend Mick McGough, who had been appointed Brexit Party treasurer. McGough had said that the Miliband brothers – who are Jewish – have 'shallow UK roots', and that Peter Mandelson – whose father was Jewish – was 'devoid of UK roots'. One of McGough's Facebook posts referred to 'someone from a bingo bongo land'.[36]

Just four days before nominations were due to close for the European elections, Farage warned Blaiklock that her name, and Mick McGough's, would be used to 'taint' the party in the media:

> Do you really want the weight of opprobrium put upon you, and

to have the press camped outside your door? This is what will happen, and it will be highly unpleasant for you and damaging for the Euro Election campaign.

This situation is doing us huge financial damage. Metro Bank will give us an immediate credit card facility but not while you are a director . . . I should be signing people up en masse but I can't: we are stuck with Paypal with its high fees and so far we have lost between £30,000–£40,000 in unnecessary costs, let alone the lost income opportunities from people who refuse to use Paypal.[37]

Farage said he understood that Blaiklock was keen to stand for election again, 'but this will take time', he said, and 'profuse apologies' from her before she could stand for the party in a general election:

but if you obstruct us from moving forwards now, that would never happen, as there would be so much anger against you from within the party . . . my view is that you and Mick [McGough] can no longer be directors.

If we can sort this out before the problem comes into the public domain and you follow Mick's example and resign, then I can give you my assurance that you can take on [Conservative MP] Brandon Lewis in Great Yarmouth and you will probably win.

I'm sorry for all of this, but the situation is urgent. Do not allow history to portray you as an obstruction to political change – it is that serious. [38]

Note how Farage seemed to offer an election opportunity to someone who had made clear racist statements, something which he purported to oppose. Blaiklock felt she had no option but to accede to Farage's demands, and she resigned as a director of The Brexit Party Limited. Lance Forman, a businessman she'd introduced to the party, advised her 'to do the honourable thing, just sign them over', she says:

So I did. And yet just before the European elections I could have said I'm going to shut it all down, and Nigel would have had to go elsewhere. I could have clicked a button and taken down the website. I could have gone to a newspaper at that point and said: 'Do you want to look at this?' There was data flying round everywhere. It was just madness. I could have handed back every donation – one million pounds of it. I could have changed history.[39]

When the first opinion polls for the European elections put the Brexit Party and UKIP neck-and-neck, Catherine Blaiklock raised the possibility that Farage and the UKIP leader Gerard Batten should make a pact. Batten was understandably worried by the advent of a rival pro-Brexit party formed by his old adversary. 'Gerard phoned me,' says Blaiklock. 'He was all over me, and he said: "I'll make you an MEP candidate if you stuff Nigel." I said, "I'm not doing that."'[40]

Looking back on that rush of events in late 2018 and the early months of 2019, Catherine Blaiklock isn't totally negative about Farage. He did have 'one positive characteristic – this unbelievable energy, which goes on and on and on,' she says. 'He's personable. He's charming. He's fun.' But she subsequently felt she had made the wrong decision to back down. 'I could see no other way. I made a mistake. I got worn down by it. It was Nigel when he was at his most ferocious. I'd never do that again. I would never do it in finance or business. I'd never be cajoled like that. I trusted them.' She still likes Farage, 'even though he shat on me from a great height. He takes advantages and opportunities. He's an amiable person, and I don't think he's an evil person. He's a political operator and I was naive in a den of sharks.'[41]

Politically, despite the debt he owed Catherine Blaiklock, Nigel Farage had no option but to forget any sentiment, be ruthless, and exclude her totally from his campaign. She had posted numerous messages on social media which most people would regard as racist. And this would have been especially damaging to the Brexit Party at a time when it was trying to avoid any suggestion that it was a racist party. That new, inclusive image was strongly reflected in the Brexit Party's work over the previous few weeks to find seventy candidates to fill its lists in the eleven electoral areas of Great Britain for the

European elections. The selection process was conducted rapidly by Toby Vintcent, a former Conservative who in 1999 had worked on Jeffrey Archer's disastrous campaign to become Mayor of London, and Lesley Katon, a TV director who had made documentaries and light entertainment programmes such as *The Weakest Link*, but ultimately, says Richard Tice, 'it was Nigel and my decision who stood where and in what order'.[42] The aim, in contrast to the past UKIP lists of MEPs, was to achieve as much diversity as possible, not just socially but politically. So they chose, for instance, the broadcaster Claire Fox, who'd been active in the Revolutionary Communist Party with Lesley Katon. She was placed top of the Brexit Party list for the North West, despite having voiced support for IRA terrorism in the past. Other candidates included John Longworth and Richard Tice from Leave Means Leave; Lance Forman, a salmon trader; and Christina Jordan, a Malaysian-born nurse.

The party put considerable effort into recruiting big names. Others made the approach to Farage. The former Conservative minister Ann Widdecombe, once a darling of the Tory conference, was on a Christian cruise round Scotland and Norway when, after fifty-five years with the Conservatives, she 'crossed a Rubicon', she says. So she got Farage's number from a journalist, and phoned him from the side of a Norwegian fjord. When Farage answered himself, he seemed to be surprised, Widdecombe recalls, as she announced her name and said she wanted to join his party. 'There was a slight pause, but then he got very enthusiastic. He asked if I wanted to stand in the European elections.' Widdecombe agreed. So when the cruise reached Poole in Dorset, Lesley Katon had come down to meet her at the quayside. 'That was where I signed the nomination forms. I docked, I think, forty-eight hours before they had to go in, or maybe twenty-four hours.' Next day, she went to see Farage at his Westminster office, and when he asked if she wanted a serious seat, or to be just one of the 'runners and riders', Widdecombe indicated that she wanted to win and wanted to get the referendum result implemented.[43]

Even though thirteen of UKIP's MEPs had followed Farage into the Brexit Party over the previous few months, only two of

them, apart from Farage, were picked to stand for the new party –
Jonathan Bullock from the East Midlands, and Farage's old ally from
Wales, Nathan Gill. UKIP MEP Mike Hookem recalls how earlier in
the year Farage and his aides had rung round the delegation saying,
'UKIP's finished, join the Brexit Party. You'll be guaranteed a seat
as a candidate.' And most UKIP MEPs gradually switched over,
only to find themselves discarded when it came to Brexit Party
selection. 'They'd been conned,' Hookem says. Some, he recalls,
such as David Coburn from Scotland, and Julia Reid in the South
West, were very upset.[44]

A few weeks before, Farage had confided in a Conservative
MEP, 'This lot don't know it yet. They're not gonna be in the next
Parliament.' One of the two survivors, Jonathan Bullock, recalls
Farage saying the other UKIP MEPs had had 'their five years', a 'fair
innings', and 'We can't all look like we're ex-UKIP.'[45] The new party
wanted a 'clean break', says Richard Tice. 'We had to be different
and be *seen* to be different.'[46] It was ruthless, but probably necessary.

Not excluded, however, was an interesting choice for the Brexit
Party list in the South East. Farage, of course, was placed top in
the region – his position for UKIP in the four previous European
elections. I received an excited call from the former UKIP communications boss, Paul 'Gobby' Lambert, pointing out that second on
the regional list – so likely to get elected – was Alex Phillips, who'd
helped set up the Brexit Party. No other journalist seemed to notice.
After Phillips's troubles with UKIP and in Wales, it would be some
consolation for her.

Nor did the Brexit Party have any connection with Arron Banks,
or receive any money from him. 'The whole point of the Brexit
Party,' says one of Farage's closest aides, 'was to broaden the appeal.
It would have queered a very important pitch. There had to be a
cooling of the ardour, as it would not be helpful. We didn't ask him
for a single bean. He got that as much as we did.' 'We wouldn't
let him get involved in the Brexit Party in any way,' says Richard
Tice. 'So much noise, and uncontrollable!'[47] Farage's decision had
echoes of the way in which Douglas Carswell tried to exclude Farage
himself from the Leave campaign for the 2016 referendum. Arron

Banks and his operation, Leave.EU – which was still very active in 2019 – 'were seen as being somewhat toxic,' says another adviser. 'We wanted to separate Nigel from the past.'

Much of the Brexit Party's work was a natural extension of what Leave Means Leave (LML) had been doing since the previous summer. In March, LML organised a march from Sunderland to London, culminating in a rally in Parliament Square on what was meant to have been Brexit Day, 29 March. Around fifty people walked the whole route, though Farage walked a few miles on the first day, dressed as if for a pheasant shoot, and a later leg in the East Midlands.

Theresa May now faced a huge threat. Until 29 March, the Conservative poll rating was around 35–36 per cent, which wasn't bad for a government party, but almost immediately after the Brexit deadline was missed – and before the Brexit Party officially got going – Tory ratings rapidly fell below 30 per cent, and stayed there. The Brexit Party sensed a new anger among Brexit supporters and developed their campaign along the lines of 'They screwed you over' (though that was never an official slogan). 'The level of anger was off the scale,' says Steven Edginton, a brilliant 19-year-old video producer who was brought across from Leave Means Leave.

> They felt betrayed by the political class. There were people who'd never voted, who then voted for Brexit, and were left saying, 'What's the point of voting?' 'Yes, you've been betrayed and humiliated,' was our message. 'This political class is useless, but there are people out there who can help.' We knew most Tories were on our side, and we had to get them thinking, 'Yes, it is acceptable to vote for Nigel.'[48]

The Brexit Party's outward election campaign consisted largely of major rallies, organised by the same events team used by Leave Means Leave, and run on similar lines. Farage, Tice and Ann Widdecombe were often the main speakers. The party's initial slogan, 'Fighting Back', polled badly, so they switched to 'Change Politics for Good', 'and that worked superbly; it really did get people excited', says Richard Tice.[49]

'Nigel had seen this electioneering done in the United States,' says David Bull, a doctor and TV presenter who was a leading candidate. 'He thought politics could have more razzmatazz. And blimey, it worked.'[50] One of the things that Farage claimed to have learned in America was that 'politics needs to be a bit less drab, a bit less dull. It needs to be lively, fun, full of energy, and that's what we're trying to do.'[51] When Ann Widdecombe spoke at the working men's club in the old mining town of Featherstone in Yorkshire, a heckler was applauded for shouting out, 'Ann for prime minister!' When Farage addressed 3,000 people at Olympia in London, they chanted 'Nigel, Nigel, Nigel.' 'Do you know what? I was loving it,' Farage admitted.[52] He was far from pleased in Newcastle, though, when a man threw a milkshake over his suit. Farage publicly blamed his security team for not spotting him, though his fury was understandable given the death threats he often received. Very unpleasantly, the comedian Jo Brand said it should have been battery acid, not a milkshake.

The rallies would be live-streamed on social media, and Steven Edginton, who'd run his own YouTube channel while still at school, was asked to produce two or three short video films each day. 'We hired a team of people who made videos for rap artists. Our goal was to make Brexit cool again,' Edginton says.[53] Farage signed off the slogans, and had a good instinct on what visuals would work, but left the technical details to others.

The Euro result was extraordinary, and way beyond anything UKIP had ever achieved. The Brexit Party won 5,248,533 votes (30.5 per cent) – almost 2 million more than the Liberal Democrats in second place, and three and a half times as many as the Conservatives who got only 8.8 per cent, well behind even the Greens. It was easily the worst vote by a main government party in the history of British elections. The Brexit Party took 29 seats; the Lib Dems 16; Labour 10; the Greens 7, and the Conservatives were left with just four MEPs.

At the South East count, held in Southampton, Farage was elected first, ahead of a Liberal Democrat, while Alex Phillips came third, elected to public office at last, if only for a few months. As the winners stood on the platform, the TV footage shows how her eyes never left Farage, as he delivered his acceptance speech. 'If we don't leave on October the 31st,' Farage warned the Conservatives and Labour, 'then the scores you've seen for the Brexit Party today will be repeated in a general election, and we are getting ready for it.'[54]

It was a spectacular moment of triumph and of history for a politician who had never even been elected as an MP, let alone been a government minister. He had done something never achieved before in Britain: he had now won two national elections for two different parties. And his Brexit Party, committed to leaving the institution at the earliest possible moment, now found itself as the biggest single party in the European Parliament. Yet the party hadn't even existed a few weeks before; indeed, it had very nearly failed to get off the ground.

The Brexit Party had clearly stolen a huge chunk of the Conservative vote. It didn't take much effort to find Tory officials and MPs who quietly admitted they'd voted for Farage's new party, in the hope that it would force Theresa May from office and bring about a harder Brexit deal, or possibly No Deal. There were almost certainly government ministers, including some in the Cabinet, who voted for the Brexit Party, too. And it would be interesting to know how Boris Johnson voted.

Donald Trump delivered his congratulations from Washington, though he ended up praising both Brexit leaders. 'Nigel Farage is a friend of mine; Boris is a friend of mine. They're two very good guys, very interesting people. Nigel's had a big victory. He's picked up 32 per cent [sic] of the vote – starting from nothing, and I think they're big powers over there. I think they've done a good job.'[55]

The nature and strength of the Brexit Party's extraordinary achievement meant that the Conservatives only really had one choice.

Nigel Farage had brought down a prime minister, and was now effectively the kingmaker. He had delivered 10 Downing Street to a man who in so many ways was rather like himself.

26

NIGEL VERSUS BORIS

It was one of the most poignant moments in modern politics. The day after polling in the European elections, but two days before the results were announced, Theresa May, clad in a striking red dress, stepped out of 10 Downing Street and stood at the lectern. She announced that in two weeks' time she would step down as Conservative leader and prime minister. 'I do so with no ill-will,' she concluded, holding back the tears, 'but with enormous and enduring gratitude to have had the opportunity to serve the country I love.'[1]

Theresa May fell primarily because Conservative MPs rejected her Brexit withdrawal deal in huge numbers. However, it had been the threat from Nigel Farage and his new party which delivered the *coup de grâce* and drove her from power.

He looked like the most powerful man in British politics. Now, after the European triumph, Farage had to keep up the momentum and maintain the pressure on the Conservatives. The problem that had always dogged UKIP was translating success in European elections into gains at the ballot box in subsequent Westminster contests. In 1999, 2004, 2009 and even 2014, that had always led to disappointment. An opportunity to show that the Brexit Party could buck that trend had already presented itself. A by-election was due to take place in Peterborough just a fortnight after the European poll, caused by new procedure. A public recall petition had been triggered by the imprisonment of the sitting Labour MP, Fiona Onasanya, for lying to the police to avoid a speeding ticket, and the petition received enough signatures to force a by-election.

On the face of it, Peterborough should have been an attractive proposition. The city voted almost two to one for Leave in the 2016 referendum, and Farage's party got almost 40 per cent of the vote there in the European election. A railway community which had experienced high immigration from eastern Europe, the constituency had long been a highly competitive marginal between Labour and the Conservatives. This time, the Brexit Party might slip through the middle.

And the party picked what looked like a good candidate, a local businessman, Mike Greene, who'd been a Tory donor in the past. But Greene was new to politics, and at the press conference to announce him, Nigel Farage admitted that they started with a 'couple of disadvantages'. Labour, knowing how things were going with Fiona Onasanya, had effectively been campaigning in Peterborough for months, while the Brexit Party had only been launched four weeks before, 'so we haven't exactly got much data on voters within Peterborough,' Farage said. 'We start with nothing in terms of electoral resource.' Farage wouldn't forecast victory. 'We're gonna give it our best shot, and that's the best I can say at this stage.'[2]

The trouble was that until the final fortnight of the Peterborough contest, Farage and Brexit Party colleagues had been concentrating on achieving the best possible result in the European polls. They were simply not prepared for the rigours and detailed on-the-ground organisation of a constituency battle. An army of keen volunteers turned up in Peterborough every day from all over the country, but most of them had no clue how to fight an election street by street. A senior figure in the Brexit team recalls how some canvassers might spend fifteen minutes on one doorstep. 'It was that basic. Enthusiastic people who believed in Brexit and would spend half a day trying to convert one person . . . Half the tally sheets came back with people having not ticked if the person was going to vote, how they were going to vote, whatever.' So while the party was spending huge sums on professional independent polling in Peterborough, 'what we weren't seeing was an on-the-ground, door-by-door, understanding of what was going on'.

And the Brexit Party was up against two experienced

rivals – Labour and the Conservatives – who had been contesting Peterborough as a tight marginal for decades, and had lots of information on individual voters.

Farage's party was also handicapped in another respect. It was only five months since the senior Conservative official, Marion Little, had been convicted of spending fraud in seeing off Nigel Farage's attempt to win South Thanet in 2015, which meant they had to be especially cautious. 'So we spent only three quarters what we could have done, since whoever's name is on the spending declaration might be in the firing line,' says one party source.

The Electoral Commission's investigations into the EU referendum had left staff in 'absolute terror of over-spending or being seen to overspend', says Steven Edginton.[3] People were especially on edge because the Electoral Commission had visited the Brexit Party headquarters in London at the end of May after the former prime minister Gordon Brown publicly expressed concerns that the party was raising large sums from overseas through PayPal, which was potentially illegal. Nigel Farage 'is not going to be remembered, as he wants, as the man of the people,' Brown joked. 'He's going to be remembered as the man of the PayPal, because that is where the money is coming from.'[4]

In the end, Peterborough was extremely tight, and Mike Greene finished just 683 votes behind Labour. Like Heywood and Middleton in 2014, where the margin was very similar, it was a great missed opportunity. Once it was clear by early to mid-May that the Brexit Party would easily win the European contest, they might have been wise to put more effort and organisation into Peterborough. Although it was still a formidable result for Farage's new party, and he declared 'the old certainties of two-party politics are now broken', it diluted the impact of the incredible European result.[5] Nigel Farage no longer looked quite so formidable.

If the Brexit Party couldn't win a promising Westminster seat while still flush with success from the Euros, it would probably never do so. Nonetheless, the next day Farage did a stunt in Downing Street where he delivered a letter to Theresa May, arguing that the Peterborough result justified giving him a role in the Brexit

negotiations. 'The electorate have asked for us to come into the negotiating team and we are ready to do so immediately', his letter said.[6]

The persistent weaknesses of Farage's parties in fighting
Westminster seats were underlined again two months later in the
Brecon and Radnorshire by-election in central Wales, when the
party came a poor third with barely 10 per cent of the vote. Farage
didn't even bother to visit Brecon, and symbolically, four days
before polling day, his party's light-blue campaign bus was found
abandoned, blocking a lay-by and crashed into a hedge.

Nine days before polling in Brecon – to no one's surprise –
Conservative Party members had elected Boris Johnson as their new
leader, after he beat his biggest rival Jeremy Hunt by almost two to
one. Farage must have had mixed feelings about the result. On the one
hand, Johnson was a Conservative for whom he had often expressed
admiration in times gone by (along with Michael Gove), and was also
the most likely contender to force through the kind of hard Brexit
which Farage wanted. And yet in style, Johnson was likely even more
than before to overshadow Farage's public guise as the populist,
cheeky-chappy, celebrity showman and master communicator of
British politics. Like Farage, Johnson knew how to make politics fun.

Conservative members had voted for Johnson as the man to 'get
Brexit done', but also as the 'Stop Farage' candidate for the next general election. The Conservative backbencher Sir Desmond Swayne
says that earlier in the year he'd quietly been 'touching people' for
Michael Gove in anticipation of another leadership ballot, but with
the European elections everything changed. 'The result was so
devastating that it was no longer a question of "Who can win?" as
"Who can beat Farage?" So I had to switch to Boris, and I went to
Gove and told him. He was quite good about it really.'[7]

'The moment Boris was elected our support started to slip away,'
says the then Brexit Party chairman Richard Tice. He and Farage
assumed Johnson would want to call an election as soon as he could,
to restore the Conservative majority at Westminster and get enough
MPs to push any withdrawal deal through Parliament. 'Our strategy
was based on a September or October election.'[8]

With Johnson's election, many people started wondering whether the Conservatives had shot Nigel Farage's fox. Was there much point to the Brexit Party any more? But Farage and Tice felt they had to keep up the pressure on Johnson over Brexit, and expressed confidence that in an election they would win seats in a way UKIP had never managed to do. Farage had been in Washington DC when the Tory leadership result was announced, at a conference for the right-wing organisation Turning Point USA. Donald Trump was present, too.

'A really good man is going to be the prime minister of the UK now, Boris Johnson,' the president said. 'He's tough, and he's smart. They're saying "Britain Trump" [sic].'

Then Trump looked up to try and spot Farage in the crowd. 'Where is he? Nigel Farage. He's here some place. I saw him . . . I'll tell you what: he got 32 per cent [sic] of the vote from nowhere, over in UK . . . And I know he's going to work well with Boris. They're going to do some tremendous things.'[9]

The next day, Farage was less optimistic, but challenged Johnson to call an election and do a deal with his party.

> If Boris was genuine about this, if Boris said, 'Right, we are going to leave on 31 October, the only way this can be done is to change the arithmetic in the House of Commons by fighting a general election, and Nigel, your party has got a much better chance of winning – for argument's sake – a seat like Pontefract than we've got.' So, you know, there is a possibility that an electoral pact could be forged. But we would need to believe them. And at the moment that's not very easy.[10]

But things were already stirring behind the scenes. A few weeks earlier, Arron Banks had helped arrange a secret meeting for Farage with the former Cabinet minister – and future home secretary – Priti Patel at Banks's Mayfair club, 5 Hertford Street, along with the Democratic Unionist MP Ian Paisley Jr. The group discussed the possibility of an electoral pact in the event of Johnson becoming Conservative leader. It was the first of many attempts over the next six months, involving numerous players, to forge an electoral alliance between the two fully fledged Brexit parties.

Richard Tice says he and Farage initially worked on the assumption 'that Labour and the Liberal Democrats would form a Remain alliance over the summer, which would then force the Tories to have to come and talk to us. Instead Jo Swinson refused to deal with Corbyn.' And that, Tice claims, 'enabled the Tories to carry on without us.'[11]

Meanwhile, the twenty-nine newly elected Brexit Party MEPs had taken their seats in the European Parliament. In theory, they would be members of the assembly for only a few months, until 31 October or whatever date Britain did finally leave the European Union, so there would not be much time to make an impact. But they still discussed the issue of whether to join an international grouping. In the past, with UKIP, Nigel Farage had negotiated such alliances pretty much on his own at the start of each Parliament, and presented it to his group as a *fait accompli*. Farage knew he had to handle his new Brexit Party colleagues much more carefully. Many, like John Longworth, Ann Widdecombe and Claire Fox, were formidable figures with substantial careers behind them, and couldn't simply be bounced into a grouping with controversial right-wingers with racist and unsavoury pasts.

One option presented by Farage was to join the new Identity and Democracy group, which would include Marine Le Pen's renamed Rassemblement National – National Rally (formerly the National Front), and the German far-right Alternative für Deutschland (AfD). The Brexit Party leader explained how joining a group would give them extra speaking time, staff and funding; it would also give Farage his old place on the front ring of the assembly, as well as the right to attend top-level meetings which he'd enjoyed for many years now – a seat at the top table.

According to Lance Forman, who is Jewish, Farage went round the horseshoe of his MEPs at a meeting in Westminster. Should they join the Identity and Democracy group?

> I said, 'Absolutely not', and that there was not a hope in hell that I could sit round the table with those people. I said I'd have to resign. We had quite a heated argument at that point. Other

people mostly agreed with Nigel, and they said: 'It doesn't mean we agree with Le Pen and the AfD.' I said we didn't really need speaking time any more. 'What do we need funding for? We're gonna be out in September.'

Farage explained that he'd got Le Pen to agree that if there was any anti-Semitism among the French party's MEPs, the culprits would be expelled from the group.

It was never likely that someone like Louis Stedman-Bryce, who is Black and gay, would vote for such a move, or Christina Jordan who is of Malaysian origin. The whole point of the Brexit Party, Lance Forman argued, was not to be another UKIP. They were different, he argued, and probably the most ethnically diverse party in the entire new Parliament. Joining with Le Pen and the AfD would undo all their great work, he further argued. 'That was the first time where there were serious differences between us.'[12]

No vote was taken, but the mood was clearly against Farage, Widdecombe relates. 'I think Nigel had the feeling of where everybody was. And he thought about it and said, "Right, we'll go *non-inscrit* [non-attached]". Which I think militated against all his instincts.' She felt Farage wanted to be down at the heart of the chamber 'giving them hell' as a group leader, as he'd long done in his UKIP days. 'But we did quite well giving them hell from the back.'[13]

Farage was exasperated by the decision, but the fact that he bowed to the will of his colleagues did reflect internal goodwill and harmony in those early days. Since British MEPs weren't likely to be there long, it wasn't worth fighting about, though Farage made it clear he would want them to join a group if the Brexit deadline was further extended by any significant amount.

The first Strasbourg session was set for 2 July, and with Farage no longer leader of an international grouping, the Brexit Party MEPs mounted a stunt to draw attention to themselves. They sat at the back due to their *non-inscrit* status, and as the EU anthem – Beethoven's Ode to Joy – was played by a band, they stood and turned their backs on the rest of the assembly. Farage had discussed the idea with his MEPs beforehand, though it was something he'd done before, with the UKIP group back in 2014. 'I don't think anybody felt particularly comfortable doing it,' recalls Lance Forman. 'There was a genuine difference between the new MEPs and the former UKIP ones. Annunziata Rees-Mogg was particularly vocal.' Another MEP recalls, though, that 'everyone was too scared to oppose it', and says that Farage had 'bounced' them into it, by tipping off the press in advance, so it was hard to stop it happening.

The new group of Brexit Party MEPs soon built up a camaraderie, aided by holding monthly dinners in Strasbourg in the way the old UKIP contingent had done. Farage 'was great fun', Ann Widdecombe recalls, and 'would lead the company in song. I can remember us doing "Cockles and mussels, alive, alive, oh". He sang quite well – more than I can do. I'm tone deaf.'[14] The MEP David Bull remembers Farage at one dinner 'pretending to play the bagpipes with a small coffee table. It was like a rugby tour. It was boisterous.'[15]

When politics resumed at Westminster in September, Boris Johnson still had to operate within a House of Commons where the Conservatives – thanks to Theresa May's disastrous general election in 2017 – were in a precarious position. The arithmetic was made worse when one Conservative MP defected to the Lib Dems, and twenty-one other centrist Tories had the party whip withdrawn for voting against the government. Labour and the other opposition parties feared that if Johnson couldn't get a deal with Europe, or couldn't get a deal through Parliament – as May had spectacularly failed to do – then Johnson would simply go ahead and leave the EU with a no-deal Brexit on 31 October. That, the opposition argued, would be disastrous for the economy. In early September, the Johnson government was defeated when MPs passed the so-called Benn Act, named after its instigator, the former Labour Cabinet minister Hilary Benn. This stipulated that unless Parliament approved a withdrawal agreement by 19 October – or alternatively voted for a no-deal Brexit – then the prime minister would be obliged to ask the EU to extend the deadline yet again – to 31 January 2020.

Boris Johnson claimed that the Benn Act would weaken his

negotiating hand with the EU, and therefore he had no option, he said, but to call an election. However, Johnson was thwarted in his attempt to override the Fixed-term Parliaments Act, and hold an election on 15 October, when the vote fell short of the two-thirds majority of MPs required under the legislation. The government's second attempt five days later met the same fate.

Nigel Farage kept warning Boris Johnson that their two parties had to do a deal, otherwise the danger was that an election would simply produce another hung parliament which would probably lead to a second referendum, and quite likely a government led by the left-wing Labour leader Jeremy Corbyn.

Progress on a deal suddenly seemed faintly possible at the end of August when Farage attended the wedding of the American conservative commentator Candace Owens in Virginia. He bumped into Jon Moynihan, the flamboyant venture capitalist who had played a role in the Vote Leave group and also given £100,000 to Boris Johnson's leadership campaign. Farage told Moynihan he'd like to talk to some of the so-called 'Spartans', the most diehard Tories from the European Research Group (ERG). Moynihan rang the former Brexit minister Steve Baker, who was about to become ERG chairman, and who feared that Farage's party might endanger seats like his own, in Wycombe. Three days later, just before lunch on 3 September, Farage and Richard Tice turned up at Moynihan's grand home in Chelsea.

Baker greeted Farage and Tice warmly and, swallowing his pride, congratulated them on the Euro elections. But then the Brexit Party leaders overplayed their hand. A pact might get them twenty seats, they claimed, but Moynihan warned they might get none. And Farage and Tice stipulated that they should both be given safe seats, where the Conservatives would stand aside. Baker said he couldn't ever see Boris Johnson agreeing to that. Yet Farage and Tice pressed on, and said they also wanted ministerial jobs – Tice spoke of being Transport Secretary; Farage was less specific. Baker was astonished by this, and asked what sort of governing arrangement the pair envisaged – a formal coalition, or a 'confidence and supply' deal where Brexit Party MPs would back the Tories in major Commons votes? 'Neither,' Farage and Tice reportedly replied. When Baker suggested there was no way they could be ministers in that case, they had no response. The meeting made no progress on a pact, but led to further discussions, and Farage and Tice were provided with regular figures from various private polls which forecast that the Brexit Party would win none of their target seats.

In mid-September, Farage then offered a non-aggression pact which would require Johnson to promise not to try to renegotiate Theresa May's withdrawal deal and go for no deal instead, together with a second pledge that the Tories would step down in ninety Labour seats to avoid splitting the Leave vote. Farage identified constituencies such as Bassetlaw, Bolsover and Mansfield in the East Midlands, and others in the northern coalfields, as places which his party could win but the Conservatives couldn't. 'If Boris Johnson really thinks he can win in those seats I don't know what he's smoking . . . It just isn't going to happen.'[16]

The big problem was that Nigel Farage and Boris Johnson couldn't simply carve up the country between them, because both parties saw many of the same seats as their targets. These were known as the Red Wall seats, long-standing Labour constituencies which had voted heavily for Leave in 2016, and where voters hated Jeremy Corbyn, and thought he and his metropolitan Labour Party were unpatriotic and took places like the North for granted.

Boris Johnson brushed aside the Brexit Party leader's demands. 'The PM will not be doing a deal with Nigel Farage,' a Downing Street spokesman said emphatically. A senior source was quoted as saying: 'Neither Nigel Farage nor Arron Banks are fit and proper persons and they should never be allowed anywhere near government.'[17] The words sounded like Dominic Cummings' or someone close to him, and the fact that Cummings and several of the Vote Leave team who were now in Downing Street detested Farage so much was bound to be a huge obstacle to any pact.

After weeks of political high drama at Westminster – and the historic and unanimous decision by the Supreme Court that it was 'unlawful' for the government to prorogue (or suspend) Parliament for five weeks – Boris Johnson did finally come to an agreement with the European Union on 17 October. Most of this divorce settlement was a rehashed version of Theresa May's deal, but it included new arrangements for the tricky situation in Northern Ireland. It ditched the controversial and complicated 'Irish backstop', the provision in Theresa May's agreement that might have entailed the UK having to remain part of the EU customs regime.

Almost before anyone had a proper chance to read the fine print of Johnson's deal, Nigel Farage rushed to denounce it. 'It's just not Brexit,' he declared.[18] While the EU had now 'accepted that the UK is leaving the customs union', he said, the 'bad bit' was that the Irish backstop had been replaced with a new regulatory border between the UK and Northern Ireland, 'something that Boris said no British prime minister would ever do'. What's more, Farage argued, Britain would have to surrender control over its fisheries, and accept regulatory alignment in areas such as environment and employment law, and also taxation.[19] Then astonishingly, in apparent support of the Benn Act, the Brexit Party leader perplexed and dismayed colleagues by saying he would rather delay leaving the EU than accept the Johnson deal. He was derided by Remainers. 'Quite right, Nigel,' tweeted his frequent radio sparring partner, Lord Andrew Adonis. 'Parliament needs to take back control!'[20]

Several of Farage's MEPs were distressed, too, by what they saw as his knee-jerk response, for which he hadn't bothered to consult any of them. Before the deal was struck, Lance Forman had said he trusted Johnson, and that his champagne 'was on ice' in expectation Johnson would get a deal 'we can live with'.[21] Now the actual agreement was 'quite positive', he told *The Times*, and one 'we can move forward with'.[22] His colleague John Longworth, former director-general of the British Chambers of Commerce, said he was also inclined to accept it. A third Brexit Party MEP, Lucy Harris, said she hoped Parliament would vote for it. This was the start of serious divisions between Farage and some of his colleagues, from which the party never really recovered.

When the Brexit Party group met in Strasbourg the following week, Nigel Farage couldn't contain his fury at what he saw as disloyalty and betrayal by his colleagues. 'You disrespected me!' Lance Forman

remembers Farage shouting at him across the room. 'It was a very
uncomfortable moment. People were in shock. It was like being told
off by the headmaster. But you can't bring experienced people in and
tell them what to do and what to think.'[23] A colleague remembers it
as the 'most severe bollocking I've ever seen', as Farage spent ten minutes attacking the three MEPs whom he felt had defied him, and he
focused on John Longworth especially. Farage furiously told the rebels:
'You are only here because of me.' It was a very difficult moment for
Longworth, who admits: 'But for Nigel, Brexit would never have been
a reality, and the country owes him a debt of gratitude for that.'[24]

Yet Farage hadn't spoken to any of his MEP colleagues before
so roundly dismissing the Johnson deal straight after its publication. The row with these MEPs exposed the huge irony that an
organisation based on upholding a democratic decision – the 2016
referendum result – was itself the least democratic of parties, in
effect the greatest one-man dictatorship in modern British politics.

Forman says others quietly agreed with him but were too nervous to say so. From then on he, Longworth, Harris and Annunziata
Rees-Mogg would operate as an internal opposition group, known
as the Gang of Four.

Two days after the latest withdrawal agreement was struck, MPs
voted it down in a special Saturday sitting, whereupon Johnson was
forced – very grudgingly – to write to the president of the European
Council, Donald Tusk, to seek an extension until 31 January, as
required by the Benn Act. On 29 October MPs voted for a specific
new law that a general election would be held on 12 December. It
was initiated by a government now desperate to unblock the impasse
by winning a majority. Fatally, Labour and the Liberal Democrats
both officially backed an early election.

Rarely can any British party leader have enjoyed such an early coup
in their election campaign as Nigel Farage did in 2019. The very day
the general election bill became law, LBC announced they would
broadcast that evening on Farage's show an interview with Donald
Trump. It was billed as a historic first. Never before had an American
president done an extended interview with a British radio station.

The timing was pure chance, in fact, and Farage only got there in the nick of time. It wouldn't have been possible a few days later when Ofcom election rules kicked in, which prohibit any party leader from broadcasting their own programme during a campaign.

Farage's producer Christian Mitchell had been trying to secure an interview with Trump for almost three years, hoping the friendship between the two politicians would clinch it. Initially, whenever he knew Farage was about to meet Trump, Mitchell urged him to mention doing an interview, without success. 'I got a sense that he didn't want to look like he was capitalising on the friendship, and obviously Trump got to fall out with so many different people over the years, and he didn't want to jeopardise that.'[25]

Mitchell took matters into his own hands, and spent over two and a half years cultivating members of the White House press team, but that wasn't easy because the officials kept changing at an incredible rate. Mitchell was delighted when Trump's early press secretary Sarah Huckabee Sanders said at one point that it could happen the following week. 'And then she left, and this happened sort of several times over, to the point where we were almost on the verge of getting him on, and then either they were fired or they left. So then I'd have to start the relationship all over again.'

Eventually, Mitchell developed contact with a junior White House press assistant who seemed 'a bit star-struck by the fact that we're going through him to organise this interview with Nigel Farage, cos he seemed a bit of a fan of Nigel'.

At last, a time was agreed in October 2019, but that day Farage and LBC were then kept waiting for more than an hour, Mitchell remembers:

They kept saying 'Nigel, please hold for the President,' every ten minutes. We had all our PR teams at LBC on standby, and then I literally had a phone call from the press team saying 'Oh, I'm so sorry, the President's been pulled away.' And they were like, 'Oh, can we try and do this maybe in the New Year?'

The reason Trump had been 'pulled away', in fact, was for an operation, initially timed for that day, to kill the leader of Isis, Abu Bakr al-Baghdadi, though the attack was then postponed for a few days. Many producers would have given in at that point and agreed to leave things until the New Year. But Mitchell simply suggested they do it the following week instead:

> I had to try and think 'How do I persuade Trump to come on LBC?' And I thought, 'He's a man who likes to have his ego stroked,' so in my email request I just said, 'Nigel would like to congratulate the President on the mission against al-Baghdadi.' They lapped that up, they bought it, cos Trump was getting a lot of stick for the operation. And Trump came on about the same time the following week and no one knew it was coming, but it was the biggest coup: a president has never phoned into a radio station in the UK, ever.[26]

Typically of Trump and Farage, the interview was full of interesting material. First Trump rubbished Boris Johnson's Brexit deal, arguing it would harm British business between the two countries: 'You can't do it. You can't trade. I mean, we can't make a trade deal with the UK . . . Because under certain ways we're precluded, which would be ridiculous.'[27]

The interview was originally meant to last only seven or eight minutes, but ended up at half an hour. Trump also floated the possibility on many people's minds – including his host's – of a Farage/ Johnson pact for the coming election: 'I'd like to see you and Boris get together, because you would really have some numbers because you did fantastically in the [European] election . . . He has a lot of respect and like for you, I just – I wish you two guys could get together. I think it would be a great thing.' Minutes later, he returned to the issue. 'I know that you and him will end up doing something that could be terrific if you and he get together as, you know, [an] unstoppable force. And Corbyn would be so bad for your country.'

Farage told Trump: 'If he drops this dreadful deal, fights the general election on the basis that we'd just have trade with Europe, but no political interference. Do you know what? I'd be right behind him.' And Farage complained once more about being excluded by Johnson from any role in negotiating with the EU. 'I'd have loved to have helped, but at the moment they've chosen not to use me in any of these negotiations.'[28]

Mitchell had been concerned the interview might be too soft, so gave Farage a list of important topics to raise, including Ukraine; Trump's impeachment case; the coming 2020 election; and the case of Harry Dunn, the 19-year-old killed in a road accident in Northamptonshire by an American woman who was claiming diplomatic immunity from prosecution. But the exchanges were all lovey-dovey. 'I know one person that's going to say Trump is going to win – that's Nigel,' the president said at one point. Such was Farage's admiration, almost infatuation, for Trump that he wasn't at all tough on his guest and failed to put the searching questions most professional broadcasters would have posed.

Nigel Farage had repeatedly said his party had recruited more than 600 candidates to stand in every seat at the election. And in the early stages of the 2019 general election contest, it was widely believed that if the Brexit Party pressed ahead with its plans, then Farage would severely imperil the chances of Boris Johnson gaining a majority. Many Conservatives feared the Brexit Party might do so much damage to their party's support as to usher in a Labour–Scottish Nationalist coalition under Jeremy Corbyn, and might also cause the Liberal Democrats to pick up Tory seats in southern England.

The day after the Trump interview, emboldened perhaps by his broadcasting coup, Nigel Farage launched his party's election campaign at Westminster. He would fight every seat, he warned, unless Johnson abandoned his Brexit deal: 'He is trying to sell a second-hand motor where he has polished up the bonnet but actually underneath nothing has changed. This is Mrs May's appalling surrender treaty.'[29] 'Drop the deal,' Farage insisted three times.[30]

Many in the Brexit Party, and other supporters of leaving the EU, felt Farage had acted far too aggressively. They feared he was endangering Brexit itself and that it should primarily be Farage who withdrew candidates, not Johnson. John Longworth publicly told his leader that it would be 'sensible' to concentrate the party's resources on just twenty or thirty seats.[31] Farage's old chum Arron Banks also attacked him in public. 'He is being very dog in the manger about

it,' said Banks. 'I think Nigel is just playing the deck of cards he has
in his hand because he wants to take part in the television debates.
But I'm on the naughty step with Nigel. He knows I disagree with
him on this.'[32]

For the second election running, Farage had announced he himself wouldn't fight a seat. That, he argued, would give him more
time to campaign elsewhere. Catherine Blaiklock, the woman who
had actually founded his new party, but had already been rejected
as a general election candidate herself, said his refusal to fight a seat
was evidence he knew the party was a 'busted flush'. His strategy
was 'kamikaze', she said.[33]

There were now less than two weeks to strike a deal between
the two parties, as the clock ticked down to 4 p.m. on Thursday
14 November, the deadline for candidates to submit their nominations. More importantly in this story, it was also the last moment at
which candidates could *withdraw* their names from the ballot paper.
Nigel Farage was by now in an incredibly difficult position. From
the exhilarating high of the Trump interview on LBC, he would
suddenly be plunged into what must have been the worst fortnight of
his political career. Over the next two weeks he came under intense
and often conflicting pressures. It was difficult to give ground to the
Tories when hundreds of candidates had already been selected, and
when he had denounced the Johnson Brexit deal so roundly.

The clamour for him to help Boris Johnson came not just from
the Conservatives and from within his party, but also from the pro-
Brexit press. The *Daily Mail* effectively mounted a campaign against
Farage for the rest of the election, with frequent front-page splash
stories, and regular pleas both from its editorials and from its various
columnists for the Brexit Party leader to help Johnson.

The *Sunday Times* described Farage as 'the man paving the way for
a hard left Labour government', arguing that 'with his absurd charge
that the Prime Minister's hardish Brexit is not really a Brexit at all,
his party will either sink without trace or, more likely, deprive the
Tories of the majority they need to ensure a smooth passage for their
Brexit deal'. Dominic Lawson in an adjacent column said Farage had
become a 'monster of egotism . . . exceeded only in Hollywood or

the current White House'. It is clear, Lawson said, that 'he is losing grip on reality'.[34]

'If I field a full slate of candidates,' Farage told a fly-on-the-wall documentary team, 'it will be a hung parliament, of that I've got absolutely no doubt at all . . . The alternative is to let Boris win. No, I've got a big decision to make. I know that and I'm weighing those things up.'[35]

On 11 November, the press were summoned to the ballroom of the Grand Hotel in Hartlepool where, beneath the chandeliers, Nigel Farage would make an announcement. 'What we're saying now will fundamentally change the election and the result of the election,' Farage boasted before he went on stage.[36] Looking tired and haggard, he announced that his Brexit Party would withdraw its candidates in the 317 seats won by the Conservatives in 2017. 'Our action, this announcement today, prevents a second referendum from happening, and that to me, I think right now, is the single most important thing in our country . . . So in a sense, we now have a "Leave Alliance". It's just that we've done it unilaterally,' he said with a grin. 'We've decided ourselves that we absolutely have to put country before party and take the fight to Labour.'[37]

He referred to taking the decision 'ourselves', but it had really been Farage's decision – Richard Tice always ceded such strategy questions to him. So why the change of heart? For weeks there had been intense contacts between Farage's party and senior Conservatives. When it was plain that the Tories were unlikely to stand any of their candidates down, Farage's emissaries pleaded that Boris Johnson had to make some concession to allow the MEP to save face. 'And it had to be public, it had to be visible,' says one Farage adviser. That concession came the night before Farage's climb-down in a public pledge by Johnson not to extend the proposed Brexit transition period any further. 'We can get the fantastic new free trade agreement with the EU by the end of 2020. And we will not extend the transition period beyond the end of 2020,' Johnson said on Twitter. Farage must have known by now that Johnson promises were worthless, and the media were sceptical. 'What these fucking cretins don't understand is I held out and got a big concession but they are too fucking stupid to get it,' he told his press aide Dan Jukes.[38]

But ditching more than half the party's candidates meant that broad-casters were no longer obliged to treat Farage as a national leader, on a par with Johnson, Corbyn or Jo Swinson of the Liberal Democrats.

And even his 'Unilateral Alliance' only intensified the drama and the pressure on the Brexit Party leader. With three days to go before the candidate nomination deadline, it left open the question of all the other seats that the Conservatives needed to pick up – mainly from Labour pro-Leave areas – to secure a big enough majority in the Commons for Johnson not to have to worry about rebellious backbenchers on the right or left.

Farage's party was now in chaos. He had lost control and was under attack from both sides. Some thought he had conceded too much to Johnson, with little in return, and many of the 317 candidates forced to withdraw were upset. They felt the huge effort, time and expense they had invested over the previous few months had been wasted.

Even Alex Phillips, who had just been stood down as a candidate in the Conservative seat of Southampton Itchen, seemed unhappy. 'I have been disenfranchised by my own party,' she said.[39] Another candidate made redundant, Robert Wheal in Sussex, said Farage was 'finished as a politician', and had 'exposed his duplicity to so many supporters who had put their faith in him'.[40] Some Brexit Party candidates even disobeyed the order, and stood as independents instead. David Bull, who admits he has 'nothing but admiration' for Farage, says the MEPs were given only a few hours' notice. 'It was like someone had let the gas out of the balloon at that point. It deflated everything. That decision was taken without us. It did pretty permanent damage to the brand and the reputation. I think it was the wrong move.'[41]

But many figures in the party – especially among its MEPs – and even some of those who were still standing in non-Tory seats, felt Farage needed to retreat much further. It posed a horrible dilemma.

Arron Banks told Farage publicly that he had '48 hours to save Brexit' and should withdraw candidates in 150 Conservative target constituencies, and instead 'smash Labour in 40 or so seats where the Tories are nowhere'.[42] 'The Conservative Party is the Brexit

Party,' Banks added. 'Boris has to win or Brexit is dead. He should do the right thing.'[43]

Behind the scenes there was feverish activity and a sense of despair. Every day more candidates were standing down of their own accord, sometimes quickly to be replaced by people who could no longer stand in the 317 Tory seats.

Right up until almost the close of nominations, the Brexit Party tried to strike a deal with the Conservatives, but the ultimate problem was that the two parties' lists of winnable targets were so similar. It no longer made sense for Farage to talk about Labour Leave seats in the North where Johnson's party stood no chance, when internal Tory polls showed they now had a very good chance. It was no longer realistic to think of winning a handful of seats to exercise a bit of clout over Johnson, and keep Brexit on track. It was more about Farage saving face, and soon got to the stage where winning just one seat would be enough.

The secret contacts between the Brexit Party and the Conservatives were numerous and grew more intense in the countdown to the nominations deadline. Farage had long been in regular communication with the Conservative co-chairman Ben Elliot. Also involved in trying to broker a deal were Dougie Smith, a backroom fixer in Downing Street who is married to Boris Johnson's policy adviser Munira Mirza, and has long been involved in Conservative intrigue. Other players were the environmentalist Ben Goldsmith, brother of the Tory minister Zac Goldsmith, and the hedge-fund boss and Conservative donor Crispin Odey, who was close to Jacob Rees-Mogg, whom Johnson had recently made Leader of the Commons, and had also known Farage for many years. Odey had once employed the Brexit Party MEP Robert Rowland, who was yet another link in this network of parallel negotiations.[44]

The Conservatives' Australian election strategist Lynton Crosby played a small part, too, as did the former UKIP treasurer and Conservative donor Stuart Wheeler. By the close of nominations there was a complex web of conversations going on in parallel, often unconnected. 'Part of the problem was there wasn't a single summit,' says a Tory source, 'but several different endeavours, some freelance. It wasn't clear who was authorised to do what.'

Among the more significant brokers was Andrew Reid, who had flitted between the Conservatives and Farage's party over the years, and had the distinction of having let part of his offices in Mayfair to both Boris Johnson and Nigel Farage – or UKIP – at one time or another. Reid was squeezed out of the process towards the end, however, and felt frustrated at the Conservatives' refusal to stand down anywhere. Farage 'was definitely expecting to be able to discuss and come up with a sensible arrangement on seats that only the Brexit party could win,' Reid said at the time. 'But the argument back from the Conservatives was that the Brexit Party cannot win any seats based on their polling.'[45] One concern was that an overt deal with Farage might give the Conservatives too hard an image, and so drive pro-Remain, left-leaning Conservative voters towards the Liberal Democrats. Reid thought the real reason was the Tories simply couldn't accept the idea of Farage having any MPs at all.

It then boiled down to whether the Conservatives might be willing instead to run 'paper' campaigns in some places, i.e. token candidates with little or no actual campaigning on the ground. The problem for Farage was that any Tory candidate, no matter how inactive, was bound to siphon off thousands of voters who might otherwise support his party. As the Brexit Party fell in the polls, Farage rapidly lost his bargaining power. In the end there was no deal.

Meanwhile, the pro-Brexit press kept up the pressure. The *Daily Mail* tried to persuade some of the Brexit Party's candidates in Labour seats to stand down of their own accord, by printing the party's email addresses for four dozen of them. 'Make your voice heard by sending them an email,' the paper urged readers.[46] The *Mail* also appealed to the Brexit Party leader's vanity. 'Mr Farage has this choice,' an editorial declared on nomination day. 'To be remembered as the man who saved Brexit – or the one who destroyed it.'[47]

A *Times* editorial was in similar vein: 'Mr Farage has played a central and historic role in helping bring about Brexit. It is no doubt galling to have to accept this role is now over but he should declare victory and retreat.'[48]

Ann Widdecombe, who was due to stand in one of the Plymouth seats, recalls as late as the day before nomination papers had to go in, Farage was trying to strike a deal, but then sent her a text saying there would be 'no agreement at all' and so she submitted her forms.

> A person, who I've never named, from Number Ten, rang me up on my mobile, and first of all tried to bully me. And said, 'You know, if you stand and the Conservatives lose' – because I was in a marginal – 'it'll be all your fault. You'll always be blamed for it.' And I said, 'So what?' . . . then a couple of hours later he phoned me back, and he said if I agreed to withdraw I would be involved in the talks. What that means, I don't know. But it was a straightforward inducement, and I just said 'No'. Come on, what sort of idiot did they think they were talking to? I was furious. I was on the television that night saying there's been an attempt to bribe me. And when they denied it, I said I would swear it on holy writ. And then there was a sudden silence, because nobody would have disbelieved me if I'd done that. It was folly, folly to try that on me.[49]

Mike Greene, standing again in Peterborough, claimed he had been offered a government 'education' role. The MEP David Bull, standing in Sedgefield, says several Tories suggested he could have a safe seat at the subsequent election if he agreed to stand down. Farage claimed that it had repeatedly been suggested to him 'that I might like a seat in the House of Lords so I can go quietly. Every time this gets said my answer is the same: I'm not for sale. I'm not interested.'[50] Indeed, Farage maintained that over the summer he had been offered a seat in the Lords by two different people. 'They thought the deal was that if I accepted that, we would only fight a few seats. That came from two very close sources – one from an adviser and one a minister, not a member of the cabinet, suggesting this was the right thing to do. I said I was not interested.'[51] Farage later issued a video alleging:

> There was a concerted attempt from people who work deep inside Number Ten Downing Street – and I'm not blaming Boris for this; I don't believe he would be part of this, but it shows you the calibre of people he's got around him, it shows you the culture that exists

in Westminster. No, they bypassed me and went to other senior figures in the Brexit Party suggesting that eight of them could go in the House of Lords, and all they had to do was come to Nigel and convince him to stand down in a whole load more marginal seats.[52]

It's thought that among the eight MEPs who would be offered peerages if Farage could be persuaded were Richard Tice, Robert Rowland, Rupert Lowe, June Mummery, Matthew Patten, Martin Daubney and Claire Fox (who, amid great controversy, did actually join the Lords in 2020). The Conservatives had clocked that some Brexit Party MEPs rather liked the legislative lifestyle, and were disappointed that their time in the European Parliament would be short. A place in the Lords was an attractive alternative, though the promises were never likely to be fulfilled. Farage also alleged on Twitter that Boris Johnson's chief adviser Sir Edward Lister 'was calling our candidates and offering them jobs if they withdraw. The system is corrupt and broken.'[53] He told Sky News:

> Today every single one of the Brexit Party candidates has come under intimidation – thousands of phone calls, emails – even officials from Number Ten ringing up candidates and offering them jobs if they stand down. Now that makes us more like Venezuela than the United Kingdom.[54]

Farage was right. This was serious criminal and corrupt activity, by the people at the highest levels of the governing party, as people were offered substantial bribes – seats for life in the upper house of the British Parliament, on generous daily allowances, with a title thrown in – in return for corrupting the election process. Several people, including the Labour peer and former justice secretary Lord Falconer, made complaints to the police about possible bribery offences.

It was the Conservative Party at its most devious and determined. Earlier, an attempt had been made at the start of November to divide the Brexit Party by targeting its chairman Richard Tice, who only the year before had applied to become Conservative candidate for Mayor of London for the election due in 2020 (and put a lot of money into his effort). When the former minister Alan Duncan announced on 30 October he wasn't standing again for his seat of Rutland and Melton, a Conservative at Westminster approached Tice about standing for the Tories in the seat. He had been a pupil at Uppingham School and now sat on the school's governing body. It may have been yet more skulduggery, since if Tice had even shown the slightest interest the fact might have been leaked and done great damage to the Brexit Party.

The biggest blow to Farage came just before the close of nominations when the Brexit Party MEP Rupert Lowe announced he was pulling out of fighting the Labour marginal of Dudley North. Farage was especially furious as he felt he'd been betrayed by Lowe and knew it was too late to find a replacement. 'I am putting country before party,' Lowe tweeted around the time of the deadline, explaining his involvement might have helped the election of a Labour MP who belonged to the left-wing group Momentum.[55]

Lowe was guilty of 'disgusting behaviour', an angry Farage told the press. 'What he probably hasn't told you is that he met a senior official from Number 10 in the middle of last week, somebody quite close to Boris, and this was obviously stitched up. If he made a decision, he went and changed course, he's entitled to. But to let everybody else down at the eleventh hour, dreadful behaviour – shocking.'[56] The party had been 'double-crossed', Farage said, and Lowe had behaved 'dishonestly'. Lowe was certainly targeted by Number Ten as a possible weakness in the Farage team.

Lowe threatened legal action, and a month later Farage apologised to him and withdrew his remarks. He hadn't realised, he said, that Lowe had told Richard Tice in advance that he was planning to withdraw. The evening after Lowe withdrew, Farage was due to address a Brexit Party rally in Willenhall, not far from Dudley. Farage had had to 'go back to London to sort out key strategic elements', I was told when I turned up and found Farage was no longer on the bill.

For Farage, it must have felt like the whole campaign – his whole party – was falling apart. Tensions grew between the old Kippers and the new Brexit Party team. Farage grew increasingly bad-tempered and irascible. People who had known him for years said they had never seen him so depressed and angry. For forty-eight hours he refused to go anywhere near journalists. A source at the centre of the party spoke to me at the time, and compared the situation to Hitler in his Berlin bunker in 1945:

> Now the whole house is coming down; now the recriminations begin; now it's an absolute bloodbath. It is like in *Downfall* where Hitler is dismissing his generals who have advised him not to carry on with his strategy. He's started only listening to his people – what I call the UKIP crowd – advice he wants to hear. Anyone with intelligence or sensible things to say was kicked out of the internal discussions. It's total chaos. The Tories have absolutely outmanoeuvred Tice and Farage. It's over. They want to go down fighting. The praetorian guard are the only ones left. It's a witch-hunt inside. They're going absolutely nuts.

For years Nigel Farage had got so used to being 100 per cent in control, and now all of a sudden he didn't feel able to control anything. It was only six months since his triumph in the European elections, barely a fortnight since the extraordinary 'high' of the Donald Trump interview. To fall from grace so quickly, to be outmanoeuvred by your opponents and betrayed by so many colleagues must have been psychologically traumatic. His close aides couldn't get him out of the bunker. He wouldn't go out and speak to the media. As an astute politician, he knew it was all over.

Eventually though, within two or three days, his friends got him up and running again. Even days afterwards, Farage couldn't hide his frustration, as he suggested some Conservatives were jealous that he had public recognition and a 'level of personal political support' that they didn't have. 'I think there is a bit of jealousy, I genuinely do.'[57] It was a strange thing to say about the party of Boris Johnson.

Yet Farage still had to suffer what he saw as the final act of treachery. The Gang of Four had decided for several weeks that they would be voting Conservative, and wanted to urge other Brexit voters to do so. They bided their time, however, according to Lance Forman.

'We felt strongly that it was best to conceal from the Brexit Party that we were splitting, and decided not to go too early, and go about a week before the election.'[58] Hoping to make the most impact, they secretly made arrangements for a press conference at the Institution of Mechanical Engineers in Westminster seven days before polling. The cat was almost let out of the bag, however, when staff put up a sign the day before saying 'Brexit Party MEPs'. But nobody noticed it.

The rebels duly announced to the press that they were leaving the Brexit Party, because the party was splitting the Leave vote in marginal seats. 'The Conservatives are the only option for Brexit supporters and democrats alike,' said Annunziata Rees-Mogg. The four urged Farage to stand down his candidates and abandon the election completely. Farage, said Forman, could be one of the greatest statesmen if he said, 'We need to get Brexit delivered, Vote for Boris Johnson.'[59]

'Never underestimate greed and stupidity' was Farage's angry response, implying the four had been bought off with what he'd called 'Christmas baubles'. 'They rode off my back. They'd been planning this ever since Boris Johnson was elected.' He was particularly upset about Annunziata Rees-Mogg, whom the party had turned into something of a star, with speaking slots at many of the rallies (the betrayal must have had echoes of Douglas Carswell for Farage). Other Brexit Party MEPs seriously thought of following their colleagues, but decided there was no need.

In reality, Brexit Party hopes now rested on a single seat, Hartlepool, where Richard Tice was standing. It came close to being the one seat the Brexit Party did pick up, thanks, it seems, to some sympathetic local Conservatives and an extraordinary fiasco whereby the Tory candidate, Arun Photay, had to pull out because, he said, of 'an administrative error'. A local Tory official had forgotten to submit Photay's forms to the returning officer, and then gone on holiday. 'Terrible coincidence,' says a Brexit Party source. 'They were that busy; they drove to Manchester Airport to fly to Amsterdam, and forgot to drop the papers off first.' The nomination forms were locked in the official's car in the airport car park.

Photay was too far away from Hartlepool to sign new forms in time, but Conservative headquarters insisted someone had to stand for the party. There was talk of flying Photay up by helicopter, before a Stockton councillor, Stefan Houghton, was pressed into fighting the seat instead. His forms were submitted with minutes to go. (From almost not having a Conservative candidate in 2019, Hartlepool would go on to have a Tory MP eighteen months later.)

Just as with UKIP and South Thanet in 2015, the Brexit Party's efforts were narrowed down to winning Hartlepool. Activists were directed there from around the country, and Farage came to help Richard Tice several times. Almost everywhere else, however, Brexit Party candidates found they were pretty much on their own, with no established infrastructure, and no support from party headquarters, as they tried to fend off questions as to why they were standing at all.

A sad example was Mike Greene, who'd come within fewer than 700 votes of winning Peterborough only six months before. In the June by-election, his campaign had been so overwhelmed with enthusiastic activists from outside that his team hadn't known how to deploy them. By the general election, however, Green found himself stuffing leaflets through letterboxes with almost nobody else to join him on the streets. 'I've got nothing,' Greene complained to a friend. It was so demoralising, especially when he must have known he was doomed.

On election night in mid-December, Greene was pushed down to fourth place in Peterborough, and he lost his deposit with just 4.4 per cent, less than a sixth of what he'd got six months earlier. And the Brexit Party's results across the country showed a similar pattern. Nigel Farage's party got just 644,257 votes – a mere 2 per cent of the national total – which meant that even if they'd stood in 600 seats, as originally promised, they would only have managed around 5 per cent. It was an extraordinary drop from the 30.4 per cent in the Euro elections in May – almost certainly the biggest ever fall by any British party between successive national elections.

Earlier that night, Farage had forecast a small Tory majority of about twenty. In fact it was eighty, and many of the Conservative gains were in those working-class Labour areas which had voted heavily for Leave in 2016 – places like Dennis Skinner's Bolsover, and Bassetlaw, the very seats which Farage had cited when he taunted Johnson that he must be smoking something if he thought the Tories could win them. In the event, the Brexit Party got around 10 per cent in both constituencies, yet the Conservatives still managed to win in each case for the first time in decades. The so-called Labour Red Wall, which Farage had targeted and tried to soften up in recent times, had fallen dramatically to Boris Johnson instead. The six-week campaign had been a traditional minority squeeze, as the Brexit Party's polling figures fell from about 10 per cent around the time the election was called in late October, to less than half that by polling day. The fall for Farage's party was mirrored by an even greater rise in the Conservative vote, and much of the increase came from former Brexit Party and UKIP voters.

Boris Johnson and his colleagues had held their nerve, and successfully called Farage's bluff all the way. The Brexit Party leader had looked increasingly forlorn and desperate as his demands diminished week by week – from the time in September when he aggressively insisted the Conservatives had to step aside in ninety Labour constituencies which voted Leave in 2016. Now many of those seats had Tory MPs.

'The victory for Boris was hugely helped by us, and is far better than the Marxist Corbyn and a second referendum,' Farage tweeted at 11.30 on election night before the results started coming through.[60] He claimed his decision to stand down in the 317 Tory-held seats had stopped a hung parliament. That was not true, though the Conservative majority would certainly have been lower had Farage not stood down half of his nominees.

And by refusing to withdraw his candidates on the other side of the ledger, in midlands and northern Labour seats, Farage probably stopped Boris Johnson getting a majority of around 100.

Indeed, several senior Labour figures – including Ed Miliband and Yvette Cooper – almost certainly owe their victories to Nigel Farage's determination to resist the pressure and carry on fighting in their constituencies.

The great kingmaker of May, June and July had been reduced to insignificance, a mere asterisk on the results table of the British general election of 2019.

27

A LOOSE END

It was 29 January 2020, two days before the official Brexit Day. Nigel Farage was in Strasbourg for the occasion of which he'd long dreamed. 'So this is it,' he declared in his last speech as an MEP, 'the final chapter; the end of the road; a 47-year-political experiment that the British frankly have never been very happy with.' His parents had signed up to a Common Market, not to a political union, he said, 'not to flags, anthems, presidents and now you even want your own army'. He continued:

> There's a historic battle going on now across the West, in Europe, America and elsewhere – it is globalism against populism. And you may loathe populism, but I'll tell you a funny thing: it's becoming very popular [laughs] . . . And it has great benefits. No more financial contributions. No more European Court of Justice. No more Common Fisheries Policy. No more being talked down to. No more being bullied. No more Guy Verhofstadt. I mean, what's not to like? I know you're gonna miss us.

At that point Farage and other Brexit Party MEPs raised an array of small desk-top Union Jacks. 'I know you want to ban our national flags,' he concluded, 'but we're gonna wave you goodbye and we look forward in the future to working with you as sovereign . . .' At that moment Farage was cut off by the president of the Parliament, on the grounds that flag-waving is banned in the chamber. As she asked for the little flags to be removed, Brexit Party MEPs stood and gave Farage three rounds of 'hip, hip hooray'.[1]

It was a symbolic moment, not just for the UK but Europe, too. For the first time in history the Parliament and the European Union itself were shrinking in size. Some MEPs were pleased to see the departure of the 'troublesome' British, especially Farage and his twenty-eight party colleagues, but not all. Later that year the Dutch Conservative MEP Derk Jan Eppink – an astute Farage-watcher – would tell the Parliament that 'without Nigel Farage over there in the corner' the assembly had become 'rather quiet, like a provincial assembly . . . Without the British, the right to dissent seems to disappear from this Parliament.'[2]

On Brexit Day itself, Nigel Farage joined a jubilant crowd in Parliament Square for a late-night party organised by Leave Means Leave. As the hand on Big Ben moved towards the moment of departure – 11 p.m. in London is midnight in Brussels – they sang the national anthem and waved Union flags. Farage, wearing a Union Jack tie, told them:

> In thirteen minutes' time we will leave the European Union. We did it. We transformed the landscape of our country and there are some that say we shouldn't celebrate tonight. Well, we *are* going to celebrate tonight . . .
>
> The only reason we are here tonight is because Westminster became utterly detached from ordinary people in this country. The people have beaten the establishment. The real winner tonight is democracy. And I am somebody who believes that we should be pro-Europe, but not pro the European Union . . . We're never, ever going back . . . This is the greatest moment in the modern history of our great nation.[3]

A few hundred yards away, the 'official' Leave forces, led by Boris Johnson, celebrated separately at 10 Downing Street. A countdown clock was projected onto the wall of Number Ten. Events had moved rapidly after Johnson secured his eighty-seat majority in the election seven weeks earlier. Nigel Farage was not invited to the Downing Street party, which mainly involved senior Conservatives and figures from Vote Leave. Even now, at their moment of jubilation, Brexit forces were still divided into rival camps.

Nigel Farage may no longer have been a parliamentarian but he was still leader of the Brexit Party. He continued to enjoy a substantial media platform, especially with his radio show five days a week on LBC, his regular columns in the *Daily Telegraph* and *Newsweek*, and his growing presence on social media. But with the achievement of Brexit, Farage and his party had an obvious quandary. What did they do now? For the party chairman Richard Tice, the dilemma was so acute that he even sounded out the former Labour Cabinet minister Andrew Adonis – a passionate Remainer – about the possibility of personally joining the project of the likely new Labour leader, Sir Keir Starmer. As they met over breakfast, Adonis thought the idea so absurd that he didn't even respond. Farage would have been horrified had he known what Tice was up to. When I interviewed Tice he dismissed the story as 'nonsense'.

If the Brexit Party was to have any hope of staying in business, Tice and Farage needed a big new cause to replace the European Union. And within weeks of Brexit Day it arrived completely out of the blue, from Wuhan in China, in the form of the coronavirus pandemic, known as Covid-19. It took a while, however, for Farage to seize the issue.

In March 2020, British citizens were told to adopt 'social distancing' – they should not stray within two metres of people from outside their own families. The Johnson government then introduced measures more draconian than anything imposed in Britain in modern times. Workplaces, schools, pubs, restaurants and all but the most essential shops were closed down and people told to stay at home with their families. Initially, Farage backed these measures. 'The first duty of any government is to protect the wellbeing of its citizens and their country,' he wrote in *Newsweek*.[4] Indeed, Farage wanted the government to follow the examples of Singapore and South Korea and be even tougher, especially with the British testing regime, and restrict people who were still arriving in the UK from overseas. 'Get a grip,' Farage told Boris Johnson, urging him to sack the Health Secretary Matt Hancock.

Yet within a few days, Farage adopted a more libertarian line. 'Are the government and police trying to prevent the spread of coronavirus, or put the nation under house arrest?' he asked.[5] As the Covid crisis dominated politics for the rest of 2020 and much of 2021, Farage became increasingly hostile to successive rounds of lockdown restrictions. Amid a general cross-party consensus on the issue, the Brexit Party became a leading champion of easing regulations and then scrapping them altogether.

In the autumn of 2020, Farage endorsed the Great Barrington Declaration, drawn up by three senior international scientists. The declaration advocated greater protection of people most vulnerable to Covid-19, such as the elderly, while at the same time argued that most of the population should be allowed to resume normal life. When the Brexit Party was reborn in November 2020, and rebranded as Reform UK, this civil liberty approach to Covid became their prime policy. 'Imprisoning people is unspeakable cruelty,' Farage and Tice declared.[6] 'Ultimately more people will die of other illnesses because they've not been diagnosed, than will die from Covid-19,' Farage warned in a video just as ministers imposed a new round of restrictions. 'This second lockdown says to me that the cure is now worse than the disease.'[7]

Almost until the end of 2020, however, Farage was sceptical that a vaccine would 'miraculously' come along, or that people would actually be willing to be vaccinated. But when several vaccines arrived almost simultaneously, and the British vaccination programme proved to be a huge success, with initial figures way ahead of any other European state, Farage hailed it as one of the great benefits of Brexit. If Britain had remained in the EU, he argued, we would still be embroiled in the internal EU squabbling and regulatory procedures which were hindering vaccination on the continent.

As the Covid crisis seemed to crowd out nearly every other news story, Nigel Farage also took an especial interest in the large numbers of foreign migrants who were now openly crossing the English Channel in small boats to seek asylum in the UK.

This issue more than any other helped turn Farage into a broadcast video reporter. On one occasion, out in the English Channel, in a small fishing boat he'd hired, he came across a grossly overcrowded dinghy with twenty-two migrants packed shoulder to shoulder. The vessel was shipping water. To stay afloat the passengers were throwing overboard all unnecessary objects, before they were eventually rescued by a boat from the UK Border Force.

Whatever your views on the issue, the accounts and pictures of asylum-seekers riskily and brazenly crossing the waters between France and England – just like the Mediterranean crossings a few years before – were a shocking story, full of political, moral and logistical dilemmas. Yet mainstream TV and radio broadcasters seemed reluctant to focus on the development. Growing numbers, mostly men, from war-torn countries like Iraq, Afghanistan and Syria, as well as several parts of Africa, were willing to pay thousands of euros and put themselves at the mercy of ruthless people-smugglers to cross the world's busiest shipping lane in perilous plastic boats. And the authorities seemed not only powerless to stop the traffic, but actively, if inadvertently, appeared to abet organised criminals by assisting these migrants across the Strait of Dover.

On another occasion, Farage watched and delivered a commentary from the deck of a fishing boat, as the French navy escorted another migrant dinghy towards the halfway point between the two shores, and then handed the precarious vessel over to the protection of the UK Border Force. Both sides, Farage alleged, had tried to stop him and his team filming the drama, and he even claimed that the skipper of his boat had been warned by the English Coastguard that they would 'commandeer' their vessel if they didn't stop filming. 'They're threatening him with his living if we tell the truth about this story,' he explained to camera. 'Home Secretary, you've got to act,' he urged Priti Patel.[8]

Just as Asian and African migrants sought a new life in Britain, Nigel Farage was looking for a new future, too. He was reinventing himself as a campaigning journalist. By the summer of 2021, Farage's personal YouTube channel had almost 270,000 subscribers. The man who had long dominated UKIP was now becoming a master of YouTube.

The figures for those crossing the Channel had risen rapidly during the early months of 2020, with more than 1,000 arrivals in the first four months of the year, and the numbers doubled again in the early months of 2021 – and those were just the official figures; others arrived on remote shores and never registered with the UK authorities. Farage was very familiar with the coastline of Kent and East Sussex, of course, not just as a South East MEP who'd twice stood for the coastal seat of South Thanet, but also as a sea angler who even at the peak of his political activity had occasionally nipped down to the coast at night and spent several hours on a boat fishing in the dark.

Farage had long belonged to the angling association in Dungeness, the remote headland and shingle beach between Folkestone and Hastings, and had recently acquired a second home in the area. Local friends and fishing contacts – his 'spotters', he called them – supplied him with regular reports on the migrant boats. Farage argued that since these journeys were organised by people-smugglers, many of the migrants would be forced into the black economy once they got to Britain so as to repay the many thousands of pounds they'd paid to the organised gangs, or they might be forced into modern slavery and the women into prostitution.

In his first video, Farage visited Pett Level, a beach not far from Dungeness which he said was a favourite arrival spot for illegal boats, and spoke to people in nearby Hastings who claimed to have witnessed numerous migrants turning up.[9] The resulting broadcast prompted several complaints to the police alleging Farage had broken Covid rules, and at ten o'clock one evening he was visited at his home by a couple of policemen. Farage claimed that he was a journalist and pointed out that, under lockdown rules, reporters were deemed to be 'key workers' and free to travel to do their work. In another video report, Farage visited a hotel in Bromsgrove in the West Midlands where the entire building seemed to be devoted to recent migrant arrivals, much to the dismay of some local residents. 'I fear we could be on the verge of something almost approaching an invasion this year,' he warned on his LBC show. 'I won't be silenced on this,' he vowed.[10] Of course, he was making a political argument, but it was also first-class video reporting.

Perhaps Farage's most striking report was unintended, however. He had gone out with a friend fishing early one November morning, five miles off the coast, when they came across two young men from Mali who had been trying to row across from France in a cheap inflatable kayak. The Africans seemed exhausted, appeared to have stopped rowing and were at the mercy of an increasingly rough sea with only one life-jacket between them. As Farage's boat tried to rescue the pair, their kayak capsized and the migrants fell into the water. They were too weak to clamber on board the fishing boat, but Farage's crew managed to turn the kayak back upright and tow it into harbour with the migrants clinging on. Without this lucky intervention, Farage claimed, the men would quickly have perished. 'They had given up rowing, it was awful weather and there was no boat around. There is no question they wouldn't have survived. One of them would have been dead after an hour with hypothermia, and the other not long after.'[11]

Farage had become more and more a social media creature. As well as his substantial YouTube following, he also had 1.6 million followers on Twitter towards the end of 2021, and more than a million followers on Facebook. The only politicians to exceed these figures were Boris Johnson, Jeremy Corbyn, David Cameron and Sadiq Khan.

His numbers became something of a fixation, as he demanded to know from aides how much response each posting prompted, how many hits his latest press columns had generated. He wanted to know which other media outlets had picked up his stories or comments, or which mainstream politicians had publicly denounced him.

'He's obsessed with his daily reach,' one colleague says. 'He's absolutely fascinated by the numbers. He has to be on top of his figures.' Throughout the day Farage would constantly have his eye on the TV news channels, or flick through his Twitter feed, to see what new stories he could respond to, where else he could make an impact. He kept pushing at the boundaries of what he might say for a headline.

In effect, he'd become a social media junkie. And his latest habit and addiction would cost him perhaps the best-paid, and probably most satisfying, job he'd ever had.

In May 2020, the world was diverted from the troubles of Covid by horrific pictures from the American city of Minneapolis of the notorious murder by a white policeman of a Black man called George Floyd. The incident sparked anger around the world, and the Black Lives Matter (BLM) movement was reinvigorated overnight. Amid numerous demonstrations around Britain, angry protestors in the centre of Bristol pulled down the bronze statue of the seventeenth-century slave trader Edward Colston. They then rolled Colston several hundred yards to the nearby dock and pushed him into the dark waters. For the demonstrators it was a symbolic moment after years in which local campaigners had tried to remove the statue. Colston had been dumped into the murky depths in the same way that many of his wretched slaves, dead or dying, would have been thrown overboard during their unspeakable Atlantic crossings. But Farage saw the felling of the Colston statue as rule by the mob. 'A new form of the Taliban was born in the UK today,' he tweeted. 'Unless we get moral leadership quickly our cities won't be worth living in.'[12]

Two days later, Farage appeared in an extremely heated debate on *Good Morning Britain* on ITV, where he was pitted against the Black activist and writer Shola Mos-Shogbamimu and the historian Kate Williams. It was not a balanced discussion, and rarely has Farage looked so uncomfortable. Not only his two fellow guests, but also the two ITV presenters, Piers Morgan and Susanna Reid, attacked him for his 'Taliban' tweet, and for arguing that Colston had been a major philanthropist as well as a slave trader. Farage didn't directly repeat the Taliban comparison but did say the Bristol protestors had been 'the most appalling example of mob rule'. The Taliban, he tried to explain, 'love to blow up and destroy historical monuments from a different time that they do not approve of'. As the discussion grew ever more bad-tempered, Farage praised the words 'Black Lives Matter' as a 'laudable aim', but argued that BLM was 'a far-left Marxist organisation whose chief aim is to defund and close down police forces'. 'That is an utter lie,' Mos-Shogbamimu shot back, and she went on to accuse Farage of being a 'racist'.

Farage looked hot and flustered; his usual composure and good humour deserted him. He could easily have conceded gracefully that comparing the Bristol protestors to the Taliban might have been a bit excessive, while still criticising their methods. Perhaps because he was doing the interview from home and on Zoom, probably with no one around to advise him, he badly misjudged the mood of the discussion, and the wider national mood. It must go down as one of the worst TV appearances that Nigel Farage has ever made.

It cost him dearly. After the broadcast, Shola Mos-Shogbamimu said that, given his comments about the Taliban, Farage's position as an LBC presenter was 'incompatible and inconsistent with any stance of solidarity a national station like LBC claims to have with its Black audience'. Two days later, LBC announced that Farage would be leaving the station immediately, and tweeted: 'Nigel Farage's contract with LBC is up very shortly and, following discussions with him, Nigel is stepping down from LBC with immediate effect. We thank Nigel for the enormous contribution he has made to LBC and wish him well.'[13]

It was all so sudden. Farage's producer, Christian Mitchell, who was preparing for his show that evening, only heard of his presenter's departure when he read it on social media, and LBC quickly had to bring forward Iain Dale's 7 p.m. show by an hour to fill the gap.

'We got our station back,' tweeted LBC's left-leaning presenter James O'Brien. Farage's comments had put LBC in a difficult position, since their parent company, Global Media, also owns several music stations, including Capital Radio, Heart and Smooth, and also Capital Xtra which claims to be the most popular Black station in the UK. And Global was already being accused of not employing enough Black people. Many staff were extremely unhappy about Farage's employment by the company, and shared their concerns on LBC's internal ethnic minority discussion group.

Farage said very little about his departure. 'I've got no wish to comment about it,' he told the rival station Talk Radio the next day. 'I've no wish to display sour grapes.' He added light-heartedly that losing his job was 'pretty small' compared with climbing out of a light aircraft after his crash in 2010.[14] Farage later alleged that some of LBC's advertisers had been 'bombarded with tens of thousands of complaints' after he had also criticised Black Lives Matter on his LBC broadcasts.[15]

Privately, Farage was 'very upset' by his dismissal, says the former Brexit Party MEP David Bull, who had become part of his inner circle. He had lost another big public platform, and it was a huge financial blow, too. His European Parliament declaration in July 2019 showed that he was making about £342,000 a year from his journalism, broadcasting and speaking engagements, income channelled through his own media company Thorn In The Side Ltd.[16] LBC must have accounted for at least half of that, perhaps between £500 and £1,000 for each of the five shows he presented every week.

But Nigel Farage will never be 'skint', the ridiculous claim he made in 2017, at least not by the standards of most British people. Although he declined the £153,000 severance pay to which he was entitled as a long-standing MEP when Britain left the European Union, he will still be due a generous EU pension when he reaches sixty-three in 2027 – worth 70 per cent of his final MEP's salary, a yield of about £63,400 a year. In addition, Farage will receive tens of thousands of pounds more each year from a secondary voluntary European Parliament pension, a highly controversial, secretive and extremely generous scheme under which the EU agreed to match MEPs' contributions by a ratio of two to one. There should also be a hefty pension from his twenty or so years in the City.

Farage quickly found new sources of income as well. In the spring of 2020, he began contributing to a free daily investment newsletter, Fortune & Freedom, working with a former Goldman Sachs banker, Nickolai Hubble. The newsletter made much of Farage's involvement, posting his picture on its online masthead. 'I have 40 years of experience in finance AND politics,' he wrote.

I will say what needs to be said (and I don't care if the woke media attack me for it). To help you forge the prosperous financial life you deserve. I have spent decades fighting for your political freedom. Now comes the next battle – to get your money and your destiny back in your hands. I have deep-rooted contacts that provide me with intelligence and a unique perspective.[17]

In 2021, Farage also enrolled with Cameo, the internet service whereby people can pay for a short, personalised video message from a celebrity, perhaps to mark a birthday or similar event. Farage initially charged £52.50 a time, though this quickly rose to £75 (on which Cameo took 25 per cent commission). Customers submit a script for the celebrity to read, though not surprisingly Farage soon fell prey to pranksters. Social media rocked with laughter, for instance, when he delivered a message saying, 'Happy birthday, Hugh Janus . . .'[18] On later occasions he was tricked into delivering Irish Republican slogans, including 'Up the Ra', a reference to the IRA. He didn't look comfortable delivering his greetings: they were rushed and stiff as he simply read from his text with forced smiles and no sense of enjoyment. He seemed embarrassed, and gave the impression he felt it was all rather demeaning.

Normally, Farage would have hoped to spend much of 2020 in America supporting the re-election campaign of his friend Donald Trump. In February 2020, he again spoke at the annual CPAC, the Conservative Political Action Conference, in Maryland, where he and his girlfriend Laure Ferrari briefly met Donald Trump. Farage hoped later in the year to return to America to act as an occasional speaker at Trump rallies, and as a media commentator. Covid largely put paid to that.

Nonetheless, in June 2020, Farage travelled to Tulsa, Oklahoma, where 100,000 tickets had reportedly been issued for a major Donald Trump rally, which, because of Covid, was the president's first public event in three months. All other visitors from Britain were banned from entering America at that time, but the US government gave Farage special dispensation in the 'national interest'. A Democrat congressman, Bennie Thompson, chairman of the House Committee on Homeland Security, complained that 'the decision . . . to enable him to attend a campaign rally at a time when most travel from the United Kingdom to the US has been suspended raises numerous troubling questions, as does the claim that such travel was in the national interest'.[19]

It was a wasted trip. The Tulsa rally was an embarrassing flop. Only 6,200 people attended, the local fire department reckoned, and the outdoor overflow stage, where Farage had been due to speak, was scrapped just hours beforehand. The poor turnout may in part have been due to Covid, but also a deliberate effort by Trump opponents to sabotage the event by booking tickets they never intended to use, thereby denying genuine Trump supporters the chance to attend.

Nonetheless, Farage publicly forecast all summer and autumn that Trump would again defy the experts. In the final week of the campaign, when it was clear that Trump faced defeat, he returned to America – this time on a media visa – and addressed a string of small Trump campaign meetings in the swing state of Arizona, all without the president. Then, at a rally addressed by Trump in Phoenix, the president spotted Farage in the crowd, summoned him up onto the stage and introduced him as 'a friend of mine – a lot of people say one of the most powerful men in Europe . . . He's a very non-controversial person,' Trump teased, adding, 'He's very shy.' Farage repaid the praise, though not the mockery. 'This is the single most resilient and bravest person, I have ever . . . met . . . in . . . my . . . life,' he boomed. But it all seemed terribly flat compared with his duet with Trump in Jackson, Mississippi, in 2016. Farage spoke for barely two minutes, and the applause lasted less than ten seconds from an audience who showed little sign of knowing who he was. Farage spent election day in Washington DC and tweeted a picture of himself on Pennsylvania Avenue, holding a betting slip showing he'd put $10,000 on a Trump victory.

He lost his stake, of course. Farage didn't echo Trump in arguing that the election had been stolen – though he complained about corrupt postal balloting in both the US and the UK. Nor did he say the election could or should be overturned in the courts. And when Trump supporters violently took over the US Capitol in January 2021, Farage was quick to condemn them. 'Storming Capitol Hill is wrong. The protesters must leave,' Farage tweeted.[20] But he said he had no regrets about backing Trump, and argued that his defeat was only 'a temporary setback'.[21]

As the second round of Brexit negotiations continued through the course of 2020 to achieve a long-term trade arrangement between

Britain and the EU, Farage argued that unless Brussels made sub-stantial concessions then Britain should simply walk away with 'no deal', or a 'clean break Brexit'. Britain would then trade with the EU on 'WTO terms' – the World Trade Organisation system of tariffs. And up until the last moment it looked as if there might well be no deal, as both sides could not agree what to do about fishing rights, or the status of Northern Ireland. 'No Deal is the only way Johnson can keep his election promises,' Farage said, and the talks, he argued, were all a 'charade'.[22] 'If Johnson wants to be remembered as a man of courage, he must stop caring what people may or may not think of him and act decisively. Too often, he wobbles like a jelly. This time, he must be as solid as a rock,' he wrote on 22 December, nine days before the formal end of the transition period on New Year's Eve.[23]

Two days later, however, in the early hours of Christmas Eve, British and EU negotiators finally struck a last-minute deal – the EU–UK Trade and Cooperation Agreement. Farage's initial response was that the agreement betrayed British fishermen, since only 25 per cent of the rights of EU boats to fish in British waters would be transferred to the UK before 2026. 'Even if after 2026 Britain wants to increase further its own quota allocation, it will have to pay compensation to the EU to do so. This is an outrageous humiliation.'[24] Yet only two days after urging the government to go for no deal, Farage claimed that it was 'never a possibility' and that the two sides were always bound to reach a settlement.[25]

After Christmas, Farage tried to be more generous towards Boris Johnson, and bury the hatchet after five years of hostilities between the two Brexit camps. 'The war is over,' he wrote in the *Mail on Sunday*. And Farage conceded that he and his parties would never have achieved Brexit alone:

> As a team acting on its own, I think that UKIP, the businessman Arron Banks, and a handful of dependable rebel Labour and Tory MPs could have scored about 43 per cent in the referendum. That is why it was so crucial that Boris Johnson, who is now finishing the job, opted to join the Leave side. Johnson's Vote Leave group, which included Michael Gove, got us over the line.[26]

In his articles, videos and interviews there was a sense that Nigel Farage knew his mainstream political career was drawing to a close. He was still officially the leader of Reform UK – as the Brexit Party was renamed in January 2021 – and the party claimed that more than 3,000 people had applied to be candidates for the local elections due in May 2021. In reality, though, Farage's party but was no longer a serious force. Covid restrictions meant that no elections had taken place in Britain – Westminster or council contests – since the 2019 general election, so the party could carry on pretending it was a credible player. Farage knew that the local elections due in May 2021 were likely to be a disaster.

On 6 March 2021, two months before polling day, Nigel Farage suddenly announced he was standing down from frontline politics. He would now become honorary president of Reform UK and hand over the leadership to Richard Tice, which seemed strangely undemocratic moves for a party whose remaining policies largely consisted of extending democracy. 'This is not me retiring,' Farage tried to reassure supporters in a video. He was merely 'getting out of active party politics':

> I'm not going away. I'm still going to fight and battle for change. We got Brexit. There's an awful lot more to do, but for me, after nearly 30 years . . . That's enough of active politics, and do you know something? I've actually achieved what I set out to do, and I don't think there are many people in politics that can ever say that . . . Probably between six and seven million people at some point voted for parties that I led. They had the confidence in me, and the team around me to do that, and that is what completely changed British politics. That is what got us back our independence.[27]

Among issues he now wanted to pursue were the global influence of the Chinese Communist Party; the 'indoctrination of children' in schools; and, surprisingly perhaps, environmental concerns. Farage's green credentials hadn't been obvious during his twenty years in the limelight. He had often been sceptical about how serious climate change was. In the 2015 election, for example, UKIP had pledged to repeal the Climate Change Act; and to encourage fracking and rejuvenate the coal industry. Farage was really a conservationist, keen to preserve the oceans, woodlands and wildlife. He announced he was joining the advisory board of Dutch Green Business, a carbon-offset enterprise which carries out reforestation projects and has the ambitious goal of planting three trillion trees by 2030, doubling the current number.

Farage was actually abroad in May when Britain held its first proper elections since December 2019. Four weeks earlier, at a time when many Britons longed for a foreign holiday, but were barred by the Covid rules from taking one, Farage made his third transatlantic trip since the pandemic started. He flew to the Caribbean island of Saint Martin, and spent a fortnight enjoying the spring sunshine with friends. He then travelled on to America for a six-week programme of speaking engagements, which encompassed at least nine states.

Rather grandly called 'America's Comeback Tour', it was organised by the grassroots conservative group FreedomWorks, and the idea was to give demoralised American conservatives a lift with heroic stories of his triumph in the 2016 referendum, and the Brexit Party's historic success in the 2019 European polls. Republicans should not get disheartened was his message; American conservatives had an excellent chance of bouncing back in the mid-term elections in 2022; and Trump could well win if he stood again in 2024. Farage visited Trump at Mar-a-Lago, his grandiose estate in Palm Beach, and in a brief thirty-minute meeting urged the former president to do so. 'You're the only guy that can do it,' Farage reportedly told him. 'No one has your charisma.'[28]

At one point Farage complained on Twitter that 'hoaxers' had been booking 'fake tickets' to events on his US tour with no intention of using them, the same ruse opponents had used against Trump in 2020. 'Over the last 24 hours,' Farage wrote in mid-May, 'some 47,000 tickets have been booked for my next event in Pittsburgh. Many of these bookings are fake. They have been made by hard-left agitators who are based in the United Kingdom.'[29]

When the local elections occurred on 6 May, Reform UK stood just 285 candidates around Britain – despite the 3,000 people who'd allegedly applied to stand. Only two were elected (both in Derby), and the party got just 1 per cent of the vote in the London Assembly elections. In the by-election in Hartlepool, where Richard Tice had got more than a quarter of the vote in 2019, Reform UK was reduced to just 1.2 per cent.

What remained of the UK Independence Party fared even worse. Neil Hamilton, who had been acting UKIP leader since September 2020 – the party's ninth leader since Farage – failed dismally to secure re-election to the Senedd (as the Welsh Assembly was now called), and UKIP lost all forty-eight council seats it was defending nationwide. Despite huge public demand for some kind of 'alternative' political force, neither body struck a chord with voters any more. (Hamilton finally became permanent UKIP leader in October 2021, though the party was hardly worth leading any more.)

In the not too distant past, the two political parties over which Nigel Farage presided – UKIP and the Brexit Party – had struck fear into the hearts of mainstream politicians, especially Conservative and Labour.

Now the band had packed up; the drinks had run out; the buffet was down to a few crumbs and the host had departed, along with nearly all his guests.

Both Nigel Farage parties were truly finished; but he wasn't.

28

FARAGE NEWS

Under a hot sun on the Côte D'Azur in early August 2020 a new 'Stop Farage' movement began to hatch. Three men were gathered at a secluded luxury home in the hills above Grasse, the medieval town not far from Cannes. The host was the renowned and long-standing Scottish broadcaster and journalist Andrew Neil, who had invited his two visitors over from London to discuss an intriguing proposal they had put to him. They wanted Neil to leave the BBC, and take the flagship role of lead presenter on GB News, a new channel they planned to launch.

As the group enjoyed lunch on the terrace by the pool, with plenty of the broadcaster's favourite rosé wine (Whispering Angel from a nearby vineyard), the talk turned to whether there might be a role for Nigel Farage on the new channel. Andrew Neil was wary – he feared that Farage's involvement, and especially giving him a prime-time slot, might send out all the wrong signals. It would only confirm growing suspicions that GB News was designed as a British version of Rupert Murdoch's Fox News for which Farage often worked. Neil may have been close to Murdoch in the distant past, but he was adamantly against trying to copy Fox.

Andrew Neil knew one of his visitors very well. Sir Robbie Gibb, who'd spent two years as Theresa May's director of communications in Downing Street, had previously been editor of the two main programmes that Neil presented for the BBC: *Daily Politics* and *This Week*. Since leaving Number Ten, Gibb had been involved in the early development of GB News, of which wooing Neil was a major part. He and Neil were agreed in wanting a channel which was centre to centre-right in outlook, and would counter what they saw as the left-leaning output of the BBC and Sky News. They believed that the new channel should cater for people who felt 'left out' by the prevalence of liberal metropolitan values in mainstream broadcasting, and that they should cover stories which other TV news outlets often neglected.

Neil's other visitor was Angelos Frangopoulos, an Australian who was chief executive of GB News. The Scotsman had never met Frangopoulos before, even though, for nearly twenty years, he had run Murdoch's Australian version of Sky News, which like Fox, but unlike the British Sky News, is opinionated and right wing.

At the meeting in Grasse, the three agreed that employing Farage in a major on-screen role would impede the channel's early impact, since he would probably deter a lot more potential viewers than he attracted. Neil said, however, that he wasn't averse to Farage holding a more minor position – perhaps as co-presenter of a Sunday political show – so long as he was balanced by a prominent Remainer from the left.

A few weeks after Grasse came the dramatic announcement that Andrew Neil was leaving the BBC after a quarter of a century to become chairman of the new channel, and its main evening presenter.

Yet Neil and Gibb didn't really appreciate that the two main founders of GB News, and most of their investors, were very keen that Nigel Farage should play a major role. Andrew Cole, an English businessman who lives in America, and Mark Schneider, an American based in Britain, were both key figures in Liberty Media, the conglomerate owned by the American billionaire and Trump supporter John Malone. Cole and Schneider were both pro-Brexit, and great admirers of the former UKIP and Brexit Party leader. They, like many conservatives in Britain and America, saw Farage as a historic and heroic figure – one of the most significant politicians of modern times.

The project had raised funding from the Dubai investment group Legatum, the Discovery Channel from America, and £10 million from the British hedge fund boss Sir Paul Marshall, who'd once been a leading player in the Liberal Democrats but had broken with them over Brexit. 'The investors, with the exception of Discovery... love Nigel Farage,' Andrew Neil would explain later. 'They regard him as huge – a big, big character. They believe it will succeed and they're ideologically driven.'[1] On the Farage issue, Angelos Frangopoulos increasingly sided with his bosses. Neil later came to suspect that well before he had joined the enterprise, the founders and investors had secretly offered Farage a substantial deal to fill a major on-screen position.

Without doubt, there were very obvious tensions at GB News from the start – broadly between those like Neil and Gibb who wanted to counter what they saw as the left-leaning, 'woke' bias of the rest of British broadcasting; and the more ideological directors and investors who wanted an aggressively right-wing channel. The divisions mirrored those that had raged within the Leave camp ahead of the EU referendum. Nigel Farage might attract a loyal hard-core of supporters to the channel, but he could also repel an even bigger group of potential viewers, and put off advertisers too.

When Robbie Gibb left the project at the end of 2020 (to become a BBC trustee), Andrew Neil grew increasingly isolated. The Scotsman had always got on well with Farage on a personal level, and thought he was good company, but his demand that they find a left-leaning presenter to balance Farage on the proposed Sunday show met with obstacles. Both Frangopoulos and Gibb's replacement – former Sky News editor John McAndrew – courted Tony Blair's former media chief, Alastair Campbell, for the job. 'I didn't think it was a totally crazy idea,' Campbell says:

> Whether you like him or hate him, Farage has always had the capacity to inject himself into the political debate and get public attention. I always enjoyed debating with him and feel his arguments have to be challenged. I spoke to him a few times about it, and the channel bombarded me for a while, but in the end I made a judgement that GB News was not a platform I wanted to support. He's always been obsessed with the media, of course, and technically is a very good broadcaster.[2]

Andrew Adonis agreed to fulfil the role instead.

Well before GB News was launched, and while Farage was still officially leader of the Brexit Party, he had clearly become a big influence behind the scenes. Two former candidates for his party, the former *Apprentice* winner Michelle Dewberry, and the 24-year-old 'anti-woke' campaigner Inaya Folarin Iman, were announced as GB News presenters. In early March 2021, coincidentally the day before Farage finally resigned as leader of his party, the channel revealed another daytime on-screen presenter – none other than Farage's close friend Alex Phillips. The GB News press release announcing her arrival also revealed that Farage's old producer at LBC, Christian Mitchell, would become an executive producer for the new project.[3] Both Phillips and Mitchell are talented broadcast journalists, but it's hard to believe that Farage played no role in either appointment.

Before the launch, there was another last-minute push to make the former politician a regular prime-time presenter. Andrew Neil and John McAndrew resisted, and succeeded in excluding Farage's name and face from the initial promotional material, even though Farage was lined up to co-present the Sunday show, entitled *The Political Correction*, along with Andrew Adonis.

GB News was a disaster from the start – a public joke, thanks largely to endless production mishaps that would have disgraced a student TV station. And when Adonis saw the initial output in June 2021 he concluded, just as Alastair Campbell had feared, that it was indeed an English version of Fox News, and he withdrew from joining Farage on *The Political Correction*. Instead it was co-hosted by the 'Blue Labour' trade unionist Paul Embery, and the young Conservative MP Dehenna Davison.

After initial public curiosity, viewing figures fell dramatically. Then, having presented only eight prime-time programmes, Andrew Neil, the channel's sole moderate ratings success, announced he was taking a long summer break. Neil insisted the channel should be relaunched that autumn, and even agreed that Farage should then get a prime-time slot. But he expected the details to be settled on his return.

Three weeks later, in Neil's absence, Angelos Frangopoulos

jumped the gun – or panicked, as Neil would say. It was announced that Nigel Farage would now present an hour-long show at 7 p.m., four nights a week, from Monday to Thursday – the slot before Neil himself – in addition to his Sunday show. Although Andrew Neil had come round to the idea of Farage, he was plainly not happy. The very day of the Farage announcement, Neil posted a tweet (later withdrawn) which said that on US election night the previous November: 'I asked N Farage for evidence of voter fraud. He couldn't provide any. Nine months later – there still isn't any.'[4] It had become a contest of two famous egos, and two major British disruptors. With growing signs that Neil would never return to GB News, Nigel Farage had suddenly become its new face.

The ideological, pro-Farage conservatives had won. That became clear with the departure of John McAndrew, over an incident involving Guto Harri – an occasional presenter for GB News who'd previously been adviser to Boris Johnson as mayor of London. GB News suspended Harri for taking the knee during a studio discussion about racism towards England footballers. When the channel issued an apology saying that Harri had breached their 'standards', McAndrew resigned in disgust. Nigel Farage, in contrast, tweeted that he would 'not be taking the knee for anyone' on his new show. Harri then resigned, asking the channel to 'please explain how [Farage's stance] does not breach editorial standards but I did'.[5]

Harri, who is a lifeboat volunteer, says that if he hadn't quit over his 'taking the knee', he might have done so when Farage caused a stir by criticising the Royal National Lifeboat Institution (RNLI) for picking up migrants off the Kent coast. 'This is the Ramsgate lifeboat today, rammed full,' Farage tweeted in early July. 'Sadly the wonderful RNLI in Kent has become a taxi service for illegal immigration, to the dismay of all involved.'[6] When he subsequently repeated his RNLI remarks on GB News, Andrew Neil tweeted directly to the RNLI: 'You are the epitome of courage and self-sacrifice. The very best of British, in fact.'[7] The RNLI said that donations soared following Farage's remarks, including more than £200,000 in a single day. Andrew Neil finally announced his departure in September 2021.

Farage's weekly timetable at GB News was quite similar to his schedule at LBC. The first half-hour of his nightly show – called *Farage* – involved him digesting and analysing that day's news, with help from guests and GB News correspondents. He also delivered his own opinions, with the ever-growing cross-Channel migration a frequent topic. The second half-hour began with 'Talking Pints', where Farage interviewed a well-known individual over drinks. His guests were mostly right-wing, pro-Brexit figures, but not always. Finally, just before 8 p.m., came the 'Barrage the Farage' segment, where he responded to questions submitted by viewers.

'Farage does do the work,' admitted a former colleague who wasn't his greatest fan. 'He makes the promotional videos and trailers. He's willing to travel round the country.' Under the title 'Farage at Large', he got out of London to present whole shows from 'left out' communities such as Sunderland and Port Talbot.

The former party leader was soon attracting better audiences than Andrew Neil had in his brief spell – somewhere between 60,000 and 80,000 a night, at a time when the GB News breakfast show barely managed 10,000. *Farage* became easily the highest-rated show on GB News, and usually boasted more viewers than Sky News during the same 7–8 p.m. time slot, and occasionally more than the BBC News channel. But Farage was less successful in creating a 'halo effect', an audience which would stay for the rest of the evening. Most of his viewers tuned in to watch him, then vanished once he had gone.

He was in clover, nonetheless. He had finally achieved his dream of a prime-time TV show. Unlike his LBC days, he had time for proper preparation, and would come into the studios several hours ahead to help research his interviews and monologues. His presence raised staff morale and, perhaps surprisingly, he insisted on the need for alternative voices to contrast with his own views. 'GB News has been the making of him,' observed a fellow presenter. 'He has learned to ask intelligent questions, and to listen.' Colleagues were also impressed at how, unlike other TV anchormen, Farage didn't use an autocue, and simply spoke to camera off-the-cuff.

He was also among friends. A couple of former Brexit Party staff joined the *Farage* production team, and his former media adviser Patrick Christys became a GB News morning presenter. His friend Isabel Oakeshott was given a weekly programme, and Gawain Towler even did a few shifts on the channel's production desk. At least ten people employed by GB News in 2021 had strong connections with Farage or his parties.

GB News was effectively now Farage News. It had become a 'UKIP tribute band', complained a very bruised Andrew Neil, and an 'irrelevance'.[8] It was astonishing that the official regulator Ofcom, which is legally meant to uphold impartiality within British broadcasting, allowed GB News to develop into the first openly partisan TV channel – conservative, pro-Brexit and anti-woke.

Farage secured a major coup for GB News with an hour-long interview with Donald Trump at his home in Florida – Trump's first interview with a non-US broadcaster since leaving the White House. GB News had enough funds to last well into 2022, but with such poor viewing figures for the channel overall, it was hard to see how 'Farage News' could survive long term. That seemed especially the case after Rupert Murdoch revived his old plans for a Fox-like news channel – to be called TalkTV – and recruited Piers Morgan as its main presenter. Murdoch, who has long been a fan of Farage, might provide him with a more stable TV platform.

Yet Farage has also suggested he's not finished with politics. In late November, at the end of a *Telegraph* column which warned of the security dangers of illegal cross-Channel migration, Farage claimed he had been 'approached by several high-ranking donors asking me if I am considering getting back into the political arena'. His 'gut instinct', Farage said, 'is not to do so, but I will have to give it some serious thought'.[9] His comments may simply have been over-excitement about a front-page report in the *Sunday Telegraph* the day before, which quoted a prominent Conservative donor warning that immigration is 'going to destroy us and there is going to be a [Nigel] Farage-style party'.[10]

Might Farage try to resume the leadership of Reform UK? The day after his column I asked Richard Tice whether he would be willing to step aside and let Farage have his old job back. Tice ducked the question, but clearly wasn't keen, and didn't seem to have been consulted about his colleague's surprise remarks. Farage was concentrating '110% on GB News', Tice said.[11]

Another move might be to try and rejoin the Conservative Party, where Farage is certainly admired by many activists.

Neither option seems likely, yet nor does the third possibility – setting up yet another party.

AFTERWORD

A DISRUPTIVE LIFE

On the day in March 2021 that Farage announced he was stepping down, the political scientist Matthew Goodwin tweeted: 'Future historians will present Nigel Farage as one of the most influential and underestimated politicians of our time who won two elections with two different parties and paved the way for Brexit.' Goodwin, who was one of the first academics to understand the significance of UKIP, added that Farage was 'one of the most consequential populists, a modern day Wat Tyler' – the leader of the famous Peasants' Revolt of 1381.[1]

'Nobody in this country has come closer than me to smashing the system,' Farage said in 2020. 'I succeeded in one way, and failed in another. It's not everything I want – but victory never is.'[2]

In the summer of 2021, another prominent political scientist, Philip Cowley, tweeted that Farage was one of the five 'most significant' politicians of the last fifty years, alongside Thatcher, Blair, Sturgeon and Johnson. I agree (though I'd substitute Salmond for Sturgeon).

Nigel Farage's first notable achievement is easily forgotten. It seems like a distant memory, but for the first three years of his leadership, between 2006 and 2009, UKIP was outflanked by the British National Party in opinion polls and at elections. Had Farage been a weak TV performer – like so many UKIP leaders before and since – and had Nick Griffin been a more attractive and charismatic figure, UKIP might never have emerged as the more dominant of the two parties. Farage's boast to have 'seen off' the BNP is not far from the truth. So long as Britain had a substantial populist and nationalist party like UKIP between 2009 and 2019, the prospects for racist and neo-Nazi parties who were well to UKIP's right, such as the BNP, would remain bleak. And the swallowing up of tens of thousands of working-class voters who had supported the BNP during the Blair/Brown government helped UKIP to advance rapidly during the Cameron era, and develop a new offensive into Labour territory. Farage and his party were helped, of course, in another direction, by picking up the mantle abandoned by the Liberal Democrats as the main party of protest.

Fortune played a part, too, such as the early death of Sir James Goldsmith; the advent of proportional representation for elections to the European Parliament; and the Blair government's decision to allow unchecked immigration from the new EU member states of eastern Europe. Then, boosted by the three great crises which beset the European Union around 2010 – the EU-wide financial crisis, the Greek debt crisis, and the southern European migration crisis – UKIP rose rapidly in the polls. That, combined with rapidly growing Euroscepticism within Tory ranks, forced David Cameron to try to lance the European boil with the promise of an In-Out referendum, a pledge from which he could not row back once the Tories unexpectedly won a small majority in 2015.

Dan Hannan, a leader of the rival and official Vote Leave campaign in 2016, says that Farage 'played an enormously important role in getting us a referendum. I think that is indisputable. Had he not been prepared to put hours of his life into fruitless arguments with some very nutty people to try and weld that inchoate force into an electoral machine, I'm not sure there would have been a referendum.'[3] Yet as both Richard North and Nikki Sinclaire have shown, Farage was actually very slow to support the referendum route to EU withdrawal; for years, he preferred the more improbable 'Westminster' route of electing and converting enough MPs to vote to leave the EU in the House of Commons.

Whether Nigel Farage was vital to winning the referendum is more open to debate. Both Hannan and his Vote Leave chum Dominic Cummings argue that, without Farage, the margin of victory for Brexit would have been significantly greater. The counter-argument is that Nigel Farage and Arron Banks and their unofficial Leave.EU gingered up their Vote Leave rivals, and pushed them to campaign more boldly. Did the Farage emphasis on immigration deter waverers from voting Leave, as Cummings feared? Perhaps, but it may also have stiffened the resolve of working-class people who had become so disillusioned with politics they had lost the habit of voting at all. For many, 2016 was their first visit to a polling station in decades. And even the supposedly more cautious Vote Leave campaign made much of immigration in the end, as seen by the huge sums they spent on targeted Facebook ads warning that Turkey, Albania, Serbia and other states might soon join the EU.

Finally, in 2019, when it looked increasingly like Brexit might be thwarted, the formation of Nigel Farage's new Brexit Party forced a prime minister from office after he humiliated Theresa May in the European elections. The continued threat from the Farage insurgency in the months that followed – the Brexit Party was top of six opinion polls in late May and June 2019 – effectively forced Conservative members to pick as May's successor a charismatic campaigner who had convinced people he genuinely believed in Brexit, and gave Tory members hope they could win outright power again. Had Theresa May remained in office with no majority, the outcome of the Brexit negotiations, in Parliament and Brussels, would probably have been further stalemate or another referendum. Once Boris Johnson was in Downing Street, however, Nigel Farage looked almost redundant, without a role.

By the autumn of 2019, the transformation of the Conservative Party brought about by Brexit was almost complete, as many of the remaining pro-EU Tory MPs were purged for defying the government in the lobbies, or they chose to jump ship and quit as MPs. These groups included several senior former ministers – Ken Clarke, Philip Hammond, Dominic Grieve, Rory Stewart, David Gauke, Amber Rudd, Justine Greening and Greg Clark, as well as Churchill's grandson Sir Nicholas Soames. Though some of them returned to the party, people of their outlook now have bleak prospects as Conservative politicians.

The former home secretary Amber Rudd said in 2021 that she

would no longer manage to become a Conservative candidate. 'People who have the same beliefs that I do can't get selected to become MPs any more,' she remarked. 'The Conservative Party has swallowed UKIP whole. I think Farage is a genius in many ways.'[4] The former chancellor Ken Clarke said he no longer recognised the party he had served in the Commons for forty-nine years: 'It's the Brexit Party, rebadged,' he complained, adding that Boris Johnson had the 'most right-wing Cabinet any Conservative Party has ever produced'. And in 2020 that Cabinet bent towards another UKIP policy – opposition to foreign aid – by ignoring the Cameron government's 2015 legislation enshrining in law the UK's commitment to spend 0.7 per cent of GDP on overseas aid. It was cut instead to 0.5 per cent.

The 2016 referendum not only radically changed the nature of the Conservative Party, but also seems to have marked a watershed in British elections. For decades the psephologists, the election experts, argued that class was the dominant factor in determining how people voted. Since 2016 the dividing issue has been Brexit.

For a hundred years the Labour Party had depended on class loyalty. People voted Labour because they'd always voted Labour, and their families and friends and neighbours all voted Labour, too. They did so without thought, or any question of choice, as an expression of class solidarity, and affinity with their relatives and communities. In the 2016 referendum, Labour officially urged people to vote Remain, yet in hundreds of traditional working-class Labour seats, especially in the Midlands and the North, Labour supporters and trades unionists voted emphatically to leave the EU. The 2016 referendum burst the rising dam of resentment in such places that Labour no longer delivered for poor people like them with insecure, lowly paid jobs, and that under Blair, Miliband and Corbyn, Labour had become just another London party for wealthy middle-class types who'd gone to university.

Of the fifty-four seats Boris Johnson took from Labour in 2019, most were old industrial working-class communities which had strongly opted to Leave in 2016 – the so-called Red Wall constituencies which had once seemed impregnable. In most cases Labour had held them for decades, often with massive majorities. But Nigel Farage and his parties can justifiably claim a huge role in the process which turned the Red Wall seats blue. Some have compared his two parties to a 'gateway drug' which leads people to stronger narcotics. 'The Red Wall voters – there's not a single person who voted Conservative [in 2019] who hadn't voted UKIP or for the Brexit Party,' Farage claimed in 2021, with obvious exaggeration, but also some truth. 'UKIP were getting 10,000 votes in those seats in 2015. We were the gateway drug when it came to the general election of 2019.'[5]

Past evidence suggests that Labour will now struggle to win the Red Wall back. Once class solidarity has been breached, once people have broken a habit, it's hard to persuade them to return to old ways.

Look what happened in 2017 when, despite the overall national swing to Labour, the Conservatives nonetheless seized six Red Wall, pro-Brexit working-class constituencies. In 2019, the Conservatives won all six seats again – in five cases with handsome majorities of more than 10,000. The long-term effects of the 2016 referendum may prove to be even more profound on Labour than they are for the Conservatives. There must be a serious chance that the Labour Party will never again govern on its own in Britain.

And Brexit could well have huge effects on the future of the United Kingdom. It must be 50-50 that Scotland will vote for independence in the next few years. The future of Northern Ireland within the UK is also in serious doubt.

This is all part of Nigel Farage's legacy.

Of course, Farage cannot take sole responsibility for Brexit and its after-effects. Others fought in the frontline of the Eurosceptic battle over many decades – Bill Cash, Michael Howard, John Redwood, Iain Duncan Smith and Dan Hannan among them, along with Tony Benn, Peter Shore, Norman Tebbit, Margaret Thatcher and Enoch Powell from a previous generation. Subsequently, Michael Gove and, famously, Boris Johnson came very late to the cause, but played major roles, too.

With the obvious exception of Johnson, nobody in modern politics boasts Nigel Farage's all-round skills as a political communicator.

Many politicians are brilliant in one medium, but less effective in another. A powerful platform orator may not always be good in the broadcasting studio or comfortable with ordinary voters on the doorstep. But Nigel Farage performs superbly across the communication range – the party platform, the parliamentary chamber, on radio or TV, and he positively relishes dialogue and banter with people on the street. Maybe it's his background at Dulwich and in the City, but Farage is comfortable with all classes, at home in a Yorkshire miners' club as much as a Pall Mall gentlemen's club. Despite the accusations of racism, he's relaxed among ethnic minorities, and especially older Black people. He's struck up a special friendship with the Zimbabwean heavyweight boxer Derek Chisora and attended several of his fights. Farage matches Tony Blair for his instinctive understanding of public attitudes, and their shifting sands. Above all, unlike many senior politicians, and as his media adviser Gawain Towler tells people, Farage 'speaks fluent human'.

Yet rarely has British politics thrown up a leader who seems so little interested in policy. Other than the issue of EU withdrawal, he's always been happy to leave the manifesto drafting to others, and rarely seems to read the outcome. He's a dreadful organiser and manager, and UKIP did best during the six years when Farage left Steve Crowther to organise the party. It's perhaps just as well he was never a minister or MP, for he would have hated the life of dull ministerial meetings, or of detailed legislative scrutiny in Parliament.

No leader in modern British history can have left so many enemies and casualties among his party colleagues. Dictators worldwide would have admired Farage's ruthlessness and ability to show no mercy in purging critics and potential rivals. The suppression of dissent may have kept a lid on internal wrangling for some years, but it left an army of angry opponents and deprived his parties of strong successors, as UKIP found so disastrously after 2016.

Yet during twenty years in the European Parliament, Farage showed himself to be a master of the dark arts of forming parliamentary groups, a process that requires patient negotiating skills, and in his case a readiness to compromise declared principles and ally with some of Europe's most unsavoury politicians. Other qualities are his extraordinary energy and stamina; and his ability both to wake up unimpaired by an evening of heavy drinking, and to survive on very little sleep.

Egotism, arrogance, duplicity, dishonesty, hypocrisy, all are attributes Nigel Farage has in abundance, but so do many other successful politicians, not least our prime minister.

Farage always presents himself as the rebel, yet part of him wants to be admitted to the club. He's spent his life trying to provoke and rile the establishment – from Dulwich schoolmasters, to Brussels bigwigs and the liberal media, yet he also yearns for establishment involvement or recognition. He loves attending Old Alleynian events; reveres decorated servicemen; and enjoys belonging to the East India Club. It rankles that Whitehall never sought his advice on Trump, or considered him as ambassador to Washington, or thought him worthy of a peerage or even a meaningless knighthood.

It's hard to think of any other politician in the last 150 years who has had so much impact on British history without being a senior member of one of the major parties at the time. You might cite Churchill's fight against appeasement and calls for rearmament in the 1930s; or Joseph Chamberlain's campaign for imperial preference for British trade; or more recently the battle for Scottish independence by Alex Salmond. Yet none of those 'outsider' campaigns was really successful. Nobody can dispute that Nigel Farage achieved his goal of leaving the European Union. Without ever being elected a Westminster MP.

Quite how far-reaching Farage's legacy will be – how damaging or beneficial, or a combination thereof – it's far too soon to judge.

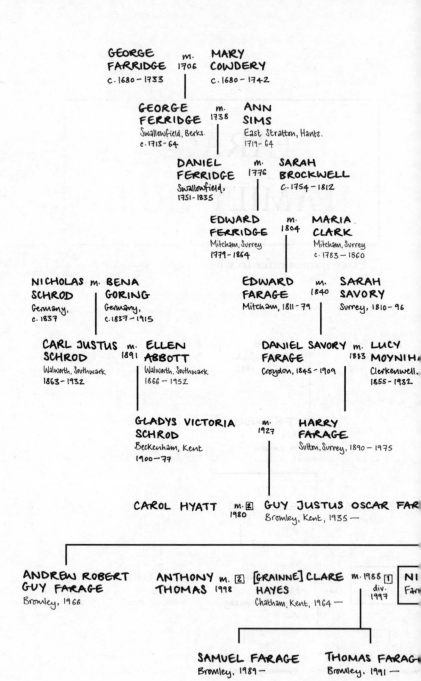

GEORGE
FARRIDGE
c. 1680 - 1733

m.
1706

MARY
COWDERY
c. 1680 - 1742

GEORGE
FERRIDGE
Swallowfield, Berks.
c. 1713 - 64

m.
1738

ANN
SIMS
East Stratton, Hants.
1719 - 64

DANIEL
FERRIDGE
Swallowfield,
1751 - 1835

m.
1776

SARAH
BROCKWELL
c. 1754 - 1812

EDWARD
FERRIDGE
Mitcham, Surrey
1779 - 1864

m.
1804

MARIA
CLARK
Mitcham, Surrey
c. 1783 - 1860

NICHOLAS
SCHROD
Germany,
c. 1837

m.

BENA
GORING
Germany,
c. 1837 - 1915

EDWARD
FARAGE
Mitcham, 1811 - 79

m.
1840

SARAH
SAVORY
Surrey, 1810 - 96

CARL JUSTUS
SCHROD
Walworth, Southwark
1863 - 1932

m.
1891

ELLEN
ABBOTT
Walworth, Southwark
1866 - 1952

DANIEL SAVORY
FARAGE
Croydon, 1845 - 1909

m.
1883

LUCY
MOYNIH

Clerkenwell.
1855 - 1932

GLADYS VICTORIA
SCHROD
Beckenham, Kent
1900 - 77

m.
1927

HARRY
FARAGE
Sutton, Surrey, 1890 - 1975

CAROL HYATT

m. 2
1980

GUY JUSTUS OSCAR FAR
Bromley, Kent, 1935 —

ANDREW ROBERT
GUY FARAGE
Bromley, 1966

ANTHONY
THOMAS

m. 2
1998

[GRAINNE] CLARE
HAYES
Chatham, Kent, 1964 —

m. 1988 1
div.
1997

NI
Far

SAMUEL FARAGE
Bromley, 1989 —

THOMAS FARAG
Bromley, 1991 —

FARAGE FAMILY TREE

Place names refer to where people were born.

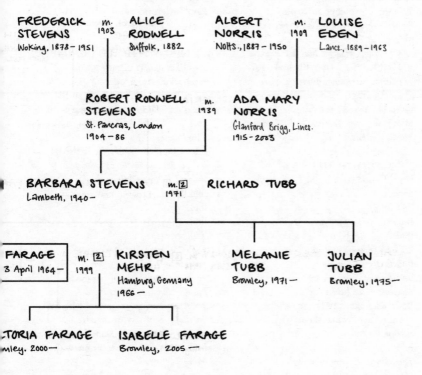

FREDERICK STEVENS
Woking, 1878 – 1951

m. 1903

ALICE RODWELL
Suffolk, 1882

ALBERT NORRIS
Notts., 1887 – 1950

m. 1909

LOUISE EDEN
Lancs., 1889 – 1963

ROBERT RODWELL STEVENS
St. Pancras, London 1904 – 86

m. 1939

ADA MARY NORRIS
Glanford Brigg, Lincs. 1915 – 2003

BARBARA STEVENS
Lambeth, 1940 –

m. 2 1971

RICHARD TUBB

FARAGE
3 April 1964 –

m. 2 1999

KIRSTEN MEHR
Hamburg, Germany 1966 –

MELANIE TUBB
Bromley, 1971 –

JULIAN TUBB
Bromley, 1975 –

TORIA FARAGE
mley. 2000 –

ISABELLE FARAGE
Bromley, 2005 –

NOTES

Key: MH – Margaret Crick (Hounsell); HD – Henry Dyer

INTRODUCTION

1 Air Accident Investigation Branch bulletin, November 2010, p.67.
2 *Daily Telegraph* video, YouTube, 13 March 2015.
3 Nigel Farage, *Fighting Bull* (later revised and retitled *Flying Free*), Biteback, 2010; *The Purple Revolution*, Biteback, 2015.
4 Owen Bennett, *Following Farage*, Biteback, 2015; *The Brexit Club*, 2016.
5 Matthew Lynn, *Independently Minded: The Rise of Nigel Farage*, Kindle, 2015.

1. DOWNE HIS WAY

1 Nigel Farage, *Fighting Bull*, Biteback, 2010, p.3.
2 Ibid., p.5.
3 *High Profiles*, 2 December 2011.
4 Ibid.
5 Farage, *Fighting Bull*, p.6.
6 Ibid., p.7.
7 Ibid., p.13.
8 *Algemeiner*, 22 July 2013.
9 *Daily Telegraph*, 22 May 2009.
10 Nigel Farage, conversation with author.
11 Ibid.
12 *The Globe*, 6 September 1870.
13 Martin Young, interview with MH.
14 Farage, *Fighting Bull*, pp.14-15.
15 Ibid., p.16.
16 Roy Thompson, interview with MH.
17 Farage, *Fighting Bull*, p.16.
18 Anna Marie Marshallsay, interview with MH.
19 Pam Taylor, interview with MH.
20 Farage, *Fighting Bull*, p.17.

2. REBEL WITHOUT A CAUSE

1 Nigel Farage, *The Purple Revolution*, Biteback, 2015, p.43.
2 Peter Petyt, interview with author.
3 Gardner Thompson, interview with MH.
4 Tim France, email to author.
5 Stuart Dunbar, interview with MH.
6 *Independent* website, 17 June 2016.
7 Farage, *Fighting Bull*, p.30.
8 Ibid., p.33.
9 Ibid., p.28.
10 Ibid., p.23.
11 Ibid., p.24.
12 *High Profiles*, 2 December 2011.
13 John Stuart Mill, *On Liberty*, OUP, 2008, p.14.
14 Farage, *Fighting Bull*, p.26.
15 Jonathan Mayne, interview with MH.
16 *Spotlight*, ITV, 23 April 2015.
17 Channel 4 News, 19 September 2013.
18 Mohan Yogendran, interview with MH.
19 *GQ*, May 2009.
20 Chloe Deakin, letter to David Emms, 4 June 1981.
21 David Emms, interview with author for Channel 4 News.

22 Channel 4 News, 19 September 2013.

23 Farage, *Fighting Bull*, p.37.

24 Channel 4 News, 19 September 2013.

25 *Independent* website, 13 May 2019.

26 Bob Jope, email to author.

27 Peter Ettedgui, email to author.

28 Nick Gordon Brown, interview with author for Channel 4 News, 2013.

29 David Edmonds, interview with author.

30 Tim France, interview with author.

31 Jonathan Mayne, interview with MH.

32 Jon Benjamin, interview with author (2013).

33 Ian Oakley Smith, interview with MH.

34 Nigel Farage, email to author.

35 Roger Gough, interview with MH.

36 *Alleynian*, Summer 1981.

37 *GQ*, May 2009.

38 *Independent*, 5 February 2012.

39 *Independent*, 9 November 2013.

40 Lord (Andrew) Adonis, interview with author.

41 Farage, *Fighting Bull*, p.37.

42 Neil Fairlamb, interview with MH.

3. CITY TRADER

1 *High Profiles*, 2 December 2011.

2 Farage, *The Purple Revolution*, p.62.

3 *Third Way*, Winter 2012.

4 Farage, *The Purple Revolution*, p.63.

5 Farage, *Fighting Bull*, p.40.

6 *Third Way*, Winter 2012.

7 *High Profiles*, 2 December 2011.

8 Farage, *Fighting Bull*, pp.40-41.

9 Farage, *The Purple Revolution*, p.66.

10 *High Profiles*, 2 December 2011.

11 Steven Spencer, interview with MH.

12 *Financial Times*, 8 April 2016.

13 *Independent*, 5 February 2012.

14 *High Profiles*, 2 December 2011.

15 *Financial Times*, 8 April 2016.

16 Farage, *Fighting Bull*, p.42.

17 *Independent*, 5 February 2012.

18 *Financial Times*, 6 February 2015.

19 *Nigel Farage: Who Are You?* Channel 4, 15 March 2018.

20 *Third Way*, Winter 2012.

21 Farage, *The Purple Revolution*, p.68.

22 Farage, *Fighting Bull*, p.44.

23 Ibid., p.50.

24 Ibid., p.51.

25 Ibid., p.52.

26 *Independent*, 9 November 2013.

27 *GQ*, May 2009.

28 *Piers Morgan's Life Stories* (Farage), ITV, 24 February 2017.

29 *GQ*, May 2009.

30 *Independent*, 7 August 2014.

31 *Profile* (Godfrey Bloom), BBC Radio 4, 4 December 2012.

32 Steven Spencer, interview with MH.

33 Breitbart News, 21 August 2015.

34 Farage, *Fighting Bull*, pp.66-7.

35 Ibid., p.79.

36 Ibid., p.80.

37 Ibid., p.81.

38 *Profile*, BBC Radio 4, 4 December 2012.

39 Malcolm Freeman, interview with MH.

40 Steven Spencer, interview with MH.

41 Malcolm Freeman, interview with MH.

42 *Financial Times*, 6 February 2015.

43 Ibid.

44 Stephen Ayme, interview with author.

4. HOOKED BY POLITICS

1 Farage, *Fighting Bull*, p.55.

2 Margaret Thatcher, Bruges Speech, 20 September 1988, Thatcher Foundation Archive.

3 Farage, *Fighting Bull*, p.66.

4 Mark Daniel, *Cranks and Gadflies*, Timewell Press, 2005, p.12.

5 *Gearty Grilling*, LSE, YouTube, 28 May 2014,

6 Robert Ford and Matthew Goodwin, *Revolt on the Right*, Routledge, 2014, p.21.

7 Alan Sked, interview with author.

8 Farage, *Fighting Bull*, p.70.

9 Alan Sked, interview with author.

10 Ibid.

11 Farage, *Fighting Bull*, p.73.

12 Ibid., pp.73-4.

13 Ibid., p.75.

14 Ibid., p.81.

15 Ibid.

16 *Daily Telegraph*, 12 December 2014.

17 *Channel 5 News*, YouTube, 4 July 2016.

18 'Nigel Farage Through the Years', RobinHoodUKIP, YouTube, posted 5 July 2016.

19   *Salisbury Journal*, 13 July 1995.
20   *UK Independence News*, October 1996.
21   Daniel, *Cranks and Gadflies*, p.29.
22   Richard North, interview with author.
23   Ibid.
24   Anthony Scholefield, interview with author.
25   Alan Sked, interview with author.
26   UKIP NEC Minutes, 11 February 1997.
27   *Mail on Sunday*, 6 June 2004.
28   Alan Sked, interview with author.
29   Other accounts include (Channel 4 News) interview with author, December 2012. Also *Mail on Sunday*, 6 June 2004.
30   Richard North, interview with author.
31   *Guardian*, 15 June 2016.
32   Norman Lamont, *In Office*, Little, Brown, 1999, p.417.
33   Daniel, *Cranks and Gadflies*, p.19.
34   UKIP party election broadcast, 21 April 1997.
35   Farage, *Fighting Bull*, p.89.
36   Alan Sked, interview with author.
37   Patrick Robertson, interview with author.
38   Peter Gardner, *Hard Pounding*, June Press, 2006, p.59.
39   Anonymous letter to editor of the *Salisbury Journal,* undated, *c.*April 1997.
40   Robert Key, interview with author.
41   Ford and Goodwin, *Revolt on the Right*, p.30.

5. TREACHERY

1   *Election 97*, BBC1, 2 May 1997.
2   *Evening Standard*, 12 May 1997.
3   Daniel, *Cranks and Gadflies*, p.21.
4   Ibid., p.40.
5   Ibid., p.34.
6   Ibid., pp.20-21.
7   Farage, *Fighting Bull*, p.91.
8   Ibid., p.95.
9   Ibid.; Alan Sked, letter to Michael Holmes, 18 June 1997.
10   *UK Independence News*, August 1997.
11   Chopper's podcast, 6 March 2021.

12   *Piers Morgan's Life Stories* (Farage), ITV, 24 February 2017.
13   Farage, *Fighting Bull*, p.81.
14   Ibid., p.99.
15   Daniel, *Cranks and Gadflies*, p.50.
16   *UK Independence*, October 1997.
17   Alastair Campbell, *The Alastair Campbell Diaries*, Vol. 2, Hutchinson, 2011, p. 567 (18 November 1998).
18   Paddy Ashdown, *The Ashdown Diaries*, Vol. 2, *1997-99*, Allen Lane, 2001, p.370 (15 December 1998).
19   Peter Gardner, *Hard Pounding: The UKIP Story*, June Press, 2006, pp.84-5.
20   Jack Straw, interview with author.
21   Nikki Sinclaire, *Never Give Up: Standing Tall Through Adversity*, Junius Press, 2013, p.166.

6. PICTURE OF A COMPROMISING THREESOME

1   Farage, *Fighting Bull*, p.94.
2   Mark Deavin, interview with author.
3   *UKIP Newsletter*, 7 February 1995.
4   Alan Sked, interview with author.
5   Farage, *Fighting Bull*, p.93.
6   *Guardian*, 13 October 1999.
7   *The Cook Report*, 'The Truth Behind the Front', ITV, 17 June 1997.
8   *Guardian*, 13 October 1999.
9   Jonathan Marcus, *The National Front and French Politics: The Resistible Rise of Jean-Marie Le Pen*, Macmillan, 1995.
10   *The Cook Report*, 'The Truth Behind the Front', ITV, 17 June 1997.
11   Alan Sked, letter to UKIP members, 19 May 1997.
12   Alan Sked, letter to UKIP members, 3 June 1997.
13   Farage, *Fighting Bull*, p.95.
14   *Spearhead*, no. 341, July 1997.
15   *The Times*, 5 June 1999.
16   Ibid.
17   *The Times*, 8 June 1999.
18   UKIP press release, 8 June 1999.
19   Affidavit, Nigel Farage v. Times Newspapers, 21 June 1999.
20   Mark Deavin, interview with author.
21   Ibid.
22   Farage, *Fighting Bull*, p.93.
23   Affidavit, Nigel Farage v. Times

24 Farage, *Fighting Bull*, pp.95-6.
25 Ibid., p.96.
26 Mark Deavin, interview with author.
27 Nick Griffin, interview with author.
28 *Sunday Times*, 26 April 2015.
29 *The Times*, 21 July 1999.
30 Alastair Brett, letter to Nigel Farage, 27 October 1999.
31 Farage, *Fighting Bull*, p.131.
32 *Spearhead*, no. 341, July 1997.
33 Mark Deavin, interview with author.
34 Gardner, *Hard Pounding*, p.87.
35 Sinclaire, *Never Give Up*, p.144.
36 UKIP campaign leaflet, 'Your Pound, Your Country, Your Chance . . .', Spring 1999.
37 UKIP *Election Bulletin*, 'A Global Future for the South East', Spring 1999.
38 *Daily Telegraph*, 18 January 1999.
39 Gardner, *Hard Pounding*, p.91.
40 Ibid., pp.93-4.
41 David Lott diary (unpublished), 8 June 1999.
42 Ibid., 13 June 1999.
43 Ibid.
44 ITV News, 17 September 2016.

7. BREAKING AND ENTERING

1 *Desperately Seeking EUtopia: The Enemy Within*, Mosaic Films, 2000.
2 Michael Holmes, letter to UKIP candidates, 22 April 1999.
3 UKIP manifesto, 1999 European election.
4 *7 Days*, ITV Meridian, 25 July 1999.
5 House of Commons research paper, SN/1A/5388, 18 March 2010.
6 *Desperately Seeking EUtopia: The Enemy Within*, Mosaic Films, 2000.
7 Ibid.
8 NEC Minutes, 17 November 1999, cited in Gardner, *Hard Pounding*, p.111.
9 *Guardian*, 20 October 1999.
10 *The Times*, 14 December 2000.
11 LBC Video, YouTube, 31 January 2020.
12 LBC, 29 January 2020.
13 YouTube, 31 January 2020.
14 'Nigel's rebellion 1993-2016', YouTube, 23 September 2016.

15 Jens-Peter Bonde, interview with HD.
16 Richard North, interview with author.
17 Daniel, *Cranks and Gadflies*, p.65.
18 Richard North, interview with author.
19 Ibid.
20 Ibid.
21 Debates, European Parliament, Strasbourg, 21 July 1999.
22 Daniel, *Cranks and Gadflies*, p.67.
23 Farage, *Fighting Bull*, p.122.
24 Ibid., p.123.
25 Ibid., p.124.
26 Rob McWhirter ('Sponplague'), Democracy Forum chat site, 2 and 3 February 2008.
27 Sinclaire, *Never Give Up*, p.145.
28 *Private Eye*, 14 January 2000.
29 Farage, *Fighting Bull*, p.125.
30 Gardner, *Hard Pounding*, p.119.
31 Farage, *Fighting Bull*, p.125.
32 Gardner, *Hard Pounding*, p.117.
33 Farage, *Fighting Bull*, p.126.

8. SLAYER OF KINGS

1 *Black Adder*, 'The Foretelling', BBC1, 15 June 1983.
2 Bill Jamieson and Christopher Booker, letter to UKIP NEC, 9 March 2000.
3 Rodney Atkinson and Norris McWhirter, *Treason at Maastricht: Destruction of the Nation State*, Compuprint, 1995.
4 Rodney Atkinson, 'A Reply to the Booker/Jamieson letter', undated (*c.*March 2000).
5 Greg Lance-Watkins, interview with author.
6 Ibid.
7 Daniel, *Cranks and Gadflies*, p.79.
8 Farage, *Fighting Bull*, p.127.
9 Statement by Rodney Atkinson and others, April 2000.
10 Bryan Smalley, note to Mike Nattrass and Jeffrey Titford, 21 July 2000.
11 Gordon Black, witness statement, 21 August 2000.
12 Hugh Meechan, email copied on UKIPList, 11 March 2000.
13 Ibid.
14 Statement by Rodney Atkinson, *Why I*

Resigned from the UK Independence Party, 20 August 2000.

15 David Lott, email to Ind-UK list, 30 March 2000.

16 Farage, *Fighting Bull*, p.136.

17 Bryan Smalley, 'Commentary and Timetable on Sale of "Pirate" Videos', 3 September 2000.

18 Adam Alexander, fax to Nikki Sinclaire, 1 September 2000.

19 Adam Alexander, fax to Nigel Farage, 31 July 2000.

20 Bryan Smalley, 'Commentary and Timetable on Sale of 'Pirate' Videos', 3 September 2000.

21 Jeffrey Titford, fax to Bryan Smalley, 24 August 2000.

22 Adam Alexander, letter to Nigel Farage, 25 August 2000.

23 Nigel Farage, letter to Adam Alexander, 5 October 2000.

24 Bryan Smalley, letter to Members of the NEC, 3 September 2000.

25 Ibid.

26 Ibid.

27 Ibid.

28 Bryan Smalley, letter to John De Roeck, 10 September 2000.

29 Bryan Smalley, letter to colleagues, 16 September 2000.

30 Phil Hornby, interview with author.

31 *Private Eye*, 14 January 2000.

32 *Essex County Standard* Online, 3 January 2000.

33 *Guardian* Online, 4 January 2000.

34 Daniel, *Cranks and Gadflies*, p.95.

35 Farage, *Fighting Bull*, p.151.

36 Daniel, *Cranks and Gadflies*, p.96.

37 Farage, *Fighting Bull*, pp.152-3.

38 *Guardian*, 3 March 2001.

39 Democracy Forum website, 29 May 2007.

40 *Rye & Battle Observer*, 18 May 2001.

41 Charles Wardle, interview with author.

42 *Rye & Battle Observer*, 11 May 2001.

43 *Daily Telegraph*, 9 May 2001

44 Charles Wardle, interview with author.

45 Ibid.

46 Ford and Goodwin, *Revolt on the Right*, Routledge, p.40.

47 Ibid., pp.38, 41.

9. KILROY WAS HERE

1 Neil and Christine Hamilton, interview with author.

2 Richard North, interview with author.

3 Farage, *Fighting Bull*, p.154.

4 Ibid.

5 Christine Hamilton, interview with author.

6 Daniel, *Cranks and Gadflies*, p.107.

7 Richard North, interview with author.

8 *Sunday Express*, 4 January 2004.

9 Ford and Goodwin, *Revolt on the Right*, p.45.

10 Farage, *Fighting Bull*, p.163.

11 Daniel, *Cranks and Gadflies*, p.133.

12 Ibid.

13 Ibid., p.134.

14 Farage, *Fighting Bull*, p.164.

15 Ibid.

16 Gardner, *Hard Pounding*, p.176.

17 Daniel, *Cranks and Gadflies*, p.135.

18 David Butler and Martin Westlake, *British Politics and European Elections 2004*, Palgrave Macmillan, 2005, p.124.

19 *The Times*, 7 June 2004.

20 Gardner, *Hard Pounding*, p.169.

21 *Evening Standard*, 23 October 2009.

22 *The Times*, 7 June 2004.

23 Ford and Goodwin, *Revolt on the Right*, p.47.

24 Daniel, *Cranks and Gadflies*, p.136.

25 *Sunday Telegraph*, 30 May 2000; email from Richard North to David Lott, 23 August 2003.

26 *Mail on Sunday*, 6 June 2004.

27 Ibid.

28 *Independent* Online, 7 January 2004.

29 Frank Maloney website, 6 January 2004.

30 BBC News Online, 29 April 2004.

31 Gardner, *Hard Pounding*, pp.173-4.

32 *Daily Telegraph*, 21 July 2004.

33 Farage, *Fighting Bull*, p.174.

34 *Evening Standard*, 14 June 2004.

35 *The Man Behind the Tan*, BBC3, 31 January 2005.

36 Ibid.
37 Daniel, *Cranks and Gadflies*, p.134.
38 Ford and Goodwin, *Revolt on the Right*, p.47.
39 Farage, *Fighting Bull*, p.164.
40 Ibid., p.179.
41 *Frost*, BBC1, 3 October 2004.
42 *The Man Behind the Tan*, BBC3, 31 January 2004.
43 Ford and Goodwin, *Revolt on the Right*, p.49.
44 *New Statesman*, 18 September 2019.
45 Ibid.
46 BirminghamLive website, 29 June 2013.
47 Farage, *Fighting Bull*, p.187
48 Helyn Clack, interview with author.
49 Sir Paul Beresford, interview with author.
50 BBC News Online, 5 December 2006.
51 Farage, *Fighting Bull*, pp.150-51.
52 Jonathan Aitken, interview with author.
53 Petrina Holdsworth, email to author, 27 November 2020.
54 UKIP Thanet newsletter, November 2004.
55 *Guardian*, 12 May 2004.
56 UKIP, 'Declaration by Party Officer' form, undated.
57 Jonathan Aitken, interview with author.
58 Stephen Ladyman, interview with MH.

10. THE AWKWARD SQUAD

1 *The Man Behind the Tan*, BBC3, 31 January 2005.
2 *Jewish Chronicle* Online, 14 November 2011.
3 World Jewish Congress website, 17 November 2011.
4 *Guardian*, 26 January 2010.
5 Farage, *Fighting Bull*, p.176.
6 Umberto Bossi Wikipedia entry.
7 European Parliament, 18 November 2004, *Euractiv* website, 26 May 2008.
8 LBC Video, YouTube, 29 January 2020.
9 *Daily Telegraph*, 28 November 2004.
10 Farage, *Fighting Bull*, p.191.

11 UKIP press release, 19 November 2004.
12 UKIP press release, 31 March 2005.
13 Derk Jan Eppink, email to author.
14 YouTube, 18 November 2004.
15 BBC Online, 22 November 2004.
16 European Parliament, 11 January 2005.
17 Derk Jan Eppink, *Empire of Little Kings*, Pelckmans, 2015, p.191.
18 European Parliament, 25 May 2005.
19 Eppink, *Empire of Little Kings*, p.192.
20 LBC, 29 January 2019.
21 Roger Knapman, letter to UKIP NEC members, 13 May 2007.
22 This author should declare he was among those making the accusations.
23 *Sunday Times*, 16 November 2003.
24 *Sunday Times*, 20 November 2009.
25 Gawain Towler, interview with author.
26 European Parliament, 20 December 2005.
27 David Cameron, *For the Record*, William Collins, 2019, p.512.
28 BBC Online, 4 April 2016.
29 *Have I Got News for You?*, BBC2, 14 April 2014.
30 Lord (Chris) Rennard, text to author.
31 Ford and Goodwin, *Revolt on the Right*, p.71.
32 *News of the World*, 26 January 2006.
33 Farage, *Fighting Bull*, p.137.
34 UKIP-vs-EUKIP website, 29 January 2006.

11. MYSTERY OF THE OLD BETTING SHOP

1 *Kentish Express*, 16 October 2003.
2 *Independence*, August 2005.
3 UKIP Finance Committee report to NEC, 3 September 2003.
4 Ibid.
5 John De Roeck, letter to Derek Clark, 5 September 2003.
6 John De Roeck, interview with author.
7 Petrina Holdsworth, Democracy Forum chat site, 23 February 2007.
8 UKIP NEC Minutes, 9 January 2006.
9 Letter from Richard Suchorzewski to David Campbell Bannerman, 5

October 2006.

10 Richard Suchorzewski, untransmitted interview for Channel 4, 24 June 2013.

11 Ibid.

12 UKIP NEC Minutes, 17 October 2005.

13 Rodney Howlett, Ind-UK chat site, 18 November 2003.

14 Brian Lee, UKIP forum, 4 October 2005.

15 Minutes of meeting between representatives of UKIP NEC and Chichester branch, 17 October 2005.

16 Ashford Call Centre, financial statement, December 2005.

17 Letter sent to *Sunday Telegraph*, 20 February 2007.

18 David Campbell Bannerman, interview with author.

19 *Sunday Telegraph*, 18 February 2007.

20 Douglas Denny, Democracy Forum chat site, 14 January 2008.

21 Business meeting report by Geoffrey Kingscott, 3 July 2007.

22 UKIP South Eastern Counties accounts, 2004.

23 Tony Ellwood, untransmitted interview for Channel 4, June 2013.

24 *The Times*, 16 April 2014.

25 Delroy Young, research interview for Channel 4, 2013.

26 Statement by Ian Gillman, undated.

27 Ian Gillman, untransmitted interview for Channel 4, June 2013.

28 Tony Ellwood, research interview for Channel 4, 2013.

29 UKIP NEC Minutes, 10 November 2003.

30 UKIP NEC Minutes, 12 May 2003.

31 *Sunday Times*, 18 February 2007.

32 Bruce Lawson UKIP resignation statement, 17 April 2007.

33 Ian Gillman, untransmitted interview for Channel 4.

12. GAME, SET AND MATCH TO FARAGE

1 Statement by Julia Langmead, 31 July 2006.

2 Richard Suchorzewski resignation letter, 5 October 2006.

3 Ford and Goodwin, *Revolt on the Right*, pp.72-3.

4 Ibid., pp.73-4.

5 *Telegraph* Online, 4 March 2007.

6 *Western Morning News*, 19 March 2007.

7 *Western Morning News*, 24 March 2007.

8 Nick Griffin, email to author.

9 UKIP press release, 5 May 2003.

10 Martin Haslam, draft address to UKIP NEC, November 2008, written 30 October 2008.

11 Buster Mottram email to Robin Collet, 11 September 2008.

12 Message included in email from Andrew Edwards to unknown person, 5 November 2008.

13 Eric Edmond report on NEC 'farce', undated.

14 Ford and Goodwin, *Revolt on the Right*, p.74.

15 Paul Nuttall, email to UKIP branch chairmen, 3 November 2008.

16 Douglas Denny email to Eric Edmond, NEC members and others, 6 November 2008.

17 David Campbell Bannerman, interview with author.

18 Buster Mottram statement, posted on Democracy Forum, 5 November 2008.

19 Paul Nuttall, email to UKIP branch chairmen, 3 November 2008.

20 David Abbott report, 4 November 2008.

21 Eric Edmond email to 12 NEC members and others, 6 November 2008; posted Democracy Forum, 8 November 2008.

22 UKIP NEC Minutes, 3 November 2008.

23 Ford and Goodwin, *Revolt on the Right*, p.75.

24 Eric Edmond, email to Douglas Denny and other NEC members, 6 November 2008.

25 David Abbott's report on the NEC 'farce', 4 November 2008.

26 UKIP NEC Minutes, 3 November 2008.

27 yourcanterbury.co.uk/kentnews, 8 November 2008.

28 BBC News Online, 3 November 2008.

29 Paul Nuttall email to UKIP branch chairmen, 3 November 2008, posted Democracy Forum.

30 Ford and Goodwin, *Revolt on the Right*, p.75.

31 Paul Nuttall, statement to author, June 2021.

32 Douglas Denny, email to Martin Haslam, 6 November 2008, posted Democracy Forum.

33 Douglas Denny, email to Eric Edmond, NEC members and others, 6 November 2008.

34 Eric Edmond, interview with HD.

35 David Abbott, Democracy Forum, 4 November 2008.

36 David Abbott, statement to UKIP NEC, 12 January 2009.

37 Eric Edmond statement to UKIP NEC, 12 January 2009.

38 David Campbell Bannerman, interview with author.

39 'Buster's report of NEC Farce', Democracy Forum, 5 November 2008.

40 Junius Blog, 11 July 2009; Douglas Denny email to NEC members and others, 6 November 2008.

41 *Daily Telegraph*, 1 March 2009.

42 Robin Page, letter to Paul Nuttall, 28 February 2009.

43 *GQ*, May 2009.

44 Clive Page, interview with author.

45 *Observer*, 24 May 2009.

46 Ibid.

13. CRASHING TO EARTH

1 BBC News Online, 4 September 2009.

2 Ford and Goodwin, *Revolt on the Right*, p.78.

3 Ibid., p.79.

4 This author inadvertently played a small role in Bercow's elevation. I bumped into him at the Commons a few days after he announced he was standing, and he was still considered an outsider. Why, I asked, was his name not in the bookmakers' lists of runners and riders? 'If I were you,' I said in half-jest, 'I'd go and get a friend to put a large sum of money on you!' Sebastian Whale's 2020 biography says Bercow took my advice, and got his friend Michael Keegan to place bets in small sums at different bookies, which quickly generated momentum. Sebastian Whale, *John Bercow: Call to Order*, Biteback, 2020, p.141.

5 BBC News Online, 11 November 2009.

6 Ibid., 12 November 2009.

7 *Spectator*, 18 October 2014.

8 *The Times*, 30 November 2009.

9 Dave Fowler, interview with MH.

10 John Stevens, interview with MH.

11 Jocelyn Phillips, letter to MH, 16 November 2020.

12 European Parliament, 11 February 2010.

13 *Daily Telegraph*, 27 February 2010.

14 *Daily Telegraph*, 2 March 2010.

15 Eppink, *Empire of Little Kings*, p.195.

16 Ibid., p.196.

17 Daniel, *Cranks and Gadflies*, 2005.

18 *Sunday Times*, 21 March 2010.

19 Gawain Towler blog, 21 March 2010.

20 *Sunday Times*, 21 March 2010.

21 *Sunday Times*, 18 April 2010.

22 *Guardian*, 3 September 2009.

23 *Daily Telegraph*, 6 May 2010.

24 Dave Fowler, interview with MH.

25 *New Statesman*, 21 April 2010.

26 *Daily Telegraph*, 6 May 2010.

27 *Sunday Times*, 18 April 2010.

28 Dave Fowler, interview with MH.

29 *Daily Telegraph* video, YouTube, 13 March 2015.

30 *Daily Mail*, 7 May 2010.

31 Nigel Farage, *Flying Free*, Biteback, 2011, p.248.

32 Air Accident Investigation Branch bulletin, November 2010, p.67.

33 Farage, *Flying Free*, p.250.

34 *Piers Morgan's Life Stories*, ITV, 24 February 2017.

35 *Independent*, 11 November 2010.

36 Neil Hall, interview with MH.

37 Farage, *Flying Free*, p.250.

38 *Piers Morgan's Life Stories*, ITV, 24

February 2017.

39 *Bucks Free Press*, 6 May 2010.
40 Bobby Friedman, *Bercow: Mr Speaker*, Gibson Square, 2011, p.223.
41 Ibid., p.224.
42 Farage, *Flying Free*, p.242.
43 Dave Fowler, interview with MH.
44 Dennis Kavanagh and Philip Cowley, *The British General Election of 2010*, Palgrave Macmillan, 2010, p.404.
45 Farage, *Flying Free*, p.258.
46 *Daily Telegraph* video, YouTube, 13 March 2015.
47 *Independent*, 6 May 2010.
48 Thom Airs, interview with MH.
49 *Oxford Mail*, 12 April 2011.
50 Ibid.
51 *Oxford Mail*, 10 May 2011.
52 *Oxford Mail*, 13 April 2011.
53 *Oxford Mail*, 10 June 2011.

14. NIGEL'S BACK

1 *Sunday Times*, 4 April 2010.
2 *Guardian*, 17 August 2010.
3 Farage, *Flying Free*, p.259.
4 Tim Congdon, interview with HD.
5 Farage, *Flying Free*, pp.259, 267.
6 Ibid.
7 *Guardian*, 3 September 2010.
8 Farage, *Flying Free*, pp.259, 241.
9 David Campbell Bannerman, interview with author.
10 Junius blog, 3 September 2010.
11 Junius website, 11 December 2012, published anonymously, but Doug Denny now says he was the author of the statement.
12 Ibid.
13 Doug Denny statement on Sir Patrick Moore, 11 February 2021.
14 Ibid.
15 Tim Congdon, interview with HD.
16 *Independence*, July 2011.
17 Reuters, 11 August 2007.
18 Sinclaire, *Never Give Up*.
19 *The Coalition: Our Programme for Government*, Cabinet Office, 2010, p.27.
20 Sinclaire, *Never Give Up*, p.188.
21 Gary Cartwright, interview with author.
22 Cameron, *For the Record*, pp.331-2.

23 Sinclaire, *Never Give Up*, p.188.
24 *The News Thing*, Russia Today, 12 August 2016.
25 *Westerham Chronicle*, 22 March 2012.
26 Interview with Andrew Gimson for conservativehome.com, 16 July 2013.

15. BLOOMBERG AND BLOOM

1 *Daily Telegraph*, 23 January 2013.
2 *Guardian* video, YouTube, 24 January 2013.
3 Cameron, *For the Record*, pp.399, 406-07.
4 Annabelle Fuller, email to Sean Howlett el al., 10 February 2013.
5 *Daily Telegraph*, 3 May 2013.
6 *Yorkshire Post* Online, 30 April 2013.
7 *Daily Mail*, 22 November 2013.
8 Off Script podcast, *The Telegraph*, 17 September 2021.
9 Sky News, 20 September 2013, YouTube.
10 *Guardian* Online, 20 September 2013.
11 BBC News Online, 21 September 2013.
12 ChatPolitics, 8 December 2013, YouTube.
13 BBC News Online, 24 September 2013.
14 *Daily Politics*, BBC2, 12 June 2014.
15 Godfrey Bloom, interview with author.
16 *Huffington Post* Online, 1 November 2011.
17 Neil Hamilton, interview with author.
18 Ibid.
19 Ibid.
20 BBC News Online, 28 February 2014.
21 Ibid., 1 March 2014.
22 *Guardian/Observer* Online 1 March 2014.
23 Neil Hamilton, interview with author.
24 Ibid.
25 *Guardian* Online, 14 December 2014.
26 Neil Hamilton, interview with author.
27 *Mail on Sunday*, 14 December 2014.
28 Neil Hamilton, interview with author.

16. A WEAKNESS FOR WOMEN

1 European Parliament, YouTube, 12 March 2014.

2 Eppink, *Empire of Little Kings*, p. 197.
3 *Birmingham Mail*, 11 July 2016.
4 BBC Online, 14 March 2014.
5 Ibid.
6 *Nick Ferrari Show*, LBC, 13 March 2014.
7 *Guardian,* 13 March 2014.
8 BBC West Midlands, YouTube, 12 March 2014.
9 *Mail on Sunday,* 22 March 2014.
10 Ibid.
11 *Have I Got News For You?*, BBC2, 11 April 2014.
12 Richard North, interview with author.
13 Mike Nattrass, interview with author.
14 *Daily Telegraph*, 26 May 2014.
15 Farage, *Fighting Bull*, p.119.
16 Richard North, interview with author.
17 *Daily Telegraph*, 27 June 2010.
18 *Daily Telegraph*, 26 May 2014.
19 *Huffington Post*, 30 September 2013.
20 BBC News Online, 12 March 2014.
21 *Mail on Sunday*, 11 November 2017.
22 Ibid.
23 Ibid.
24 *Daily Express*, 7 June 2014.
25 *Mail on Sunday*, 11 November 2017.
26 *Daily Mirror*, 15 March 2014.
27 *Mail on Sunday*, 11 November 2017.
28 Gregg Beaman blog, 'More on Leaving UKIP', 30 January 2009.
29 *Mail on Sunday*, 14 March 2014.
30 BBC News Online, 12 March 2014.
31 *Daily Mail*, 16 January 2016.
32 *Mail on Sunday*, 11 November 2017.
33 *Daily Express*, 7 June 2014.
34 Trixy Sanderson (Annabelle Fuller), interview with author.
35 *Mail on Sunday*, 11 November 2017.
36 *Daily Telegraph*, 11 March 2014.
37 *The Times*, 13 March 2014.
38 *HuffPost* website, 21 May 2014.
39 *Euractiv*, 21 May 2014.
40 Godfrey Bloom, interview with author.
41 *Euractiv*, 21 May 2014.
42 Godfrey Bloom, interview with author.
43 Alex Phillips, interview with author.
44 *Euractiv*, 21 May 2014.
45 Alex Phillips, interviews with author.
46 ConservativeHome website, 20 September 2016.

47 Alex Phillips, interview with author.
48 Ibid.
49 Ibid.
50 Roger Bird, interview with author.
51 Ibid.
52 Trixy Sanderson (Annabelle Fuller), interview with author.
53 Ibid.
54 Ibid.
55 Jay Beecher, *UKIP Exposed*, 2017, chapter 6, p.5
56 Ibid., p.4.
57 Trixy Sanderson (Annabelle Fuller), interview with author.
58 *Daily Telegraph*, 26 May 2014.

17. TOP OF THE POLL

1 *King of Chaos: Nick Clegg interviews Nigel Farage,* podcast, 18 April 2018.
2 *Daily Telegraph*, 5 March 2014.
3 *Times* Online, 26 March 2014.
4 Ibid.
5 *Guardian* Online, 2 April 2014.
6 Ibid.
7 James O'Brien programme, LBC, 16 May 2014.
8 John Lyndon Sullivan, Twitter, 17 February 2014.
9 *Evening Standard*, 28 February 2014.
10 *Guardian* Online, 26 May 2014.
11 *Daily Telegraph*, 29 May 2014.
12 ITV News, 15 November 2013.
13 *Independent*, 24 June 2014.
14 The last had been in 1989 in Richmond, Yorkshire, where William Hague won because the new Social and Liberal Democrat Party and the remaining SDP both fought the seat and split the main anti-Tory vote.
15 The only cases over the previous sixty years I know of are Harold Macmillan in Stockton in 1962; Tony Blair, Uxbridge, 1997; and Gordon Brown, Glenrothes, 2008.
16 Arron Banks, *The Bad Boys of Brexit*, Biteback, 2016, p.xxv.
17 BBC News Online, 28 August 2014.
18 Ibid.
19 Owen Bennett, *Following Farage*, Biteback, 2015, p.63.

20 *Guardian* Online, 28 August 2014.

21 Douglas Carswell, *Rebel: How to Overthrow the Emerging Oligarchy*, Head of Zeus, 2017, p.34.

22 *New Statesman*, 3 April 2014.

23 Carswell, *Rebel*, p.5.

24 Tim Shipman, *All Out War*, William Collins, 2016, p.29.

25 Carswell, *Rebel*, p.37.

26 Shipman, *All Out War*, p.30.

27 *Guardian* Online, 28 August 2014.

28 *Guardian* Online, 10 October 2014.

29 Matthew Goodwin and Caitlin Milazzo, *UKIP: Inside the Campaign to Redraw the Map of British Politics*, OUP, 2015, p.176.

30 Bennett, *Following Farage*, p.73.

31 Carswell, *Rebel*, p.42.

32 Ibid., pp.42-3.

33 britishfuture.org, 9 October 2014.

34 *Newsweek Europe*, 9 October 2014.

35 Carswell, *Rebel*, p.41.

36 *Today*, BBC Radio 4, 10 October 2014.

37 Bennett, *Following Farage*, p.74.

38 Ibid., p.76.

39 Carswell, *Rebel*, p.41.

40 Goodwin and Milazzo, *UKIP: Inside the Campaign to Redraw the Map of British Politics*, pp.180-81.

41 Ibid., pp.164-5.

42 *Guardian* Online, 12 November 2014.

43 Clive Page, interview with author.

44 BBC News Online, 27 September 2014.

45 Cameron, *For the Record*, p.557.

46 Conservative Party channel, YouTube, 1 October 2014.

47 *Today*, BBC Radio 4, 1 October 2014.

48 ConservativeHome website, 14 October 2014.

49 Channel 4 News, 8 February 2016.

50 Goodwin and Milazzo, *UKIP: Inside the Campaign to Redraw the Map of British Politics*, pp.170-71.

51 Ibid., pp.171-2.

52 Ibid., p.173.

53 Ibid., p.174.

18. THE BATTLE OF THANET

1 Bennett, *Following Farage*, p.337.

2 Nigel Farage, *The Purple Revolution*, Biteback, 2015, p.223.

3 *Daily Telegraph*, 16 March 2015.

4 Bennett, *Following Farage*, p.250.

5 Goodwin and Milazzo, *UKIP: Inside the Campaign to Redraw the Map of British Politics*, p.227.

6 *Meet the UKIPpers*, BBC2, 23 February 2015.

7 Goodwin and Milazzo, *UKIP: Inside the Campaign to Redraw the Map of British Politics*, p.231.

8 *Guardian* Online, 23 March 2015.

9 Goodwin and Milazzo, *UKIP: Inside the Campaign to Redraw the Map of British Politics*, p.203.

10 Alex Phillips, interview with author.

11 *Spectator*, 7 March 2015.

12 Farage, *The Purple Revolution*, pp.300-01.

13 *Question Time*, BBC2, 8 May 2014.

14 *Steph and Dom Meet Nigel Farage*, Channel 4, 15 December 2014.

15 *Independent*, 16 December 2014.

16 *Nigel Farage Swings for Europe*, Paddy Power, YouTube, 25 September 2014.

17 *Guardian* Online, 24 April 2015.

18 Paul Lambert, conversation with author.

19 Alex Phillips, interview with author.

20 *Independent*, 6 April 2015.

21 Sentencing judgement, R v Mackinlay, Gray & Little, 9 January 2019.

22 *Guardian* Online, 24 April 2015.

23 *Guardian*, 12 March 2015.

24 *Guardian*, 16 March 2015.

25 Philip Cowley and Dennis Kavanagh, *The British General Election of 2015*, Palgrave Macmillan, p.175.

26 *Leaders' Debate*, ITV, 2 April 2015.

27 Ibid.

28 Bennett, *Following Farage*, p.259.

29 Ibid., p.258.

30 Ibid., pp.253-5.

31 BBC Election Debate, 16 April 2015.

32 *Daily Telegraph*, 24 April 2015.

33 *Daily Telegraph* rolling blog, 8 April 2015.

34 MailOnline, 6 May 2015.

35 Ibid.

36 Bennett, *Following Farage*, p.331.

37 Ibid., p.324.
38 Ibid., p.326.
39 Sky News, 8 May 2015.
40 Will Scobie, interview with author.
41 Alex Phillips, interview with author.
42 Banks, *The Bad Boys of Brexit*, 2016, p.xxv.
43 Ibid., p.xxvi.
44 Douglas Carswell, email to author.
45 Cowley and Kavanagh, *The British General Election of 2015*, pp.372, 374.
46 Matthew Goodwin, interview with author.

19. QUITS OR DOUBLE?

1   BBC News Online, 8 May 2015.
2   Ibid.
3   Bennett, *Following Farage*, pp.330-31.
4   Suzanne Evans, interview with author.
5   David Soutter, interview with author.
6   Goodwin and Milazzo, *UKIP: Inside the Campaign to Redraw the Map of British Politics*, p.290.
7   Paul Oakley, *No One Likes Us, We Don't Care: A UKIP Brexit Memoir*, NER Press, 2019, p.188.
8   David Soutter, interview with author.
9   Goodwin and Milazzo, *UKIP: Inside the Campaign to Redraw the Map of British Politics*, p.290.
10 Suzanne Evans, interview with author.
11 Ibid.
12 Goodwin and Milazzo, *UKIP: Inside the Campaign to Redraw the Map of British Politics*, p.290.
13 Ibid., p.293.
14 Shipman, *All Out War*, p.32.
15 Goodwin and Milazzo, *UKIP: Inside the Campaign to Redraw the Map of British Politics*, p.294.
16 Suzanne Evans, interview with author.
17 Owen Bennett, *The Brexit Club*, Biteback, 2016, p.1.
18 BBC News Online, 13 May 2015.
19 Carswell, *Rebel*, p.61.
20 *The Times*, 16 May 2015.
21 Ibid.
22 Daniel Hannan, interview with author.
23 *Guardian Politics live*, 14 May 2015.
24 ITV News, 14 May 2015.
25 *The Spectator*, 23 May 2015.

26 BBC News Online, 19 May 2015.
27 Christine Hamilton, interview with author.
28 Neil Hamilton, interview with author.
29 Ibid.
30 Piers Wauchope, interview with HD.
31 Alex Phillips, interview with author.
32 Anonymous anti-Hamilton leaflet, *c*.10 February 2016.
33 Piers Wauchope, email to UKIP members in Wales.
34 Elizabeth Jones et al., letter to Steve Crowther, 14 February 2016.
35 Kirsten Farage, email to NEC members, 15 February 2016.
36 Breitbart News, 1 August 2016.
37 BBC News Online, 24 February 2016.
38 WalesOnline, 17 March 2016.
39 Gareth Bennett, interview with author.
40 BBC News Online, 4 April 2016.
41 Ibid., 13 May 2016.
42 Breitbart News, 3 October 2016.

20. A DESIGNATION MATTER

1   Bennett, *Following Farage*, p.351.
2   Dominic Cummings blog, 19 June 2015.
3   Shipman, *All Out War*, p.43.
4   Ibid.
5   Banks, *The Bad Boys of Brexit*, 2017 edn, p.xxi.
6   Ibid., p.xxvi.
7   *Sunday Telegraph*, 21 June 2015.
8   Banks, *The Bad Boys of Brexit*, 2017, p.5 [1 July 2015].
9   Ibid., p.19 [20 July 2015].
10 Shipman, *All Out War*, p.211.
11 *Profile* [Arron Banks], BBC Radio 4, 10 December 2016.
12 Ibid.
13 Banks, *The Bad Boys of Brexit*, 2017, pp.9-10 [5 July 2015].
14 Shipman, *All Out War*, p.43.
15 Banks, *The Bad Boys of Brexit*, 2017, p.11 [7 July 2015].
16 Shipman, *All Out War*, p.44.
17 Ibid.
18 Banks, *The Bad Boys of Brexit*, 2017, p.35 [23 August 2015].
19 Shipman, *All Out War*, pp.44-5.
20 Banks, *The Bad Boys of Brexit*, 2017,

p.95 [4 November 2015].

21 Ibid., p.15 [14 July 2015].

22 Goodwin and Milazzo, *UKIP: Inside the Campaign to Redraw the Map of British Politics*, p.116.

23 *Guardian*, 21 May 2019.

24 Ibid.

25 Shipman, *All Out War*, p.209.

26 *The Economist*, 21 January 2016.

27 Dominic Cummings speech, Ogilvy Nudgestock conference, YouTube, 4 September 2017.

28 Bennett, *The Brexit Club*, p.151.

29 *Mail on Sunday*, 27 December 2015.

30 Daniel Hannan, interview with author.

31 *Guardian*, 5 February 2016.

32 *The Times*, 6 February 2016.

33 Banks, *The Bad Boys of Brexit*, 2017, p.207 [22 March 2016].

34 *Daily Telegraph*, 14 July 2017.

35 Ibid.

36 Daniel Hannan, interview with author.

37 Suzanne Evans, email to author, 12 March 2020.

38 ITV News website, 27 February 2016.

39 Bennett, *The Brexit Club*, pp.225-6.

40 Matthew Elliott, interview with author.

41 Bennett, *The Brexit Club*, p.232.

42 *Profile* [Arron Banks], BBC Radio 4, 10 December 2016.

43 Oakley, *No One Likes Us, We Don't Care*, p.238 [13 April 2016].

21. INDEPENDENCE DAY

1 yahoo!news, 15 April 2016.

2 Banks, *The Bad Boys of Brexit*, 2016, pp.228-9 [15 April 2016].

3 Ibid., p.232 [18 April 2016]

4 Ibid., p.246 [29 April 2016].

5 *Off Script* podcast, *Telegraph*, 17 September 2021.

6 Matthew Elliott, interview with author.

7 Bennett, *The Brexit Club*, p.277.

8 Russia Today, 29 April 2016.

9 *Sunday Telegraph*, 5 June 2016.

10 Craig Oliver, *Unleashing Demons: The Inside Story of Brexit*, Hodder &

Stoughton, 2016.

11 *The Times*, 12 May 2016

12 Banks, *The Bad Boys of Brexit*, 2016, p.280 [8 June 2016].

13 Ibid.

14 Commons Home Affairs Select Committee, YouTube, 7 June 2016.

15 Shipman, *All Out War*, p.327.

16 BBC News Online, 7 June 2016.

17 Banks, *The Bad Boys of Brexit*, 2016, p.269 [23 May 2016].

18 Ibid.

19 Ibid., pp.269-70 [23 May 2016].

20 Dominic Cummings blog, 27 April 2018.

21 Banks, *The Bad Boys of Brexit*, 2016, p.287 [15 June 2016].

22 Gawain Towler, interview with author.

23 MailOnline, 15 June 2016.

24 Bennett, *The Brexit Club*, p.309.

25 Banks, *The Bad Boys of Brexit*, 2016, p.289 [15 June 2016].

26 Gawain Towler, interview with author.

27 Banks, *The Bad Boys of Brexit*, 2016, p.282 [13 June 2016].

28 *Guardian* Online, 16 June 2016.

29 *Scotsman*, 16 June 2016.

30 Matthew Elliott, interview with author.

31 Banks, *The Bad Boys of Brexit*, 2016, p.293 [17 June 2016].

32 Ibid., p. 295 [19 June 2016]; *Today*, BBC Radio 4, 20 June 2016.

33 *Guardian* live, 20 June 2016

34 Banks, *The Bad Boys of Brexit*, 2016, p.300 [17 June 2016].

35 Ibid., p.302 [23 June 2016].

36 Sky News, 22.00, 23 June 2016.

37 *Sunday Times*, 8 July 2018.

38 Banks, *The Bad Boys of Brexit*, 2016, p.305 [23 June 2016].

39 *Daily Telegraph*, 14 July 2017.

40 Banks, *The Bad Boys of Brexit*, 2016, p.305 [23 June 2016].

41 *Daily Telegraph*, 14 July 2017.

42 @Nigel_Farage, Twitter, 24 June 2016.

43 *Guardian* News, 24 June 2016.

44 *Daily Telegraph*, 14 June 2017.

45 Matthew Elliott, interview with

46 Alex Phillips, interview with author.
47 Matthew Elliott, interview with author.
48 Dominic Cummings blog, 9 January 2017.
49 *Andrew Marr Show*, BBC1, 12 May 2019.
50 *Newsnight*, BBC2, 24 July 2016.

22. TRUMP THAT

1 European Parliament debates, 28 June 2016.
2 Banks, *The Bad Boys of Brexit*, 2016, p.321.
3 *AMI magazine*, 10 February 2021.
4 *Farage Against the Machine*, LBC podcast, 12 July 2018.
5 *The Trump Card* podcast, part 1, 29 September 2020.
6 Ibid.
7 *Guardian*, 27 February 2015.
8 *Independent*, 8 December 2015.
9 Video of the *Express* Debate, 3 June 2016.
10 Isabel Oakeshott, interview with author.
11 *Mother Jones*, 6 June 2017 (updated).
12 *Guardian*, 25 November 2018.
13 Banks, *The Bad Boys of Brexit*, 2016, p.325 [21 July 2016].
14 *Washington Post*, 28 November 2018.
15 InfoWars, 4 August 2016.
16 *The Trump Card* podcast, part 1, 29 September 2020.
17 Video of Goddard Gunster inauguration party, 20 January 2017.
18 Isabel Oakeshott, interview with author.
19 *Guardian* Online, 7 June 2017.
20 *The J. T. Show*, SuperTalk Mississippi, 24 August 2016.
21 *The Trump Card* podcast, part 1, 29 September 2020.
22 Michael Wolff, *Siege: Trump Under Fire*, Little, Brown, 2019, p.157.
23 CBS News, 24 August 2016.
24 *The Trump Card* podcast, part 1, 29 September 2020.
25 Video of Goddard Gunster inauguration party, 20 January 2017.

26 ITV News, 25 August 2016.
27 Sky News, 20 January 2014.
28 *The Times*, 26 August 2016.
29 Banks, *The Bad Boys of Brexit*, 2017, p.340.
30 *Daily Express*, 3 September 2016.
31 *Piers Morgan's Life Stories*, ITV, 24 February 2017.
32 *The Times*, 26 August 2016.
33 InfoWars, 30 August 2016.
34 *Washington Post* website, 8 October 2016.
35 Fox News, 8 October 2016.
36 Sky News, 10 October 2016.
37 *The Trump Card* podcast, part 1, 29 September 2020.
38 Bloomberg Media, 7 November 2016.
39 *Sunday Times Magazine*, 8 October 2017.
40 *Andrew Marr Show*, BBC1, 15 October 2017.
41 *Fox & Friends*, Fox News, 16 October 2017.
42 *Spectator* website, 2 November 2016.
43 *The Agenda*, ITV, 8 November 2016.

23. FRIENDS OF VLADIMIR

1 *New Yorker*, 30 November 2016.
2 Tim Shipman, *Fall Out: A Year of Political Mayhem*, William Collins, 2017, p.105.
3 *The Trump Card* podcast, part 2, 6 October 2020.
4 Banks, *The Bad Boys of Brexit*, 2017, p.xxx.
5 Shipman, *Fall Out*, p.105.
6 Banks, *The Bad Boys of Brexit*, 2017, p.354.
7 Breitbart News, 22 November 2016.
8 Kim Darroch, interview with author.
9 Twitter, @realDonaldTrump, 22 November 2016.
10 *The Trump Card* podcast, part 3, 6 October 2020.
11 Banks, *The Bad Boys of Brexit*, 2017, p.359.
12 *Guardian*, 22 November 2016.
13 Guardian News, YouTube, 24 February 2017.
14 Jens-Peter Bonde, interview with HD.
15 Conservativehome.com, 16 July 2013.

16 Twitter, @carolecadwalla, 20 August 2020.
17 Breitbart News Daily, 29 March 2017.
18 *Newsweek* video, 15 May 2018.
19 *The Brink*, AliKlay Productions, 2019.
20 *Guardian*, 22 May 2019.
21 ABC News (Australia), 27 April 2016.
22 *Guardian*, 31 March 2014.
23 *LBC Leader's Debate: Nick Clegg v. Nigel Farage*, LBC, 26 March 2014.
24 BBC News Online, 27 March 2014.
25 *Guardian*, 31 March 2014.
26 *Sam Delaney's News Thing*, RT, 13 August 2016.
27 Sam Delaney, interview with HD.
28 *Sam Delaney's News Thing*, RT, 3 March 2017.
29 Disinformation and 'fake news': Interim Report, DCMS Committee, Fifth Report of Session 2017-19, HC 363, 28 July 2018, paras 185 & 186.
30 Electoral Commission, Investigation into payments made to Better for the Country and Leave.EU, 1 November 2018.
31 Peter Geoghegan, *Democracy for Sale*, Head of Zeus, 2020, p.48; Bloomberg, February 2019.
32 Alastair Sloan and Iain Campbell, openDemocracy, October 2017.
33 National Crime Agency, Public Statement on NCA Investigation into Suspected EU Referendum Offences, 24 September 2019.
34 Statement by Electoral Commission, Robert Posner, Arron Banks and Elizabeth Bilney, 29 April 2020.
35 BBC News Online, 1 May 2019.
36 Mueller Report, p.1.
37 *Guardian*, 23 April 2017.
38 BuzzFeed.com, 9 March 2017.
39 Glenn Simpson, testimony to House Intelligence Committee, 17 November 2017.
40 *The Nigel Farage Show*, LBC, 29 October 2017.
41 Christian Mitchell, interview with author.
42 *This Week*, BBC2, 26 January 2017; Twitter, @Nigel_Farage, 27 January 2017.
43 Theodore Malloch, *Hired: An Insider's Look at the Trump Victory*, WND Books, 2017.
44 *Guardian*, 28 November 2018.
45 Ibid., 13 November 2018.
46 *Washington Post*, 29 June 2018.
47 Report On The Investigation Into Russian Interference In The 2016 Presidential Election [Mueller Report], Vol. 1, p.55.
48 *Die Ziet* Online, 19 May 2017.

24. BREAKING UP

1 Banks, *The Bad Boys of Brexit*, 2017, p.344 [October 2016].
2 *Guardian*, 31 March 2014.
3 *New Statesman*, 6 June 2018.
4 Christian Mitchell, interview with author.
5 *The Nigel Farage Show*, LBC, 20 April 2017.
6 Beecher, *UKIP Exposed*, chapter 5, p.7.
7 Oakley, *No One Likes Us, We Don't Care*, p.263 [3 August 2016].
8 *HuffPost* website, 29 July 2016.
9 Beecher, *UKIP Exposed*, chapter 5, p.8.
10 *Daily Politics*, BBC2, 9 September 2016.
11 Reeders Cunningham, interview with author.
12 *Profile* [Arron Banks], BBC Radio 4, 10 December 2016.
13 *Daily Mirror*, 17 September 2016.
14 Banks, *The Bad Boys of Brexit*, 2017, pp.341-2 [September 2016].
15 *Any Questions?*, BBC Radio 4, 16 September 2016.
16 *Profile* [Arron Banks], BBC Radio 4, 10 December 2016.
17 BBC News Online, 16 September 2016.
18 ConservativeHome.com, 20 September 2016.
19 BBC News Online, 5 October 2016.
20 Shipman, *Fall Out*, p.450.
21 *Telegraph* Online, 21 November 2016.
22 BBC News Online, 17 October 2016.
23 Sajjad Karim, interview with HD.
24 BBC News Online, 17 October 2016.
25 Channel 4 News website, 1 February

2017.

26 *Daily Telegraph*, 24 February 2017.
27 Shipman, *Fall Out*, p.540.
28 *Evening Standard* website, 20 April 2017.
29 *Daily Telegraph*, 20 April 2017.
30 *Telegraph* Online, 5 May 2017.
31 Investigation by The Overtake website, 11 April 2019.
32 Sky News website, 17 November 2016.
33 *Politico*, 21 November 2016.
34 Electoral Commission, *Investigation: UK Independence Party*, 18 September 2018.
35 *Euractiv*, 7 November 2019.
36 *Daily Telegraph*, 1 July 2017.
37 *Mail on Sunday*, 13 January 2018.
38 *Daily Telegraph*, 22 January 2018.
39 *Question Time*, BBC1, 17 January 2013.
40 *Mirror* Online, 18 May 2016.
41 BBC News Online, 17 May 2016.
42 *The Wright Stuff*, Channel 5, 11 January 2018.
43 Sky News, 18 August 2018.
44 Ibid.
45 John Longworth, interview with author.
46 BBC News Online, 6 February 2017.
47 Channel 4 News website, 26 June 2019.
48 *Politico* website, 26 June 2019.
49 *Sunday Times*, 10 June 2018.

25. THE MASSACRE OF MAY

1 *Eastern Daily Press*, 15 February 2019.
2 Catherine Blaiklock, interview with author.
3 *Guardian*, 29 April 2017.
4 *Independence Daily*, 16 October 2018.
5 *Daily Telegraph*, 23 November 2018.
6 Press Association video, 23 November 2018.
7 *Telegraph* website, 23 November 2019.
8 Richard Ford interview.
9 Ibid.
10 Minutes of UKIP NEC, 2 December 2018.
11 *The Nigel Farage Show*, LBC, 4 December 2018.
12 *Independence Daily*, 5 December 2018.
13 Catherine Blaiklock, interview with author.
14 Ibid.
15 *Sun on Sunday*, 20 January 2019.
16 Catherine Blaiklock, interview with author.
17 Catherine Blaiklock, email to Alexandra Phillips, 5 February 2019.
18 Catherine Blaiklock, interview with author.
19 Ibid.
20 Catherine Blaiklock, email to Electoral Commission, 11 February 2019.
21 *Guardian*, 21 May 2019.
22 *Guardian* Online, 22 January 2019.
23 Ibid.
24 *Salisbury Review*, 7 August 2018.
25 BuzzFeed News, 11 February 2019.
26 *Guardian* Online, 22 January 2019.
27 *Guardian*, 20 March 2019.
28 Catherine Blaiklock, interview with author.
29 *Guardian*, 20 March 2019.
30 Ibid.
31 Channel 4 News, 12 April 2019.
32 Catherine Blaiklock, interview with author.
33 Catherine Blaiklock, letter to Farage, McGough and Basey, *c.*14 April 2019.
34 Catherine Blaiklock, interview with author.
35 Nigel Farage, letter to Catherine Blaiklock, 20 April 2019.
36 *Guardian*, 3 April 2019.
37 Nigel Farage, letter to Catherine Blaiklock, 20 April 2019.
38 Ibid.
39 Catherine Blaiklock, interview with author.
40 Ibid.
41 Ibid.
42 Richard Tice, interview with author.
43 Ann Widdecombe, interview with HD.
44 Mike Hookem, interview with HD.
45 Jonathan Bullock, interview with HD.
46 Richard Tice, interview with author.
47 Ibid.
48 Steven Edginton, interview with author.
49 Richard Tice, interview with author.

50 David Bull, interview with HD.
51 Sky News, 24 May 2019.
52 Chopper's podcast, 6 March 2021.
53 Steven Edginton, interview with author.
54 BBC News Online, 26 May 2019.
55 C-Span, 30 May 2016.

26. NIGEL VERSUS BORIS

1 BBC News Online, 24 May 2019.
2 Brexit Party press conference, 9 May 2019.
3 Steven Edginton, interview with author.
4 *Guardian* Online, 20 May 2019.
5 BBC News Online, 7 June 2019.
6 *The Times*, 8 June 2019.
7 Sir Desmond Swayne, interview with author.
8 Richard Tice, interview with author.
9 Donald Trump, remarks at Turning Point USA's Teen Student Action Summit, 23 July 2019.
10 BBC News Online, 24 July 2019.
11 Richard Tice, email to author.
12 Lance Forman, interview with author.
13 Ann Widdecombe, interview with HD.
14 Ibid.
15 David Bull, interview with HD.
16 *The Times Guide to the House of Commons 2019*, Times Books, 2020, p.13.
17 *Guardian* Online, 11 September 2019.
18 *Evening Standard* Online, 17 October 2019.
19 Twitter, @LBC, 17 October 2019.
20 *Telegraph* Online, 17 October 2019.
21 Brexit Central website, 15 October 2019.
22 *The Times*, 17 October 2019.
23 Lance Forman, interview with author.
24 John Longworth, email to author.
25 Christian Mitchell, interview with author.
26 Ibid.
27 *The Nigel Farage Show*, LBC, YouTube, 31 October 2019.
28 Ibid.
29 *Mail on Sunday*, 3 November 2019.
30 *The Times*, 2 November 2019.
31 *Telegraph* Online, 5 November 2019.

32 *Mail on Sunday*, 3 November 2019.
33 *Daily Mail*, 4 November 2019.
34 *Sunday Times*, 3 November 2019.
35 *Farage: The Man Who Made Brexit*, Channel 4, 29 January 2020.
36 Ibid.
37 Sky News, 11 November 2019.
38 *The Man Who Made Brexit*, Channel 4, 29 January 2020.
39 *Evening Standard*, 12 November 2019.
40 *The Times*, 13 November 2019.
41 David Bull, interview with HD.
42 *Telegraph* Online, 12 November 2019.
43 *The Times*, 13 November 2019.
44 Rowland drowned in a diving accident while on holiday in the Bahamas in 2021.
45 *Telegraph* Online, 14 November 2019.
46 MailOnline, 10 November 2019.
47 *Daily Mail*, 14 November 2019.
48 *The Times*, 13 November 2019.
49 Ann Widdecombe, interview with HD.
50 *Guardian*, 14 November 2019.
51 *Sunday Times*, 3 November 2019.
52 *Guardian*, 14 November 2019.
53 Twitter, @Nigel_Farage, 14 November 2019.
54 Sky News, 14 November 2019.
55 Twitter, @RupertLowe10, 14 November 2019.
56 Birmingham Live, 15 November 2019.
57 *Farage: The Man Who Made Brexit*, Channel 4, 29 January 2020.
58 Lance Forman, interview with author.
59 *Telegraph* Online, 5 December 2019.
60 Twitter, @Nigel_Farage, 12 December 2019.

27. A LOOSE END

1 European Parliament, YouTube, 29 January 2020.
2 ECR channel, YouTube, 18 December 2020.
3 LBC, YouTube, 31 January 2020.
4 *Newsweek* Online, 9 March 2020.
5 *Daily Telegraph*, 30 March 2020.
6 *Daily Telegraph*, 1 November 2020.
7 Twitter, @Nigel_Farage, 1 November 2020.
8 YouTube, 21 May 2020.

9   Twitter, @Nigel_Farage, 4 May 2020.
10 *Nigel Farage Show*, LBC, YouTube, 13 May 2020.
11 MailOnline, 1 December 2020.
12 Twitter, @Nigel_Farage, 7 June 2020.
13 Twitter, @LBC, 11 June 2020.
14 Talk Radio, 12 June 2020.
15 *Daily Telegraph*, 18 May 2021.
16 European Parliament, Declaration of Members' Financial Interests, 1 July 2019.
17 Fortune and Freedom website, 'Our Mission', *c.*14 October 2020.
18 Kent Online, 15 April 2021.
19 *Evening Standard*, 23 June 2020.
20 Twitter, @Nigel_Farage, 6 January 2021.
21 *Independent* Online, 7 November 2020.
22 Twitter, @Nigel_Farage, 13 December 2020.
23 *Daily Telegraph*, 22 December 2020.
24 Ibid.
25 LBC, 24 December 2020.
26 *Mail on Sunday*, 27 December 2020.
27 Twitter, @Nigel_Farage, 6 March 2021.
28 *Daily Telegraph*, 27 April 2021.
29 *Daily Telegraph*, 18 May 2021.

28. FARAGE NEWS

1   *Financial Times*, 9 October 2021.
2   Alastair Campbell, interview with author.
3   GB News press release, 5 March 2021.
4   Twitter, @afneil, 17 July 2021 (since deleted).
5   BBC News Online, 19 July 2021.
6   Twitter, @Nigel_Farage, 4 July 2021.
7   Twitter, @afneil, 29 July 2021.
8   *i* Online, 17 November 2021.
9   *Telegraph* Online, 22 November 2021.
10 *Sunday Telegraph*, 21 November 2021.
11 *mailplus* website, 24 November 2021.

A DISRUPTIVE LIFE

1   Twitter, @GoodwinMJ, 6 March 2021.
2   *Daily Telegraph*, 11 January 2020.
3   Dan Hannan, interview with author.
4   *Prospect* website, 11 March 2021.
5   Off Script podcast, *The Telegraph*, 17 September 2021.

BIBLIOGRAPHY

Allen, Nicholas and John Bartle (eds), *None Past the Post: Britain at the Polls, 2017* (Manchester University Press, 2018)

Ashcroft, Michael, *Jacob's Ladder: The Unauthorised Biography of Jacob Rees-Mogg* (Biteback, 2019)

Banks, Arron, *The Bad Boys of Brexit* (Biteback, 2016 & 2017)

Beecher, Jay, *UKIP Exposed* (2017)

Bennett, Owen, *Following Farage* (Biteback, 2015)

Bennett, Owen, *The Brexit Club* (Biteback, 2016)

Booker, Christopher and Richard North, *The Great Deception: The True Story of Britain and the European Union*, 4th edn (Bloomsbury, 2021)

Butler, David and Dennis Kavanagh, *The British General Election of 1997* (Palgrave Macmillan, 1997)

Butler, David and Dennis Kavanagh, *The British General Election of 2001* (Palgrave Macmillan, 2002)

Butler, David and Martin Westlake, *British Politics and European Elections 1999* (Palgrave Macmillan, 2000)

Butler, David and Martin Westlake, *British Politics and European Elections 2004* (Palgrave Macmillan, 2005)

Cameron, David, *For the Record* (William Collins, 2019)

Carswell, Douglas, *The End of Politics and the Birth of Democracy* (Biteback, 2012)

Carswell, Douglas, *Rebel: How to Overthrow the Emerging Oligarchy* (Head of Zeus, 2017)

Clarke, Harold, Matthew Goodwin and Paul Whiteley, *Brexit: Why Britain Voted to Leave the European Union* (Cambridge University Press, 2017)

Cowley, Philip and Dennis Kavanagh, *The British General Election of 2015* (Palgrave Macmillan, 2016)

Cowley, Philip and Dennis Kavanagh, *The British General Election of 2017* (Palgrave Macmillan, 2018)

D'Ancona, Matthew, *In It Together: The Inside Story of the Coalition Government* (Viking, 2013)

Daniel, Mark, *Cranks and Gadflies: The Story of UKIP* (Timewell Press, 2005)

Eppink, Derk Jan, *Empire of Little Kings* (Pelckmans, 2015)

Farage, Nigel, *Fighting Bull* (Biteback, 2010)

Farage, Nigel, *Flying Free* (Biteback, 2011)

Farage, Nigel, *The Purple Revolution* (Biteback, 2015)

Farrell, Jason and Paul Goldsmith, *How to Lose a Referendum: The Definitive Story of Why the UK Voted for Brexit* (Biteback, 2017)

Ford, Robert, Tim Bale, Will Jennings and Paula Surridge, *The British General Election of 2019* (Palgrave Macmillan, 2021)

Ford, Robert and Matthew Goodwin, *Revolt on the Right: Explaining Support for the Radical Right in Britain* (Routledge, 2014)

Friedman, Bobby, *Bercow: Mr Speaker* (Gibson Square, 2011)

Gardner, Peter, *Hard Pounding* (June Press, 2006)

Geoghegan, Peter, *Democracy for Sale: Dark Money and Dirty Politics* (Head of Zeus, 2020)

Goodwin, Matthew and Caitlin Milazzo, *UKIP: Inside the Campaign to Redraw the Map of British Politics* (Oxford University Press, 2015)

Hutchins, Chris and Dominic Midgley, *Goldsmith: Money, Women and Power* (Neville Ness House, 2015)

Kavanagh, Dennis and David Butler, *The British General Election of 2005* (Palgrave Macmillan, 2005)

Kavanagh, Dennis and Philip Cowley, *The British General Election of 2010* (Palgrave Macmillan, 2010)

Lamont, Norman, *In Office* (Little, Brown, 1999)

Marcus, Jonathan, *The National Front and French Politics: The Resistable Rise of Jean-Marie Le Pen* (Macmillan, 1995)

Morris, Dick, *50 Shades of Politics* (Triangulation Publishing, 2018)

Mount, Harry, *Summer Madness: How Brexit Split the Tories, Destroyed Labour and Divided the Country* (Biteback, 2017)

Oakley, Paul, *No One Likes Us, We Don't Care: A UKIP Brexit Memoir* (NER Press, 2019)

Oliver, Craig, *Unleashing Demons: The Inside Story of Brexit* (Hodder & Stoughton, 2016)

Seldon, Anthony, *May at 10* (Biteback, 2019)

Seldon, Anthony and Peter Snowdon, *Cameron at 10* (William Collins, 2015)

Shipman, Tim, *All Out War: The Full Story of Brexit* (William Collins, 2016)

Shipman, Tim, *Fall Out: A Year of Political Mayhem* (William Collins, 2017)

Simpson, Glenn and Peter Fritsch, *Crime In Progress: The Secret History of the Trump-Russia Investigation* (Allen Lane, 2019)

Sinclaire, Nikki, *Never Give Up: Standing Tall Through Adversity* (Junius Press, 2013)

Swire, Sasha, *Diary of an MP's Wife: Inside and Outside Power* (Little, Brown, 2020)

Whale, Sebastian, *John Bercow: Call to Order* (Biteback, 2020)

Wheeler, Stuart, *Winning Against the Odds: My Life in Gambling and Politics* (Quiller, 2019)

Wolff, Michael, *Siege: Trump Under Fire* (Little, Brown, 2019)

INDEX